CONTENTS

PREFACE

This seventh volume of *The Papers of John C. Calhoun* includes documents of the year that began on April 1, 1822, and ended on March 31, 1823. Chiefly but not exclusively official in nature, they comprise a record of part of Calhoun's long stewardship in the office of Secretary of War—a record that is rich in amplifying details. These letters and other writings have been assembled from scores of different sources. Many of them are published for the first time. Their impact is to confirm and to strengthen an impression given in five preceding volumes of the series—an inescapable conclusion that the young South Carolinian, by this time approximately forty years old, was proving himself to be an outstandingly able administrator. He worked indefatigably and with visions of national honor and strength and glory as his motivating force, but not without hope also that he would be enabled to ride the tide of national progress to personal advancement.

Calhoun's purposes may have been reasonably noble, but easy his pathway to fame during 1822–1823 certainly was not. These twelve months constituted a year of incessantly difficult struggle against obstacles that ever loomed high, if not insurmountable. Because the documents that appear within these covers do not tell the whole story, the editor's Introduction has been added to them as a means of providing readers with insights from other sources that will supplement and complement the words written by Calhoun and his correspondents. That essay is not exhaustive. It is intended merely to hint at some of the relationships that existed among the documents and among their writers.

Letters are not always self-explanatory. Often they are exchanged by persons who share a certain body of knowledge. The writers do not bother to explain fully what they write, because they can confidently take it for granted that their words will be understood by recipients whose observations and experiences will serve to fill the gaps. It is conspicuously true of Calhoun's papers that many were not written for posterity. In order that readers of such mail can be enabled to "read between the lines," they need to acquire an understanding comparable to that of the authors and of their addressees.

There is, in addition, a somewhat different reason for offering an Introduction to letters that were largely official rather than personal. Speaking generally, most of the documents that appear within these covers originated in a workaday world. They were written by and to governmental officers about public business of a usually ordinary or normal kind. A cryptic style calculated simply to get the job done as briefly or quickly as possible was considered sufficient. (In contrast, recent decades have witnessed the development of governmental "gobbledegook," a clumsy, much more expansive, quite befuddling patois that fails to convey clear meaning because it says too much rather than too little.) But writers who strive for clarity through conciseness can sometimes fall short of conveying their meaning fully. And even within the compactness of their businesslike language a subtle nuance of expression can occasionally be detected by the knowing. Readers will be well advised, therefore, if they are aware of the likes and the dislikes, of the agreements and the conflicting views, of correspondents whose pathways converged as coöperative colleagues, ran parallel courses as distant partners, or even crossed as detesting rivals.

Once more in 1822–1823, as in preceding units of this series of Calhoun's *Papers,* the mail that he dispatched and received was so voluminous that it would be impracticable for the whole to be published. Sheer necessity has compelled the editor to be selective, omitting perhaps four in every five of the extant manuscripts written by, addressed to, or considered by Calhoun within the year. Even so, more than 1,100 documents are included. About one-third of these appears in full-length transcriptions. The other two-thirds has been summarized in paragraphic abstracts. More than 2,200 manuscript and printed versions of these documents are cited in the 1,100 abstracts and transcriptions. Such figures are, however, comparatively unimportant. The more significant accomplishment of this book is to be found in the light that it sheds upon times in which our national heritage was developing some new and even somewhat modern facets.

The editor and his associates would prefer to present in print the whole of the contents of the unique collection of photocopies of Calhoun papers that has been assembled in the South Caroliniana Library of the University of South Carolina. That collection, begun twenty years ago, is still being enlarged; it has grown in every month of the editor's association with the project. Familiarity with such a large collection is the best qualification that can be urged for the making of selections that have been admittedly subjective in part. Exclusion of the omitted documents has been based chiefly on the editor's evaluation of the usefulness of their contents. But only certain manuscripts preserved in the National Archives—those of most nearly routine nature recording the day-by-day, financial, and "housekeeping" functions of the United States government—have been omitted. All known Calhoun documents of the relevant months of 1822–1823 that are preserved in scores of other repositories and in private hands have been either transcribed or abstracted, no matter how insignificant their contents appear. That fact enhances the value of this book, if only as a "finding aid." The staff's office files, which are open to researchers, increase the helpfulness of the project.

The staff has undergone two changes in personnel during the year since it sent Volume VI of *The Papers of John C. Calhoun* to press. Mrs. Mary Catherine Lever typed some of the printer's copy for this seventh volume, and Mrs. Shirley Gail (Bolin) Adkins has prepared the remainder. Dr. Clyde N. Wilson, Jr., of the University of South Carolina's History Department has begun to collaborate with us on a part-time basis. Miss Shirley Ann Bright, Research Assistant, continues to help with increasing effectiveness in variegated chores that range from accessioning documents to proofreadings. To each of these colleagues the editor expresses an appreciation that he feels daily. And they join him in acknowledging the continuing support of the State of South Carolina through the South Carolina Department of Archives and History, of the National Historical Publications Commission, of the University of South Carolina, and of the South Caroliniana Society.

W. Edwin Hemphill

South Carolina Department of Archives and History
Columbia, South Carolina
August 1, 1972

INTRODUCTION

John C. Calhoun served as Secretary of War throughout almost seven and one-half years of the two administrations of James Monroe as President of the United States. Those two men kept constantly in mind some major objectives and sought with much consistency to attain them. They labored together with impressive harmony—so much so that their relationship was rarely ruffled, despite extreme provocations from others. One example of national policy about which they never disagreed fundamentally, although perhaps occasionally in respect to details, was their common belief that a strategically sound system of coastal fortifications should be constructed for defense against possible invasion by any enemy force. How otherwise could they prevent a repetition or counterpart of the humiliating experience during the War of 1812 in which the nation's capital had been captured and many of its buildings burned?

But patriots can disagree. Changing times can lead to opposite conclusions men of intelligent minds and worthy motives. And it became obvious even to Monroe's and Calhoun's fellow citizens of the 1820's that the government in which they were leading figures was divided against itself. What those two statesmen wanted and what they could obtain became two different things.

The twelve months comprehended within this volume of *The Papers of John C. Calhoun* made that fact more openly, more blatantly clear than ever before. Some reminders as to specific issues that were discussed in Calhoun's correspondence within the year will serve as a setting for what he and others wrote. Few of these issues originated or were concluded within the year. It may be all the more desirable, accordingly, that they should be placed in perspective.

The Reduction of the Army

One question that the United States has never decided with finality is how big its defense forces should be. A long-term tendency has been to keep them small. That inclination was given a major impulse when the Panic of 1819 and its longer-lasting aftermath reduced the government's revenues below the level of its expenditures and compelled it to borrow money for several years. Those who sought to achieve economy for its own sake had an additional motivation: by portraying the administration as a spendthrift, extravagant, wasteful government that was tilting at a windmill by preparing for defense against dangers that were more imaginary than real, the critics' own political aspirations might be promoted.

The ingredients for a bitter contest were inherent in the situation. Impressed for the rest of his life by lessons learned from the War of 1812, Secretary of War Calhoun was a sincere advocate of preparedness and of an adequately strong Army. Monroe's Secretary of the Treasury, William H. Crawford, could win a creditable reputation if he could boast of economy in the public finances and prevent a return to the direct, excise tax of wartime and the first postwar years. These men were rival candidates to succeed Monroe as President. And each had admirers, friends, followers, and converts in Congress, which held the purse strings and could enact laws that would magnify or curtail the powers of Cabinet members.

Crawford's ideas won a majority in each house of Congress. On March 2, 1821, that majority imposed upon the administration a stringent law reducing the authorized personnel of the Army from 10,000 men to 6,000, exclusive of the 2,000 who comprised the Corps of Engineers. Congress had requested Calhoun's suggestions how such a diminution could be achieved but had made the pill much less palatable by ignoring in important particulars his recommendations.

The mere enactment of any such drastic measure at all was destined to become one of the major setbacks in Calhoun's entire career. Adopted just two days prior to the end of Monroe's first administration, it set the stage for increasing discord throughout his second.[1] And its effects lasted even longer, in that the Army was not allowed to regain its lost strength even when the government's income became embarrassingly large.

Unwelcome task though it was, Calhoun and his subordinates

[1] W. Edwin Hemphill, ed., *The Papers of John C. Calhoun,* Volume V, *1820–1821* (Columbia: University of South Carolina Press, c. 1971), pp. xx–xxi. Hereafter, within this book, volume and page numbers will be cited in numerals (usually Arabic) separated by a colon, for example, 5:xx–xxi.

resolutely reduced the Army's manpower with remarkable rapidity, largely within three months. Officers had to be discharged, demoted, transferred. That anguished protests would result was predictable. Equally so was it that Congressmen would hear outcries and that repercussions would follow. Many a legislator would be convinced that he could have made better executive decisions for the retention or even the promotion of one or more officers for whom he would confess no favoritism whatsoever. Congress's chicken came home to roost. Or, to change the metaphor, the flight of Congress's fancy had boomeranged. Inevitably, Congress demanded, Calhoun helped to prepare, and Monroe dutifully submitted reports concerning the way in which the Army reduction law had been put into effect.[2]

This contest between legislative and executive branches of the government remained quite unsettled on Monday, April 1, 1822, the date with which this volume opens. As long ago as two days before the preceding Christmas the House of Representatives had directed its Committee on Military Affairs to investigate the reduction of the Army. That group, filled with Crawford-minded men rather than with partisans of Calhoun, had questioned fully a dozen of the dismissals, transfers, and appointments that had been meted out in 1821 to Army officers—such men as Henry Atkinson, Daniel Bissell, Robert Butler, James Gadsden, William Lindsay, Alexander Macomb, Daniel Parker, and Nathan Towson. On April 2, 1822, the Committee reported that "the Army has been reduced according to the provisions of the act" of March 2, 1821. Considering the bias of the Committee's members, that conclusion by it was strong evidence that Calhoun and his colleagues had performed an extremely difficult task almost unassailably well. But a member of the Committee, Representative John Cocke of Tennessee, who was usually aligned against Calhoun, informed the House that the Committee had reached its decision by a majority of only one and only after a change in its membership. It had been initially, Cocke asserted, "decidedly of opinion that the act had been disregarded."[3] The administration had no cause to congratulate itself prematurely.

The issue was joined more pointedly in the Senate. That body

[2] *Ibid.*, 6:ix–xii *et passim.*

[3] *Annals of Congress,* 17th Cong., 1st Sess., cols. 1455–1458; Washington, D.C., *Daily National Intelligencer,* April 12, 1822, p. 2, cols. 1–2. The statute of March 2, 1821, can be found, for example, in *Annals of Congress,* 16th Cong., 2nd Sess., cols. 1798–1799.

had the Constitutional power to confirm or to reject Presidential appointments. To the Senate, sitting in executive session in order that its proceedings would be kept secret until it should decide otherwise, Monroe had submitted on January 22 a list of about 60 promotions and appointments of Army officers made under the Army reduction law, together with Calhoun's letter of January 2 on that subject.[4] Senator John Williams of Tennessee, Chairman of the Senate Committee on Military Affairs, who was as much a Crawfordite as Cocke, reported in March the Committee's recommendation that the appointments that had been given to Nathan Towson to be the Colonel and commanding officer of the new 2nd Regiment of Artillery and to Col. James Gadsden to be the new Adjutant General of the Army should not be confirmed. The Senate approved the new appointments given to Henry Atkinson and to Alexander Macomb by not-reassuring margins of about five and six against three. It rejected the appointments of Towson and Gadsden by votes equivalent to the approximate ratio of four in favor against five in opposition.[5] Despite the fact that scores of changes in the Army were approved, those two rebuffs hurt.

Typically, Monroe discussed the rejections with his Cabinet. He sought its advice concerning a message that he proposed to send to both houses of Congress in defense of his right to nominate Towson, who had recently been a staff officer, and Gadsden, a line officer, to newly created positions in the line and staff, respectively. Monroe believed that his Constitutional right to make appointments should not be limited, especially not in respect to two "original" or new positions. He wanted to state publicly his belief that "every instance" of changed duties assigned during the reduction of the Army was perfectly legal. Calhoun agreed heartily. Secretary of State John Quincy Adams and Secretary of the Navy Smith Thompson concurred also but raised minor questions of expediency. William H. Crawford was "very decidedly" against the message, pronounced the appointment of Towson to have been "not warranted by the Law" and "in violation of the Constitution," and counseled against further Presidential action as likely to be

[4] An abstract of Calhoun's letter appears in Hemphill, ed., *The Papers of John C. Calhoun,* 6:666. The Senate's record of Monroe's submittal appears in the *Annals of Congress,* 17th Cong., 1st Sess., cols. 471–474, and in the Washington, D.C., *Daily National Intelligencer,* May 4, 1822, p. 2, col. 1.

[5] *Annals of Congress,* 17th Cong., 1st Sess., cols. 475–478; Washington, D.C., *Daily National Intelligencer,* May 4, 1822, p. 2, col. 2.

considered "extremely offensive" by Congress. These views Crawford "maintained with great pertinacity against the President, and against Calhoun." So ran the discussion for two hours, inconclusively.[6]

Three days later, on April 11, 1822, Monroe announced to his Cabinet that he had decided to submit the proposed message to the Senate only, as some had suggested, and to renominate Towson and Gadsden to the same positions. It was generally agreed that this would be proper. But "Mr. Crawford expressed doubts of the expediency of the measure, as tending to excite irritation in the Senate—and thought it probable they would reject the nominations again." Monroe was being apparently stubborn not only because a principle of Presidential powers was involved. He wanted to counteract a political objective of Crawford's Congressional friends, which was to censure and embarrass "the administration of the War Department, with a view to promote Mr. Crawford's election to the Presidency." John Quincy Adams, an observer who was himself not totally disinterested, recorded his impression that Crawford had formerly "been somewhat cautious" in leading his partisans but had recently become "decisive and explicit—at the same time repeating with iteration more anxious than prudent, that he had no communication with any members of the Senate upon the subject, and did not know upon what grounds they had rejected the nominations of Towson and Gadsden."[7]

The Senate received on April 12 the President's two messages—one defending his past actions, the other making the renominations.[8] The two matters were immediately referred to the hostile Committee on Military Affairs, presided over by Crawford's partisan, Williams. He reported adversely once more in about two weeks, and on April 29 the Senate voted again its disapproval of the two appointments, by 17 ayes against 25 noes.[9]

[6] Entry of April 8, 1822, in the Diary of John Quincy Adams, Massachusetts Historical Society (published microfilm of the Adams Family Papers, roll 35).

[7] Entry of April 11, 1822, in *ibid.*

[8] *Annals of Congress,* 17th Cong., 1st Sess., cols. 479–486; Washington, D.C., *Daily National Intelligencer,* May 4, 1822, p. 2, col. 5. Monroe's self-justifying message appears (erroneously under the date of April 13, 1822) also in James D. Richardson, *A Compilation of the Messages and Papers of the Presidents, 1789–1902* (10 vols. [Washington:] Bureau of National Literature and Art, 1903), 2:129–136.

[9] *Annals of Congress,* 17th Cong., 1st Sess., cols. 489–502 and 509–510;

Monroe and Calhoun could probably find small comfort indeed in the fact that this second defeat was "wholly of a technical nature," as a Marylander had explained Towson's first rejection in March.[10] And each of the two displaced officers felt it necessary, even a year later, to publish letters concerning the Senate's refusal to let them serve in the reduced and reorganized Army where their superiors wanted them to be.[11] If there had ever been any doubt that the Senate's course had been politically motivated, that question was answered affirmatively when that body's executive proceedings since January in respect to the realignment of Army officers were made public, contrary to ordinary practice, at the time of the announcement of the second rejections.[12]

The Senate's adamancy had long-term effects. One was that the administration was made willing, in respect to a minor question, "to avoid further conflict." Monroe pointed out to his Cabinet that nominations of certain Army officers to certain ranks had been confirmed but not as of the dates on which he had proposed that the new commissions should become effective. The Cabinet decided to yield: the new commissions should be issued as of the day of the Senate's approval.[13] A second effect was that the two positions that Towson and Gadsden were not allowed to occupy remained vacant throughout the three remaining years of Monroe's second administration.[14] To be without an Adjutant

---

Washington, D.C., *Daily National Intelligencer,* May 4, 1822, p. 3, col. 5; entry of May 5, 1822, in the Diary of John Quincy Adams, Massachusetts Historical Society (published microfilm of the Adams Family Papers, roll 35).

[10] Washington, D.C., *Daily National Intelligencer,* April 3, 1822, p. 3, col. 5.

[11] *Ibid.,* February 24, 1823, p. 2, cols. 2–3, and April 7, 1823, p. 2, cols. 1–4.

[12] Harry Ammon, *James Monroe: the Quest for National Identity* (New York: McGraw-Hill Book Company, c. 1971), p. 661. Compare the entry of May 5, 1822, in the Diary of John Quincy Adams, Massachusetts Historical Society (published microfilm of the Adams Family Papers, roll 35).

[13] Entry of June 28, 1822, in the Diary of John Quincy Adams, Massachusetts Historical Society (published microfilm of the Adams Family Papers, roll 35).

[14] Ammon, *James Monroe,* p. 501. See also the blanks that appeared where the names of the Adjutant General and of the Colonel of the 2nd Regiment of Artillery could have been printed in the Army Registers dated August, 1822, February, 1823, January, 1824, and January, 1825, in William A. Gordon, *A Compilation of Registers of the Army of the United States, from 1815 to 1837 (Inclusive) . . .* (Washington: James C. Dunn, printer, 1837), pp. 221, 224, 233, 237, 247, 251, 263, and 267.

General, who could serve as the Army's chief personnel officer and more, was indubitably a serious handicap, because Calhoun's concept of efficient administration emphasized the value of staff bureaus under qualified chieftains directly responsible to himself, each supervising a distinct and cohesive function of Army services. The bureau survived, of course, with a few Clerks, because it was necessary, but without an ideal administrator. Maj. Gen. Jacob Brown, the military commander of the whole Army, devoted some of his time to personnel matters and sometimes even signed letters as "Adjutant General"; and Capt. Charles J. Nourse is reported to have served as Acting Adjutant General from May 8, 1822, to March 7, 1825.[15]

What became of the unfortunate men who had been pawns in Crawford's and Congress's political chess game? James Gadsden left the Army, without even the formality of writing a letter of resignation, because he had no office to relinquish. He settled in Florida for 16 years, returned to his native South Carolina, utilized his knowledge of engineering in connection with transportation developments, and served the United States in diplomacy.[16] He left Calhoun in 1823, but he did not leave Calhoun's career forever. In contrast, Col. Nathan Towson spent the remainder of his life, until 1854, in the Army. Calhoun managed to retain Towson's services by appointing him, as of May 8, 1822, to be the Paymaster General of the Army—the headship of the staff bureau from which Towson had been removed almost one year earlier to take the command position in the line that the Senate had later denied to him.[17] And therein hangs a tale, one in which the alert John Quincy Adams saw political implications, as usual.

In order to make room for Col. Towson's appointment as Paymaster General, Brig. Gen. Daniel Parker of Massachusetts had to be dismissed from that office. That was a step not to be taken lightly. He had been the Chief Clerk of the War Department, virtually Undersecretary of War, during the War of 1812. In 1814 he had begun to serve for seven years as the Adjutant and Inspector

[15] Francis B. Heitman, *Historical Register and Dictionary of the United States Army, from Its Organization* . . . (2 vols. Washington: Government Printing Office, 1903), 1:753.

[16] *Ibid.*, 1:441; J. Fred Rippy, "James Gadsden," in Allen Johnson and Dumas Malone, eds., *Dictionary of American Biography* (22 vols. New York: Charles Scribner's Sons, 1928–1944), 7:83–84.

[17] Heitman, *Historical Register*, 1:968.

General of the Army, and for almost a year he had been the Paymaster General. Lightly or not, Calhoun and Monroe had decided to dispense with Parker even before the Senate's refusal to approve the Artillery appointment to which they had assigned Towson. In May of 1821, when Andrew Jackson was exchanging a military office for a civil one, he had warned Calhoun quite pointedly that Parker was a man who lacked "talents and magnanimity," one who had specifically given aid and comfort to Calhoun's Congressional enemies when a report made by the South Carolinian was under attack.[18] In February, 1822, Calhoun had summoned Parker into the Secretary of War's office and had asked point-blankly whether or not Parker "had spoken in a spirit of ridicule or censure" about any of Calhoun's reports. Parker had refused to answer the question, although Calhoun had insisted that certainly Parker "knew whether he had so spoken." Calhoun considered himself as having been "ill-treated," John Quincy Adams was told by Monroe. "I suppose," Adams decided, that "this was the decisive cause" of Parker's removal from his office.[19] But there were other reasons as well. For one, mutual dislike had existed between Monroe and Parker since 1813.[20]

The dismissed Parker, "deeply exasperated at the treatment he had received," promptly poured out his soul for many hours in repeated interviews with Adams, not simply because he wondered if he could obtain a Clerkship in the Department of State. He had already received and declined an offer of such a position in the Treasury Department, on the very day of his dismissal, from William H. Crawford, who had sent to Parker in advance a warning "that there was an intrigue for turning him out of office." (Crawford might well have used for political advantage Parker's knowledge of War Department affairs.) Adams listened sympathetically, with the avidity of a man who suspected one of his rivals of making a mistake, to Parker's recital of Calhoun's self-contradictory and allegedly insincere explanations to Parker why he had been discharged. The reasons attributed by Parker to Calhoun, Adams concluded, sounded "addly"—that is, addle-brained—"to

[18] Andrew Jackson to John C. Calhoun, May 22, 1821, in Hemphill, ed., *The Papers of John C. Calhoun,* 6:142–143.

[19] Entry of May 13, 1822, in the Diary of John Quincy Adams, Massachusetts Historical Society (published microfilm of the Adams Family Papers, roll 35). Monroe told Adams early in April, 1822, that "Parker had treated Mr. Calhoun ill" and was to be dismissed. Entry of April 4, 1822, in *ibid.*

[20] Entry of June 2, 1822, in *ibid.*

me." More was at stake than a staff position in the War Department. Rivalries for the Presidential office itself were involved. Parker feigned "an air and tone of indifference" but would probably in the future revive agitation over his having been replaced. Adams foresaw no immediate repercussions upon himself but decided to be on guard.[21]

As if the statute for reduction of the Army in 1821 had not been drastic enough, the House of Representatives considered in the spring of 1822 a bill for a further reduction of the military establishment. Debate on this new proposal consumed a large majority of the House's time on April 15 and 16. The proposed crippling of the Army, if approved, would limit the military establishment to a yet smaller number of high officers and would assign to them lower ranks. For example, the office held by Maj. Gen. Jacob Brown as the military commander of the whole Army would be abolished, plus those of his two aides-de-camp; in lieu of these three positions, the bill would permit one Brigadier General with one aide. Proponents of the bill, identifiable chiefly as partisans of Crawford, pictured staff officers as a swarm of supernumeraries having so little to do that they were to all intents and purposes unemployed. Calhoun's friends portrayed them as being busy in the performance of necessary and useful duties. Moreover, Representatives Edward Fenwick Tattnall of Georgia, George McDuffie and Joel R. Poinsett of South Carolina, and Micah Sterling of New York argued that ruinously weakening the Army would result in quite small economies at best: the reduction of staff salaries would save less than $22,500 annually and all other provisions of the bill less than $80,500. Even William Eustis, the Chairman of the House Committee on Military Affairs, which had offered the bill, conceded that perhaps it should be killed.[22] That concession seems all the more remarkable when one considers the fact that Eustis avowed later that "he would have broken down Calhoun at the last Session of Congress" if he could have "and that he might yet do it at the next."[23]

If the bill had been voted by both houses of Congress, Monroe

[21] *Ibid.*

[22] *Annals of Congress,* 17th Cong., 1st Sess., cols. 1565–1611; Washington, D.C., *Daily National Intelligencer,* April 22, 1822, p. 2, col. 4, through p. 3, col. 1, and May 1, 1822, p. 2, cols. 1–4.

[23] Entry of June 2, 1822, in the Diary of John Quincy Adams, Massachusetts Historical Society (published microfilm of the Adams Family Papers, roll 35).

would have vetoed it. Indeed, he drafted reasons, in case they should be needed, that "he intended to assign" for his disapproval. He considered the proposed further reduction to be "most pernicious" and might as well "say so" publicly. In both houses of Congress opponents of the administration "were already as inveterate as they could be"; to give them one more bone of contention, Monroe believed, would make their influence "no greater nor more mischievous."[24]

Another economy move also failed in Congress. The House Committee on Retrenchment offered on April 24 a bill under which the salaries of employees in the executive branch of the government would be lowered substantially. The annual compensation received by the Secretaries of the State, Treasury, War, and Navy Departments would each be reduced, by $1,000, to $5,000 for 1822. All Clerks in the government's service would receive one-fifth less than in 1821.[25] But the annual act for civilian salaries, approved on April 30 (at the end of the fourth month after the fiscal year had begun), maintained Calhoun's salary at the $6,000 level and provided him with almost $75,000 for the men other than soldiers who were employed in the War Department's bureaus and for such supplies as fuel and stationery.[26] Thus financed, the staff could function at approximately its recent pace.

Appropriations and Fortifications

To readers of the preceding pages one conclusion must have become clear: some members of both houses of Congress were really at war against Calhoun. To John Quincy Adams, who was also subject to attacks because he was also a loyal supporter of the policies of Monroe's administration, it seemed that almost every member of Congress could be classified as an adherent of one or the other of three men. These three were William H. Crawford, Henry Clay, and Calhoun—and Adams felt confident that Crawford's faction was the strongest, Calhoun's the weakest. In order to prevent any victory by Calhoun's, the other two were likely

[24] Entry of April 22, 1822, in *ibid.*

[25] Washington, D.C., *Daily National Intelligencer,* April 26, 1822, p. 3, col. 3.

[26] *Ibid.,* May 3, 1822, p. 2, col. 2; *Annals of Congress,* 17th Cong., 1st Sess., cols. 2592–2599, especially 2595–2596.

to combine their strength.[27] Crawford was generally known to have become himself at war against his colleagues of the administration. Clay had rarely been aligned with it since its beginning in 1817. The executive branch of the government had little chance to win in Congress.

From Calhoun's viewpoint, this Congressional picture must have been disheartening indeed. Not only were his friends outnumbered; they were also misplaced, in that they did not hold key positions. Men who often opposed Calhoun served as the chairmen of practically every committee in each branch of Congress with which he had to deal. Examples are William Eustis of the House Committee on Military Affairs and John Williams of the Senate's corresponding committee. When Philip Pendleton Barbour of Virginia was elected Speaker of the House in December, 1821, conservative Republicans or antiadministration factions of the party gained control of that body for the first time since 1807. The irony was that Calhoun had been influential, for reasons that seemed good to him at the time, in elevating Barbour. Calhoun had not foreseen that the new Speaker would make the committee appointments that he did and would soon identify himself with the partisans of Crawford.[28] John Quincy Adams, a fellow sufferer from the same developments, repeatedly reminded Calhoun about his blame and that he had made his own bed.[29]

Crawford's so-called Radical faction of the Republican party predominated and had key positions in Congress, but it did not succeed in changing things as radically as one might expect. Congressmen talked much about extravagance and mismanagement in the War Department, but they made appropriations for its operations at roughly the levels of recent years.[30] Approved on March 15, 1822, were appropriations to it for that year totaling almost $3,900,000. Within that sum were individual items such as almost $1,000,000 for the pay of the soldiers and the subsistence of officers and almost $2,000,000 for pensions.[31] Added on May 7 of and

[27] Entry of June 2, 1822, in the Diary of John Quincy Adams, Massachusetts Historical Society (published microfilm of the Adams Family Papers, roll 35).

[28] Hemphill, ed., *The Papers of John C. Calhoun,* 5:xxvii–xxviii and 6:xvii; Ammon, *James Monroe,* p. 499.

[29] Entry of May 8, 1822, in the Diary of John Quincy Adams, Massachusetts Historical Society (published microfilm of the Adams Family Papers, roll 35).

[30] Ammon, *James Monroe,* p. 499.

[31] *Annals of Congress,* 17th Cong., 1st Sess., cols. 2576–2577.

for the same year were supplementary appropriations of nearly $1,000,000 more for the Department's use in respect to Indian affairs and for various other needs plus a total of $370,000 for eight of the coastal fortifications upon which it had begun construction.[32]

Nor did the financial limitations of the War Department become drastically truncated in 1823. This proved to be true despite the fact that the economy bloc continued to maintain its strong grip upon Congress during the session of 1822–1823. In vain, for example, did the former Speaker of the House who professed to have become friendlier to the administration, John W. Taylor, seek to displace Barbour.[33] Several appropriation bills were enacted by the session on the day of its adjournment, March 3, 1823. That for civilian salaries included $56,850 for the War Department, including $6,000 for Calhoun's own compensation.[34] The major statute for the military service itemized a total of more than $4,132,000, with its two largest items reduced by only about $100,000 because some Revolutionary pensioners would die.[35] Allotments for Indian affairs totaled approximately $200,000, the level that had proved to be necessary during the past two years despite efforts to economize.[36] Expenditures for eight fortifications were authorized at more than $500,000, and almost $50,000 were added for two unrelated items.[37] A separate act authorized the making of a survey, at a cost not exceeding $5,000, to discover the best location for a proposed national armory in the West and required a report to Congress on that subject.[38]

[32] *Ibid.,* cols. 2618–2620; Washington, D.C., *Daily National Intelligencer,* May 16, 1822, p. 2, cols. 1–2.

[33] Entry of November 30, 1822, in the Diary of John Quincy Adams, Massachusetts Historical Society (published microfilm of the Adams Family Papers, roll 35).

[34] *Annals of Congress,* 17th Cong., 2nd Sess., cols. 1382–1388.

[35] *Ibid.,* cols. 1370–1372; Washington, D.C., *Daily National Intelligencer,* March 13, 1823, p. 2, col. 5.

[36] *Annals of Congress,* 17th Cong., 2nd Sess., cols. 1372–1373; Washington, D.C., *Daily National Intelligencer,* March 13, 1823, p. 2, col. 5, through p. 3, col. 1.

[37] *Annals of Congress,* 17th Cong., 2nd Sess., col. 1411; Washington, D.C., *Daily National Intelligencer,* March 17, 1823, p. 2, col. 2.

[38] *Annals of Congress,* 17th Cong., 2nd Sess., col. 1416. For bits of information relevant to the growing demand in the Senate and in the House that a third, Western armory should be considered see the Washington, D.C., *Daily National Intelligencer,* December 6, 1822, p. 3, col. 2, and Richardson, *Messages and Papers of the Presidents,* 2:136 and 198.

The totals of such figures meant that funds in the neighborhood of $5,000,000 were placed at the Department's disposal in each of the years 1822 and 1823. Those totals were not markedly different from what had been available in 1821. But all three of those stringent years were in sharp contrast to the more than $9,500,000 that it could have spent during twelve months that preceded slightly the date on which Calhoun had assumed the duties of its Secretary.[39] In keeping with the belt-tightening times of the early 1820's, the Army was forced to live on reduced financial rations. Its creativity was curtailed. It could adopt no such new, pioneering, nation-building ventures as Calhoun had sponsored recently in establishing Army posts, for example, at Council Bluffs on the Missouri and at St. Peters on the Mississippi.

The funds voted for the Army were in some instances more than Calhoun in his gloomiest moods may have expected. Among the appropriations for fortifications in 1822 and 1823 that have been mentioned were included $175,000 for Fort Monroe and $130,000 for Fort Calhoun. Those two construction projects were to become the twin bastions that would guard the entrance into the Chesapeake Bay, the route by which the British navy had transported the enemy soldiers who had burned the nation's capital so ignominiously in 1814. Each was destined to be useful for about a century, until improvements in military and naval aircraft and in other weapons began to make them potentially obsolete. In a nation whose national anthem glorifies the successful resistance of Fort McHenry, near Baltimore, against those War of 1812 invaders, the strategic importance of Forts Monroe and Calhoun does not need to be explained.

Appropriations for their continued construction probably seemed to Calhoun, however, to be anything but assured. The House of Representatives voted on April 22, 1822, to launch an investigation—not the first—of the contract under which Elijah Mix had obligated himself in 1818 to deliver building stones that were being used at both of the two sites.[40] Ingredients out of which political hay could be made were plentiful in what had developed since; but the story does not need to be retold in these pages. A few aspects of the matter should suffice. Calhoun was not a party to the contract; his former subordinate, Bvt. Brig. Gen. and Chief Engineer Joseph G. Swift, had signed it for the United States. Calhoun's Chief Clerk, Christopher Vandeventer, also

[39] Hemphill, ed., *The Papers of John C. Calhoun,* 2:51.

[40] *Annals of Congress,* 17th Cong., 1st Sess., cols. 1629–1630.

signed the document as a witness. More implicating were the facts that Vandeventer was a brother-in-law of Mix and purchased a share of Mix's interest. Vandeventer's investment in the contract was condemned by Calhoun promptly and in no uncertain terms. Vendeventer sold his share "within a few months," but it had already exposed him "to improper insinuations," he confessed in a public apology. "To me it has been a source of deep regret, not because I violated any law, or that the public has sustained any loss, but because it has been a source of misrepresentation and much vexation."[41] An act of such poor judgment by an associate so close to him must certainly have been scarcely less embarrassing to Calhoun.

Over a less sordid focal point of attack Calhoun could have had no direct control whatsoever. The contract was alleged by his enemies to be unduly costly to the public and enormously profitable to Mix and to those who became associated with him. Such accusations were possibly true, although not fully so. When the purchasing power of a dollar amid the prosperity of 1818 is taken into account and when rival bids are considered, the payments promised to Mix were low. But the Panic of 1819 and consequent increases in the buying power of money made the contract become by 1822, as Vandeventer admitted, less favorable to the government and more so to businessmen, although even then it seemed "only moderately profitable to the contractors."[42]

The House committee proceeded industriously for more than two weeks with its investigation. Its extensive report, widely published when newspaper editors could manage, filled many a newspaper column.[43] Not until May 7, the day preceding adjournment, did it submit to the House its report, which urged in vain that no further appropriations should be made for expenditure under the Mix contract.[44] The fact that the report also vindicated all persons who were involved in the matter may have been counterbalanced in public opinion by the mere fact that there had been an investigation of possible wrongdoing among public employees.

[41] Christopher Vandeventer to the Editor of the Washington, D.C., *City Gazette,* April 20, 1822, reprinted in the Washington, D.C., *Daily National Intelligencer,* April 24, 1822, p. 3, col. 3.

[42] *Ibid.*

[43] See, for example, *ibid.,* June 7, 1822, p. 2, cols. 1–5; June 8, 1822, p. 2, cols. 1–4; June 11, 1822, p. 2, cols. 1–3; and June 12, 1822, p. 2, cols. 1–3. Other, related documents appeared in *ibid.,* June 15, 1822, p. 2, cols. 1–3, and June 19, 1822, p. 2, cols. 3–4.

[44] *Ibid.,* May 8, 1822, p. 3, col. 3.

What was probably the nation's most powerful newspaper, not conspicuously a supporter of Calhoun, twice felt it desirable to publish corrective editorials. One emphasized the injustice that had been done to the government by overly suspicious observers.[45] The other, much more specific, pronounced as "preposterous" any charge that Calhoun had participated criminally in the contract and declared, as that embattled executive doubtless wished quite devoutly, that such accusations would be remembered "only with contempt" until they should pass soon into "oblivion."[46] But people sometimes have long memories. Calhoun had not heard the last of the Mix contract. Neither had Vandeventer. Monroe nominated him twice in 1823 to be the Navy Agent at New York City, and twice the Senate refused to confirm him. What he had done was "neither contrary to law nor injurious to the public interest"; in two investigations he had been fully exonerated; but his complicity with his brother-in-law had been neither forgotten nor forgiven, a newspaper reported.[47]

If there had not been malfeasance in office in connection with Fort Calhoun, perhaps there had been culpable inefficiency. The House Committee on Military Affairs proposed to send two of its members early in 1823 to investigate at the site. So wrote its Chairman, William Eustis, to Calhoun. Feeling concerned over the implications, Calhoun shared the request with President Monroe; he, in turn, discussed with Cabinet members a proposed reply that he had drafted for Calhoun. It would respond affirmatively by giving assurance that the requested facilities for accommodation of the junketing Congressmen would be provided by the commanding officer at Hampton Roads. But larger issues were also involved in the proposition. Committees of Congress might make personal investigations in connection with appropriations or with impeachments; but Monroe doubted their right to do so at public expense for such a personal inspection of progress being made by the executive branch of government. And he was led directly into a discussion with John Quincy Adams about the political ramifications suggested by such a trip and about the "double dealing" that he saw in the conduct of the Radicals.[48]

[45] *Ibid.*, May 28, 1822, p. 3, col. 2.

[46] *Ibid.*, June 7, 1822, p. 3, col. 1.

[47] *Ibid.*, April 4, 1823, p. 2, col. 4.

[48] Entry of January 2, 1823, in the Diary of John Quincy Adams, Massachusetts Historical Society (published microfilm of the Adams Family Papers, roll 37).

Congress's grants of funds to the War Department said plainly that the War Department could not expand its program. A pointed and repeated denial of funds told the Army unmistakably that it could not even resume a halted project. Construction of a fort on Dauphin Island in Mobile Bay had been arrested in 1821, because Congress had flatly denied any money for that installation. President Monroe and the Army's Board of Engineers considered the proposed fortification to be essential for the defense of Mobile and of strategic importance for the protection of New Orleans; to remove that link in the chain of coastal fortifications was to vitiate the value of a unified whole that was one of Monroe's favorite objectives. He pleaded repeatedly with Congress for resumption of progress at Dauphin Island.[49]

Presidential pleas and the informed advice of military and naval experts were ignored once more. As Chairman of the House Committee on Military Affairs, William Eustis rejected all importunities and counsel pointing out the crucial nature of the unfinished Dauphin Island project. He argued that the program for fortifications was an expense that the nation could ill afford: more than twelve percent of the government's borrowings totaling $8,000,000 in 1820 and 1821 had been appropriated to fortifications in those years. He contended that large sums of money had been paid in advance to, but used inefficiently by, contractors both at Dauphin Island and at Mobile Point. And he concluded, without reservation, "that it is inexpedient to construct the projected fortification on Dauphin Island."[50] That became Congress's decision as well. Not one cent was appropriated in 1822 or in 1823 for expenditure at that site. For three consecutive years, therefore, the project was pointedly rejected.

The administration thus suffered another setback. John Quincy Adams discussed it at length with Eustis on a Sunday. Adams's diary recorded the conference, complete with even some gossipy revelations about attitudes that lay behind the stalemate. "I told him I was exceedingly concerned at this misunderstanding, growing up between the President and both Houses of Congress; and that he ought to use his endeavours to conciliate." Eustis answered that he had offered, as a compromise, to seek money for a smaller fortification on Dauphin Island than had been proposed. But he had been assured that the House "would never give a dollar for

[49] Hemphill, ed., *The Papers of John C. Calhoun,* 6:xiii–xiv.

[50] *Annals of Congress,* 17th Cong., 1st Sess., cols. 1540–1544. Compare Ammon, *James Monroe,* pp. 499–500.

it." The opposition had been angered because women "were making themselves very busy" in the contest; Eustis named Mrs. [John C.] Calhoun and two Army wives, Mrs. [Joseph] Lovell and Mrs. [John E.] Wool, and indicated that other petticoat lobbyists were also involved. Representative John Cocke of Tennessee felt that President Monroe had tried, with arrogance, to appeal from Congress to the people at large.

Nor did it sit well, as the saying goes, with some humiliated but defiant legislators that progress had been halted toward construction of the companion fort on Mobile Point. Samuel Hawkins, the contractor there, had died after having received large advances, had done little but begin to assemble some materials, and had left an insolvent estate. One of the bondsmen under Hawkins's contract was Nicholas Gouverneur of New York, and Samuel L. Gouverneur of the same State was a son-in-law of James Monroe. So, if good money were poured after bad into the Mobile Point fortification, such funds might rescue Hawkins's bondsmen, who were distantly connected with the White House itself.[51]

Could anything be done to break the stalemate? Calhoun and Adams advised Monroe in 1822 that, in order to protect the public from loss, the government had only one recourse. The United States should sue Hawkins's bondsmen for the funds that had been advanced without comparable value having been received in return. The bondsmen could then petition Congress for recovery of any judgment against them, perhaps making their appeal on the ground that they had suffered some breach of contract. Monroe saw no other alternative but decided to obtain an official opinion from Attorney General William Wirt before resorting to any such distressing course.[52]

The Abolition of the Factory System

Congress was cruel in destroying, also, another long-term part of the War Department's program. Since the last years of the eighteenth century the United States had maintained trading establishments, often called Factories, for the benefit of the Indians. Through them it provided, at prices usually considered to be lower

[51] Entry of April 14, 1822, in the Diary of John Quincy Adams, Massachusetts Historical Society (published microfilm of the Adams Family Papers, roll 35).

[52] Entry of May 30, 1822, in *ibid.*

than private enterprisers would have adopted, blankets and other necessities upon which the aborigines were dependent. Moreover, the Factories served to reduce, although by no means to prevent, illicit traffic in alcoholic beverages. And, because each Factory was likely to be located near both an Army post and an Indian Agency, it helped such other governmental services to maintain peace between the tribes and between them and their nearest white neighbors. A fourth advantage was that the Factories afforded a steady market at fair prices for the furs that the Indians frequently offered in exchange for goods. In other words, the motivation of the Factory system had been largely humanitarian from the first, and this remained conspicuously true of its purposes and operations about 1820. Calhoun and Monroe viewed it in benevolent terms, and nobody can doubt the sympathetic attitude toward the Indians of the former merchant who served during 1816–1822 as the Superintendent of Indian Trade, Thomas L. McKenney.

But some others judged the Factory system in the hard-boiled terms of businessmen. Were the approximately 20 government trading establishments, they asked, too few in number and so immobile that some Indians preferred to exchange furs for blankets with roving British traders? Was the government losing all or part of the capital that it had invested in purchasing the goods that the Factories offered? Were the salaries of the Factors too expensive? Were the stores making a profit or losing money? Were records being kept with sufficient efficiency for such questions to be answered at all? Were the private fur traders who coexisted with the Factory system being denied by that near-monopoly a capitalistic system's chance to earn profits? John Jacob Astor of New York and his subordinates in the American Fur Company sought for years to eliminate their governmental competition. So did the Missouri Fur Company.

To discern the strengths and weaknesses of such conflicting views is not essential here. It is enough simply to report that Congress showed more concern for private businessmen than for the Indians. The Missourians found a relentless champion in one of their Senators, Thomas Hart Benton; and the New Yorkers had the joy of seeing one of theirs, Martin Van Buren, make common but less boisterous cause with Benton in attaining success in 1822.[53]

[53] Ammon, *James Monroe,* p. 500. For much more information about the Factory system see Francis Paul Prucha, *American Indian Policy in the Formative Years: the Indian Trade and Intercourse Acts, 1790–1834* (Cam-

The Factory system, Senator Benton declaimed, "grew out of a national calamity, and had been one itself." It was, he insisted, "worse than useless."[54] It mattered little that the public heard also respectable testimony, from persons who had an eyewitness knowledge of the actual value of the government trading houses, to diametrically opposite effect. For example, George C. Sibley, who knew much also about both the Indians west of the Mississippi and the Missouri Fur Company, contributed to a newspaper in mid-April, 1822, a stout defense of the Factory system, although he was confident that he was doing so in a losing cause.[55]

His despair was justified. Monroe felt that he was compelled to sign on May 6, 1822, a bill that abolished the government trading houses. The suddenness with which the law was to be put into effect was shocking. Monroe was to appoint persons who were to receive from Thomas L. McKenney and all of his subordinates "all the goods, wares, and merchandise, furs, peltries, evidences of debt, and property and effects of every kind" that belonged to the United States—and this transfer was to be made on or before June 2, 1822, or as soon thereafter as possible. All such property was to be sold; the accounts of McKenney, his Factors, and his Sub-Factors were to be closed; and all proceeds were to benefit the United States treasury. Monroe was required to report, soon after the convening of the next session of Congress, how and with what results the government had been extricated from the Indian trade.[56]

Not conspicuously unnatural but doubtless galling to Calhoun was the fact that the newly appointed receivers of the Factory system were not to serve under and to report to him; they would be agents of Secretary of the Treasury William H. Crawford. Something was said in at least one Cabinet meeting about the disposal of such goods; but for some reason John Quincy Adams barely mentioned that development without adding in his diary

---

bridge, Mass.: Harvard University Press, c. 1962), especially pp. 84–93, 109–110, 215–216, 219–221, and Hemphill, ed., *The Papers of John C. Calhoun*, vols. II–VI.

[54] Benton's speech in the Senate, March 25, 1822, in the Washington, D.C., *Daily National Intelligencer*, April 10, 1822, p. 2, cols. 1–5.

[55] *Ibid.*, April 18, 1822, p. 2, cols. 1–3. For praise and criticism in the House of Representatives on May 4, 1822, of the existing programs for the Indian trade and for the civilization of the Indians, see the *Annals of Congress*, 17th Cong., 1st Sess., cols. 1792–1801.

[56] *Annals of Congress*, 17th Cong., 1st Sess., cols. 2606–2608.

any other details.[57] The textual pages of this book include evidence that Calhoun directed his Indian Agents to buy from Crawford's men as much of the goods of the former Factories as could be used properly for gifts to the Indians.

If the government was removing itself from the Indian trade, it should do something to regulate the private businessmen whose activities might be expanded accordingly. A companion statute to that for abolition of the Factories was enacted on the same day, May 6, 1822. Superintendents of Indian Affairs and Indian Agents, who were responsible to Calhoun, were authorized to issue licenses to citizens of the United States to trade with Indians. Licenses could be effective for not more than two years east of the Mississippi and seven west of that river. Licensees were to post bonds of as much as $5,000. If a trader had alcoholic beverages among his goods, all of his stock in trade could be seized, with half to be given to any informer who might have suggested the search and the remainder to benefit the government; a guilty trader was also to have his license canceled and his bond put in suit. The profits of traders were protected by a requirement that all purchases of goods by the government to be used for annuities and gifts to the Indians were to be made locally by the Superintendents and Agents of Indian Affairs.[58]

This new law gave legal status to two new Superintendents of Indian Affairs—to one because Missouri's status had changed from that of a Territory, to the other because Florida's provisional Territorial government was being regularized. The jurisdiction of William Clark as the Superintendent of Indian Affairs resident at St. Louis extended far beyond the boundaries of the State of Missouri. As following pages show, Calhoun relied upon one of the men who had been discharged in the reduction of the Army, former Lt. Col. Gad Humphreys, to assume the duties of Superintendent of Indian Affairs in the Territory of Florida. The salary of each of these men was $1,500 annually.[59]

[57] Entry of June 3, 1822, in the Diary of John Quincy Adams, Massachusetts Historical Society (published microfilm of the Adams Family Papers, roll 35).

[58] *Annals of Congress,* 17th Cong., 1st Sess., cols. 2610–2612.

[59] *Ibid.* When Missouri relinquished its Territorial status, Clark lost automatically the position of Territorial Superintendent of Indian Affairs. For some information about his retention in a similar capacity during a transition year, 1821–1822, until the new law created a Superintendency for someone who would be resident in St. Louis, see the index entries under Clark's name in Hemphill, ed., *The Papers of John C. Calhoun,* vol. VI.

As had been required, Monroe did assure Congress promptly that the administration had fulfilled all "injunctions" of the law that closed the business of the trading houses.[60] In response to a House resolution requesting more specific information, he transmitted to that body two reports by Crawford.[61] Because promises had been made in treaties with the Osage and the Sauk Indians that Factories would be maintained for their benefit, Calhoun's subordinates had been forced to negotiate with those tribes new treaties that would eliminate that obligation. These new agreements were submitted to the Senate for ratification early in 1823.[62] A report by the House Committee on Indian Affairs about the execution of the law for the exit of government from the Indian trade very nearly wrote *finis* to the voluminous Congressional documentation concerning the Factories.[63] If Calhoun ever indulged in bitter thoughts about the demise of a program that he and many enlightened persons both in and out of the administration had supported heartily, a loose analogy may have occurred to him: the system was murdered in 1822, and its obituaries were written in 1823 by its murderers.

Other Indian Affairs

Calhoun and the War Department still remained, however, in charge of Indian affairs. Indian Agents and the Army still labored together, combining persuasion and force, respectively, for the accomplishment of United States objectives in regard to the tribes. Among the chief of these was to keep peace—a task not so easy as it sounds. Another was to promote emigration by Eastern tribes to reservations west of the Mississippi and, as in the case of the Choctaws, to provide them with definable boundaries for such a Western reservation.[64] Treaty obligations needed to be respected

[60] Monroe's sixth annual Message to the Senate and House of Representatives, December 3, 1822, in Richardson, *Messages and Papers of the Presidents,* 2:189.

[61] James Monroe to the House of Representatives, January 6, 1823, and February 19, 1823, in *ibid.,* 2:197–198 and 204.

[62] James Monroe to the Senate, January 6, 1823, in *ibid.,* 2:198.

[63] Washington, D.C., *Daily National Intelligencer,* March 22, 1823, p. 3, cols. 1–2.

[64] Monroe relayed a report by Calhoun about the Choctaws' Western boundaries. James Monroe to the House of Representatives, February 6, 1823, in Richardson, *Messages and Papers of the Presidents,* 2:201.

on both sides, annuities paid under those agreements with the Indian "nations," and new understandings negotiated. Long-unsettled disputes remained to be resolved—for example, the claims of Georgians against the Creeks for losses suffered and payable under treaties antedating 1800.[65] New funds were appropriated in 1822 with which the land hunger of Georgia might be satisfied by negotiating with the Creeks and the Eastern Cherokees for cessions of their lands that still lay within the boundaries of that State.[66] A projected treaty with those Cherokees was delayed throughout the remainder of the year by resignations of men who had been appointed to meet with the Indians. And, as the following pages also show, those Indians positively refused even to enter upon any negotiation early in 1823 that might end in their relinquishing their claim to any lands.[67] The situation was further complicated by the illness and death, near the same time, of the Eastern Cherokee Indian Agent, the veteran Return J. Meigs. To replace him, Monroe appointed, with the Senate's consent, Joseph McMinn,[68] the recent Governor of Tennessee.

To such setbacks Calhoun had probably grown accustomed. Five years of experience in supervising Indian affairs, the distance and slow communications between his headquarters and the tribes, and other factors would have inured him to delays. Impatient though he often seemed, he could scarcely have expected utopia to arrive overnight in that facet of his responsibilities anyway. Certainly he and others who were familiar with the Indians did not count upon quick results from their program for educating and Christianizing thousands of native Americans whose languages and habits and superstitions and religious ideas were so totally foreign to the white man's equivalents. What was being done

[65] Calhoun advocated in a Cabinet meeting a generous but legalistic and not extravagant attitude toward the Georgians' claims. Entry of May 25, 1822, in the Diary of John Quincy Adams, Massachusetts Historical Society (published microfilm of the Adams Family Papers, roll 35).

[66] *Annals of Congress,* 17th Cong., 1st Sess., cols. 2618–2620; Washington, D.C., *Daily National Intelligencer,* May 16, 1822, p. 2, cols. 1–2.

[67] The Washington, D.C., *Daily National Intelligencer,* March 25, 1823, p. 3, col. 3, reprinted from two Georgia newspapers stories about how adamant the Cherokees had been in refusing to meet the United States commissioners. For documents relevant to Indian lands in Georgia and in Missouri see James Monroe to the Senate and House of Representatives, February 3, 1823, and James Monroe to the Senate, February 14, 1823, in Richardson, *Messages and Papers of the Presidents,* 2:200 and 202, respectively.

[68] Washington, D.C., *Daily National Intelligencer,* March 15, 1823, p. 3, col. 3.

for the civilization of the Indians was deliberately beamed chiefly at Indian children. The success of the effort would depend upon results that would span not less than a generation.[69] The reaching of intermediate milestones would be nonetheless gratifying, however, and the textual pages of this book include heartening signs that the government-aided schools for Indians were growing both in numbers and in effectiveness.

The abolition of the Factory system left Calhoun more exclusively responsible for Indian affairs than he had been previously. The former, semi-independent Office of Indian Trade was no more; its final Superintendent, McKenney, Calhoun's personal friend, was out of a job. The War Department, which had been responsible previously for administration of the laws governing private trade with the Indians, had to absorb the new duty of licensing additional private traders. And this was true despite its having been given neither new funds nor additional personnel for service in Washington headquarters or in the field. With his characteristic concern for efficiency and direct responsibility in governmental organization, Calhoun was destined to do all that he could to improve this situation: he created in 1824 a Bureau of Indian Affairs in the War Department.

Calhoun in the Cabinet

That there was outright friction between the legislative and executive branches of the United States government in 1822 has already been revealed. Calhoun commented to John Quincy Adams, on the day of the adjournment of Congress, that "there had never been such a state of things in this Government before." Indeed, to Adams it seemed that "Calhoun spoke to me with great bitterness of the proceedings of both houses of Congress."[70] Friction existed also within the executive branch itself—so much so that it became public knowledge that members of President James

[69] Compare Hemphill, ed., *The Papers of John C. Calhoun,* vols. IV–VI, and Prucha, *American Indian Policy,* especially pp. 213–224. Representative Thomas Metcalfe of Kentucky tried to persuade the House of Representatives that the Indians derived no benefits from the civilization program and that the government grants to mission schools should be discontinued. Washington, D.C., *Daily National Intelligencer,* May 11, 1822, p. 2, cols. 1–2, and p. 3, col. 1.

[70] Entry of May 8, 1822, in the Diary of John Quincy Adams, Massachusetts Historical Society (published microfilm of the Adams Family Papers, roll 35).

Monroe's Cabinet were rivals and were working at cross-purposes. And this was embarrassing, because disharmony prevailed in the very place that unity was most diligently cultivated and was most nearly attainable. What is more, the discordant situation raised, in the minds of some observers, a question of loyalty, because one member of the administration seemed to be so much at odds with his chieftain and with his peers.

Calhoun's papers include almost no references to Cabinet meetings. Those consultations of the government's other chief executive officers with Monroe were supposed to be confidential, and Calhoun kept well the tradition of secrecy that promoted free exchanges of opinions. For that matter, so did others of the President's counselors; but John Quincy Adams wrote extensively in his diary about the Cabinet's quite frequent meetings—a practice that violated no obligation, because his comments were long kept private. Only within the past two decades has that record become available in unexpurgated length, in a microfilm edition.

It confirms emphatically some earlier impressions. Monroe avoided one-man decisions; he believed in the value of multiple viewpoints. He tried to rule democratically; he often sought and usually followed the advice of the Secretaries of the State, Treasury, War, and Navy Departments and of the Attorney General, in order that he and they might reach and maintain what would be truly *administration* policies. As frequently as several days within a week and for as many as 20 hours per week, he assembled his colleagues for exhaustive consideration of problems that seem to later generations to have been in some instances obviously major ones but in others quite minor. Thus Calhoun contributed to decisions concerning diplomatic relationships, economic questions, executive appointments, and a wide range of other issues.

The unity of the administration was maintained symbolically. As his wont was, Monroe had Cabinet members join him at the Capitol for his signing of the bills that Congress enacted in the closing days of its sessions.[71] Ceremonial appearances by Cabinet members were not limited to such rare occasions; once, for example, they went together to the Navy Yard to observe a partially successful trial of an invention by Commodore John Rodgers for cradling a ship out of water.[72]

[71] *Ibid.*; entries of March 1 and 3, 1823, in *ibid.* (published microfilm of the Adams Family Papers, roll 38).

[72] Entry of May 9, 1822, in *ibid.* (published microfilm of the Adams Family Papers, roll 35).

The topics that Monroe posed to his Cabinet were varied. On the Monday with which this volume of Calhoun's *Papers* opens the question was whether Monroe should pardon or reprieve a murderer who had been sentenced to be hanged on the next Thursday. William H. Crawford denied any Presidential right to pardon. Calhoun and Secretary of the Navy Smith Thompson took a rather different stance. It was decided that Monroe should seek advice from some judges.[73] While he was preparing to send to Congress a veto message, he tested the reactions of at least two of his Cabinet members, Adams and Calhoun.[74] When the question was whether to take any action because a Navy officer had captured a Spanish privateer, Calhoun thought that the officer's excuse was slender, but Adams discovered a justification for it.[75] When Spain offered a liquidation, Calhoun argued in "clear and unhesitating" terms that it could not properly be received.[76] In another Cabinet meeting the issue posed was whether or not Monroe had ample authority to effect the return of fugitive slaves. Calhoun agreed entirely with Attorney General William Wirt that such power belonged to the Presidential office "but felt more the difficulty of carrying it into execution. Calhoun has no pretty scruples about constructive Powers, and State Rights. His opinions are at least consistent." Adams, yet more politic, thought that "perhaps a Law of Congress may be necessary, providing the process, by which the power should be exercised."[77] At another time, when some proposed commercial arrangements with France were under discussion, Crawford argued, rather typically, against the views of Calhoun, Adams, and Monroe.[78] At Monroe's insistence, Adams sought Calhoun's overnight judgment about the provisions and wording of a Presidential proclamation that would open United States ports to trade from the British West Indies. Calhoun approved an expanded interpretation that was embodied in the text of the document but, unlike Monroe and Adams, suggested a means by which it could be determined, without undue delay, whether the liberal interpretation was within the limits of what Congress had authorized or intended. A Senator's approval was

[73] Entry of April 1, 1822, in *ibid.*

[74] Entry of May 4, 1822, in *ibid.*

[75] Entry of September 17, 1822, in *ibid.*

[76] Entry of March 10, 1823, in *ibid.* (published microfilm of the Adams Family Papers, roll 38).

[77] Entry of October 1, 1822, in *ibid.* (published microfilm of the Adams Family Papers, roll 35).

[78] Entry of May 21, 1822, in *ibid.*

also secured, therefore, although not before Monroe fretted a bit with impatience to initiate an economic arrangement that was vital to the national welfare. And within two weeks the proclamation was published—a step that could be taken by the administration with increased confidence because several possible objections had been anticipated, with resultant revisions in the document.[79]

Calhoun's counsel was often given in relation to other kinds of foreign affairs. Although Adams saw some reasons to advocate the sending of Ministers from the United States to the newborn Latin-American republics, Calhoun and Smith Thompson opposed that idea, and such recognition of them was not then given.[80] Should the United States acquire the Spanish island of Cuba? Several times that question came to the Cabinet in different forms. A secret letter from the island invited United States intervention there, wrote that faithful diarist, John Quincy Adams. "Mr. Calhoun has a most ardent desire that the Island of Cuba should become a part of the United States, and says that Mr. [Thomas] Jefferson has the same. There are two dangers to be averted by that event. One [is] that the Island should fall into the hands of Great Britain; the other that it should be revolutionized by the Negroes. Calhoun says Mr. Jefferson told him two years ago, that we ought at the first possible opportunity to take Cuba, though at the cost of a War with England; but as we are not now prepared for this, and as our great object must be to gain time, he [that is, Calhoun] thought we should answer this overture, by dissuading them from their present purpose, and urging them to adhere at present to their connection with Spain." Adams urged giving to the Cubans "no advice whatever."[81] In four additional sessions of the Cabinet, Adams's policy of noninterference in Spanish affairs prevailed. An answer of that kind was approved.[82]

Later in 1822, in the autumn, the Cabinet discussed a possibility of sending a secret observer to Cuba, chiefly to promote commerce with the United States. Calhoun, "who has a Candidate always ready for every thing," Adams commented with wry humor, im-

[79] Entries of August 14, 15, 20, and 23, 1822, in *ibid.* For the first publication of the proclamation see the Washington, D.C., *Daily National Intelligencer,* August 24, 1822, p. 3, col. 5.

[80] Entry of June 20, 1822, in the Diary of John Quincy Adams, Massachusetts Historical Society (published microfilm of the Adams Family Papers, roll 35).

[81] Entry of September 27, 1822, in *ibid.*

[82] Entries of September 26, 28, 30, and 31, 1822, in *ibid.*

mediately suggested former Lt. Col. William McRee of the Army—a man whom Calhoun characterized as being as "secret as the grave," one who would by temperament "prefer concealing such an appointment to disclosing it." But, it was objected, a confidential role would depend upon other factors. Could such an agent maintain successfully the guise of representing only a commercial firm? The idea died.[83] In 1823, when a citizen of the United States was prepared to go to Cuba without even the cloak of posing as a businessman, the subject was resumed in debates that seemed to Adams to be "almost warm." Calhoun was willing to declare war against Great Britain if that nation intended to take Cuba. Smith Thompson wanted to urge the Cubans to declare their independence if they could maintain it. Adams contended that they could not do so and that, if England wanted to take possession of Cuba, the United States neither could nor would prevent that intervention in New World affairs. Calling Congress into a special session was considered, but three days of such debating ended inconclusively.[84]

Presidential appointments could also provide fuel for the flames of rivalry among Cabinet members. Offices in the Territorial government of Florida, under a statute for replacement of the former provisional establishment there with a regular one,[85] became a bone of contention. Former Governor John Branch of North Carolina was urgently recommended, as a candidate for the Governorship of the Territory, by friends of William H. Crawford. Indeed, their support for Branch was pressed upon Monroe as a test of Crawford's influence over appointments in the administration. A former Representative from Kentucky, William P. DuVal, who was already in Florida as a United States Judge under the provisional government, was also recommended for the same gubernatorial office by other factions of the party. Calhoun doubtless favored DuVal. Monroe nominated DuVal for the Governorship and Branch to be a federal judge in Florida, and the Senate so confirmed them. The entire North Carolina delegation in Congress reacted "in high dudgeon" and with "a concentration of rage" because Branch had not been preferred for the top position. So plain was the North

[83] Entry of November 28, 1822, in *ibid.*

[84] Entries of March 14, 15, and 17, 1823, in *ibid.* (published microfilm of the Adams Family Papers, roll 38).

[85] Statute of March 30, 1822, in *Annals of Congress,* 17th Cong., 1st Sess., cols. 2578–2583; Washington, D.C., *Daily National Intelligencer,* April 4, 1822, p. 2.

Carolinians' resentment that Monroe "considered himself personally insulted by them."[86]

Later in 1822, while Crawford was enjoying a four-months-long absence from Washington,[87] Monroe showed once more a friendship toward Calhoun. To succeed Josiah Meigs, who had died, Monroe chose John McLean, a former Representative from Ohio, to be the new Commissioner of the General Land Office, which was a part of Crawford's Treasury Department. Monroe's motive may have been, in part, to give a sop to a Western State. But the suspicious Adams supposed also that McLean was a friend of Calhoun and that the South Carolinian "has probably suggested the expediency of filling the place, without delay"—that is to say, without even consulting Crawford, under whom McLean would work.[88]

Behind almost all such maneuverings lay the rivalry of Crawford and Calhoun for preferment in the Presidential election that was yet to come in 1824. A third member of the Cabinet, Adams, was also in the race, but not so prominently in that early stage of it. Knowing observers perceived how divisive the contest had become. Former President James Madison, for example, deplored in 1822 "the state of Mr. Monroe's Cabinet, and the personal factions, which have been struggling against each other in Congress"; Madison branded such discord "as a grave and alarming symptom

[86] Entries of April 4, 15, 16, and 20, 1822, in the Diary of John Quincy Adams, Massachusetts Historical Society (published microfilm of the Adams Family Papers, roll 35).

[87] Entry of November 5, 1822, in *ibid.* Smith Thompson was also away from Washington for about an equal amount of time ending a week later. Entry of November 11, 1822, in *ibid.* A Washington newspaper had announced in August that Calhoun, Crawford, and Governor John Clark of Georgia, who was a friend of the former and a political enemy of the latter, had been expected to attend the commencement exercises of Franklin College (now the University of Georgia) in Athens. But the news story added the Calhoun had remained in the capital throughout the summer. Washington, D.C., *Daily National Intelligencer,* August 24, 1822, p. 3, col. 2.

[88] Entry of September 10, 1822, in the Diary of John Quincy Adams, Massachusetts Historical Society (published microfilm of the Adams Family Papers, roll 35). When McLean assumed his duties, it was not Crawford but First Comptroller Joseph Anderson of the Treasury Department who introduced McLean to Adams. Entry of November 14, 1822, in *ibid.* Under the pseudonym of "Benjamin Franklin," McLean had contributed to an Ohio newspaper eight letters published during February–April, 1822, that praised Calhoun and criticized his Presidential rivals. James F. Hopkins and Mary W.M. Hargreaves, eds., *The Papers of Henry Clay* (3 vols. to date. [Lexington:] University of Kentucky Press, c. 1959, 1961, 1963), 3:259.

in our public affairs."[89] Another opinion was that Calhoun's prospects had grown better during the winter of 1821–1822, that Crawford's Congressional friends then adroitly turned the tables upon Calhoun's during the early spring of 1822, that each side would ultimately prostrate the other because of the public disgust engendered by their warfare, and that any President whose Cabinet was so rent by internal dissension should not hesitate to dismiss all of its members.[90]

Whether or not Monroe ever considered, in the inner recesses of his secret and outwardly neutral mind, any such clean sweep of the entire Cabinet cannot be learned now. But three related facts are known. One is that John Quincy Adams predicted to friends in the spring of 1822 that the Cabinet could not remain intact through the next session of Congress, which would end in March, 1823. "Mr. Crawford or Mr. Calhoun, and most probably the latter," Adams expected, "would be compelled to resign. Very probably the case might be my own."[91] A second known fact is that Monroe considered quite seriously removing Crawford but was advised not to do so, lest his dismissal should convert an enemy into a martyred enemy.[92] And a third fact has already been revealed: Monroe often gave to Calhoun stalwart support, not in the political contest itself but in respect to issues that became political footballs. Those two men played as teammates against Crawford's partisans when James Gadsden and Nathan Towson were being denied their appointments, when no funds were appro-

[89] Entry of May 26, 1822, in the Diary of John Quincy Adams, Massachusetts Historical Society (published microfilm of the Adams Family Papers, roll 35).

[90] John Speed Smith to Henry Clay, April 30, 1822, in Hopkins and Hargreaves, eds., *The Papers of Henry Clay,* 3:202–203. Public weariness "with the intrigues of the Cabinet" candidates for the Presidency would provoke people to turn from them to some citizen "unconnected with the administration or Congress," predicted another of Clay's correspondents. William Creighton, Jr., to Henry Clay, May 2, 1822, in *ibid.,* 3:205. Another sign of the self-defeating nature of carping criticisms by partisans that were too overt and unproved was an "indignant" protest against attacks in Congress upon Cabinet members. Such outbursts endangered public confidence in the government, argued the contributor of this public letter. Communication signed "Aristides," in the Washington, D.C., *Daily National Intelligencer,* April 26, 1822, p. 2, col. 3.

[91] Entries of May 9 and June 2, 1822, in the Diary of John Quincy Adams, Massachusetts Historical Society (published microfilm of the Adams Family Papers, roll 35). The quoted words appear in the latter of these two entries.

[92] Ammon, *James Monroe,* pp. 501–502.

priated for the strategically essential fortifications on Dauphin Island, when William P. DuVal was chosen over John Branch for the Governorship of the Territory of Florida, and when other inevitably political issues arose.

Crawford vs. Calhoun as Candidates

During 1822 the Presidential race seemed to be primarily a contest between William H. Crawford and John C. Calhoun. Other candidates and potential candidates were quite numerous enough, but those two were the early front-runners, with John Quincy Adams and Henry Clay reasonably close behind and others far in the rear. Because this volume includes many letters from Calhoun that were written to his supporters in order to stimulate and to maintain their confidence and their exertions in his behalf, it may be helpful to place such correspondence in the setting of its own times.

The South Carolinian's political letters of the year were focused very largely against the Georgian. Calhoun's conversations with some people were even more pointed and were less objective in tone and in content. To Adams, himself an interested party who could not muster complete objectivity, Calhoun spoke of Crawford "with great bitterness." They had both watched Crawford's designing "manoeuvering and intrigues." There "had never been a man in our History," Calhoun declared, "who had risen so high, of so corrupt a character, or upon so slender a basis of service." And this was Calhoun's opinionated judgment after he "had witnessed the whole series of Crawford's operations from the Winter of 1816 to this time."[93]

Two cautioning correctives to such an estimate can be mentioned in fairness. To no man is it given to see himself without some degree of myopia. Crawford could write early in the campaign to a man who corresponded also with Calhoun, "I shall avoid the contamination of faction and intrigue."[94] And to Adams it

[93] Entry of April 22, 1822, in the Diary of John Quincy Adams, Massachusetts Historical Society (published microfilm of the Adams Family Papers, roll 35).

[94] William H. Crawford to Charles Tait, September 4, 1821, in J.E.D. Shipp, *Giant Days, or the Life and Times of William H. Crawford, Embracing Also Excerpts from His Diary, Letters and Speeches . . .* (Americus, Ga.: Southern Printers, c. 1909), p. 149.

seemed that both Crawford and Calhoun played the political game, while Adams himself lacked "any faculty" for its finesses and was rather above such tactics. Crawford was "a much superior artist" in the manipulations of the contest to the younger Calhoun, "whose hurried ambition will probably ruin himself and secure the triumph of Crawford."[95]

In Calhoun's letters written to encourage his followers it was appropriate for him, as their leader, to take an optimistic stance. He exuded confidence; he coupled it sometimes with realistic appraisals of discouraging signs or handicaps; but he contrived never to appear disheartened and was willing to see even in setbacks, if he possibly could, some kind of victory for "the cause," if not for himself. When a visitor told Adams in June, 1822, that "Calhoun was very sanguine in his expectations of succeeding to the Presidency," Adams replied that the Secretary of War was "too sanguine."[96]

Letters were not a candidate's only means of seeking support. Newspapers were another medium for informing and persuading the public. Crawford and his friends had an organ in the capital that raised the pitch for a nationwide anti-administration chorus. That paper was the Washington, D.C., *City Gazette*. Its attacks upon the executive branch of government were not merely vigorous; they were considered by many to be abusive, scurrilous, ribald, vitriolic, insidious. Its support of Crawford, not professed publicly until the latter part of the summer of 1822, was discernible to the perceptive. Its columns were "known to be under the management of Clerks in the Treasury" Department, Calhoun told Adams one Sunday afternoon while they were riding in Calhoun's carriage to a dinner.[97] Indeed, some of its articles were suspected of being written by Crawford's employees.

To Calhoun it seemed that the capital's other newspaper, the *National Intelligencer*, was also dependent and also objectionable. Published by the public printers, it might be expected to support the administration; but it received the revenues that accompanied its issuance of the proceedings of Congress by vote of that body,

[95] Entry of May 9, 1822, in the Diary of John Quincy Adams, Massachusetts Historical Society (published microfilm of the Adams Family Papers, roll 35). Compare the entry of May 2, 1822, in *ibid.*, in which Adams denominated the rival sides as "two unprincipled factions."

[96] Entry of June 2, 1822, in *ibid.*

[97] Entry of July 28, 1822, in *ibid.* Compare the entries of July 8 and 11, 1822, in *ibid.*

in which Crawford and Henry Clay held dominant influence. While its editorial policy was explicitly neutral in respect to the campaigners, its editorial policy and news content tended to be critical of the administration and implicitly favored the objectives of Crawford and Clay as Presidential aspirants aligned against the pro-administration pair, Calhoun and Adams.

In order to "expose the intrigues" of Crawford and Clay, an *independent* newspaper in Washington was indispensable, Calhoun assured Adams.[98] With the demise of the Factory system of Indian trade, Calhoun's cordial friend, Thomas L. McKenney, became unemployed and hence available to edit such a journal. And in June, 1822, McKenney issued a prospectus of the Washington, D.C., *Republican and Congressional Examiner,* to be issued as a semiweekly on and after August 7 (but it appeared as a daily when Congress was in session). McKenney's preview promised that the *Republican* would defend the United States Constitution, would support the administration "so long as it shall continue to discharge the high duties entrusted to it with fidelity and economy," would oppose the "desolating, all-sweeping retrenchment . . . of the Radicals," and would print accurate accounts of Congressional proceedings (without a subsidy) and reliable analyses of the qualifications of Congressmen.[99]

Adams, who saw himself as the secondary target of the *City Gazette,* thought well of McKenney's prospectus and hoped that the new venture would consummate its promises. But the editor, Adams told Calhoun, "must have a heart of oak, nerves of iron and a Soul of Adamant to carry it through. His first attempt would bring a Hornet's Nest upon his head, and if they should not sting him to death or blindness, he would have to pursue his march with them continually swarming over him, and beset on all sides with slander, obloquy and probably assassination." The South Carolinian replied that Adams had drawn a "high coloured" picture but conceded that McKenney would probably have "a stormy career" in journalism.

But Adams did not welcome the proposed rebuttal sheet with admiration unalloyed. To his diary he confided the possibility that the *Republican* was intended to be less a pro-administration organ than a pro-Calhoun one. "I doubt much," he wrote, "whether Mr. McKenney's paper will be Independent. I think

[98] Entry of July 28, 1822, in *ibid.*

[99] Washington, D.C., *Daily National Intelligencer,* June 12, 1822, p. 2, cols. 4–5.

it originated in the War office, and will be Mr. Calhoun's Official Gazette, as long as it lasts. Whether it will live through a Session of Congress, is to be seen; but if it fulfills the promise of its prospectus it will pass through more than fire if it does" outlast a Congressional session. Adams discerned that Calhoun "evidently considers his future prospects, and even his continuance in the present Administration as depending upon it."[100] Other newspapers favorable to Calhoun, in addition to those that espoused Crawford, had already begun "to degrade me in the public opinion," Adams observed.[101] Calhoun's new *Republican* was, from Adams's viewpoint, to be feared also.

The first issues of the *Republican* proved to be distinctly a relief to the apprehensive Adams. He was not its target. McKenney's initial series of seven articles, "very well written" in temperate language, "unfolded . . . with much moderation and decorum . . . the opposition against the present administration, which has been forming itself under the auspices of Mr. Crawford, and with a view to promote his election to the Presidency."[102] But any war—even a newspaper war—tends not to remain mild. The *City Gazette* was pushed into open advocacy of Crawford's candidacy. Democracy, Economy, and Reform become the slogans of his supporters and of his chain of newspapers—Democracy as a weapon against Adams, Economy against Calhoun, and Reform against both.[103] The *Republican* countered with an analysis of reductions in expenditures by the War, Navy, and Treasury Departments to show that the Treasury had "the least pretension to boast of its economy."[104] Less factual but adept at in-fighting, the *City Gazette* struck back with such jabs as a perversion of a McKenney announcement into an imitative bit of heavy-handed humor containing "vulgarity and venom" without any wit. Its articles were "infamously scurrilous and abusive, not only upon Mr. Calhoun," but even in respect to his mother-in-law, Floride Bonneau Colhoun. "This is Mr. Crawford's mode of defensive warfare."[105]

Throughout the autumn of 1822 the deadly conflict continued with increased intensity. McKenney's successes in attacking Craw-

[100] Entry of July 28, 1822, in the Diary of John Quincy Adams, Massachusetts Historical Society (published microfilm of the Adams Family Papers, roll 35).

[101] Entry of July 8, 1822, in *ibid.*

[102] Entry of August 24, 1822, in *ibid.*

[103] Entry of August 26, 1822, in *ibid.*

[104] Entry of September 11, 1822, in *ibid.*

[105] Entry of September 9, 1822, in *ibid.*

ford's reputation and in exposing, with at least some reserve, the practices of his partisans "has thrown them," Adams observed, "into a paroxysm of rage." They reacted by publishing not only "personal invective and menace" but also "the foulest abuse" upon both McKenney and Calhoun "personally."[106] The *Republican's* reason and facts brought forth from the *City Gazette* scurrility and billingsgate. The latter struck a telling blow when it told the world a fact, however, that had first been exposed in New York—the fact that some copies of McKenney's prospectus had been distributed through the mails under a frank. McKenney confessed that postage had not been paid for some copies but retorted that they had been sent as enclosures in a farewell letter from him as Superintendent of Indian Trade to persons to whom he could properly frank letters about government business. McKenney added that, as soon as that practice had been "made known to Mr. Calhoun, he disapproved it, and directed its discontinuance."[107] The very next day after Adams dismissed a Clerk from the State Department, for ample reasons, Adams "saw his hand" in the *City Gazette,* which then continued with a series of articles twisting truth to hurt Adams's Presidential candidacy.[108]

However much or little the nation may have been set agog by such skirmishes in printer's ink, their effectiveness seems to have declined as the year 1822 expired and the next year began. "These Engines" of war, Adams predicted, "will counteract each other."[109] He discontinued reading in his office all newspapers except the *National Intelligencer,* as a means of avoiding "the waste of Time."[110] That journal did not enter the fray but remained outwardly uninvolved, although it occasionally expressed mild disapproval of McKenney's tactics.[111] Calhoun continued to tell Adams privately that Crawford's career represented "a very singular instance" of a not even admirable man rising to undeserved eminence—that none other in the history of the Union "with abilities so ordinary, with services so slender, and so thoroughly corrupt" had ever "contrived to make himself a Candidate for the

[106] Entry of September 14, 1822, in *ibid.*

[107] Entry of September 21, 1822, in *ibid.* Compare the entry of four days later.

[108] Entry of November 7, 1822, in *ibid.*

[109] Entry of August 26, 1822, in *ibid.*

[110] Entry of November 4, 1822, in *ibid.*

[111] Washington, D.C., *Daily National Intelligencer,* August 31, 1822, p. 3, cols. 1–2; September 4, 1822, p. 3, cols. 1–2; September 21, 1822, p. 2, cols. 2–3.

Presidency." And, still optimistic, Calhoun thought that it was impossible for Crawford's campaign to succeed.[112]

A newspaper war was not the only result of the rivalry between Crawford and Calhoun. Their personal battle spilled over and involved two of their partisans in another in which actual shots were fired. Former Col. William Cumming of Georgia, a follower of Crawford, took offense at remarks made in another newspaper war by George McDuffie, a Representative from South Carolina and steadfast supporter of Calhoun. Cumming challenged McDuffie to a duel. They fought it in June, 1822. McDuffie emerged from it with a wound that did not prove to be mortal, as was at first reported, and Calhoun's comments in letters to his friends reveal both extraordinary concern and infinite relief; but the effects of McDuffie's spinal injury were to plague him for the remainder of his life. What was called "honor" had been satisfied, but the feud between the two was resumed in additional printed attacks. A second duel was once avoided, in what seemed to John Quincy Adams to have become by then a "burlesque." But it was also more than that: Cumming and McDuffie fired at each other again about the time that Congress convened for the session of 1822–1823. McDuffie was again wounded. Amputation of one of his arms was at first expected and then proved to be unnecessary; but his slow recovery cost Calhoun the advantage of having McDuffie present on the floor of the House of Representatives.[113]

What had opened as primarily a two-man contest, between Crawford and Calhoun, for the Presidency was destined to develop, after the autumn of 1822, into a campaign having, as is widely known, more than twice that many serious contenders. Of its later stages more will be said later.

Congress in Session, 1822–1823

Despite the campaign, the workaday business of the War Department had to proceed. As was true annually, that obligation reached another period of peak work load for Calhoun when

[112] Entry of August 27, 1822, in the Diary of John Quincy Adams, Massachusetts Historical Society (published microfilm of the Adams Family Papers, roll 35).

[113] Entry of October 5, 1822, in *ibid.*; Washington, D.C., *Daily National Intelligencer,* June 18, 1822, p. 3, col. 2; June 19, 1822, p. 3, col. 1; December 10, 1822, p. 3, col. 4; December 23, 1822, p. 3, col. 3.

Congress convened on December 2, 1822, for a session that was adjourned on March 3, 1823. Typically, too, the climb toward the peak began two months or more in advance, when Calhoun began to assemble from his staff subordinates their budget estimates for 1823 and the various reports demanded by Congress.

Also typical was it that President James Monroe solicited from his Cabinet members suggestions about the sixth annual message that he would have to deliver to Congress. He began about six weeks in advance to invite their help in drafting that document. Characteristically, William H. Crawford, back in the capital after a four-months absence, viewed pessimistically the probable amount of the government's income; he submitted to Monroe an estimate less favorable than those that the President had already obtained from two of Crawford's Treasury Department subordinates. But Monroe was not fooled: he decided that the receipts for the year 1822 would exceed its estimate by more than $4,000,000.[114] A passage drafted by Crawford that seemed to discount the revenues likely to be received in 1823 was deleted.[115] Exhibiting more acumen in political economy than Crawford, Calhoun persuaded Monroe to change a word in a paragraph drafted by Crawford concerning freight, so that the reference would be to its *value* rather than its *cost*.[116]

Monroe's draft of his message included a long passage about the Military Academy and the discipline of Cadets. Adams and Crawford felt that no such discussion was necessary, but Monroe and Calhoun contended that it was quite proper, because Newton Cannon, a Representative from Tennessee, had proposed in the last previous session of Congress to abolish the Academy entirely. By questioning the inclusion of that topic in the message, Adams, who really was in favor of the Academy, learned the two things that he wanted to know: that Calhoun was "sensitive" in respect to the institution and that Crawford would willingly see it disappear, because its death would reduce the patronage that Calhoun was able to dispense.[117]

Thus hewed, the message became unusually long but also more

[114] Entry of November 12, 1822, in the Diary of John Quincy Adams, Massachusetts Historical Society (published microfilm of the Adams Family Papers, roll 35). Compare the entries of October 22 and 29 and November 1 and 8, 1822, in *ibid.*

[115] Entry of November 27, 1822, in *ibid.*

[116] Entry of November 26, 1822, in *ibid.*

[117] *Ibid.*

than customarily informative. Monroe used it as an opportunity for an administration that had been under attack to defend itself. The government's income during the first nine months of 1822 had exceeded $14,745,000; its expenditures within the same period had approximated $12,280,000; some indebtedness had been retired; and yet the unexpended balance at the end of the year would probably be almost $3,000,000. The Army had established two new frontier posts, one at the Sault de Ste. Marie between Lakes Superior and Huron, the other on the Red River in Arkansas Territory—thus extending into a half-moon of protection the recent posts at St. Peters on the upper Mississippi and at Council Bluffs on the Missouri. The War Department was accorded complimentary remarks in respect to many aspects of its administration and results.[118]

In reference to some matters, Congress itself treated the War Department well during the session of 1822–1823. Col. George Gibson had performed advantageously his duties as Commissary General of Subsistence; he had purchased and distributed rations for the Army at economical prices but had also improved their quality. There was little thought of reverting to the pre-1818 system of permitting individual, regional contractors to assume responsibility for delivering provisions. But Gibson's statutory authority was about to expire. So Congress extended it for another five years and until the end of the next session of Congress thereafter.[119]

Needed legislation for veterans' benefits was also enacted. Congress extended into 1825 the deadline before which bounty land warrants could be issued to Revolutionary soldiers and the latest date on which a recipient could locate his tract.[120] The House of Representatives refused, by a large majority, to accept

[118] James Monroe to the Senate and House of Representatives, December 3, 1822, in Richardson, *Messages and Papers of the Presidents,* 2:185–195. The message appears also in such places as the *Annals of Congress,* 17th Cong., 2nd Sess., cols. 12–21, and in the Washington, D.C., *Daily National Intelligencer,* December 4, 1822, pp. 2–3.

[119] Statute of January 23, 1823, in *Annals of Congress,* 17th Cong., 2nd Sess., col. 1338. Compare Hemphill, ed., *The Papers of John C. Calhoun,* 2:lxi–lxix. Monroe had recommended a renewal of the commissary system of supplying rations. James Monroe to the Senate and House of Representatives, December 3, 1822, in Richardson, *Messages and Papers of the Presidents,* 2:190.

[120] Statute of March 3, 1823, in *Annals of Congress,* 17th Cong., 2nd Sess., cols. 1402–1403.

a Senate amendment to a Revolutionary pensions bill that would have reduced all such pensions by one-fifth.[121] And Congress lifted from Calhoun's shoulders the burden of an injustice that he had been compelled by law to practice. Under a statute of 1818 he had been able to grant Revolutionary pensions on the basis of his judgment as to the "reduced circumstances" of the applicants.[122] Under an 1820 law new applicants and even those who were already receiving pensions had to submit sworn, public evidence that they were, in effect, paupers[123]—a term that carried more stigma in Calhoun's generation than it does now. Some recipients were removed from the pension rolls as a result, and it was discovered that their pensions could not be restored in instances in which they subsequently fell into impoverished circumstances. So Congress authorized Calhoun to restore the pension of any such veteran who had become indigent.[124] Quite promptly Calhoun had new regulations published, in order to inform such victims how to make application for a resumption of their benefits.[125] A cloud appeared on the pensions horizon near the end of March, after Congress had adjourned. Stephen Cantrell, the Pension Agent in Nashville, was accused of paying pensioners not in specie having full value but in depreciated local banknotes.[126] The next volume of *The Papers of John C. Calhoun* is expected to reveal how thoroughly and typically Calhoun, ever sensitive to any hint of fraud, reacted to that report.

Despite some constructive treatment of the War Department by Congress, not everything done on its floors could be considered by Calhoun to be favorable. John Floyd, Representative from Virginia, alleged that the War Department twice failed to submit information requested by Congress. That accusation was refuted categorically by the writer of an anonymous letter to a newspaper. He asserted: "It can be affirmed, without the possibility of contradiction, that the Department of War has never neglected to answer

[121] *Ibid.,* cols. 1141–1142.

[122] Hemphill, ed., *The Papers of John C. Calhoun,* 2:li–lii.

[123] *Ibid.,* 5:xix–xx.

[124] Statute of March 1, 1823, in *Annals of Congress,* 17th Cong., 2nd Sess., cols. 1409–1410; Washington, D.C., *Daily National Intelligencer,* March 11, 1823, p. 3, cols. 4–5.

[125] Among many printings of these regulations, datelined at first simply March, 1823, and later March 8, 1823, are those in the Washington, D.C., *Daily National Intelligencer,* March 11, 1823, p. 3, cols. 4–5, and April 3, 1823, p. 4, cols. 4–5.

[126] *Ibid.,* March 29, 1823, p. 3, col. 2.

any call of Congress made upon it, and to furnish all the information required, if within its control."[127] A set of resolutions offered by Newton Cannon, Representative from Tennessee, was adopted by the House. They sought increased reliance upon the militia, rather than the Army, for national defense; less exclusive dependence upon the Military Academy for Army officer recruitment and training; and the construction of fortifications by the labor of soldiers rather than by contractors.[128]

But Calhoun doubtless rejoiced over some other developments. Third Auditor Peter Hagner, the chief keeper of War Department accounts (other than those for Indian affairs), told Congress that unpaid claims owed by the United States since the War of 1812, which had once totaled about $45,000,000, were reduced by more than $2,000,000 within approximately the year 1822, leaving little more than $3,500,000 worth of such claims yet to be settled.[129] And, in an election that would become effective on March 4, 1823, South Carolina's voters chose Robert Y. Hayne, who could be expected to support Calhoun, to replace United States Senator William Smith, who was known to be a partisan of William H. Crawford.[130]

The Personal Lives of the Calhouns

Amid serious sallies at statecraft and even the bitter factionalism of political rivalries John C. Calhoun managed to find some opportunities for relaxation. He and members of his household maintained some of the amenities of society. John Quincy Adams, for example, found that his relationship with Calhoun became by the summer of 1822, for obvious reasons, "delicate and difficult"—one

[127] *Ibid.*, February 24, 1823, p. 3, col. 5.

[128] *Annals of Congress,* 17th Cong., 2nd Sess., cols. 470–471.

[129] Washington, D.C., *Daily National Intelligencer,* April 10, 1823, p. 3, col. 3.

[130] *Ibid.*, December 9, 1822, p. 3, col. 1. Compare Smith's letter "to the Good People of South Carolina" in *ibid.*, February 6, 1823, p. 3, cols. 1–2. Smith complained to John Quincy Adams that the administration never gave appointments to persons whom Smith recommended. Entry of January 12, 1823, in the Diary of John Quincy Adams, Massachusetts Historical Society (published microfilm of the Adams Family Papers, roll 37). That Smith's defeat had implications bearing upon the Presidential aspirations of Calhoun, Clay, and Crawford was realized immediately by some observers. Letters of Francis Johnson and of Henry R. Warfield to Henry Clay, December 10, 1822, in Hopkins and Hargreaves, eds., *The Papers of Henry Clay,* 3:335–337.

characterized by "civility" more than by "confidence."[131] But the two of them attended together such functions as the annual Fourth of July celebration and a dinner for about 20 guests given by the British Minister to the United States, Stratford Canning.[132] Calhoun invited Adams to ride in Calhoun's carriage, with a Senator from Louisiana who was Calhoun's guest, to Georgetown, in the western part of the District of Columbia, for the funeral of Mrs. Alexander Macomb.[133] When Calhoun's wife, Floride, saw Adams walking, she gave him a ride.[134] Moreover, at least thrice within six months Adams and those with whom he lived were invited to attend dances or parties at the Calhouns' residence. During one of these evenings Calhoun introduced Adams to several guests, one of whom was an Englishman who had become associated with Thomas L. McKenney in editing the Washington *Republican and Congressional Examiner* and who "spoke to me of the righteous cause which they are maintaining, and of the extraordinary success of their paper."[135]

The Calhouns' social life may have been somewhat curtailed during the late summer and early autumn of 1822 by an epidemic. Yellow fever, cholera, or some similar dread disease became widespread. At Pensacola it claimed the life of former Assistant Surgeon General James C. Bronaugh, a member of the Legislative Council of the Territory of Florida, and delayed some important Territorial arrangements.[136] In the capital area it caused a frightening number of deaths, made people become unusually careful about their diets, and led many persons to show concern also for their souls. These last dared to risk catching the prevailing contagion in revival meetings that enjoyed an unprecedented popularity that was approved by only some of the physicians and

[131] Entry of July 8, 1822, in the Diary of John Quincy Adams, Massachusetts Historical Society (published microfilm of the Adams Family Papers, roll 35).

[132] Entries of July 4 and November 28, 1822, respectively, in *ibid.*

[133] Entry of September 20, 1822, in *ibid.*

[134] Entry of July 4, 1822, in *ibid.*

[135] For the quotation see the entry of November 6, 1822, in *ibid.* For other evidences of the Calhouns' hospitality see the entries of August 26, 1822, in *ibid.* and of February 13, 1823, in *ibid.* (published microfilm of the Adams Family Papers, roll 38).

[136] Entry of November 6, 1822, in *ibid.* (published microfilm of the Adams Family Papers, roll 35); James Monroe to the Senate and House of Representatives, December 3, 1822, in Richardson, *Messages and Papers of the Presidents,* 2:190.

preachers in the District. Most fervently evangelistic was Calhoun's mother-in-law, Floride Bonneau Colhoun. She was not deterred even by a hard rain from visits intended *"to beat up recruits"* for evening services. Her daughter, the younger Floride, an Episcopalian rather than a Presbyterian in inclination, she could not persuade, however, to attend the night meetings, because the daughter did not approve of such evangelism. What Calhoun himself thought of this temporary revival is not recorded. His deism or Unitarian preference probably did not respond to any appeals that young missionaries or his mother-in-law may have made.[137]

The Calhouns acquired in 1822 a new focal point for their living in the capital, John C. Calhoun announced cryptically in a letter that he wrote on October 8 to one of his brothers-in-law, John Ewing Colhoun. (It appears within these covers.) Not much explanation was offered: simply to state the barest facts was a sufficient report in a family whose members commonly tolerated perplexingly intermixed business transactions without misunderstandings. The home, a large mansion with spacious grounds on a height in the Georgetown section of the District of Columbia, was doubtless considered to be a healthy site, comparatively remote from any miasmic lowlands. It was purchased with money that belonged to Calhoun's mother-in-law, but the title was placed in the name of her younger son, James Edward Colhoun. The Calhouns, who moved to their new estate in the summer of 1823, named it "Oakly"; in recent times it has been the showplace known as "Dumbarton Oaks."[138]

Calhoun's Candidacy during 1822–1823

To maintain the momentum of a political campaign throughout two or three years, Calhoun was to learn, is quite a feat. He had been led to become openly a candidate for the Presidency

[137] Margaret Bayard (Mrs. Samuel Harrison) Smith to Jane (Mrs. Andrew) Kirkpatrick, August 17 and October 12, 1822, in Gaillard Hunt, ed., *The First Forty Years of Washington Society, Portrayed by the Family Letters of Mrs. Samuel Harrison Smith (Margaret Bayard), from the Collection of Her Grandson, J. Henley Smith* (New York: Charles Scribner's Sons, c. 1906), pp. 155–162. The quoted phrase appears on p. 159. Compare Gerald M. Capers, *John C. Calhoun, Opportunist: a Reappraisal* (Gainesville: University of Florida Press, c. 1960), pp. 75–76.

[138] Charles M. Wiltse, *John C. Calhoun: Nationalist, 1782–1828* (Indianapolis: The Bobbs-Merrill Company, c. 1944), pp. 269–270.

almost three full years before voters would go to the polls in 1824. Could his appeal survive so long an interval?

Through more than half of the year 1822 it appeared that Calhoun was a front-runner in the race. Pennsylvania, which he himself considered to be the most pivotal State, seemed to favor him. Such Pennsylvania Representatives in Congress as Thomas J. Rogers and John Sergeant were known to be on his side; his friend Samuel D. Ingham, who returned in 1822 to the United States House of Representatives, was loyally active in his behalf; and the influential *Franklin Gazette* of Philadelphia advocated him.[139] Such manifestations of public support almost persuaded Pennsylvania and the nation at large that the State would lead the Calhoun bandwagon.[140] As late as mid-November, 1822, a newspaper editor in Pennsylvania who wanted Calhoun to succeed wrote to Henry Clay, "My impression is still very decided, that Mr. Calhoun is the favorite of Pennsylvania." But, the editor added, if it should be found that Calhoun could not prevail, the State would unite in support of any other one of his rivals in preference to William H. Crawford.[141] Indeed, even in February, 1823, a former Representative from Massachusetts felt that Calhoun rather than John Quincy Adams could certainly carry that Commonwealth and that the Commonwealth of Pennsylvania seemed also to prefer Calhoun.[142]

Nevertheless, the Presidential race became more complex during the winter of 1822–1823, and Calhoun's prospects appear to have declined. One cause was a natural reaction to the newspaper war between Crawford's *City Gazette* and Calhoun's *Republican and Congressional Examiner*. They drubbed each other so thoroughly that some people were inclined to reach a quite human conclusion. If one-tenth of what the embattled editors alleged was true, some readers decided, "it is time we make choice of a man unconnected with the administration."[143]

[139] Entry of July 8, 1822, in the Diary of John Quincy Adams, Massachusetts Historical Society (published microfilm of the Adams Family Papers, roll 35).

[140] Langdon Cheves to Henry Clay, November 9, 1822, in Hopkins and Hargreaves, eds., *The Papers of Henry Clay*, 3:313–314.

[141] John Norvell to Henry Clay, November 14, 1822, in *ibid.*, 3:321. In respect to Norvell's earlier support of Calhoun see Henry Toland to Henry Clay, August 8, 1822, in *ibid.*, 3:273.

[142] Henry Shaw to Henry Clay, February 11, 1823, in *ibid.*, 3:373.

[143] John Sloane to Henry Clay, October 16, 1822, in *ibid.*, 3:294–295. Compare Peter B. Porter to Henry Clay, September 30, 1822, in *ibid.*, 3:290.

And other eager candidates were certainly available, They included John Quincy Adams and Henry Clay, two beneficiaries of the fact that Crawford and Calhoun weakened not only each other but also themselves.[144] Clay was nominated by about half the members of the Ohio legislature; they gave him 50 ballots, while five voted for De Witt Clinton of New York, one for Adams, and one for Calhoun.[145] The death of William Lowndes in November, 1822, removed from the field the candidate who had been nominated by a caucus of South Carolina legislators.[146] But even a fourth member of the Cabinet, Secretary of the Navy Smith Thompson, made an overture to ascertain whether he should enter the contest, in return for which he was counseled not to do so.[147] A newcomer who was persuaded to participate in the race was Andrew Jackson. Much to the astonishment of many, he was nominated by the legislature of Tennessee, unanimously. President James Monroe considered appointing Jackson to be the United States Minister to Mexico. Could such a choice be interpreted as an underhanded device to get a candidate out of the way? Besides, did not Monroe know from experience that Jackson was prone to commit indiscretions? So the President hesitated,[148] but the nomination was made and confirmed in January, 1823. The appointment was also declined.[149] Jackson was fully committed to the Presidential race.[150]

In the light of such new developments, Calhoun's problem became to combat rumors that he would withdraw from the contest. Letters of the winter of 1822–1823 that appear within these covers include his own pleas with his followers to keep him prominently before the public as a contestant. These appeals do not reveal how pointedly he knew that people were beginning to count him out of the race. But a Representative from Maryland could write

[144] One of many testimonies to this effect is in Henry Clay to Amos Kendall, February 16, 1823, in *ibid.*, 3:382–383.

[145] Henry Clay to Francis T. Brooke, January 8, 1823, in *ibid.*, 3:350–351; Washington, D.C., *Daily National Intelligencer*, January 17, 1823, p. 3, col. 3.

[146] Washington, D.C., *Daily National Intelligencer*, January 20, 1823, p. 2, col. 4. Compare Hemphill, ed., *The Papers of John C. Calhoun*, 6:xv–xvi.

[147] Hopkins and Hargreaves, eds., *The Papers of Henry Clay*, 3:377.

[148] Entry of January 12, 1823, in the Diary of John Quincy Adams, Massachusetts Historical Society (published microfilm of the Adams Family Papers, roll 37).

[149] Washington, D.C., *Daily National Intelligencer*, April 1, 1823, p. 3, col. 1.

[150] *Ibid.*, February 12, 1823, p. 3, col. 3.

from Washington about a week after Congress had reconvened, "It is generally understood and believed here that Calhoun will withdraw from the contest—His friends speak of it in that way, and I have no doubt of [its truth]."[151] One speculation was that the South Carolinian would throw his support to John Quincy Adams and would become Secretary of State in the administration of his older colleague.[152] Representative James Hamilton, "the best informed, most active and most influential member of Congress" from South Carolina, assured Clay, on the other hand, that South Carolina would prefer to support Clay rather than Adams.[153]

For present purposes it does not matter which of these guesses may have been the more nearly true. It is enough now to reflect that, at the beginning of the spring of 1823, Calhoun was yet a long way from relinquishing his Presidential candidacy and still more than a year and half short of being elected the Vice-President of the United States.

[151] Henry R. Warfield to Henry Clay, December 10, 1822, in Hopkins and Hargreaves, eds., *The Papers of Henry Clay,* 3:336.
[152] Henry Shaw to Henry Clay, February 11, 1823, in *ibid.,* 3:375.
[153] Henry Clay to Peter B. Porter, June 15, 1823, in *ibid.,* 3:433.

THE PAPERS
of
JOHN C. CALHOUN

Volume VII

APRIL 1822

Congress continued to be in session. Calhoun continued, therefore, to be quite busy, and on the 10th Lewis Cass announced that Calhoun might be compelled to forego his intended trip to the Northwest. On the 3rd and the 19th Calhoun wrote to correct erroneous impressions in the minds of Congressmen. On the former date he submitted a draft that he had written for inclusion in a bill to be enacted by Congress. Some old problems remained, among them the New York militia court-martial and the Factory system of Indian trade. In the last ten days of the month the Elijah Mix contract began to be discussed anew. Paymaster General Daniel Parker praised on the 29th the new regulations given by Calhoun for the guidance of that bureau. To serve the people honestly, Calhoun assured a close friend on the 5th, "is the way to win their favour."

From M[icah] Sterling, [Representative from N.Y.]

[Washington, April, 1822]

Before I could see Judge [Hugh] Nelson [Representative from Va.] he had sent a petition in circulation for [the appointment of] Major Hamilton [as a Military Storekeeper]. I could do no less than sign it. I conclude you will not be in haste in making the appoen[tmen]t [*sic*]. Qualification is all essential but next to that *considerations connected with the good of the Gov[ernmen]t* may well have influence[;] how that may be in this case I know not[;] still I know that affairs in N[ew] York are in a state some what delicate & it is all important that the discontent towards the Cabinet *should not be increased.*

[P.S.] Can you reconsider any case under the claims law upon new evidence[?]

ALS in DNA, 1, S-434 (M-221:94).

To C[HARLES] S. TODD

[*Ca.* April 1822]

Mr. Calhoun's respects to Mr. C.S. Todd and agreeably to his request informs him that the Artist employed on the [medals] reported in January last, that he had in han[d t]he Battle for the reverse of [the medal for] Governor [Isaac] Shelby & had made great progress in it, and that the likeness of the Governor [on the observe] was completed. It may be expected to be finished shortly.

LU in DLC, Shelby Family Papers, 6:2366. NOTE: This manuscript is somewhat mutilated. The artist's report mentioned by Calhoun is a letter to him from Mority Fürst dated 1/14 [LS in DNA, 1, F-70 (M-221:92)]. Charles S. Todd was a son-in-law of Isaac Shelby and was diplomatic representative of the U.S. in Colombia during 1820–1823.

From [JOHN HAYS]

Indian Agency, Fort Wayne, April 1st 1822

At sight please pay Lewis Cass Esq. Governor of Michigan Territory or order Nine hundred and fifty dollars, and Seventy-five cents, being on account of the expenditures for the Indian Department at this Agency.

$950.75 (Signed Triplicate)

CC in In.

From Law[rence] Taliaferro, [Indian Agent, St. Peters,] 4/1. He applies for the position of principal Indian Agent for the Mississippi if the Department of War finds it necessary to hire one. FC in MnHi, Lawrence Taliaferro Papers, Journals, 6:99 (published microfilm, roll 3, document 363, frame 72).

From Law[rence] Taliaferro, 4/1. He acknowledges Calhoun's letters of 11/13 and 11/17/1821. He informs Calhoun that three Indians escaped from jail. Taliaferro has issued a draft in favor of James Kennerley for $555. LS in DNA, 1, T-181 (M-221:94); FC in MnHi, Lawrence Taliaferro Papers, Journals, 6:102 (published microfilm, roll 3, document 363, frame 74).

From Joseph Anderson, First Comptroller, Treasury Department, Washington, 4/2. He received on 3/31 the letter [of 3/28] from James Buchanan, [Representative from Pa.,] to Calhoun [LS in DNA, 1, B-309 (M-221:92); LS in DNA, RG 233, 17A-C27.1]. Anderson reports that his office contains no information about the amount of militia fines in Pa. other than what was sent to Calhoun on 2/10/1821 [FC in DNA, 59, 20:143–145; PC with Ens in Senate Document No. 100, 16th Cong., 2nd Sess.; PC with Ens in *American State Papers: Military Affairs*, 2:315–319]. The difference of $51,364.59 between the totals of Pa. militia fines assessed upon delinquents as reported by Calhoun on 2/14/1821 ($243,609.41) and by the Secretary of the Commonwealth of Pa. ($294,974) results, apparently, "from an omission on the part of some of the Courts-Martial to make returns to this Office." Anderson discusses the collection of militia fines and the accountability of Marshals; he states that a lawsuit has been brought against John Smith, the former Marshal of Pa., on several charges, including the unlawful appropriation of militia fines collected by his office to his personal use. LS with DU in DNA, RG 233, 17A-C27.1; FC in DNA, 59, 20:420–422.

From Gershon P[hilip] Cohen, Charleston, [S.C.,] 4/2. "It is with pleasure I acknowledge the receipt of the appointment for West Point. My cordial acceptance will perhaps be the best testimony of my appreciating it. And I cannot refrain from tendering my most unfeigned thanks, and trust that my conduct will be such as to merit your approbation." ALS in DNA, 15, 1820, 17 (M-688:13), with an AES by his father: "I concur."

To William Eustis, Chairman, House Committee on Military [Affairs], 4/2. Calhoun encloses a report [of 3/30 (PC under that date in *The Papers of John C. Calhoun*, vol. VI) by Alexander Macomb] that provides the information requested by a House resolution of 2/19, as communicated by Eustis's letter of 2/21 [LS in DNA, 1, E-119 (M-221:92)]. LS with Ens in DNA, RG 233, 17A-E4; FC in DNA, 4, 2:238 (M-220:1); CC with Ens in DNA, RG 233, Record of Reports from the Secretary of War, 17th Cong., 1st Sess., 240:148–161; PC with Ens in House Document No. 104, 17th Cong., 1st Sess.; PC with Ens in *American State Papers: Military Affairs*, 2:380–387; PC in *Niles' Weekly Register*, vol. XXII, no. 15 (June 8, 1822), pp. 232–234.

To J[ohn] T. Johnson, [Representative from Ky.,] 4/2. In regard to Johnson's request of 3/30 [ALS in DNA, 1, J-142 (M-221:93)] that additional time be given to [former Deputy Commissary of Purchases] John "McKenney [*sic*; McKinney]" to pay what McKinney owes to the U.S., Calhoun states that "there is very little discretion allowed to this Department in such a case. I have however advised the Auditor to suspend reporting his account for suit for three months—at the expiration of which time, if it be not paid, the balance will be reported to the 5th Auditor [Stephen Pleasonton] for suit, to whom Col. McKenney [McKinney] must thereafter address himself as this Department will then have no further control over the subject." FC in DNA, 3, 11:373 (M-6:11).

From Samuel L. Southard, [Senator from N.J.]

Trenton, 2 Ap[ri]l 1822

The mail will be closed in a few moments & permits me merely to say, that I have rec[eive]d your letter [of 3/31] & sincerely thank you for it & the enclosed message. I look to the deliberations & decision of the Senate on the subject of the message with much anxiety—but fear I shall not be able to take part in them. Mrs. Southard & our little boy are both better—but she is not entirely out of danger & my situation is such that I do not expect to reach Wash[ingto]n before Monday next [April 8]. On that day I hope to be in the Senate.

Autograph draft in NjP, Samuel L. Southard Papers. Note: A PC of Calhoun's letter of 3/31 to Southard can be found in *The Papers of John C. Calhoun,* vol. VI.

To Daniel P[ope] Cook, Chairman, [House] Select Committee [to Examine Land Offices, etc.]

Department of War, April 3, 1822

I have received your letter of the 2d inst[ant (LS in DNA, 1, C-359 [M-221:92])] enclosing a copy of the report of the Select Committee upon the subject of examining the land offices in Ohio &c. and in reply to inquiries, I have to state, that the Committee is under a mistake in stating that Mr. [Caesar Augustus] Rodney and Mr. [Henry] Baldwin, the former a member of the Senate, and the latter of the House of Representatives were "employed and paid as counsel under the direction of the present Secretary of War." The precise period at which the former was employed cannot be ascertained, but it was previous to July 1820. He was paid for his service the 8th November 1820, before he became a member of Congress. Mr. Baldwin was employed by Major [Abram R.] Woolley of the Ordnance [Corps] in the Spring of 1817 before I came into the War Department and previous to taking of his seat in Congress, in the case of Daniel Deker[,] a soldier in the United States service who had been indicted for murder, for which service Mr. Baldwin has not been yet paid. He was also employed before I came into the Department, and it is believed about the same time by General Tannehill and Major Woolley (who had been appointed commissioners in 1815 to sell certain lots of land belonging to the Government at Pittsburg[h]), in an indictment of the Commonwealth of Pennsylvania against John Young[,] the Auctioneer[,] for selling the lots without paying the auction fees. For this service he was paid in 1820 one hundred dollars. It cannot be ascertained from the records of this office that any part of the service was rendered subsequent to the time of his taking his seat in Congress.

In relation to the employment of Mr. [Jeremiah] Morrow and Gen[era]l [Thomas] Worthington in 1812 I herewith enclose a copy of the letter of instruction to them, and a letter from the 3d Auditor [Peter Hagner dated 4/4 (LS in DNA, RG 233, 17A-E4; FC dated 4/3 in DNA, 53, 25:135–136)] which will give all of the information in relation to it which can be obtained from this Department.

In the case of a member of the House of Representatives in the present Congress who is employed under the authority of the War Department as a Superintendent of a fortification of the United States for which he receive[s] an annual compensation and which I understand from your letter refers to Mr. [Mark Langdon] Hill from Maine, I find on examination that he was employed by [Brig.] General [Eleazer W.] Ripley in 1816 to take charge of the Fort and other publick property at Phip[p]sburg in Maine and that he was to receive a compensation averageing [*sic*] $—— per annum. The enclosed communications from the 2d and 3d Auditors [William Lee dated 4/3 (LS in DNA, RG 233, 17A-E4; FC in DNA, 51, 7:270) and Peter Hagner] of the Treasury Department contain all of the facts in relation to it within the knowledge of this Department. It is proper to observe that it does not appear that the account was ever submitted to the War Department for its approval as the Auditors considered the authority of the Commanding Officer sufficient for its allowance, and that I had no knowledge that Mr. Hill was so employed.

FC in DNA, 4, 2:239 (M-220:1); LS with Ens in DNA, RG 233, 17A-E4; PC in the Washington, D.C., *Daily National Intelligencer,* April 8, 1822, p. 3, col. 4; PC with Ens in House Document No. 106, 17th Cong., 1st Sess.; PC in *Annals of Congress,* 17th Cong., 1st Sess., cols. 1470–1471; PC with Ens in *American State Papers: Public Lands,* 3:543–544.

From Return J. Meigs, Cherokee Agency, 4/3. He submits his estimate for the present quarter; he has received no remittance of funds for last quarter; floods and other causes have made mail deliveries to him particularly late or uncertain during the past winter. [Senator] John Williams has sent to Meigs a copy of a bill approved by the House of Representatives in 1/1822 under which Meigs's salary would be $1,800 and that of any Sub-Agent under him $600; Meigs comments at length about these figures, the high cost of living at the Agency, and the caliber of public servants obtainable at such salaries. Draft in DNA, 75 (M-208:9).

From Henry R. Schoolcraft

Washington, April 3rd 1822

In fullfilling [*sic*] the duties of my appointment, as mineralogist to the expedition [of 1820] for exploring the country adjacent to the Great Lakes, and the sources of the Mississippi, I have the honor to transmit, with this communication, a report on the mineralogy of that section of country.

In presenting this paper to the Department of War, I must take the occasion to express the deep sense I feel of the indulgence which has been extended to me, in regard to the time for preparing it; and of the ready disposition which has been manifested to comply with the terms of my engagement, both by the War Department, and by the executive officer [Lewis Cass] under whose personal orders the flag of the United States was carried through the Indian territories of that remote frontier. It is indeed owing to the excellent arrangements of this officer to meet, and provide for, every exigency—to the facilities which he constantly furnished for accomplishing every object of utility connected with the expedition, and to that fertility of resource, personal energy, and a suavity of deportment peculiar to himself under the most untoward circumstances, that the labour of exploration, has been continually rendered a pleasure, rather than a duty.

It is proper that I should also acknowledge the liberal feelings which have governed, in conceding, at my request, compensation for preparing my report, and/or travelling expences to, and from, Detroit—a point which, it is believed, was submitted for decision by Governor [Lewis] Cass. In regard to the latter item of compensation, I cannot, however, speak with confidence, circumstances not having, as yet, permitted a final settlement of my account. But I ought not to conceal the fact, that with every allowance paid, or expected to be paid to me, and every attention to economy consistent with the circumstances, the amount of compensation falls far short of the sum actually expended in travelling—in drawing up my report, and in other contingent disbursements demanded of me by the expedition.

It is not however with a view to solicit further compensation, or an equivalent for any loss thus sustained, that these facts are mentioned, since I have no reasonable claim for such remuneration, and since more has already been allowed to me, than was originally stipulated. But justice to myself, and the importance of the subjects discussed in the report, both in a national and scientific point of view, seem to require of me, that I should solicit from the government, the publication of it. These expressions are sustained by obvious facts, and could be strengthened by citing from the report itself many instances illustrative of the mineral character and resources of those regions. It will, however, be sufficient to adduce those which are furnished respecting the existence of copper, lead, gypsum, plumbago, coal, salt, alum, and ochres—substances which not only constitute important means of profitable manufacture in themselves, but upon whose existence the value of the contiguous public lands, must, in a greater or less degree, depend. If it was expedient to institute a survey of the mineralogy of those regions, it must be equally so, to spread the result of that survey before the public eye, and to disseminate throughout the country the knowledge of those varied natural resources, which invite employment. It is not conceived necessary to dwell upon this point; but if there ever is a time when portions of the revenue of a government can be appropriated with wisdom to the encouragement of the sciences and arts, it is surely that, when the national councils, and the executive departments, are employed in devising means of public economy, and in founding a system of revenue upon the permanent basis of domestic industry.

I have considered that it would not be thought improper to make these remarks, or to solicit that a reply to this point, may be given to me, intimating whether under the circumstances, my request can be complied with, and if not, whether any aid, in any shape, can be given by the Department of War, to promote this object.

I also transmit with this letter duplicates of my account for services in preparing the accompanying report, in conformity with your letter of May 28th 1821.

ALS in DNA, 24, 160.

To Samuel Smith, Chairman, House Committee on Ways and Means, 4/3. As Smith requested on 4/1 [ALS in DNA, 1, S-397 (M-221:94)], Calhoun encloses a copy of his letter of 2/19 "with a draft of a section of a bill for annuities to the several Indian Tribes mentioned therein. I have not included any provision to pay the claims against Gov[ernmen]t which may be established under the Creek Treaty. Should you desire it a section will be prepared for that purpose." FC in DNA, 4, 2:240 (M-220:1).

To Joseph Vance, [Representative from O.,] 4/3. When Vance's resolution [of 1/9] was received, Calhoun directed [William Lee] to prepare as quickly as possible the required report [concerning employees of the Indian branch of the War Department, their salaries and by whom they were appointed, and the amounts of money paid to the Territorial Governors and to the Superintendents and Agents of Indian Affairs since 12/31/1819]. Vance's letter of 3/29 [Abs in *The Papers of John C. Calhoun*, vol. VI] was also referred to [Lee], whose enclosed reply will show that the report "will be prepared for transmission to Congress in a few days." (Calhoun sent the report to Philip Pendleton Barbour on 4/11.) FC in DNA, 3, 11:374 (M-6:11).

From Eli Whitney, New Haven, [Conn.,] 4/3. He encloses vouchers for a delivery of 500 muskets under his contract and requests a remittance of $6,000. (An EU indicates that the muskets were inspected by J. Newbury and were received by Laban Smith, [Military Storekeeper]. The EU indicates also that the account was certified and was handed to the 2nd Auditor, [William Lee,] on 4/8.) ALS in DNA, 31, 1822, W.

To James Buchanan, Chairman, House Select Committee [to Examine Pa. Militia Fines], 4/4. In reply to Buchanan's letter of 3/28, Calhoun encloses the letter [dated 4/2] from First Comptroller [Joseph Anderson]. LS with Ens in DNA, RG 233, 17A-C27.1; FC in DNA, 4, 2:241 (M-220:1).

To Rufus King, Senator [from N.Y.], 4/4. In reply to John L. Lawrence's letter [of 3/30] to King, Calhoun observes that Mrs. [Eleanor] Lawrance has been told repeatedly that "the most natural and equitable adjustment" of her claim would be for the U.S. to buy the land at the 1814 price and to pay interest for the time during which it was occupied by troops. Because this is impossible without an act of Congress, "the next most equitable arrangement was that, of allowing a just compensation for the occupation and damages done the premises; which, after much investigation[,] was fixed at $3,500." Mrs. Lawrance could have disposed of the land in any manner she wished after the troops were withdrawn in 1816; the government "has no right to interfere in any disposition which she may think proper to make of it." An AES by Rufus King on the LS states: "Enclosed to Mr. John L. Lawrence with his letter to me of March 30, to which this letter is an answer." LS in DNA, 25, 134; FC in DNA, 3, 11:375 (M-6:11).

To W[INFIELD] SCOTT, New York [City]

Department of War, April 4th 1822

I have received your letter of the 27th Ultimo [ALS in DNA, 1, S-395 (M-221:94)], concerning your claim to the pay of your Brevet Rank of Major General, and requesting me to lay your statement before the Military Committee of the House of Representatives to whom was referred the decision of the Attorney General [William Wirt].

In relation to the request I have to observe that it is not usual for this Department in cases of private claims, and such I deem yours to be, to be the channel of communication with Congress.

The customary course is for the person having such claims to make the application direct to that body through one of its members, or its proper Committee. It is however due to candor to state that from the disposition manifested by many of the members of Congress in relation to brevet pay, excited by the construction given to the laws on the subject by the Attorney General to which you refer, there is but little prospect of obtaining a result favorable to your wishes, and that the application will probably increase the excitement.

You are mistaken in supposing I sent the opinion of the Attorney General to Congress [on 1/21/1822] as an appeal to that body against his decision [of 12/29/1821], for you may remember I stated last spring when you desired the opinion of the Attorney General to be taken, that I did not consider it to have been the intention of Congress to allow the pay of Brevet Rank of Major General to you or General [Edmund P.] Gaines, and that should it be his opinion upon a technical construction of the law that you were entitled, I should under my impressions feel it to be my duty to lay the subject before Congress in order that, that body might take such measures as might be judged proper in relation to it. In transmitting the Attorney General[']s opinion to the Military committee, I have but pursued the course then indicated.

FC in DNA, 3, 11:374–375 (M-6:11).

To [1st] Lt. Thomas J. Baird, 4/5. "A furlough is granted to Lieut[enant] Thomas J. Baird, of the 3d Regiment of Artillery until the 5th day of July next, when he will join his Command. Lieut[enant] Baird will report his address monthly to the Adjutant General's office." LS in PHi.

To [Samuel D. Ingham, former Representative from Pa.]

War Dep[artmen]t, 5th April 1822

I have received your several favours of the 15th, 22d & 25th March, [*not found,*] which have been prevented from being answered, till this time, only by a pressure of official duties. The tone of feeling which you found strong at Harrisburgh [*sic*] & else where, in relation to the subject which now excites so much interest, I would say was highly gratifying to me, were it not, that I might be thought too much personally interested, to express my feelings. With you however, I am under no restraint, and I may frankly express the great pleasure which it has afforded me. It would be [*one word canceled and* "mere" *interlined*], affectation, not to acknowledge, that there is some thing of mere personal gratification in the pleasure which it has excited, but I would be wholly unworthy of the preference, which my friends have given ["me" *interlined*] for the highest trust of the nation, if the preponderance of pleasure ["was" *canceled and* "were" *interlined*] on that account. I know I am, without any self deception, much more attached to *the cause* than to my personal advancement. I would much rather go down in pursuing, that system of policy, to which I am attached, than ["to" *interlined*] rise by persuing [*sic*] any other. The happiness and greatness of ["this" *canceled and* "our" *interlined*] country have, from early youth, been my first object. These are best advanced, by what I consider the highest Republican principle, a fixed confidence in the virtue and intelligence of the people. With such a confidence, a conviction must follow, that the best way to rise is to do right, to pursue with *prudence* the *lasting interest* of the country. This I have endeavoured to do, and the favour, with which as a publick man, I am regarded by the American People, is, on no account more gratifying to me, than that it affords additional evidence, that to serve them honestly is the way to win their favour. The information of the stage passenger is curious and interesting. It corresponds with appearances here. I have a good deal of reliance on Vermont, tho the delegation from that State, is perfectly silent. MacLean [Louis McLane, Representative from Del.,] is hostile, I do not doubt. His connection with the Custom house through his father, and opposition to Rodney [probably Caesar A. Rodney, Senator from Del.], will, at least in part, account for it. [Martin] Van Buren has not yet decided on his course. Since his return from Richmond appearances are more favourable. The Republicans of New York in Congress, still continue very [*or* "my"; *and here this incomplete letter ends.*]

ALU (incomplete) in ScU-SC, John C. Calhoun Papers.

From W[illiam] Eustis, [Chairman, House Committee on Military Affairs,] 4/6. As instructed by the Committee, Eustis requests a reply to his "notes" of 3/25 and 3/28. In addition to the information requested in the latter, "you will be pleased to add, thro' whose hands the contracts for the works on Dauphine [*sic*] Island and Mobile Point have passed, and who is at this time responsible for them." ALS in DNA, 30, 297.

To E[BENEZER] HERRICK, [Representative from Me.]

War Department, April 6th 1822

In compliance with your request, I have to state to you, that the principles by which I have been governed in the investigation of pension claims under the act of May 1st 1820, you will find generally laid down in the opinions of the Att[orne]y Gen[era]l, [William Wirt,] to which I would respectfully refer you, as well as to my letter to the Hon. John Cocke, of the 17th Dec[embe]r last, accompanying them, all of which have been laid before the House of Rep[resentative]s & published. David Paul, to whose case, you particularly allude, was dropt from the roll because his property, although inconsiderable, was considered sufficient, with his own labor & that of his family, none of whom were unable to work, to keep him from becoming an object of charity. In addition to these circumstances, it may be proper to remark, that his service was not of sufficient duration nor at such a period of the war, as to give him a claim to an exemption from the general rule. He enlisted in Dec[embe]r 1781, & served to the end of the War. However reduced he now may be, there is no authority vested in this Dep[artmen]t to restore his name to the List.

FC in DNA, 91, 12:80.

To A[ndrew] Jackson, Nashville, 4/6. Having reëxamined the claim of [Samuel] Houston for pay as a 1st Lt. of Infantry from 10/21/1817 to 3/1/1818 while serving also as an Indian Sub-Agent, Calhoun concurs with the opinion expressed by Jackson in his letter of 3/13 to [James] Gadsden. Whereas previously Calhoun had viewed the appointment as a Sub-Agent as a permanent appointment, he sees that it was temporary and approves Houston's claim. FC in DNA, 3, 11:377–378 (M-6:11).

To John Langdon, Portsmouth, N.H., 4/6. "I have received your letter of the 28th Ult[im]o [ALS in DNA, 1, L-139 (M-221:93)] on the subject of interest [paid by Langdon on money borrowed by him as a Deputy Commissary of Purchases for government use during the War of 1812]. I cannot authorize the allowance of any account for Interest paid, unless the expense was incurred by order of this Department." LS in MHi; FC (dated 4/9) in DNA, 3, 11:378 (M-6:11). (Heitman, *Historical Register,* 1:614, apparently states incorrectly that Langdon had died on 3/12/1819.)

From [Bvt. Maj. Gen.] Alexander Macomb, [Chief Engineer,] 4/6. "The unusual press of business in this Dep[artmen]t particularly that arising from the appointment of the Cadets has prevented a completion of the several reports required by the Military Committee of the House of Representatives by the letters of their Hon. Chairman [William Eustis] of the 25th & 28 Ult[im]o addressed to you." The materials are being prepared as quickly as possible, as is the information requested by [Eustis] today. FC in DNA, 21, 1:254–255.

To Stephen Pleasonton, 4/6. "In reply to your letter of yesterday[']s date [LS in DNA, 1, P-240 (M-221:94); FC in DNA, 215, 3:70–71], requesting copies of the contracts and bonds of James Johnson, I have to inform you that the originals conformably to law, have been deposited in the Office of the 2d Comptroller [Richard Cutts]." LS in DNA, 211; FC in DNA, 3, 11:375 (M-6:11).

From [former Capt.] George H. Richards, "Private"

April 6th 1822

Respected Sir, Permit me, once more, & for the last time, to trouble you with ["a" *canceled and* "my" *interlined*] personal affairs.

You know from the conversations, which I have held with you, that, of any provision under the Government to which I am entitled to look, I should prefer the place of *Secretary of Legation.* Under the circumstances with which you are acquainted, Mr. [James?] Lanman, [Senator from Conn.,] if appointed to an embassy, could not but be pleased to have me attached to his mission; & I think

I have the express authority of the Candidate from your State, for saying that I should be acceptable to him in that capacity, in the event of his appointment.

I shall not presume to instruct you in the nature of my services & claims, with which I believe you are already acquainted. Mr. Lanman, at my request, has addressed a letter to the President [James Monroe] in my behalf; and I have also had the honour to present in person to the President a very full & strong [letter] in my favour from Col. Joseph L[ee] Smith, which letter, I understood the President to say, he had submitted to you.

Hence you must have had a favourable opportunity for advancing my interests; and believe me, Sir, I do confidently rely, & extremely depend upon your justice, your generosity, your humanity, & (shall I say), your friendship.

There can be no doubt that a word from you would secure my object; for your influence, like your character, notwithstanding the extraordinary & violent efforts of your political enemies, is not only unimpaired, but the more powerful from the trial of its strength.

Though I have thus freely expressed the object of my desire, for which I ["think" *canceled*] have the vanity to think myself ["both" *canceled*] sufficiently qualified, & strongly recommended by powerful friends, as well as having respectable claims from past military & civil services; yet, Sir, my *absolute poverty* at this moment compels me to say that I would accept, with a lasting sense of gratitude & obligation, any provision that you can, *in a spirit of charity,* be able to confer on me. *In extreme distress,* Geo. H. Richards.

ALS in DLC, Personal Papers—Miscellaneous.

To Henry R. Schoolcraft, 4/6. "I have received your interesting report on the Mineralogy of that Section of the Western Country, embraced by the late expedition under Governor [Lewis] Cass, and although I have not had it in my power, as yet, to peruse it with attention, I will see you at any time you please on the Subject of your letter respecting it." LS in DLC, Henry R. Schoolcraft Papers, vol. 3, 460.

To Samuel Smith, Chairman, House Committee on Ways and Means, 4/6. In reply to Smith's letter of 4/5 [ALS in DNA, 1, S-400 (M-221:94)] "requesting to be informed whether the sum of $18,107.10 will be required to be appropriated to meet the disburs[e]ments growing out of the late Indian Treaty at Chicago," [negotiated in 1821,] Calhoun states that that sum must be appropriated and refers the Committee to Calhoun's letter of 2/19 concerning its necessity. FC in DNA, 4, 2:241 (M-220:1).

To Robert Tillotson and N[icholas] Gouverneur, [sureties for deceased contractor Samuel Hawkins,] New York [City], 4/6. The enclosed copy of a letter from [Lewis S.] Coryell to Calhoun [dated 3/29 (ALS in DNA, 30, 281)] reveals Coryell's decision not to enter into a contract for construction of the fort at Mobile Point. "The indulgence you were to have received under the arrangement contemplated to have been made with him will still be extended to you under any other arrangement of the same nature. But you will perceive the necessity of its being done promptly as so much time has already been lost. The appropriation will shortly be made, and unless the arrangement can be made within a reasonable time the [War] Department will be under the necessity of declaring the contract to be forfeited." To enable Tillotson and Gouverneur to effect quickly proper arrangements by which the contract can be executed, the papers previously submitted have been altered in order "to make them correspond with the views of the Department." Calhoun encloses these and other papers relating to the contract. FC in DNA, 3, 11:376 (M-6:11); CC in DNA, RG 233, 18A-C10.3; PC in House Report No. 62, 18th Cong., 2nd Sess.

From W[illiam] G.D. Worthington, Secretary and Acting Governor of East Fla., St. Augustine, 4/6. An Indian Chief named Oponey who visited Worthington on 4/6 is anxious, as are the other Indians, to learn what to expect from the U.S. Worthington requests that a talk with the Indians be authorized; reports the arrest of a Spaniard suspected of smuggling the Indians' Negroes to Havana; and announces that he has drawn upon the War Department for $1,000. Complaining of ill health and insufficient salary, Worthington asks that he be sent on a mission to South America. LS in DNA, 1, W-282 (M-221:94).

[2nd] Lt. C[lark] Burdine, [Edwardsville,] Ill., to [George] Bomford, 4/7. Burdine recounts his movements in taking provisions to the lessees who will work the lead mines in Ill. and in Mich. Territory that belong to the U.S. He has been told that

several white men, particularly Frenchmen, have been working the mines. He requests that troops be made available to oust these intruders if force should prove necessary to protect U.S. rights at the mines. ALS in DNA, 31, 1822, B.

From CALLENDER IRVINE, [Commissary General of Purchases]

Philad[elphi]a, April 8th, 1822

I have received Elias Peck's letter of the 18th of March last, [*not found,*] addressed to the Department of War. Mr. Peck, after alluding to the appropriation of seventy-five thousand dollars for the procurement of woollens for the Army, for the service of the year 1823 [*sic*] expresses a belief that the principal object of Congress in making the appropriation is to afford relief to manufacturers who are destitute of Capital, & whose establishments are upon rather a limited scale; and in expressing a desire to obtain a contract, he asks whether money is to be advanced or wool is to be furnished by Government to Manufacturers. As I find there are other manufacturers who are similarly circumstanced with by the discussions of the bill, upon its passage in the House of Representatives, & the subsequent remarks of Editors of News-papers, I will be happy to receive your instructions as to the manner, & description of Manufacturers with whom it is expected and intended the contracts for woollens for the service of 1823 shall be concluded. I would not trouble you at this time, well knowing how much you are occupied, but for remarks made on the floor of Congress, that sufficient notice to, and time to put in bids by Western Manufacturers had not been afforded, tho' I feel satisfied the remarks were not well founded, because those Manufacturers who had furnished woollens on contract with the Deputy Comm[issar]y of P[urchase]s, [John McKinney,] up to the period when his services were discontinued by an act of Congress, were specially written to by me, & were furnished with samples of the Clothes required. But one or two of them replied to my communications, and their proposals were much higher than those of other persons with whom contracts were made, as will be seen on reference to the statement of proposals transmitted by me to the War Department. The answer from the Steubenville [O.] Factory, and the Factory no doubt alluded to when it was stated that "one establishment West of the Mountains could furnish all the woollens required for the Army" was, that they did not wish to make the coarse Kerseys, their gears & Machinery not being calculated therefor, and their proposal to furnish blue cloth was at $2.75 p[e]r yard 6/4 wide; whereas the contracts made for that article were at $2.00 p[e]r yard east of the mountains. I will not add on this head.

We have now attained that perfection in the quality and uniformity in the colour & appearance desired & necessary in the Army supplies generally, and particularly so in regard to the woolens. And notwithstanding the additional Garments furnished, and amongst the number a Great Coat, an important & essentially requisite article, and the improved quality of all the supplies, the Army, since I have had any knowledge of its supplies, has not been so cheaply clothed as it is at the present time. The question which now presents itself is, in my opinion, shall we run the risque of losing these advantages, and at the same time risque the loss of the public money by distributing it in the way of advances upon contracts with numerous manufacturers whose establishments are upon a limited scale, who acknowledge that they are without capital? I owe it to Government & to myself to state explicitly that it is unnecessary to make advances of money on contracts to be concluded in this Department for Army supplies; and to state, generally, that those persons who have not required advances of money have executed their contracts much more satisfactorily & promptly, than the persons who have received money in advance. The practice is a dangerous one, and it is attended with much trouble to all & frequently with loss to government. Witness the contracts & advances of 1808.

If the contracts are distributed amongst numerous manufacturers who are engaged in a small way, there cannot be uniformity in the quality & appearance of the supplies thus procured; nor will there be certainty in the execution of the contracts. The moment a contract is found to be a losing or an unprofitable one, the manufacturer will discontinue his operations, & will throw himself upon the clemency of the Government. Putting a Bond in suit, under such circumstances, will not clothe the Army, nor is it likely that any advantage would result to Government from that course. You are aware Sir, that there is no agent of this Department west of the mountains, or any authority to employ one & to incur the expences attendant upon a clothing establishment there. Admitting that the materials for Clothing could be got west of the mountains as cheaply, and of as good quality, as they can be procured East of them, from the experiment already made I doubt if they could be well, uniformly & cheaply made up to any considerable extent. This is to be accomplished only I think where there is a very dense population, & consequently many very poor people, who are willing and anxious to work at very low rates. Submitting the foregoing remarks for your consideration, I request your instructions generally upon the subject which has given rise to them, & particularly to the following points.

1st. Whether advances are to be made, & if so, what proportion they shall bear to the amount of a Contract.

2dly. The nature of the security to be given, & who is to judge of the sufficiency thereof?

3dly. In the event of losses from advances to be made, who is to be held responsible therefor?

4thly. What is considered to be sufficient notice, in regard to time, to domestic manufacturers in remote parts of the United States?

On the first point I have stated my opinion, which is founded in experience, also the probable consequences of making advances of money, and of distributing the contracts amongst manufacturers who are engaged in a small way, who are destitute of capital, & some of them, perhaps, much embarrassed. But, if it shall be determined to make advances, I request precise instructions as to the 2d & 3d points; and I beg to be exonerated from responsibility for monies to be thus advanced, and for the timely procurement of Army supplies to be drawn from sources upon which, generally, judging from the past, little reliance is to be placed.

ALS in DNA, 1, I-149 (M-221:93); FC in DNA, 45, 389:294–296. NOTE: Calhoun wrote on 3/22 to Elias Peck, Jr., at Plainfield, Conn., that Peck's letter of 3/18 was being referred to Irvine. FC in DNA, 3, 11:370 (M-6:11). Calhoun answered Irvine on 4/12.

From [THOMAS S. JESUP, Quartermaster General]

April 8th 1822

In relation to the claim of Colo[nel James] Johnson for the transportation of the cargo shipped on board the keel boat General Wolf during the year 1820, I have the honor to report, that the claim was disallowed at this office in consequence of the boat, with her whole cargo, having been entirely lost.

The reasons for the disallowance were, that the Government

did not stipulate to insure the safe arrival of the vessel of Colo[nel] Johnson, but that the contract provided for the payment of freight on the supposition that the voyage would be a prosperous one, and that the cargo would be actually delivered agreeably to the bill of lading, for "a contract for transportation of stores or merchandize, is in its nature an entire contract; and unless it be completely performed, by the delivery of the goods or stores at the place of destination, no compensation can be claimed"; but that the transportee is accountable for the value of the cargo, unless he be able to shew by adequate evidence, not only that the loss did actually occur, but that it took place without any fault on his part or that of the crew.

The deposition furnished by Colo[nel] Johnson, is in my opinion, sufficient to exonerate him from liability for the value of the cargo. But so far from establishing his claim to freight, it proves that even wages could not be recovered from him by the hands employed, unless in his engagement with them there has been an express stipulation to that effect because the whole profits of the voyage have been lost; and it is a well established maxim of law, not only that "the safety of the vessel is the mother of freight," but that "freight is the mother of wages," and, in this case, no freight being due, consequently no wages are due.

FC in DNA, 42, 3:477–478 (M-745:2, frame 262); FC in DNA, 50, vol. 2.

From Francis Kinloch

Near Georgetown, S.C., Ap[ril] 8th 1822

Permit me to recall myself to your recollection in asking a favor of you.

Dr. Myers, a respectable Physician of this neighbourhood, is persuaded, notwithstanding all I can say to the contrary, that it might promote his views in favour of his son Mr. Mordecai Myers of Savannah, that I should mention his name to you as a candidate for employment in one of the expected missions to Spanish America, & I really believe, that the young man's acquirements & personal respectability are such, that he would fill with credit the place of Secretary on such an occasion.

Sensible of the impropriety I commit in thus intruding upon you, I have thought it preferable to the seeming insensibility I should have incurred the reproach of, had I refus[e]d the request of an old friend in favour of his son, whom I thus beg leave to recommend to your notice & protection.

When Dr. Myers applied to me, I immediately recollected Horace's epistle upon a somewhat similar occasion, but when in looking for it I stumbled upon the

O Navis, referent in mare te novi
Fluctus &c.

I could not help considering it as ominous of the event, which has occasion[e]d you the trouble of this letter. God grant I may be mistaken, or that the Prosperity & repose of the United States may not be endangered.

Adieu—dear Sir—& believe me to be with every good wish for your success & for your happiness in publick & in private life & with sentiments of the greatest respect & Esteem, Your humble Obedient S[ervan]t, Francis Kinloch.

ALS in DNA, 103, Myers (M-439:12, frames 453–456). NOTE: An AEI by Calhoun reads: "Submitted for the consideration of the Sec[re]t[ar]y of State [John Quincy Adams]. Mr. Kinloch, the writer, is a gentleman of great respectability." Mordecai Myers served as a Capt. in the "regular Army" during 1812–1815. Heitman, *Historical Register,* 1:740.

From the Rev. Robert Bell, "Charity Hall, Chickasaw Nation," 4/9. He has received Calhoun's letter of 12/18/1821 (PC in *The Papers of John C. Calhoun,* vol. VI). Bell answers that his school is located "within the limits of the Chickasaw Nation." The Cumberland Missionary Board was establishing a school in the white settlements near the Tombigbee River in 1820, but the Board ordered it to be discontinued when [Robert] Donnell learned of the requirement as to the location of Indian schools. Bell expects to complete the buildings and to open the school fully next autumn. He is astonished that Calhoun has not received the Chickasaw Agent's certificate as to the buildings, but he will have a new certificate sent soon to Calhoun. ALS in DNA, 77 (M-271:4, frames 9–12). Agent Robert C[arter] Nicholas certified on 4/20 that the school "has been in partial operation for more than a year past, that the necessary buildings were long since commenced," that Nicholas sent a certificate to this effect to Calhoun on 4/4/1821, that the school deserves patronage, and that "its location & superintendent are unexceptionable." 2 ALS's in DNA, 77 (M-271:4, frames 181–184).

From BENJAMIN O'FALLON, Indian Agent

Saint Louis[,] April 9th 1822

I have the honor to inform you that I reached this place on the 5th instant with the Indians all well, and they are now on the eve of setting out by land to the Council Bluffs, from whence they will diverge to their respective homes.

They are all in fine health and spirits, and most favourably impressed with the stren[g]th, wealth, and magnanimity of our Nation.

I am happy to state that the Indians of the Tribes of this Deputation, have conducted themselves well towards us, during my absence; but regret the continuence [*sic*] of a war between the Pawnis [*sic*; Pawnees] and Kanzas [*sic*], the last of whom, killed eleven (warriors) of the former a short time since, and are now trembling for their safety. I have never made peace between those two nations, because they were not prepared to preserve it. They have been so long at war, as to view each other almost in the light of natural enemies, and from that circumstance have been slow to make a permanent peace, which I am in hopes soon to effect.

The Indians high up the Missouri (Sioux) continue to insult our traders; but I hear of no late depredations.

I understand that License has been granted Messrs. [William H.] Ashley & [Andrew] Henry to trade, trap, and hunt, on the Upper Missouri. I have not seen it, but am in hopes that limits have been prescribed to their hunting and trap[p]ing on Indian Lands, as nothing is better calculated to alarm and disturb the harmony so happily existing between us and the Indians in the vicinity of the Council Bluffs.

As I can see no probability of the Military expeditions progressing up the Missouri this year; I think there is no impropriety in allowing hunting and trap[p]ing above the Mandans, on the lands of Indians who are unfriendly to us, and under foreign influence; but, as soon as we have an opportunity of counteracting that influence, and producing a good understanding between us and those Indians, then, hunting and trap[p]ing should be prohibited and our traders confined above to a fair and equitable trade with them.

This trading, hunting and trap[p]ing Company calculating surely on obtaining License, equip[p]ed, and set out a short time before my arrival here.

ALS in DNA, 1, O-5 (M-221:96).

To [Bvt. Brig. Gen. HENRY] ATKINSON, St. Louis

Adj[utan]t Gen[era]l[']s Office, 10 April 1822

In approving of the right wing of the Western Department being assigned to your command, it was not the intention of the Dep[artmen]t of War that the command should be considered to entitle you to the pay and emoluments of your Brevet rank.

The assignment however has been such, and the command of such an extent as to give effect under the regulations to your Brevet rank; the pay & emoluments charged have therefore been legally awarded you.

FC in DNA, 12, 6:159 (M-565:6, frame 375); CC in DNA, 1, G-178 (M-221:92).

Lewis Cass, [Governor and Superintendent of Indian Affairs, Mich. Territory,] Detroit, to George Boyd, [Indian Agent,] Mackinac, 4/10. "It [is now] somewhat doubtful whether Mr. [John C.] Calhoun will be able to visit this country agre[e]ably to his intention last fall. I will thank you, however, to send down in the Decatur or Jackson one of those canoes you may have engaged, together with the necessary appendages. You can send the bill properly drawn and receipted, and the amount shall be remitted. Should the other Canoe be wanted, I will write to you in season to have it sent down. If not, I shall not wish to purchase it." LS in DNA, 76 (M-1:70, pp. 285–286).

To William Eustis, Chairman, [House] Committee on Military Affairs, 4/10. In reply to Eustis's letter of 3/28 [LS in DNA, 1, E-118 (M-221:92)], Calhoun encloses reports from [Alexander Macomb dated 4/10 and Peter Hagner dated 4/2 (FC in DNA, 53, 25:120)]. Calhoun discusses the War Department balance as of 1/1/1821 and refers Eustis to his letter of 2/2/1821 to [Philip Pendleton Barbour]. The balance on hand on 1/1/1821 for the construction of fortifications during 1821 was $100,000. For the reasons given by Macomb, Calhoun did not learn of the transfer of funds from Gulf Coast fortifications to those in the Chesapeake Bay until after Congress adjourned. At that time, the matter was referred to [James Monroe], who decided that the sums should be "applied in the manner stated in the report of the Chief Engineer." LS with En (by Macomb) in DNA, RG 233, 17A-E4;

FC in DNA, 4, 2:243–244 (M-220:1); PC with En in House Document No. 114, 17th Cong., 1st Sess.; PC with En in *Niles' Weekly Register*, vol. XXII, Supplement, pp. 44–46.

To [Bvt.] Maj. Gen. [Edmund P.] Gaines, Louisville, Ky.

Adj[utant] Gen[era]l[']s Office, 10 April 1822

General [Henry] Atkinson has made a charge for his Brevet pay & emoluments as Brigadier General in virtue of the command assigned him by you. The nature and extent of the command exercised, seems under the existing regulations for the government of the Army, to entitle him to the emoluments claimed, & they have consequently been awarded him.

In approving of the right wing of your command being assigned to General Atkinson, it was distinctly stated in a letter from the Adj[utant] Gen[era]l[']s office to you of the 3d August last, that the command would not be considered of a nature to entitle him to the pay & emoluments attached to his brevet rank. The assignment however has been such as under the regulations, to operate contrary to expectations, involving an expense not anticipated or provided for. It is necessary that General Atkinson be assigned exclusively to the command of his Regiment, and that in future no disposition be made of officers under your command or district or department created with a view to give effect to Brevet rank. The existing state of affairs, does not seem imperiously to demand any other organization of your Department, than that into Posts, Battalions or Regiments; in case of necessity requiring the concentration or coöperation of Troops on the same frontier, General Atkinson may in virtue of his Brevet rank exercise command over the Troops on the Mississippi or Arkansas rivers, and where the occasion demands such an exercise, his brevet rank will necessarily take effect, & no reasonable objections can be urged against the pay & emoluments accompanying it. But in times of general tranquility like the present, when a reduced revenue imposes the necessity of economy of expenditure in all departments, it is indispensable to restrict the pay & emoluments of officers to the ordinary rank, which seems to be the intention of the provisions of the act of Congress of the 2d of March 1821 awarding the brevet pay & emoluments only in such cases where the public good alone imperiously demands the exercise of a command equal to such rank.

FC in DNA, 12, 6:159–160 (M-565:6, frames 375–376); FC in DNA, 17, 1:21; CC in DNA, 1, G-178 (M-221:92).

From Peter Hagner, Third Auditor, Treasury Department, Washington, 4/10. He reports that proceedings have been instituted against 12,000 militia delinquents in N.Y., that 5,569 have been tried, that fines totaling $141,599 have been imposed, and that fines totaling $26,551.20 have been collected. He reports also how this revenue has been allocated for expenses associated with the trials. Deputy marshals have encountered resistance in attempting to collect the fines, and the N.Y. Superior Court has "decided against the legality of the fines"; accordingly, "all further collection is suspended until an appeal can be had to the highest court of the State." DS in DNA, RG 233, 17A-E4; PC in House Document No. 107, 17th Cong., 1st Sess.

From J[acob] Lewis, New York [City], 4/10. Having been refused the return of some papers that he "accidentally left" in the War Department, he requests certified copies. ALS in DNA, 30, 301.

From Alexander Macomb, 4/10. He replies at length to the request of 3/28 from [William Eustis] for information about disbursements for fortifications during 1821, "the authority under which [former Bvt. Brig.] Gen. [Joseph G.] Swift formed contracts for the Construction of Fortifications at Mobile & Lake Pontchartrain," whether those contracts are still in force, and the losses sustained under them. Macomb reports that $302,000 were available for fortifications in 1821, but that it was discovered only in 3/1821, through the slowness of the mails, that $104,000 remained unexpended from the 1820 appropriation for fortifications along the Gulf of Mexico. Since this balance was "applicable to the service of the year 1821 it was determined to appropriate a portion of it to the Chesapeake, and leave the residue for the Gulf service." The device of transferring funds among Engineer officers was adopted rather than suffer the delay of appealing to the U.S. Treasurer [Thomas Tudor Tucker] for formal transfers. The arrangement by which $60,000 were transferred among officers for use on the Chesapeake "was submitted to the Sec[retar]y of the

Treasury [William H. Crawford] last summer, during your absence and being sanctioned by him, was carried into effect." In regard to the contracts let by Swift for Mobile Point and Lake Pontchartrain, Macomb reports that, "previous to the year 1821, the appropriations for fortifications were made in a Gross sum, without designating any special sum for any particular Work. Under the Authority of the General Appropriation, the President [James Monroe] having determined to commence the work in question, Gen. Swift[,] then Chief Eng[inee]r[,] recommended that construction should be by contract under a belief that they could be executed more economically by that than by any other mode. This opinion was founded in part, on the belief, that in a country so destitute of resources necessary for the erection of such works, that [*sic*] the enterprize & individual interest of a Contractor, would be the best means of overcoming the difficulties which would be presented . . . . It is proper to observe that those contracts were formed before the passage of the law prohibiting the formation of Contracts unless upon existing appropriations adequate to their fulfil[l]ment." In each case, the "periods stipulated for the completion of the Contracts have expired," but suitable arrangements with the sureties are being negotiated. Suit will be instituted if these efforts fail, but in no cases are losses anticipated. Macomb reports, in answer to a query by [William Eustis] on 4/6, that "the Contract for Dauphine [*sic*; Dauphin] Island is still in the hands of the Original Contractors[,] Messrs. [Richard] Harris & [Nimrod] Farrow, who together with their sureties are responsible for it. The Contract for Mobile Point, was originally made with Col. [Benjamin W.] Hopkins, and at his death with the consent of the Department, was transferred to Col. [Samuel] Hawkins, who being also deceased, his Representatives & Sureties [Robert Tillotson and Nicholas Gouverneur] are responsible for its execution." LS in DNA, RG 233, 17A-E4; FC in DNA, 21, 1:255–257; PC in House Document No. 114, 17th Cong., 1st Sess.; PC in *Niles' Weekly Register*, vol. XXII, Supplement, pp. 45–46; PEx in House Report No. 69, 18th Cong., 2nd Sess.

To Samuel Smith, Chairman, House Committee on Ways and Means, 4/10. Calhoun replies at length to Smith's letter [of 3/18 (LS in DNA, 1, S-379 [M-221:94])] requesting a statement of the accounts of the late Maj. Gen. [Gerard] Steddiford and of Col. Jonathan Varian [for services in the court-martial for N.Y. militia delinquents]. A balance of $2,253.49 is due to Col. Varian, but Steddiford's accounts have been returned to his executors in N.Y. "The principle adopted in the settlement of Col. Varian's account has been applied to those of all the other members of the Court." Calhoun discusses the daily allowances of the members and explains why the allowances were considered necessary during peacetime. "A very rigid construction of the law and the rules and regulations of this Department relative to charges for forage and servants was applied to the settlement of these accounts, in consequence of which nearly the whole of these allowances have been deducted from the accounts of each member. It has tended to equalize their pay" and has saved a considerable sum in reducing their claims. The President of the court, [Steddiford,] and its Judge Advocates have been allowed pay and emoluments for threee months subsequent to its adjournment in 3/1815 for completion of its proceedings. The court was dissolved on 1/11/1819, "and the President and Judge Advocates [Hugh] Maxwell and [Henry B.] Hagerman were retained in service until the 29th March following for the purpose of completing the records of the Court and of examining and reporting to this Department such delinquents in extraordinary cases of hardship or poverty as might be presented to them." LS in DNA, RG 233, 17A-E4; FC in DNA, 4, 2:242–243 (M-220:1); PC in House Document No. 107, 17th Cong., 1st Sess.

To William H. Ashley, 4/11. Calhoun authorizes Ashley to trade with the Indians "up the Missouri" during the next 12 months. (Notations indicate that a similar license was granted on the same date to Andrew Henry.) FC in DNA, 72, E:226 (M-15:5); CC in DNA, RG 233, 18A-D1, vol. 257; PC's in Senate Document No. 1 and House Document No. 2, 18th Cong., 1st Sess.; PC in *American State Papers*: *Indian Affairs*, 2:428.

To Philip P[endleton] Barbour, [Speaker, House of Representatives,] 4/11. Pursuant to a House resolution of 1/9 [DS in DNA, 1, R-187 (M-221:94)], Calhoun encloses reports from [William Lee dated 4/8 (LS with Ens in DNA, RG 233, 17A-E4) and Thomas L. McKenney dated 1/19] concerning the number of persons employed in the Indian branch of the War Department and their salaries. Calhoun discusses the relatively high salaries of blacksmiths and encloses a letter [of 10/4/1820] from [David B.] Mitchell explaining why the salaries of blacksmiths and strikers are so high. Calhoun explains that the $10,000 appropriation for the civilization of the Indians has been applied in the form of grants to benevolent societies or individuals who teach Indians; "in no instance have teachers or agriculturalists been employed by this Department." For a fuller explanation of expenses in civilizing the Indians, Calhoun refers the House of Representatives to a report already submitted by [James Monroe] during this session to Congress. LS with Ens in DNA, RG 233, 17A-E4; FC in DNA, 4, 2:244–245 (M-220:1); PC with Ens in House Document No. 110, 17th Cong., 1st Sess.; PC with Ens in *American State Papers*: *Indian Affairs*, 2:364–371.

To Samuel Smith, Chairman, [House] Committee on Ways and Means, 4/11. In reply to Smith's letter of 3/25 [ALS in DNA, 1, S-419 (M-221:94)], Calhoun encloses a report [of 4/11 from Alexander Macomb (FC in DNA, 21, 1:258), stating that $77,899.80 will be required to complete Fort Delaware and $64,419.91 for Fort Washington]. FC in DNA, 4, 2:245 (M-220:1).

To J[ames?] Gibbon, Richmond, 4/12. Calhoun thanks Gibbon for his letter "of the 11th [*sic*; 4/10 (ALS in DNA, 30, 319)] informing me of your having sent a barrel and a keg of water proof cement." Calhoun has forwarded the "letter with the directions for using the cement to" [Alexander Macomb], who "will take proper measures for having it fairly tried both here and at [Old] Point Comfort." FC in DNA, 3, 11:380 (M-6:11).

To C[allender] Irvine, Philadelphia

Department of War, April 12th 1822

I have received your letter of the 8th instant, concerning the advance of any portion of the sum of $75,000 appropriated [by] the present session of Congress for procuring woollen supplies for 1825 [*sic*] to such persons as may form contracts with you for that purpose. As I consider the appropriation to have been made to enable the Government to procure the supply of woollens advantageously and not in the nature of a loan to manufacturers, you will not advance any portion of it to contractors. The customary rule of paying on delivery is to be observed in this case as well as in all others.

FC in DNA, 3, 11:379 (M-6:11).

To V[IRGIL] MAXCY, Baltimore

War Dept., 12th April 1822

I have bearly [*sic*] to say to you, that Maj[o]r [George] Peter formerly in Congress from Maryland called on me day before yesterday, and opened the subject of the next Presidential election fully and freely. He takes great interest in it, and is a decided friend to my election. He says it is of great importance that [Roger B.] Taney should go right, and that there is no man, who has more influence with him than your self, & that ["He" *canceled and* "he" *interlined*] speaks of you in the highest terms. He also says that it [is] very important, that the paper edited at Fredericktown by [Samuel] Barnes should take the right side. The editor, it seems on the discussion in relation to renewing the charter of the old U[nited] States Bank, took much offence at some observations of Mr. [William H.] Crawford in relation to himself. He was at that time an editor in Baltimore. The Maj[o]r said that he would take such measures as were in his power to put the editor right. He thinks that Taney might be of some use through some of his friends to effect the same thing. I told him, I would write to you, and would hear from you on it in a few days.

You, I suppose, know the character of the Maj[o]r. While in Congress, he stood very high as a man of strict honor and integrity. He spoke in very favourable terms of you, but said he was not particularly acquainted with you. If you can get a favourable opportunity you had better extend your acquaintance with him. In great haste. Yours sincerely, J.C. Calhoun.

ALS in DLC, Galloway-Maxcy-Markoe Papers, vol. 32. NOTE: George Peter served as a Representative from Md. during 1816–1819 and 1825–1827. Samuel Barnes's newspaper was the *Political Examiner & Public Advertiser.*

From Capt. D[AVID] B[ATES] DOUGLASS, Professor of Mathematics

Military Academy, West Point, April 13, 1822

A mutual agreement having been concluded between Professor [of Engineering Claudius] Crozet and myself to make an exchange of Professorships in this Institution provided that such an arrangement would meet the approbation of the Secretary of War, I take occasion on my part, and in the understanding that a similar communication will be made by Professor Crozet, to express my wish for such an exchange.

ALS in DNA, 14, 280. NOTE: No such exchange was effected promptly.

From Goodman G. Griffin, Tuscaloosa, Ala., 4/13. He requests Calhoun's aid in obtaining the Postmastership in Tuscaloosa. "Although I once had the honour of being examined by you at the Pendleton [S.C.] Ac[a]d[em]y, yet I cannot flatter myself that you have any recollection of me." ALS in DNA, 1, G-154 (M-221:92).

JAMES MONROE to the Senate

Washington, April 13th 1822

Having cause to infer, that the reasons, which led to the construction, which I gave, to the Act of the last session, [approved on 3/2/1821,] entitled "An Act to reduce & fix the peace Establishment of the U.S." have not been well understood, I consider it my duty, to explain, more fully, the view which I took of that Act, and of the principles, on which, I executed, the very difficult and important duty, enjoined on me, by it.

To do justice to the subject, it is thought proper, to show, the actual state of the Army, before the passage of the late act, the force in service, the several corps, of which, it was composed, and the grades, and number of officers, commanding it. By seeing distinctly, the body, in all its parts, on which, the law operated; viewing, also, with a just discrimination, the spirit, policy, and positive injunctions of that law, with reference to precedents, established in a former analogous case, we shall be enabled to ascertain, with great precision, whether, these injunctions, have, or have not, been strictly complied with.

By the act of the 3d of March 1815, entitled an "Act fixing the military peace Establishment of the U.S." the whole force in service, was reduced to 10,000 men, Infantry, Artillery, & Riflemen, exclusive of the Corps of Engineers, which was retained, in its then state. The Regiment of Light Artillery, was retained, as it had been organized, by the Act of 3d March 1814. The Infantry, was formed into 9 Regiments, one of which consisted of Riflemen. The Regiments of Light Artillery, Infantry, Riflemen, and Corps of Engineers, were commanded, each by a Col., Lt. Col., & the usual Battalion & Company officers: and the Battalions of the Corps of Artillery, of which there were Eight, four for the Northern, & four for the Southern Division, were commanded by Lt. Colonels, or Majors, there being four of each grade. There were, therefore, in the Army, at the time, the late law was passed 12 Colonels, belonging to those branches of the Military establishment. Two Major Generals, and four Brigadiers were, likewise retained, in service, by this act: but the Staff in several of its branches, not being provided for, and being indispensable, and the omission inadvertent, proceeding from the circumstances, under which the Act was passed, being at the close of the session, at which time, intelligence of the peace was received, it was provisionally retained, by the President, & provided for, afterwards, by the Act of the 24th of April 1816. By this act, the Ordnance Department was preserved, as it had been organized by the Act of Feb[ruar]y 8th 1815, with one Col.[,] one Lt. Col.[,] 2 Majors[,] 10 Captains, & 10 first, second, and third Lieutenants. One Adjutant and Inspector General of the Army, two Adjutant Generals—one for the Northern, and one, for the Southern Division, were retained. This Act, provides, also, for a Pay Master General, with a suitable number of Regimental & Battalion paymasters, as a part of the General Staff, constituting the military peace Establishment; & the Pay Department, and every other branch of the Staff, were subjected to the rules & articles of war.

By the act of March 2d, 1821, it was ordained, that the military peace Establishment, should consist of 4 Regiments of Artillery, & of 7 of Infantry, with such officers of Engineers, Ordnance, and Staff, as were, therein, specified. It is provided, that each Regiment of Artillery, should consist, of 1 Col.[,] 1 Lt. Col.[,] 1 Major & 9 Companies, with the usual Company officers, one of which, [was] to be equipped as Light Artillery, and that, there should be attached, to each Regiment of Artillery, one supernumerary Captain to perform ordnance duty; thereby merging the Regiment of Artillery, and Ordnance Department, into these 4 Regiments. It was provided, also, that each Regiment of Infantry should consist of 1 Col.[,] 1 Lt. Col.[,] one Major & 10 Companies, with the usual Company officers. The Corps of Engineers, Bombardiers excepted, with the Topographical Engineers, and their Assistants were to be retained, under the existing organization. The former establishment, as to the number of Major Generals, and Brigadiers was curtailed one-half, and the office of Inspector and Adjutant

Gen[era]l to the Army, and of Adjutant General to each Division annulled: and that of Adjutant General to the Army instituted. The Quarter Master, Pay Master, and Commissary Departments, were also specially provided for, as was every other branch of the Staff, all of which received a new modification & were subjected to the rules and articles of war.

The immediate & direct operation of this Act, on the military peace Establishment of 1815 was that of reduction, from which, no officer, belonging to it, was exempt, unless it might be, the Topographical Engineers, for in retaining the Corps of Engineers, as was manifest, as well by the clear import of the section relating to it, as by the provisions, of every other clause of the act, reference was had, to the organization, and not, to the officers, of the Corps. The Establishment of 1815 was reduced, from 10[,000] to about 6,000 men. The 8 Battalions of Artillery, constituting what was called, the Corps of Artillery, and the Regiment of Light Artillery, as established by the act of 1815 were to be incorporated together, and formed into 4 new Regiments. The Regiments of Infantry were to be reduced from 9 to 7, the Rifle Regiment, being broken. Three of the General officers were to be reduced, with very many of the officers, belonging to the several corps of the Army, and particularly of the Infantry. All the provisions of the Act, declare, of what number, of officers, and men, the several corps, provided for, by it, should thenceforward consist; and not, that any corps, as then existing, or any officer of any corps, unless the Topographical Engineers were excepted, should be retained. Had it been intended, to reduce the officers, by corps; or to exempt the officers of any corps from the operation of the law; or, in the organization of the several new corps, to confine, the selection of the officers, to be placed, in them, to the several corps of the like kind, then existing, and not extend it, to the whole military Establishment, including the Staff; or to confine the reduction to a proportional number of each corps, and of each grade in each corps, the object, in either instance, might have been easily accomplished, by a declaration, to that effect. No such declaration was made, nor can, such intention, be inferred. We see on the contrary that every corps of the Army and Staff, was to be reorganized; and most of them reduced in officers and men; and that in arranging the officers from the old, to the new corps, full power was granted to the President, to take them from any & every corps, of the former Establishment, & place them in the latter. In this latter grant of power, it is proper, to observe, that the most comprehensive terms, that could be adopted, were used, the authority, being, to cause the arrangement to be made, from the officers of the several *corps*, then in the service of the U.S. comprizing, of course, every corps of the Staff, as well as of Artillery & Infantry, & not from the *corps of troops*, as in the former act, & without any limitation, as to grades.

It merits particular attention, that although the object of this latter act, was reduction, & such its effect, on an extensive scale, five new officers, were created by it—4 of the grade of Col., for the 4 Regiments of Artillery, and that of Adjutant General, for the Army. Three of the first mentioned, were altogether new, the Corps having been newly created; & although one officer of that grade, as applicable to the Corps of Light Artillery, had existed, yet as that Regiment was reduced, and all its parts reorganized, in another form, and with other duties, being incorporated into the 4 new Regiments, the commander was manifestly displaced, and incapable of taking the command, of either of the new Regiments, or any station, in them, until he should be authorized, to do so, by a new appointment. The same remarks, are applicable, to the office of Adjutant General to the Army. It is an office, of new creation, differing from that of Adjutant and Inspector General, and likewise, from that of Adjutant General to a Division, which were severally, annulled. It differs from the first, in title, rank, and pay, and from the two latter, because they had been created by law, each, for a Division, whereas, the new office, being instituted, without such special designation, could have relation only, to the whole Army. It was manifest, therefore, that neither of those officers, had any right to this new station, nor to any other station, unless, he should be, specially, appointed to it, the principle of reduction, being applicable, to every officer, in every corps. It is proper, also, to observe that the duties of Adjutant General, under the existing arrangement, correspond, in almost every circumstance, with those of the late Adjutant & Inspector General, and not, with those, of an Adjutant General of a Division.

To give effect to this law, the President, was authorized by the 12th Section, to cause the officers, non commissioned officers, artificers, musicians, and Privates, of the several corps, then in the service of the U.S., to be arranged in such manner, as to form, and complete out of the same, the force, thereby provided for, and to cause the supernumerary officers, non commissioned officers, artificers, musicians & Privates, to be discharged from the service.

In executing this very delicate and important trust, I acted, with the utmost precaution. Sensible, of what, I owed to my country, I felt strongly, the obligation, of observing the utmost impartiality, in selecting, those officers, who were to be retained. In executing the law, I had no personal object to accomplish, or feeling to gratify; no one, to retain; no one, to remove. Having on great consideration, fixed, the principles, on which, the reduction, should be made, I availed myself of the example of my predecessor, by appointing, through the proper Department, a board of general officers, to make the selection, and whose report, I adopted.

In transferring the officers, from the old to the new corps, the utmost care was taken, to place them, in the latter, in the grades & corps, to which, they had respectively belonged in the former, so far, as it might be practicable. This, though not enjoined by the law, appearing to be just and proper, was never departed from, except in peculiar cases, and under imperious circumstances.

In filling the original vacancies, in the Artillery, and in the newly created office of Adjutant General, I considered myself at liberty, to place in them, any officer, belonging to any part of the whole military Establishment, whether of the staff, or line. In filling original vacancies, that is, offices newly created, it is my opinion, ["as a general principle" *interlined*] that Congress have no right, under the Constitution, to impose any restraint, by law, on the power, granted to the President, so as to prevent, his making, a free selection of proper persons, for these offices, from the whole body of his fellow citizens. Without, however, entering here, into that question, I have no hesitation, in declaring it, as my opinion, that the law fully authorized a selection, from any branch of the whole military Establishment, of 1815. Justified, therefore, as I thought myself, in taking that range by even the highest sanction, the ["whole" *canceled and* "sole" *interlined*] object, to which, I had, to direct my attention, was the merit of the officers, to be selected, for those stations. Three Generals of great merit, were either to be dismissed, or otherwise provided for. The very gallant, & patriotic defender of N[ew] Orleans, [Maj. Gen. Andrew Jackson,] had intimated his intention, to retire, but at my suggestion, expressed his willingness, to accept, the office of Commissioner, to receive the cession of the Floridas, and of Governor, for a short time, of that Territory. As to one, therefore, there was no difficulty. For the other two, provision, could only be made in the mode, which was adopted. [Brig. Gen. and Bvt. Maj.] Gen[era]l [Alexander] Macomb, who had signalized himself, in the defense of Plattsburg, was placed at the head of the Corps of Engineers, to which, he had originally belonged, and, in which, he had acquired great experience, Col. [Walker K.] Armistead, then at the head of that Corps, having voluntarily accepted, one of the new Regiments of Artillery, for which he possessed, very suitable qualifications. [Brig.] Gen[era]l [Henry] Atkinson, likewise an officer of great merit, was appointed, to the newly created office of Adjutant General. Brev[e]t [Brig.] Gen[era]l [Moses] Porter, an officer of great experience, in the Artillery, and merit, was appointed to the command of another of those Regiments; [Bvt.] Col. [John R.] Fenwick, then the oldest Lt. Col. of Artillery, and who had suffered much, in the late war, by severe wounds, was appointed to a third; and [Bvt. Lt.] Col. [Nathan] Towson, who had served with great distinction, in the same Corps, and been twice brevetted for his gallantry, in the late war, was appointed, to the last remaining one. Gen[era]l Atkinson, having declined the office of Adjutant General, Col. [James] Gadsden, an officer of distinguished merit, & believed to possess qualifications, adapted to it, was appointed, in his stead. In making the arrangement, the merits of Col. [Robert] Butler, & Col. [Roger] Jones, were not overlooked. The former, was assigned to the place, which, he would have held in the line, if he had retained his original lineal commission; and the latter, to his commission in the line, which he had continued to hold, with his Staff appointment.

That the reduction of the Army, & the arrangement of the officers, from the old to the new Establishment, and the appointments referred to, were in every instance, strictly conformable to law, will, I think, be apparent. To the arrangement, generally, no objection has been heard; it has been made, however, to the appointments, to the original vacancies, and particularly to those, of Col. Towson & Col. Gadsden. To those appointments, therefore, further attention, is due. If they were improper, it must be, either, that they were illegal, or, that the officers, did not merit the offices conferred on them. The acknowledged merit of the officers, and their peculiar fitness for the offices, to which, they were respectively appointed, must preclude all objection, on that head. Having already suggested my ["opinion" *canceled and* "impression" *interlined*], that in filling offices newly created, to which on no principle whatever, any one, could have a claim, of right, Congress could not, under the Constitution, restrain the free selection of the President, from the whole body of his fellow citizens, I shall only further remark, that if that ["opinion" *canceled and* "impression" *interlined*] is well founded, all objection to these appointments, must cease. If the law imposed such restraint, it would, in that case, be void. But, according to my judgment, the law imposed none. An objection to the legality of those appointments, must be founded, either, on the principle, that those officers, were not comprized, within the corps, then in the service of the U.S., that is, did not belong to the peace Establishment, or that the power, granted by the word "arrange," imposed, on the President, the necessity, of placing in these new offices, persons of the same grade, only, from the old. It is believed, that neither objection, is well founded. Col. Towson, belonged to one of the corps, then in the service of the U.S., or in other words, of the military peace Establishment. By the act of 1815.16 [*sic*] the Pay Department, of which, the Pay Master General, was the chief, was made one of the branches of the Staff, and he, and all those under him, were subjected to the rules & articles of war. The appointment, therefore, of him, and especially to a new office, was strictly conformable to law.

The only difference, between the 5th Section of the Act of 1815, for reducing the Army, and the 12th section of the Act of 1821, for still further reducing it, by which, the power to carry those laws into effect, was granted to the President, in each instance, consists, in this, that by the former, he was to cause the arrangement to be made, of the officers, non commissioned officers, musicians & Privates, of the several *corps of troops*, then in the service of the U.S., whereas, in the latter, the term, [of] *troops*, was omitted. It cannot be doubted, that, that omission, had an object, and that, it was, thereby, intended, to guard against misconstruction, in so very material & important a circumstance, by authorizing the application of the Act, unequivocally, to every corps of the staff, as well as, of the line. With that word, a much wider range was given, to the act of 1815, in the reduction, which then took place, than under the last act. The omission of it, from the last act, together with all the sanctions, which were given by Congress, to the construction of the law, in the reduction, made under the former, could not fail, to dispell [*sic*] all doubt, as to the extent of the power, granted, by the last law, and of the principles, which ought to guide, and, on which, it was thereby, made the duty, of the President, to execute it. With respect to the other objection, that is, that officers of the same grade, only, ought to have been transferred, to these new offices, it is equally unfounded.

It is admitted, that officers, may be taken from the old corps, & reduced, & arranged in the new, in inferior grades, as was done, under the former reduction. This admission, puts an end to the objection, in this case, for if an officer, may be reduced, and arranged, from one corps to another, by an entire change of grade, requiring a new commission, and a new nomination to the Senate, I see no reason, why an officer, may not be advanced, in like manner. In both instances, the grade, in the old corps, is alike disregarded. The transfer from it, to the new, turns, on the merit of the party; and, it is believed, that the claim, in this instance, is felt, by all, with peculiar sensibility. The claim of Col. Towson, is the stronger, because, the arrangement of him, to the office, to which, he is now nominated, is not, to one, from which, any officer, has been removed, and to which, any other officer, may, in any view, of the case, be supposed, to have had a claim. As Col. Gadsden, held, the office of Inspector General [in the Southern Division], and as such, was acknowledged, by all, to belong to the Staff of the Army, it is not perceived, on what ground, his appointment, can be objected to.

If such a construction is to be given to the Act of 1821, as to confine the transfer of officers, from the old to the new Establishment, to the *corps of troops*, that is, to the line of the Army, the whole Staff of the Army, in every branch, would not only be excluded, from any appointment in the new Establishment, but altogether disbanded, from the service. It would follow, also, that all the offices of the Staff, under the new arrangement, must be filled by officers, belonging to the new Establishment, after its organization, and their arrangement, in it. Other consequences, not less serious, would follow. If, the right of the President, to fill these original vacancies, by the selection of officers, from any branch of the whole military Establishment, was denied, he would be compelled, to place in them, officers, of the same grade, whose corps, had been reduced, and, they with them. The effect, therefore, of the law, as to those appointments, would be, to legislate into office, men, who had been already legislated, out of office, taking from the President, all agency, in their appointment. Such a construction, would not, only, be subversive of the obvious principles of the Constitution, but utterly inconsistent, with the spirit of the law itself; since it would provide offices, for a particular grade, and for every member of that grade, in those offices, at a time, when every other grade, was reduced, & among them Generals, and other officers of the highest merit. It would also defeat every object of selection, since Colonels of Infantry would be placed, at the head of Regiments of Artillery, a service, in which, they might have had no experience, & for which, they might, in consequence, be unqualified.

Having omitted in the message to Congress, at the commencement of the session, to state the principles, on which, this law, had been executed, and having imperfectly explained them, in the message to the Senate of the 17th of Jan[uar]y last, I deem it, particularly incumbent on me, as well, from a motive of respect to the Senate, as to place, my conduct, in the duty imposed on me, by that act, in a clear point of view, to make this communication, at this time. The examples, under the law of 1815, whereby officers were reduced, and arranged from the old corps to the new, in inferior grades, fully justify all that has been done, under the law of 1821. If the power to arrange, under the former law authorized the removal of one officer, from a particular station, & the location of another, in it, reducing the latter from a higher, to an inferior grade, with the advice and consent of the Senate, it surely justifies, under the latter law, the arrangement of these officers, with a like sanction, to offices of new creation, from which, no one had been removed, & to which no one had a just claim. It is on the authority of these examples ["supported by the construction which I gave to the law" *interlined*] that I have acted, in the discharge of this high trust. I am aware, that many officers, of great merit, having the strongest claims on their Country, have been reduced, and others dismissed, but under the law, that result, was inevitable. It is believed, that none have been retained, who had not, likewise, the strongest claims to the appointments, which have been conferred on them. To discriminate, between men, of acknowledged merit, especially, in a way, to affect so sensibly and materially, their feelings and interests, for many of whom, I have personal consideration & regard, has been a most painful duty, yet, I am conscious, that I have discharged it, with the utmost impartiality. Had I opened the door, to change, in any case, even where error, might have been committed, against whom, could I afterwards have closed it, and into what consequences might not, such a proceeding have led? The same remarks, are applicable, to the subject, in its relation to the Senate, to whose calm & enlightened judgement, with these explanations, I again submit, the nominations, which have been rejected.

LS in DNA, RG 46, 17B-A1. NOTE: No evidence has been found that bears directly upon the point, but it is probable, considering Monroe's usual deference to his Cabinet officials in matters that concerned their respective branches of the administration, that this report to the Senate was prepared for Monroe's signature under Calhoun's direction or even by Calhoun himself. In organization, phraseology, and other stylistic details it embodies similarities with Calhoun's writings.

To [James Monroe], 4/13. Pursuant to a Senate resolution [of 4/9 (DS in DNA, 1, S-421 [M-221:94])] requesting information about the best site for the erection of an arsenal "on the Western Waters," Calhoun replies that all relevant information "to be found in this office is embraced in a report of Major Gen[era]l [Andrew] Jackson of January 1818, the original of which was transmitted to the Chairman of the Committee of Public Lands of the Senate, [Jeremiah Morrow,] on the 4th February, 1818 [Abs in *The Papers of John C. Calhoun*, 2:120]. No copy has been retained in this Department." LS in DNA, RG 46, 17A-E6; FC in DNA, 6, 2:53 (M-127:2).

From W[illiam] G.D. Worthington, Secretary, Acting Governor, and Superintendent of Indian Affairs for East Fla., St. Augustine, 4/13. He suggests that better materials, such as clay bricks and wood, be used in any new construction work there, rather than the usual concrete blocks, and that old, dilapidated buildings made of concrete be torn down. Concrete "is unfit for the upper parts of buildings where people reside or sleep." It produces a "disagreeable effluvia" in damp, hot weather. With regard to the repairs and improvements made to Fort St. Marks and the convent of St. Francis for use by troops, Worthington encloses a copy of a letter dated 8/24/1821 from [Andrew] Jackson to Worthington, [actually addressed to Capt. John R. Bell or the commanding officer,] and Worthington's reply of 10/4, for the purpose of showing that Worthington's role in requisitioning for the repairs was quite small. (A note from T[rueman] Cross that is found in this file indicates that the papers were borrowed by the Quartermaster General's Department and were returned and that Cross disagreed with Worthington's supposition that some material other than concrete would produce a better effect.) ALS with Ens in DNA, 1, W-301 (M-221:94).

Lt. Col. George Bomford to N[INIAN] EDWARDS, [Senator from Ill.]

Ordn[an]ce Dep[artmen]t, 15 Ap[ri]l 1822

The applications addressed to you by Mess[rs.] Duff Green & others, of Missouri, for leases of Lead mine lands from the U.S. & communicated by you to the Hon[orable] Sec[retary] of War, have been laid by him before this Dep[artmen]t in whose Charge the issuing of such Leases, under the sanction of the Dep[artmen]t of War, & the Presid[ent] of the U.S. [James Monroe] has recently been placed.

I have therefore the honor to state to you, for your information, that, until the Business of the Lead mine lands can be revived under new & better regulations, and more full & direct Information attained in regard thereto (and for which measures are now taking) the Gov[ernmen]t has concluded to grant leases of small extent, say of 160 Acres of Land to each applicant or Company on certain privileges & conditions, the principal of which are: To continue for 3 years, the 2 first to be free from Rent, & on the 3d a Rent of 1/10th of the Mineral raised to be paid to Gov[ernmen]t; the Lessees to have the privilege of wood [*one word canceled*] to erect their works, use of water &c. usual in such cases; to be paid at a certain valuation for the improvements they shall have made at the Close of the Lease, if not renewed by them, on the Land located & worked; the selection of the Land & the Commencement of the works, (of mining) to be within 9 months from the date of the Lease under penalture [*sic*] of forfeiture thereof; & no sub-leases allowable.

Should you think proper to direct Leases for the applicants now named, this Office will be prepared under the direction of the Sec[retary] of War to take such further measures as may be deemed requisite.

FC in DNA, 33, 1:6.

To [James Monroe], 4/15. Pursuant to a Senate resolution of 4/12 [DS in DNA, 1, S-424 (M-221:94)] "requesting the President [James Monroe] . . . to cause to be laid before the Senate the original proceedings of the Board of General Officers, charged with the reduction of the Army under the Act of the 2nd of March 1821; together with all communications to and from said board on the subject of reducing the Army including the case submitted to the Attorney General, [William Wirt,] and his opinion thereon," Calhoun encloses the requested papers, with the exception of two whose originals cannot be found: "one of which provides for the contingency of General [Henry] Atkinson's declining the place of Adjutant General, ["and the other" *canceled*] and the other, in the event of his declining recommends Col. [James] Gadsden to be selected to fill his place." Nevertheless, a copy of the former has been taken from the Army Register and is enclosed. Calhoun explains that the members of the Board "were influenced in their selection by their personal knowledge of the Officers with the characters of whom . . . it is believed the Board was intimately acquainted." He encloses a copy of the only correspondence with [William Wirt, dated 5/16/1821], dealing with soldiers under sentences of courts-martial. Wirt was consulted frequently while the reduction of the Army was under consideration, but he "gave no other written or official opinion." Calhoun considers it important that the enclosed original and confidential papers be preserved in the [War] Department. LS with En in DNA, RG 46, 17B-A1; FC in DNA, 6, 2:57 (M-127:2). The En found in DNA, RG 46, 17B-A1, is a copy of the actions of three sessions of the Board. An apparently related DU, listing seven groups of documents submitted to Monroe in regard to "the late reduction of the Army," can be found in DNA, 77 (M-271:4, frame 877).

From Brig. Gen. D[aniel] Parker, Paymaster General, 4/15. When Calhoun "handed the original papers [for publication with the *Army Register*] to me on the 14th of May last directing me to prepare the reduced Army list accordingly, there were three papers of which the enclosed are copies." While Parker was returning with them to Calhoun for additional instructions, [Jacob] Brown asked for them and failed to restore them to Parker. "I reported the facts [to Calhoun] and afterwards received the paper [from Brown] which was published in Gen[era]l orders with the Army list of the 17th of May 1821." LS in DNA, RG 46, 17B-D2; FC in DNA, 291, 15:409; CC in DNA, 1, P-304 (M-221:94). (Compare Parker's deposition to the Senate Committee on Military Affairs, printed herein under date of 4/23.)

To Jasper Parrish, Sub-Agent of the Six Nations, Canandaigua, N.Y.

Department of War, 15 Ap[ri]l 1822

I have received your letter of the 11th Jan[uar]y last [Abs in *The Papers of John C. Calhoun*, vol. VI].

I enclose herewith a copy of my answer to a letter from the Chiefs of the first Christian party of the Oneida Nation with extracts of letters to S[olomon] U. Hendricks [*sic*; Hendrick], which contain the views of the Government relative to the Treaty with the Menomeenees and Winnebagoes and the removal of the Six Nations to the lands ceded by it. These views you will communicate to the Indians in the way you may judge best calculated to make a favorable impression.

I have directed the amount of the annuity due to the Six Nations to be remitted to you, to be applied agreeably to the wishes of the Chiefs.

When Hendricks was here, he at the request of Cornelius Beard applied for a medal for him and at the same time stated that there was but one medal owned by any of the Stockbridge tribe, in answer to which he was informed that you would be requested to furnish an estimate of the number of medals that would be required to supply those who were entitled to them, and I have now to request that such an estimate may be forwarded.

[Enclosure]

Brothers, I have received your letter of the 14th inst[ant; actually 3/14: LS (with their marks) in DNA, 1, O-74 (M-221:93)] and enclose herewith extracts of my answers to two communications which I received from Solomon U. Hendricks, who lately visited the seat of Government in the capacity of a Deputy from the Stockbridge tribe which contain answers to your 1st 2nd & 3d inquiries.

In answer to the 4th inquiry, I have to state that if Schools should be established among you after your removal, for the purposes of instructing you in agriculture & letters, the government will give to them the same aid toward the construction of the necessary buildings and for tuition that it has given to establishments of a similar description elsewhere.

You will observe by my answer to S.U. Hendricks that permission has been granted for another party from from [*sic*] the Stockbridge tribe and ["from" *interlined*] the Oneida or the other tribes of the Six Nations, consisting of six, to visit Green Bay, to procure an extension of the cession from the Menomeenees & Winnebagoes, in the way you desire, who will be furnished with letters as heretofore, and with one ration each ["a" *interlined*] day.

The reports which you state are in circulation "that if you ratify the Treaty which has been concluded with the Menomeenees & Winnebagoes you will be immediately obliged by the government to remove to the Country ceded by it, in a general body" are without foundation. Your Great Father the President [James Monroe] thinks it would be better for the respective tribes of the Six Nations to dispose of their lands in Newyork [*sic*] and to remove to the lands which have ["been" *interlined*] or may be ceded to them by the Menomeenees and Winnebagoes, because they could then concentrate their now scattered population, and being removed to a distance from the white settlements, they would be more secure against the effects of violence and injustice and the efforts of the government to improve their condition would be ["rendered" *canceled*] less difficult and expensive. With these views your Great father the President approved of the treaty which had been made with the Menomeenees and Winnebagoes, and it would be pleasing to him to see it ratified by the Six Nations generally; but whether the treaty be ratified or not, he by no means intends to adopt any measures for the removal of the Six Nations, or any part of them, nor will he suffer it to be done, without their free assent.

Given under my hand & Seal of the War Office of the U.S., the 15th day of April 1822. J.C.C.

LS in N, no. 7236; FC with En in DNA, 72, E:234–235 (M-15:5). Note: The En was addressed to Anthony Ascregoioa, John Brant, Hendricks Poulis, John Scanandow, Nedy Alriquest, John August, Cornelius Beard, Thomas Scanandow, Peter August, John Cornelius, and John Peter as "Chiefs of the 1st Christian party of the Oneida Nation."

To W[illiam] B[eatty] Rochester, [Representative from N.Y.]

Dep[art]m[en]t of War, 15 April 1822

For the information of Mr. [Robert] Troup I herewith enclose copies and extracts of letters which indicate the views and measures of the government in relation to the removal of the Six Nations from the State of New York. By these it will be seen that the Government has endeavoured to impress upon the Indians the advantages of changing their present residence for one further [*sic*] West, and it will continue to do so upon every suitable occasion; but no steps for their removal can be taken without their consent.

I have enclosed a copy of my answer to the letter of the Chiefs of the 1st Christian party of the Oneida nation to Capt. [Jasper] Parrish, with instructions to make known to the Indians generally the views which it contains relative to the Treaty concluded with the Menominees & Winnebagoes and their removal to the country ceded by it, but no immediate answer to the communication from him upon the subject was deemed necessary as the substance of these views had been already communicated to the Indians through Capt. Parrish & various other channels.

FC in DNA, 72, E:233–234 (M-15:5). NOTE: How this letter was received is revealed, herein, in that of 6/10 from Troup to Calhoun.

From THOMAS HEMPSTEAD, Acting Partner of the Missouri Fur Company

Saint Louis, April 17, 1822

Having just seen the printed documents relative to the Indian Trade, Submitted to the Senate by the Committee on Indian Affairs, I was much astonished to read the letters of Mr. G[eorge] C. Sibley, United States Factor at Fort Osage, to Thomas L. McKinney [*sic*], Superintendant [*sic*] of Indian Trade. The first is dated Fort Osage, April 16, 1819, and the second May 16, 1820. The language he uses, and the charges ther[e]in mentioned against the Missouri Fur Trader, are unwarranted and unjust. As the Acting Partner of the Missouri Fur Company, I am bound for myself and that company to notice those letters.

In the first letter, in the appeal which this Factor would make to the American Farmers he says, "you who may emphatically be called the pioneers of civilization, you have to remove your families to the borders; you have purchased lands there from the government, and have been led to beleive [*sic*] that your government possessed, and meant to retain the power to controll your enemies, the *Savages* and the *Traders*, and thus afford you protection, and such truly and such truly [*sic*] was the intention of government; but it is now different—the clamorous cupidity of the traders will no longer be restrained; the Indian trade must be given up to 'Individual enterprize,' *to merciless men who feel not for your sufferings and care not for your wrongs*, to intriguing foreigners, who thirst for the blood of your wives and little ones[,] to the unprincipeled [*sic*] pioneers of commerce of every shade and hue.["] Again, "your property must be sacrificed, yourselves murdered, and your farms desolated; but these men insist upon their rights & the fur and the fur trade left open to them." In the same frothy language, he says, "your arms must defend the frontiers, and the blood of your wives and children appease the savage propensities of your Indian neighbours. Who must be left in the present unhappy state a scourge to our frontier, a reproach to the government, profitable to those *few* highly favoured, because meritorious Citizens—the Indian Traders." He[,] Mr. Sibley, adds, that he fondly hopes for better things, and although we are left for another year powerless and unprotected from the malice and galling insults of every *renegade trader*, although the Agents of the government are still subjected to the derision and open op[p]osition of the traders, without any official power to compel those people to treat the institutions of the government, with a becoming respect.

In the letter of May 16, Mr. Sibley says, "but if those ped[d]lers are not kept from among the Indians, they will most inevitably all be totally ruined, cruel wars will be excited[,] our frontiers will again bleed, and the wretched Indians crushed. Mark me Sir, these things are near at hand.["]

At the date of the first letter, the present Missouri Fur Company was not formed—it was shortly after—but the Missouri Indian trade was chiefly in the hands of the late Mr. Manuel Lisa (of whom it may be truly said the government nor the inhabitants of the frontiers, had not a better supporter, or a more sincere & efficient friend with the Indians,) and of several highly respectable citizens of Saint Louis. Mr. Manuel Lisa was the founder of the present Missouri Fur Company, and I conceive Mr. Sibley must refer to him as one of the "merciless Indian traders.["] In justice to the memory of that enterprising citizen, let me assure you that if he is meant, Mr. Sibley[']s letter is, as regards him, a most unwarranted calum[n]y; and here let me refer you to Gen[era]l [William] Clark, late Superintendant of Indian Affairs, at St. Louis, for the conduct and character of Manuel Lisa.

The last extract of Mr. Sibley[']s letter I consider applies to the Missouri Fur Company—and in reply I have but to answer that the Company is composed of men, whose characters for integrity and unimpeachable patriotism, are "*above suspicion*," and however lowly the patriotic Factor may deem them, would not even exchange characters with him. I would invite and boldly challange [*sic*] any man to point his finger to that act of the Missouri Fur Company which is not strictly correct and just, towards the government or the Indians[,] and I am ready and willing to be accountable to the government for every act of the Company or its agents, or to any man that will not degrade himself by making false misrepresentations. For the character & conduct of the members of the Missouri Fur Company, permit me to refer you to Maj. Benj[amin] O'Fallon, Indian Agent for the Missouri, Gen-era]l Wm. Clark, [Bvt. Brig.] Gen[era]l [Henry] Atkinson[, former Brig.] Gen[era]l D[aniel] Bissell, and every honest man in the Country. I cannot express my astonishment, at the boldness, or insanity of this little pretended champion of Missouri, when I recollect how insignificantly he acted during the late war: cooped up in good quarters with perhaps a Company of U.S. [soldiers] to guard him and who never saw the smoke of a hostile gun during the War.

I have taken the liberty of addressing this communication to you as the Immediate Superior of the Indian trade, and because I know that for[?] you it will be treated in its proper light, with a single eye only to the dignity of the government, and Justice to us. I cannot think of confideing [*sic*] in any of the dependants on the Factory system whose interests it is to support by *all means* their offices.

A list of the gentlemen[']s names who compose the Missouri Fur Company at this time and in 1820 shall be forwarded to you, together with a copy of the articles of association for your perusal.

ALS with En in DNA, 1, H-288 (M-221:92).

From the Rev. J[EDIDIAH] MORSE

N[ew] Haven, Apr. 17th 1822

I arrived here the 8th inst[ant] & have ever since been confined by extreme debility, from wh[ic]h I am, by good nursing, fast recovering. I found my family well, except a fine ["ba" *canceled*] infant grand daughter a fortnight old, who has since sunk into the arms of death—& yesterday was consigned to the grave. The event afflicts us, but we have our comforts from our undoubting faith in her present & everlasting happiness.

I am preparing, as I gain stren[g]th, to commence the printing of my Report. I wish to be favored with copies of all your printed communications to Congress on the subject of Ind[ia]n Affairs—particularly that announced by the Speaker the 12th inst[ant] on the No. &c. of Superintendants [*sic*], Agents &c.—& with any Reports of Ind[ia]n Agents & others wh[ic]h come into your office, & wh[ic]h may be of use to me.

With kind regards to the Ladies of your good family, in wh[ic]h Mrs. M[orse] joins me, I am, D[ea]r Sir, very truly yours[,] J. Morse.

ALS in DNA, 1, M-342 (M-221:93).

From WINFIELD SCOTT

Governors Island, [N.Y.,] Ap[ri]l 17th 1822

The melancholy duty has devolved on me to report that Brevet Brigadier General [Moses] *Porter*, Colonel of the 1st Regiment of Artillery, who passed thro' two wars with honour to himself & signal utility to his country, has at length paid the debt of nature. He died on the morning of the 14th instant near Boston. Brevet Lieutenant Colonel [John De Barth] Walbach, the nearest commander reports—"he shall make every arrangement which his small command will permit to inter the deceased with military honours as the last respect we can pay to this departed meritorious soldier & patriot."

If it shall be thought necessary to issue an order for officers on duty to wear crape on the hilts of their swords for [*here a space was left blank*] month, I beg leave to suggest that it be issued from general head quarters so that it may include the whole Army.

As this death may affect the position of Brevet Lieutenant Colonel [Abram] Eustis, & as I *know* it to be his wish to remain in East Florida, permit me to suggest whether it be not possible to give him some equivalent civil appointment, under the general government which will retain him in that quarter? He has six small boys whose translation to Detroit would be extremely inconvenient & detrimental. The merits of the Lieutenant Colonel are known to be of the first order as a soldier, to which I will take the liberty to add, that his talents for most civil employments are but little less, if any thing inferior. I am aware that this suggestion is aside from the ordinary course of official correspondence; but shall confidently rely on your liberality for my apology.

ALS in DNA, 16, 1822, S-27 (M-567:5, frames 74–77); FC in DNA, RG 393, Records of U.S. Army Continental Commands, 1821–1920, Eastern Division and Department, 1818–1861, Letters Sent, Eastern Division, 1817–1823.

To John Williams, [Chairman,] Senate Committee on Military [Affairs], 4/17. In answer to Williams's letter of 4/15 [ALS in DNA, 1, W-270 (M-221:94)], Calhoun encloses "copies of the correspondence of Generals [Jacob] Brown & [Henry] Atkinson relative to the appointment of the latter to be Adjutant General" and copies of letters by [1st] Lt. [John A.] Dix and by the [War] Department, all of which have been sent to the House Committee on Military Affairs. Calhoun observes that "previous to the meeting [in 1821] of the Board [of Army officers to consider the reduction of the Army] I was directed by the President [James Monroe] to offer [Brig.] Gen[era]l [Alexander] Macomb the command of the Engineer Corps, and [Brig.] Gen[era]l Atkinson the command of his former Regiment or any other he might choose with the Brevet rank of Brig. General[,] to which he assented. His letter signifying it, was laid before the Board and is transmitted to the President with ["the" *interlined*] original proceedings of the Board in answer to the call of the Senate on that subject. The Board[,] notwithstanding[,] thought he might be more useful in the Office of Adjutant General for which his qualifications peculiarly fitted him, and accordingly arranged him to that station, believing it ["would be" *interlined*] equally acceptable to him as the command of a Regiment." LS in DNA, RG 46, 17B-D2; FC in DNA, 4, 2:246 (M-220:1).

From C[LAUDIUS] CROZET, Professor of Engineering

West-Point, April 18th 1822

Captain [David Bates] Douglass having Communicated to me his wish to be transferred into the Department of Engineering and accordingly proposed a mutual exchange of our Professorships, as I had no personal reason to prefer either Department, I agreed to take charge of that of Mathematics, if your Excellency had no objection to this arrangement, which we respectfully submit to your Consideration.

ALS in DNA, 14, 280.

To P[atrick] Farrelly, [Representative from Pa.,] 4/18. "The assertion that $300,000 in addition to the sum appropriated had been expended last year on account of fortifications to which your note of this morning [ALS in DNA, 1, F-102 (M-221:92)] refers, is incorrect." Calhoun refers Farrelly to War Department reports of 4/10 to [William Eustis], Chairman of the House Committee on Military Affairs, and of 3/8 to [Benjamin] Hardin, Chairman of a Select Committee [to Study Retrenchment in Public Expenditures]. FC in DNA, 3, 11:382 (M-6:11).

From Winfield Scott, Governors Island, [New York Harbor,] 4/18. He recommends that the detachment of the 3rd Infantry Regiment stationed at Chicago be ordered to return to its headquarters. "This recommendation is founded on the belief, that the keeping of troops at Chicago has no important influence on the neighbouring Indians; that the post affords no essential protection to any white settlement; that the route from Lake Michigan, to the Mississippi, via the Chicago & the Illinois rivers is but little used; that the concentration of the Regiment will promote public economy; the discipline &c., of the corps; & that the force at Green Bay ought to be augmented." Feeling that the subject of transferring a portion or the whole of the 2nd Infantry Regiment to a new post is within the sphere of his responsibility, Scott offers his opinion. "I trust that the Regiment will not be divided for some of the reasons already suggested in respect to the *third*. Division would impair its present high character for pride & efficiency." Scott agrees with a proposal to transfer the Regiment to Sault Ste. Marie. "A strong force at the Sault of St. Mary would certainly operate as a strong moral restraint, in time of peace, on the Indians of the North-west, in their passage to & from Drummond's Island where the British annuities & presents are distributed; and, in a more direct manner, exclude British Indian traders from our territory." Scott feels that Sackets Harbor, "as a military station," has little value. "In the contingency of war with Great Britain, our regular forces, in my humble judgement, ought to be assembled on the frontier of Lower Canada for offensive operations, & Madison Barracks used only for the lodgement of militia till the end of a successful campaign. The moment our Army is established in some point on the St. Lawrence (the lower down the better) all the positions above, ships &c., both American & British, will be useless. The more important of these views were urged by me during the late war; but I had not, in time, rank or influence, to effect our plans of campaign; & the late expenditure at Sacketts Harbour was principally made before the post came under my command. Neither was I consulted on the subject of the military road commencing at the same point. The order for the work was issued by higher authority." If the whole Regiment moves from Madison Barracks, the Company of Artillery at Plattsburg or the Company at Michilimackinac might be ordered to Madison Barracks to take care of the buildings. "It is presumed, that when Green Bay & the Sault of St. Mary, are strongly occupied that Island may be evacuated." ALS in DNA, 1, S-458 (M-221:94).

To Samuel Smith, Chairman, House Ways and Means Committee, 4/18. Calhoun requests that appropriations for four constant expenses incurred under Indian treaties be provided on a permanent basis: $2,400 annually to the Choctaws, as stipulated by treaties of 11/16/1805 and earlier dates; $750 to pay the annuity and other expenses "relative to Light Horse" incurred by the Choctaw treaty of 10/18/1820; the $500 annuity of the Kaskaskias, as specified by a treaty of 8/13/1803; and $2,000 to employ a blacksmith and someone "to aid in agriculture," as was arranged at Saginaw on 9/24/1819. Calhoun thinks that standing appropriations for these recurring expenses will lessen confusion and promote uniformity. FC in DNA, 72, E:237–238 (M-15:5).

To Samuel Smith, Chairman, House Committee on Ways and Means, 4/18. Calhoun encloses a letter from [Alexander Macomb dated 4/18 (LS in DNA, RG 233, 17A-E4; FC in DNA, 21, 1:258–259)] suggesting an appropriation [of $30,000] for the collection of materials for construction of a fort on the right bank of the Mississippi, opposite Fort St. Philip. Calhoun suggests that the wording be altered to include the expense of constructing a levee. LS with En in DNA, RG 233, 17A-E4; FC in DNA, 4, 2:246 (M-220:1).

From Samuel L. Southard, [Senator from N.J.]

18 Ap[ri]l 1822

The enclosed Papers were received by me, yesterday. I am acquainted with the persons named in the Papers as Officers & Physicians—they are respectable men.

May I beg the favor of an early attention to the case of Clarkson, & information whether any thing can be done for him?

ALS in ScU-SC, John C. Calhoun Papers. NOTE: An AEI by Calhoun indicates that this letter was referred to [James L.] Edwards of the Pension Office. An AEU indicates that this letter was answered, probably by Edwards, on 4/22.

To John Williams, Chairman, Senate Committee on Military Affairs, 4/18. In reply to Williams's letter of 4/17 [ALS in DNA, 1, W-271 (M-221:94)], Calhoun encloses a copy of Robert Brent's commission in 1809 as Paymaster General. No copies can be found of the commissions as Paymasters General of [Caleb] Swan, dating from 1792, and of [Nathan] Towson, dated 8/28/1819, but Towson has been requested by mail to send his commission for the perusal of the Committee. FC in DNA, 4, 2:246–247 (M-220:1).

Lewis Cass, Detroit, to [George] Boyd, [Mackinac,] 4/19. "I have only a moment to say that, if you have not already made such arrangements with respect to a canoe that you cannot recede from them, that [*sic*] I wish you would not send me one. I received yesterday a letter from Mr. [John C.] Calhoun in which he says that the unexpected length of this session of Congress will prevent him from making the tour he had anticipated. No news yet of an appropriation." LS in DNA, 76 (M-1:70, p. 289).

To Lewis Cass, Detroit, 4/19. Cass will receive $14,800 with which to pay annuities of $4,300 to the Ottawas, $3,800 to the Chippewas, $5,700 to the Potawatomies, and $1,000 to the Ottawas, Chippewas, and Potawatomies residing on the Illinois and Milwaukee Rivers. Funds for current expenses of the Agencies under Cass's supervision and the annuities specified in the Treaty of Chicago [of 1821] will be forwarded when Congress appropriates the money. LS with En in DNA, 76, 5:166–173 (M-1:10, pp. 166–173); FC in DNA, 72, E:239–240 (M-15:5).

To Richard Graham, [Indian Agent,] St. Louis, 4/19. He will receive $10,300 to cover annuities as follows: $4,300 to the Delawares, $3,000 to the Weas, $2,000 to the Kickapoos of the Vermilion, $500 to the Great Osages, and $500 to the Little Osages. Of the Delaware cash annuity of $5,500, the remaining $1,200 have already been sent to [John] Johnston to pay for horses used by the recent emigrants. When Congress makes funds available, the following sums will be remitted: the $2,000 due to the Kickapoos under the Treaty of Edwardsville, the annuities due to two Delaware Chiefs, and the cash in lieu of salt due to the Delawares. [James] Miller has informed Calhoun that [George C.] Sibley has $2,500 worth of goods withheld from the Osages' annuities of 1817–1820 (the FC cited below says 1817–1821); Sibley will be directed to distribute these goods generally among the Osages and will be informed that in the future the annuity for the Osages of Clamore's Village will be remitted separately. Calhoun has sent $500 for those Osages this year, and the balance due to the Osages will be paid by Graham as instructed above. Calhoun thinks that this is a fair division of the tribes's income. Congress has not yet appropriated expense funds for Indian affairs, and Calhoun fears that the public interest may suffer because Agents lack funds. He directs Graham, therefore, to use the $10,792.61 that he is obtaining by cashing a draft as follows: [Pierre] Menard, [Nicholas] Boilvin, [Thomas] Forsyth, and [Lawrence] Taliaferro are to be given $2,000, $2,000, $1,500 (the FC says $1,300), and $2,500, respectively, for their Agency expenses, and the balance of $2,792.61 should cover Graham's Agency expenses through the first half of 1822. "It would be proper for you and Mr. Menard to correspond with each other, in order that you may have a perfect understanding, during the emigration of the Delawares, as to your respective proceedings in relation to them, to prevent mistakes and unnecessary expense. It is presumed that the attention of Mr. Menard to these Indians will not be much longer required, and that it will not be necessary to make any expenditure on their account except what may be made through you." Calhoun cannot now answer Graham's inquiry concerning the annuity due to the Shawnees but has requested information from [John] Johnston, within whose Agency the Shawnees east of the Mississippi reside. Calhoun will answer within a few days Graham's letters concerning the Delawares and the war between the Osages and the Cherokees. LS in MoSHi, Richard Graham Papers; variant FC in DNA, 72, E:240–242 (M-15:5).

To J[ames] Noble, [Senator from Ind.]

War Department, April 19th 1822

In answer to your letter of the 15th inst[ant; *not found*] I have to state that you are under a mistake as to the time of passing the military appropriation act. It did not pass "early in February"—but on the 15th March 1822. The funds were transmitted immediately thereafter to all the Agents for paying Pensioners. The Agent in Indiana [Thomas Posey] has been furnished with funds for the purpose of paying the arrearages due to Pensioners up to the 4th March last.

FC in DNA, 91, 12:108.

From E. Robins "of Ohio"

Washington City, April 19th 1822

It has occurred to me that it might not be improper, before leaving the City to hand you a note expressive of my views and wishes, relative to an appointment under government.

It will be seen by the various letters of my Western friends to gentlemen here, that some of those letters have in view an appointment as Register of one of the Land Offices, while others refer, generally, to important public trusts. I have already intimated to you that I was induced to relinquish the idea of an application for a Land Office appointment, having ascertained satisfactorily, by conversation with many gentlemen here, that the circumstance of my being a citizen of a different State, would, in all probability, be urged in the Senate as an objection. I determined, therefore, with the advice of my friends, to apply for the situation of Secretary of Legation to Mexico, or to one of the new Governments of South America. Mexico would be greatly preferred, but as, in the present incipient state of things, in reference to these Embassies there are more than ordinary contingencies incident to such an appointment, and which cannot at this early period be guarded against, my next object, *and the one in which, in fact, I place the greatest reliance* is an appointment as Consul in one of the considerable ports of the new governments of South America—my choice would, of course, be, *a healthy port.*

In conformity with a suggestion of the President, [James Monroe,] I have handed to the Secretary of State the papers relating to my application.

Permit me to add, Sir, that your frank and polite attentions since my arrival here have inspired me with confidence, that I may calculate on your personal and I trust successful influence in accomplishing an object, which will be so gratifying to my own feelings, and to an extensive circle of friends who feel a warm interest in the result of my application.

P.S. Should a failure attend the application in both instances referred to, *which, however, I trust may not be the case*, a Consular agency in one of the European ports, should a vacancy exist, would meet my views—or an Agency in the Indian Department.

The Secretary of State [John Quincy Adams] assured me yesterday that he would call on the President immediately and place my application before him—it would be exceedingly gratifying if it were in your power to avail yourself of an early period to advise with the President in my behalf. Respectfully, E.R.

ALS in DNA, 103, Robins (M-439:14, frames 733–737).

WINFIELD SCOTT to [Christopher] Vandeventer

Eastern Department, Gov. Island, Ap[ri]l 19th, 1822

But for the pendency of the Bill further to reduce the Army, I should take the liberty to set out immediately for Washington, as my character, for aught I know, may have been involved in the late discussions in the Senate on the subject of my labours as Editor of the Army Regulations. I am prepared to show that [*one or two words canceled*] the book was reprinted in the most perfect good faith. No other person has the means of justifying me or perhaps would take the necessary trouble to do so. I am therefore desirous of obtaining permission to visit Washington, as soon as practicable—also for the further purpose of looking to my accounts which, I dare say, are exhibited in a manner not altogether as favourable to me as they might be exhibited. I of course have not seen the last report of the 3rd Auditor [Peter Hagner]; nor do I mean to insinuate any thing against him or any body else. I mean, however, to say that I am not a public debtor & that I have too long neglected my interests in respect to those accounts.

If permission be accorded to me to visit Washington, little minds, I am aware, will attribute my presence, ["at the seat of government," *canceled*] at this time, to the motives which are most familiar to their own breasts. I believe I can afford them that advantage, & whether in, or out of the service, still remain much beyond the reach of their censures. Those who are now in the government, as well as those who have lately retired, can bear witness, that I made no solicitation to be retained, either by myself or friends, at the last two reductions; & so help me God, I will not, in respect to that which impends. Let some of the individuals alluded to, say as much if they can. Of course, I do not include my friend [Bvt. Maj.] Gen[era]l [Edmund P.] Gaines among the number; & I might further except hundreds ["of" *interlined*] other honourable men—some who asked, & some who were silent as to their *wishes* to remain in service. *I*, however, shall not even express a wish, on the approaching question.

I write in great haste not to lose the mail. Have the goodness *verbally* to mention my proposition to the Secretary [of War, Calhoun], & if he thinks my presence for a day or two will not be prejudicial to *the interests of the Army* write to me at Phila[delphia] whither I shall go tomorrow or the next day, on a little visit (of two days) to my family. This letter is not official, & will not do to be shown. Yours with great regard, Winfield Scott.

ALS in DNA, 2, S-1822 (M-222:23).

To Peter Hagner, 4/20. Calhoun encloses a letter from Rufus King, [Senator from N.Y.,] a receipt of Mrs. Eleanor Lawrance for $3,500, "the amount allowed to her for damages &c. done" to her farm near Hell Gate, [Long Island, N.Y.,] and a copy of a letter to King "on that subject. You will adjust the claim conformably to this decision." FC in DNA, 3, 11:383 (M-6:11).

From J[oseph] McIlvaine, [U.S.] District Attorney for N.J., Burlington, N.J., 4/20. He informs Calhoun that Dr. Henry Gale has suspended his action of ejectment against Maj. [Samuel] Babcock [as representative of the U.S.] for possession of the Pea Patch Island. Gale intends to institute another lawsuit, in the N.J. Supreme Court with the State as a party to it. McIlvaine and [Richard] Stockton urge the necessity of persuading the N.J. legislature "to pass an act corresponding with that passed by . . . Delaware." McIlvaine states briefly the claims of Gale, Del., and N.J. to the island and requests early payment of Stockton's charges as attorney for the U.S. in the suit. PC's in *American State Papers: Military Affairs*, 5:485–486, and *Public Lands*, 6:439.

From Alexander Macomb

Engineer Department, April 20th 1822

The Contract with Mr. [Elijah] Mix for supplying stone for the Fortifications at Hampton Roads was made in July 1818.

Mr. Mix's proposal was for $3 per perch & was the lowest. There were two other proposals for delivering at Hampton Roads—one of them from Havre de Grace, [Md.,] the other from Port Deposit [Md.] nearly opposite to it on the Susqu[e]hannah, both at $3.50. There was also a proposal for delivering the stone on the bank of James River 25 miles above Richmond at $1.25 p[er] perch. Besides these a proposal of $4 was received a few days after the contract was concluded. The two proposals from the Susquehannah were founded upon experiments to ascertain the Cost, which had been authorized by this Department.

Mr. Mix arrived here early in July, and having intimated his intention to make a proposal for the contract, departed shortly after to examine the quarries, and collect other information requisite to aid him therein. He did not return until so long a time had elapsed, that it was supposed he had abandoned his intention, and the other proposals were about to be considered. And it is probable, if his absence had been delayed a few days longer, that one of them would have been accepted as according to the best information $3.50 appeared to be a reasonable price. Mr. Robert Leckie, a respectable & intelligent Stone Mason, who, as an Agent of this Department, had examined the Quarries on the Susquehannah, Potomac, York & James Rivers to collect such information, had reported that Stone could not be delivered at Hampton Roads for less than $3.50. In addition to this it was estimated that a quantity of Stone which had been quarri'd by the Government, and delivered at Old Point Comfort in the year 1817, & also in 1818 had cost about that price.

There had been no advertisement in the Newspapers for this Contract. It was deemed that the intention of the Government to make it, had received such publicity, and particularly at the quarries on the Susquehannah, Potomac, York & James Rivers, from which Proposals were most likely to be made, as would ensure proper competition. Nevertheless advertisements would have been issued, but it was found that those requiring proposals for materials &c. for the Fortifications on the Gulf of Mexico, had failed to produce the competition which had been expected, the only proposals received being from individuals in the immediate vicinity of this place.

It is proper to remark that it was proposed by the Engineer Department to add 50,000 Perches to the quantity embraced in the Contract, and that Mr. Mix declined it, in consequence of his doubts with respect to the adequacy of the price. Those doubts were founded upon the facts, that freight at that time could not be obtained for less than $2 per perch, and Quarriers for less than $1 & [$]1¼ p[er] day. The rate of freights has since been reduced to $1.50, and the hire of quarriers in a still greater proportion[;] from these adventitious circumstances, the Contract has become profitable.

FC in DNA, 21, 2:264–265.

To William Ward, [Choctaw Indian Agent, in Miss.,] 4/20. He will receive $9,300 in part payment of the Choctaw annuity for 1822. The balance, including the annuity due to Mushulatubbee "and the sum to be paid for the support of Light horse in each District of the Choctaw nation," totaling $3,150, will be sent as soon as Congress shall have appropriated the money. Ward will that he will render essential services to the government of his Agency. FC in DNA, 72, E:242–243 (M-15:5).

From V[IRGIL] MAXCY

Annapolis, April 21, 1822

Many of the Friends of General [William H.] Winder (and they are very numerous in Maryland) are desirous that he should be appointed Minister to one of the Spanish-American Governments & particularly to Mexico and one of them having written me to request, that I would address a letter to you on the subject, I take sincere pleasure in adding my testimony in his favour. His talents are too well known to all the members of the administration to require any remark. And having several times in conversation spoken of his personal character to you I have very little to add on that head. I can say with the greatest sincerity that no man in Maryland is more distinguished for enlightened & ardent patriotism & attachment to & confidence in our institutions, for a high sense of honour and for integrity & elevation of character. He would not only fill, but adorn the situation, which his friends are desirous he should be placed in. His appointment would I think be acceptable to all parties in this State, except perhaps a small squad of violent ultra Federalists. From an intimate personal acquaintance for many years & having served with him in the Senate [of Md.], I can say with truth, that no one, within my knowledge habitually acts from purer, more elevated or disinterested motives. Such men do honour to the country in all situations and, if he should be appointed, I shall feel a sincere gratification not only from my personal friendship for him but from a conviction that he will render essential services to the government of his country.

ALS in DNA, 103, Winder (M-439:19, frames 268–271).

From [Capt.] John R. Bell, [Acting Indian Agent in Fla. Territory,] Washington, 4/22. He has learned why the Indians west of the Suwannee River did not attend the meeting that was to have been held at Alachua on 11/20/1821. He doubts the wisdom of a license issued by [William G.D.] Worthington, Secretary of East Fla., to a white man allowing him to purchase 60 horses and 100 cattle from the Indians; if the U.S. should concentrate the Indians, they will be forced to turn their attention to agricultural pursuits and will need livestock. The Indians east of the Suwannee should be required to move to land between that stream and the Apalachicola River; their Agency should be established within that area, at Fort Gadsden, or at St. Marks; Bell suggests that someone should be sent from St. Augustine through Indian country to Pensacola to determine "the most practicable route for carrying the mails" and the best location for the Agency. ALS in DNA, 1, B-101 (M-221:95); PC in Carter, ed., *Territorial Papers,* 22:409–410.

From Thomas Forsyth, [Indian Agent,] St. Louis, 4/22. He criticizes the practice of giving as presents to the Indians any articles that cannot be sold in U.S. Factories. "Better and Cheaper Goods can be purchaced [*sic*] from individuals in this Country, than from the Factories." In addition, the British give a much greater quantity of presents to the Indians. ALS in DNA, 1, F-123 (M-221:92); two FC's in WHi, Draper Collection, Thomas Forsyth Papers, 4:118 and 7:83.

From [Col.] R[OGER] JONES

Fort Severn, [Md.,] April 22d 1822

For the reasons stated in the letter I have the honor herewith to transmit, I willingly unite my voice with the Officers whose names are therein subjoined.

I believe it may be received as an axiom in sound policy, when an individual or thing proves on actual trial to answer all the ends designed, that there can be but little wisdom or advantage in attempting experiments with new agents: It is in this practical point of view therefore, that I now feel authorized to express the hope that Mr. [Bennet] Hurst may receive the appointment as Sutler.

ALS owned in 1960 by Harvey S. Teal of West Columbia, S.C.

From ALEXANDER MACOMB

Engineer Department, 22nd April 1822

I have the honor to transmit herewith a Table showing the present Condition of the Fortifications at Mobile P[oin]t & Dauphine [*sic*] Is[lan]d.

The contracts for those fortifications were formed three months after advertisements for proposals had been circulated throughout the country, upon terms considered at the time very advantageous, being for each upwards of $50,000 within the estimate of the Board of Engineers. That for Dauphine Island was in a prosperous condition at the time the appropriation was withheld, and from the means applicable to its prosecution, as shewn in the table, there is every reason to believe, its progress would have continued to be entirely satisfactory, and that it would be erected within the estimate. The progress of that at Mobile Point, although retarded by the successive deaths of two contractors, yet it is believed that the securities who are gentlemen possessing ample means, would have made arrangements entirely satisfactory for their completion agreeably to the terms of the Contract, but for a fear that adequate appropriations would not be made to fulfil[l] them. In fact, arrangements had been nearly consummated with an individual [Lewis S. Coryell] of excellent character and business habits, and well supported by ample capital, but who, after the report of the [House Military Affairs?] Committee in relation to Dauphine Isl[an]d declined to complete them. It is believed that no other difficulty but the want of confidence, that the necessary appropriation would be made, would prevent the work from being completed under the Contract.

FC with En in DNA, 21, 1:265–266; CC in DNA, RG 233, 17A-F2.1.

To V[IRGIL] MAXCY

War Dept., 22nd April 1822

I received through Mr. [John Pendleton?] Kennedy your very agreeable favour of the 15th Inst[ant; *not found*]. Should it be in my power to render Mr. Kennedy any service, it will afford me much pleasure to do so. From what I have seen of him, I have formed a very favourable opinion, and have no doubt, that he is well qualified for the place which he solicits.

I return the letters of Gen[era]l [Robert Goodloe] Harper which you enclosed. I have read them with much pleasure. He will have a very important bearing on the coming contest, which in all probability will readjust the political elements of our country.

The indications are very favourable in North Carolina, and I doubt not with a little effort ["it" *canceled and* "the State" *interlined*] will be brought entirely right.

I have no doubt that your decision in regard to yourself has been judiciously formed; and altho' I would be much gratified to see you in the Legislature of your State, yet nothing ought to be put to hazard. I will converse with [Joseph?] Kent in relation to your M[anu]s[cript].

Things are coming rapidly to a crisis here. Few now doubt the hostility of ["on" *canceled*] the friends of one of its members [William H. Crawford] to the administration. The assault in the house on ["their" *canceled*] part ["of his friends" *interlined*] has been, within the last few days, fierce, but has been meet [*sic*] by those of the administration with complete effect. The more heat the better. It will bring the fever to the surface, and fully develop what has been so long concealed from the knowledge of the publick. I wrote you a few days since [on 4/12] in relation to Maj[o]r [George] Peter. I hope you have received my letter and that I shall soon hear from you.

Mrs. [Floride Colhoun] Calhoun & her mother [Floride Bonneau Colhoun] join their best respects to you and the ladies of your family. Yours truely [*sic*], J.C. Calhoun.

ALS in DLC, Galloway-Maxcy-Markoe Papers, vol. 32.

General order No. 22 by Calhoun, 4/22. "As a testimony of respect to the memory of [Bvt.] Brigadier General Moses Porter, a soldier of the Revolution and an officer of distinguished merit, the officers of the Army will wear crape on the hilt of their swords for the space of thirty days." FC in DNA, 19, 3:20; CC in DNA, 17, 1:23; CC in DNA, RG 98, Western Department, Orders and Letters Received by Gen. Henry Atkinson, 1821–1827, p. 45; CC in DNA, 186, 1821–1822:308–310; CC in DNA, 188; PC in Washington, D.C., *Daily National Intelligencer,* April 25, 1822, p. 3, col. 5. (Porter had died on 4/14. Heitman, *Historical Register,* 1:800.)

To Samuel Smith, Chairman of the House Committee on Ways and Means

Dep[art]m[en]t of War, April 22, 1822

I have received your note of this morning [ALS in DNA, 1, S-433 (M-221:94)] relative to the appropriations to carry into effect certain Indian treaties which is the first intimation I have had of the wish of the Committee of Ways and Means upon the subject.

All of the Indian treaties for which specific appropriations have been asked, are to be found in the first & sixth volumes of the laws of the United States, except the treaty concluded at Chicago, which was ratified by the Senate during the present session of Congress and published in the National Intelligencer of the 30th ult[im]o.

The treaty of Chicago was, after its ratification lodged in the Department of State, where all treaties are lodged and if the Committee deem it material to have the original, it will be necessary to make application to that Department for it, which I have no doubt will be readily complied with.

FC in DNA, 72, E:242 (M-15:5).

From Bvt. Lt. Col. Joseph G. Totten

New York [City], April 22d 1822

A letter from Mr. S[tephen] Pleasonton "agent of the Treasury" informs me that as respects a balance of $1,068.96 due from me to the United States some arrangement must be made before the

1st of June for its liquidation within a reasonable time, or suit will be commenced. My uneasiness under the reproach of being a public debtor, induces me to offer to you a relinquishment of my pay, subsistence &c. until the proper am[oun]t be retained.

ALS in DNA, 1, T-182 (M-221:94); FC in DNA, 230, 1822:7.

To Richard Graham, St. Louis, 4/23. Calhoun acknowledges Graham's letters of 11/12 and 12/28 in last year and of 1/3, 1/21, 2/7, and 3/4 in this [Abs's in *The Papers of John C. Calhoun*, vol. VI, except that of 1/21/1822, of which there is an ALS with Ens in DNA, 1, G-121 (M-221:92), and a PC with En in Carter, ed., *Territorial Papers*, 19:395–396]. Graham's salary as Indian Agent while he served in the survey of the Indian boundary has been allowed. James Latham has been appointed Sub-Agent at Peoria. Graham is to use his own discretion about supplying food to the emigrating Delawares; Calhoun thinks that an adequate supply of corn should be sufficient until they can become self-supporting. Graham is also to use his own judgment in choosing the site of permanent settlement for the Delawares, but Calhoun advises that it should be as far away from the Osages' lands as possible, in order to reduce friction. The lead mines in the area that has been intended for the Delawares must be reserved for the U.S. The warlike tendency of the Indians is a matter of concern to the government, and it is hoped that outbreaks can be avoided. If it is impracticable for Graham to submit his accounts and vouchers quarterly, he can do so semiannually. His advances to [Nicholas] Boilvin and to [Lawrence] Taliaferro are approved. His suggestion that a Sub-Agency be established for the Kansas [and Iowa] Indians will be considered when Calhoun has more time. LS in MoSHi, Richard Graham Papers; FC in DNA, 72, E:243–244 (M-15:5).

Alexander Macomb to [Bvt.] Maj. Gen. E[dmund] P. Gaines, Louisville, Ky., 4/23. The Secretary of War directs that the steamboat "Western Engineer now lying at Cash River five miles above the mouth of the Ohio" be sold on the best possible terms. FC in DNA, 21, 1:266–267.

Alexander Macomb to Zach[aria]h Wilson, [Pilot,] "Steam boat Western Engineer[,] Cash River," 4/23. The Secretary of War has directed that the *Western Engineer* "should be disposed of."

Wilson will conform with [Bvt.] Maj. Gen. [Edmund P.] Gaines's instructions. FC in DNA, 21, 1:267.

[Josiah Meigs, Commissioner, General Land Office,] to C[hristopher] Vandeventer, 4/23. "In answer to your enquiry as to the manner of disposing of Lead mines or Salt springs on the Public Lands, I have to state that the practice has been to apply to the Register & Receiver of the Office in whose district the mine or spring is, or to the Recorder of land titles in Missouri for leases, which leases were submitted to the appropriation or rejection of the President of the United States [James Monroe]. It has not been customary to advertise for the disposal of Mines or Springs." FC in DNA, 82, 11:359 (M-25:11).

Deposition of Daniel Parker, 4/23. He restates the substance of his oral testimony to the Senate Committee on Military Affairs concerning the destruction by [Maj.] Gen. [Jacob] Brown of certain papers concerning the reduction of the Army in 1821 and concerning the refusal by [Brig.] Gen. [Henry] Atkinson of the office of Adjutant General. PC in Senate Document No. 91, 17th Cong., 1st Sess.; PC in *American State Papers*: *Military Affairs*, 2:410.

From C[ornelius] P. Van Ness

New York [City], April 23d 1822

I am desirous to obtain an appointment as a Cadet at the Military Academy at West Point for Henry E. Theyes of Vermont. He is a young Gentleman whom I consider well qualified for that situation. It would be agre[e]able to me, if you would have the goodness to inform me, by letter directed to Burlington Vt. whether it will be probable that Mr. Theyes and his friends will be gratified.

ALS in PHi.

To William Ward, Choctaw Agency, 4/23. Calhoun acknowledges Ward's letters of 3/19 [*not found*] and 3/25 [ALS in DNA, 77 (M-271:4, frames 230–232)], which were received after money had been sent to Ward [on 4/20] for the Choctaw annuity in accordance with Ward's promise to the Indians. Ward can purchase the goods desired by the Choctaws from this sum. "If you should deliver any of the goods which you have received from the Chickasaw Bluffs in payment of the annuity of this year, you will retain the value thereof out of the money remitted to you for said annuity and report the amount so retained to this Department for further orders." The U.S. "will take measures for the execution of the 7th & 8th articles of the late treaty [of 10/18/1820] with the Choctaws and securing to them the full amount of their annuity as soon as it can possibly be done. In the mean time it is presumed the Choctaws would not wish to withdraw from the Schools established among them for the education of their children the support which the Chiefs have so liberally & voluntarily extended to them & which could not now be done without materially embarrassing the opperations [*sic*] of these institutions and diminishing their capacity to do good in the nation." As soon as time allows "the report of the Commissioners appointed to value the improvements of the Choctaws under the late treaty will be taken up, and if approved, the money will be remitted to you to be paid accordingly." A postscript instructs Ward to pay the annuities as quickly as possible. FC in DNA, 72, E:244 (M-15:5).

To John Williams, [Chairman, Senate Committee on Military Affairs,] 4/23. Calhoun transmits the commission of Col. [Nathan] Towson to be the Paymaster General [as of 8/28/1819] and asks that the document shall be returned when it is "no longer required by the Committee." FC in DNA, 3, 11:384 (M-6:11).

To Philip P[endleton] Barbour, 4/24. The enclosed letter [of 4/23 from William Lee (LS in DNA, RG 233, 17A-E4; FC in DNA, 51, 7:310)] will show that the House resolution of 1/8 [concerning Ordnance Department expenses, 1817–1821 (DS in DNA, 1, R-101 [M-221:94])] cannot be answered during the present session of Congress [because requests for data from the House and its committees have been so frequent that Lee's Clerks cannot compile the information before adjournment]. LS with En in DNA, RG 233, 17A-E4; FC in DNA, 4, 2:247 (M-220:1).

From [Col.] George Gibson, [Commissary General of Subsistence]

Subsistence Office, Washington, April 24th 1822

I have the honor to lay before you, a statement shewing the cost of subsisting the Army for one year, commencing on the 1st of June 1820, and ending on the 31st of May 1821. This year has been selected in preference to the one preceding, because of the expense necessarily attendant on the first operations of the new system. The contract year commencing 1st of June 1816, has been selected to contrast with the 2nd year of the new system, because the contractor's [that is, contractors'] accounts for the subsequent years, are not finally adjusted, as appears by the letter of the 3rd Auditor [Peter Hagner]; and the amount may be hereafter affected by decisions which may take place on them. In ascertaining the number of men, subsisted in the contract years, under the former and present system, I have deemed it most equitable to take the number of men in service, in the month of December in each year, that period being the middle of the contract year.

In furnishing this statement, it may be proper to remark, that, altho' the price of provisions was considerably lower in the year commencing on the 1st of June 1820, yet the contracts were necessarily made in the fall of 1819, when provisions were not so much reduced in price as during the period embraced in the statement. It may, also, be proper to remark, that considerable expense has accrued from the regular issue of fresh beef at the posts on the Missouri, Upper Mississippi, and at Green Bay, by reason of the great distance Cattle had to be driven, and the loss sustained in wintering them at those cold and remote points. I beg leave, also, to draw your attention to the subject of the commutation of the hospital rations, by which a supply of fowls, milk, vegetables, and other necessaries, is furnished to the sick, at considerable cost to the subsistence fund. The greatest expense, however, has accrued from the improvement in the quality of the ration issued under the new system. The pork is rather better than prime, but not so good as Navy mess; and the flour is fine, and sometimes superfine. Under the old contracts, pork and flour of inferior brands could be issued, provided it was pronounced "merchantable" by two citizens; and I know of no instance wherein this was not the case.

LS with DS in DNA, RG 46, 17A-E6; FC in DNA, 191, 2:661–662; PC with En in Senate Document No. 92, 17th Cong., 1st Sess.; PC with En in *American State Papers*: *Military Affairs*, 2:416.

From Peter Hagner, 4/24. Pursuant to a Senate resolution [of 12/20/1821] concerning subsistence of the Army, Hagner reports that nearly all of the War Department accounts that were settled through the year 1812 "were lost or destroyed at the burning of the public buildings in 1814." Records dating from 1813 cannot yield the information requested "without an investigation almost equal to another settlement of the accounts of all the Paymaster's [*sic*] & Contractors during the late war & requiring therefore a great length of time." The cost of provisioning the Army from 6/1/1817 to 6/1/1819 was $1,561,076.25, of which $370,364.35 remain to the debit of the contractors and for the recovery of which lawsuits have been instituted. LS in DNA, RG 46, 17A-E6; FC in DNA, 53, 25:232–233; PC in Senate Document No. 92, 17th Cong., 1st Sess.; PC in *American State Papers: Military Affairs*, 2:415–416.

From [former Bvt. Brig. Gen.] J[OSEPH] G. SWIFT

New York [City], 24th April 1822

The commissioners to fix the Boundary line between Canada & the Un[ited] States operate this year between Lake Superior and the Lake of the Woods. The Commission want much a good Surveyor & Draughtsman & have requested my Brother-in-Law [2nd] Lieut[enant George W.] Whistler to accompany them. This operation would, in my opinion, bring Mr. Whistler forward prominently & do him a very material service & as the duty to be performed is of a Public nature, I hope you will be pleased to allow Mr. W[histler] a furlough & permission to accept the invitation of the Commissioners.

Mr. Whistler has consulted Major [Sylvanus] Thayer, who, in consequence of not being able to make Whistler's functions at the Academy as agreeable in a pecuniary way, as was expected, has advised to ask permission of the Gov[ernmen]t for Whistler to accompany the Commission.

I hope a compliance with Whistler[']s wishes may be found compatible with the public interest & remain . . . .

ALS with Ens in DNA, 16, 1822, W-22 (M-567:5, frames 618–626).

From A[lbert] G[allatin, U.S. Minister to France,] Paris, 4/25. "I have the honor to enclose [John,] Viscount de Lomagne's receipt for his Warrant for four hundred acres of land as Major in [Charles Treflin] Armand's Legion, and his original commission as such. He sends the Warrant to Mr. Petry with request to locate it. The Patent may be sent under cover of this legation." FC in NHi, Gallatin Papers.

From Howes Goldsborough & Co., Havre de Grace, [Md.,] 4/25. Although this firm has been recognized by [the War Department] as owner of a contract "to deliver at Fort Calhoun [Va.] as our proportion not less than 9,000 perches of stone p[e]r year," Congressional appropriations have been so small that "we were prohibited from delivering not [*sic*] more than 1,600 [to] 1,700 perches, thereby obliging us to discharge our vessels and men, at a heavy loss and leaving on our hands a large quantity of stone, quarries, &c." This has injured the company's credit by its having to forfeit contracts with individuals and has resulted in very heavy damages. "We therefore beg leave to observe to you [*two words canceled*], that for all these breaches of Contract on the part of the Government, we shall expect to be paid damages, such as shall be consistent with strict Justice." LS in DNA, 30, 311.

To John T. Johnson, [Representative from Ky.,] 4/25. Calhoun acknowledges Johnson's letter of 4/10 [ALS in DNA, 1, J-154 (M-221:93)]. Calhoun replies that [Isaac] McCoy's request will be complied with if "the necessary appropriations to carry into effect the stipulations of the treaty of Chicago relative to the employment of teachers &c. are made by Congress." LS in KHi, Isaac McCoy Papers (microfilm edition, roll 2, frames 466–467); FC in DNA, 72, E:246 (M-15:5).

To R[ICHARD] RUSH, [U.S. Minister to Great Britain, London]

Washington, 25th April 1822

I take the liberty of making you acquainted with Dr. [William R.] Waring of Savannah Georgia, who will hand you this letter. The Doctor is alike distinguished for his excellent qualities as a citizen and great proficiency in his profession. He visits Europe with the intention to advance still farther [*sic*] his medical skill and acquirements.

From your known urbanity and attention to such of our citizens as visit England, I have assured the Doctor that he may calculate on every facility on your part which may be in your power to enable him to effect the objects of his visit to Europe.

ALS in NjP, Rush Family Papers.

From G[eorge] C. Sibley, [Sub-Agent to the Osage Indians,] Washington, 4/25. As requested by the Osages, Sibley discusses certain aspects of their affairs. "The Osage Annuities have heretofore been paid from The Osage Factory in Merchandise at first cost, selected by the Chiefs. It has been my uniform practice to deliver them very publicly, to have the articles carefully examined and compared with the Invoices in the presence of the Indians." "After the Chiefs had distributed the Goods among families and individuals in their own way, I have permitted those who were not satisfied with the articles they had received, to exchange them at The Factory for such as they liked better, cost for cost." Therefore, it is not likely that any complaint exists against the government. "The last payment I made them was in April last, for the years 1820 and 1821. The Osages are entitled to *$1,500* per annum. When the Treaty was made with them, they were divided into Three distinct Tribes—The Great Osages of The Osage River—The Great Osages of the Arkansas, and The Little Osages. Each Tribe had its own Chiefs, and altho they were all a good deal united by intermarriages &c. they were (and still are) considered as Nations independent of each other." "When I paid the first Annuity under the Treaty, the Chiefs agreed that each Tribe should receive an equal part, and I have ever since divided the Annuity, by their desire, in the same manner. The Arkansas Tribe has not been paid their part for the last five years, because they would not go to F[or]t Osage for it—they have been regularly notified and invited to attend with the other two Tribes, but have been prevented by various causes from doing so—chiefly I believe in consequence of their unfortunate difficulties with The Cherokees. It seems that the Deputation of Osages from the Osage river, who visited the seat of Government in 1820, requested (or were understood to have done so) that the future payment of their Annuities should be made in Silver Dollars instead of Merchandise." Unaware that the annuities for 1820 and 1821 had been paid, the Agent at St. Louis procured the money and "proceeded last Summer to the Osages, and there discovered that two of the Tribes had nothing due them. Deeming it best however not to take the Money back to St. Louis, and considering it unsafe perhaps to leave it in the Indian Country, he paid it to the Osages as an advance for the year 1822." [Richard] Graham realized that "this Money would be of little or no use to the Osages (who are nearly as ignorant of its value as the Buffalo) unless he took some measures to assist them." The Chouteaus were engaged to "furnish the Osages with Goods in exchange for their Dollars on fair and reasonable terms." Sibley does not "doubt that so far as Major Graham's influence and interference could effect the object, that [*sic*] those Traders did furnish Goods on as reasonable terms as could have been effected, and probably as low as could be afforded. Still they could not have been any thing like as low as the Cash Prices of the Goods at the U.S. Factory, nor could Mr. [Auguste Pierre] Chouteau's very limited Stock, have afforded much room for choice." Six Osage Chiefs ask in an enclosed petition to James Monroe for annuity payments in goods and complain, "and very justly, of the conduct of the Strolling Peddlers that find their way, unlicensed, into the Villages and Hunting Camps of the Osages. The greater number of those Peddlers are sent out by the licensed Traders. My communications to The Indian Office and to Governor [William] Clark on the pernicious effects of this practice would almost make a volume. The Osage, have long been sensible of the evil, and have repeatedly desired me to represent the matter for them to the proper authority, which I have repeatedly done. It can only be repressed by our Gov[ernmen]t." "I am fully persuaded that unless this practice is speedily forbidden and effectually stopped, the Osages will be totally ruined and destroyed." "They complain also, that the Blacksmith employed by the Gov[ernmen]t (agreeably to Treaty) does not render them any service—and in this I know they are correct." "I found him a drunken worthless wretch, utterly incapable of rendering any Service, and even unwilling to make an exertion to be useful." "Major Graham you know Sir, has been but recently charged with the Osage Affairs—when he took them in hand last Summer, he was an entire Stranger to those Indians and their concerns. He found Mr. [Paul L.] Chouteau among them acting as a Sub-Agent, and very naturally relied on him for every necessary information in the details of his Agency. Major G[raham] has been grossly deceived and abused by Mr. Chouteau, in relation to Osage Affairs, as others have been." Sibley encloses a copy of a letter dated 1/25 from Paul Baillio, U.S. Factor, to Thomas L. McKenney that discusses the improper conduct of the Chouteaus toward the Indians. Also enclosed is a copy of a letter dated 1/21 from an unnamed individual to McKenney that shows irregularities in trade among the Indians. ALS with Ens in DNA, 1, S-83 (M-221:96).

To Nicholas Boilvin, Indian Agent, Prairie du Chien, "via St. Louis," 4/26. Calhoun encloses an extract from his letter [dated

4/26] to [Lawrence] Taliaferro. "Should overtures of Peace be made on the part of the Sioux to the Sacs & Foxes you will prepare the latter to receive them favorably and coöperate with Mr. Taliaferro." FC in DNA, 72, E:246 (M-15:5).

From Stephen Elliott, [Commissioner for the U.S.]

Charleston, So[uth] Car[olina,] 26 April 1822

At the request of Mr. [William] Lowndes I have on the part of the United States met the referee appointed by the State of South Carolina to "ascertain the damage done to the holders of the Land through which the fortification across the neck passes" and I have the honor to enclose you the award. [The amount agreed to by Elliott and John Robinson, Commissioner for S.C., is $18,215.94.]

There has been no delay on my part in the conclusion of this business. I attended whenever the agent of the State was ready to produce his vouchers, and the documents prepared left little room for hesitation in deciding ultimately on the claims.

The sum allowed for buildings destroyed in order to clear the space necessary for the Fortifications is exactly that which the State of South Carolina paid for them according to valuations made by the Commissioners at the time, and the Estimate of injury to the Land was made by Major [John] Wilson, a gentleman of unexceptionable probity and who was the acting Engineer of the United States when these works were constructed.

The damage to the land I should have been disposed as a planter somewhat accustomed to the labour of embanking[,] levelling &c. to assess rather lower than has been done in our award, but as I was aware that labour near a City is more expensive than in the Country, as I had great confidence in the experience and judgement of the Engineer to whom we referred[,] and as the claims on the part of the State were to a much more considerable amount[,] I thought it on the whole adviseable [*sic*] to abide by the Estimates of Major Wilson.

ALS with En in DNA, 262, 10354.

To Thomas Forsyth, Indian Agent, Fort Armstrong, "via St. Louis," 4/26. Calhoun encloses an extract from his letter [of 4/26] to [Lawrence] Taliaferro and directs Forsyth to prepare the Sauks and Foxes to receive favorably any peace overtures that the Sioux may make. "Altho' the Winnebagoes are not within your Agency but as it is believed they are nearer to you than any other Agent you are authorized to make an arrangement with the relations of the two men who were delivered up for the murder of our men at Fort Armstrong, to relieve from the distress which it is represented they have suffered in consequence thereof. The compensation to be allowed, however, must be moderate. The arrangement which you make you will report to this Department." FC in DNA, 72, E:246–247 (M-15:5).

From Alexander Macomb, 4/26. "On reviewing the Table that accompanied the report of this Department dated the 22d inst[ant], I discovered that the amount paid to the Contractor of Dauphin Island [Richard Harris, Nimrod Farrow, and Turner Starke] had been set down at $152,251.37," which was $10,000 too low. Accordingly, "the balance for which the contractor is accountable" should be increased by $10,000 to $113,352.22. FC in DNA, 21, 1:267.

From H[enry] Robertson, Fayett[e]ville, Tenn., 4/26. He encloses a copy of the report [dated 4/14] by [Samuel Smith and B.C. Barry] as inspectors of the road constructed by Robertson [in Miss.]. Robertson is much in need of funds and wants to be paid for his work. He believes that the U.S. should pay the costs of the inspection. ALS with En in DNA, 1, R-209 (M-221:94).

From G[EORGE] C. SIBLEY

Washington, April 26, 1822

I beg leave to call your attention a moment to my claim to the ground at Fort Osage on the Missouri. The matter stands thus.

In August 1819 F[or]t Osage was broken up and abandoned, agreeably to an order from the War Department. Very soon afterwards I discovered that certain land speculators were about to locate a New Madrid certificate upon the scite [*sic*], and knowing that I should in that event be very seriously embarrassed and annoyed in my public office, and not a little affected in my own rights, I took the necessary steps to locate the place myself. In December of the same year, I entered a N[ew] Madrid Certificate for 640 Acres at the surveyor's office in St. Louis and directed it to be located, agreeably to Law, at Fort Osage, so as to embrace the Fort, public Buildings and Fields there.

I apprised the Sup[erintenden]t of Indian Trade [Thomas L. McKenney] immediately of this fact, and advised him that my location should not in any event affect the property of the Government in the public buildings &c. or interfere at all with their occupancy so long as they were wanted for public use. I made a similar communication to [Brig.] General [Henry] Atkinson in relation to the stockade and Military Buildings.

Being myself a public officer, I felt bound to secure the place from the embarrassments that would necessarily follow its location by any of the land speculators; and I felt an unwillingness from the same consideration, to speculate myself. I therefore satisfied myself with securing my right to occupancy whenever the Government might think it no longer necessary to use the place as a Military Station. In the spring of 1820 (in April) F[or]t Osage was reoccupied as a kind of Hospital for the sick Troops that it was thought necessary to remove from the Council Bluffs. On this occasion, I believe I requested Gen[era]l Atkinson to consider my claim as formally asserted, and to enquire of the proper authority when I might expect to be left in the quiet possession, or something to that amount.

I was, I know excessively harrassed [*sic*] at the time, being crowded with my family in a very small stockade, amidst about *300* men literally putrid, the greater number of them, with the scurvy.

Since that time it has been thought necessary to keep military possession of F[or]t Osage, not for any Military purpose, but as Gen[era]l Atkinson tells me, merely to prevent my getting possession again. Gen[era]l Atkinson is desirous of withdrawing the present command from F[or]t Osage, which is not only useless there but expensive, and desired me to tell you so a few days before I left St. Louis. He says he cannot remove the garrison without your permission. Such being the state of the matter, I think I am at liberty to request that Gen[era]l Atkinson may be instructed to give up the place to me, subject only to such legal objections as may or may not be set up against my claim by the Treasury Department, or in other words, leaving me on the same footing with others, who have similar claims upon the National domain.

Since I have been in this City, I have been informed by a

Letter from F[or]t Osage, that a part of the building in which I left my family, has tumbled down—it will be necessary for me to occupy for a short time (when I return) the old Barrack rooms that I formerly fitted up; and I must request the favor that I may be put in possession of *them* without delay.

I beg that nothing I have said on this subject may be considered as proceeding from any wish in me to give trouble or to ask for any thing unreasonable or improper. If the War Dep[artmen]t has no further use for F[or]t Osage, I shall be very glad to have it given up to me, that I may proceed to perfect my title under the provisions of the Law.

General Atkinson would no doubt make a proper use of any discretionary power that may be given him in this matter. I shall be perfectly satisfied to have it refer[r]ed to him.

ALS in DNA, 1, S-453 (M-221:94); variant FC in DNA, 181, pp. 196–199.

To Lawrence Taliaferro, Indian Agent, St. Peters

Dep[art]m[en]t of War, 26 April, 1822

I have received your communication of the 1st Ultimo [ALS with En in DNA, 1, T-180 (M-221:94); FC in MnHi, Lawrence Taliaferro Papers, Journals, 6:127–131 (published microfilm, roll 3, document 363, frames 67–69)] relative to certain recent occurrences among the Indians and traders on the Mississippi.

It is difficult, under the present laws, to prescribe any particular course of conduct to be pursued towards [Edward] Pizan & Mayrand, who appear from your statement to be in the employment of the American Fur Company. You will, however, keep your eye upon them, and [Joseph] Rolette, whose character is well known here, and report their proceedings to this Department. Their conduct in selling spirituous liquors to the Indians is very reprehensible, and if you should have sufficient evidence of the fact, you are authorized to seize all such liquor in their possession, and destroy it, if it cannot be sold without danger of its falling into the hands of the Indians. Montry and Boushon, both of whom you state are British subjects and trading without license with the Indians within our territory, ought to be forthwith ordered to depart, and if the order be not obeyed within a reasonable time, force must be used to compel obedience. The part which the Sioux Chief, the Leaf, has acted towards Mr. Grigrion, a trader whom you state to be regularly licensed by the Indian Agent at Green Bay, [John Biddle,] is viewed as unfriendly to the Government, and you will represent to him in strong and spirited terms the impropriety of his conduct and the consequences to which a repetition of it may lead.

The Act of Congress passed 29 April 1816 supplementary to the Act of 1802 points out the mode in which the goods of foreigners trading without license, and which may be seized, are to be disposed of.

This Department has been informed that the Sacs & Foxes complain that they have suffered by the interference of the Government in the war between them and the Sioux, as relying upon such interference for protection, they were attacked by the latter when they were unprepared to defend themselves. The Government is very desirous that peace should be made between these tribes, and as the Sioux have been the aggressors it is deemed proper that they should move first in the business, and you will accordingly use your exertions to induce them to do so. The Agents at Prairie du Chien [Nicholas Boilvin] & Fort Armstrong [Thomas Forsyth] have been instructed to coöperate with you in effecting a peace between the Sioux and the Sacs & Foxes, by preparing the latter to receive the overtures of the former favorably.

Colo[nel] [R.] Dixon [or Dickson] will be able to give you some useful information in relation to the best mode for the settlement of the difference between the tribes above mentioned, of which you will avail yourself; but as he is a foreigner it is not considered proper that he should have any personal interference in the business.

Colo[nel] Dixon has applied to this Department for a passport to go to & from the English settlement on Red river; but as it is a case in which this Department has no knowledge of the circumstances connected with it, and with which it is presumed you are well acquainted, I have therefore referred him to you to act upon his application. You will accordingly exercise your discretion, and if you should think it proper grant him the passport he desires.

LS owned by Floyd Risvold, Minneapolis, Minn. [photostat in MnHi, Lawrence Taliaferro Papers (published microfilm, roll 1, document 41)]; FC in DNA, 72, E:247–248 (M-15:5); CCEx in WHi, Draper Collection, Thomas Forsyth Papers, 5:14. Note: Taliaferro's enclosure of 3/1 was a copy of a letter dated 1/29 that he had received from Michael Dousman, who reported upon some illegal trading activities in the area.

S[ylvanus] Thayer to Alexander Macomb

Military Academy, West Point, 26th April 1822

I have the honor to enclose herewith a letter [of 4/26] from [2nd] Lieutenant George W. Whistler, Acting Assistant Teacher of Drawing at the Military Academy, requesting a Furlough for the purpose of accepting the situation of Surveyor & Draftsman to the Board of Commissioners for establishing the Bound[a]ry Line between Lake Superior & the Lake of the Woods. As the offer made him is a very advantageous one & as his services at the Academy are not indispensably necessary at the present time, I beg leave to recommend his application to the favorable consideration of the Secretary of War. Another reason for my consenting to this application is that Lieut[enant] Whistler, who has a family to provide for, joined the Academy in the expectation of receiving the extra compensation which at that time was allowed to Acting Ass[istan]t Professors but which was immediately thereafter discontinued.

ALS with En in DNA, 14, 283. Note: The letter from Whistler appears immediately below.

From 2nd Lt. George W. Whistler, 2nd Artillery Regiment

Military Academy, West Point, Ap[ri]l 26th 1822

Having been invited to join the commission for establishing the Northern Boundary line between Lake Superior and the Lake of the Woods, I am desirous of obtaining a furlough for that purpose. Tis a duty that I hope will prove highly advantageous to my individual interest, and as the service is for the government, I hope you will find it in your power to grant me the requisit[e] permission.

As to my duties at the Military Academy and how I can be spared from those duties, I refer you to the opinion and remarks of the Sup[erintenden]t, Major [Sylvanus] Thayer, who will forward my application.

ALS in DNA, 14, 283. Note: Thayer's letter appears immediately above.

From WINFIELD SCOTT

Washington, April 27th, 1822

In compliance with your request, I will state, to the best of my memory & belief, the material circumstances known to me, relative to the recommendation of Brevet Brigadier General [Henry] *Atkinson* for the office of Adjutant General, made by the Board of General Officers, of which I was a member, assembled for the purpose of assisting in the late reduction of the Army.

It is not deemed material for me to say what were my own wishes or opinion on that recommendation; tho' I am free to declare that I entertain for Gen[era]l Atkinson, the greatest respect as an officer, & hold him in the closest esteem as a man.

On taking a view of the whole Army list, & the general effect of the impending reduction, it very early occurred to the Board (I mean at least a *majority* thereof, either including or excluding myself, individually) that it would be desirable, in order to save the greatest number of valuable officers for the service, generally, to retain Gen[era]l *Atkinson* as Adjutant General. Before, however, any decision was taken on the question, I understood, from [Maj.] Gen[era]l [Jacob] *Brown*, that he had written to Gen[era]l A[tkinson] intimating what would probably be done by the Board, relative to the latter; and, afterwards, when the arrangement had been definitively made in that case, & in the others of importance connected therewith, I learnt from Gen[era]l *Brown*, that he had received a letter from Gen[era]l A[tkinson], expressing a preference for his then situation, & a desire to be continued in it—with the reduced rank of Colonel of the 6th infantry, & the brevet of Brigadier in the Army. Now there was an official letter of Gen[era]l A[tkinson] addressed to the War Department, before the Board, at that time, in which it was distinctly seen what was his ["opinion" *canceled*] meaning as *to his then situation* (for he was already advised, at the time of writing the letter, of his reduction to the rank of Colonel)—viz. the command of a department with, of course, the pay & emoluments of his brevet-rank. But understanding, from you, that he could not be continued in that command, that is, that you would be obliged, under the law, to have but two great departments, for myself & [Bvt. Maj.] General [Edmund P.] Gaines, the Board concluded that when General *Atkinson* should become acquainted with that decision (of which he was then ignorant) he would prefer the office of Adjutant General to the immediate & sole command of the 6th Regiment—particularly, as all the difficulties in ["making" *interlined*] the establishment at the Council Bluffs had been already overcome & there was no longer room for ["further" *canceled*] activity or enterprize in that quarter. I feel myself at liberty to say, that this was my own opinion, & ["appeared to be" *interlined*] that of the other members of the Board, down to the period of my leaving Washington to attend to other duties. I, however, never saw Gen[era]l *Atkinson's* letter to General *Brown*, nor do I know that it was shown to either yourself or Gen[era]l *Gaines*. I am confident it was not laid before the *Board*. There were other considerations which contributed to the persuasion last expressed above; such as Gen[era]l *Brown's* declared intention to write a second time to urge Gen[era]l A[tkinson] to accept; to inform him of the important contingencies which would depend on his decision, &c., &c. I was, at the time, in question, not unacquainted with the opinion entertained by my friend [Brig.] Gen[era]l [Daniel] Parker on this subject, & the reasons on which it was founded, but nevertheless confidently expected a different result.

ALS in DNA, RG 46, 17B-A3; PC in Senate Document No. 91, 17th Cong., 1st Sess.; PC in *American State Papers*: *Military Affairs*, 2:412–413; PC in *Annals of Congress*, 17th Cong., 1st Sess., cols. 507–508.

To [Isaac H. Williamson], Governor of N.J.

Department of War, April 27th 1822

The State of Delaware believing it possessed the right to do so, by [an] act of its Legislature[,] ceded to the United States, a small Island in the Delaware River called the Pea Patch, on which the United States commenced the Erection of a Fort for the defence of that River, and the adjacent Country—which Fort is now in a state of considerable forwardness. Since the United States has been in possession of the Pea-Patch, a person by the name of Henry Gale of New Jersey has set up a claim to this property and has brought an action of ejectment against the Engineer of the United States [Maj. Samuel Babcock] who is superintending the works. Mr. [Joseph] McIlvaine District Attorney who is fully acquainted with the whole circumstances of the case, is of opinion, that to obtain a cession from the State of New Jersey would still further confirm the title of the United States. I have submitted the subject to the consideration of the President [James Monroe] who approving of the suggestion of the District Attorney directed me to communicate with [your] Excellency in relation thereto. Believing that the position is a very valuable one, not only as it regards the defence of the State of New Jersey, but the Country bordering on the Delaware, I have to request, if it will meet your approval that a recommendation be made at the next session of the Legislature of the State of New Jersey to cede to the United States the right and [title?] which still may remain in the State. Mr. McIlvaine has been requested to communicate with your Excellency on this subject, and from his knowledge of all the details connected therewith, he will be enabled to afford such explanations as may be requisite. If Doct[or] Gale or any other individual have any claim to the property, it is unnecessary to observe that the cession on the part of the State would not invalidate such right.

FC in DNA, 3, 11:386–387 (M-6:11).

From JOHN P[ENDLETON] KENNEDY, [later a Representative from Md.]

Washington, Ap[ri]l 28, 1822

Being constrained to leave town to day, on account of my professional engagements in Baltimore, I have taken the liberty to trespass on your kindness so far as to beg you to present the enclosed letters to the President, [James Monroe,] if you should think of it, when the subject of the appointments is brought before him, as additional testimonials to those I have lately had the honour to submit. The first is from the Governor [Samuel Sprigg] and Council of our State, being now in session at Annapolis, who have favoured me with this mark of their regard, and the second from my friend and fellow citizen Gen[era]l [Robert Goodloe] Harper. In the letters I have thought it necessary to collect, I have endeavoured to unite political recommendations with the private evidences of esteem from our most distinguished citizens whose friendship it has been my good fortune to share. I hope, as such, they will be regarded by the President. In addition to the recommendatory letter of the Maryland representation [in Congress], and the enclosed note from the Executive of the State, I have presented letters from Gen[era]l Strickler, Mr. [William] Wirt, Gen[era]l [William Henry] Winder, Col. [Benjamin Chew?] Howard, Mr. [Charles?] Carroll [of Carrollton?] and a joint letter from the most conspicuous Republicans of Baltimore, to which I shall add in a few days Judge Duvall's [Gabriel Duval's], Gov[erno]r Sprigg's and the Chancellor's, with that also of Mr. Stewart the President of the Maryland Senate; after this I do not conceive it necessary to take any other step in regard to the appointment but leave it to that disposition of things which I am sure will be regulated by a reference to the publick good, and a just estimate of the claims of individuals. I think it probable that my future life will be very much occupied with political pursuits, and I should not be solicitous to leave the country at this era, (in my view about to become highly interesting,) if I did not feel persuaded that the absence of a few years from my profession and my home were ["not" *canceled*] necessary to the reëstablishment of my health, at present too much impaired to allow me for some time to appear before the people.

In case the Senate should not concur in the views of the Executive in regard to the recognition of the Independence of the Spanish colonies, I should have no objection to be considered an applicant for the secretary[ship] in the Lisbon embassy, for which post I have not yet understood there was any particular person in view. In this purpose I should be happy in your friendship which I fear I have already too far intruded on.

I have perused the report you were so polite as to furnish me and need not say how much I was gratified with such triumphant vindication of the department against the charges of prodigality and extravagance so freely echoed through the representative hall. It will give me great pleasure, whenever your leisure may bring me to your remembrance, to receive from you any document of interest relating to your branch of the government, for which I have always felt a zealous concern, and for [*mutilated*; your?] administration the most sincere respect.

ALS in DNA, 103, Kennedy (M-439:10, frames 113–116). NOTE: Numerous recommendations are in the same file.

From JOHN KEITH

Keithfield, [S.C.,] 29th April 1822

My friend Dr. Myers of Georgetown, [S.C.,] learning that I had the honor of being acquainted with you, has requested me to mention to you the wish of his son, Col. Mordecai Myers, for the appointment of Secretary of Legation, to the Embassy to South

America about to be instituted. Should you by your influence, promote the views of this young Gentleman, I can assure you that he would do credit to the station to which he aspires. I have known Col. Myers from his infancy. He is well educated, & has always been esteemed for his merits & his talents, & he has ["been" *interlined*] for some years a resident of Savannah, where he is highly respected as a Gentleman, & a member of the Bar.

ALS in DNA, 103, Myers (M-439:12, frames 457–458). NOTE: An AEI by Calhoun reads: "Submitted for the consideration of the Sec[re]t[ar]y of State," [John Quincy Adams].

From Alexander Macomb, 4/29. As directed by Calhoun, Macomb explains why his report of 3/30 [on the Military Academy] did not cover the entire period of time between 1802 and the date of the report, as called for by a House resolution of 2/19. Since the academic year ends on 6/30, accounts have been rendered for the sums paid to Cadets only through 6/30/1821. Fifty-two Cadets have left the Academy between 2/1/1821 and 3/30/1822: 13 failed to pass their final examinations; eight were allowed to resign "because they could not proceed with their classes"; six were "obliged to resign to avoid dismission"; 15 were permitted to resign at the request of their parents or guardians or resigned because they would not agree to serve for five years; and 10 were dismissed. FC in DNA, 21, 1:269–270. (An incomplete report dated 4/27 [FC in DNA, 21, 1:269] was superseded by the above report and was therefore not sent to Calhoun.)

From Alexander Macomb, 4/29. Macomb submits a lengthy report on the Elijah Mix contract, signed [on 7/25/1818,] when [Joseph G.] Swift was the Chief Engineer, in answer to [Josiah Butler's] inquiry of Calhoun dated 4/23/1822. Prior to 1818 the Department did not always advertise for contracts, and it was apparently not done in this instance; nevertheless, extensive investigations were undertaken, and the contract was considered highly advantageous at the time. Stone from the first quarry used by Mix proved to be inferior in quality, and Mix, under protest, acquiesced in Swift's demand that superior stone be supplied, although Mix had to bear the expense of transporting it for greater distances. The contract was accompanied by a penal bond for $20,000; copies of the contract and bond are enclosed. Mix has delivered 87,964¾ perches of granite, mostly from quarries near

Georgetown, [D.C.]. The stone was weighed by marking the waterline of vessels containing it. Howes Goldsborough & Co. purchased one-fourth of the contract, with Mix remaining responsible to the U.S. for it. A private subcontract for one-half the contract is understood to have been made by [Christopher] Vandeventer, but it was not accepted by the Department, and Mix remains responsible to the government for the whole contract. Among other documents, Macomb encloses statements from Mix showing the expense involved in freighting and quarrying this stone. LS with Ens in DNA, RG 233, 17A-C27.1; FC in DNA, 21, 1:270–276; CC with Ens in DNA, RG 233, 17C-B1, 241:210–215; PC with Ens in House Report No. 109, 17th Cong., 1st Sess.; PC with Ens in *American State Papers: Military Affairs*, 2:435–440; PC with Ens in *Niles' Weekly Register*, vol. XXII, no. 16 (June 15, 1822), pp. 254–256, and no. 17 (June 22, 1822), pp. 257–259.

To [James Monroe], 4/29. Pursuant to a Senate resolution [of 12/20/1821] requesting information about the subsistence of the Army under the act of 4/14/1818 and a comparison of the present and former modes of supply, Calhoun submits reports from [William Lee dated 4/25/1822 (LS with DS, dated 4/24, in DNA, RG 46, 17A-E6; FC in DNA, 51, 7:311), Peter Hagner dated 4/24, George Gibson dated 4/24, and James Gadsden dated 1/9 (DS abstracting the general returns of the Army, 1801–1821, in *American State Papers: Military Affairs*, 2:417–418)]. LS with Ens in DNA, RG 46, 17A-E6; FC in DNA, 6, 2:58 (M-127:2); PC with Ens in Senate Document No. 92, 17th Cong., 1st Sess.; PC with Ens in *American State Papers: Military Affairs*, 2:415–418.

From D[aniel] P[arker, Paymaster General,] 4/29. "The new regulations which you have given to this department are found highly beneficial to the economy of the service while they afford all reasonable facilities to Paymasters as well as to Officers of the Army in relation to their individual accounts. No regulation however affording such facilities can guard against false certificates as explicit as that of 1st Lieut[enant] N[athaniel] G. Wilkinson of the 7th Inf[antr]y [Regiment] which [is] herewith enclosed with an official report from the Com[missar]y Gen[era]l of Subsistence [George Gibson]. A certified copy of the Pay account has been filed as a voucher with the accounts of Paymaster B[enjamin] F. Larned. I feel it a duty to make this report believing the evidence will fully support a charge for a violation of the 14th article of the rules and articles of War. I am convinced nothing will more efficiently enforce a uniform adherence to the laws and regulations affecting this department as exemplary punishment for their violation." FC in DNA, 291, 15:414–415.

To J[ohn] Williams, Chairman, [Senate] Committee on Military Affairs, 4/29. Calhoun encloses a deposition [of 4/29] by Bvt. Maj. Gen. [Winfield] Scott and a letter [of 4/28] from Alexander Smyth to Scott, both of which explain the difference between the Army regulations as printed under Scott's direction and the manuscript laid before the House of Representatives and printed by that body prior to its adoption by Congress. The War Department version agrees with the one adopted by Congress, but it differs in some respects from the printed House copy. Article 75, relating to transfers, is correct as printed by the War Department. Calhoun also encloses a letter [of 4/27] from Scott stating his reasons for believing, when he served on the board of Army officers for reduction of the Army, that Brig. Gen. [Henry] Atkinson would accept the position of Adjutant General "in preference to the command of a Regiment which had ["been" *interlined*] offered him by the President [James Monroe] through this Department." Calhoun did not believe that Atkinson would accept, "yet I did not believe it to be certain; particularly, as I Knew, that the Maj[o]r Gen[era]l, [Jacob Brown,] to whom the Adjutant was immediately attached, took a deep interest in his acceptance of that office and would use his personal influence with him to its full extent to induce him to accept." LS in DNA, RG 46, 17B-D2; FC in DNA, 4, 2:247–248 (M-220:1); PC with Ens in Senate Document No. 91, 17th Cong., 1st Sess.; PC with Ens in *American State Papers: Military Affairs*, 2:412–413; PC with Ens in *Annals of Congress*, 17th Cong., 1st Sess., cols. 506–509; PC with Ens in *Niles' Weekly Register*, vol. XXII, no. 26 (August 31, 1822), pp. 422–423. Calhoun wrote also on 4/29 a hasty ALS to Williams, enclosing the materials "accidentally omitted" from his earlier letter. All of the enclosures are found with this ALS in DNA, RG 46, 17B-A3, and in the above-mentioned printed sources.

To Josiah Butler, Chairman, House [Select] Committee to Investigate the Contract between the Engineer Department and Elijah Mix, 4/30. Calhoun answers Butler's inquiry of 4/23 [ALS in DNA, 30, 310; CC in DNA, RG 233, 17A-C27.1; CC in DNA,

RG 233, 17C-B1, 241:209; PC in House Report No. 109, 17th Cong., 1st Sess.; PC in *American State Papers: Military Affairs,* 2:433–434; PC in *Niles' Weekly Register,* vol. XXII, no. 16 (June 15, 1822), p. 254]. Calhoun encloses a copy of the letter to himself from Alexander Macomb dated 4/29 answering several specific questions concerning the Mix contract of 7/25/1818 and developments under it. LS with Ens in DNA, RG 233, 17A-C27.1; FC in DNA, 4, 2:248 (M-220:1); CC with Ens in DNA, RG 233, 17A-B1, 241:209–215; PC with Ens in House Report No. 109, 17th Cong., 1st Sess.; PC with Ens in *American State Papers: Military Affairs,* 2:434–440; PC with Ens in *Niles' Weekly Register,* vol. XXII, no. 16 (June 15, 1822), pp. 254–256, and no. 17 (June 22, 1822), pp. 257–259.

To Josiah Butler, 4/30. Calhoun encloses an additional letter [dated 4/30] from [Alexander Macomb] to Calhoun concerning the Mix contract [of 7/25/1818]. LS with Ens in DNA, RG 233, 17A-C27.1; FC in DNA, 4, 2:248 (M-220:1); CC with Ens in DNA, RG 233, 17C-B1, 241:229–232; PC with Ens in House Report No. 109, 17th Cong., 1st Sess.; PC with Ens in *Niles' Weekly Register,* vol. XXII, no. 17 (June 22, 1822), pp. 259–260; PC with Ens in *American State Papers: Military Affairs,* 2:441–442.

To Peter Hagner, 4/30. "The deposits made by Col. James Johnson conformably to the enclosed requisitions, were considered as made under his contract ending the 31st of May 1819, and not under the contract commencing 1st June 1819." FC in DNA, 3, 11:388 (M-6:11).

To J[oseph] McIlvaine, [U.S.] District Attorney [for N.J.], Burlington, N.J., 4/30. Calhoun agrees with McIlvaine's recommendation of 4/20 [that N.J. should cede to the U.S. any right or title that N.J. may have to the Pea Patch Island in the Delaware River] and approves the amount charged by [Richard] Stockton for his legal services. Calhoun encloses a copy of his letter [of 4/27 to Isaac H. Williamson,] Governor of N.J., in which [Williamson] is referred to McIlvaine for additional information. FC in DNA, 3, 11:388 (M-6:11).

From Alexander Macomb, 4/30. At Macomb's request [on 4/30 (FC in DNA, 21, 1:277), Joseph G.] Swift has examined Macomb's report of 4/29 regarding the contract of [Elijah] Mix [to deliver stone to Forts Calhoun and Monroe]. Macomb encloses Swift's reply and deposition dated 4/30 (FC in DNA, 21, 1:277) and a statement concerning [Henry] Denison's proposals [for the delivery of the stone] made by Commodore [John] Rodgers, U.S.N., [in answer to Macomb's letter to Rodgers of 4/30 (FC in DNA, 21, 1:276–277)]. Macomb observes that the deliveries are up to date and that the quality of the stone is entirely satisfactory. LS with Ens in DNA, RG 233, 17A-C27.1; FC in DNA, 21, 1:277; CC with Ens in DNA, RG 233, 17C-B1, 241:229–232; PC with Ens in House Report No. 109, 17th Cong., 1st Sess.; PC with Ens in *American State Papers: Military Affairs*, 2:441–442; PC with Ens in *Niles' Weekly Register*, vol. XXII, no. 17 (June 22, 1822), pp. 259–260.

Special order no. 36 by Calhoun, 4/30. He relieves [2nd] Lt. George W. Whistler of his duty at the Military Academy and assigns him to service "in the survey of the North West boundary line"; Whistler "will therefore report to Mr. James Delafield of New York whose directions he will obey." FC in DNA, 261, 1:13; CC in DNA, 186, 1821–1822:310.

To William Plumer, Jr., [Representative from N.H.,] 4/30. In reply to Plumer's letter of 4/23 [ALS in DNA, 1, P-257 (M-221:94)], Calhoun remarks that, although [John] Langdon, [former Deputy Commissary of Purchases,] was authorized to purchase certain articles, he was not given permission to do so on credit. Langdon's accounts and vouchers for the purchases have been approved, but Calhoun cannot refund the interest paid by Langdon on his loan. FC in DNA, 3, 11:387 (M-6:11).

MAY 1822

"MY FRIENDS HAVE HAD A SIGNAL TRIUMPH." THUS DID Calhoun announce on the 6th the failure of William H. Crawford's friends in Congress to weaken Calhoun by insinuating that he was culpably involved in the Elijah Mix contract. But they were persistent: on the 31st he complained that their newspaper in Washington "keeps a constant attack on me." He did not dare to leave the capital for a trip to South Carolina, he had decided by the 14th, or even to an agricultural exhibition in Maryland, although he wanted to demonstrate his belief that those who contribute to the improvement of agriculture are "among the greatest public benefactors"; besides, his wife was "very ill." The Factory system of Indian trade was abolished—too precipitately for proper accountability, thought Thomas L. McKenney. That was at least one major defeat for Calhoun.

From [Capt.] John R. Bell, Washington, 5/1. Having been unsuccessful in his attempts to see Calhoun "during the morning," Bell submits this letter before his return to Fla., reporting that no instructions were given for the disposal of the money that he possesses. "I am therefore under the impression that if the Bill for regulating trade &c. &c. with the Indians which provides for an Agent in Florida, and which has passed the Senate, becomes a law at the present Session of Congress, I may expect to receive the appointment. But should no provision be made at this Session, I will receive instructions to deliver over to Capt. [Peter] Pelham the am[oun]t of cash now remaining in my hands . . . as also all property[,] papers & documents relative [to] the Indian Dept. in Florida." ALS in DNA, 1, B-102 (M-221:95).

To Josiah Butler, Chairman, House [Select] Committee to Investigate the Elijah Mix Contract, 5/1. In reply to Butler's letter of 4/30 (ALS in DNA, 30, 315), Calhoun encloses a report [of 5/1 from Alexander Macomb]. LS with Ens in DNA, RG 233, 17A-C27.1; FC in DNA, 4, 2:250 (M-220:1); CC with Ens in

DNA, RG 233, 17C-B1, 241:232–234; PC with Ens in House Report No. 109, 17th Cong., 1st Sess.; PC with Ens in *American State Papers: Military Affairs*, 2:442; PC with Ens in *Niles' Weekly Register*, vol. XXII, no. 17 (June 22, 1822), p. 260.

[Lt. Col.] H[ENRY] LEAVENWORTH to Col. James Gadsden, "Adj[utan]t Gen[era]l"

Fort Atkinson, [Council Bluffs,] May 1, 1822

By the return of our last express I had the honour to receive your favour of the 4 of March last for which I thank you. It is highly gratifying to learn that the supposed cause of injury to the feelings of [Lt.] Col. [Willoughby] Morgan has been remov[e]d. My command is very agreeable to me. I have sufficient employment which is the most agreeable of any part of my situation. We suffer by the prevalence of severe winds and dust. Other wise the post is a pleasant one.

While so strong a disposition ["prevails" *interlined*] to reduce the various establishments of the government, and to bring about as much retrenchment as possible, I am surprised that Indian Agencies & presents to the Indians have not received a more close examination. It would not, I think, be difficult to point out a mode of having all the duties of the whole fraternity as well performed as they now are, and at the same time effect to the government a saving equal to the expence of the whole family.

Presents, as such to Indians, do more harm than good. Ev[e]ry man who knows any thing of the subject & who is not interested in the distribution (that is concerned in the distribution) of them will say so.

If sinecures are desireable [*sic*] the Indian Agencies & Factories too, should be preserved. They approach nearer to that thing than any ["other" *interlined*] thing to me known.

I have neither said [n]or written any thing on this subject before & you have my permission (if that is necessary) to consider this letter either public or private.

I can prove what I have here said to the full satisfaction of any unprejudiced mind.

ALS in DNA, 2, L-1822 (M-222:23). NOTE: EU's indicate that this letter was mailed at Chariton, [Mo.,] in May and that it was received in Washington on 6/22. Leavenworth's letter to Gadsden dated 1/2, which can be found in the same file and microfilm, had discussed Morgan's injured feelings and had asked for Gadsden's intervention.

From Joseph Lovell, [M.D., Surgeon General,] 5/1. He makes his quarterly financial and sick report, the latter for the final quarter of 1821. He analyzes in detail the causes of deaths and the frequency of various diseases. He condemns the high mortality experienced in moving the 7th Infantry Regiment to the Red River. He deplores the practice of moving soldiers on ships so laden with stores that the sick are confined to the deck without protection from the weather. ALS (incomplete) with Ens in DNA, 16, 1822 (M-567:3, frames 744–756); FC in DNA, 243, 1:132–136.

From Alexander Macomb, 5/1. In reply to inquiries from [Josiah Butler], Macomb encloses a letter [dated 5/1] to himself from [Joseph G.] Swift [concerning Swift's failure to obtain recommendations of Elijah Mix]. A full examination of departmental records does not provide information regarding a Mr. Perley's offer to furnish stone [at Forts Calhoun and Monroe]. The contract with Mix has invariably been construed to mean stone of the proper description and size required at any particular time; consequently, Mix is not allowed to deliver to the Rip Raps Shoal any stone weighing less than 150 pounds. Macomb points out that the heavier stone entails considerable expense to the contractor and involves much wear and tear on the contractor's vessels. LS with Ens in DNA, RG 233, 17A-C27.1; FC in DNA, 21, 1:278; CC with Ens in DNA, RG 233, 17C-B1, 241:232–234; PC with Ens in House Report No. 109, 17th Cong., 1st Sess.; PC with Ens in *American State Papers*: *Military Affairs*, 2:442; PC with En in *Niles' Weekly Register*, vol. XXII, no. 17 (June 22, 1822), p. 260.

From Return J. Meigs, Cherokee Agency, 5/1. He acknowledges Calhoun's letter of 11/3/1821 [PC in *The Papers of John C. Calhoun*, vol. VI] relative to charges against [Sub-Agent James G.] Williams. Williams has denied charges made by Capt. [Richard Keith] Call and has stated that statements by [Charles R.] Hicks and [John] Ross carry no weight because "the law has never recognized them as legal men." "If Mr. Williams could be permitted to retain his place until the next autumn it would be of great service to him & his family." Williams's mother is the wife of [former] Governor [Joseph] McMinn of Tenn. Even though Capt. Call's statement is "incontrovertible," Meigs urges "the exercise of the Magnanimity of the Government" towards Williams. ALS in DNA, 1, M-8 (M-221:96).

To Bvt. Maj. Gen. [Winfield] Scott

War Dept., 1st May 1822

In answer to your note of this morning, [*not found,*] I have to state that I have a perfect recollection of the discussion which took place between [Bvt. Maj.] Gen[era]l [Edmund P.] Gain[e]s and yourself in my presence on Art. 3 P[aragraph] 3 [of your compilation of general regulations for the Army], in June, 1820 or some time in that summer. The discussion, I think, took place on a suggestion from me while the manuscrip[t] was under consideration, that I had experienced some difficulty in the Department in applying the terms "seperate [*sic*] command" [in connection with the regulations' statement of qualifications for brevet pay?] and that I thought that the paragraph, as it then stood, was not sufficiently explicit. The result of the discussion was ["to make" *canceled and* "that" *interlined*] some additions or al[t]erations were made, which as far as my memory serves me modified the paragraph as it now stands.

ALS in DNA, 2, C-1822 (M-222:23). NOTE: One EU dates this letter, evidently by inadvertent error, as being of 5/21. Another indicates that Scott may have been in Washington on 5/1.

From [former Capt.] H[opley] Yeaton, Portsmouth, Va., 5/1. "Your favour [of] 25 April appointing me Sutler for Norfolk Harbor I had the honor of receiving this day and herewith report my acceptance of the same." ALS owned in 1960 by Harvey S. Teal of West Columbia, S.C.

To William Carroll, Governor of Tenn., 5/2. Pursuant to Carroll's letter of 4/5 [LS in DNA, 1, C-382 (M-221:92)], Calhoun reports that [Nathan] Starr has delivered the swords [that are to be presented to Andrew Jackson and Edmund P. Gaines] to [Newton] Cannon, [Representative from Tenn.]. "The swords have been examined at the Ordnance Office, and are pronounced to be at least equal, if not superior, to that made by Mr. Starr for Col. [Richard M.] Johnson." FC in DNA, 3, 11:389 (M-6:11).

From Andrew Jackson

Hermitage, May 2d, 1822

I have the pleasure to acknowledge the receipt of your letter of the 6th Ult[im]o advising me that the account of Gen[era]l [Samuel] Houston for pay, &c., as 1st Lieut[enan]t of [the 1st] Inf[antr]y [Regiment during 10/21/1817–3/1/1818], enclosed by me to Col[one]l [James] Gadsden to be laid before you, was ordered to be paid. This is gratifying to me, as I believe it to be just and well founded in law, and the General though poor is one of those noble-minded fellows, that in a military capacity will always deserve well of his country; and his feelings were sore, as he beleived [*sic*] it had been through the influence of Col[one]l [John] Williams of the Senate (who is his enemy) that his acco[un]t was suspended, that he General Houston might appear a public defaulter.

I take the liberty of enclosing a letter to Col[one]l Gadsden with a request that you will have the goodness to hand it to him if [he is] in the City; if not to give it a direction to him.

CC with Ens in DNA, 1, J-163 (M-221:93). Note: One of the enclosures is a CCEx of a letter from Second Auditor [William Lee] to John H. Eaton dated 2/15/1821 [CCEx in DNA, 1, J-146 (M-221:93)] returning Houston's account unpaid, "the Secretary of War having decided against its allowance in consequence of Mr. Houston having been paid for the same term as Sub Indian Agent." Another enclosure is a CC of a letter from Jackson to Gadsden dated 3/13/1822, explaining various details as to Houston's application for the pay in question and incorporating various orders received by Houston. For comments in regard to Houston's claim, see Marquis James, *The Raven: a Biography of Sam Houston* (Indianapolis: The Bobbs-Merrill Company, c. 1929), pp. 50–51. An ALS of this letter of 5/2/1822 was offered as Item 80 in Sale 2268 on 3/31/1964 by the Parke-Bernet Galleries, Inc., 980 Madison Ave., New York City.

To Samuel Smith, Chairman, [House] Committee on Ways and Means, 5/2. Having observed that an appropriations bill now before Congress provides only $50,000 for the payment of the claims of citizens of Ga. under the recent treaty with the Creeks, Calhoun requests that the sum be raised to at least $91,770.32, the amount awarded for that purpose by the commissioners. [James Monroe] has not yet decided upon the question of interest, but, if that should be allowed, the total would approximate $250,000. FC in DNA, 4, 2:249 (M-220:1).

To W[ILLIAM] D. WILLIAMSON, [Representative from Me.]

Depart[men]t of War, 2nd May, 1822

I have the honor to acknowledge the receipt of your letter of the 29th Ult[im]o [ALS in DNA, 1, W-283 (M-221:94)].

I take great interest in the defence of the State of Maine, for which so little has been done heretofore. The Topographical Engineers will be put in motion as soon as possible, to resume the survey of the coast of Maine. They will be instructed to ascertain the practicability and advantages of a road parallel to the coast within the distance you mention, viz., 10, 15, or 20 miles, provided that a reconnaissance of the coast to that distance can be made without essentially interfering with their other duties. The Board of Engineers will be stationary in the City of New York for a considerable time, to complete the details of what has already been undertaken, and will not visit Maine this season. Agreeably to your desire, I have directed the Cheif [*sic*] Engineer [Alexander Macomb] to notify you of the time when the Topographical Engineers will set out for Maine, and the part of the Coast they will first visit.

LS in CtY; FC in DNA, 3, 11:388 (M-6:11).

From Lt. Col. G[EORGE] BOMFORD

Ordnance Department, May 3d 1822

In obedience to your directions I have the honor to submit, herewith, copies of all the documents on record in this Office, which have relation to the Lead mine-lands of the United States; and furnishing all the information called for by the House of Representatives, on the 23d of April, which this Department is, at this time, enabled to give upon the subject.

The papers referred to, are as follow[s]:

Those marked A, containing the letters addressed from this Office to the persons applying for leases of a portion of the above lands; with instructions to sundry officers, issued by the Dep[artmen]t of War and this Office, for aiding in locating and surveying the lands embraced in said leases.

That marked B being a copy of the Report made by this Office to the Department of War, furnishing all the information received, respecting those mine-lands; with the proposal of a plan for rendering them more productive to the public revenue.

The paper marked C, containing a copy of a conditional lease, proposed by this Dep[artmen]t in the cases of [Thomas D.] Carneal and [James] Johnson, and others; to be finally acted upon hereafter.

LS with Ens in PU, Bloomfield Moore Manuscripts; FC with Ens in DNA, 33, 1:1–12; PC with Ens in House Document No. 129, 17th Cong., 1st Sess. NOTE: Another version of this letter (LS with Ens in DNA, RG 46, 17A-E6; PC with Ens in Senate Document No. 94, 17th Cong., 1st Sess.; PC with Ens in *American State Papers*: *Public Lands,* 3:561–565) differs only in its reference in the first sentence to a Senate resolution of 4/25. The Ens in group A are letters from George Bomford to R[ichard] M. Johnson on 1/4 and 2/1, to [2nd] Lt. Clark Burdine on 2/13, to N[inian] Edwards on 4/15 and 4/20, and from Calhoun to Thomas Forsyth, Alexander Wolcott, Jr., and Nicholas Boilvin dated 2/13. Paper B is Bomford's report dated 3/30 to Calhoun about lead mines.

To the Rev. [Obadiah B.] Brown, Washington, 5/3. Calhoun notifies Brown of his decision to increase the government allowance to the Rev. J[ohn] Peck's school in the Oneida nation to $500 for 1822. The money will be paid quarterly to Brown as the Society's agent. FC in DNA, 72, E:251–252 (M-15:5).

To WILLIAM LEE and PETER HAGNER, [Second and Third Auditors, respectively]

Department of War, May 3d 1822

The 2d section of the Act making appropriations for the support of the Government for the year 1822 and for other purposes passed the 30 of April last, prohibits the payment to any person for his compensation who is in arrears to the United States, until such person shall have accounted for and paid into the Treasury all sums for which he may be liable. It is therefore necessary that you furnish to the Pay Master General, [Daniel Parker,] and the Quarter Master General [Thomas S. Jesup] as soon as practicable a list of all Officers and Agents, now entitled to receive compensation from them, who are indebted to the United States.

FC in DNA, 3, 11:389 (M-6:11).

To [James Monroe]

War Department, 3 May 1822

In reply to the call of the House of Representatives, of the 22d [*sic*; 23rd] of last month [DS in DNA, 1, R-198 (M-221:94)], relative to the Lead mines of Missouri, and referred to this Department, I have the honor to transmit, herewith, sundry papers (marked A, B, & C) received from the Office of Ordnance [with George Bomford's letter of 5/3], which embrace all the information which this Department is, at this time, enabled to give upon a subject which was referred to it, on the 29 Nov[embe]r last, from the Departm[en]t of the Treasury.

The papers, received from that Department were transferred to that of the Ordnance, with instructions to report thereon; it being intended, when the business of the Departm[en]t will admit, to investigate the subject: and, after maturing the necessary arrangements, to invite by public advertisement under the leading features of the report, settlers and workmen upon the mine lands of the U[nited] States: under a conviction that, with suitable aid, and strict attention, they may be made a productive source of revenue.

In the interim, the parties applying for leases, have been furnished with a sufficient outline for their direction in locating the grounds, and effecting a completion of their leases, subject to the final decision of the Executive.

LS with Ens in PU, Bloomfield Moore Manuscripts; PC with Ens in House Document No. 129, 17th Cong., 1st Sess. Note: Calhoun wrote also to Monroe on 5/3 a letter that was identical, with the exception that its first sentence referred to a Senate resolution of 4/25 [DS in DNA, 1, S-452 (M-221:94)]. LS with Ens in DNA, RG 46, 17A-E6; FC in DNA, 6, 2:58 (M-127:2); PC with Ens in Senate Document No. 94, 17th Cong., 1st Sess.; PC with Ens in *American State Papers*: *Public Lands,* 3:560–565.

To the Rev. J[ohn] Peck, [President, Hamilton Baptist Missionary Society,] Cazenovia, N.Y., 5/3. Calhoun acknowledges his receipt from the Rev. [Luther?] Rice of Peck's letter of 4/21 to Calhoun and Peck's letter to the Rev. [Obadiah B.] Brown [*neither found*]. Because of the success of Peck's school in the Oneida nation and of its extension into "the Mechani[c] Arts and Agriculture," Calhoun has agreed to increase the aid from the government to $500 for 1822. The money "will be paid to Mr. Brown as the Agent of the Society." FC in DNA, 72, E:251 (M-15:5).

To Josiah Butler, Chairman, House [Select] Committee to Investigate the Elijah Mix Contract, 5/4. Calhoun encloses a report of 5/4 and accompanying documents from [Alexander Macomb (LS with Ens in DNA, RG 233, 17A-C27.1; FC in DNA, 21, 1:279; CC with Ens in DNA, RG 233, 17C-B1, 241:234–238)] in regard to the Mix contract. LS with Ens in DNA, RG 233, 17A-C27.1; FC in DNA, 4, 2:250 (M-220:1); CC with Ens in DNA, RG 233, 17C-B1, 241:234–238; PC with Ens in House Report No. 109, 17th Cong., 1st Sess.; PC with Ens in *American State Papers: Military Affairs*, 2:442–444; PC with Ens in *Niles' Weekly Register*, vol. XXII, no. 17 (June 22, 1822), pp. 260–261.

By Reod[olphus] Malbone, Chickasaw Agency, 5/4. He explains that Levi Colbert and other Chickasaw Chiefs dislike their Agent, R[obert] C[arter] Nicholas, and have made charges against him because he is utterly fair and does not cater to the selfish interests of the Chiefs. In a separate statement, dated 5/2, Malbone testifies also that Nicholas acted properly in the recent distribution of the Chickasaws' annuity. 2 DS's in DNA, 1, B-418 (M-221:92).

From W[illiam] G.D. Worthington, Secretary, Acting Governor, and Superintendent of Indian Affairs of the Province of East Fla., St. Augustine, 5/4. He encloses papers concerning several men and a document that discussed the conduct of [Horatio S.] Dexter. "And now Sir, in winding up my last official hour with your department . . . suffer me to return you the homage of my respect & gratitude for the confidence placed in me—and to assure you that at all times, either here or elsewhere it will give me pleasure to render you any humble service in my power." (An EU indicates that the enclosures were sent to the [newly appointed] Governor of Fla. Territory, [William P. DuVal]. Calhoun corresponded with Worthington through much more than an additional year about the latter's accounts.) LS in DNA, 1, W-83 (M-221:96).

From [former Bvt. Brig. Gen.] D[anie]l Bissell, Franklinville Farm, near St. Louis, 5/6. He requests an inquiry into his discharge as a supernumerary, in the reduction of the Army in 1821. ALS in DNA, 1, B-14 (M-221:95); ALS in DNA, 1, B-425 (M-221:101).

To Josiah Butler, Chairman, [House Select Committee to Investigate the Elijah Mix Contract,] 5/6. Answering Butler's question of 5/4 [ALS in DNA, 30, 317; CC in DNA, 21, 1:280; PC in *Niles's Weekly Register*, vol. XXII, no. 18 (June 29, 1822), p. 281] whether invitations to bid on the fortifications on the Gulf Coast and at Hampton Roads were advertised, Calhoun transmits a report to himself from [Alexander Macomb] of 5/6 [FC in DNA, 21, 1:280; PC in *Niles' Weekly Register*, vol. XXII, no. 18 (June 29, 1822), p. 281], who answered that the Gulf Coast contracts were advertised and that some of the contracts for the Hampton Roads area were advertised but that some were not. FC in DNA, 4, 2:250 (M-220:1); PC with En in *Niles' Weekly Register*, vol. XXII, no. 18 (June 29, 1822), p. 281.

Alexander Macomb to Josiah Butler, Chairman, [House Select] Committee [to Investigate the Elijah Mix Contract], 5/6. In reply to Butler's letter of 5/6 inquiring about the proportion of the 1821 appropriation applied to the Mix contract during 1821, Macomb replies that $40,806 were allotted and presumed used for that purpose, because "the balance in the hands of the agent, was but 8 dollars on the last Settlement." Macomb cannot now refer to the accounts, because they are in the hands of the [House?] Committee on Military Affairs. FC in DNA, 21, 1:279–280; CC in DNA, RG 233, 17C-B1, 241:238–239; PC in *Niles' Weekly Register*, vol. XXII, no. 17 (June 22, 1822), p. 261; PC in *American State Papers: Military Affairs*, 2:444.

From William Clark, St. Louis, 5/6. He acknowledges Calhoun's letters of 3/6 [FC in DNA, 3, 11:360 (M-6:11)] and 3/13 [FC in DNA, 72, E:228 (M-15:5)] to Clark. Some of the public arms mentioned in Calhoun's letter of 3/6 have not been turned over to Governor [Alexander] McNair because a depository has not been procured for them. In reply to Calhoun's doubt that Sans Nerf is one of the principal Chiefs of the Osage nation and that the two Indians who accompanied Sans Nerf to Washington in 1820 were considered "Warriors" by the Osages, Clark states his belief that Sans Nerf is considered to be a Chief by the Osages. Clark has observed this opinion of Sans Nerf in the various councils he has had with the Osage Chiefs during the last 18 years. "If San[s] Nerf has lost his influence, and produced jealousy among the Chiefs of his Nation, since his return from Washington, it arrises [*sic*] most probably from his having effected more for the interest of the Nation, than other Chiefs of greater pretention [*sic*]." Clark encloses a letter from [Richard] Graham, the Osage Indian Agent, which shows Sans Nerf's present standing, as well as the rank and standing of the two men who accompanied him to Washington in 1820. It is possible that "imposition may have been practiced on me, as well as the government," by [Paul L.] Chouteau, Sub-Agent, in maintaining that Sans Nerf and the two others were authorized agents of the Osage. If that be the case, Chouteau "would certainly forf[e]it all sort of confidence as a public officer; yet I am inclined to believe he has not intentionally practiced an imposition." Clark will continue to make further inquiries into the conduct of Chouteau and will report "every violation which I learn he may have commi[t]ed." ALS in DNA, 1, C-433½ (M-221:92).

To [Mority] Fürst, Philadelphia, 5/6. In reply to Fürst's letter of 5/4 [LS in DNA, 2, F-1821 (M-222:22)], Calhoun directs him to apply to [Joseph] Hopkinson for further instructions [concerning medals for heroes of the War of 1812]. "The appropriation bill containing an item for the medals has passed the House and will, no doubt[,] pass the Senate in a few days when a remittance will be made to you." FC in DNA, 3, 11:390 (M-6:11).

To Joseph Hopkinson, Philadelphia, 5/6. "Mr. [Mority] Fürst has reported to this Department that he has completed five pair[s] of dies, and states his readiness to proceed with the execution of the remaining ones concerning which I have directed him to apply to you for instructions." FC in DNA, 3, 11:390 (M-6:11).

From Alex[ander] Macomb, 5/6. In answer to Josiah Butler's letter of 5/4 to Calhoun (ALS in DNA, 30, 317; CC in DNA, 21, 1:280), Macomb reports that "there were advertisements for proposals for the Contracts for the fortifications at Mobile Point, Dauphine [*sic*] Island and at Lake Pontchartraine [*sic*]; and that since July 1818 of the contracts made for the works at [Old] Point Comfort & elsewhere there were twelve made on public notice for proposals & seven that were not so made." FC in DNA, 21, 1:280.

To V[IRGIL] MAXCY, Annapolis, Md.

War Dept., 6th May 1822

Your three last favours with their enclosures came safe to hand. I have read with much pleasure Williams' letter. I hold his friendship in high estimation. He is an honest, fair & sound-judging man. The course which he indicates in his letter is very judicious. It would be a great point for him to be elected Speaker and Dwight President of the Senate.

I am glad to hear that [Roger B.] Taney's health is better, and I hope it may be entirely restored. Tho' not personally acquainted with him, I have a very great esteem for his character. I have not seen M[a]j[o]r [George] Peter since I received your letter, and cannot tell what part Barne's [*sic*; Samuel Barnes's Fredericktown] paper took in [John?] Nelson's election. I deem it very important, that some respectable press should be prepared to come out in that quarter. You can best judge as to the means of effecting it.

My friends have had a signal triumph. The Radicals, after failing in all of their attempts to [*one word canceled*] impair my standing, laid their plan to come out suddenly and in full force on [Elijah] Mix's contract, made by the Eng[inee]r Dept. shortly after I came into office. They so managed as to make a deep impression in the house against it, by insinuations and misstatements. A Com[mit]tee of 3 was named to investigate it. Contrary to every parliamentary rule, all who were appointed were known to be deeply prejudiced against the contract. They proceeded in their investigation wholly ex parte, without any one being present on the part of the Department to explain or cross examine ["the witnesses" *interlined*]. Neither the name[s] of the witnesses nor the substance of their testimony was communicated to the Dept. I saw no time was to be lost, and determined at once to make a full communication to the Com[mit]tee with such documents and information as could be obtained. The appropriate bill in the mean time ["is" *canceled and* "was" *interlined*] taken up, and the members of the Committee rose and state[d] that there were supecious [*sic*] circumstances, and that the appropriation for the contract ought to be withheld at least till the next session. The House adjourned without taking a question, and I found my friends very anxious about the result. I asked, if the Com[mit]tee had brought my communication before the house, and was told not. I said, I had but one request, that it might be read, and the next morning furnished a copy to Mr. [George] McDuffie. When the question came up he called for the reading of the ["papers" *canceled*] "communication" from the Dept. to the Com[mit]tee, and finding that the members of it were indisposed to bring it forward, he offered the copy which he held to be read. This forced out the reading. The result was instantaneous and decisive. Mr. [Cadwallader D.] Colden, who had his mind prejudiced against the contract, rose as soon as the reading was finished, and declared that every doubt was removed, and that the proof was so clear and satisfactory as to the fairness of the contract and its expediency, that farther [*sic*] debate was useless. He moved the previous question, accordingly, which being sustained by an overwhelming majority, the question was taken on reading the bill a 3d time by yeas and nays 131 to 20. It was felt on all sides to be an effort to impair my political standing, and that my Radical friends based their future prospects very much on defeating the appropriation. Their mortification and the gratification of my friends may be very well conceived from so decisive a vote. I have given you the facts as I know they will afford you pleasure, particularly as one of the Baltimore papers the Patriot, without knowing the true state of the facts, made some very hasty observations, which were calculated to have a pernecious [*sic*] effect.

I find I cannot go south without very great inconvenience, and have declined the journey. My remaining here, will give me some leisure, which I will endeavour to turn to advantage.

Mrs. [Floride Colhoun] Calhoun & her mother [Floride Bonneau Colhoun] desire to be remembered with much affection to you all. Yours sincerely, J.C. Calhoun.

ALS in DLC, Galloway-Maxcy-Markoe Papers, vol. 32.

From Henry R. Schoolcraft, Washington, 5/6. "With respect to the contemplated Agency at the Sault Ste. Marie, you will judge the necessity, or expediency of an immediate nomination. I shall only add, what is my sincere conviction from the observations I have been enabled to make upon that frontier, that the state of the Indian tribes, & the public service, demand that the authority of the United States, should be established as early as is consistent, among those tribes, and a proper intercourse opened." The Chippewa Indians who will be placed under this Agency number about 20,000 "nearly one-half of the entire Indian population of Michigan & the North west Territories, and extending over a district of country more than one thousand miles from south-east to north-west. This is exclusive of the contiguous Chippeway bands, who inhabit the Canadian borders of Lake Superior, and to whom the Agent at the Sault will be compelled to act as the interpreter of the wishes of the President [James Monroe]. The duties therefore of that Agent will be arduous in their execution, while the insular position of the Agency, will impose risques & inconveniencies [*sic*], which are unknown to more favoured positions; and it is hoped these considerations will have a proper weight in deciding upon the compensation, and the perquisites, to be allowed." ALS in DNA, 1, S-463 (M-221:94); PC in Carter, ed., *Territorial Papers*, 11:237–239.

From Josiah Butler, [Representative from N.H.,] 5/7. He states that Calhoun's reply [of 5/6] to Butler's letter of 5/4 arrived after noon and after the committee had reported. ALS in DNA, 1, B-354 (M-221:92).

To N[INIAN] EDWARDS, [Senator from Ill.]

Department of War, 7: May, 1822

I have received your letter of the 6th instant [*not found*].

The Department has great confidence in the talents and integrity of Gen[era]l [Duff] Green and would cheerfully give him the appointment to which you refer, and which it is believed would be advantageous for the government; but as the appropriation for the Indian Department, has been reduced very nearly $30,000 below the estimate, for this year, and will not without great economy be sufficient to meet the present expenditures of the Department, it is not deemed advisable to make any new appointments at this time.

LS in NcU, Duff Green Papers (published microfilm, roll 1, frame 75); FC in DNA, 72, E:252 (M-15:5).

Resolution by the House of Representatives, 5/7. "Resolved, That the practice which has obtained in the Public Offices in this City [Washington] (of not attending to business until 9 or 10 o'clock in the morning, and closing the offices at 3 o'clock in the evening) is inconvenient to those who have business to transact in them; is not such reasonable attention to the public service as should be given, nor such attention as the salaries allowed by law are entitled to command and that the said practice ought to be abolished." Resolved, that [James Monroe] shall cause five Department heads, including Calhoun, to report on the second day of the next session of Congress how many active and well-qualified Clerks and Accountants will be necessary to perform the duties of their respective offices if "a reasonably constant and diligent attention to business" is required, And resolved, that [Smith Thompson] be required on the same day to propose maximum limits for the Navy and for the Marine Corps during peace. DS (signed by Thomas Dougherty) in DNA, 138, 1820–1825:102.

To [James Monroe], 5/7. Calhoun submits for approval the appointments of William Clark as Superintendent of Indian Affairs at St. Louis, Gad Humphreys as Indian Agent in Fla. [Territory], and Henry R. Schoolcraft as Agent at Vincennes, "but to be transferred under the Act of the 3d March 1819 to the Sau[l]t of St. Mary." FC in DNA, 6, 2:59 (M-127:2).

To the Assistant Commissaries of Subsistence in Mich. Territory, 5/8. "The Assistant Commissaries of Subsistence stationed at posts in the Michigan Territory will issue to the Rev[eren]d Eleazer Williams and his companions, forming a party of seven, (delegates from the Stockbridge tribe, and from the Oneida and other tribes of the Six Nations of Indians) a sufficient quantity of provisions, not exceeding one ration each per day, for their subsistence on their journey to and from Green Bay, and during their stay at that place." FC in DNA, 72, E:254 (M-15:5); Abs in DNA, 192, vol. 2.

To [Bvt.] Brig. Gen. H[enry] Atkinson, St. Louis, 5/8. "I enclose herewith a Copy of a letter from Mr. [George C.] Sibley [dated 4/26] respecting the occupation of Fort Osage. The Policy of evacuating Fort Osage is left wholly to your discretion, having regard always to the public Interest. Whatever treaty you may find it necessary to enter into with regard to the evacuation of the Fort, or whatever arrangements you make on the subject, you will communicate the same to this Department. Should it be your determination to withdraw the Troops from that Post, you will take measures to secure the public property against injury." FC in DNA, 181, pp. 195–196; FC in DNA, 12, 6:166 (M-565:6, frame 379).

From C[hurchill] C. Cambreleng, [Representative from N.Y.,] 5/8. Because certain papers were not in the War Department, he "was unable to adjust the account" [of Gerard Steddiford for his services as president of the court-martial for N.Y. militia delinquents] with [Peter Hagner]. "You will very much oblige me by enclosing under cover to Mr. Peter Stagg a warrant payable at New York [City] for the balance due General Steddiford's Estate." If [Henry B.] Hagerman intends to travel soon to that city, send the warrant by him; if not, "have it sent by mail." ALS in DNA, 2, C-1822 (M-222:23).

To Lewis Cass, Detroit, 5/8. Calhoun explains that the bearer, the Rev. Eleazer Williams, heads a deputation from the Six Nations and the Stockbridge tribe. This group seeks an extension of the land near Green Bay that was ceded to its tribes by the Menominees and the Winnebagoes on 8/18/1821. The deputation will explain its wishes, and the enclosed extracts from letters to S[olomon] U. Hendrick will show the War Department's views, with which Cass will comply. LS in DNA, 76, 5:200–203 (M-1:10); FC in DNA, 72, E:254–255 (M-15:5).

From J[ames] L. Edwards, Principal Clerk, Pension Office, 5/8. He submits his quarterly report on the business of the Pension Office during the quarter that ended on 4/30. It shows, among other data, a cumulative total of 46,764 applications received and a cumulative total of 31,916 pensions granted under more than 11 statutes. Among the latter total are 19,812 Revolutionary pensions. Applications for Revolutionary pensions that remain to be granted or denied number 12,281. DS in DNA, 2, E-1822 (M-222:23); FC in DNA, 91, 12:174–175.

To the Indian Agents and other U.S. officials in Mich. Territory, 5/8. "The Rev[eren]d Eleazer Williams, who bears this, and his companions, forming a party of seven, visit the Michigan Territory as Delegates from the Stockbridge tribe and from the Oneida and other tribes of the Six Nations of Indians residing in the State of New York for the purpose of obtaining from the Menominees & Winnebagoes, in the neighbourhood of Green Bay an extension of the cession of land which was made by the latter to the former tribes in a treaty concluded between them the 18th day of August 1821, which has received the sanction of the President of the United States [James Monroe]. The object of their visit is approved and they are hereby recommended to the attention and kindness of all officers of Government." FC in DNA, 72, E:254 (M-15:5).

Order no. 24 by Calhoun, 5/8. "Major [Charles J.] Nourse is detailed to act temporarily as Adjutant General of the Army. He will repair to General Head Quarters [in Washington] with as little delay as practicable." [1st] Lt. P[atrick] H[enry] Galt of the Artillery will report for orders to Bvt. Maj. Gen. [Winfield] Scott. FC in DNA, 19, 3:21; CC in DNA, 188; CC in DNA, 186, 1821–1822:314–316; CCEx in DNA, 17, 1:23.

Report by the Committee on Military Affairs, U.S. Senate, 5/8. The Committee recommends that Lt. Col. James House and Bvt. Col. John R. Fenwick be promoted to Col. and that Maj. Ab[ra]m Eustis be promoted to Lt. Col. The Committee also recommends other promotions and appointments in the Army. DU in DNA, 1, S-22 (M-221:96).

From Bvt. Lt. Col. JOSEPH G. TOTTEN

New York [City], May 8th 1822

In a letter from Major [Christopher] Vandeventer of the 26th ult[im]o I am informed that my proposition, to have my full pay, subsistence &c. retained until the balance of $1,068.96 due by me be cancelled, had not been submitted to Mr. [Stephen] Pleasonton on the supposition that I was not aware that I should not be entitled, during my employment here, to the per diem of $4.50. I feel very much obliged by the consideration, which withheld that proposition; and I hope my present proposition—to have half my allowance of pay, subsistence &c. stopped—may be made acceptable.

I confess I was taken by surprise by the late decision as regards the per diem, for as the regulation give it as a commutation for transporatation, *fuel* and *quarters*, which two last are only allowed to an Officer while stationary, I imagined it would be continued while the Board [of Engineers] might be stationary.

ALS in DNA, 1, T-187 (M-221:94); FC in DNA, 230, 1822:11.

From Eli Whitney, New Haven, 5/8. He encloses vouchers as evidence that he has delivered 500 muskets and requests a remittance of $6,000. ALS in DNA, 31, 1822, W.

To the Rev. Eleazer Williams, Oneida, N.Y., 5/8. Calhoun acknowledges Williams's letter of 4/26 and the enclosed communication from the Oneida Chiefs [ALS with En in DNA, 1, W-297 (M-221:94)]. "I am pleased to learn that my communication" of 4/15 "to the Chiefs of the first Christian Party of the Oneida nation has given general satisfaction." No objection will be made by the War Department if French settlers, related by marriage to the Indians in the Northwest, shall be permitted to live on the lands that the Six Nations have obtained or may yet obtain from the Menominees and Winnebagoes; but Calhoun refuses to intervene in the proposal, asserting that the tenure of the French "must be entirely a matter of arrangement between yourselves." Calhoun would like to yield to the Six Nations' request that a deputation of at least 12 shall be permitted to visit the Northwest tribes, but limited funds compel him to authorize payment of the expenses of only seven, including Williams; even so, this number is one more than Calhoun had told [Solomon U.] Hendrick that Calhoun would permit to go. Calhoun encloses authorization for supplying rations for the seven, a circular letter to all Indian Agents and other U.S. officials enlisting their aid for the Indians' mission, and an unsealed letter to [Lewis] Cass dated 5/8. FC with Ens in DNA, 72, E:253–255 (M-15:5).

From Joseph Hopkinson, Philadelphia, 5/9. He informs Calhoun that [Mority] Fürst has completed the dies for five of the medals and that they have been sent to Calhoun for his examination. Hopkinson encloses Fürst's account showing a balance due to Fürst of $2,250. Hopkinson suggests that $2,000 be remitted to Fürst and that $250 be retained "to keep the account open. I have no doubt of his intention to go on with the work on the terms of his contract, but still it is best to keep a reasonable security over him." Hopkinson reports that a likeness of [Eleazer W.] Ripley has not been received. ALS in DNA, 1, H-271 (M-221:92).

From David A. Ogden, [Judge of the Court of Common Pleas of St. Lawrence County, N.Y.,] New York [City], 5/9. Having received a copy of Jasper Parrish's letter dated 1/11 [Abs in *The Papers of John C. Calhoun,* vol. VI] to Calhoun concerning the frictions within the Six Nations over ratification of the treaty their deputies had negotiated with the Menominees and Winnebagoès, Ogden expresses his desire for the Indians to ratify the treaty. "From all the information I have been enabled to collect, the communication of Mr. Parrish exhibits a very faithful representation of the present situation of the Six Nations of Indians. The Christian Party among the Senecas, altho the most respectable, are numerically in the Minority, and being generally possessed of small Improvements, are fearful in Case their Nation should not recognize the Treaty that their Removal might not only involve the loss of such Improvements, but also deprive them of any participation in the Monies which might eventually arise from a future sale of their Lands in this State. The Pagan Party, being the most numerous, and being led by Red Jacket, whose Talents give him a powerful ascendency, ["They" *canceled*] control the affairs of the Seneca Nation. He lays it down as a principle, that no Indian Nation has ever adopted Civilization, without becoming merged, in the White Population, & losing their National Character and respectability. He asserts that an Indian is incapable individually of providing for himself, or of taking care of his Property, & he Cites himself as an Instance of this." Ogden and his associates want to coöperate with the U.S.; he requests a copy of Calhoun's reply to Parrish. ALS in DNA, 1, O-83 (M-221:93).

Henry R. Schoolcraft, Washington, to C[hristopher] Vandeventer, [Chief Clerk, War Department,] 5/9. "In compliance with the request contained in your letter of yesterday, [*not found*,] inclosing a resolution of the Senate on the subject of Copper Mines, I shall have the honour, in due time, to communicate to the Secretary of War, a revised copy of my report of November 6th 1820." ALS in DNA, 1, S-464 (M-221:94).

To H[ORATIO] SEYMOUR, [Senator from Vt.]

Washington, May 9th 1822

I have received I have received [*sic*] y[ou]r note covering the resolutions adopted by the members of Congress who have been pupils of the Law School at Litchfield [Conn.] & I have added my name to the subscription attached to the resolutions with the greatest pleasure.

For the Venerable Judge [Tapping Reeve] I have the most sincere esteem, & will at all times take much pleasure in doing any act, which may tend to cheer the evening of his days. Few men have passed through life more usefully & none with a more spotless reputation.

The period which I spent at Litchfield under his instruction will be long remembered by me. No period of my life of equal duration has been spent more advantageously to myself. I love to look back on it & to dwell on all the objects Connected with its remembrance. I must ask of you the favour to tender to our venerable preceptor my most sincere esteem & to remember me affectionately to your Father[,] y[ou]r Brother & his family & my other friends in Litchfield.

Copy in DLC, Galloway-Maxcy-Markoe Papers, box 13; PEx in Samuel Herbert Fisher, *The Litchfield Law School, 1775–1833* (*Tercentenary Pamphlet Series* No. 21. [New Haven:] Yale University Press for the [Connecticut] Tercentenary Commission, 1933), pp. 15–16. NOTE: Calhoun was responding to an appeal by Seymour and other Congressmen that Reeve's former students should each subscribe $10 for the financial relief of the famous Judge. Unfortunately, "only a few hundred dollars were raised." Fisher, *ibid.*, p. 15. In the same file with the above-cited copy of Calhoun's letter is a letter dated 6/2 in Washington that seems to have been written to Maxcy by an unknown correspondent. This second document states that "the good old man [Tapping Reeve] had written to me" in "terms of heartfelt gratitude" for the appreciative comments made by Calhoun to Seymour about Reeve. It discussed also a possible publication of Calhoun's letter. It reported also: "I called to see Mr. C[alhoun]. Mrs. [Floride Colhoun] C[alhoun] I did not see though she is much better—to him I mentioned I had got [from Reeve] the Copy of his [Calhoun's] letter [to Seymour]." A footnote printed with the PEx states that Calhoun's letter was published in "the circular issued by former students of the school, August 26, 1822." Fisher, *ibid.*, p. 16.

From William Carroll, [Governor of Tenn.,] Nashville, 5/10. "The inclosed papers are forwarded at the request of James Orr, a pensioner residing in this State, who is anxious to be transfer[r]ed to the Tennessee agency for payment of his pension. If consistent with the rules . . . the transfer can be made, it will be a great accommodation to an infirm old man, who will soon cease to be an expence to his Government." LS in TKL.

From John Brannan, Washington, 5/11. He requests permission to copy certain letters in the War Department for inclusion in his proposed publication, *Official Letters of the Military and Naval Officers of the United States, during the War with Great Britain in the Years 1812, 13, 14, & 15* . . . (Washington: published by the editor, 1823). These letters will make his book "more complete as a historical document." He encloses a letter dated 3/20 to himself from [former] Maj. Thomas M. Nelson, a former Representative from Va. and a former soldier under [Brig.] Gen. [Wade]

Hampton. Nelson claims that a certain campaign in 10/1813 under Hampton was so mismanaged that it was not disclosed to the public. Brannan requests specifically permission to see the official report of Hampton's campaign, "as I am very desirous to do justice to every officer of whatever grade who risked his life in defence of his country." A letter dated 5/15, also found in this file, from Smith Thompson to Brannan indicates that Brannan was given access to the files of the Navy Department. ALS with En in DNA, 1, B-12 (M-221:95).

From [1st Lt.] JOHN A. DIX, A[ide-]D[e-]Camp

Brownville, [N.Y.,] 12th May 1822

I have the honor to enclose by direction of Major General [Jacob] Brown his accounts for quarters from the 1st July to the 31st Dec. 1821, and to request your order for their payment. He claims an exemption from the operation of the general rule, depriving officers of a pecuniary allowance for quarters when absent from their stations, on the ground that the regular duty, of inspecting the Army, which belongs to his office, requires him to be absent from his Head Quarters a large portion of the year, and that the rule applied to him would have the effect of excluding him almost totally from a participation in the benefit of the Law authorizing these allowances. Although his own case comes under the general regulation referred to, it is so modified by circumstances, he cannot doubt that you will see the justice of exempting him from its operation. He would also remind you that the house, which he rented in Washington, was taken with your assurance that the allowance for quarters should be regularly furnished in consideration of the expenditure for rent. The subject is susceptible of other views, but he conceives it unnecessary to present them.

FC in DLC, Jacob Brown Papers, Letterbooks, 2:214.

To JOHN P[ENDLETON] KENNEDY, [Baltimore?]

Washington, 12th May 1822

I duely [*sic*] received your note of the 1st Ins[tan]t [*not found*] but have been prevented from answering it, as early as I desired, by the pressure of official duties incident to the termination of a session of Congress.

The President, [James Monroe,] after mature deliberation, determined not to make the appointments of the ministers to South America for the present; and it is not improbable that appointments will be made, at least to Mexico & Colombia.

I am under obligations to you for the interest you take in my young friend [George] McDuffie. My solicitude on his account has been very great. His life ought to be considered as publick property. I fear, however, that Col. [William] Cum[m]ing will revive the contest from what I observe in the publick papers. He appears to be actuated by a spirit not common on such occasions.

I have been deprived of the pleasure of my intended visit to Carolina by the lateness of the session of Congress and the accumulation of business which required my attention at the close of the session.

ALS in MdBP. NOTE: Below Calhoun's signature he wrote: "Washington, 29th June 1822." There is no obvious explanation, unless it be that this letter was not signed and mailed promptly because of a doubt as to where it would reach Kennedy. Compare the letter from Kennedy to Calhoun dated 4/28.

To R[ICHARD] RUSH, Minister [to Great Britain, London]

Washington, 12th May 1822

Dr. James M. Staug[h]ton of this city is about to visit Europe to enlarge and perfect his scientifick acquirements, and to facilitate his object has requested letters to you. I have with pleasure complied with his request, knowing that it would gratify you to give him any aid in your power in effecting the laudable object which he has in view. He is one of the professors in a college of much promise lately established in this District, and has the reputation of much zeal and ability for the sciences.

ALS in NjP, Rush Family Papers. NOTE: Calhoun's reference to a "college of much promise" is doubtless to Columbian College (later George Washington University), of which Dr. William Staughton, probably the father of Dr. James Staughton, was the President.

To [Brig. Gen. Simon] Bernard, Brig. Gen. T[homas] Cadwalader, [Philadelphia,] Gen. George Izard, Philadelphia, Capt. [John] Le Conte, Professor [Eugenius] Nulty, [Philadelphia,] Commodore John Rodgers, [U.S.N., Washington, Winfield] Scott, Professor [Benjamin] Silliman, [New Haven, Joseph G.] Swift, New York [City], and [Bvt.] Lt. Col. [Joseph G.] Totten, New York [City], 5/13. Calhoun invites these men of the Army, the Navy, the militia, and institutions of higher learning to serve as members of the Board of Visitors of the Military Academy for this year, beginning on 6/1. LS (Rodgers's copy) in DNA, 135, vol. 10; LS (Swift's copy) in NWM; FC in DNA, 3, 11:391 (M-6:11); FC in DNA, 13 (M-91:1, pp. 130–131); 2 drafts in DNA, 222, F-71. (The several versions of these letters are variant; they may not all have been written actually on the same date. Comparison of them seems to indicate that Calhoun first intended for Rodgers to serve as the President of the Board, that he next intended to utilize the services in that capacity of Izard, and that he decided finally to appoint Cadwalader to that position—an action possibly taken on 5/13, according to a letter of that probably inaccurate date that appears in M-91:1, pp. 130–131, but on 5/24, according to a similar letter of that later date that appears herein. See also herein Cadwalader's letter of 5/27 accepting the office of President. Calhoun's LS of 5/13 to Le Conte was in 1953 in the possession of George R. Loeb of Philadelphia and was offered by Charles Hamilton Autographs, 25 E. 53rd St., New York City, as part of Lot No. 38 in its Auction No. 3 on 3/19/1964.)

To Henry D. Downs, Warrenton, Miss., 5/13. Calhoun directs Downs to sell "on the best terms you can" the articles that "you purchased while acting as Commissioner for running the Choctaw boundary line west of the Mississippi for the use of the Commission and which you stated while in Washington remained on hand." Calhoun also instructs Downs how to deposit the proceeds to the credit of the U.S. "in any safe Bank that may be convenient to you." FC in DNA, 72, E:255–256 (M-15:5).

To Nathaniel Frye, [Jr., Washington,] 5/13. [Brig.] Gen. [Daniel] Parker, "being relieved as Pay Master General, has been directed to turn over to you such books, papers and public property as pertain to the Pay Department. You will take charge of the same, and will perform the duties of the office until Col. [Nathan] Towson, who is appointed Pay Master General assumes the duties of the Pay Department." FC in DNA, 3, 11:392 (M-6:11).

From [Maj.] Charles J. Nourse

Governors Island, N[ew] York, May 13, 1822

I have the honor of acknowledging the receipt by this morning[']s mail of the order of the 8th instant, by which I am detailed to act temporarily as Adjutant General of the Army.

Permit me to express the high sense I entertain of the confidence reposed in me, and though diffident of my abilities, to add, that they will be exerted to a correct performance of the duties with which I am temporarily charged.

I shall leave this [place] for General Head Quarters [in Washington] as soon as Lt. [Patrick Henry] Galt arrives, and I can have turned over to him the official records of the Department, which will be in the course of tomorrow or the day following.

ALS in DNA, 16, 1822, N-33 (M-567:4, frames 588–589).

From [Brig. Gen.] D[aniel] Parker

Pay Department, May the 13th 1822

It is said I am superceded [*sic*] as a Paymaster General. If such is the fact I will hope to be advised and relieved as soon as your leisure will permit. Once enlisted the expiration of the term of service does not justify desertion.

LS in DNA, 1, P-269 (M-221:94); FC in DNA, 291, 15:418.

To Daniel Parker, former Paymaster General

Department of War, May 13th 1822

I have received your letter of to day, and in reply have to inform you that Col. [Nathan] Towson has been appointed Pay Master General which supersedes your functions in that Office, and you will accordingly turn over to the Chief Clerk Mr. [Nathaniel] Frye [Jr.] the books and papers and property pertaining to it.

You would have been earlier relieved, but the confirmation of Col. Towson[']s nomination by the Senate was not communicated by the Secretary of the Senate [Charles Cutts] until Saturday last [5/11].

LS and CC in PHi; FC in DNA, 3, 11:392 (M-6:11).

To Stephen Pleasonton, [Fifth Auditor, Treasury Department]

Department of War, May 13th 1822

I have to inform you that the contract for building a Fort on Mobile Point, which was on the 13th day of May 1818 entered into between the War Department and Benjamin W. Hopkins (since deceased), and subsequently transferred by the administrator on the estate of said Hopkins to the late Col. Samuel Hawkins, has not been fulfilled, but has failed.

Robert Tillotson and Nicholas Go[u]verneur of New York as sureties for the said Col. Samuel Hawkins deceased are bound for the faithful execution of the said contract, and also for the amount of advances which have been made upon it. You will forthwith cause their bonds to be put in suit in order to [procure] the recovery of the amount for which they are liable.

FC in DNA, 3, 11:392–393 (M-6:11).

To Henry Robertson, Fayetteville, Tenn., 5/13. Calhoun acknowledges Robertson's letters of 4/15 [2 ALS's in DNA, 1, R-203 and R-204 (M-221:94)] "transmitting the report of the Inspectors appointed to examine the road opened under a contract with you from the old Natchez road to Columbus [Miss.]." That report [by Samuel Smith and B.C. Barry] is satisfactory, and Calhoun has ordered $5,000 to be sent to Robertson. Because that sum was appropriated to cover all expenses in connection with the road, Robertson is to pay the Inspectors out of it. FC in DNA, 72, E:255 (M-15:5).

To Henry Sherburne, [former Chickasaw Agent,] Newport, R.I., 5/13. In answer to Sherburne's inquiry of 5/6, [*not found,*] Calhoun states that there is no vacancy to which Sherburne can be appointed in the War Department but that he might find some occupation with "the Indian Department—on the frontiers." Calhoun has no control over the Treasury Department's legal proceedings against Sherburne to recover money due from him to the government, but Sherburne's letter has been referred to [Stephen Pleasonton]. FC in DNA, 3, 11:392 (M-6:11).

To John E[wing] Colhoun, [Pendleton, S.C.?]

Washington, 14th May 1822

Dear John, You will call us very fickle when I inform you that we have declined our journey to the South. On the adjournment of Congress, I found so much business on hand that, on calculation, I could not complete it and get off before the mid[d]le of June, which we consider too late to make so long a journey with our family. It is a source of deep regret to us as we anticipated much pleasure in seeing you all. But I must surrender every consideration to the duties of my office. The sacrifice is great but it must be made, particularly as my friends the Radicals have selected me as the object of their peculiar favour, as you no doubt have seen by the papers. I must be prepared for them. They have gained nothing yet but defeat, and I am determined that they shall gather no other harvest. You see how easily I slide into politicks, but I will resist the tendency, as you will through [George] McDuffie learn all that is interesting here. I will only add that I hope that you will send us [Warren R.] Davis [Representative from S.C., 1827–1835] from Pendleton at your next election [as a member of the U.S. House of Representatives] and some sound[,] good member in the place of Judge [William] Smith for the Senate. [John] Wilson [Representative from S.C., 1821–1827] appears to be an honest[,] good man but we require something more at present, and Smith, I fear, is united with the [Radical] faction in Congress. This, however is for yourself only, and must go no farther.

Your mother [Floride Bonneau Colhoun] says she intends to go South this summer, but I think it very uncertain as she has not fixed the time. She wishes you, however, to have Clergy Hall put in order for her reception.

We have been projecting an arrangement for you & Mrs. [Martha Maria Davis] Colhoun next winter, to which we hope you will make no objection. It is for you to make a visit to Washington after the adjournment of the [S.C.] Legislature and spend the winter with us. If you will do so, we will certainly return ["it" *interlined*] by spending the ensuing summer with you in Pendleton. We are so intent on this arrangement, that we will not let you off on a slight excuse; and altogether interdict before hand your old one, "that you have no time."

Your mother and the family join their love to you & Mrs. C[olhoun]. We are all well. Yours affectionately, J.C. Calhoun.

ALS in ScCleA; PC in Jameson, ed., *Correspondence,* pp. 202–203.

To Samuel Dakin, New Hartford (Oneida County), N.Y., 5/14. Calhoun answers Dakin's letter of 4/26 [ALS in DNA, 1, D-139 (M-221:92)]. The Stockbridge Chiefs have already been informed through their deputy, Solomon U. Hendrick, to what maximum extent the U.S. can afford to cover the expenses of a deputation representing that tribe and the Six Nations in the planned trip to Green Bay, and the promised authorizations have been sent to the Rev. Eleazer Williams. FC in DNA, 72, E:256 (M-15:5).

From T[homas] Cadwalader, Philadelphia, 5/15. He accepts Calhoun's invitation of 5/13 and promises that he "will attend the examination of the Cadets at West Point on the first of June." ALS in DNA, 222, F-71.

From Capt. T[rueman] Cross, Quartermaster General's Office, Washington, 5/15. Having been shown, by Calhoun, [Joseph Lovell's] report [dated 5/1], which discussed the "inconvenience and mortality which attended the sick in the movement of the 7th [Infantry] Regiment" from Fort Scott, [Ga.?,] to New Orleans to the Red River, Cross argues that no fault is attributable to deficient arrangements by any Quartermaster. An especially bad storm [in the Gulf of Mexico?] hampered part of the movement; nobody has alleged that Quartermasters furnished insufficient ships; and it was a physician, not a Quartermaster, who chose to move the sick from New Orleans with the well rather than to let the ill remain in that city until they had recovered. ALS in DNA, 16, 1822 (M-567:3, frames 757–759); FC in DNA, 42, 4:47–48 (M-745:2, frames 321–322); FC in DNA, 50, vol. 2.

John H. Hall, Harpers Ferry, to George Bomford, 5/15. Hall explains the reasons for some of the expenses incurred in the manufacture of his patented rifles. ALS in DNA, 31, 1822, H.

To David A. Ogden, New York [City], 5/15. Pursuant to Ogden's request of 5/9, Calhoun encloses "an extract of my answer with the papers to which it refers to the letter of Capt. [Jasper]

Parrish of the 11th January last. The letter to the Oneida Chiefs I am informed by ["a" *interlined*] communication lately rec[eive]d from ["them" *interlined*] has given general satisfaction." FC in DNA, 72, E:257 (M-15:5).

C[hristopher] Vandeventer to DANIEL PARKER, "(Unofficial)"

Department of War, May 15th 1822

On the subject of the enclosed letter, you may remember that I applied to you last winter with a request that you would furnish a list of such Pay Masters as should have been nominated to the Senate under the law of the 15th of May 1820. According to my best recollection, you replied that the subject had or would be attended to, but you did not know whether there were any cases in your Department which demanded attention. Will you do me the favor to state the cause of the omission, that I may report the facts to the Secretary of War[?]

FC in DNA, 3, 11:393 (M-6:11). NOTE: The "enclosed letter" has been neither identified nor found.

D[ANIEL] PARKER to C[hristopher] Vandeventer

Washington, May 15th 1822

I have just received your note of this morning & have to inform you, that, under the act of the 2nd of March 1821 [for reduction of the Army], the Pay Dep[artmen]t was organized anew. It consists of one Pay Master General & fourteen Paymasters, exclusive of the Pay Master of the Corps of Engineers. All these, except the first & the last, therefore, became new Officers, not before known to the law: as such they gave new bonds, & their appointments required the sanction of the Senate, as well as other appointments made in the recess. I presume they must have been submitted with the Army list in which they were published on the 17th of May 1821.

Never having had charge of the Army list, since the first of June last, I cannot tell what has been done in relation to appointments, further than that by some process I have been put out. This may be the case with all the Paymasters for aught I know.

ALS in DNA, 1, P-273 (M-221:94).

From Commodore John Rodgers, [U.S.N.,] Washington, 5/15. "I tender you my thanks for the honor which you have been pleased to confer upon me, by your letter of the 13th ins[tant]; but as my official duties will probably call me to visit the Navy yard at Boston, about the time proposed for the meeting of the Board of Visitors at West Point, I am constrained, tho' reluctantly, to request that you will excuse my acting as one of the Visitors." LS in DNA, 222, F-71.

From Bvt. Maj. Gen. Edmund P. Gaines

H[ea]d Q[uarte]rs, Western Department,
Louisville, Ky., May 16, 1822

On my return to this place the 12th instant Captain [Daniel E.] Burch handed to me your several communications up to the 29th of the last month, the receipt of which he had acknowledged.

My aid[e]-de-camp [1st] Lt. [Henry R.] Dulany, who I had left at this place for the purpose of distributing orders, making returns, forwarding my letters &c. was attacked with severe illness and has been unable to do any duty for the last four months; nor was it until the 18th of March that I received a report of his illness. I immediately directed Captain Burch to take charge of the office and to attend to the duties confided to Lt. Dulany. These circumstances, added to the distance and difficult routes I have travelled (through woods and wilderness, and having been often delayed by high waters, and for want of regular means of conveyance where it was necessary to travel by water) will account for my not having sooner received your letters. They shall receive my immediate and particular attention.

After leaving Fort Seldon, [Fort Selden, La.,] from whence I last addressed the Adjutant General, I travelled by land to the mouth of the Kyamesha [*sic*; Kiamisha], on Red River, and thence across the hills and vallies of the Kyamesha and Poto, to Fort Smith, Arkansaw, where I arrived on the 22nd of the last month.

A sketch of this very interesting border of Louisiana and Arkansaw will form a part of my report, when my tour of inspection is completed. But considering the subject as one of no ordinary concernment, as it is connected with our Indian relations, on an important section of the frontier; I take this occasion to submit to you such views as my tour through the country, added to the information derived principally from officers and agents of the government have enabled me to bring together, upon the subject of the Choctaw claim; the practicability of roads being opened through the country, & of supplies being obtained for the troops.

It was my intention on visiting Fort Smith to have assembled a few of the principal Chiefs of the Cherokee and Osage Nations, with a view to warn them of the danger to which they expose themselves in continuing to carry on a war against each other on the border of our frontier settlements, and to urge them to abstain from further hostilities. But on my arrival, finding that Governor [James] Miller had but recently failed in a similar in a similar [*sic*] attempt, of which you have doubtless received his report; I did not deem it advisable or proper to renew the subject, without specific authority from your Department authorising me to say to the Chiefs that the President of the U.S. [James Monroe] requires and directs that they shall desist from further hostilities; and in this case I have no doubt but they would make peace forthwith.

Enclosed you will receive a copy of General [Henry] Atkinson's report upon the subject of Indian hostility supposed to exist among the N.W. tribes. I enclose likewise copies of my orders to General Atkinson & other commanding officers, of this date, in relation to Indians, and to brevet commands.

ALS with Ens in DNA, 1, G-177 (M-221:92); unsigned, variant FC in DNA, RG 98, Western Department, Letters Sent, 1:242–243. NOTE: One of the enclosures is an extract from Gaines's journal describing the land of the Choctaw claim and the Red River frontier. Another is a letter dated 5/2 at St. Louis from Atkinson to Gaines; another is Gaines's reply dated 5/16. Another is a copy of some orders issued for Gaines by Burch on 5/16. Calhoun replied on 5/30.

From Amos B. Eaton, n.p., 5/17. He accepts his conditional appointment of 4/27 to become a Cadet and will report next month. His father, Amos Eaton, appends his consent. (According to Heitman, *Historical Register,* 1:395, Amos B. Eaton rose to the rank of Brig. Gen. in 1864 as the Commissary General of Subsistence.) ALS in DNA, 15, 1822, 42 (M-688:20). (In the same file is a letter of recommendation written on 4/18 by Amos Eaton, who was teaching a course in Botany to the Cadets, to Stephen Van Rensselaer and to John D. Dickinson, [Representatives from N.Y.]).

From E.C. Izard, Philadelphia, 5/17. "[Former Maj.] General [George] Izard is in North Carolina, and will not return to this part of the world for several months. I therefore give you this information that another President [of the Board of Visitors of the Military Academy] may be appointed to investigate the Military Establishment at West Point." ALS in DNA, 30, 320.

To Thomas Newton, [Jr., Representative from Va.,] Norfolk, 5/17. In response to Newton's letter of 5/14 (ALS in DNA, 8, 1823, 262), Calhoun states that no vacancies for a Clerk are anticipated soon in the War Department. The "one or two Clerks recently reduced" would have preference over William Simmons should a vacancy arise, but Calhoun will be pleased to appoint Simmons when the situation permits. LS owned in 1952 by Dr. Louis A. Warren, Lincoln National Life Foundation, Fort Wayne, Ind.; FC in DNA, 3, 11:394 (M-6:11).

From Bvt. Lt. Col. Joseph G. Totten, New York [City], 5/17. He has been honored by Calhoun's letter of 5/13 [inviting Totten to be a member of the Board of Visitors of the Military Academy] and promises that he will "not fail to attend at West Point in compliance with its requisition." ALS in DNA, 222, F-71; FC in DNA, 230, 1822:12.

From [Brig. Gen. Simon] Bernard, New York [City], 5/18. He accepts Calhoun's invitation [of 5/13] to him to serve in the Board of Visitors of the Military Academy. ALS in DNA, 222, F-71.

From T[RUEMAN] CROSS, A[ssistant] Q[uarter]m[aster] G[eneral]

Q[uarter] M[aster] General['] s Office, May 18, 1822

In the year 1819, the [Assistant Deputy] Q[uarter] Master [General] at Pittsburgh [Capt. Hezekiah Johnson] made expenditures connected with the outfit of Major [Stephen H.] Long[']s exploring party, to the amount of $4,247.53, for which in consequence of the expenditure of the appropriation for that object, neither the department nor the Q[uarter] Master has ever received a credit. I deem it proper to report the case to you, in order that some arrangements, if practicable, may be made, by which the officer will be enabled to close his accounts and the department obtain a credit that is due to it.

ALS in DNA, 30, 322; FC in DNA, 42, 4:59 (M-745:2, frame 327); FC in DNA, 50, vol. 2.

From Mority Fürst, Philadelphia, 5/18. He repeats his request for funds, because he is "now in very poor circumstances" and because it is impossible for him to proceed with his work [on the medals honoring heroes of the War of 1812]. LS in DNA, 1, F-118 (M-221:92).

From A[lbert] S[idney] Johnston, n.p., 5/18. He accepts his appointment to be a Cadet; his father, [Dr.] John Johnston, appends his consent. (Albert Sidney Johnston rose to the rank of a Bvt. Brig. Gen. in the United States Army. Heitman, *Historical Register*, 1:577–578. For a sketch of his life, including his Confederate career, see the *Dictionary of American Biography*, 10:135–136). ALS in DNA, 15, 1822, 39 (M-688:20).

From B[enjamin] Silliman

New Haven, May 18, 1822

In accordance with the invitation, contained in your favor of the 13th Instant, I will repair to West Point, as near the time mentioned as possible, & will attend a part of the examination of the Cadets. My own public duties here will prevent my remaining through the whole period.

With a due sense of the honour done me by this invitation I remain with the greatest respect your very ob[edien]t serv[an]t, B. Silliman.

ALS in DNA, 222, F-71.

From Mority Fürst, Philadelphia, 5/19. He reports that he has received a check for $2,280, the amount due to him [for his work on the medals honoring the heroes of the War of 1812]. LS in DNA, 1, F-119 (M-221:92).

From [Capt.] John R. Bell, St. Augustine, 5/20. He reports that Capt. [Peter] Pelham is too ill to attend to his Indian duties; Bell states that he will be more than glad to accept the position of Temporary Agent, if he is requested to do so. "The pretended proprietors or their Agents for the Alachua country are quarrelling among themselves, and I fear the Indians will become implicated in some of the depredations committed. Already a house has been burnt, and [there are] complaints of Cattle & hogs having been killed." Pelham requests $150 for his salary and other expenses. ALS in DNA, 1, B-385 (M-221:92).

From Joseph Lovell, New York [City], 5/20. He has been informed by a friend of [Maj.] Gen. [Jacob] Brown that Brown is now rapidly recovering from his illness. Before his medical treatments were materially changed during the last five weeks, Brown had been "much depressed"; he was "fully convinced" that he would not recover. All symptoms of his illness are gone, with the exception of "debility in his arm & hand. It is expected that he will be in this city by the first week of the next month on his way to Washington." From the information that Lovell has received, it is probable that Brown will soon be completely restored to health. ALS in DNA, 1, S-480 (M-221:94).

From Thomas L. McKenney

Office [of] Indian Trade, May 20th 1822

I have the honour to enclose you a letter [*not found*] to the President of the United States [James Monroe] conveying my views of the mode of winding up and transferring the U.S. property connected with the Indian Trade, to another set of agents who are to be appointed to receive it.

I beg leave to add further for your information and the information of the President that it could not have been the object of Congress to put it out of my power to see to the bringing to *one point* the distant concerns for which *I alone* am responsible, and for the faithfull [*sic*] attention to which I have bonded and taken an oath; and if not, then it is impossible for any period to arrive bringing with it a rightfull [*sic*] dissolvement of my compact short of that which shall put me in possession of the evidences on which my accounts can alone be settled. Any other view would sever the obligation I am under, & cancel my bonds and the bonds of the Factors, and release us from the obligation imposed by our oaths, for it is not reasonable to expect that our bond[s] and oaths should be made to involve or to force us by the acts of others.

The bill I presume contemplates no more than a stoppage of the business and a surrender of the property, but this surrender cannot be made till the property is embodied and Invoiced *for that purpose.* All this could be accomplished in a short period were it here, but its being at a distance and scattered, and some more time being therefore required to get in the accounts will not, it is presumed, be considered as a reason why those who have it in charge now, should be disposs[ess]ed of it before they received the vouchers on which alone they are to rest their claims of faithfulness, and cancel their bonds &c. by a fair and proper adjustment of their charge.

As to myself I see no way but the one I have suggested that will not involve my rights, for I must first get in from the Factors their several returns, before I can bring the business at this office to its proper close, and before a transfer can be rightfully made *to any person,* unless indeed with such sudden abandonment I have delivered up to me my bond and receipts &c.

The moment the returns are all made by the Factors, I shall be ready at this office to recognize the agent & prepare to invoice the stock on hand here, and to surrender to him the books & accounts &c., on doing which and having got his receipt, I shall pass the whole body of receipts to the credit of the Trade fund in the Treasury of the United States.

All which is respectfully submitted. Thomas L. McKenney.

LS in DNA, 1, M-382 (M-221:93); FC in DNA, 73, F:348–349 (M-16:6).

From [Joseph] Gales, [Jr.,] and [William W.] Seaton, Office of the *National Intelligencer,* [Washington,] 5/21. [Former Brig.] "Gen. [Joseph G.] Swift, who borrowed the Report on [Elijah] Mix's Contract, informs us he left it with you. Having occasion to commence its publication, you will oblige us by directing it to be sent to us." Have any new appointments for War Department positions been made? If so, "we shall be obliged by being furnished with a List thereof for publication, having received requests from New York to publish them." LS in DNA, 1, G-163 (M-221:92).

From Thomas L. McKenney

Off[ice of] In[dian] Trade, May 22, 1822

It appears the Treasury Department is acting in the affair of winding up the affairs of this office. *A Clerk* from the office of the 5th Auditor [Stephen Pleasonton] brought a verbal [that is, an oral] message to my Clerk, purporting to be from the Sec[retar]y of the Treasury, [William H. Crawford,] and requesting to have sent in the returns as they may be received from the Factors—also an invoice of the property &c. in my hands as S[uperintendent of] I[ndian] Trade. Will you have the goodness to say if the President [James Monroe] have [*sic*] thus decided?

LS in DNA, 1, M-374 (M-221:93).

J[ames] M[onroe] to [John C. Calhoun, 5/22]. Monroe inquires "how many & what tribes have claims by treaty to the establishment of trading houses among them[?]" ALI in DNA, 1, P-277 (M-221:94).

From Eugenius Nulty

Philadelphia, May 22, 1822

It is with extreme regret that I find myself obliged to decline the honour of attending the examination of the Cadets at West-Point [as a member of the Board of Visitors of the Military Academy]. The present state of my health renders it imprudent in me to purpose travelling any distance from the City; and, indeed, my engagements hardly admit my absence.

Accept, Sir, my sincere thanks for the honour you have conferred on me, and my assurance of the pleasure I should take in witnessing the progress of sciences to which I have always been attached.

ALS in DNA, 222, F-71.

From the Rev. Humphrey Posey, Valley Towns, [Eastern Cherokee Nation,] 5/22. At the request of the Sarepta Mission Society of Ga., Posey reports the progress of the school at Tensawattee. It has been in operation for one year and has averaged about 25 students; they have done well under the Joseph Lancaster plan of instruction. A U.S. grant would be appreciated. Postscripts indicate that about $300 have been spent at Tensawattee this year, that more buildings need to be erected, and that the school at the Valley Towns, which has recently opened a "female school," has an average enrollment of 65 to 70. ALS in DNA, 77 (M-271:4, frames 186–188).

From Smith Thompson, Secretary of the Navy, 5/22. The U.S. schooner *Porpoise* has been ordered to St. Marys, Ga., to assist the revenue cutter that is attached to the Savannah Naval station in the survey of the coasts of Fla. [Territory]. The Navy officers who will help the Topographical Engineers in the survey will meet the Engineers at St. Marys on or about 7/1. LS in DNA, 30, 1822, 324; FC in DNA, 136, 1:129.

From Lewis Cass

Detroit, May 23rd 1822

Not having seen the act which has been passed for the abolition of the Factories, I am ignorant of its details. But presuming that provision has been made for issuing gratuitously to the Indians such part of the goods on hand as may not be necessary for other purposes, I take the liberty of suggesting that, from circumstances which are fully known to you, there is probably no section of the Country in which for some years the wants of the Indians will be more pressing than here, and as there is little probability that any appropriation which may be made will be adequate to the relief of their necessities, a strong inducement is furnished for devoting to this object as large a portion of these goods as may be consistent with other claims.

LS in DNA, 1, C-43 (M-221:92); FC in DNA, 76 (M-1:5, p. 3).

To James E[dward] Colhoun, Philadelphia

Washington, 23d May 1822

Your note of the 18th Inst[ant; *not found*] was duly received in which you state that the dividends of 1820 were transmitted to Mr. [*one name illegible*] of Charleston [S.C.]. Will you inform me of the amount in order that I may take measures to draw from him what is due to me[?]

I have declined my visit to the South this summer. I could ["not" *interlined*] get off till the season was too far advanced to take the journey with my family. I suppose you may negotiate a draft on Augusta through the U.S. Bank. Mr. [Langdon] Cheves can give you information in relation to it.

Your sister [Floride Colhoun Calhoun] has been very ill but is now much better. The rest of the family is well. With affection, J.C. Calhoun.

ALS in ScCleA. NOTE: This letter was franked: "War Dept., J.C. Calhoun."

From J[AMES] L. E[DWARDS]

Pension Office, May 23d 1822

In conformity with your orders [*not found*] accompanying the resolution of the House of Representatives of the U[nited] States of the 16th ult[im]o I have the honor to inform you, that in addition to the undersigned, seven Clerks have been employed in this Office for more than a year past, and some times an eighth, (Mr. F[rancis] Wright) now in the Secretary's own office. Three of the nine are unnecessary. The business, I think can be performed by six well qualified Clerks, including the one who superintends the business. A reduction might have been made during the Session of Congress, had it not been supposed that the Bill which passed the House of Rep[resentative]s authorising the Secretary of War to restore certain names to the pension roll, would have also passed the Senate. Had that Bill become a law, there would have been ample employment for as many as are now attached to the office. Col. [David] Henley, from his age and infirmities, is not qualified for a recording Clerk. The buiness of examining the old records of Revolutionary service, having nearly ceased, he is now without employment. None who are employed in this Branch of the Department, are to my knowledge, engaged in any other pursuit for a livelihood.

FC in DNA, 91, 12:187.

From T[HOMAS] L. McK[ENNEY]

Indian Trade Office, 23d May 1822

In reply to your letter of yesterday [*not found*] requesting to be informed how many & what tribes have claims by treaty, to the establishment of trading houses among them, I have the honor to state that with the Sac and Fox Indians a treaty stipulation exists, tho' they have no house specially allotted for them, but they do their business at Pra[i]rie du Chien & Fort Edwards. This and those with the Osages and the Chaktaws [*sic*] make up the number of trading houses stipulated for by treaty. I know of no others.

FC in DNA, 73, F:353 (M-16:6).

From Peter Stagg, New York [City], 5/23. He reports that he has forwarded the accounts and vouchers comprising the claim of his deceased father-in-law, [Gerard Steddiford]. As "the accounts are now made out in conformity with the instructions of the War department," Stagg hopes that there will be "no further obstacle to a settlement." ALS in DNA, 1, S-483 (M-221:94).

To [Brig.] Gen. THOMAS CADWALADER, Philadelphia

Department of War, May 24th 1822

I have been duly favored with your letter notifying this Department of your intention to repair to West Point in June next, agreeably to the invitation which was sent you [on 5/13]. The following is a list of the Visitors who will constitute the Board [of Visitors of the Military Academy this year], and at which I have to request you will preside. Gen[era]l Cadwallader [*sic*; as] President, Gen[era]l [Joseph G.] Swift, [Brig.] Gen[era]l [Simon] Bernard, Col. [Joseph G.] Totten, Professor [Benjamin] Silliman, Professor [Eugenius] Nolte [*sic*; Nulty], Capt. [John] Le Conte.

FC in DNA, 3, 11:391 (M-6:11).

From Winfield Scott, Washington, 5/24. He requests a review of and a final decision about his accounts. ALS in DNA, 1, S-15 (M-211:96).

From Lt. Col. George Bomford, Chief of Ordnance, 5/25. He proposes a plan under which the federal obligation to supply arms to the militia of the States and Territories under an 1808 statute providing $200,000 annually for that purpose can be fulfilled for the years 1816–1821. It will mean the distribution of 80,000 stands of arms (muskets, bayonets, and ramrods), or their equivalent in other forms, to the States and Territories, with subtractions for the 24,000 stands that were delivered during the six years. The allotment to each recipient, in proportion to the imperfect returns of the strength of its respective militia, is itemized. Bomford seeks Calhoun's approval. FC in DNA, 32, 3:233–236; CC in DNA, 332, pp. 27–30.

To William Carroll, Governor of Tenn., Nashville, 5/25. In reply to Carroll's letter of 5/10, Calhoun encloses a notification for James Orr that Orr has been transferred from the Ky. pension roll to that of Tenn. Upon Orr's compliance with the law of 5/1/1820 requiring an oath concerning pensioners' pecuniary circumstances, the [Pension] Agent in West Tenn., [Stephen Cantrell,] will be instructed to pay the arrearages that are owed to Orr. FC in DNA, 91, 12:192.

From [Peter Hagner, Second Auditor,] 5/25. In response to the request written to Hagner today from C[hristopher] V[andeventer (FC in DNA, 3, 11:396 [M-6:11]), Hagner] states that the claims of the State of N.Y. against the U.S. presented by [Ferris] Pell total $316,349.51. Of that amount, $126,509.60 have been paid. The unpaid balance of $189,939.91 "has been disallowed or suspended." FC in DNA, 53, 25:395–396.

From Return J. Meigs, Cherokee Agency, 5/25. The remote [Eastern] Cherokees of Hightown, adjacent to the Creek boundary, 200 families in number, feel that they did not receive their proportionate share of agricultural and domestic tools before the recent retrenchment deprived them of these gifts. They have requested $500 worth of spinning wheels, ploughs, hoes, axes, etc. Meigs seeks authority to make these gifts. ALS in DNA, 1, M-29 (M-221:96); draft in DNA, 75 (M-208:9).

From [Capt.] John R. Bell, St. Augustine, 5/26. He expresses his disappointment in not having been appointed to serve as the Indian Agent in Fla. Territory. The appointment of [former Lt.]

Col. Gad Humphreys came as a complete surprise to Bell. ALS in DNA, 1, B-419 (M-221:92).

From [2nd] Lt. W[illia]m Theobald Wolfe Tone

London, 26 May 1822

I arrived a few days ago in this city, from whence I shall proceed in the course of next week to Paris. My first care was to deliver the dispatches intrusted to me for Mr. [Richard] Rush, [U.S. Minister to Great Britain,] and to give the chronometer of the Topographical Dep[artmen]t to Mr. Brockbank—for repairs &c. That gentleman told me it would take six weeks to put it in order, by which time I shall be returned from Paris. I have written to the [Acting] Adj[utan]t General [Charles J. Nourse] to inform him how to address me, in case you had any further orders to send. Any letters addressed to the care of Mr. Rush will reach me.

I must acknowledge this city to be the most splendid and beautiful of any I have ever seen. In monuments of architecture and collections of the Fine Arts it is inferior to Paris, in neatness to Philadelphia, but in magnitude, in the general elegance and beauty of its buildings & accommodations, the splendour & richness of the shops, streets &c., the public works & manufacturies[,] docks &c. I have never seen anything to equal it, nor had I any conception of it. The British troops are superb. Their appearance &c. is totally altered and entirely copied from the French. It is remarkable that the reductions which they have made in their Army are exactly on the principles of your report [of 12/12/1820 offering a plan for reduction of the U.S. Army (PC in *The Papers of John C. Calhoun,* 5:480–491)], and the parliamentary debates on this subject present a repetition of the arguments used in Congress by MMS. [*sic*; that is, Messrs. Charles Fenton] Mercer, [Representative from Va., Newton] Cannon [Representative from Tenn.] &c. I visited in the Isle of Wight an encampment of 4,000 or 5,000 men embarking in a few days for the East & West Indies & shall bring back with me the latest regulations & Army list I can procure.

In Paris I shall procure for General [John] Mason answers from the first authorities to a series of questions on casting guns &c. which he gave me. These I shall forward first to the War office, in order that you may take copies of them if you think fit.

My mother and Mr. Wilson beg to be kindly remembered to Mrs. [Floride Colhoun] Calhoun. Allow me also to present my respects to her and to subscribe myself with all possible deference . . . .

ALS in DNA, 1, T-8 (M-221:96).

From T[homas] Cadwalader, Philadelphia, 5/27. "I have to acknowledge your Letter of the 24th with a List of the Visitors at the approaching Examination at West Point—and to thank you for the honour conferred upon me by designating me as President of the Board." ALS in DNA, 1, C-406 (M-221:92).

To William Clark, St. Louis, 5/28. Calhoun commissions Clark to be the "Superintendent of Indian Affairs at St. Louis" and asks him to file a bond for $20,000. "Enclosed is a copy of the act of Congress passed at the late Session, under which you have been appointed. Altho' the act does not appear from the face of it, to make it a part of your duty, to exercise a superintending control over the Indian Agencies on the Mississippi and Missouri, yet it is believed that such was the intention of Congress in authorizing the appointment of a *Superintendent* of Indian Affairs at St. Louis." Clark is to supervise Agents [Benjamin] O'Fallon, [Richard] Graham, [Nicholas] Boilvin at Prairie du Chien, [Thomas] Forsyth at Fort Armstrong, and [Lawrence] Taliaferro at St. Peters, and Sub-Agent [Pierre] Menard at Kaskaskia. "The enclosed act contains several new and important provisions, to which it will be necessary that the attention of the Agents should be immediately and particularly drawn. In the execution of the 1st section of this act, which authorizes the issuing of licenses to trade with the Indians, the words, 'remote tribes' will be considered as applicable to those tribes of Indians who may occupy the Country beyond the chain of our military Posts. The Indian Agents will furnish you with returns of all licenses issued by them, under this section, and you will as soon after the 1st of Sept[embe]r in each year as practicable, transmit an abstract of all licenses issued by them or by yourself, within the year ending on that day, made out in the manner and form prescribed, to be laid before Congress. A punctual compliance with the 3d section relative to the settlement of accounts will be rigidly exacted. The law is imperative, and a failure on the part of those concerned to comply with its requisitions in this respect, will render it necessary to report them as delinquents, and to withhold from them any further advance of funds, until their accounts shall have been settled." Their accounts are to be submitted through Clark, who will transmit them, with his own, at least one month before each winter session of Congress. These accounts are to itemize as specifically as practicable the nature of all disbursements, so that few outlays will be comprehended within the general term contingencies; every employee is to be named, and the amount paid to each is to be revealed. The appropriations for Indian affairs this year total $123,638. Of this sum, $22,300 are available for the pay of Agents, $11,338 for that of Sub-Agents, $15,000 for presents to Indians under a law of 1802, and $75,000 for contingencies. Allotted to Clark are $6,800 for the pay of Agents, $2,000 for that of Sub-Agents, $5,350 for presents, and $12,150 for contingencies. Clark is to use his judgment in apportioning these four sums among his subordinates; "every economy consistent with the public interest will be used, to reduce the expenditures under each head as much below" the four maximums "as possible, particularly those for contingencies." If Graham has made advances, under the authorization written to him by Calhoun on 4/19, to Taliaferro, Forsyth, Boilvin, and Menard, those advances will have to be deducted from the total funds at Clark's disposal. Remittances will be made to Clark on the basis of quarterly estimates by him, based upon requests by his subordinates. The annuities for 1822 have all been remitted except $2,000 due to the Kickapoos under the Treaty of Edwardsville, $500 due to the Kaskaskias under an 8/13/1803 treaty, and private annuities due to two Delaware Chiefs, which were delayed for want of an appropriation; these are now being sent. If the tribes want goods instead of money, the Agents should try to buy from the Factories; and those trading houses should also be given a preference in purchasing goods for presents. But, [because the Factory system has been abolished,] no money is to be paid to the Factors; instead, the amount of such purchases is to be retained and reported by Clark, who will be given instructions what to do with it. Copies of the recent law are sent to Clark for distribution to his Agents; he is to add "such instructions as you deem it necessary to give to insure a just & faithful execution of its several provisions. Officers commanding military posts will receive orders thro' the proper officer in relation to the execution of the duty required of them by the 2nd Section of the act. It is deemed unnecessary to enlarge upon all the points to which your attention will be directed by the act of 1802 and the amendatory act now transmitted. Great confidence is reposed in your judgment and experience in the management of Indian Affairs, & it is believed that nothing on your part will be omitted which may be essential to the due execution of the laws & regulations upon the subject." FC in DNA, 72, E:258–261 (M-15:5).

To E[DMUND] P. GAINES, Louisville, Ky.

Dep[art]m[en]t of War, 28 May 1822

I enclose copies of an Act passed at the late session of Congress [concerning Indian trade] by the 2nd Section of which it is made the duty of Military Officers, "to cause the Stores and packages of Goods of all Indian traders, upon suspicion or information that ardent spirits are carried into the Indian Country by said Traders, to be searched"; and prescribes the penalty, if any such spirits shall be found. You will enclose a copy of the Act to each of the officers commanding military posts in & adjacent to the Indian Country within your command and order them to attend to the execution of the duty thereby imposed upon them.

FC in DNA, 72, E:258 (M-15:5); CC in DNA, 111, no. 561; CC in OClWHi, Mich. Territory, Circuit Court for Irwin and Crawford Counties, Joseph Renville vs. William R. Jouett, October Term, 1834; PC in *American State Papers: Military Affairs*, 5:507–508.

To Capt. GEORGE N. MORRIS, Commanding Fort St. Marks, West Fla.

Dep[art]m[en]t of War, 28th May 1822

I have received your letter of the 2nd Inst[ant (ALS in DNA, 1, M-378 [M-221:93])]. The expense of rations issued to the Indians must not exceed $200 per month. As the season is now far advanced, it is presumed the Indians will soon be able to supply themselves, and the necessity to issue rations to them will cease. You will accordingly stop the issues at the post as soon as it can be done without injury to the public interest.

The Indians will be permitted to live on the lands they now occupy and cultivate them for their support. In the fall, measures will be taken to concentrate them as has been contemplated, and which would have been done last fall if they had met Capt. [John R.]

Bell agreeably to his invitation. In the mean time you will treat them friendly and give them every aid in your power in repairing their tools and implements of husbandry.

FC in DNA, 72, E:258 (M-15:5). NOTE: Morris replied on 8/2.

To Nicholas Boilvin, Thomas Forsyth, Richard Graham, B[enjamin] O'Fallon, Lawrence Taliaferro, Indian Agents, and Pierre Menard, Sub-Agent, 5/29. "General William Clark late Governor of Missouri Territory has been appointed under an act of Congress passed at the late session Superintendent of Indian Affairs at St. Louis, and, by direction, of the President [James Monroe] his Superintendency will embrace the several Indian Agencies on the Mississippi and Missouri. You will therefore upon rec[e]ipt of this correspond with him in relation to your duties and take his instructions upon all points connected with them. He will transmit ["to" *interlined*] you a copy of an act passed at the late session of Congress, amending the act of intercourse of 1802 which contains several new & important provisions, and in relation to which he is directed to give you full instruction." FC in DNA, 72, E:262 (M-15:5); LS (Taliaferro's copy) in MnHi, Lawrence Taliaferro Papers (published microfilm, roll 1, document 42).

To Lewis Cass, Detroit, 5/29. Calhoun announces the appointment of Henry R. Schoolcraft to be the Indian Agent at Sault Ste. Marie. Schoolcraft will report to Cass for instructions. Calhoun encloses copies of a new statute [of 5/6 concerning Indian trade] and explains its key provisions. In the first section, authorizing issuance of licenses to trade with the Indians, the words "remote tribes" apply to those Indians living "beyond the chain of our military posts." Agents reporting to Cass must furnish him with reports of all licenses they issue. As soon as possible after 9/1 of each year, Cass is to submit to the War Department abstracts of all licenses issued within his Superintendency. Calhoun stresses that every Agent must comply rigidly and punctually with the third section of the act, which deals with the settlement of accounts. Those who fail to comply will be reported as "delinquents," and further funds will be withheld until their accounts have been settled. Agents will render their accounts quarterly, "or at all events" within a reasonable time after 9/1. Cass must send his and their accounts to the War Department at least one month before the fall session of Congress convenes. All accounts "must be accompanied by a *general abstract* of *all disbursements*" during each quarter prior to 9/1. Expenses must be detailed under distinct headings, for example, "pay of Agents, Sub-Agents, Interpreters & Blacksmiths, presents, transportation of annuities, rations issued at the Agencies and at the distribution of annuities." As few items as possible should be placed under the general head of "Contingencies." There must be annexed to the abstract a statement revealing the names of all employees for each quarter and their wages. "These abstracts and statements are indispensably necessary to enable the Department" to render its annual report to Congress. Cass will examine and send, with necessary explanations, the accounts, abstracts, and statements to the War Department, which will then pass them along to the Second Auditor [William Lee] for settlement. The Indian Department has received the following appropriations for 1822: $22,300 for the pay of Indian Agents; $11,338 for that of Sub-Agents; $15,000 for presents to Indians under the act of 1802; and $75,000 for contingencies. Of the total appropriation of $123,638, $31,400 have been alloted to Cass's Superintendency: $6,600 for the pay of Indian Agents; $5,000 for that of Sub-Agents; $4,500 for presents; and $15,300 for contingent expenses, which include the wages of other employees, the allowances for Cass, and the salary of the newly-appointed Agent at Sault Ste. Marie, [Schoolcraft]. Cass may apportion the funds for presents and contingencies among Agencies under his supervision as he thinks best. Cass must not operate outside his budget and must practice strictest economy, in order to reduce all expenditures, particularly those for contingencies. Because "of the temper manifested in Congress at the late session in relation to the allowances made to Governors of Territories as Superintendents of Indian affairs," and because of the Indian Department's reduced appropriation, Calhoun thinks it advisable to reduce the allowances. Cass's 10 rations daily will be discontinued, but he will receive $1,500 for "Clerk hire, Office rent &c." Calhoun sends $15,000 to Cass as an advance for expenses but reminds him that his general estimate for the year has not been received. He instructs Cass to make it out in great detail, using quarterly estimates of the Agents as its basis. Annuities for 1822 have been sent to the proper Agents, except for those provided for by the Treaty of Chicago. Cass will receive and pay these through the proper Agents. If the Indians should prefer the payment of annuities in goods, Agents should purchase the goods from a local U.S. Factory, if possible. Goods for presents may be bought in the same manner. All Agents who disperse more than $10,000 in annuities are required under the fifth section of the new statute to give new bonds in the amount of $20,000. Since annuities paid through [John] Johnston and [John] Hays amount to much more than $10,000, Calhoun encloses two blank bonds to be executed by them for $20,000 each. Each must have two or more securities, the sufficiency of which must be certified by a U.S. District Judge or U.S. Attorney. The executed bonds must be sent to the War Department. Cass is instructed to send copies of the enclosed statute and necessary instructions to the Agents under his control. Officers commanding military posts will receive orders through channels in regard to duties required of them by the second section of the act. Expressing "great confidence" in Cass's "judgement and experience in the management of Indian affairs," Calhoun entrusts to him proper execution of the acts of [3/30]/1802 and [5/6]/1822. A postscript directs that funds shall not be paid to the U.S. Factories for the goods that may be received from the Factories for annuities but that such money shall be held until instructions are given as to its disposition. LS in DNA, 76, 5:253–260 (M-1:10, pp. 253–260); FC (without the postscript) in DNA, 72, E:265–267 (M-15:5); CCEx in DNA, 111.

From R[ichard] Graham, Louisville, 5/29. He acknowledges Calhoun's letters of 4/19 and 4/23, with a draft for $10,300. Graham has paid to [Nicholas] Boilvin $2,000 and to [Lawrence] Taliaferro $2,500; Graham left $1,500 for [Thomas] Forsyth and has not yet paid [Pierre] Menard, who is now among the Delawares. Calhoun may have misunderstood a Graham report about the Delawares' annuity for 1821; no annuity is due to them until 1823. Graham will try to keep peace among the Western tribes. He sees no threat of any attack by a coalition of them against the U.S. He discusses the personal and salt annuities due to two Delaware Chiefs. He encloses claims by U.S. citizens against the Osages for destroyed property. ALS in DNA, 1, G-8 (M-221:95); draft in MoSHi, Richard Graham Papers.

Lt. Col. C[harles] Gratiot, Fort Monroe, to Alexander Macomb, 5/29. Gratiot explains that payments from the 1821 appropriation have been made totaling about $50,000 under the [Elijah] Mix contract for stone delivered at Forts Monroe and Calhoun. ALS and CC in DNA, 223, 921.

From P[ETER] H[AGNER, Third Auditor]

29th May 1822

I have the honor to state in reply to the letter [*not found*] of Mr. G.W. Adams agent for James Johnson referred by you to this office, that there are no disallowed vouchers in the account of James Johnson under his Contract dated 6th December 1817. On the first settlement of that account a number of Items were disallowed and others suspended, which on settlement made the 5th of January last were either in whole or in part allowed to his credit agreeably to a statement transmitted to him by letter from this office dated 9th of that month. The vouchers being thus disposed of, they cannot be returned though in some instances only a part of the charge has been allowed, but it is believed that the statement furnished of the Items allowed and rejected will be sufficiently explicit to shew the amount claimed, that allowed and the reasons for not allowing the balance.

The copy of the statement of the account of James Johnson under Contract with the Commissary General dated the 25th November 1818 is herewith furnished agreeably to the request of Mr. Adams. No vouchers in this account were disallowed or suspended and consequently there are none to return to Colonel Johnson.

A like copy of the statement of his account under his Contract with the same officer dated 1st January 1820 is also herewith sent as requested, together with the letter of Mr. Adams herein referred to.

FC in DNA, 53, 26:18.

To R[ichard] M. Johnson, [Senator from Ky.,] Great Crossings, Ky., 5/29. As Johnson requested on 5/14 [ALS in DNA, 1, J-180 (M-221:93)], Calhoun sends vouchers relating to suspended items in an account of James Johnson. FC in DNA, 3, 11:398 (M-6:11).

To James Miller, [Governor of Ark. Territory,] Little Rock, 5/29. Calhoun gives instructions similar to those issued on 5/28 to William Clark concerning the new statute regulating trade with Indians. The sum of $5,500 has been allotted to Miller's superintendency, to be apportioned as follows: $1,500 for pay of the Indian Agent, [David Brearley]; $500 for pay of the Sub-Agent [Nathaniel

Philbrook]; $500 for presents to Indians; and $3,000 for contingencies. Miller will place the sums allowed for presents and contingencies in the hands of the Agent to be spent under Miller's direction. Every economy must be practiced. Only one Sub-Agent is provided for, because it is not thought expedient at present to replace the deceased Quapaw Sub-Agent, [Jacob Miller]. If, however, an appointment to the vacancy should be made later, B. Smith, whom Miller recommended, will be named. "In consequence of the temper manifested in Congress at the late Session in relation to the allowances made to Governors of Territories as Superintendents of Indian Affairs and also of the reduced appropriation which has been made for the Indian Department it is deemed advisable to reduce these allowances. You will accordingly be allowed from the last settlement $750 for Clerk hire, Office Rent &c. instead of $1,500 heretofore allowed for the same objects. A reduction of equal amount has also been made in the allowance to the Governor of the Michigan Territory," [Lewis Cass]. Calhoun remits to Miller $3,000 for the expenses of his Superintendency through 6/30. Annuities have already been sent to Miller, and Calhoun authorizes him upon request by the Indians to pay annuities in merchandise secured from the Factories. FC in DNA, 72, E:262–264 (M-15:5); PC in Carter, ed., *Territorial Papers*, 19:435–437.

To C. Ridgely "of Hamp[ton, Baltimore]"

Washington, 29th May 1822

I received by this day's mail your favour of the 27th Ins[tan]t, containing an invitat[ion] from the Committee of arrangement to attend the exhibition of the Maryland Agricultural Society on the 30th & 31st Inst[ant]s.

I am prevented by the severe indisposition of Mrs. [Floride Colhoun] Calhoun from doing myself the pleasure of accepting the invitation. Agriculture is my favourite persuit [*sic*], in which I take the deepest interest. I consider those among the greatest publick benefactors, who contribute to its improvement. I must request of you to make known to the Committee the regret, which I feel, that it is not in my power to accept their invitation; and to make my acknowledgement to them for their polite attention.

ALS in MdHi, Custis-Law-Rogers Letters.

Lewis Cass, Detroit, to George Boyd, Mackinac, 5/30. "I had hoped that the two canoes which I requested you to procure were not as absolutely contracted for as to render it necessary to receive them on the part of the United States, as the principal reason for procuring them has failed [in that Calhoun is unable to make his intended tour of the Northwest]. But if it is so, the case admits of no remedy. We must take them. One of them you can retain for the use of your Agency, and an additional sum, equal to the cost, shall be assigned to you for the payment. The other I will thank you to forward to this place by the first opportunity. They will probably be wanted both by you and me, when the final instructions are received respecting the exclusion of our Indians from Canada." LS in DNA, 76 (M-1:70, pp. 297–300).

From Edmund P. Gaines

Louisville, Ky., May 30th, 1822

A review of your letter of the 10th of last month in relation to the command assigned to General [Henry] Atkinson sug[g]ests to me the propriety of stating, what I had not before deemed it necessary to state, that I did not omit to apprise General Atkinson of the Instructions given to me through the Adjutant General[']s office under date the 3rd of August last. On the contrary I furnished him shortly after the receipt of the letter of instruction, with an Extract, embracing that part relating to him, to which I called his attention, expressly stating in an accompanying letter that the extract was enclosed for his information and government. I considered it to be my duty to do this, because it is my duty to "obey the orders of the President of the United States, and the orders of the officers appointed over me according to the rules and articles of war." But since I am thus reminded of the instruction refer[r]ed to, I take this occasion to say, that I have been able to view the order prohibiting General Atkinson from receiving Brevet pay in no other light than, as among the very few orders I have ever received which did not appear to me to be conformable to law.

This apparent collision between military orders and military law, could not fail to produce in a mind habituated to passive obedience, a degree of pain and embarrassment which I have learned how to feel but not to describe. In all such cases of collision I earnestly endeavor to consult the best lights that reason and experience afford to guide me through the labyrinth which such collisions seldom fail to produce. In cases that appear at all doubtful the *order* demands always unhesitating obedience, because the right of construing and settling all doubtful questions of military law necessarily belongs to the commander-in-chief—but when the law is so clear and explicit as to admit of no doubt whatever, and the order at variance with such a provision of law, I think myself bound to conclude that as there must have been a mistake either in the printing of the law or the copying of the order, it would seem most likely to have occur[r]ed in the order; and that if the one or the other be entitled to precedence it must be the law. Yet notwithstanding these are my settled convictions as regards the case refer[r]ed to, I could not think myself justified in withholding from an officer of my command any views or instructions emanating from the General in chief or the Department of War affecting such officer or his command. And permit me further to state that my having called General Atkinson[']s attention to the right wing of my command was strictly conformable to long established military principles (as well in Europe as in the United States), without regard to his *brevet rank*: his rank in the line was quite sufficient to justify the selection. As a proof that I was governed by military usage and military law alone, and not (as the Department of War seems to suppose) by a disposition to create Districts or departments with a view to give effect to brevet rank merely it will be found that the attention of several other of my field officers had been directed to such stations and sections of my command as appeared to me most convenient and conducive to the interests of the service, where brevet rank was manifestly out of the question. It will be seen, too, by the enclosed extract of my letter to General Atkinson that I did not lose sight even of a verbal [that is, oral] suggestion made by you and repeated by the General in chief, as to the principle upon which commands were to be assigned. But I should be unfaithful to the trust with which I am honored, were I to withhold from you the respectful declaration of my conviction that, the changes which I have made pursuant to your instructions of the 10th of April are not well adapted to the primary purposes of an inland frontier defence, where the forces to be guarded against consist of savages; and I consider this view of the subject as strongly supported by the authority given to General Atkinson, under your sanction, to command in virtue of his Brevet rank, when the occasion may demand it:—namely whenever the Indians shall make war upon the frontier near him. If hostilities upon the frontier heretofore assigned to him would render it proper to give the usual extension to his command, I cannot but think it essential to the service that he should possess all the advantages the command would previously afford him, of ascertaining and keeping himself informed of the state and condition of the frontier, its resources and means of defence, as well as the strength[,] character and conduct of the Indians to be guarded against.

Upon the subject of brevet pay, I do assure you that this is a consideration to which I attach very little importance; and I am assured that General Atkinson likewise regards it as unworthy of estimation compared with considerations of rank and usefulness in the great scale of national defence. And whenever Congress may see fit to reduce the pay, it will produce not a murmur on my part—especially when a reduced revenue shall urge the propriety of the measure.

But until Congress shall deem it proper to make such reduction of pay I must be permitted to decide in my own case whether to receive or relinquish any part of the pay allowed me by the law—and I certainly shall not be disposed to make any such relinquishment so long as the Treasury Department claims of me a balance which I am convinced I do not justly owe, and which I have no means of paying at this time other than by receiving the full amount due to me; and I take this occasion to request that you will order the Paymaster General [Nathan Towson] to make payments allowed to me by law.

The above mentioned enclosure refer[r]ed to is numbered 1. I enclose also a copy of my letter [of 1/28] to Col. [John R.] Fenwick, No. 2—which contains my views in relation to Departments.

ALS with Ens in DNA, 1, G-178 (M-221:92); variant FC in DNA, RG 98, Western Department, Letters Sent, 1:244–247. NOTE: The first enclosure mentioned by Gaines is an extract from his letter of 7/14/1821 to Atkinson. Other enclosures include CC's of Calhoun's letters of 4/10/1822 to Atkinson and to Gaines, of James Gadsden to Gaines on 1/21, of Gadsden to Atkinson on 1/19, and of E[dmund] Kirby to Gaines on 8/3/1821.

To EDMUND P. GAINES, Louisville, Ky.

Department of War, May 30, 1822

I have received your letter of the 16th instant, announcing your return to your habitual Head Quarters at Louisville, stating the causes of your not earlier noticing my several communications, enclosing copies of your orders to General [Henry] Atkinson as well as for the regulation of seperate [*sic*] commands in the Western Department—also, a copy of a report from General Atkinson to you respecting the disposition of the North Western Indians, and an extract of your journal touching the claim of the Choctaw Indians on the Red River.

The circumstances which prevented your earlier notice of my communications satisfactorily account for the delay.

The orders which you have issued to Gen[era]l Atkinson, and relative to seperate Commands are correct and approved. The account which Gen[era]l Atkinson gives of the state of the upper posts as well as the tem[per] of the adjacent Tribes of Indians is very satisfactory; and there is no doubt but so long as the present appearance of efficiency be maintained in their vicinity we shall have peace with them. The extract of your journal is interesting. Information of that character is very useful and I shall be glad to receive such reports in relation to the interior as your observations may enable you from time to time to make.

In relation to the existing hostilities between the [Western] Cherokees and Osages, the President [James Monroe] takes great interest in having [them] properly and permanently adjusted, and he directs that you say to the Chiefs of both nations that he requires and directs that they shall desist from further hostilities, and that they make peace on just principles immediately.

FC in DNA, 3, 11:398–399 (M-6:11).

To V[IRGIL] MAXCY, Baltimore

Washington, 31st May 1822

I received your favour of the 29th Inst[ant; *not found*] by this day's mail, and I assure you that I would have been greatly gratified by attending the agricultural exhibition near Baltimore. I did not receive the invitation of the Committee till the 29th Inst[ant], but the shortness of the notice, would not have prevented ["me" *interlined*] from attending. Agriculture, as you know, is my favourite pursuit; and I would doubtless [have] been much gratified with the exhibition, in addition to the pleasure, which it would have afforded ["me" *interlined*], to enlarge the sphere of my acquaintance in your State. All this, however, I had to forego on account of the state of Mrs. [Floride Colhoun] Calhoun's health. Till to day, she has been confined to her bed for the last 10 days. She is now considerable [*sic*] better, but very weak. I fear the state of her health will deprive us of the pleasure anticipated from a visit to West River. The Physician advises us, that great care will be necessary to avoid a relapse in her particular case; and, as the season is now considerably advanced, she will not be in a condition to meet the fatigue of the ride till it will be too late. I regret that I had not the pleasure of seeing Mr. [Benjamin or Beverly?] Chew. It would have afforded me much pleasure to have made his acqua[in]tance.

The miserable paper in this place, the City Gazette, keeps a constant attack on me. He [the editor] is anxious to combine the interest of the other Gentlemen against me, and particularly to excite the ill will of Mr. [John Quincy] Adam[s]'s friends. I doubt not, however, the paper is under the influence of the [Secretary of the] Treasury, [William H. Crawford,] which is concealed for the present to give more effect to his [the editor's] attacks. The impression here is, that he does no harm. Present information from the West is very flattering, but publick sentiment cannot be ["so" *canceled*] considered to be so far settled, as to form any accurate estimate. The greatest danger is in New York. Her politicks are so much a matter of calculation of personal interest and ["is subject to such" *interlined*] sudden combinations, that it is impossible to form any satisfactory opinion of the course which she may adopt. I have, however, been conversing with a gentleman from Utica to day, ["so" *canceled and* "who" *interlined*] says, that he thinks the sentiment of that part of the State is settling down very fast and so favourably as could be desired.

Mrs. Calhoun and her mother [Floride Bonneau Colhoun] desire their best regards to yourself & Mrs. Maxcy. Yours truly, J.C. Calhoun.

ALS in DLC, Galloway-Maxcy-Markoe Papers, vol. 32.

JUNE 1822

ACTION BREEDS REACTION. CRAWFORD HAD AN ANTI-Calhoun newspaper. So Calhoun solicited on the 8th subscribers for a proposed journal to advocate his own Presidential candidacy, under the editorship of the soon-to-be-displaced Thomas L. McKenney. And Andrew Jackson suggested confidentially on the 28th a way to confound the political intriguers who had prevented James Gadsden from continuing to be the Adjutant General; but the proposal proved to be in vain. Calhoun wrote on the 17th and the 18th with concern about the duel forced upon one of his friends by a Crawfordite. The provisional government of the Territory of Florida was replaced with something better, under Governor William P. DuVal. Jedidiah Morse's *Report* about Indian affairs was published at last. And Samuel Houston protested on the 4th against government red tape.

To Capt. JOHN R. BELL, St. Augustine

Department of War, June 1st 1822

When the appointments of Indian Agents were made, at the close of the late session of Congress I laid your name, and that of [former] Lieut[enant] Col. [Gad] Humphreys who was also an applicant, before the President [James Monroe] for the appointment of Agent in Florida. After due consideration the President nominated Col. Humphrey[s]. His recent disbandment [as of 6/1/1821,] which was one of the hardest cases at the late reduction [of the Army], and his present restricted means of support, of himself and family gave him high claims to the patronage of the government. His selection was induced wholly by these considerations, and not upon any idea of superior fitness over yourself. On the contrary the President would have availed himself of your capacity and experience in the affairs of the Indians in Florida, but for the reasons above mentioned. The President considered that your present command in the Army did not throw you so peculiarly upon the patronage of the government. Under this view you will see that the appointment of Col. Humphrey[s] was in a degree unavoidable, and was not made in preference to yourself, or from any diminution of confidence in your capacity and integrity.

FC in DNA, 5, 1:130–131 (M-7:1); PC in Carter, ed., *Territorial Papers,* 22:450.

From JOHN McKEE, [former Choctaw Agent and later a Representative from Ala.]

Tuskaloosa [*sic*] (Ala.), June 1, 1822

Mr. [Thomas Hill] Williams of the U.S. Senate, from Mississippi, has requested me to communicate to you direct, my opinion of a new site for the residence of the Choctaw Agent. The subject was frequently spoken of at the Treaty at Doaks, and the opinion I then gave, is one I still entertain, that Nannawya Hill, or some place within twenty to twenty-five miles of ["it" *interlined*], will be most central to the population, and convenient for intercourse with the nation. It is situated on one of the highest branches of the Pearl River, and near the sources of Noxubbee, one of the western branches of Tombigbee. The only objection to this site, is its distance from Navigation, but this will apply to any other in the interior. If navigation is important it must be sought either on Tombigbee or Yazoo, and the choice will necessarily be determined by the ulterior views of the Government in relation to the Choctaws.

ALS in DNA, 1, M-14 (M-221:96).

From H[enry] Robertson, Fayetteville, [Tenn.,] 6/2. He has received Calhoun's letter of 5/13, is pleased that payment for the construction of the road was being initiated, but still believes that he is entitled to a refund of what he paid to the inspectors of the road. ALS in DNA, 1, R-7 (M-221:96).

To John Crowell, Creek Agency, 6/3. Calhoun gives to Crowell instructions under the new statute regulating trade with Indians. Crowell has been allotted $5,100, to be apportioned as follows: $1,800 for his pay; $500 for the Sub-Agent's pay; $100 for presents to Indians; and $2,700 for contingencies. Expenditures must not exceed these sums, and every economy should be practiced to reduce expenses to a smaller total. Calhoun remits $2,375 for the Agency's needs during the first two quarters of 1822. Because Crowell pays more than $10,000 annually in annuities, he must execute in the proper manner an enclosed blank bond for $20,000. FC in DNA, 72, E:267–269 (M-15:5).

To George Gray, [Indian Agent,] Natchitoches, La., 6/3. Calhoun gives to Gray instructions under the new statute regulating trade with Indians. Of the $4,000 that have been allotted to Gray's Agency, $1,200 are for his salary, $800 are for presents to Indians, and $2,000 are for contingencies. He will receive $2,000 to cover his Agency's expenses during the first two quarters of 1822. FC in DNA, 72, E:272 (M-15:5).

To R[eturn] J. Meigs, [Eastern Cherokee Agent,] Calhoun, Tenn., 6/3. Calhoun sends to Meigs a copy of the new statute concerning the licensing of Indian traders; it "contains several new and important provisions, to which your attention is particularly called." Calhoun itemizes the $4,760 that have been allotted to Meigs's Agency for this year and remits $2,380 (less than Meigs has estimated that he needs) for the first half-year; what Meigs wanted for blacksmiths has been considered to be excessive. Calhoun remits also $1,000 as tuition allowances through 6/30 to the Cherokee Indian schools, including an increase of $50 per quarter in the grant to the school at Brainerd. LS and CC in DNA, 75 (M-208:9); FC in DNA, 72, E:269–270 (M-15:5).

To R[obert] C[arter] Nicholas, Chickasaw Agency, 6/3. Calhoun gives to Nicholas instructions under the new statute regulating trade with Indians. The Chickasaw Agency has been allotted $4,600 for its expenses this year: $1,300 are for Nicholas's salary, $500 are for the Sub-Agent's salary, $100 are for presents to Indians, and $2,700 can be used for contingencies. Nicholas cannot exceed these amounts, and he should spend less if possible. Calhoun remits $2,300 to Nicholas for the first half-year and explains that Nicholas's estimate had to be reduced by half because of the small appropriation for Indian affairs. Because Nicholas handles more than $10,000 in annuities each year, he must execute in the proper manner an enclosed blank bond for $20,000. FC in DNA, 72, E:271–272 (M-15:5).

To William Ward, Choctaw Agency, 6/3. Calhoun sends to Ward a copy of and instructions concerning the new statute governing Indian trade. The allotment to Ward's Agency for its expenses in 1822 is $4,760; half of that amount is being remitted now for the first half-year. This remittance is less than Ward has requested, but it "is as much as the limitted [*sic*] appropriation made by Congress will admit of. The expenses therefore must be reduced to that amount." The costs of neither presents to Indians nor contingencies can exceed the year's allotment. Calhoun encloses $600 in payment of a grant to the Indian school at Elliot[t, Miss.]. He authorizes Ward to purchase goods for the Choctaw annuity from the nearest U.S. Factory if Ward does not have them in hand or from other sources if he cannot secure them at reasonable prices from the Factory. The new law requires that Ward shall execute a new bond for $20,000, and Calhoun encloses a form for that purpose. FC in DNA, 72, E:270–271 (M-15:5).

To William Wirt

Department of War, June 3d 1822

The leasing of the lead-mines in Missouri having been lately transferred by order of the President [James Monroe] from the Treasury Department to this, and as some doubts have been expressed in the Senate in relation to the power of making leases, I have to submit the following questions for your opinion, viz.

Has the President of the United States power to make leases of Lead-mines? and if so, to whom and for what time? and can he prescribe conditions in the leases, provided they be not inconsistent with existing laws?

I transmit herewith the laws in relation to the lead-mines, with a report of the Ordnance Department made in obedience to a resolution of the House of Representatives at the last session of Congress, and the Speeches of Col. [Thomas Hart] Benton and Gov[erno]r [Ninian] Edwards thereon.

Your opinion on the foregoing questions is desired as soon as convenient.

LS in DNA, 111, 120; FC in DNA, 3, 11:399 (M-6:11). Note: Wirt answered on 6/6 that a statute of 3/3/[1807] authorized leases of lead mine lands for terms not exceeding three years and under any conditions that the President might think proper. LS and PC in DNA, 31, 1822, War Department, 1; FC in DNA, 113, B:76 (T-412:2); CC in DNA, 33, 1:16.

From [1st Lt.] John A. Dix, Albany, [N.Y.,] 6/4. He reports the arrival of Maj. Gen. [Jacob] Brown at that place. Brown will proceed to Washington by way of New York City in two or three days. "As he finds his health very much benefitted by exercise, he bids me to state to you his intention of performing the whole journey in his own carriage." ALS in DNA, 1, D-155 (M-221:92); FC in DLC, Jacob Brown Papers, Letterbooks, 2:214.

From T[homas] F[orsyth], St. Louis, 6/4. As Calhoun ordered on 2/14 [Abs under date of 2/13 in *The Papers of John C. Calhoun*, vol. VI], Forsyth has accompanied [James] Johnson and other lessees to the lead mines on Fever River and now reports at length. Enroute to the mines, he paid to the Sauks and the Foxes at Fort Armstrong their annuities for 1821; but the merchandise was deficient to the extent of $20.50, and he hopes that the Indians will not lose even that small an amount. He apologized as best he could for the fact that he had not received answers to the Indians' appeals of last year concerning their lands, their annuities, and a blacksmith. He assured them that the government was pleased with their good conduct. When he informed them about its leases of the lead mines on Fever River and advised them to work in the future only their lead mines on the west side of the Mississippi, the Sauk Indians disclaimed any interest in the Fever River mines, but the Foxes protested that they had never sold to the U.S. any lands on the east of the Mississippi above the mouth of the Rocky River. Forsyth told them that he was not *asking* permission for the lessees to work any lead mines on the east of the Mississippi and informed them that the lessees would assuredly proceed on the morrow to the Fever River. The Foxes left the Fort while they were much irritated and were murmuring. In a later, two-day conference at the Fever, attended by such men as Johnson, Nicholas Boilvin, and [Lt.] Col. [Willoughby] Morgan, Forsyth and the Foxes reached the same impasse again; but Forsyth assured both the Foxes and the lessees that neither must interefere with the other and mollified the Foxes somewhat by giving them a little whiskey. While Forsyth was traveling to St. Louis, he was informed that the Sauks, Foxes, and Iowas had retaliated against the Sioux for past murders or wars. Forsyth has found the Indians to be generally unwilling to disclose the extent and locations of lead deposits, but one trader and former soldier believes that they are to be found everywhere north of Rocky Island, east of the Mississippi, south of the mouth of the Wisconsin River, and west of the Rocky River. The Winnebagoes have long mined lead beside the northern branches of the Rocky River. This country, stretching about 180 miles between Rocky Island and the Wisconsin and maybe 30 miles eastward from the Mississippi to the Winnebagoes' land, is claimed by the Chippewa, Ottawa, and Potawatomi Indians, and Forsyth urges that their title should be extinquished. As many as 1,000 miners may be at work within a year, and immense wealth can result. FC in WHi, Draper Collection, Thomas Forsyth Papers, 4:126–135 (published microfilm, series T, vols. 1–9).

From SAM[UEL] HOUSTON

Nashville, 4th June 1822

A few mails since I was favoured with an acknowledgement of a ballance [*sic*] in my favor, on a final settlement of my accounts of $170:[0]9 c[en]ts. At the same time I am required by Mr. [William] Lee, 2d Auditor, to send on a voucher from the Treasury Agent, "that costs of a suit have been paid" [and am told] that until then I cannot draw the ballance due me.

I am at a loss Sir to account for this requisition. If a suit had been instituted against me on improper grounds; when the United States owed me a ballance of $170:[0]9 c[en]ts, my accounts too, had been forwarded, but treated with contempt, and myself with injustice; ought I to pay costs? Perhaps this is a rule established at the City [of Washington], but it does not fit our Backwoods notions of Justice.

As often as three different times, have I sent my accounts to Washington. Once as early as 1819, or [18]20, and at all times there were blank receipts annexed to them. Wherefore is the necessity of my sending, a power of atto[rney] as a voucher to Mr. Lee? It is not necessary, nor can it be required upon any other ground, than to produce delay!

I feel sore on the subject of *formality* & *etiquette*. My accounts have once been returned to me as "inadmissible" (to this place). Afterwards they were acknowledged to be "*Strictly legal.*" How this ever took place, I am unable to determine; but to those engaged in the transaction, I suppose all is fair and clear.

I write to you Sir that I may at some period, not very remote obtain my right. I wish to have no further business with Mr. Lee, but would be glad that the business could work into the hands of T[homas] T[udor] Tucker Esquire Treasurer [of the United States]: *he is an honest and honorable man*! I wish a Draft forwarded to me; payable at Washington, Baltimore, or Philadelphia. No suit has ever been instituted against me!! Respectfully, Sam: Houston.

ALS in DNA, 2, H-1822 (M-222:23). NOTE: An undated AES by Lee explained that the $170.09 were withheld upon request of a Treasury agent "who represented to us that he had a claim against him [that is, Houston] for costs of suit. The agent[']s claim having been withdrawn in consequence of a letter from Col[one]l [James] Gadsden the money was remitted a few days ago to Mr. Houston."

From the Rev. Cyrus Kingsbury, Mayhew, [Miss.,] 6/5. He announces the opening of his new school named Newell, which is located on the Natchez Trace. He encloses a sketch of its buildings, some of which have been constructed and others of which are still unfinished. He requests a grant from the fund for the civilization of the Indians to cover two-thirds of the costs of construction. He reports that there are now 34 students at the mission school at Mayhew. ALS with En in DNA, 77 (M-271:4, frames 153–157).

To William H. Crawford, [Secretary of the Treasury,] 6/6. Calhoun answers Crawford's request of 6/4 [ALU in DNA, 2, T-1822 (M-222:23)]. Most annuities are now paid in money to the Indians and have been sent, "with the exception of the Chickasaw annuity and those for which appropriations were made at the late ["session of" *interlined*] Congress." The following annuities, totaling $24,000, are paid in goods: Cherokees, $6,000; Sauks and Foxes, $1,000; Creeks, $11,000, to cease in 1823; Choctaws, $5,000; and Quapaws, $1,000. "It is proper to observe in relation to the Cherokee, Creek & Choctaw annuities, that the above sums are but a part of them; and that an option is given by treaty to the two latter as to the mode of payment which must, however, be seasonably signified thro' their Agents to the War Department; but as no such option was thus signified, it was therefore inferred that they wished the payment of the whole of their annuities to be ["paid" *canceled and* "made" *interlined*] in money, and they were accordingly ["remitted" *interlined*] to their respective Agents." Calhoun believes that most of the Indians can be induced to receive "at least a part of their annuities in goods, provided they can be obtained on suitable terms." Calhoun has already instructed those Agents near [U.S.] Factories to secure goods for annuities and presents from the Factories. Calhoun cannot "state even the probable amount of goods that may be taken from each Factory for annuities; but I would respectfully suggest as an inducement to the Indians to take the whole or greater part of their annuities in goods, that the Agents employed by the Government in winding up the Factory business, under the direction of the Treasury Department, may be instructed to make a reasonable reduction in the invoice prices of the goods, where they appear to be high in comparison with the prices of the same articles at other places." Calhoun estimates that $10,450 will be spent for presents, apportioned as follows: $4,500 in [Lewis Cass's] Superintendency; $500 in [James Miller's] Superintendency; $5,350 in [William Clark's] Superintendency; and $100 at the Choctaw Agency. Without a list of the Factories before him, Calhoun cannot designate "those from which annuities & presents can be most conveniently supplied," but he supposes that the goods will be secured from the Factory nearest the individual Agency. FC in DNA, 72, E:272–274 (M-15:5).

From the Rev. Jedidiah Morse

New-Haven, June 6, 1822

In the last and preceding winters, I had the honor of presenting to the President of the United States, [James Monroe,] through your hands, a Report, in part, of the results of my several visits among the Indian Tribes of our country, and of my inquiries concerning their past history and present actual state. This Report, in compliance with a Resolution of Congress, has been submitted to that honorable body, and, at my request, returned for the purpose of completing, and publishing it, under my own inspection. After some unexpected, but unavoidable delays, I now, with much diffidence, and under a deep sense of responsibility, present it to the public, as complete in matter and form, as my means, my time, and my health, and the nature of the work itself will admit. If it shall, in any measure, meet the feelings and expectations of those who are interested and engaged in promoting the welfare of Indians, prove instrumental in awakening the attention of other[s] to the state of this neglected and oppressed people, and of laying foundations for their future civil, social, and religious improvement and happiness, I shall not regret my arduous and long continued labors, nor the considerable sacrifices, I have made at my advanced age, of time, of property, and of domestic comforts, in obtaining and preparing for use, the facts and information comprised in this Report. These facts, with the remarks, and plans of improvement, which, on much reflection, they have suggested to my own mind, I now respectfully submit to the candor and consideration of the President and Congress; to the various benevolent Institutions, engaged in imparting the blessings of civilization and Christianity, to these untutored heathen tribes, and to the people generally, in this favored country.

PC in Jedidiah Morse, *A Report to the Secretary of War of the United States, on Indian Affairs . . .* (New Haven: printed by S. Converse, c. 1822), pp. 9–10.

To William Clark, St. Louis

Dep[art]m[en]t of War, 7 June 1822

By the act of Congress passed at the late session, to abolish the United States Trading Establishment with the Indian tribes &c. the President [James Monroe] is authorized to procure the abrogation of the treaty obligations on the part of the U[nited] States to keep up trading houses among the Indians and to apply a portion of the goods which may be delivered over by the Factors to the Agents appointed to receive them, to effect that object.

On examination it appears that the 9th article of the treaty with the Sacks & Foxes, of the 3d of November 1804 & the 2nd Article of the treaty with the Great & Little Osages of the 10th November 1808, contain the only treaty obligations on the part of the U[nited] States to keep up trading Houses, that are now binding, (except that contained in the late Treaty with the Choctaw nation which has not yet been carried into effect,) and as the Sacs & Foxes and the Great & Little Osages are within the limits of your Superintendency, you will, as soon as practicable, take such measures as you may think necessary by yourself or thro' the proper Indian Agents, to obtain the assent of these tribes to the abrogation of the 9th & 2nd Articles of the Treaties above referred to. In order to satisfy the Indians and to induce them to give their assent freely to this measure you are authorized to distribute among them, presents, in goods to such amount as may be necessary to produce that effect taking care to obtain the abrogation on as reasonable terms as possible. The goods for this purpose will be furnished from any of the Factories, within your Superintendency, that may be most convenient, by the Agents having charge of them, upon your requisition, which they will be instructed by the Treasury Department to comply with.

FC in DNA, 72, E:274 (M-15:5).

From Alexander Macomb, 6/7. "In pursuance of your instructions," Macomb summarizes the history of the contract for construction of a fort on Dauphin Island. The initial contract was signed on 7/17/1818 by Joseph G. Swift, then Chief Engineer, and Richard Harris. Harris and N[imrod] Farrow gave their bond for $100,000 on 8/14/1818 "to secure" the "faithful performance" of the contract. Farrow gave to Swift, as the agent of the U.S., a deed of trust to 2,200 acres of land, two mills, and 60 or 70 slaves in Fauquier County, Va., as collateral security for an advance of $45,000. Harris and Farrow established on 11/4/1818 a partnership in respect to the contract. On 8/2/1819 a bond was submitted to Col. W[alker] K. Armistead, then Chief Engineer, as agent of the U.S. by Farrow, N[athaniel] Grigsby, Josiah Tidball, and and John Ashby for $111,951.11 to secure an additional advance of $50,000 and to serve as collateral security for the faithful execution of the contract. A letter of Capt. [James] Gadsden dated 4/20/1820 "states that the concerns of Harris & Farrow had become [so] much deranged in consequence of the distrust ["of" *interlined*] each of the other and the incompetency of both ["and" *canceled*] that they had at length accommodated their differences by admitting Gen[era]l Turner ["Starke" *interlined*] of South Carolina as a partner in the contract with a share of one-half thereof and the sole management and controul of the whole; and that he [Gadsden] had recognized Gen[era]l Starke as the irrevocable agent of Harris & Farrow but not as a partner." The two men had become associated with Starke by an instrument dated 4/10/1820. On that same day Harris and Farrow conveyed to Gadsden, in trust for the U.S., "all the property in that country connected with the contract and consisting of a tract of land called the Red Bluffs, 81 Negroes besides, vessels, boats, tools, implements and other property, to be held" as security for the "advances made by the Government on the contract" to that time. "Before this arrangement was known here" Macomb wrote on 5/6/1820 to Gadsden and "declared that the contractors on the Gulf of Mexico should receive no farther [*sic*] indulgence unless their operations should inspire confidence in them that did not then exist." "The operations of the contract under the judicious management and with the additional means furnished by General Starke were almost instantly reanimated. In a short time they were efficiently organized, in conformity to the advice of the Engineer [that is, Gadsden] which had been neglected by Harris & Farrow, and by a course of steady & vigorous prosecution were about to develop the successful results which had been anticipated when they were suddenly and unexpectedly arrested by the refusal of Congress to make the appropriations requisite for their continuance." Macomb informed Gadsden by a letter of 3/20/1821 about that refusal, and Calhoun also wrote to Gadsden (see *The Papers of John C. Calhoun,* 5:690–692). Gadsden replied on 5/2; "Gen[era]l Starke was sanguine in the hope that Congress at their next session would reconsider, and upon the additional information that would be furnished them, would reverse their decision" to withhold any appropriation for Dauphin Island; "he determined patiently to await that issue and in the meantime to continue the operations with his own means. This however he discovered could not be effected without the aid of a small sum of money and accordingly he applied for the appropriation of $10,000 to the contract to enable him to continue the operations thereof until the final determination of Congress could be known. His application was rejected"; he was told, in reply on 8/25/1821, that the decision announced on 3/20/1821 was conclusive. The deed of trust from Harris & Farrow dated 4/10/1820 embraced 81 Negro slaves, 35 of whom were purchased in New Orleans on 4/26/1820, 16 days after the deed had been signed. Those 35 were later claimed by [Nathaniel] Cox of New Orleans, under a mortgage on them "which he had obtained on becoming security for the payment" that was due for them. "His claim did not succeed." "Before he had claimed the Negroes . . . Mr. Cox had charged the amount of their purchase to the Gov[ernmen]t as an advance made by him, as the agent of fortifications, on account of the Contract—but as his agency did not extend to Dauphine [*sic*] Island and at any rate he had not been authorised to make such an advance & moreover as there appeared to be the most palpable evidence of its having been a private transaction between him & Mr. Farrow, his charge was not admitted. Persisting in his refusal to account for that amo[un]t to the Gov[ernmen]t together with some other items—he was reported as a public defaulter and a suit for the recovery thereof was brought against him and tried in the last term of the circuit court of New Orleans & strange as it may appear the jury gave a verdict in his favor." Advances to the contractors total $162,251.37. They have delivered materials and have performed work that are worth $48,899.15. They are still accountable, therefore, for $113,352.22. The two bonds held by the U.S. as security for this balance have a total value of $219,951.11; and the nation has the additional security of the property embraced in the deeds of trust issued to Swift and to Gadsden. ALS in DNA, 111, 232; FC in DNA, 21, 1:292–295.

To J[OEL] R. POINSETT, [Representative from S.C.,] Charleston, S.C.

Department of War, June 7th 1822

I have the honor to acknowledge the receipt of your letter of the 30th Ultimo [LS with En in DNA, 30, 327] in relation to William Florance, late a Cadet, who was dismissed from the Military Academy under sentence of a Court-Martial in March last. It would give me pleasure were it in my power, and consistent with the interest of the Academy to restore Mr. Florance to the place he has recently forfeited; but I find, upon a review of all the facts in his case, that he cannot be reinstated without a sacrifice of discipline essential to the prosper[i]ty of that institution.

With a view to remove an impression which you appear to entertain that the punishment of Cadet Florance was disproportioned to his offence, I will ask your attention to the enclosed extract from the order approving the sentence ot the Court before which he was tried, and to an extract of a letter upon the subject from the Superintendent of the Military Academy [Sylvanus Thayer]. To these extracts it is unnecessary to add any thing, except that the number of Offences in the report referred to by Major Thayer, which embrace a period of 15 months is 103, and that 20 Offences are noted against him during the 3 subsequent months.

FC in DNA, 3, 11:402–403 (M-6:11). NOTE: The enclosure in Poinsett's letter of 5/30 is a letter dated 5/[1822] from Florance to Poinsett, in which Florance asks for assistance in obtaining his reinstatement.

From W[illiam] Ward, "(Confidential)," Choctaw Agency, 6/7. Many disputes occur because the Choctaws' livestock strays into lands owned by white people. Ward is visited daily by Indians who want to be paid for their improvements. Mississippians tell the Indians insistently that Ward has funds with which to pay for their improvements. He reports a conversation with [Thomas] Hinds, who contended first that Ward has the money and then that [Calhoun] has it. Such incidents keep the Choctaws "uneasy and troublesome to me." ALS in DNA, 77 (M-271:4, frames 233–235).

From N[athan] Towson, Paymaster General

City of Washington, June the 8th 1822

I have examined the papers you did me the honor to refer to me and respectfully submit the following opinion on the claim of [Bvt. Brig.] General [Alexander] Macomb [to compensation at his brevet rank].

I have ever thought that the act of the 6th of July 1812 authorising the President to confer brevets in certain cases, should be viewed in the light of a contract between the government, and the officers who should hazard their lives, and perform services, important in their consequences, although not strictly injoined on them by order; I believe it was so considered by the Army generally, and I am confident that many noble & gallant officers lost their lives in attempting to deserve and obtain the distinction which that act promised as a reward.

The too free use of the authority to confer brevets no doubt occasioned the passage of a subsequent act by which the pay and emoluments are restricted "to commands according to brevet rank." The abuse of a law is not a good argument against the law itself, and as there must, under any construction, be many hard cases, I think the most liberal one should be given of which the act will admit.

It is evident that the 18th paragraph of the 71st article of "Army regulations" restricts the allowance of brevet compensation to very few indeed, if taken as it has been construed and acted on by the Pay Department, that is that the command of a brevet Major or Lieut[enant] Colonel must be a *full battalion* and not any number of Companies *greater* than a Captain's command but *less* than a full battalion, and so of other ranks: I am of opinion that the act is susceptible of a more liberal construction but *have strong doubts as to the policy of giving such a one*: I believe that it would be strictly just, but I fear it might lead to the passage of other laws less favorable to brevet rank than even this rigid construction of the present one is.

I am of opinion that it would be competent to the President [James Monroe] under the act of April the 16th 1818 to allow brevet compensation in all cases embraced in the 2nd paragraph of the 3d article of the "Army regulations" except that of officers serving on courts-martial, which I think cannot be considered as giving command according to the meaning of the law; and I am further of opinion that such an allowance would embrace General Macomb's case, but I have never considered the regulation defining the commands which shall entitle officers to brevet compensation in any way changed or enlarged by the regulation just referred to; it is true it was subsequently adopted, but if intended to apply to compensation, then the one *expressly relating* to that subject, to wit, the 18th paragraph of the 71st article, might have been omitted in the publication of the Army regulations, as it would be wholly superfluous.

The case of General Macomb is certainly a very strong one. The department of which he is the head is a most important one. An assistant in that department [Assistant Engineer Simon Bernard] is in the receipt of the full pay and emoluments of a Brigadier General which are all that the head claims, and it would seem that the Senate intended that the chief should at least be placed on a footing with the assistant in regard to compensation, or why decide that he should be entitled to the Brevet rank of a Brigadier General? It could not be for the purpose of giving him rank without compensation, as he would have been entitled to that without any act of the Senate's, and to rank of a higher grade.

Upon the whole I am of opinion the President may *justly and without violating law* authorize the allowance of a Brigadier's pay and emoluments to General Macomb, but as the regulations at present stand I do not think the Pay Department would be justified in paying him more than the compensation of a Colonel.

LS in DNA, 292, 1-1733; FC in DNA, 291, 15:436–438.

To William Wirt

Department of War, June 8, 1822

The omission of Congress to make an appropriation, at the last Session, for carrying on the work at Dauphine [*sic*; Dauphin] Island, has terminated the operations at that point, and it now becomes necessary to determine what legal steps ought to be taken by the Government in relation to the contractor. I have therefore to request of you to state what, under all the circumstances of the case, that course should be. To facilitate your investigation I enclose herewith a report [dated 6/7] from the Chief Engineer [Alexander Macomb] affording a succinct statement of the facts connected with the case & accompanied by various documents and extracts of correspondence having reference to it.

LS with En in DNA, 111, 232; FC in DNA, 3, 11:403 (M-6:11). NOTE: Wirt answered on 6/11.

To V[IRGIL] MAXCY

Washington, [Sunday,] 9th June 1822

You will see by the enclosed prospectus that Col. [Thomas L.] McKenney, with whom I believe you are acquainted, proposes to edit a newspaper in this place. I know him well and he is a man of the strictest honor and considerable talents. He intends, I understand, to associate a gentleman of distinguished abilities as a writer with him. We greatly want in this place a paper which will give an able & zealous support to the administration. Such I believe this paper will give, if properly supported by a respectable list of subscribers. *The cause* depends in a considerable degree on its success. ["Now" *canceled.*] I have said to the editor, that I would endeavour to enlist my friends in his support. You can do much for him. I have enclosed 5 ["of" *canceled*] copies of the prospectus to be distributed as you may think proper. The friends to whom you send them, had better be requested to return them to you with the list of subscribers to be ["forwarded" *canceled and* "returned" *interlined*] to this place.

Mrs. [Floride Colhoun] Calhoun is much better but not fully recovered. She thinks her health is not sufficiently restored for a journey to West River, or we would doubtless make you a visit. I hope that we may have the pleasure of seeing you & Mrs. Maxcy in the city during the summer.

I had quite forgot the Rip Rap[s] contract, which has figured so much in the Radical paper in this place. The Int[elligence]r is now publishing the report and documents. Nothing can be more unfair than the former [that is, the Radical newspaper entitled the Washington *City Gazette*]. That its object is political and to implicate me can scarcely be doubted by any one, who will read it with care. That the contract was made in the usual way at the time, with due care, on favourable terms, and has been faithfully executed cannot be doubted. Why the clamour? The false quotation of Maj[o]r [Christopher] Van Deventer's statement, as far as it refers to me, will explain. The report will be examined I see in detail by [former Bvt. Brig.] Gen[era]l [Joseph G.] Swift but some short notice of the temper and object ought to appear in most of the papers. The paper here, the Washington City Gazette, is supposed to be under Mr. [William H.] C[rawfor]d's influence, and such I believe is the fact. I doubt not that it was a deliberate attempt through his suggestion to impair my standing, if possible, by abuse and slander. There is reason to believe that it has had an effect different from what was intended. The character of [Elijah] Mix and the imprudent step on the part of Maj[o]r Vandeventer [in purchasing one-fourth of the Mix contract] were supposed to afford great advantages to assault me. In speaking of contracts made without advertising, you will see, that [Bvt. Brig.] Gen[era]l McComb [*sic*; Alexander Macomb] refers to two made by the War Dep[artmen]t, the one for embanking at the Pea Patch and the other for arms with Mr. [George] Boyd. The former was on the most exorbitant terms, and the latter with *a Clerk* in the War Dep[artmen]t at the time, made without bond or security for its faithful execution, without advertisement, for the delivery of arms and amounting at least in value to $120,000 ["and one" *canceled and* "which" *interlined*] has not been executed and on which an advance of $6,000 has been lost. This Mr. Boyd's name, for this very advance, is on the list of defaulters! Of all this the Radicals say not one word.

The information from the West is very favourable since the return of the members of Congress. Several of my friends think that my popularity is to the full as great as that of Mr. [Henry] Clay in that section. In New York nothing yet is settled, but [Micah] Sterling thinks the prospect is not unfavourable.

Mrs. Calhoun & her Mother [Floride Bonneau Colhoun] desire their best respects to you, Mrs. Maxcy and Mrs. Galloway. Yours truely [*sic*], J.C. Calhoun.

[P.S.] I have not heard from you since I wrote you in Baltimore. I have sent Dr. [Joseph] Kent several of the prospectus. My name must not be used in connection with the paper.

Monday morning

I see the Int[elligence]r of this morning attempts to cover the blunders of Mr. Crawford by a tabular statement, [attempt]ing to show that his estimates [*illegible*; proved] more correct than his predecessors[']. He omits to state that the [*illegible*; revenues] being abundant a greater part of the time of his predecessors since 1802, but little more was attempted than to show there would be enough under the most moderate estimate; and that none of them ever made such blunders as Mr. C[rawfor]d or ever made so erroneous a general estimate of our means as he did in 1817, rating it 7 or 8 millions more than it turned out to be. This fatal error where the greatest caution ought to have prevailed has caused most of our embar[r]assments. Hence the repeal of the internal taxes, the pension act &c.

ALS in DLC, Galloway-Maxcy-Markoe Papers, vol. 32.

To Thomas J. Rogers, [Representative from Pa.]

War Dept., 9th June 1822

The pressure of official duties has prevented me from acknowledging your favour of the 14th of May [*not found*] till this time. The unanimity which prevails in Pennsylvania is very gratifying; but you may rest assured, that every effort will be made to distract the State. The moment, at which the greatest effort will be made, will be at your next election for Governour. I hope that our friend [Samuel D.] Ingham will be the Republican candidate. No one will administer the State more safely or virtuously. If Pennsylvania stands firm, the hopes of the opposers of the administration must be blasted.

Information from all quarters still continues favourable. It is particularly so from the West. The [Washington, D.C., *City*] Gazette continues to pour ["his" *canceled and* "its" *interlined*] torrent of filth against me, but with effects very different from what it intends. After clamoring for the documents on the Rip Rap[s] contract, he [the editor] has not had the candour to publish them. He has given what he calls extracts, but they consist almost wholly of such parts as ["it" *canceled and* "is" *interlined*] supposed to be favourable ["to his slander" *interlined*]. We want a paper here to expose such villainy. You will see by the prospectus, of which I enclose you copies, that Col. [Thomas L.] McKenney proposes to publish such a paper. He is a most honest man, & of considerable talents, and has taken the precaution to associate, I understand, with him a very able writer. Subscribers now are only wanting, which, if a respectable list can be obtained, will go far to decide the contest. You can do much in your State. I will send copies to Ingham and Judge Gibson and Col. J[ohn] Findl[a]y [Representative from Pa.]. You will give the best distribution to yours and make your arrangement to return the list of subscribers as early as practicable.

The meeting between [George] McDuffie & [William] Cumming probably took place on the 7th Inst[ant] on the Carolina side of Savannah River. I trust in God he [McDuffie] is safe. Few lives are so valuable as his. Every thing appears to have been done by his friends to avert ["the meeting" *interlined*] but I fear without ["effect" *canceled and* "success" *interlined*]. A few days will now decide.

Let me hear from you often, and believe me to be your friend, J.C. Calhoun.

[P.S.] I send a Lexington [Ky.?,] paper which takes some very sound views of those politicians who wish to use Mr. [Thomas] Jefferson's name. It might appear and I would suppose to advantage in some of your papers.

My name ought not to appear in connection with the [proposed] paper in writing friends except the most confidential.

ALS in DLC, John C. Calhoun Papers; variant PC in *The Collector,* vol. XIII, no. 11 (October, 1900), p. 133.

S[ylvanus] Thayer, West Point, to Alexander Macomb, 6/9. "After the termination of the present General Examination, I am desirous of having it in my power to leave here for a few weeks partly for the benefit of my health & partly for the purpose of visiting some near relations whom I have not seen for many years. If you will have the goodness to mention this subject to the Secretary of War & let me know his pleasure thereupon as early as practicable, I shall esteem it a very particular favor." ALS in DNA, 14, 299.

From T[homas] Cadwalader, Philadelphia, 6/10. He attended some of the final examinations of Cadets at the Military Academy, names the members of the Board of Visitors who were present, and promises to submit its report. ALS in DNA, 1, C-437 (M-221:92).

To C[harles] Caldwell, [M.D.,] Philadelphia

War Department, June 10th 1822

I have to acknowledge the receipt of your letter of the 7th inst[ant; *not found*]. It would give me pleasure to see you, and I regret that it is not convenient for you to visit the seat of government. Were it in my power, I would cheerfully afford you the information you request, as I am persuaded that great injustice has been done to our climate in regard to the longevity of the people of our country. The whole numerical force of the Revolutionary Army cannot be ascertained, the rolls being incomplete. Of those who were in the service at the close of the war, however, there are complete lists; but of that number those who are now living cannot be ascertained, as those only who are in indigent circumstances are admitted on the Pension roll. The birth places of the pensioners cannot be ascertained from any records or documents in the Department. So soon as the Clerks in the Pension Branch of this Department can complete a laborious work in which they are now engaged, I will direct them to be employed in obtaining and reducing to writing all the information on this subject in our possession. This information will embrace the number of those in service at the end of the War, and who are now on the pension list—the States to which they belonged during the Revolution, and where they reside at present.

Allow me to suggest as a subject of interesting enquiry, the respective ages attained by those who signed the declaration of Independence, as affording a source of information calculated I think, to throw additional light on the subject, from the circumstances of their being men of different habits of life.

FC in DNA, 91, 12:213. Note: Dr. Caldwell was serving in 1822 as a professor in the Medical Department of Transylvania University at Lexington, Ky. He was and became the author of a comparatively large number of books and pamphlets on biographical and medical topics. Sabin, *Bibliotheca Americana,* 3:217–218. Compare, herein, Calhoun's letters to Dr. Caldwell dated 11/29/1822 and 1/7/1823.

From Robert Troup

Geneva, Ontario County, State of New York, 10 June 1822

My friend Mr. W[illiam] B[eatty] Rochester, one of the members of Congress from this section of country, has kindly transmitted me your obliging letter to him, of the 15 April last, with the copies and extracts of letters accompanying it. These copies and extracts, as you justly observe, "indicate the views and measures of the Government, in relation to the removal of the Six Nations from the State of New York."

I beg leave, as well for myself as for Mr. [David A.] Ogden [former Representative from N.Y.] and the other gentlemen with whom I am associated in the purchase of the Indian Reservations in this State, to express to you, our most grateful acknowledgements, for your very prompt and satisfactory communication to Mr. Rochester.

The proprietors of the Reservations have no interests or views but what are in perfect coincidence with the policy adopted by the Government towards the Indians. While that policy, with equal wisdom and humanity, aims at promoting the permanent welfare of the Indians, it is happily calculated to effect their ultimate removal to a "residence further [*sic*] west"; an object which the proprietors, as may naturally be presumed, have much at heart. But however desirous the proprietors may be of inducing the Indians to remove, I hope the President [James Monroe] will be persuaded, that we are too mindful both of our duties as citizens, and of the respect we owe ourselves, ever to take a single step for the removal that will tend either to obstruct the course of the Government, or to violate the rights, or to disturb the tranquility of the Indians.

LS in DNA, 1, T-4 (M-221:96).

To William P. "Duvall [*sic*; DuVal]," Governor of Fla. Territory, Pensacola, 6/11. Calhoun discusses at length the duties of DuVal as Superintendent of Indian Affairs in Fla., with [Gad] Humphreys as Agent and with [Peter] Pelham as Sub-Agent. Calhoun explains the compensation to which each is entitled and the system under which DuVal is to receive remittances after having submitted quarterly estimates. An initial remittance of $2,500 is being sent to cover the following categories of expenses: $500 for Pelham's salary, $1,000 for presents to Indians, and $1,000 for contingencies; these funds include no allotment for Humphreys' salary, because "it is uncertain at what time he will be ready to commence his duties." Calhoun directs DuVal to make certain that [William G.D.] Worthington, former Secretary and Acting Governor of Fla., delivers to Pelham an unexpended balance of Indian funds in his hands. Calhoun encloses a copy of the statute of this year regulating trade with Indians and discusses its provisions. FC in DNA, 72, E:275–277 (M-15:5); PC in Carter, ed., *Territorial Papers*, 22:452–455.

From William Wirt, 6/11. He answers Calhoun's letter of 6/8, in which Calhoun inquired what course should be pursued by the U.S. in the light of [Alexander Macomb's] report that the contractors for the fort at Dauphin Island owe $113,352.22 to the U.S. "As my official function, under the act of Congress, is to answer *questions of law* when propounded by the Heads of either of the Departments I must consider the question as propounded in reference only to any legal function; and on an inspection of the bonds" and of the one deed of trust that was submitted to Wirt "I find them so worded as to authorize the U.S. to rely upon these securities to reclaim all the advances which have not been satisfied by work done or materials furnished by the contractors. This is" the government's "legal right. But whether under all the circumstances of this case this course should be pursued by the U.S. is an enquiry which involves questions of feeling, of honor and of national dignity which it is not my province to decide." LS in DNA, 30, 329; FC in DNA, 113, B:77 (T-412:2).

To N[INIAN] EDWARDS, [Senator from Ill.]

Washington, 12th June 1822

I have received your favour of the 22d May [*not found*] with its enclosure for Mr. [Samuel D.] Ingham, to which I gave the direction that you required. The information which you communicate as to publick sentiment is very agreeable, and accords with that, which I have received from others from the West. Mr. [William H.] C[rawfor]d it seems to me has now but a single circumstance to hang his hope on, the gaining over ["to his interest" *canceled*] the Bucktails of New York to his interest. To effect this, his friends in that State are making great efforts to prove that he is more purely of the Jefferson school of politicks than any other candidate. If [Martin] Van Buren can see his way clearly, either as to him, or [Henry] Clay, he will doubtless come out on that side, which may do much mischief in that State. I think [Mordecai M.] Noah gives some indications on that side, but I am told his standing with the party in the city is such, as to make it critical for him to make a bold stand. The information from the State is, that her course is not yet taken, but that at present my hold on the publick sentiment is much the strongest, particularly out of the city. I understand that [Joseph C.] Yates, who will be governor, has expressed himself favourably. It is quite probable that the State will not take a very decided stand for any one, but that she will ultimately unite with Pennsylvania in her course.

Great changes are taking place in Mass[achuset]ts which will terminate in the entire prostration of the Federal interest in that State, in all probability. A mid[d]le interest has grown up. The fruits already are a Republican Speaker and a partial Republican representation from Boston itself. This change must have in New England a very considerable bearing on the Presidential election. It will give to that section more weight, which I should suppose would be in the first instance in favour of Mr. [John Quincy] Adams, and if he can not be elected, in my favour. Mr. Crawford or Clay I suppose have very little hold on the publick sentiment in that portion of the Union.

From South Carolina the information is favorable. Mr. [William] L[owndes]'s friends have not yet yielded all hopes, but they are willing to pledge themselves in favour of a candidate from the State. [Robert Y.] Hayne, the Attorney Gen[era]l & one of the first men in the State, will oppose [William] Smith, and, it is said, will doubtless be elected [a Senator from S.C.]. This is a great point. The election for Senators, which will take place before the 4th of March next, is of the utmost importance. Most of the vacancies will occur in the South & West. [George] Poindexter, I understand, will oppose [Thomas Hill] Williams of Miss[issipp]i. What is [Jesse Burgess] Thomas's prospect. Will you leave him out? Tho' he is a man of moderate talents, yet much depends on his being left out.

The Radical paper in this place [the Washington, D.C., *City Gazette*] continues its attacks on me with great violence. He [the editor] is doubtless under the influence of Mr. Crawford, who I perceive gives it the Treasury advertisements, tho its circulation is so limited. It is perhaps as well, that they should spend their am[m]unition at long shot. The necessity of a paper here, however, becomes more appearent [*sic*] even from these feeble attacks. The establishment of an able and active paper in the city is almost every thing in fact in the coming contest. Col. [Thomas L.] McKenn[e]y, who is a very honest and honorable man, has proposed to establish such an one. He informs me, that he has associated with him a first rate writer, and that he will be devoted to the cause of the administration. I send you several copies of his prospectus which you will percieve is written with sperit [*sic*]. I believe nothing but a respectable list of subscribers is wanting to put a powerful engine in action. In this you can do much in the West, particularly in your State, Kentucky & Missouri. I have written to most of my friends with whom I [*illegible*; correspond] to speak on a subject, which requires so much prudence, as my name ought not to appear as giving aid to the establishment of the paper, except with my friends. The arrangements ought to be so made that, whatever subscribers are obtained may be returned in due time.

Our friend [George] McDuffie met, in all probability, Col. [William] Cum[m]ing on the 7th Inst[ant] between Augusta and Savannah on the Carolina side of the [Savannah] river [to fight a duel]. God grant that he [McDuffie] may be safe. I have, however, a strange foreboding, which I put to the account of great solicitude for him. We will hear the result in three days at the fartherest [*sic*].

I am glad to hear that Col. [William] McRee remains sound. Spain declines running the line for the present, of which he has been apprized, with the strongest assurance, that the President [James Monroe] will be glad of any opportunity of promoting his wishes.

I will be anxious to hear from you after your arrival at home. Much will depend on the West.

The Ministers to our Southern neighbours will not in all probability be selected till the meeting of Congress. I am decidedly of the opinion that one ought to be from the West, and that you ought to be the man. I will act accordingly.

My best respects to Mr. [Daniel Pope] Cook and believing me to be yours truly, J.C. Calhoun.

ALS in ICHi.

To William Ward, Choctaw Agency, 6/12. He will receive $3,150 to cover the balance of the Choctaws' annuity for 1822, "including $150 for the annuity of Mushulatubbee." Calhoun is also sending $10,985 to indemnify the Choctaws for improvements on lands ceded by them, but Calhoun cautions that no payment is to be made "unless the improvements shall have been previously abandoned." [Peter Hagner] is examining the Choctaws' claims for services rendered during the Pensacola campaign. Calhoun directs Ward to withhold from the amounts to be paid to individual Indians any debt owed by them to the U.S. FC in DNA, 72, E:278 (M-15:5).

From Isaac H. Williamson, [Governor of N.J.,] "Elizabeth Town," [N.J.,] 6/12. Pursuant to Calhoun's letter of 4/30, [probably that which was dated 4/27 and perhaps received on 4/30,] Williamson explains that the participation of the State of N.J. in the suit brought by Dr. Henry Gale for title to Pea Patch Island in the Delaware is based upon a boundary dispute with Del. and not upon any desire of N.J. to oppose the U.S. government. The legislature of N.J. has proposed to Del. a method of arbitration, but Del. has refused to participate. Williamson believes the N.J. legislature will cede the title of N.J. to the Pea Patch to the U.S., as Calhoun requested, "if it can be done without prejudice to the question of boundary between" the two States. Williamson also will "direct that all further proceedings in the action now depending [*sic*], so far as this State has any control over them, be suspended until after the next Session of the Legislature." ALS in DNA, 1, W-6 (M-221:96).

2nd Lt. C[lark] Burdine, Fever River, [Ill.,] to [George] Bomford, 6/13. Burdine reports the progress of his expedition to open the lead mines there. The Indians, once they were convinced that the Americans intend to be firm and to stay there to work the mines, agreed to work in them. Burdine's report [of 4/7] that Frenchmen were working the mines has been proved to be false, "except their trading for minerals." ALS in DNA, 31, 1822, B.

From Alexander Macomb, 6/14. "Major [Isaac] Roberdeau is very competent to direct the manner in which the conduit at the President[']s House should be constructed. He is absent at present but will be ready to morrow to make the proper examination & to project the plan." ALS in DNA, 1, E-147 (M-221:92); FC in DNA, 21, 1:297.

To the Rev. John Sergeant, "Verner [Vernon]," N.Y., 6/14. Calhoun answers Sergeant's letter of 6/3 [ALS in DNA, 1, S-3 (M-221:96)]. It has always been the government's desire that Indian tribes should live in peace and in "good understanding." If the Stockbridge Indians and the Six Nations should move to the Green Bay area, the friendship and protection of the government will go with them; the U.S. will do all that it can do to promote their prosperity and happiness. [Lewis] Cass has already been instructed to help them to get established upon the lands they have or may acquire around Green Bay, but limited Indian funds do not permit any additional expense, as [Solomon U. Hendrick] has been informed; consequently, the government can pay no part of the expenses of the agency to which Sergeant referred. The Indians have already been told that the government has no objection to arrangements that they may make with the French settlers near Green Bay, "provided these settlers" occupy "the lands precisely upon the same terms" as do the Indians. The government has tried always to prevent the use of alcohol by Indians and will continue to do so, but such efforts can never be effective "without a determined and persevering coöperation on the part of the Indians themselves." There is no objection to the inclusion, in future arrangements among the tribes concerned, of a provision such as Sergeant proposed in relation to the white settlers, but the arrangements must be left entirely to the Indians. Necessary papers have been issued for a new deputation from the Stockbridges and Six Nations and have been sent to Eleazer Williams, whose intention to accompany the Indians caused the number of delegates to be increased to seven. FC in DNA, 72, E:279–280 (M-15:5).

From [Lt. Col.] George Bomford, 6/15. He encloses and discusses a copy of a public invitation dated 6/15 to individuals and companies to lease the lead mine lands of the U.S. that is being sent today for publication in eight Western newspapers. FC (with the ad and related materials) in DNA, 3, 1:15–19.

To John Floyd, Freeman Walker, and John A[lfred] Cuthbert, 6/15. Calhoun appoints them to serve as commissioners to hold a treaty with the [Eastern] Cherokees for the extinguishment of their title to lands in Ga. An appropriation of $30,000 has been made available for negotiations for the Ga. lands of both the Cherokees and the Creeks. This sum is expected to be inadequate for those purposes; [James Monroe] has decided to apply toward negotiations with the Cherokees alone all of that sum plus the $4,989.57 that were left from a recent treaty with the Creeks. The price paid for the ceded lands cannot exceed $200,000, to be paid in installments. If Ga. should appoint commissioners "to claim property of the citizens of that State," the U.S. commissioners "will coöperate with them in the fullest manner, in promoting to the extent of your powers the interests and views of the State." Moreover, if the Ga. commissioners should arrange for payment of the property claims of citizens of Ga., there should be inserted in the proposed treaty a provision similar to one in the recent Creek treaty, but the U.S. obligation cannot "exceed $89,000, to be paid in five annual installments." The Ga. legislature wants all Cherokee land titles within the State to be extinguished; the U.S. commissioners will coöperate, but not more than $2 per acre, plus reasonable allowances for improvements, can be made payable. LS in DNA, 75 (M-208:9); FC in DNA, 72, E:281–283 (M-15:5); CC in DNA, RG 46, 17B-C2; CCEx in DNA, RG 46, 18A-E2; CCEx in DNA, RG 233, 18A-D1, vol. 263; PEx's in Senate Document No. 63 and House Document No. 127, 18th Cong., 1st Sess.; PEx in *American State Papers: Indian Affairs*, 2:464–465. (An incomplete copy of this letter was owned in 1953 by Caroline Lewis Lovett of Philadelphia.)

From Peter Hagner, 6/15. In accordance with Calhoun's request "communicated to me by Col. [Charles John] Steedman," Hagner encloses "an estimate of the probable state of the account of the State of South Carolina." LS in DNA, 1, H-310 (M-221:92); FC in DNA, 53, 26:104.

From [1st. Lt.] John A. Dix, Aide-de-Camp, New York [City], 6/16. He reports that Maj. Gen. [Jacob] Brown has arrived there. ALS in DNA, 1, D-160 (M-221:92).

To J[ohn] A[lfred] Cuthbert, [former Representative from Ga.,] Eatonton, Ga., 6/17. Calhoun informs Cuthbert about his appointment to be a commissioner to negotiate a treaty for the [Eastern] Cherokees' lands in Ga. and explains that correspondence about this business will be quickest through Freeman Walker in Augusta. FC in DNA, 72, E:283 (M-15:5).

To John Floyd, [later a Representative from Ga.,] 6/17. Calhoun informs Floyd that his commission to serve with Freeman Walker and with J[ohn] A[lfred] Cuthbert in negotiating a treaty with the [Eastern] Cherokees [for their lands in Ga.] has been sent to Walker at Augusta and that correspondence concerning the business should be sent through Walker as a means of attaining "greater facility." FC in DNA, 72, E:283–284 (M-15:5).

From George Izard, "Cascade Creek near Leaksville" (Rockingham County), N.C., 6/17. A letter from Philadelphia dated 5/22, which he received yesterday, informed Izard of Calhoun's invitation to Izard to serve as the President of the Board of Visitors of the Military Academy. Because he will be away from his home for a considerable time, he declines regretfully. ALS in DNA, 1, I-182 (M-221:93).

To M[ICAH] STERLING, [Representative from N.Y.]

Washington, 17th June 1822

The fatal meeting between [George] McDuffie and [William] Cumming has taken place, and I fear that our friend [McDuffie] is no more. We have but few particulars. The ball entered the right hip and lodged in the backbone. The wound was considered mortal. Thus has terminated ["probably" *interlined*] a life most precious to the country. He has not left behind him one of his age of equal promise. It has over whelmed us all with grief. It falls on us as a deep national calamity. I now experience the consolation resulting from the efforts, which I made at an adjustment. It was continued by friends to the last. A most judicious effort was made by my friend Judge [Henry W.] DeSaussure as late as the 4th instant, just as they were preparing to set out for the fatal spot. He visited Augusta for the purpose and obtained the aid of two of Cumming's friends of the highest standing. They addressed a letter to each, urging a reference of the subject of dispute to honorable men. Our friend acceded in terms which will for ever honor his memory. Cumming refused the reference, and the fatal consequence has followed.

ALS in CtY. NOTE: George McDuffie (1790–1851) had entered the House of Representatives in 1821 as successor to his law partner, Eldred Simkins of S.C. The famous duel fought by McDuffie against William Cumming of Ga. was related to the rivalry between Calhoun and William H. Crawford for election to the Presidency in 1824. Contrary to Calhoun's impression when he wrote the above report about the duel, the spinal wound received by McDuffie did not prove to be mortal; but it did result in an injury that affected the remaining 29 years of McDuffie's life. Compare Calhoun's corrective letter to Sterling dated 6/18/1822.

To Freeman Walker, [former Senator from Ga.,] Augusta, Ga., 6/17. Calhoun informs Walker of his appointment [on 6/15] to be a commissioner to negotiate a treaty for the [Eastern] Cherokees' lands in Ga. Calhoun asks that correspondence about the business shall be routed through Walker for expeditious deliveries to Washington and to the Cherokee Agency. FC in DNA, 72, E:283 (M-15:5).

To J[oseph] McIlvaine, [U.S. District Attorney for N.J.,] Burlington, N.J., 6/18. "I transmit herewith a copy of a letter [dated 6/12] from the Governor of New Jersey, [Isaac H. Williamson,] concerning the claim of Doctor [Henry] Gale to the Pea Patch [Island] in the Delaware, in order that you may be apprized of the views of the Governor upon the subject." FC in DNA, 3, 11:405 (M-6:11).

To V[IRGIL] MAXCY, Annapolis, Md.

Washington, 18th June 1822

The mail of this morning has spread joy over our city. Mr. [George] McDuffie is not only alive, but is believed to be safe. He so considers himself, in a letter written by him four hours after the meeting [in his duel with William Cumming]. The ball entered the small of his back obliquely. Never have my feelings undergone so great a change in so short a time. Your friend, J.C. Calhoun.

ALS in DLC, Galloway-Maxcy-Markoe Papers, vol. 32.

To R[eturn] J. Meigs, Calhoun, Tenn., 6/18. Meigs is to do everything possible to promote the cession of land by the Cherokees that is to be sought by three U.S. commissioners, all of Ga., John Floyd, Freeman Walker of Augusta, and J[ohn] A[lfred] Cuthbert. President [James Monroe] "is anxious that such a cession should be made . . . as will be satisfactory to Georgia." Meigs is to correspond with the commissioners through Walker, "whose residence affords greater facilities for communication both with you & this Dep[artmen]t." LS in DNA, 75 (M-208:9); FC in DNA, 72, E:284 (M-15:5).

To M[ICAH] STERLING, Watertown, N.Y.

Washington, 18th June 1822

The mail of this morning has spread joy over the city. Our friend [George] McDuffie is not only alive but believed to be safe! He so considers himself in a letter written four hours after the affair. The ball entered the small of the back obliquely. I trust so valuable a life is spared to the country. Never did my feelings undergo so great a change in so short a time. Your friend, J.C. Calhoun.

ALS in CSmH; PC in Jameson, ed., *Correspondence*, p. 203.

From N[icholas] Boilvin, Prairie du Chien, 6/19. In compliance with Calhoun's instructions of 2/14, Boilvin met in council with the Fox and Sauk Indians relative to Col. [James] Johnson's leasing of the lead mines on Fever River; [Lt.] Col. [Willoughby] Morgan and [Thomas] Forsyth accompanied Boilvin. At first, the Indians "appeared to be highly displeased & insinuated that Gov[ernmen]t had no right to grant such privileges to the whites, as the land belonged to them." According to them, the U.S. purchased the land from Indians who had no claim to it. However, when they were told that the U.S. government was determined to occupy the land "& that any attempts they might make to prevent the accomplishment of this design would only draw upon them the displeasure of their Great Father," they consented to give up their claim. In fact, they assured Johnson that their intentions toward him were entirely friendly. "Veins of Lead Mineral may be found no doubt in every part of the hills bordering on the Mississippi." A small stream below Fever River is thought to be extremely rich in lead deposits. "I have no doubt there are also very rich copper mines in the vicinity of this place, as the Indians have frequently brought me specimens of that mineral almost in a pure state. I have never been able . . . to learn to a certainty" where the copper mines are. Certain information acquired from the Indians "induces me to believe there is one not far in the country directly east from this [place] & another on Rock River, both on the lands occupied by the Winnabagoes." LS in DNA, 1, B-63 (M-221:95).

From Lewis Cass

Detroit, June 19, 1822

I have the honour to acknowledge the receipt of your letter of the 29th Ult[im]o. The various subjects embraced in it shall receive immediate attention, & your instructions shall be carried into full effect.

I beg leave to refer to my letter of Dec[embe]r 27, 1821 [FC with En in DNA, 76 (M-1:4, pp. 358–367)], for the estimates for the first half of the year 1822. Those for the last half of the year shall be forwarded as soon as I receive the estimates of the several Agents.

I have no doubt but [that], in apportioning among the several Superintendencies & Agencies the sum appropriated at the last session of Congress for the Indian Department, an equal regard has been paid to the claims of each & full justice done to all. But I trust I shall be pardoned for stating that for the year 1821 $24,000 were assigned for the expenditures of this Superintendency. To this sum was added $7,000, which was the balance of a former apportionment due to us. It will therefore be observed that for that year nothing more was received than the amount actually due to us, except the sum of $2,858 paid to the Agency of Mr. [John] Johnston.

The instructions of August 3, 1821 [LS in DNA, 76 (M-1:9, pp. 69–72); FC in DNA, 72, E:139 (M-15:5); CC in DNA, 76 (M-1:70, pp. 249–250)], were acted upon at some of the Agencies, but nothing has yet been received for the payment of these claims. This circumstance, together with others, has left the Agencies in arrears about $5,000. I should be extremely glad to have this additional sum, or any part of it, remitted, if the state of the general fund would admit. It would enable us without difficulty to discharge all necessary duties & to keep within the sum assigned to us. But at all events the expenditures shall be kept within the limitation you have prescribed.

At the request of the Chippeways, I have made arrangements to furnish them with some cattle, hogs, ploughs &c., and two persons are now engaged in ploughing & conducting their farming operations. A Blacksmith has also for the last two years been stationed at Saginaw in conformity with the provisions of the treaty. These sources of expenditure will, I presume, be met by the appropriation of $2,000 intended to carry into effect the stipulations of that treaty. I have the honour to request that it may be remitted for this purpose.

The appropriation of $1,500 for farming purposes, agre[e]ably to the treaty of Chicago, had better be expended by the Agent at that place, and the appropriation of $1,000 for the same objects by the same treaty should be expended here.

I shall probably soon be applied to by the Indians on these subjects and therefore request your instructions in relation to them.

LS in DNA, 1, C-31 (M-221:95); FC in DNA, 76 (M-1:5, pp. 13–14).

To RICHARD CUTTS, Second Comptroller

Dep[art]m[en]t of War, 19 June 1822

I have received your letter of this day's date, [*not found*,] enclosing a form adopted for the requisitions to be made by the War Department on the Secretary of the Treasury [William H. Crawford] in conformity to the 3d section of the act relative to the Treasury, War, and Navy Departments approved 7 May 1822.

I would suggest whether a form for refunding money to the Treasury ought not also to be prepared.

I have to request that you will prepare as soon as practicable and transmit to this Department a state[men]t of its accounts with the Treasurer of the United States [Thomas Tudor Tucker] as its Agent, specifying the several appropriations &c.

LS in NRU; FC in DNA, 3, 11:405 (M-6:11).

From Winfield Scott, Washington, 6/19. He discusses his plans for revising the General Regulations of the Army. He has collected materials to help in the revision, including a recently published book entitled *Principles of War*. "It is not my wish or expectation to be allowed any further compensation for the proposed revision." "The revision is necessary to my own literary & military standing. The subject is now brought before you in its present shape, as it may have some influence on the President[']s [James Monroe's] decision on the claim [made by me that is] before him. If he prefers to withhold his decision till I have prepared the work for a second edition, I am willing to withdraw the claim for the present." ALS in DNA, 1, S-16 (M-221:96).

To Robert Tillotson, New York [City], 6/19. Calhoun encloses a copy of his letter of 5/[13] to [Stephen] Pleasonton, in which Pleasonton was directed to initiate a lawsuit against Tillotson. In order to expedite the suit, Calhoun suggests that Tillotson might confer with Pleasonton, who is now at West Point, during Pleasonton's return trip. FC in DNA, 3, 11:406 (M-6:11).

To Eden Brashears, Port Gibson, Miss., 6/20. Calhoun thanks Brashears for his prompt and "very satisfactory" report of 5/15 [ALS in DNA, 1, B-415 and B-418 (M-221:92)] about the charges of Levi Colbert against [Robert Carter] Nicholas, the Chickasaw Agent. Calhoun sends to Brashears $192 for his services and expenses, at the daily rates of $5 and $3, respectively. FC in DNA, 72, E:285 (M-15:5).

From William H. Crawford, 6/20. He encloses an extract from the instructions that have been given by him to the agents appointed by the President, [James Monroe,] to supersede the Factors and to close the Indian trading establishments. These instructions concern the delivery of merchandise to Indian Agents for use in paying annuities and in making other payments. ALS with En in DNA, 1, C-435 (M-221:92).

To Joseph Hopkinson, Philadelphia

Department of War, June 20th 1822

I have received your letters of the 12th [ALS in DNA, 1, H-311 (M-221:92)], 15th [ALS in DNA, 1, H-312 (M-221:92)], and 17th [ALS in DNA, 1, H-313 (M-221:92)], instant, and on turning to the Resolution of Congress [of 11/3/1814] I find "Erie" named among the Battles for which medals were awarded to the Generals [Jacob] Brown, [Edmund P.] Gaines, [Peter B.] Porter, [Eleazer W.] Ripley and [James] Miller. But to divest the medals of the ambiguity of the Resolution, I approve of your suggestion to affix the date of the Battle of "Erie" properly so called, to wit, the 14th of August 1814 to the medal of General Gaines, and that of the 17th of September 1814 to those of the other Generals who have Erie inscribed on their medal[s], if it can be done without making new dies.

As to the price of General [Alexander] Macomb[']s medal, the subject is left to your discretion, to decide.

As nothing further has been heard from Generals [Andrew] Jackson and Miller, respecting the reverses of their medals, it is to be feared that they are lost, and you will consequently apply to Mr. [Thomas] Sully for new drawings. General Ripley[']s attention has again been called to his profile likeness, which it is hoped he will forward without delay.

FC in DNA, 3, 11:407 (M-6:11).

To R[eodolphus] Malbone, [Chickasaw Agency,] 6/20. Calhoun appoints him to be Sub-Agent to the Chickasaws, to serve under the supervision of Agent [Robert Carter Nicholas], at $500 per year. FC in DNA, 72, E:285 (M-15:5).

To R[OBERT] C[ARTER] NICHOLAS, Chickasaw Agency

Dep[art]m[ent of] War, 20 June 1822

I have received the report of Mr. [Eden] Brashears who was appointed to investigate the charges made against you by Levi Colbert, and also your letter of the 14th Ult[im]o [ALS in DNA, 1, N-2½ (M-221:96)] containing your remarks upon said charges.

The report is very favorable to you and entirely satisfactory to this Department. A copy of the report is herewith enclosed for your information. The investigation has terminated as was anticipated by the Department; but it was considered due to you that it should be made. The result will place you on higher ground in the estimation of the Indians generally and prevent groundless complaints against you in [the] future.

I have directed the sum of $35,100 to be remitted to you for the annuity due to the Chickasaw Nation including the annuity of $100 due to Gen[era]l W[illia]m Colbert, which you will pay in the usual mode.

As to the place of payment, you are authorized to exercise a sound discretion, having regard to convenience & economy in fixing upon it.

In addition to the annuity the sum of $200 is remitted to you to purchase two horses for the use of the Agency, in the place of the two formerly belonging to the Agency, and which died in December last.

Your accounts for the last year have been settled.

I observed from the accounts that a considerable expenditure had been made on the Agency house. As the house must now be in a comfortable state of repair, you will not incur any further expense on it without express authority from this Department.

The expense of the Blacksmith[']s establishment, I also observed[,] had been higher, than I should suppose under present circumstances it ought to be. The annuity of the Chickasaws is now ample, and they ought to pay the expense of this establishment themselves, at least they ought to supply all the Iron & Steel worked up at it for their own use; and you will endeavor to make an arrangement with them to this effect, for this year.

As it is not usual to allow for a Clerk, in which character Mr. [Reodolphus] Malbone appears in your accounts, I herewith enclose an appointment for him as your Sub-Agent.

I regret your determination to resign. I have no doubt your situation has been a very unpleasant one; but it is probable on a further acquaintance with the Indians it will become less so, which I hope may be the case and that it will be agreeable to you ultimately to remain.

FC in DNA, 72, E:285–286 (M-15:5).

C[hristopher] V[andeventer] to [former Bvt. Maj.] Gen. E[leazer] W. Ripley, New Orleans, 6/20. [Joseph] Hopkinson reports that no further work can be done on Ripley's medal [voted to him by Congress for his service in the War of 1812] until a profile likeness is received. Ripley should forward the likeness without delay. FC in DNA, 3, 11:406 (M-6:11).

To William Ward, [Choctaw Agency,] 6/20. [Peter Hagner] has approved payment of $1,792.40 to the Choctaws under the eleventh article of the treaty [of 10/18/1820] with them. That sum will be remitted, with instructions from [Hagner] stipulating how it is to be applied. FC in DNA, 72, E:285 (M-15:5).

From [Col.] John E. Wool, Inspector General, Michilimackinac, Mich. [Territory], 6/20. He discusses the conditions at the military post at Detroit. The appearance and discipline of the troops there are good. "I regret, however, to be compelled to report, that, I discovered in the men an entire ignorance of the Artillery drill, and in their Commander, Capt. [John] Mountford [*sic*; Mountfort], of the 2d Artillery [Regiment], a culpable want of knowledge in that branch of his duty, as well as in the general regulations of the Army." Wool "found none of the harmony existing among the officers, at Detroit, which is so essential to the respectability and efficiency of a Military Post." Mountfort and the Assistant Surgeon, Dr. [Benjamin] Delavan, "appear to be principally concerned in the difficulties, now prevailing there, the blame of which, each takes every opportunity of laying upon the other." Wool recommends that the conduct of both Mountfort and Delavan be investigated by a court-martial and that they be separated. "I am convinced their dissentions [*sic*] will continue, so long as they are together." While Wool was in N.Y., he recommended the use of steamboats to Capt. [*sic*; 1st Lt. Robert M.] Harrison, the Assistant Quartermaster who is in charge of providing transportation for a detachment of the 2nd Infantry Regiment to the Sault Ste. Marie. The advantages of steamboats over sailing vessels will compensate for the additional expense. LS in DNA, 1, W-14 (M-221:96).

From Brig. Gen. H[enry] Atkinson, St. Louis, 6/21. He encloses a copy of a letter [dated 6/13] from [Lt.] Col. [Willoughby] Morgan to Atkinson. Morgan "descended from Prairie du Chein [*sic*] to Fever River, agreeably to instructions from me, to join Messrs. [Thomas] Forsyth & [Nicholas] Bo[i]lvin in council with the Saucks & Foxes, relative to Col. [James] Johnson[']s being put in possession of the Lead Mines, conformably to the terms of his lease." [Morgan reported that it "was distinctly explained to the Sauks & Foxes that they owned no land on the east side [of] the Mississippi. They acquies[c]ed after some explanation and are now perfectly satisfied. There is not the slightest ground to apprehend any difficulty with the Indians on account of leasing the mines" at Fever River.] "As the result must be very satisfactory to you I hasten to lay it before you, reserving the original letter for Gen[era]l [Edmund P.] Gaines, who I expect to arrive here today, in the steam Boat Calhoun, from Louisville." "On his arrival, I presume, we shall immediately depart" for the Council Bluffs. "The return of several provision Boats from the Bluffs give[s] us advices to the 2nd & 8th inst[ant]. Things were progressing very favorably there, and the country perfectly tranquil." LS with En in DNA, 1, A-6 (M-221:95).

From Mority Fürst, Philadelphia, 6/21. He has engraved in some of the medals erroneous dates for some of the battles in the

War of 1812; but he gives assurance that the mistakes can be corrected if Calhoun should request corrections. Fürst has almost completed engraving the likeness of [Alexander] Macomb, will proceed with the reverse of that medal, and has "no drawings for the other reverses." ALS in DNA, 1, F-130 (M-221:92).

To Edmund P. Gaines, Louisville, Ky.

Department of War, June 21st 1822

I have received your letters of the 30th Ultimo, [ALS with Ens in DNA, 1, G-178 (M-221:92); variant FC in DNA, RG 98, Western Department, Letters Sent, 1:244–247,] and of the 4th instant [*not found*].

By reference to the several letters addressed to you relative to the assignment of the command of the Right wing of the Western Department to [Bvt.] Brig. Gen[era]l [Henry] Atkinson, you will perceive the objections to that measure were not on account of its being considered improper either in a military point of view or in policy. But there were objections to the exercise of the command as a Brigadier General, carrying with it the right to the pay and emoluments of that grade. These objections were founded on what was considered the intention of Congress of the law of the 2d of March 1821 for reducing the Army. The act provides only for two Brigadier Generals; consequently the Army was organized as one Division consisting of two Brigades; the former commanded by a Major General, [Jacob Brown,] the latter each by a Brigadier General, and provision was accordingly made for the pay &c. of this limited number of General Officers only, and it was believed, consistently with the act, under any permanent arrangement, no great number of General Officers of the line, could receive [brevet] pay and emoluments.

This construction of the act as respects pay and emoluments was I believe fully understood by yourself and [Bvt. Maj.] General [Winfield] Scott before you repaired to your respective commands under the General order of the 17th of May 1821 and in conformity both to the supposed intention of the Legislature of the act of the 2d of March 1821, and to the understanding had with you and Gen. Scott on that point, the Department could not sanction the assignment of the command of the right wing of the Western Department to Gen. Atkinson, so far as to entitle him to the pay and emoluments of his brevet rank. But the difficulty of assigning such command without involving the right to Brevet pay becoming apparent, the Department determined to allow the pay for the time the command had been exercised, but ordered command as a Department to be discontinued. There is a sensibility in Congress upon Brevet pay which renders it a duty not to allow it, but in cases clearly within the law and regulations and to provide against the recurrence beyond the accidents of service.

Upon the subject of your own brevet pay as Bvt. Major General, I have to observe that, it is a question of the law which refers itself to the law officers of the government. As far as this Department under orders of the President [James Monroe] could act in the matter, every thing has been done that could be by submitting the subject to the Attorney General [William Wirt] for an opinion which he has given (a copy of which is enclosed) and which is referred to the 2d Comptroller of the Treasury, [Richard Cutts,] whose duty it is now to act finally upon it. Hence you will perceive that this Department has no longer the power, if it had the option, to interfere either to obtain its allowance or rejection. The Department in no instance requires of an officer the relinquishment of a claim for pay or for any thing else to which he may think he is entitled. But it is its duty to see that no claim be allowed which is not strictly conformable to law or regulations.

General Scott is now here, advocating on his part, a similar claim for brevet pay &c. and whatever decision may be made by the 2d Compt[rolle]r in his case will be extended to yours.

FC in DNA, 3, 11:408–409 (M-6:11).

From Maj. Gen. ALEXANDER MACOMB, Chief Engineer

Engineer Department, Washington, 21 June 1822

I have the honor to report to you, that the Board of Engineers have examined & inspected the works at the Narrows of New York Harbour called Fort Diamond, who state that the work is finished & well executed.

The Board further reports "that although the work is completed, yet the quarters for the Troops cannot be considered as ready for their reception. The quarters are casemates the masonry of which being not yet dry the moisture might prove very injurious to the health of the Troops. In the summer the garrison might be quartered in the batteries, but in the winter they would be exposed to the severest cold. Therefore the Board think that the fort should be occupied by a detachment, whose duties it would be to guard the fort and to air the quarters by keeping open, during the warm season, the doors & windows. This detachment might in summer be quartered in the Batteries and in the winter in two or three casemates used as kitchens during the summer in order to get them sooner dry."

The board of Engineers have not mentioned the comfortable quarters which exist on the Island (Long) where the garrison could be quartered should it be found unhealthy in the fort. I therefore recommend that the work be put in possession of the Commander of the Troops as soon as convenient.

ALS in DNA, 16, 1822, M-39 (M-567:4, frames 104–107); FC in DNA, 21, 1:300–301.

George Bomford to the Governors of the States and Territories, 6/22. Because the required, annual militia returns are quite "defective," Calhoun is unwilling to permit at this time a distribution of arms under the statute of 1808. From some States and Territories not one return has been received for the years 1816–1821; from none has a return been submitted for every year. Bomford informs each Governor which returns are missing for his unit and asks that these returns shall be submitted as soon as practicable. CC in DNA, 332, pp. 30–31.

From T[homas] Cadwalader, Philadelphia, 6/22. As a member of the Board of Visitors of the Military Academy, he reports at length and favorably about the progress of that school. ALS with En in DNA, 222, F-64.

To [William H. Crawford], 6/22. Calhoun informs [Crawford] that $34,989.57 should be deposited in the Bank of Darien, [Ga.,] for the use "of the Commissioners appointed to hold a treaty with the [Eastern] Cherokees." FC in DNA, 72, E:287 (M-15:5). In reply on 7/3 [ALS in DNA, 1, C-12 (M-221:95)], Crawford invited Calhoun to issue a warrant under which the transfer could be made.

To W[illiam] H. Crawford

Dep[art]m[en]t of War, 22 June 1822

In answer to your note of today [ALU in DNA, 1, C-436 (M-221:92)], I have the honor to state that the Money for the Georgia claims, [made by Ga. citizens against the Creeks,] by stipulation in the late Creek treaty, is to be paid to the State of Georgia, in five annual instalments and that as soon as the Attorney General [William Wirt] returns and his opinion on the question of interest can be fully obtained one-fifth of the amount of the award of the Commissioners, appointed to ascertain the amount of these claims, will be remitted to the Governor of Georgia [John Clark] to be paid to the claimants conformably to said award, a copy of which will be transmitted to him.

I had received a letter myself from Major [Joel] Crawford upon this subject, but delayed answering it until I received the final orders of the President [James Monroe] upon the claims.

FC in DNA, 72, E:288 (M-15:5). Note: Compare, herein, the Abs of Calhoun's letter of 6/27 to Joel Crawford answering his of 4/27.

To Richard Cutts, Second Comptroller

Department of War, June 22d 1822

The contract for building a fort on Mobile Point which was on the 13th day of May 1818 entered into between this Department and Benjamin W. Hopkins (since deceased) and subsequently transferred by the Administrator on the estate of said Hopkins to the late Colonel Samuel Hawkins, has not been fulfilled but has failed.

Messrs. Robert Tillotson and Nicholas Gouverneur of New York, as sureties for the said Colonel Samuel Hawkins, deceased, are bound for the faithful execution of the said Contract and also for the amount of advances which have been taken upon it. I have therefore to request that measures may be taken forthwith for putting in suit their Bonds, which are now in possession [of] the fifth Auditor, [Stephen Pleasonton,] in order to [make possible] the recovery of the amount for which they are liable.

LS in DNA, 63, 1822, 130; FC in DNA, 3, 11:409 (M-6:11).

To George Graham, [former Acting Secretary of War,] "Principal Agent &c., Indian Trade Office," Georgetown, D.C., 6/22. "As medals are frequently required for presents to Indian Chiefs, if there are any on hand at the Indian Office in Georgetown, I have to request you will furnish me with an estimate of the number and cost of them, with a view to have them turned over to this Department." FC in DNA, 72, E:287 (M-15:5).

To Solomon U. Hendrick, Vernon, N.Y., 6/22. Calhoun acknowledges Hendrick's letter of 5/23 [ALS in DNA, 1, H-309 (M-221:92)]. [Jasper] Parrish has been directed to refund the $100 that he deducted from the Stockbridges' annuity as a result of erroneous instructions from [William Lee]. Papers concerning the deputation from the Six Nations [and its intention to seek a cession of land in the Green Bay area] have been sent to Eleazer Williams, whose addition to the group has necessitated Calhoun's increasing the number of delegates authorized [to receive rations] to seven. No copies of these papers are being sent to Hendrick, because the deputation will probably travel as a group. The War Department has no medals on hand, but the number requested by [Parrish for use as presents to Chiefs] will be secured and forwarded to him for distribution. FC in DNA, 72, E:287 (M-15:5).

From Jasper Parrish, Canandaigua, [N.Y.,] 6/22. He has been informed by the Chiefs of the Six Nations that they will "have nothing to do with the Green Bay purchase of land." If "the Stockbridge tribe with a few individuals of the Six Nations should think proper to receive, ratify and pay for the land purchased at Green Bay, they may do so, with their private money." The Chiefs of the Six Nations have stated that "no part of their national annuity should be applied to make any part of the payments." LS in DNA, 1, P-12 (M-221:96).

From Edmund P. Gaines

Louisville, Ky., June 24th 1822

I have received your letter of the 30th of last month, [PC herein,] by which I am gratified to find that my conduct, in a case I deemed to be doubtful, and in other cases in regard to which I felt considerable solicitude, had been approved.

After mature reflection upon the subject of the war between

the Cherokees and Osages, and the wishes of the President of the United States, [James Monroe,] as expressed by you upon the subject, I have deemed it advisable to address the principal Chiefs of the two nations a letter of which I have the honor to enclose herewith a copy. The style in which I have addressed them being somewhat unusual, my first intention was to submit my letter to you before I should send it, and not to visit them until September next, on my return from Council Bluffs. But having just now learned that Governor [James] Miller (with whom I promised at his request to coöperate) had made arrangements to meet the Chiefs at Fort Smith on the 29th of July, next month, I have concluded to send on my letters immediately, to touch at Fort Smith on my way to Council Bluffs, and if necessary to unite with the Governor in an effort to terminate a war, which though apparently inconsiderable, cannot but tend, if persisted in, to harrass [*sic*] and endanger the frontier settlements.

From the long acquaintance and frequent intercourse I have had with the Southern and some of the Western Indians, in the public service as well as in private affairs, I am convinced that upon all just and reasonable occasions, they will yield more certainly and more promptly to a mild but authoritative demand, than to a mere persuasive solicitation or request—especially when the nation addressing them is known to be firm, strong, and just. And no statesman or civillian [*sic*] can doubt, that upon principles of national law, the President of the United States has a right even *to use force* to put a stop to a war carried on within our own limits. But you will perceive that I have carefully avoided uttering any thing like a threat; to utter a threat indeed, under any circumstances, without being fully authorised promptly to redeem or execute it, is something worse than useless; but as it regards the Indians, an empty threat is considered by them in the light of an empty promise; which tends but to destroy confidence in the person making it.

I cannot positively promise success in the proposed effort; but as the experiment will be productive of no extraordinary expence beyond the price of two or three thousand rations, and as there is great reason to believe it will succeed, and moreover as it will be likely in this event to produce a most salutary effect on the minds of the neighboring Indians, I shall take great pleasure in contributing as much as possible to accomplish the desired object.

ALS with En in DNA, 1, G-5 (M-221:95); PC in Carter, ed., *Territorial Papers,* 19:441–443.

From Thomas L. McKenney, "Indian Office," Georgetown, [D.C.,] 6/24. Answering Calhoun's letter of 6/22 [to George Graham], McKenney reports that in "the transfer of the property of this Office to Mr. Graham, the Medals, on account of their forming no part of the trade effects, were left in my hands. I will present you with a statement of the Medal accounts and return you those which are yet in hand, in a few days." ALS in DNA, 1, M-12 (M-221:96).

To R[ETURN] J. MEIGS, Calhoun, Tenn.

Department of War, 24 June 1822

I observe from your accounts for the last year and the 1st Q[uarte]r of this year, which have been laid before me by the 2d Auditor, [William Lee,] that your disbursements have very considerably exceeded the sum to which you are limited by this Department. As it appears, however, that this excess has been, in some measure, caused by the removal of the Agency from the former to the present site, and by the removal of intruders from the Indian lands, the accounts have now been admitted; but your expenditures must, positively, in future not exceed the sum to which you are limited, without the express authority of this Department; otherwise, the amount of such excess will be charged to your personal account. A considerable reduction ought to be made in the expense for Blacksmith's work and for agricultural and manufacturing implements. It is time that the Cherokees should furnish the greater portion of these articles for themselves, as, independent of the annuity, many of them are wealthy and perfectly able to purchase every article necessary for their own use and convenience. The friendship and protection of the government will always be extended alike to every class; but the poor and destitute Indian only should experience its benevolence in this way. The expense too which you have incurred, by the employment of Mr. [Jacob] Hindman in the transaction of business which ought to have been done by the Sub-Agent, [James G. Williams,] is irregular and must not be continued. The Sub-Agent is paid by the government to aid you in the execution of your duties, and no other person ought to [be] employed, at an additional expense to it, for that purpose. If the Sub-Agent has not your confidence, you ought to report the fact to this Department, in order that another may be appointed in his place.

I understand from the 2d Auditor that in the settlement of your accounts, you appear to be in arrears to the government to a very considerable amount. By the act of Congress passed at the late session making appropriations for the several branches of the public service, under the control of this Department, it is provided, "that no money appropriated by this act shall be advanced or paid to any person on any contract, *or to any officer who is in arrears to the U[nited] States*, until he shall have accounted for and paid into the Treasury, all sums for which he may be liable." Consequently no further advances can be made to you, until this provision of the act is complied with. You will therefore see the necessity of giving the earliest attention to the settlement of your accounts.

LS in DNA, 75 (M-208:9); FC in DNA, 72, E:290 (M-15:5).

To Lewis Cass, Detroit, 6/25. In view of a prospective survey and sale of public lands near Fort Wayne, the Commissioner of the General Land Office, [Josiah Meigs,] has asked whether the public reservation there has any future usefulness for military or Indian purposes. Before deciding whether that reservation should or should not be sold, Calhoun requests the counsel of Cass. LS in DNA, 76, 5:412–415 (M-1:10, pp. 412–415); FC in DNA, 72, E:291 (M-15:5). Cass replied on 7/17.

To V[IRGIL] MAXCY

Washington, 25th June 1822

I have read with great interest your agreeable favour of the 17th Inst[ant; *not found*], which has almost tempted me to pronounce an eulogy on your caution, prudence and [*one word, which looks like* "peritution" *or* "penetration," *illigible*]. Nothing can be more judicious than your ["reflections" *canceled*] observations and arrangements on the various points on which you touch. Dr. [Joseph] Kent, who you know is very cautious, is in high sperits [*sic*], which gives ["much ground" *canceled and* "strong reason" *interlined*] to hope that the sentiment of Maryland will be much more favourable than was at first expected. I am very much gratified to learn that [Stevenson] Archer [former Representative from Md.] is favourable. He is a most worthy man, for whom I have always entertained the highest respect. Your hold on the Eastern Shore appears to me to be very powerful, so much so as to keep Mr. [Edward] Lloyd in complete check.

I have a very favourable opinion of Mr. [John Leeds] Kerr, [later a Representative from Md.,] but do fear, that I have given him some grounds of offence for the want of that attention, which would have comported with my regard for him, but which on reflection, I fear, I have been negligent in extending to him. I will profit by your hint.

Col. [Nathan] Towson is zealous and perfectly confidential. You may correspond with him with perfect safety, ["and" *canceled and* "which" *interlined*] may be of great service in the State, particularly in Baltimore. I have a very high opinion of [Roger B.] Taney, and hope, as his health returns and he becomes more fully acquainted with the real state of things, ["that he will be zealous" *interlined*]. Another session, ["with" *canceled and* "&" *interlined*] an able paper here, will go far to unfold to the nation the points on which the election must turn. If Mr. T[aney] is favourable (as I doubt not Gen[era]l [Samuel] Ringgold [former Representative from Md.] and the leading Republicans in that portion of the State will be) it will secure the populous western counties. I think he has formed an erroneous opinion of Mr. [Thomas L.] McKenney. He has some vanity but not the least obstinacy in his character, as far as I have ever noticed. His honor and honesty cannot be questioned. I have not seen Maj[o]r [George] Peter [former Representative from Md.] for some time. When I see him next, I will urge the importance of securing [Samuel] Barnes, who from the position of his [Frederick, Md.,] paper must have great weight.

Your western tour will put much in your power. One so prudent as yourself ["who is" *canceled*] & so fully master of the whole ground has the power, in the present state of the publick mind, to make strong and lasting impressions.

I enclose a sketch in reply to the piece of the Int[elligence]r in relation to the Treasury. I do not think it necessary to go fully into the subject, but to present a few strong points only.

I fear ["you" *canceled*] that it will not be in our power to make the contemplated visit to West River. Since the more favourable news from Mr. [George] McDuffie, which has again put me in a disposition of mind to enjoy the company of my friends, several intervening causes have deterred me in the city. We have had the French negotiation before us, which would have rendered it improper in me to be absent. [*One sentence canceled.*] We ["are on the eve of closing" *canceled and* "have concluded" *interlined*] a commercial arrangement with France. We do not get all that we want, but a foundation is laid to place in a short time the commerce of the two countries on that perfect freedom, which is the basis of our system.

We hope that when you take your tour west, that you will make your arrangements to spend some time with us, as Washington will be in the direct route. I will be glad to see you on many accounts; and I think that Mrs. Maxcy would find our summer society not less agreeable than ["that of" *interlined*] the winter.

Our last accounts from Mr. McDuffie continue very favourable. He has a prospect of a speedy recovery, without any inconvenience from his wound. Should any change take place as to his ["speedy" *interlined*] recovery I will inform you of it.

26th June

This morning I received your favour of the 21st inst[ant; *not found*] and am much gratified ["as to" *canceled and* "by" *interlined*] its contents. A correspondence between you and Archer will be very important. There is not any where a more estimable man. His worth is not fully appreciated in the State, as high as he stands. Tho' indolent he is very capable when roused of making vigorous exertions.

[Bvt. Maj.] Gen[era]l [Winfield] Scott is now here and if any thing can be done for Maj[o]r [Francis Smith] Belton it will afford me much pleasure. I will see the Gen[era]l in relation to him, and will ascertain what can be done.

I cannot think that Gen[era]l Ringgold will go [*one word, possibly* "awry" *or* "wrong" *illegible*]. In fact I understand that he expressed himself very distinctly when here last winter. To make sure[?] work, I will speak to Mr. [George?] Hay if a good opportunity offers to write to him. He has much weight with him.

I have just seen Gen[era]l Scott who informs me, that in consequence of a recent order which puts Col. [Jacob] Hindman in the command of the [2nd Artillery] Regiment, Maj[or] Belton will have a [*one word, possibly a misspelling of* "separate," *illegible*] command with the usual advantages attached to it.

I enclose an extract from a leading Kentucky paper, which shows the sperit in that quarter. My information from that State if very flattering. Can you get the extract inserted in the Annapolis paper?

I have scratched off some remarks in the midest [*sic*] of the hurry of the office without regard to style on the ["observation of" *canceled and* "statement of" *interlined*] the Int[elligence]r, which I have not time to reduce to better form. They are intended ["in the" *canceled and* "as" *interlined*] hints by which you may draw out something calculated for the papers, if you can decipher what is written. Yours truly, J.C. Calhoun.

ALS in DLC, Galloway-Maxcy-Markoe Papers, vol. 32.

To Josiah Meigs, 6/25. In view of the prospective survey and sale of public lands near Fort Wayne, Calhoun has asked [Lewis] Cass whether the public reservation there can be spared and hence sold. Meigs will be notified when a decision shall have been reached. FC in DNA, 72, E:291 (M-15:5).

From Solo[mon] Betton, Milledgeville, [Ga.,] 6/26. He submits his claim for horses lost during the Seminole War of 1817–1818 and requests information about obtaining a balance due to him from a Capt. for transporting supplies. Betton states that [William H.] Crawford's friends [in Ga.] are resentful that Calhoun did not appoint certain gentlemen to serve as commissioners [to negotiate the proposed treaty with the Eastern Cherokees]. Milledgeville newspapers "do not fail to notice it & to insinuate an understanding between yourself & some high in office in this State. The current is certainly strong ag[ainst] you, in Mr. Crawford['s] friends at least[,] as our next President." If [John Quincy] Adams is not elected, Betton hopes that Calhoun will be. ALS in DNA, 1, B-29 (M-221:95).

To Lewis Cass, Detroit, 6/26. Calhoun acknowledges Cass's letter of 5/23. Contrary to his supposition, the abolition of the Factory system does not involve a gratuitous issuance of goods to Indians; instead, "the Indian Department will be charged with all goods taken from the Factories for its use." Calhoun's letter of 5/29 informed Cass that he can present to the Indians goods worth [$4,500], this amount being "as liberal as it could be made, as Congress appropriated but $15,000 for that object" in the nation as a whole. Cass's letter of 4/25 [LS in DNA, 1, C-433 (M-221:92); FC in DNA, 76 (M-1:4, pp. 403–404); PC in Carter, ed., *Territorial Papers,* 11:236–237] recommending the construction with Army labor of a small military post beside the Saginaw River reached Calhoun after a decision to build such a post had already been reached, "and measures are in preparation for effecting it." LS in DNA, 76, 5:420–423 (M-1:10, pp. 420–423); FC in DNA, 72, E:292 (M-15:5).

From Edmund P. Gaines, [Louisville, Ky.,] 6/26. He encloses a letter of 6/25 from Henry W. Conway, who joins Gaines in believing that the U.S. should attempt to purchase the Quapaws' land on the south side of the Arkansas River above Little Rock. Gaines suggests that 1,600,000 acres might be bought now for $50,000 and sold in 20 years for $3,200,000. He recommends this as a profitable investment, although he is aware that "the present may be considered as an inauspicious period, particularly by those who profess to be exclusive friends of economy, for attempting to extinguish Indian claims. ALS with En in DNA, 1, G-6 (M-221:95); PC in Carter, ed., *Territorial Papers,* 19:444–446.

To R[ETURN] J. MEIGS, Calhoun, Tenn.

Department of War, 26 June 1822

Your letter of the 17th ultimo [ALS in DNA, 1, M-9 (M-221:96); draft in DNA, 75 (M-208:9)] has been received.

It would perhaps be the best means of preventing disturbances between the Indians and the whites on the Georgia frontier, to appoint a Sub-Agent to reside in that quarter, who would promptly attend to the complaints of either party and apply the remedy; but as a treaty is to be held with the Cherokees in the course of the summer, I deem it advisable to defer taking any steps for this purpose until the result of the negotiation is known.

I do not think it would be advisable for the Indians to attempt to remove intruders entirely of themselves, as resistance might perhaps be made to them and unpleasant consequences ensue. You will, for the present, direct the Sub-Agent [James G. Williams] to notify the intruders that they must remove before the fall, or by the time the season for securing the crops is over, and that if they do not remove by that time, steps will be taken to compel them. In case it should ultimately be necessary to use force, the tender of services by the militia will be accepted, which, with the aid of the Cherokee troops, will be fully competent to effect the object. The delay until the fall is not intended as a mark of lenity towards the intruders, but for the convenience of the militia, which could not turn out before that time without much inconvenience.

LS in DNA, 75 (M-208:9); FC in DNA, 72, 2:291–292 (M-15:5).

To JOHN CLARK, [Governor of Ga.,] Milledgeville

Dep[art]m[en]t of War, 27 June 1822

Knowing the deep interest which you take in the affairs of the State over which you preside, the proposed treaty with the [Eastern] Cherokee nation under the appropriation made at the last session, and the award of the Commissioner under the late Creek treaty [James P. Preston] were brought immediately after the adjournment of Congress to the notice of the President [James Monroe] for his orders in relation to both subjects. The great pressure of business, which usually follows the termination of a session, ["with" *canceled and* "and" *interlined*] the indisposition of Mr. [William H.] Crawford and the indisposition and absence of Mr. [William] Wirt has [*sic*] prevented, as early a decision as was desired; but I hope that no serious inconvenience will result from the delay.

The President has appointed Mr. [Freeman] Walker, Mr. [John Alfred] Cuthbert, and Gen[era]l [John] Floyd as Commissioners to hold the proposed treaty with the Cherokees. I enclose for your informatoon a copy of the instructions to the Commissioners, by reference to which you will percieve [*sic*] that they are instructed to coöperate with the Commissioners of the State, should any be appointed, and that there is no other restriction on their power to conclude a treaty than that the price of the lands which may be purchased and the amount stipulated to be paid for it [*sic*] are not to exceed the price & sum given in the late Creek purchase.

The President has examined with great care the decision of Gen[era]l Preston on the claims arising under the treaty with the Creek Indians and altho' he thinks the value of the property in almost all of the cases very high and the proof in many instances not such as to bring the claims strictly within the provisions of the treaties under which they rise, yet on due consideration he has confirmed the decision of the Commissioner in favor of the claims. He has also allowed the claims in all of the cases which he recommended to the favorable notice of the President with the exception of [*a blank occurs here*] which was not supported by the depositions of the original claimants, nor their representations as required by the regulations established by the President. The whole amount of the claims so allowed is $88,702.62 of which I enclose a certified list of the names of the claimants and the amount which has been awarded to each; and a remittance is made to you for the first instal[l]ment agreeably to the stipulations of the treaty.

On the question of interest [on the amount of those claims], the President took the opinion of the Attorney General, [Wirt,] who reported unfavorably to its allowance, which after much consideration, the President has approved. The opinion of the Attorney General, which has not yet been formally drawn out, will be transmitted to you when it is completed and will disclose the ground on which the claim for interest has been disallowed.

FC in DNA, 72, E:293–294 (M-15:5); CCEx in DNA, 75 (M-208:9).

To Joel Crawford, [former Representative from Ga.,] Milledgeville, 6/27. Calhoun would have answered sooner Crawford's letter of 4/27 [ALS in DNA, 1, C-443 (M-221:92)] but has had to await approval by [James Monroe] of [James P.] Preston's delayed report, as commissioner, about how the claims [by Ga. citizens] under the recent Creek treaty should be settled. The first payment against the claims has been sent to Governor [John Clark] of Ga. FC in DNA, 72, E:292–293 (M-15:5).

2nd Lt. C[lark] Burdine, Fever River, [Ill.,] to [George] Bomford, 6/28. He reports that several discoveries of lead deposits have been made and that mining has already begun at the most favorable site. A great flood has hampered operations. The Indians are friendly and say that they are happy that the Americans have come. ALS in DNA, 31, 1822, B.

From Thomas Forsyth, St. Louis, 6/28. He discusses his issuance of tobacco and gunpowder at Fort Armstrong to Winnebagoes who reside on Rocky River. He reports that other Indians object to such provisions being furnished to the Winnebagoes. He suggests that a Sub-Agent be appointed to reside at the lead mines on Fever River and recommends John Connolly for that position. ALS in DNA, 1, F-9 (M-221:95); FC's in WHi, Draper Collection, Thomas Forsyth Papers, 4:138–140, 6:8–10, and 7:94 (published microfilm, series T, vols. 1–9); EU in DNA, 8, 261.

From A[NDREW] J[ACKSON], "Private"

June 28th, 1822

Being absent vissitting [*sic*] my little farm near Florence, [Ala.,] when your letter of the 16th of May reached Nashville, I did not receive it untill the 22d Instant[,] the day of my return, and [this] will account to you for the delay of my acknowledging its receipt.

It will at all times afford me sincere pleasure to interchange with you my sentiments on any, and all subjects that may be interesting to you, or in which the interest of our common country may be involved. There is no one[']s welfare & prosperity, I have more at heart than yours. This was the reason, ["why" *canceled*] I have wrote [*sic*] you with the frankness I have done, and hastened as soon as advised to lay before you, the conduct of Gen[era]l [Thomas S.] Jessup [*sic*] at Pensacola. I believed you, like myself, to have held ["in estimation" *interlined*] the Gen[era]l free from duplicity or, dishonourable conduct, ["but as to myself" *canceled and* "From information rec(eive)d some time since" *interlined*] I was fully convinced of my Error [*several words canceled*] and I am happy you are now guarded with respect to him—he is unworthy of confidence, & capable ["in my opinion" *interlined*] of betraying it. As to our mutual friend [Col. James] Gadsden, you may rely on it, there is neither deception [n]or duplicity in his composition, ["and" *canceled*] the longer you are acquainted with him, the more you will be convinced ["of" *canceled*] that I have formed a Just Estimate of him.

It is certainly true, that the military committee of the Senate ["are" *canceled and* "have" *interlined* been] and ["have been" *canceled and* "will be" *interlined*] wielded by the ["Senate" *canceled*] present Secretary of the Treasury [William H. Crawford]; Mr. [James] Monroe ["cannot but have long" *canceled and* "must have long since" *interlined*] known of his intrigue, and I do assure you his best friends have shewed ["it" *canceled*] with regret and astonishment, that he [Monroe] still retains him [Crawford] in his Cabinet. Mr. Crawford if I mistake not, has not abandoned his intrigue and it is probable, the military committee may at the next session of Congress renew their attack against Mr. Monroe. Their object [is] to effect [*sic*] you, and draw the attention of the nation from ["the" *canceled and* "his" *interlined*] corruption, and intrigue, ["of Crawford" *canceled*]. His friends will know they can neither justify or defend him, and it is plain that this is their course from the game that is played ["off" *canceled*] by ["the red jacketts through" *interlined*] the city Gazzett [*sic*].

The right mode is to meet an enemy with his own weapons, and if Mr. [Daniel Pope] Cook could meet with ["that" *interlined*] support ["that virtue ought to elicit" *interlined*] and at the next session call up the report of the committee on the subject of the employment of ["Mr." *canceled and* "Senator" *interlined*; Jesse B.] Thomas, unfold Mr. Crawford[']s conduct fully, and his false statement to the chairman of that committee, on which the chairman founded his er[r]oneous reports, it will put the Sec[retary] and his friends down forever. Mr. Crawford ["cannot" *canceled and* "will not in my opinion" *interlined*] get a vote in this State. I have said that I am induced to believe, that Crawford, through the military committee of the Senate, will at the next session of Congress, make another effort against the Executive, to injure you. Colo[nel Thomas Hart] Benton [Senator from Mo.] will wield Williams [*probably* John Williams, Senator from Tenn.] and Crawford will wield them both like a shewman does his puppets. I know they men [*sic*; these men *or* they mean] well, and from a front view can well judge of their ["hands"? *canceled and* "interior" *interlined*]. Benton has laid a resolution on the table [on 3/8] calling for information whether Colo[nel Robert] Butler has resigned ["or not" *canceled*] &c. &c. This is not acted on, but ["it" *canceled*] is left for further operations, at the next session. If these men expect any thing from Colo[nel] Butler to aid their views they are widely mistaken; he is too honourable a man to have any thing to do with such men. I must be frank; it beho[o]ves you and Mr. Monroe to act with ["great" *interlined*] caution, and give to those men no opportunity of advantage by any act that you may do, that relates to the Army. You have no Adjutant Gen[era]l. This will ["involve" *canceled*] create for you great labour. Should you detail one to perform the duties, and allow him compensation they will endeavour to assail you for having applied the public money, ["to uses" *canceled*] not appropriated by law, alledging [*sic*] that the fault was with the President [Monroe] in leaving the office unfilled, and if Colo[nel] Gadsden should be detailed it will be handled by them as a contemptuous conduct ["of the President" *interlined*] to the Senate, that body having rejected his renomination. Permit me to remark Colo[nel] Gadsden is too valuable to the Army & his country for his services to be lost ["to it" *canceled*]. Permit me to sug[g]est a course, that will disappoint your enemies, silence them and bring Colo[nel] Gadsden into the Adjutant General[']s office, his feelings untouched, and the President free from blame. Let it be remembered, that the military committee contend, that the Adj[utan]t Gen[era]l[']s office of right ought to have been filled by [Col. Roger] Jones or Butler. Butler has tendered his resignation, which ["as yet" *interlined*] has not been accepted ["of" *canceled*]. He is under permission by Gen[era]l [Edmund P.] Gain[e]s to remain in Tennessee or untill he receives information whether his resignation is accepted or not. [*Several words canceled.*] In point of law he is still in the Army & the P[resident] in pursuing the intimation of the military committee by reappointing [Nathan] Towson [to be the] Paymaster [General] has shewn an inclination to adopt the course pointed out by them. Let Butler ["then" *interlined*] be ordered to the city [of Washington] as Adj[utan]t Gen[era]l ["but have" *canceled*]. He will obey the order, and continue to perform the duties to the next meeting of Congress with an understanding that he is permitted then to resign, and that Colo[nel] Gadsden ["will" *canceled*] be nominated by the President to the Senate to fill the office of Adjutant Gen[era]l. This will ["stop the mouths of the" *and one illegible word and* "of Crawford, Williams & Benton" *canceled and* "silence the opposition of the military committee" *interlined*] and ensure Gadsden an unanimous confirmation by the Senate. I well know that Colo[nel] Butler will make this sacrafice [*sic*] of absence from his family, to secure his friend Gadsden the appointment ["& his country his services and to relieve the administration from the present embarrassment" *interlined*] believing as he does that Mr. Monroe will provide for him by giving him the appointment of ["Adj(utan)t" *canceled*] Surveyor Gen[era]l of the Floridas when that appointment is made. Major [John H.] Eaton [Senator from Tenn.] reached me last night. This sug[g]estion I have made to him which he approves. Colo[nel] Butler[']s account goes on by this day[']s mail ["addressed to Maj. (Christopher) Vandeventer" *interlined*]. Should these sug[g]estions be approved and adopted ["his account can be suspended" *interlined*]. I ["will" *canceled*] pledge myself, for Colo[nel] Butler[']s compliance with with [*sic*] the ar[r]angement above sug[g]ested.

Present me to Mr. Monroe and say to him I have rec[eive]d his letter with the enclosure which shall be answered so soon as I have time to peruse with attention the enclosure. In haste I am Sir with great respect y[ou]r mo[st] ob[edien]t . . . .

Autograph draft, initialed, in DLC, Andrew Jackson Papers, 11417–11418 (Presidential Papers Microfilm, Jackson Papers, Reel 31); PC in Bassett, ed., *Correspondence of Andrew Jackson*, 3:164–166.

Alexander Macomb, Washington, to [John] Le Conte, New York [City], 6/28. Macomb discusses some business of the Army Engineers. ALS (franked "Free J.C. Calhoun") in PPAmP.

S[ylvanus] Thayer, West Point, to Alexander Macomb, 6/28. Thayer opposes Calhoun's wish that the Cadets should march to Carlisle, [Pa.,] for their summer encampment of 1822. Thayer argues two reasons: (1) the new Cadets who arrived late this month cannot be prepared for so long a march, and without them the Battalion, "reduced as it is by furloughs, would be too small"; (2) the Academy's appropriation is too small to cover the expense of so long a march. Thayer suggests, as an alternative, "some excursions" into Orange and Dutchess Counties, N.Y. If, however, Calhoun still insists and provides funds, Thayer will begin preparations immediately after returning on 7/6 from a vacation. ALS in DNA, 14, 306.

To Thomas [Cadwalader], Philadelphia, 6/29. Calhoun acknowledges Cadwalader's "highly satisfactory" and "very interesting" report [of 6/22] about the recent "examination of the Military Academy." FC in DNA, 3, 11:414 (M-6:11).

To Jeremiah Evarts, Corresponding Secretary, American Board [of Commissioners for] Foreign Missions, Boston

Dep[art]m[en]t of War, 29 June 1822

In answer to your letter of yesterday [*not found*] I have to state that the allowance for the education of four Indian youths at Cornwall in Connecticut, for the year ending in August next amounting to $316.67 will be advanced to you, and is the last payment to be made on account of such allowance, being the completion of four years as at first agreed to in my letter of the 18th July 1818.

Two-thirds of the expense of the buildings, as estimated by Mr. [Cyrus] Kingsbury for the new establishment at the French Camp or Newell in ["the" *interlined*] Choctaw Nation will be allowed, and a further allowance at the rate of $350 a year commencing from the 1st July next is made for tuition, to be paid through the Indian Agent [William Ward] quarter yearly. The payments on account of the buildings, will be made upon ["the" *interlined*] certificate of the Agent as prescribed by the regulations, of which Mr. Kingsbury is apprized.

Two-thirds of the expense of the buildings for the contemplated establishment in the South East part of the Choctaw Nation in the vicinity of the six towns agreeably to your estimates will also be allowed, to be paid conformably to the regulations; and an additional allowance will be made for tuition after the establishment is in actual operation, and that fact with the number of pupils belonging to it shall be certified to this Department as required by the regulations.

Nothing has as yet been advanced on account of the buildings for the school among the Cherokees on the Arkansaw [*sic*]; but $1,000 will be immediately remitted to Col. [David] Brearl[e]y, the Agent for the [Western] Cherokees, to be paid to the Superintendent of that establishment. The Agent will be directed to forward his certificate of the completion of the buildings as soon after they are completed as practicable, with an estimate of the actual cost of them, upon the receipt of which, a further allowance if necessary will be made for them, and remitted to the Superintendent thro' the Agent. An allowance for tuition will be made as in other cases, upon the Department being certified of the necessary facts, conformably to the regulations.

The allowance to the Schools at Elliot[t] & Brainerd has been increased for this year to $1,200 each, and a remittance for the two first quarters of the year has been made to the Cherokee and Choctaw Agents, [Return J. Meigs and Ward, respectively,] to be paid to the respective superintendents of these schools.

P.S. A copy of the regulations referred to in this letter is enclosed.

FC in DNA, 72, E:294–295 (M-15:5). NOTE: A PC of the letter dated 7/18/1818 appears in *The Papers of John C. Calhoun*, 2:397.

From [1st Lt.] E[DMUND] KIRBY, A[ide-]D[e-]Camp

Philadelphia, June 29th 1822

I am directed by Maj[or] General [Jacob] Brown to report to you his arrival in this city. Though still an invalid, his health has considerably improved since leaving Brownville [N.Y.].

He has consulted Doctors [Philip Syng] Physick & [Nathaniel] Chapman of this city, who are decidedly of opinion that his restoration will be perfect. To effect this will occupy some ["little" *canceled*] time—yet, placing as he does implicit confidence in the professional skill of these gentlemen, he deems it his duty to abide by their advice—which is, for him to remain stationary for the present, avoiding as much as possible company & exercise. What delay in his journey to Washington may take place cannot be foreseen—but the moment any thing definitive is known on the subject he will advise you.

ALS in DNA, 1, K-4 (M-221:96); FC in DLC, Jacob Brown Papers, Letterbooks, 2:215.

From [Brig. Gen. Simon] Bernard and [Maj.] Joseph G. Totten, [*ca.* 6/30]. They submit "Some Notes on a [proposed] School of Application" [such as that which was actually established at Fort Monroe about 1824]. DS in DNA, 222, F-70.

From Lewis Cass, Detroit, 6/30. He encloses "the Official Bond executed by Henry R. Schoolcraft, Indian Agent at the Sault St. Mary." LS in DNA, 1, C-32 (M-221:95); FC in DNA, 76 (M-1:5, p. 23).

By [former Capt. and former Military Storekeeper] James Gibson, [*ca.* 6/30?]. This undated document, [possibly belonging to the year 1821,] is a statement of clothing issued to Maj. [Stephen H.] Long for a Western expedition. DU in DNA, 47.

"Proportional Times employed on the several branches of Instruction at the United States Military Academy," [*ca.* 6/30]. This document, [probably submitted to Calhoun as a part of the report of the Board of Visitors of the Academy,] tabulates the hours and ratios of time that are allotted to each subject in the curriculum. DU in DNA, 222, F-67.

From William Wirt, [*ca.* 6/30]. "I have found the [pension] papers of Colo[nel Richard M.] Johnson and would thank you to send me the act of Congress on which the question arises—the act I think of 15 May 1820." LS in DNA, 1, W-11 (M-221:96).

JULY 1822

"I AM SORRY TO SEE, THAT YOU ARE SO DEEPLY DISGUSTED with political life," Calhoun wrote on the 1st to one of his brothers-in-law. "It is the duty of those, who have the means and capacity, to serve the country; and we ought to resist that tendency to disgust which is so apt to be excited by the many proofs, which we daily see, of the want of candour and integrity." Letters of the 15th and the 22nd reflected the fears that had been caused by Denmark Vesey's slave insurrection in South Carolina. Samuel Houston wrote bitterly on the 5th that a Nashville bank would cash a United States check only at a discount of 27%. Jacob Brown was recovering markedly on the 14th from the stroke that had postponed his arrival in Washington to serve as the commanding General of the Army. Amid the summer's heat there was a threatened renewal of a duel.

To William Clark, St. Louis, 7/1. Calhoun acknowledges Clark's letter of [5]/14 [ALS in DNA, 1, C-6 (M-221:95)] informing Calhoun of Capt. [John] Ruland's dismissal as Sub-Agent at St. Louis. Calhoun will send Ruland's salary to Clark as soon as he learns the amount. Maj. [Benjamin] O'Fallon has informed Calhoun by letter of his belief that Gen. [William H.] Ashley and Maj. [Andrew] Henry have received a license to trade, trap, and hunt on the Upper Missouri. O'Fallon is worried about the bad effect trapping and hunting in Indian territory will have upon Indian relations. Calhoun encloses a copy of a talk of the Shawnee Chiefs, to which Clark will reply as he thinks proper. He directs Clark to end the reportedly "vexatious and predatory conduct of the Indians on the frontiers of Missouri." An amount equal to the property stolen by members of tribes receiving annuities will be deducted from the annuity unless the property is returned satisfactorily. The Chiefs must also be informed that continued outrages by Indians will cause the annuities to "be altogether withheld." In cases where the tribe receives no annuity, "a restoration of the property will be expected in every case; if that be impracticable the surrender of the offenders, to be punished agreeably to our laws; if one of these conditions be not complied with, the whole tribe will be held responsible and made to feel the just indignation of the Government. In all cases, if the offenders can be arrested within the limits of Missouri, it ought to be done and exemplary punishment inflicted upon them." FC in DNA, 72, E:295–296 (M-15:5); CCEx in DNA, RG 233, 18A-D1, vol. 257; PEx's in Senate Document No. 1 and House Document No. 2, 18th Cong., 1st Sess.; PEx in *American State Papers*: *Indian Affairs*, 2:428–429.

To JAMES E[DWARD] COLHOUN, [Philadelphia?]

Washington, 1st July 1822

I have delayed answering your letter of the 13th June, [*not found*,] expecting to hear from my brother [William?], whether I might draw on my factors and to what amount. On Saturday I received a letter from him from Augusta of the 20th June, [*not found*,] in which he informs me, that he has declined making sales of our cotton [*one word canceled*] as the price was very low from the pressure on the money market. He says, however, that he would sell in a few weeks, till which time, I must decline drawing on my own account. I wrote to my factors to know whether they were in funds on your account, and whether I might ["draw for" *interlined*] $900 for you. As soon as I hear from them I will draw, if they are in funds, and remit you the money. I thought the precaution necessary in order to avoid the effects of a protested draft with the expense and damage charged on it. In the mean time you had better write to Speed or your agent to send down cotton and have it sold, if they have not already done "it" *interlined*], so as to avoid delay. I will direct the factors to inform me of any funds deposited on your account.

I do not intend to go north as you suppose, but will probably take a short excursion to the mountains. I have nothing new from the South. The small grain crop has failed, but the cotton and corn are very promising. ["We" *canceled and* "My family" *interlined*] are all well, and desire their love to you. Yours sincerely, J.C. Calhoun.

ALS in ScCleA.

TO JOHN E[WING] COLHOUN, Pendleton, S.C.

Washington, 1st July 1822

Dear John, I have received your favour of the 17th June [*not found*] and am very happy to hear that you have so flattering a prospect as to your corn and cotton crop. The information from every part of the South concur[s] in representing the prospect of those two leading articles to be very promising, so that, if the price is low, there is ["at least" *interlined*] ground to hope, that the product will be abundant.

I am sorry to see, that you are so deeply disgusted with political life. It is the duty of those, who have the means and capacity, to serve the country; and we ought to resist that tendency to disgust which is so apt to be excited by the many ["evidences" *canceled*] proofs, which we daily see, of the want of candour and integrity. You would be wrong to decline at present. The next legislature will be very important. It will take all the good sense and moderation, which can be brought forward, to prevent the State [of S.C.] from being distracted. Under these circumstances, I hope, you will not hesitate to continue in public ["life" *interlined*].

I am glad to see a disposition to leave [William] Smith [Senator from S.C.] at home. I do not think that he fairly represents the State. He is narrow minded and I believe wedded to the Georgia politicians. If reëlected, I doubt not that he will come out openly, which would do much mischief. [Robert Y.] Hayne is the man that ought to be elected. He has talents & eloquence and will honor the State. It would be imprudent ["however" *interlined*] to utter these sentiments as coming from me.

You do not mention whom you intend to send to Congress. I hope it will be [Warren R.] Davis. [John] Wilson [Representative from S.C.] is a good honest man, but certainly very little calculated for the post which he occupies.

I send you the prospectus of a new paper to be edited here. It will be conducted with zeal and abilities, and I hope will be well supported. We have need of such a paper. You must subscribe for it and get as many others as you can conveniently. By putting it [that is, the prospectus] into the hand of Joseph Gresham, or some other active person at the court house, I dare say many ["other" *canceled*] subscribers might be obtained. Should any be obtained care must be taken to have the list returned.

We are all well. I sent your letter to Andrew [Pickens Calhoun,] who is at school in the country. He has grown much and is very stought [*sic*] & hearty. I have not heard from James [Edward Colhoun,] who is at Philadelphia, for some time. He rarely writes. He speaks of going to sea in the fall, and I believe expects promotion about that time.

Floride [Colhoun Calhoun] & her mother [Floride Bonneau Colhoun] desire their love to you and Mrs. [Martha Maria Davis] Colhoun. Let me hear from you often. Sincerely, yours &c., J.C. Calhoun.

ALS in ScCleA; PC in Jameson, ed., *Correspondence*, pp. 204–205. NOTE: The newspaper about which Calhoun wrote was the proposed Washington, D.C., *Republican*, and its editor was to be Thomas L. McKenney. This letter was franked "War Dept., J.C. Calhoun" and was postmarked in Washington on 7/2.

From [Richard Graham], St. Louis, 7/1. He has forwarded to [William Lee] his accounts for the first half of 1822; he explains various details in his handling of funds, particularly an item of $750 that he paid to [Benjamin] O'Fallon out of an Osage annuity. He encloses an estimate of the costs of moving the Kickapoos. Draft in MoSHi, Richard Graham Papers.

To [Maj. Gen. JACOB] BROWN, [Philadelphia]

Washington, 2nd July 1822

I was very happy to learn by a letter from Lt. [Edmund] Kirby of the 29th June that you had arrived in Philadelphia with your health sensibly improved, and that so eminent physicians as D[octo]rs [Philip Syng] Physick & [Nathaniel] Chapman, confidently anticipate your entire restoration.

I entirely approve of your arrangement to remain in Philadelphia, in order to avail yourself of the distinguished medical skill of the place. In fact I wish you to be fully assured that such is the interest I take in your restoration both as a friend and a distinguished and useful public servant, that I shall at all times be much gratified in giving any indulgence or aid, which may be in my power, to so desirable an object.

I shall be happy to hear frequently from you & trust that each succeeding communication will add to the cheering prospect of your complete restoration; and I hope that you will by no means think of leaving Philadelphia till you have had the full benefit of its medical skill.

CC in DLC, Jacob Brown Papers, Letterbooks, 2:215.

From Thomas Forsyth, St. Louis, 7/2. As requested by an agent of William Morrison of Kaskaskia, Forsyth has presented two accounts to the Sauk and Fox Indians for cattle belonging to Morrison—cattle alleged to have been killed by some of those Indians in 1816, when Morrison was a contractor for the Army. The Sauk and Fox Chiefs have admitted that the charge is partially correct, but they know that the Winnebagoes killed many more of the animals. Forsyth believes that the Winnebagoes were responsible for the killing of some cattle while those Indians were camping on Sauk and Fox land. In addition, the Winnebagoes robbed the Sauks and the Foxes of their corn. ALS in DNA, 1, F-18 (M-221:95); 3 FC's in WHi, Draper Collection, Thomas Forsyth Papers, 4:140–141, 6:10–11, and 7:95 (published microfilm, series T, vols. 1–9).

To Duff Green, St. Charles, Mo.

Dep[art]m[en]t of War, 2 July 1822

Your letter of the 9th of December last [*not found*] relative to the vexatious and predatory conduct of the Indians on the frontier of Missouri, was duly received.

Your letter would have received an earlier answer, but as it was believed that an active Sub-Agent for Indian Affairs stationed at some suitable [*one word canceled*] point on the frontiers of Missouri would afford the most effectual protection to our Citizens against the insults and depredations of the Indians, it was intended to appoint one, and confer the appointment on you, after the passage of the appropriation for the Indian Department, if it would admit of it; the answer was therefore delayed for that event, which did not take place until the day before the adjournment of Congress. And it has been further delayed by the great press of business on the Department since, growing out of the acts of Congress which required its immediate attention.

The appropriation which was made for the Indian Department provides for those Sub-Agents only that are now in service, consequently the intended appointment could not be made. I have however instructed Gov[erno]r [William] Clark, who has been recently appointed Superintendent of Indian Affairs at St. Louis, under an act of Congress passed at the late Session, to take such measures as he may judge necessary to restrain the Indians and bring about a more friendly understanding between them and our Citizens.

FC in DNA, 72, E:296–297 (M-15:5).

From John H. Hall, Harpers Ferry, 7/2. He describes alternative sizes and forms of powder flasks that can be manufactured for use with his model of rifles; and he estimates the cost of each such flask. ALS in DNA, 35, In-7-5.

From William Wirt

Office of the Attorney General, July 2, 1822

On the subject of Colo[nel Richard M.] Johnson's pension I cannot see how it can be withdrawn from the sweeping provision of the 2d section of the Act of 15 May 1820; which directs that all pensions, in virtue of any law of the U.S. shall be considered to commence at the time of completing the testimony. This provision is so direct and so universal that the ground on which your doubts are founded is not discerned and I should be glad to confer with you on the subject before you act on this opinion.

FC in DNA, 113, B:81 (T-412:2); CC in DNA, 114; CC in DNA, 111.

To [James Monroe]

War Dep[artmen]t, 3d July 1822

Since you left the City I have received the annual report of the Academick Staff, which is highly honorable to the ["state of the" *canceled*] Military Academy. It may with confidence be affirmed that the institution never was in as high condition and is nearly as perfect as it can be rendered under the existing ["acts" *canceled*] legal provisions.

The enclosed list exhibits the names of those, who have not been found qualified to proceed with their respective classes, and have been recommended by the Staff to be discharged, in conformity with the 54th parag[rap]h of the 78th Art[icle] of the Gen[era]l regulations, which provides that, if "any Cadet of either class at that examination (June) shall be found deficient in the proper studies of the preceding year, he shall be ["reduced" *interlined*] to class next following; or, if in the opinion of the Aca[demic]k staff, he shall be evidently incapable of proceeding with that class, his case shall be recommended to the Sec[re]t[ar]y of War to the end, that he may be discharged."

If you have come to a final decision on the Military nominations, I would ["be" *interlined*] happy to be favoured with it, as some inconvenience to the service is experienced, and much anxiety is felt in the Army to know the decision.

Mr. [William] Wirt returned a few days since; and agreeably to your direction, I again consulted him on the subject of the Dauphin Island contract. He is of the opinion, that on the original bond, which was for the fulfil[l]ment of the contract, that [*sic*] the question of damages may be let in, but on a subsequent bond, with new securities, which stipulated that the advances should be accounted for, no question as to damages could be made. I have finally determine[d] to pass over the whole of the papers to the Second Comptroller of the Treasury, [Richard Cutts,] with a statement, that the work has been discontinued for the want of an appropriation, in order that he may take such legal measures as he may judge necessary to secure the publick interest. Should you, however, think that no proceedings ought to be instituted for the present, it will not be too late to give the necessary orders for some time, as the account must be audited and transmitted to the 5th Auditor [Stephen Pleasonton] before any legal step can be taken against the contractor [Richard Harris]. I, however, am inclined to think, that it would be better to permit it to take the usual course. Should the executive interfere, Congress might throw the blame on it, tho' it has through out been of the opinion, that a different course ought to have been adopted, from that which has been ultimately embraced by that branch of the Governm[en]t. If on the contrary, there should be no interference, whatever loss may accrue ["either" *canceled and then interlined*] to the gov[ernmen]t or ["oppression" *canceled*] the contractor would be referred to its true source. Yours truely [*sic*], J.C. Calhoun.

ALS in PHi; FC in DNA, 6, 2:59–60 (M-127:2).

From B[ENJAMIN] SILLIMAN

Yale College, July 3d 1822

My avocations since my return from West Point have prevented my stating at an earlier period the few ideas that occurred to me forespecting [*sic*] the improvement of the Institution.

I would remark in the first place, that I was exceedingly pleased with my visit there, and found the Institution as I expected to find it, an honour to the nation. The apparatus in the department of Chemistry appears not to be adequate to the full course of instruction expected in such an Institution. There are a considerable number of good Instruments but many more are needed to make the demonstrations complete. The same remark is applicable to chemical substances and preparations.

I conceive also a good cabinet of minerals including not only mineralogy but geology to be a very important desideratum and the sooner such a collection is commenced the better. A great many minerals may be collected in this country.

The philosophical apparatus also, although containing a number of very good instruments, requires enlargement in several departments.

A hospital appears also to be a desireable [*sic*] appendage of the Institution as it is scarcely possible for the sick Cadets to be well accommodated without.

A Modeller or person to prepare machines and facilitate improvements would be very useful as an auxiliary to the Engineer department.

In an institution where there is so little to corrupt the morals of the youth it appears proper to remove every source of seduction, and therefore the purchase by the government, of a contiguous private territory & establishment whose influence is said to be unhappy could not fail to be useful. I have great pleasure in stating that the appearance of the Cadets, as far as I had opportunity to hear them examined, was such as to do honour to them & their teachers & governors.

ALS in DNA, 222, F-65. NOTE: This letter was relayed to Calhoun as an enclosure in one dated 7/16 from T[homas] Cadwalader. ALS with En in DNA, 222, F-65.

From Cornelius Beard and other Chiefs and warriors of the First Christian Party of the Oneida nation, Oneida, [N.Y.,] 7/4.

They request that the Oneida annuity for this year be divided equally between the two parties of the Oneida nation; this policy would enable the First Christian Party's members to pay for the land that they intend to purchase near Green Bay. LS (with their marks) in DNA, 1, O-13 (M-221:96).

From Jere[miah] W. Bronaugh, Indian Office, Georgetown, [D.C.,] 7/5. At the "request of the late Superintendent of Indian Trade, [Thomas L. McKenney,]" Bronaugh returns to Calhoun all of the James Monroe medals that have not been distributed and accounts for those that were. ALS in DNA, 1, B-13 (M-221:95); CC in DNA, 77 (M-271:4, frame 33).

From Thomas Forsyth, St. Louis, 7/5. He encloses a statement showing that he will need $432 for expenses during the third quarter of 1822. ALS with ADS in DNA, 1, F-24 (M-221:95); FC's in WHi, Draper Collection, Thomas Forsyth Papers, 4:141 and 6:11 (published microfilm, series T, vols. 1–9).

From Samuel Houston, [in Tenn.,] 7/5. He has received a draft on a Nashville bank for $170.09, completing payment of his claim for pay as a 1st Lt. in the 1st Infantry Regiment during 1817–1818. The bank has offered to cash the draft, but only at a discount of 27%. Angered, Houston returns the draft to Calhoun. "I can see no reason for the conduct pursued by you . . . unless it is that I am the same man against whom you conceived so strong a prejudice in 1818 . . . . Sir I could have forgotten the unprovoked injuries inflicted upon me if you were not disposed to continue them. But your reiteration shall not be disregarded . . . . Your personal bad treatment, your official injustice . . . was to oblige a Senator [John Williams of Tenn.]—secure his interest and crush a Sub-Agent . . . . All this will I remember as a man." Quoted in Marquis James, *The Raven: a Biography of Sam Houston* (Indianapolis: The Bobbs-Merrill Company, c. 1929), pp. 50–51, from a manuscript then owned (as pp. 439 and 469 indicate) by Houston Williams of Houston, Texas.

From JOHN CLARK

Milledgeville, 6th July 1822

Congress having appropriated fifty thousand dollars for the citizens of Georgia, pursuant to the 4th article of the late Treaty with the Creek Indians, and that sum being the one-fifth of the whole amount of claims contemplated by the Treaty, it is presumed that claims to the amount of two hundred and fifty thousand dollars have been allowed. I have been waiting with some anxiety under a hope of hearing, from you, the President[']s [James Monroe's] final decision upon the subject. I am the more solicitious [*sic*] from the circumstance of being frequently called on by the claimants to know if their accounts have passed, as well as when and where, they are to get their money. By the Treaty it is to be paid to the State, and I am desirous that the persons entitled to it, should receive it with as little delay as possible. I therefore request that you will be so good as to lay this before the President, and let me have, as soon as practicable, an answer by which I may be able to give the information required by the individuals interested.

LS in DNA, 1, C-24 (M-221:95); FC in G-Ar, Governors' Letterbooks, 1821–1829:50.

From Lewis Cass, Detroit, 7/9. "I have the honour to suggest the propriety of requesting the Secretary of the Treasury [William H. Crawford] to instruct the Register & Receiver of the Land Office here to withhold from the Publick Sales which will take place in September next the site which may be selected for the military post about to be established at Saginaw, together with such land as may be necessary for the military defences & for the requisite supplies of the Garrison. Unless this measure be adopted, much difficulty will be experienced. Persons enough will be found to claim as a right the purchase of any land not reserved from market by the competent authority." LS in DNA, 1, C-36 (M-221:95); FC in DNA, 76 (M-1:5, p. 42); CC in DNA, 87, Mich. Military Reservations, box 107; CC in DNA, 282, Mich. (Saginaw). (Compare Calhoun's letter to Josiah Meigs dated 7/29.)

To J[ohn] A[lfred] Cuthbert, Eatonton, Ga., 7/9. Freeman Walker has declined to serve as a commissioner to negotiate a treaty for the [Eastern] Cherokees' lands in Ga.; Walker has been asked to relay to [John] Floyd the commission's papers. FC in DNA, 72, E:298 (M-15:5).

To John Floyd, [later a Representative from Ga.,] 7/9. Freeman Walker has declined to serve as a commissioner to negotiate a treaty with the [Eastern] Cherokees. He has been instructed to send to Floyd all of the papers concerning the proposed treaty. The sum of $34,989.57, which is available "to defray the expenses of the treaty," will be deposited in the Bank of Darien. FC in DNA, 72, E:297–298 (M-15:5). (A marginal notation indicates that this letter was sent to Walker for forwarding to Floyd, whose "immediate" address was unknown to the War Department.)

To F[reeman] Walker, Augusta, 7/9. His letter of 6/29 [LS in DNA, 1, W-12 (M-221:96)] has been received, and his reasons for declining to serve as a commissioner to seek a treaty for the [Eastern] Cherokees' lands in Ga. are understood. Calhoun asks Walker to forward to [John] Floyd all of "the papers which were transmitted to you relative to the treaty." FC in DNA, 72, E:297 (M-15:5).

From HAR[MA]N[U]S BLEECKER, [former Representative from N.Y.]

Alban[y, *ca.* July 10,] 1822

Mr. Robert R. Henry of St. Marys in Georgia is an applicant for the office of Collector of that port. He removed from this City to St. Marys four or five years ago. I have known him a long time. He was a merchant here & was always considered a fair & honest man. His connexions in this State are highly respectable. He can & probably will obtain from the most respectable persons here very favorable testimonials of his character.

FC in NcD, Robert R. Henry Papers.

To EDMUND P. GAINES, Louisville, Ky.

Department of War, July 10th 1822

I have received your letter of the 23d ultimo [ALS with En in DNA, 1, G-4 (M-221:95), the En being an ALS of 6/23 to Gaines from Capt. Daniel E. Burch, who requested extra compensation for his services as Acting Assistant Adjutant General of the Western Department,] relative to the allowance of extra compensation to an officer whom you may detail to perform the duties of Assistant Adjutant General for the Western Department under your command, and have laid the subject before the President, [James Monroe,] who directs me to say that he concurs with you in opinion and views respecting the importance and necessity of the measure, but considering the provisions of the law of the 2d of March 1821, he does not feel himself authorised to make the allowance of extra pay to any Officer whom you may detail for that duty. Considering too the temper of Congress on the subject of the Army, such an allowance would be construed not only as an illegal application of money, but as a means of evading the provisions of the law which abolishes that essential portion of the General Staff, and would be used by those opposed to the present Military Establishment to effect a further inefficiency in the organization of the Staff, if not to obtain a greater reduction of the Army generally.

I have also received your letters of the 24th [*PC herein*] and 26th [*Abs herein*] Ultimo, the former containing a speech to the Chiefs of the Osages and Cherokees, which it is hoped may have a salutary tendency upon their minds and feelings; the latter enclosing a letter from Mr. [Henry W.] Conway respecting the Quapaw Lands in the Arkansaw [*sic*] Territory. I have no doubt from the location and quality of those lands, but that they would be a desirable and valuable acquisition, still nothing can be done in the business without an appropriation by Congress.

FC in DNA, 3, 11:415 (M-6:11).

To V[IRGIL] MAXCY, "Private"

Washington, 11th July 1822

The return of the President [James Monroe] from the country, which made it necessary to give my attention immediately to such business as had been postponed on account of his absence, has prevented as prompt an answer to yours of the 5th Inst[ant], as I had intended.

I would furnish you the annual reports of Mr. [William H.] C[rawfor]d ["with pleasure" *canceled and* "as you request," *interlined*] but I have no other copies except those, which are bound up in large volumes of the publick documents. I would, however suppose the dates alone would be sufficient to satisfy Mr. [Roger B.] T[aney]. Mr. C[rawfor]d came into the treasury in 1817 and the first report he ever made ["was" *canceled*] in that Dept. was ["in the" *canceled*] the one which I referred in the Sketch. Its fal[l]acious views were the real cause for repealing the system of Int[erna]l taxation, which Mr. [Alexander James] Dallas had spared no pains to retain. He has never in one of his reports made a manly fair stand, and has so managed his Department as to endanger the whole system of the adm[inistratio]n.

If Mr. T[aney] has any doubt on this or any other particular point, by suggesting it, I will cause such a statement of facts, as will put him right. You might I think refer him with advantage to the Register as to the management of the Treasury.

I doubt not that you make a very judicious selection under the advice of your Physician of Long Branch, as a summering place. Its fine air and bathing I trust will completely restore Mrs. Maxcy's health. I would be glad [if] we could join you but am inclined to think, that if I can get off, traveling towards the mountains would be more serviceable to us, as we require exercise more than anything else.

Judge [Samuel L.] Southard resides in ["New Jersey" *canceled and* "Trenton" *interlined*]. I think you are acquainted with him. If you are not I would be glad to make you acquainted.

The letter of Mr. Key to Mrs. Maxcy which you mention that you had enclosed, was not in your letter. I suppose you had forgot to enclose it.

I fear from what I learn that the affair between [George] McDuffie & [William] Cumming will revive. The former will be out in a day or two with a counter statement founded on the certificates of his surgeon & physician. If C[umming] wrote the piece, which appeared in the Augusta paper, they will of course be at issue in their statements, from which I fear but one result can follow.

We are all well & Mrs. [Floride Colhoun] Calhoun & her mother [Floride Bonneau Colhoun] join their best regards to yourself and the ladies. Yours truly, J.C. Calhoun.

ALS in DLC, Galloway-Maxcy-Markoe Papers, vol. 32.

From John Floyd, St. Marys, Ga., 7/12. He accepts his appointment to be a commissioner to negotiate a treaty with the [Eastern] Cherokees. ALS in DNA, 1, F-26 (M-221:95).

From John Hays, Indian Agent, Fort Wayne, [Ind.,] 7/12. He encloses the answer by Mitujea, one of the principal Potawatomi

Chiefs, to a speech of [James Monroe], presented to the Potawatomies by Hays, concerning visits made by the Indians to British settlements. ALS with En in DNA, 1, H-44 (M-221:95).

From Ro[bert] C[arter] Nicholas, Chickasaw Agency, 7/12. He acknowledges Calhoun's letter of 6/3 and its enclosed copies of the law [regulating trade with the Indians that was enacted by Congress during its recent session]. "All that part of the law that has reference to white men's trading with the Indians I consider as a dead letter in this Nation; the Agent of the Chickasaws being expressly forbidden by the 7th Article of the treaty of [9/20/]1816 . . . [to grant licenses to trade with the Indians]. This treaty I consider paramount to the law, & will not act under the law unless specially directed by you. I understand the said 7th Article to bind & refer to the Agent alone. You I apprehend would be fully authorized to give licenses to trade in this Nation. The monopoly [held by the Chickasaw Chiefs], of which I have so often written, & its consequences which I have so earnestly endeavored to deprecate, is daily developing its baleful effects. Should it be found out by investigation & reflection that any body has authority to grant licenses to trade in this Nation, I urge that it may be done immediately, & thereby produce the needful competition—a thing indispensably necessary to secure the common people of any country from imposition." Nicholas complains that a draft for $2,300 on the U.S. Branch Bank at Louisville, some 400 miles away, will entail much difficulty and expense in cashing it. Having received only two letters during 1822 from Calhoun, Nicholas waits "with solicitude to hear from you." Nicholas requests that the annuity be "drawn for in Kentucky," because a trip there will be safer, cheaper, and healthier than one to the low country. Under the impression that he has already given bond for $20,000, Nicholas points out that to get an additional $10,000 in security would entail a trip to Ky., where "the fatality of the times" has rendered many of his friends unable to assist him in securing the bond. "You state that it will be imperatively demanded of me to close & forward my accounts up to the 1st Sept[embe]r. I now beg leave to say that, as a matter of course, they will be in blank unless I am furnished with the funds. I have not forwarded my accounts for the 1st & 2d Quarters for want of funds. Several days after the expiration of the 2d Quarter, I received the Treasurer's [Thomas Tudor Tucker's] draft on a Bank distant 400 Miles, & no possibility of realizing the money short of that distance. There are demands hanging over this Agency that will swallow up every cent of this remittance leaving me destitute of a cent to pay the current expences up to September. From the fact of your taking no notice of the monies due the people at or near the Chickasaw Bluffs amounting to $1,892," Nicholas requests information. He also reproves Calhoun for not having acted upon other claims. "Your letter speaks in [such] positive terms of the amount allotted for this Agency, that I see no necessity of transmitting an Estimate, but from long habit of obeying orders, I do myself the honor of enclosing an Estimate for the two last quarters of the present year. You seem to contemplate my being supported & enforcing the late law by the Military force of the U.S., as far as I am informed the nearest garrison is New Orleans or Pensacola. The Chickasaw Chiefs has [*sic*] not yet got ready to go with me to ascertain the fact whether any white people are over the [Indian boundary] line." Calhoun failed in his letter to enclose a blank bond, and Nicholas requests that it be sent to him. "I state a fact that seems to me, in the woods, to be singular. Your letter notifying me of the remittance of $2,300, bears date June 3d, that of the Aud[ito]r communicating the same fact June 8th & that of the Treasurer June 13th, & an additional fact that the letter of the Aud[ito]r is addressed to my brother Carey Nicholas." Nicholas deplores the inhuman treatment accorded to some of the 200 to 300 slaves held by the Indians. "I am told, unless their passions are roused, they are the best master in the world, when this happens they have no check or control." The Indians consider slaves to be property to be treated by the owner as he pleases. Nicholas has heard that three Negroes were killed prior to his arrival at the Agency and that one was killed recently by Col. George Colbert, "one of the wealthiest, most intelligent & influential men in the nation," whose "example will go far to fix the principle & seal it for a length of time." Nicholas hopes that Calhoun can "interfere as your better judgement may dictate. I have upon previous occasions informed you that a letter from you would be much respected & attended to. I hope most Earnestly that something may be said or done." ALS with En in DNA, 1, N-12 (M-221:96).

From JOHN O'FALLON, Adjutant General [of the Militia of Mo.]

Adjutant Gen[era]l[']s Office, St. Louis, 12 July 1822

By direction of the Govornor [*sic*; Alexander McNair], I have the honor to enclose two General orders in relation to the organization of the militia of this State which is now in progression, having been retarded by the lameness of former militia laws devolving that duty upon the Major Generals, who were not elected untill some time the last spring.

I anticipate much difficulty in obtaining correct returns of the strength ["and" *canceled*] condition &c. of the militia in consequence of the thin and scattered population of many sections of the State, the ignorance of the Officers, and the great irregularity of our mails to and from the interior of the State.

ALS with 2 Ens in DNA, 16, 1822, O-5 (M-567:4, frames 618–623).

From Ferris Pell, Washington, 7/12. He submits a statement of "General Principles" that should be followed "as a basis of settlement for injuries, done to State munitions." The principles will not "indemnify the State of New York, but will approach nearer to justice than any before proposed." "Under them the difficulty hitherto presented by the State claims, will come into consideration as peculiarities, and will not bind future cases except upon a recurrence of the same circumstances." LS with En in DNA, 1, P-18 (M-221:96).

From [1st Lt.] JOHN A. DIX

Philadelphia, 14th July 1822

Major General [Jacob] Brown had the pleasure to receive your kind favor of the 2nd Inst[ant] and feels with deep sensibility the friendly interest you take in his restoration. He intended to have acknowledged the reception of your communication with his own hand, but he has been so reduced under the new course adopted by D[octo]rs [Philip Syng] Physick & [Nathaniel] Chapman, that he has felt incapable of the exertion of writing.

His strength is very much diminished by the powerful medicines, that have been applied, and by a rigid confinement to low diet; but his head has become more calm, & his pulse is restored to the standard of health without the aid of the lancet. With these results, the fruit of a course not yet completed, and with the confident assurances of the eminent men, whose counsels he receives, neither the Gen[era]l nor his friends can doubt that time and prudence will perfect his cure. How long his physicians may think necessary to detain him here he cannot foresee. He has understood with great pleasure that you will soon pass through Philadelphia, as it will afford him an opportunity of communicating with you personally.

In closing this communication he bids me express to you how highly he values your friendship and to assure you of the deep interest, which he feels in your prosperity.

ALS in DNA, 1, D-44 (M-221:95); FC in DLC, Jacob Brown Papers, Letterbooks, 2:216.

From Thomas Bennett, [Governor of S.C.,] Charleston, 7/15. "The State of alarm which has for some time pervaded this community consequent on the discovery of insurrectionary movements [under the leadership of Denmark Vesey, a free Negro who had plotted mass murders of whites for 7/4], has elicited anxious inquiry and awakened the most extroardinary [*sic*] vigilance." Bennett presents a detailed enumeration of the troops available to maintain order and laments that only five men are available at Fort Johnson to guard "a few implements of *War*" and 140 barrels of partially damaged gunpowder. "The peculiar character of a Large proportion of our population, and the evidence of a timper [*sic*] hostile to the peace and welfare of society which has so recently been manifested, will continue for some time to excite vigilance, and elicit anxiety." The lack of troops in the city increases the alarm, and Bennett asks Calhoun to remedy the situation. ALS in DNA, 1, B-30 (M-221:95). (Calhoun replied on 7/22.)

To [John Quincy Adams], 7/17. Calhoun encloses copies of letters [dated 7/17 from himself] to [William P. DuVal] and to [Duncan Lamont] Clinch "relative to a distribution of the publick buildings at Pensacola between the Civil and Military Departments." LU with Ens in DNA, 101 (M-179:54); FC in DNA, 3, 11:416 (M-6:11).

From [Lewis Cass]

Detroit, July 17, 1822

I have the honour to enclose herewith the extract of a letter from Mr. [John] Hays, Indian Agent at Fort Wayne, respecting the mills contracted by Mr. [Benjamin] Leavell to be built for the Miamies at Massassineway, agre[e]ably to the treaty of Saint Mary's. It will be seen by the report of Mr. Hays that these mills are now completed agre[e]ably to the contract and that Mr. Leavell is entitled to his pay.

Mr. Hays has drawn two drafts in favour of Mr. Leavell, one for $1,000 and the other for $2,600, which, added to the sum of $2,000 heretofore received by him, makes the amount stipulated by his contract to be paid to him.

Not knowing the situation of the funds of the department and having no specifick instructions to draw for the amount due to Mr. Leavell, I have stated these facts upon the drafts and have directed that they be not negociated until they have been submitted for your approbation. Under these circumstances, the drafts are merely evidence of the liquidation of the claim, and [if] you will be pleased to direct their payment, the transaction will be closed. But should you decide otherwise, Mr. Leavell must wait until his demand can be paid.

It is scarcely necessary to add that it is impossible from the funds allotted to this Superintendency to meet their payments.

FC in DNA, 76 (M-1:5, p. 56).

From Lewis Cass

Detroit, July 17th 1822

I have the honor to acknowledge the receipt of your letter of the 25th ult[im]o.

It is not probable that any circumstances can occur which will render it necessary again to establish a military post at Fort Wayne. A compact settlement will doubtless soon be formed in its vicinity, adequate to all the purposes of self-defence.

But the publick buildings there are considerable and, from their situation and form, would sell for a very small sum. They are occupied by the Officers of the Indian Department and, at present, by Mr. [Isaac] McCoy's school. It would be necessary, should these buildings be sold, to erect or to rent others. I would therefore recommend that the site of the Fort, together with thirty acres of land adjoining and which shall not interfere with the building lots or with the proper location of a village, be reserved from the publick sale. It is proper there should be some land for the encampment of the Indians, without rendering it necessary for them to trespass upon private property.

This arrangement cannot injure the publick interest. A village will be established where the settlers now reside, and the land in its vicinity will increase rapidly in value. The quantity reserved can be sold at any time hereafter, when a dense population will render it improper for the Indians to resort there and when, of course, there will be no further reason for its occupation on the part of the United States.

LS in DNA, 77 (M-271:4, frames 40–42); FC in DNA, 76 (M-1:5, pp. 56–57); CC in DNA, 87, Ind. Military Reservations, box 97; CC in DNA, 282, Mich. (Fort Wayne).

To Col. D[uncan] L[amont] Clinch, Pensacola, 7/17. Because Calhoun has no inventory of the buildings there that were received from the Spanish authorities, he cannot direct a division of them between civil and military officers; consequently, he has asked Governor [William P. DuVal] to confer with Clinch about the matter. Clinch will surrender to [DuVal] "such buildings as are not clearly military as he may think necessary for the Civil Department. If it should be necessary to rent additional buildings in consequence of this order, the Quarter Master will receive the necessary directions from the proper Department." FC in DNA, 3, 11:416 (M-6:11); CC in DNA, 101 (M-179:54); CC in DNA, 43, Pensacola; CC in DNA, 2, A-1825 (M-222:23); PC in Carter, ed., *Territorial Papers*, 22:488–499.

To William P. [DuVal], Governor of Fla. Territory, Pensacola, 7/17. Calhoun acknowledges DuVal's letter of 6/21 [LS in DNA, 1, D-11 (M-221:95), with the last paragraph in DuVal's script and with a lengthy AEI by T(rueman) Cross concerning public buildings in Pensacola; PC in Carter, ed., *Territorial Papers*, 22:471–473]. Calhoun encloses a copy of his letter [of 7/17] to Col. [Duncan Lamont] Clinch, whom Calhoun has instructed concerning allotments of the Pensacola buildings. Calhoun responds to DuVal's request for instructions as to his "powers and duties as Superintendent of Indian Affairs": (1) Calhoun refers DuVal to the letter written to him by Calhoun on 6/11; (2) Calhoun tells DuVal that the War Department intends to have the Indians settle near the Apalachicola in the northern part of East Fla.; (3) an enclosed copy of a letter of 5/28 to Capt. [George N.] Morris will answer DuVal's question about issues of rations; and (4) copies of instructions to DuVal's predecessor, [Andrew Jackson,] will be mailed as soon as they can be prepared. FC in DNA, 3, 11:415–416 (M-6:11); CCEx in DNA, 101 (M-179:54); CCEx in DNA, 43, Pensacola; PC in Carter, ed., *Territorial Papers*, 22:488. The promised copies of letters to Jackson were enclosed by Calhoun to DuVal on 7/23. FC in DNA, 72, E:303 (M-15:5).

To Edmund P. Gaines, Louisville

Department of War, July 17th 1822

I have received your letter of the 28th ultimo with its enclosures [ALS with Ens in DNA, 1, G-9 (M-221:95), the Ens being a CC of 6/8 from Surgeon Benjamin F. Harney to Col. Talbot Chambers, a CC of 6/12 from Chambers to Gaines, and an LS of 6/28 from Gaines to Chambers] proposing to substitute windows for the loup [*sic*] holes in the exterior wall of the Baton Rouge Barracks. It is considered inexpedient to make the alteration. Those barracks were built on the plans designed by the Engineer, and are believed to combine as much comfort, with a capacity for defense as a proper regard for the latter would allow. It is hoped, that rigid attention to the police of the quarters, and timely medical precaution and assistance will be found to obviate the inconvenience apprehended from the want of a freer ventilation.

FC in DNA, 3, 11:417 (M-6:11); CC in DNA, 43, Baton Rouge.

From Lewis Cass

Detroit, July 18th 1822

I have the honour to acknowledge the receipt of your letter of the 26th ult[im]o.

I was under a misapprehension respecting the provisions of the act for closing the Factory Establishment of the United States. I supposed the goods on hand, after satisfying certain specified objects, were to be distributed gratuitously to the Indians. By an arrangement made last fall Mr. [Thomas L.] McKenney instructed the Factors at Green Bay and Chicago to transmit to this place such goods in their stores as were not suited for the establishment then contemplated at St. Peters. In conformity with this arrangement goods to the invoice amount of twelve thousand dollars have been forwarded from those Factories to this place. A few of them have been distributed under the impression I have stated, but nearly all of them remain on hand. These goods were selected, I presume, as the worst and most unsaleable in the Factories, and certainly they well deserve this character. They are not fit for distribution, and three-fourths of them in amount are common blankets. I shall therefore merely retain them in possession, subject to the orders of the person who may be sent to close the Factory Establishment. For I cannot consent that they shall be charged to the Department and issued to the Indians on account of the annual appropriation for presents.

The best plan that can be adopted with respect to them is to sell them at public auction.

LS in DNA, 1, C-71 (M-221:95); FC in DNA, 76 (M-1:5, pp. 59–60); PC in Carter, ed., *Territorial Papers*, 11:253–254.

To Richard Graham, St. Louis, 7/18. Calhoun acknowledges his letter of 5/29. "Your letters in which you mentioned the payment of a part of the Osage annuity by Mr. [George C.] Sibley, created an impression that the payment had been made in goods from the Factory and the annuities charged with the amount; and consequently the money for the annuity this year was remitted to you, in order that you might settle with the Factory and pay the balance, if any, to the Osages. As, however, the remittance appears to be unnecessary, you will apply the amount to the current expenses of your Agency, of which [former] Governor [William] Clark is apprized." Some claims sent by Graham have been referred to Clark for a report. LS in MoSHi, Richard Graham Papers; FC in DNA, 72, E:298–299 (M-15:5).

To John Hays, Indian Agent, Fort Wayne

Dep[art]m[en]t of War, 18 July 1822

Your letter of the 15th May [ALS in DNA, 1, H-21 (M-221:95)] reporting the number of Weas & Kickapoos remaining on the

Wabash and requesting instructions relative to their annuities, was duly received.

By the late treaties with the Wea & Kickapoo Tribes it is expressly stipulated that their annuities shall be paid at Kaskaskias [*sic*]; consequently I cannot direct any part to be paid at Fort Wayne without the consent of those tribes. Besides, it appears from your report that there is but a small part of these tribes remaining on the Wabash, and even were there no treaty stipulations upon the subject, as a general rule, it is proper that the annuities should be paid at or near the residence of the body of the respective tribes, where detached parties belonging to them should attend to receive their portion, if they should wish it; as in most cases it would be very difficult to divide the annuities so as to give satisfaction to all. It is very desirable that all the Indians belonging to the Wea & Kickapoo tribes respectively, should reside together & form one people, and you will endeavor at every suitable opportunity to induce those on the Wabash to join their brethren beyond the Mississippi, which would put an end to the difficulty in relation to their annuity.

FC in DNA, 72, E:295 (M-15:5); CC in DNA, 76 (M-1:13, pp. 92–99).

From J[ohn] A[lfred] Cuthbert, Putnam County, [Ga.,] 7/19. He declines to serve as a commissioner [to negotiate a treaty for the Eastern Cherokees' lands in Ga.] and recommends Gen. Daniel "Nunan [or Newnan]" as being "better qualified to maintain a salutary influence over Indians." ALS in DNA, 1, C-65 (M-221:95).

To John Floyd, Savannah, 7/19. Calhoun sends to Floyd a copy of a letter of 6/5 from [Return J.] Meigs containing "proposals [by Turk & McCarty] to furnish rations at the treaty" that is to be held soon with the [Eastern] Cherokees "and other views in relation to the treaty which it may be important should be known to the Commissioners." FC in DNA, 72, E:299 (M-15:5).

To William Lee, 7/19. Calhoun directs Lee to prepare "as early as practicable" certain statements of the "accounts of the disbursing Officers of the Pay, Ordnance, Medical, and Indian Departments" and to report "what progress has been made in the preparation of the information called for by the Resolutions of the House of Representatives" dated 1/8, 2/15, 3/9, and 5/7. FC in DNA, 3, 11:417 (M-6:11). (Lee replied on 7/26.)

To R[eturn] J. Meigs, Calhoun, Tenn., 7/19. Calhoun answers Meigs's letter of 5/25 by authorizing him to supply tools to the [Eastern] Cherokees at Hightown only if the tools can be bought from the funds allotted for the current expenses of his Agency. Calhoun answers Meigs's letter of 6/5 [LS in DNA, 1, M-30 (M-221:96)] by assuring him that the proposal by [James] Turk & McCarty to supply rations during the coming treaty negotiations is being forwarded to the treaty commissioners, who are empowered to buy the rations. LS in DNA, 75 (M-208:9); FC in DNA, 72, E:299–300 (M-15:5).

To B[ENJAMIN] SILLIMAN, New Haven, [Conn.]

Department of War, July 19th 1822

I had the pleasure to receive your report as a visitor to the Military Academy thro General [Thomas] Cadwallader [*sic*; Cadwalader]. I am obliged to you for the pains you have taken in the examination of this institution, and shall avail myself of your suggestions for improving the condition of certain branches of the sciences taught at West Point. It affords me much satisfaction that the establishment generally has met your approbation.

FC in DNA, 13, 1:144 (M-91:1).

Contract of M[arine] T. Wickham, 7/19. With Calhoun's consent, George Bomford and Wickham, a Philadelphian, agree that Wickham is to deliver within two and a half years, beginning on 1/1/[1823], 5,000 stands of arms—muskets, bayonets, and ramrods—for $12 each; but the price can be adjusted downward if costs decline. FC in DNA, 331, 1:155–160.

From WILLIAM WIRT

Office of the Attorney General, July 19, 1822

I now understand that the doubt with regard to Colo[nel] Richard M. Johnson's claim of pension relates to the time of its commencement. The 2d section of the Act of 15 May 1820 declares "that the right any person now has or may hereafter acquire to receive a pension in virtue of any law of the U.S. be considered to commence *at the time of completing his testimony* pursuant to the act hereby revived and continued in force." The affidavits which prove Colo[nel] Johnson's title to a pension were taken before Jeb Stevenson, a Justice of the peace of Scotts [*sic*; Scott] County, in the State of Kentucky, on the 1st day of August 1816—but it was not until the 5 Nov. 1820 that the certificate of the Clerk of Scott County, that Jeb Stevenson was a magistrate, was obtained & annexed to those affidavits. The question is when was the evidence complete—on the 1 August 1816 when the affidavits were taken; or on the 5 Nov. 1820 when the certificate of the Clerk was added?

In the short personal conference which we had on this subject, the predisposition which it is almost impossible to avoid feeling in favour of so meritorious a claim, led me to take the earliest date, in favour of the claimant—but on reflection, I must recede from this opinion and abide by those old and plain rules with which we are all familiar, and from which it is always unsafe to depart. The word *complete* is a strong one—nothing is *complete* while anything of form or of substance is wanting. Testimony is never *complete* until it comes in such a shape that it's [*sic*] *admissibility is unquestionable.* If it be inadmissible in the form in which it is presented; if it want anything of authentication to render it admissible, it *is incomplete*—and never is it *complete until every objection to its reception is removed.*

Would Colo[nel] Johnson's evidence have been received at the [War] Department without the certificate of the Clerk that Jeb Stevenson was a justice of the peace of Scott County? If it would not, it is not complete—and such, I understand, is the fact according to the rules of evidence in these cases adopted by the Department. I also understand that according to these rules, this certificate of the Clerk *removed all objection to* the testimony—hence, I am constrained to conclude that the testimony was not *complete until this certificate was procured*—to wit 5 Nov. 1820—My regret, however, is diminished by the consideration that there can be no moral doubt that Congress would, on application, carry back the pension to the time of the wounds which will be better for the petitioner than to assume the earliest date which these laws could, by any possible construction, permit.

FC in DNA, 113, B:83–84 (T-412:2); CC in DNA, RG 46, 17A-F4; PC in *American State Papers: Claims,* 1:893; PC in Senate Document No. 43, 17th Cong., 2nd Sess.

From Alexander Hamilton, St. Augustine, 7/20. He introduces Moses Elias Levy, "a gentleman of much respectability . . . from whom you will receive the most satisfactory account of this Territory." Levy is "justly entitled to much consideration," especially because of "his useful exertions in introducing [into Fla.] the fruits and plants of the W[est] Indies, at a very considerable expense." ALS in DNA, 1, L-31 (M-221:96).

To James Turk, Maryville, Tenn., 7/20. Calhoun answers Turk's solicitation of 7/2 [ALS in DNA, 1, T-12 (M-221:96)] of a contract to supply rations during Indian treaty negotiations by stating that no treaty will be held soon with the Creeks and by referring Turk to the commissioners for the negotiations with the [Eastern] Cherokees, because those officials can contract for rations. FC in DNA, 72, E:301 (M-15:5).

To J[ames] E[dward] Colhoun, [Philadelphia?]

War Dep[artmen]t, 21st July 1822

Dear James, Your letter with its enclosure of the 5th Inst[ant; *not found*] has been received. Having no genius myself for mechanicks, I placed your sketch of the self moving [or "mowing"] machine in the hands of ["the" *canceled*] Capt. [William] Wade of the Ordnance [bureau of the War Department], and I herewith return you his observations on it.

I have heard from my factors. They inform me that, tho they have no orders as to your cotton, that [*sic*] I may draw for the amount which you mentioned in your former letter, but as the B[ranch] Bank [of the United States] here declines ["negotiating bills" *interlined*] drawn on Georgia except payable at the Branch at Savannah and as that Branch will not receive Georgia paper, the factors say, that it will be almost impossible to pay at the Savannah Branch, without giving a high premium for U.S. paper specie. To avoid this, I have written to know if they could pay in Charleston. If you can you had better wait their answer, but if you ["are" *canceled*] prefer it, I can draw at once, and take the hazard as to the amount of premium.

We are all well. The duel between [George] McDuffie and [William] Cum[m]ing has revived. The latter challenged and the former promptly accepted. It will be fought, I presume immediately. It is to be deeply deplored that so valuable a life as McDuffie's should be thus pursued. With affection, J.C. Calhoun.

ALS in ScCleA.

From J[OEL] R. POINSETT, [Representative from S.C.]

Charleston[,] 21 July 1822

When the Commissioners [that is, the Board of Engineers] were here to examine the defences of Charleston they privately expressed an opinion, that the Lines of our city were useless. I have been long impressed with the beleif [*sic*], that they are worse than useless and am anxious to have them removed. They retard the progress of our city; the ditches contain a great deal of stagnant water and render that part of the Neck unhealthy. By removing the Lines and cutting a canal from river to river a distance of three-quarters' [*sic*] of a mile, the land would be well drained, a water communication established for the upper part of our City, and a better line of defence formed than the present one.

I shall address the Legislature on the subject and would be glad to have the opinion of the Commissioners whether the Lines across the neck of Land above the City of Charleston are necessary for the defence of the City.

ALS in DNA, 30, 334. NOTE: Calhoun replied on 7/29 and on 8/9.

To Maj. JAMES BANKHEAD "or Officer Com[man]d[in]g at Charleston[,] S.C."

Department of War, July 22d 1822

Upon the representation of the Governor of South Carolina [Thomas Bennett, dated 7/15,] requiring an additional military force to be stationed at Charleston, the enclosed order [dated 7/22] has been given to Lieu[tenan]t Colonel [Abram] Eustis for the removal of one Company from St. Augustine to that place, with orders, on its arrival to report to you.

You will consult with the Governor of South Carolina upon the distribution to be made of the Company on its arrival and co-operate with him upon such measures as may be deemed adviseable [*sic*] in quelling the disturbances at Charleston [that arose from the Denmark Vesey conspiracy].

FC in DNA, 3, 11:418 (M-6:11).

To Thomas Bennett, Governor of S.C.

Department of War, July 22d 1822

I have received your letter of the 15th instant in relation to the state of the Garrisons in Charleston Harbour, and have ordered without delay a reinforcement of one Company from St. Augustine, which I hope will be sufficient to remove the uneasiness in the publick mind on account of the inadequacy of the Garrisons. I would add another Company, but the Military Establishment is so reduced in proportion to the number of posts which we are compelled to occupy that it cannot be done with propriety. At no point on the Atlantic Coast is there more than one Company, except at Boston, New York [City], Norfolk, Charleston and St. Augustine, at the latter of which there are three, and at all the others but two each. To reduce the Garrison by withdrawing a Company from Boston, New York [City], or Norfolk, would I fear produce much excitement, and make an impression which ought if possible to be avoided. The recruiting depots, are, however[,] now opened and the recruiting will be pushed with activity in the principal Northern Cities, and I have given orders to fill the Companies at Charleston Harbour so soon as the recruits are made. I have also ordered the Officer Commanding in the Harbor [Maj. James Bankhead] to consult with you, and to co-operate to the extent of his means in such measures as may be thought advisable to be adopted. I enclose you a copy of the orders [dated 7/22] to him.

I hope these measures will be satisfactory. I wish you to be assured that if more ample means existed, it would have afforded me much pleasure to have added to those which have been adopted.

FC in DNA, 3, 11:417–418 (M-6:11).

To Lt. Col. A[bram] Eustis "or Officer Comm[an]d[in]g at St. Augustine"

Department of War, July 22d 1822

Orders, Lieutenant Colonel Eustis, or Officer Commanding at St. Augustine will cause to be embarked immediately from that place one effective Company of Artillery under the Command of a suitable subaltern Officer to proceed to Charleston South Carolina, and report for orders to Major [James] Bankhead or Officer Commanding.

The Company on its arrival at Charleston, will be turned over to the command of Captain [Matthew M.] Payne who is now at that place.

The Quarter Master's Department will provide the necessary transportation in the above case.

FC in DNA, 3, 11:418 (M-6:11); CC in DNA, 186, 1822–1823:83–84. NOTE: Eustis replied on 8/6.

To [Thomas S. Jesup, 7/22]. A Company of Artillery is to be transported immediately from St. Augustine to Charleston, S.C., for new duty in the latter place. FC in DNA, 49, 1:108; CC in DNA, 48, 185.

To Jasper Parrish, Canandaigua, [N.Y.,] 7/22. Calhoun answers Parrish's letter of 6/30 [LS in DNA, 1, P-29 (M-221:96)] by giving assurance that Parrish's salary and the requested annuity payments are being remitted. Calhoun inquires whether Parrish thinks it practicable and fair to divide the Oneidas' annuity between the First Christian Party and the others, as has been requested by a Chief of the First Christian Party. FC in DNA, 72, E:302 (M-15:5).

To W[INFIELD] SCOTT, New York [City]

Department of War, July 22d 1822

You will perceive by the enclosed order [of 7/22 to Abram Eustis] that one Company of Artillery at St. Augustine, has been directed to proceed to Charleston. This order was given direct from this Department, upon the urgency of the case, and upon the requisition [of 7/15] of the Governor of South Carolina [Thomas Bennett] for an additional military force.

FC in DNA, 3, 11:419 (M-6:11).

From W[illiam] Ward, Choctaw Agency, 7/22. He has received Calhoun's letter of 6/12, but the remittances of $3,150 and of $10,985 have not yet arrived. Ward has obtained money from a bank to pay the claims for Indian improvements and will do so on 7/25, believing that the annuity can be paid in 8/1822 in cash. He encloses his bond [*not found*] and an estimate of expenses during the third quarter of 1822. ALS with En in DNA, 77 (M-271:4, frames 236–238). (Calhoun replied on 8/26.)

Capt. John R. Bell, St. Augustine, to [Christopher] Vandeventer, 7/23. Bell introduces Charles Vignoles, "Topographical Engineer," who is "preparing a map and descriptive account of Florida for publication." He has "contributed liberally" to the Topographical office, and Bell recommends that Vignoles be granted "access" to it. ALS in DNA, 228.

To John Clark, [Governor of Ga.,] Milledgeville

Dep[art]m[en]t of War, 23d July 1822

Your letter of the 11th inst[ant (LS in DNA, 1, C-33 [M-221:95]; FC in G-Ar, Governors' Letterbooks, 1821–1829:51)] has been received.

"The President [James Monroe] is now absent—as soon as I have an opportunity, your letter, agreeably to your request, will be laid before him for his decision in relation to keeping open the Commission for adjusting the claims against the Creek Nation under the late treaty as proposed by you."

I avail myself of this opportunity of transmitting to you the opinion of the Attorney General [William Wirt] on the question of Interest referred to in my letter of the 27th Ult[im]o[—an opinion] which I received this morning.

Major [Freeman] Walker who was appointed one of the Commissioners to hold the contemplated treaty with the [Eastern] Cherokees has declined acting; and the President does not deem it necessary to appoint another in his place; so that the treaty will be held by Gen[era]l [John] Floyd & Mr. [John Alfred] Cuthbert.

FC in DNA, 72, E:303 (M-15:5).

From Lt. Col. G[eorge] Bomford, 7/24. As directed by Calhoun, Bomford submits this report about the expense of repairing small arms. From "the various data collected in this Office, together with the results of investigating the cost of repairs, and injuries to Small Arms in the hands of the regular Troops, it appears that a sum, not exceeding One Dollar per Annum, may be estimated as the annual cost of each. But, as the same care and system cannot be expected to have been used, on the part of the Militia, it is deemed but just and equitable that a greater allowance, than the foregoing, should be credited, for such injuries and repairs, to the States who furnished Arms to Militia whilst in services of the U[nited] States. The sum of One Dollar and twenty cents, per annum for each musket, or Ten Cents per month, is accordingly recommended to be allowed." ALS in DNA, 1, O-18 (M-221:96); FC in DNA, 32, 3:244–245.

To John Crowell, Indian Agent, Creek Agency, Ga.

Dep[art]m[en]t of War, July 24, 1822

Your letter of the 6th instant [*not found*] enclosing your accounts has been received.

Your accounts appear to be regular and have [been] passed to the 2nd Auditor [William Lee] for settlement. The expense incurred on the Agency house will be allowed.

It will not be necessary for you to transmit copies of the licenses issued by you to Indian traders, or of the bonds taken of them, with the abstract required of you by the 1st section of the act to regulate trade and intercourse with the Indian tribes passed at the late session of Congress. The licenses will of course be recorded and the bonds filed in your office, to be acted upon in the event of a failure on the part of any of the traders to comply with the conditions of the latter.

A mistake was made in stating that the sum of $2,375 was remitted to you. The sum actually remitted was $2,550.

FC in DNA, 72, E:303 (M-15:5).

From F[reeman] Walker, Augusta, 7/24. He would have placed the papers concerning the proposed treaty with the [Eastern] Cherokees in the hands of [John] Floyd promptly, as Calhoun requested in his letter to Walker of 7/9, but for the fact that Floyd has asked Walker to retain them "a little longer." Walker believes that Floyd will not accept his appointment to serve as a commissioner. ALS in DNA, 1, W-38 (M-221:96).

From the Rev. Andrew Yates, Corresponding Secretary, N[orthern] Missionary Society of New York, Schenectady, 7/25. Some missionaries were sent last autumn by the Society to Saginaw but have not been able to reach that point. Instead, they are at Fort Gratiot, [Mich. Territory,] have gained the confidence of the Indians there, and would like to remain there. Yates asks that the missionaries be allowed to occupy and to care for the public property there, which would help the Society and would also provide the best possible care of the land and buildings. ALS in DNA, 30, 336; CC in DNA, 76 (M-1:11, pp. 110–114).

From [William Lee], 7/26. As Calhoun directed on 7/19, [Lee] submits statements that show, in part, the financial information about accounts of officers in the Paymaster, Ordnance, Indian, and Medical Departments, pursuant to House resolutions of 1/8, 2/13, 3/9, and 5/7. Five Clerks have been assigned the duty of preparing two statements that are not yet completed. FC in DNA, 51, 8:20–21.

To Benjamin O'Fallon, Council Bluffs, 7/27. Calhoun has received O'Fallon's letter of 7/1 [ALS in DNA, 1, O-17 (M-221:96)]. O'Fallon's expense account for the Indian deputation's trip [of the past winter and spring] to Washington has been relayed to [William Lee]. O'Fallon's estimates for the last two quarters of 1822 have been sent to William Clark, through whom such requests for funds should be submitted. Calhoun is glad to know of the safe return of the Indians to their villages, hopes that they will convey a favorable impression of the U.S. government to their tribes, and expresses regret that O'Fallon's health was affected adversely by the fatigues of the journey and hope that he is now well again. FC in DNA, 72, E:305 (M-15:5).

To Thomas Forsyth, Indian Agent, Fort Armstrong, [Ill.]

Dep[art]m[en]t of War, 26 July 1822

Your letters of the 24th [ALS in DNA, 1, F-8 (M-221:95); FC's in WHi, Draper Collection, Thomas Forsyth Papers, 6:1–6 and 7:89–93 (published microfilm, series T, vols. 1–9)] & 28th [*Abs herein*] ultimo have been received.

I am happy to learn that Col. [James] Johnson has been put

in peaceable possession of his [lead-mine] lease, and hope he will meet with no interruption in his operations from the neighboring tribes of Indians.

The deficiency which you state there was in the annuity of the Sacks and Foxes for 1821 will not be their loss as the Trading Department by which the Merchandize for the annuity was forwarded is responsible for the amount.

The Win[n]ebagoes should apply to the Indian Agent to whose Agency they belong for such articles as they are in need of and which it is his duty to supply but whenever any of them visit your Agency you will continue to treat them civilly, and furnish them with any small presents they may want, to a moderate amount, which will be allowed provided it is approved by Gen[era]l [William] Clark, Superintendent of Indian Affairs at St. Louis.

I transmit to you an extract from Gen[era]l Clark's report relative to the lands of the Sacks & Foxes, which contain all the information in this Department on the subject. It appears by this report that the Sacks & Foxes have a very questionable title to the lands below the River des Moines, whatever they may have to those above it. Measures however would be adopted for quieting the claim of these Indians and that of the Ioways agreeably to the suggestion of General Clark, but as it would incur some expense, for which there is no appropriation it cannot be done without the sanction of Congress. Whenever this is obtained, there will be no delay in acting upon it.

FC in DNA, 72, E:304 (M-15:5).

To John Scott, [Representative from Mo.]

Department of War, July 27th 1822

Your letter of the 2d inst[ant; *not found*] recommending Mr. Thomas McKnight for a lease of a part of the Lead Mine Lands up the Missouri has been received.

I am happy to perceive gentlemen of his character and standing coming forward with a disposition to work those mines, which I have no doubt will prove productive of advantage to the United States, and highly beneficial to the Western Country. Previous to Mr. McKnight[']s obtaining a lease it will be necessary for him to make a selection of the site he intends to locate; and to transmit a survey thereof with the other corresponding papers as pointed out in the notice of the 15th June last from the Ordnance Office. Major [John] Anderson of the Topographical Engineers and [2nd] Lieu[tenan]t C[lark] Burdine of the Ordnance have been directed to have such surveys made, and will repair to that part of the Country for that purpose.

FC in DNA, 3, 11:420 (M-6:11).

To Richard Cutts, 7/29. Pursuant to a statute of 7/16/1798, Calhoun encloses the bond of Henry R. Schoolcraft, Indian Agent at Sault Ste. Marie, dated 6/29/1822. LS in DNA, 63, 1822:159; FC in DNA, 3, 11:420 (M-6:11). Cutts acknowledged the bond and Calhoun's letter on 7/30. LS in DNA, 1, C-44 (M-221:95).

To Josiah Meigs, 7/29. Calhoun requests that one square mile of land surrounding the fort at Saginaw shall be reserved for that military post, as was suggested by Lewis Cass in his letter to Calhoun of 7/9. LS with En in DNA, 87, Mich. Military Reservations, box 107; FC in DNA, 3, 11:421 (M-6:11); CC in DNA, 282, Mich. (Saginaw). Meigs replied on 7/30 that this reservation would be made and also that, pursuant to Calhoun's request of 6/15 [*not found*], one section of land would be reserved for Fort Smith in Ark. Territory. LS in DNA, 1, M-36 (M-221:96); FC in DNA, 82, 11:472 (M-25:11); PC in Carter, ed., *Territorial Papers*, 11:255.

To J[oel] R. Poinsett, Charleston, S.C.

Department of War, July 29, 1822

I have had the honor to receive today your communication of the 21st Ins[tan]t upon the subject of the present lines for the defence of Charleston, & expressing a wish to have the opinion of the Board of Engineers whether the lines across the neck of land above the City are necessary for its defence. The B[oar]d of Engineers have not yet reported their plans for the defence of the Coasts of So[uth] Carolina & Georgia, and it will be necessary to refer the subject of your communication to them. A Copy of your letter will be immediately dispatched to the Board, who are in New York [City,] with direction to make a report upon the subject thereof as soon as practicable, which will be transmitted to you without delay.

FC in DNA, 21, 1:309.

From Thomas Bennett, [Governor of S.C.,] Charleston, 7/30. Calhoun's letter and enclosures of 7/22 have been received, and his "prompt attention given to my request [for additional troops to maintain order in Charleston], has proved highly gratifying to the Citizens of this place, and the arrival of the forces will no doubt contribute greatly, to allay the public excitement" [occasioned by the abortive Denmark Vesey insurrection]. Bennett proposes the removal of gunpowder from Fort Johnson to Castle Pinckney following construction of a magazine at the latter post. "Fort Johnson can no longer be regarded as a Military Post; except the officers' Quarters and the Barracks, no appearance of its having once been so exists. [Bvt.] Major Bird [*sic*; John A. Burd] with a laudable zeal to give effect to our health Laws, has constructed . . . a small platform, on which he has placed a couple of pieces of Ordnance. Understanding that another site has been selected by the Engineer Department, on which it is proposed to construct permanent and extensive works, I should be much gratified to learn at what time it is probable these will be commenced, and whether in time to anticipate a communication to the Legislature of this State, having for its object the adoption of efficient measures to enforce the Quarantine Regulations." Bennett is confident that S.C. would like to receive Fort Johnson, should it be abandoned by the U.S., as "a site for a Lazaretto and Ware Houses." Bennett regrets that Calhoun was unable to increase "the force on this station to three Companies; such an augmentation at this particular juncture, would tend not only to tranquillize the public mind, but produce the happiest effects upon that class of persons who have caused the present excitement [that is, Negroes]. I am very confident however that the causes of disappointment are very remote from any sentiment connected with your inclination to serve this community." LS in DNA, 1, B-55 (M-221:95). (Calhoun replied on 8/13.)

From James Eakin, Chief Clerk, Second Auditor's Office, 7/30. In compliance with Calhoun's instructions of 7/19 [to William Lee], Eakin encloses statements showing "the situation of the Accounts of the Disbursing Officers" of the Pay, Ordnance, and Indian offices. "In the Medical & Hospital Department there is no Disbursing Officer, all accounts of that description being rendered direct to, and paid by requisition at this Office." Eakin also reports the progress made toward compliance with the resolutions of the House of Representatives of 1/8, 3/9, and 5/7. The information required by the resolution of 2/13 "must be furnished from the late Office of [the] Superintendent of Indian Trade." LS with 2 Ens in DNA, 1, L-14 (M-221:96).

To Lewis Cass, Detroit, 7/31. Calhoun sends to Cass a copy of the letter from [Andrew Yates dated 7/25]. If Fort Gratiot is vacant, "there is no objection to Mr. Hudson occupying it, and taking charge of the property, provided there result therefrom no expense to the public." Because "you are on the spot, it is thought adviseable [*sic*] to refer the application to you for your decision thereon, which you will be pleased to communicate to Mr. Hudson." FC in DNA, 21, 1:309–310.

From W[illiam] W[irt, *ca.* 7/31]. "'The day on which the evidence was closed' is not sufficiently explicit. The question is, when the evidence is closed: is it at the date of the deposition, or the date of the certificate as to the justiceship or authority of the person before whom the depositions were taken? To settle the practice, reference must be made to cases in which the date of the depositions and the date of these certificates is different; if, in such cases, the long-standing practice has been to take the date of the depositions in contradistinction to the date of the certificates, I should have no hesitation in yielding my former opinion to such settled practice. If the Secretary of War will make a new statement, with the additional fact of this standing practice, I will give a formal answer to this effect, if it is desired; and, as my former opinion is recorded, it would be better that this course should be taken." PEx in *American State Papers*: *Claims*, 1:894.

To [the Rev.] Andrew Yates, [Corresponding] Secretary, Northern Missionary Society of New York, Schenectady, 7/31. Calhoun answers Yates's letter of 7/25. "A person was last fall appointed to take charge of" Fort Gratiot "and is probably yet in the occupation of it." Lewis Cass has been instructed, "if the fort should be vacant, to allow Mr. Hudson to take possession of the premises, and the care of the property, provided no expense shall ensue therefrom to the public." FC in DNA, 21, 1:310.

AUGUST 1822

WAS PRESIDENT JAMES MONROE ERRING IN HIS APPOINTMENTS by ignoring "the distinction between friends and foes"? So Calhoun complained on the 20th to Ninian Edwards. Was there an increasing tendency among Army officers "to cavil about orders and instructions"? So Alexander Macomb wrote on the 24th. Were William H. Crawford, Martin Van Buren, Spencer Roane and others attempting to win votes in 1824 for Crawford as a strict constructionist? Would the "unauthorized proceedings among the Indians" in Florida of Horatio S. Dexter be halted? Who was entitled to be the commanding officer of the Military Academy when Sylvanus Thayer was away? Which commissioners, if any, appointed to negotiate a treaty for cession of the Eastern Cherokees' lands in Georgia would serve? Calhoun pondered these and other problems.

To JOHN HAYS, Indian Agent, Fort Wayne, Ind.

Department of War, August 1st 1822

Your letter dated at Cahokia 22d April [ALS in DNA, 1, H-35 (M-221:95)] has come to hand but a few days ago.

No representation against you on account of your absence from the Agency has been made to this Department. The Department entertains a favorable opinion of you as a public officer, and should any representation be made against you, you will be notified thereof before it is acted upon. The cause you have assigned for your absence [that is, illness] is a very sufficent one.

FC in DNA, 72, E:308 (M-15:5).

From Joseph Lovell, [M.D., Surgeon General,] 8/1. He encloses his quarterly report through 3/31 about the Army's sick. "The troops have been so remarkably healthy during the present quarter & the complaints so slight that no particular remark is required." Drugs have been delivered to the posts in generally good condition. Most of the Surgeons and Assistant Surgeons are on duty. Lovell summarizes his financial transactions for the quarter that ended on 6/30. LS with En in DNA, 1, S-53 (M-221:96); FC with En in DNA, 243, 1:138–139.

To Gad Peck, Cincinnati, 8/1. Calhoun answers Peck's request of 7/20 (ALS in DNA, 30, 359) for a reëxamination of his son, Robert T. Peck, who failed to qualify last June for admission into the Military Academy, by saying that [Sylvanus Thayer] will choose which candidates will be given a new examination next month. FC in DNA, 13, 1:146 (M-91:1).

To William Ward, Choctaw Agency, 8/1. Calhoun acknowledges Ward's letter of 7/8 [ALS in DNA, 1, W-34 (M-221:96)] and encloses the blank bond then reported not to have been enclosed in Calhoun's letter of 6/3. Ward's accounts to the date on which the bond shall be executed should be transmitted promptly for settlement. The Indian who seeks compensation for lost horses must look to State laws for indemnity or for the punishment of the thief. FC in DNA, 72, E:307–308 (M-15:5).

To William Lee

Department of War, August 2d 1822

I have received your report of the 30th Ultimo, [*not found,*] and regret to see that so many of the accounts, particularly in the Indian Department, have remained so long in the Office unsettled. The prompt settlement of accounts is essential to the proper administration of the Department, and all should be settled within the quarter in which they are rendered, which with the force of your Office may it is believed be done without difficulty. You will accordingly in future take the most prompt measures for the settlement of the accounts, and in no event permit any to remain unsettled beyond the period mentioned.

FC in DNA, 3, 11:421–422 (M-6:11).

To V[irgil] Maxcy, Annapolis, Md.

Washington, 2d Aug[us]t [1822]

I received this morning your favour of the 30th Inst[ant; *sic; not found*] with the enclosed letters, which as requested, I herewith return.

Gen[era]l H's indicates the experienced and profound observer, and if he can induce the leading men who have heretofore acted with him, to pursue his course, it will result not only in having a decided influence on the event, but in producing a new and better political organization than now exists.

I am glad to see [Hezekiah] Niles so sound. It will be better for him to select his own time and occasion to bring out his views; and in the mean time, the piece might appear in the paper which you suggest.

I send you the additional prospectus. The paper will appear on the 7th, and I have furnished the editor with some reflections which he is to bring out in his own language in a series of Nos. commencing with his first paper. It will at once display the talents, character and the course of the paper. I have seen his first No.; and think it able and well executed. It is important that it should be republished and favourably noticed as far as possible. You will be able to do something that way at various points both ["by yourself &" *interlined*] through your friends.

[William H.] C[rawfor]d's game begins to develope [*sic*] itself more and more. He intends to rest on a single ground, that of being a thorough partisan. The two points of operations will be the Nat[ional] Advocate of New York [City] and the Richmond Enquirer; the first under the direction of Mr. [Martin] Van Buren, and the latter Judge [Spencer] Roan[e]. However discordant the material, a coöperation will be attempted between the Constitutionists of Virginia and the political managers of New York. I do not think it can succeed, but this is the only hope to Mr. C[rawfor]d and his partisans. I have watched the process closely, and know the whole arrangement; and I have greatly mistaken the American people, if it cannot be completely foiled.

I have not been able to do any thing as to [Samuel] Barnes, as I have not seen Maj[o]r [George] Peter. If an opportunity should present, it shall not be omitted.

The affair between [George] McDuffie and [William] Cumming has revived. The latter challenged and the former promptly accepted. It is not known when the meeting will take place, but will doubtless as soon as McD[uffie]'s ["health" *canceled*] wound will permit.

It is so healthy in Washington that it is quite uncertain when we will leave here. When you write direct to this place, and put your letter under two covers the inner marked private, which if I should not be here will be forwarded.

I am glad to hear that Mrs. Maxcy had experienced benefit from the bathing and trust her health will be fully restored.

It may not be amiss to state to you that [Charles Jared] Ingersoll is said to be friendly to Mr. C[rawfor]d. Yours truly, J.C. Calhoun.

[P.S.] I am glad to hear that [Stevenson] Archer is roused. There is no better man, and none that ought to be more influential. Col. [George E.] Mitchel[l] if right will have great weight, and he, [Ezekiel Forman?] Chambers [later a Senator from Md.] and ["Mitchel" *canceled and* "Archer" *interlined*] ought to out weigh [Edward] Lloyd on the Eastern Shore. Col. [Thomas L.] Mc-Kenney is an intimate friend of Chambers, they having been at school together. J.C.C.

ALS in DLC, Galloway-Maxcy-Markoe Papers, vol. 32. NOTE: The Gen. "H." mentioned by Calhoun at the beginning of his second paragraph was probably Robert Goodloe Harper.

From Capt. George N. Morris, Fort St. Marks, 8/2. In reply to Calhoun's letter of 5/28, Morris states that the "average quantity of rations issued to Indians has probably exceeded the am[oun]t authorized by you." In addition to the rations already issued, Morris plans to issue a small amount to the Indians on the coast, because crops there are harvested much later than those inland. LS in DNA, 1, M-56 (M-221:96).

From Jasper Parrish, Canandaigua, [N.Y.,] 8/2. In reply to Calhoun's letter of 7/22, Parrish states "that it has been the invariable practice of this Agency, both by myself and my predecessors, since the treaty of 1794 to divide the annuity among the Six Nations of Indians according to their respective numbers." "As the Oneidas are divided into two parties and have requested a division of their annuity, I see no impropriety in making such a division, as it is in merchandize, which I will attend to with pleasure to please them, altho they reside at the same place." LS in DNA, 1, P-71 (M-221:96).

[2nd] Lt. L[ouis] A. Rigail, Cantonment Sand Hills near Augusta, Ga., to [George] Bomford, 8/4. Rigail has been informed that [at Adam Carruth's former armory] in Greenville, [S.C.,] there are about 1,400 gun stocks, of which approximately 700 or 800 are suitable for the "stocking of guns" at the Augusta Ar-

senal. Rigail asks for permission to purchase these stocks, especially in view of the difficulty experienced in obtaining seasoned wood in Augusta. ALS in DNA, 31, 1822, R. (Compare the letter from Rigail to Bomford dated 8/11.)

From George Bomford, 8/5. He encloses an offer by John Mason [of D.C.] on 8/2 to exchange eight of the 24-pound, heavy guns of the new pattern for as many guns of the same caliber and of the old pattern. A large number of the old-pattern cannons is at Greenleafs Point, [D.C.]. "The weight of cannon of the old pattern, is about the same, as of the new; an exchange of the one, for the other, will be advantageous to the U[nited] States; I therefore recommend that the proposition be accepted." (An AEI by Calhoun states: "Approved.") LS with En in DNA, 31, 1822, War Department; FC in DNA, 331, 1:160–161, with notations indicating that 10 guns were actually exchanged.

To Ferris Pell, O'Neale's [Hotel], Washington

Dep[art]m[en]t of War, 5th August, 1822

I have received your letter of the 25th July [LS in DNA, 1, P-39 (M-221:96)], and find on the perusal of it that you have misapprehended my observations in our last conversation.

The difficulty in adjusting the claim of the State of New York for the repair of arms is not in establishing a rule by which the claim ought to be adjusted, but in substantiating the claim under it. The United States are unquestionably liable for all damages done to the arms which were issued by the State to Militia in their service, or which were called out by the State and afterwards recognized by the U[nited] States, and consequently the State ought to be paid for all the sums which she has expended in repairing such damages. This principle was established, I think, in our first conference on this subject. The difficulty which has occurred arose in auditing the account. The vouchers offered to support the claim of the State under the rule are not deemed sufficient. To remove the difficulty, I informed you, that I was willing to assent to any relaxation in the usual rules, that governed in the auditing of accounts, which on full consideration should be deemed safe; and among many others, suggested that, if it would facilitate the settlement of the account and you should desire it, I would allow the State at the rate of ten cents per month for each stand for the number actually issued, deducting for those which were lost and paid for by the United States, provided the sum expended by the State on repairs should not exceed the sum which it would give. The object of the suggestion was, if possible, to get clear of the difficulty of ascertaining that the repairs, for which the State had paid, were for damages actually done while the arms were in the service. It was thought damages to that amount might be fairly presumed for arms issued to Militia.

Finding from your observations, that the relaxation would not facilitate the settlement of the account, I have no disposition to make it. Should any suggestion occur to you, which would facilitate the settlement, I will give it due consideration, with a strong disposition to adopt the most liberal course, which I can with propriety.

No arrangement has been made with the Agent for the State of South Carolina [Charles John Steedman] for a similar claim, as you suppose. He has been informed, that the decision would be postponed until the claim of the State of New York was adjusted, and that whatever rule was adopted in the settlement of the claim of that State would be extended to that of So[uth] Carolina.

I do not think that the suggestion made by Colo[nel George] Bomford can be adopted as it goes on the supposition that all of the Militia called out were armed by the State, which, it is manifest, does not correspond with the fact.

LS in MWiW-C; FC (dated 8/3) in DNA, 3, 11:422–423 (M-6:11). NOTE: Pell's letter of 7/25 was a 22-page-long presentation of N.Y.'s claim. He had been seeking since as early as 1818 to obtain U.S. payments to N.Y. in compensation for War of 1812 services. See, for example, *The Papers of John C. Calhoun*, 2:214 and 219.

Alexander Macomb to [Bvt.] Maj. W[ILLIAM] J. WORTH, West Point

Engineer Dept., Washington, 5th Aug[us]t 1822

I enclose for your information a copy of a letter from this department to [1st] Lieutenant [George] Blaney of the Corps of Engineers containing the decision of the Secretary of War upon a question recently submitted by Lieut. Blaney as to the officer at West Point entitled to the command during the absence of Major [Sylvanus] Thayer. This decision should have been communicated to you at the time it was made, but the matter was inadvertently neglected.

CC in DNA, 30, 340. NOTE: For related letters see, herein, some dated 8/11, 8/20, and 8/24. Worth held the lineal rank of a Capt. in the 1st Regiment of Artillery, was the Instructor of Tactics in the Military Academy, and was serving as Acting Superintendent of the Academy. Blaney was a member of the Corps of Engineers, from which it was customary for the commandant of the Academy to be chosen.

Pension certificate of Leonard Bleecker, 8/6. Calhoun certifies that Bleecker, formerly a Maj. in the Revolutionary Army, is to be paid $20 per month from 3/25/1818 through the N.Y. pension agency. DS in PPL.

From [Lt. Col.] Abr[a]m Eustis, St. Augustine, 8/6. In compliance with Calhoun's order of 7/22, Eustis has directed Capt. [Matthew M.] Payne, who has been on duty in St. Augustine, to proceed with his Company to Charleston, S.C. "Fortunately a suitable vessel is now lying in this harbour. She has been engaged to transport the Company, & weather permitting, will sail from this port on Thursday the 8th inst[ant]." ALS in DNA, 1, E-21 (M-221:95).

To GEORGE BOYD, Mac[k]inac, and Seven Others

Dep[art]m[en]t of War, August 7, 1822

It appears by a report of the 2nd Auditor [William Lee] which has been made to me, that your accounts have been rendered only to the 30th of September 1821. You will without delay on the receipt of this transmit your accounts up to the 30th of June last through this Department to the 2nd Auditor for settlement; and in future, render them punctually immediately after the close of every quarter as heretofore directed.

LS in WHi, George Boyd Collection; FC in DNA, 72, E:308 (M-15:5). NOTE: This transcription follows the LS. The FC indicates that the same letter was written to John Biddle, David Brearl[e]y, John Johnston, Lawrence Taliaferro, and Alexander Wolcott and that letters were written also to John Crowell and to R[obert] C[arter] Nicholas that were identical except that accounts through 12/31/1821 from these two were acknowledged.

From Ferris Pell, Washington, 8/7. He has received Calhoun's letter of 8/5. Pell discusses at length N.Y.'s claim against the U.S. for repairs of arms furnished to the N.Y. militia during the [War of 1812]. He urges, in particular, that the U.S. should require less strict evidence for settling the claim and that a set of "rules of Audit," which he elaborates, should be adopted. LS in DNA, 262, 7786.

To J[OEL] R. POINSETT, Charleston, S.C.

War Department, August 8th 1822

I have the honour to acknowledge the receipt of your letter of the 28th ultimo [ALS in DNA, 15, 1823, 300 (M-688:27, frames 312–315)], repeating the wishes of the friends of Mr. Oliver Cromwell, who was recommended last year to be appointed to the Military Academy. Mr. Cromwell's name was regularly entered with those of the other applicants from South Carolina; but as there were a considerable number of candidates of more suitable age, it was thought best, on account of his extreme youth, to transfer Mr. Cromwell to the list for the ensuing year, when he will be duly considered.

FC in DNA, 13, 1:148 (M-91:1).

To J[OEL] R. POINSETT, [Representative from S.C.,] Charleston, S.C.

[August 8, 1822?]

. . . from you while you are there. All of our accounts represent the state of the country as very unsettled. Yours truly, J.C. Calhoun.

Fragment of an ALS in ScHi. NOTE: It is possible to assign a reasonably probable date to this fragment. The fact that it was franked by Calhoun over his autograph as a War Department official, considered in conjunction with the month of the postmark, narrows the possible years to 1818–1824, inclusive. The postmark is legible enough to show that the letter was mailed in Washington on some day in an August, probably the 8th but perhaps the 3rd or the 5th. Poinsett's two major travels during 1818–1824 were to Europe in 1821 and to Mexico during 8/1822–1/1823. He wrote from New York City to a Charlestonian on 7/10/1821 that he was sailing for Liverpool. Grace E. Heilman and Bernard S. Levin, eds., *Calendar of Joel R. Poinsett*

Papers in the Henry D. Gilpin Collection (Philadelphia: Historical Society of Pennsylvania, c. 1941), p. 8. That fact makes it unlikely that Calhoun would write to Poinsett in Charleston in 8/1821. As Calhoun may have learned in a Cabinet meeting or otherwise, President James Monroe commissioned Poinsett in 1822 to investigate the stability or instability of the new, revolutionary government of Mexico. Poinsett began his journey to Mexico by leaving Charleston on 8/28/1822. Dorothy M. Parton, *The Diplomatic Career of Joel Roberts Poinsett* (Washington: Catholic University of America, c. 1934), p. 49. These facts make it quite probable that Calhoun closed a personal letter written to Poinsett early in 8/1822 by assuring him that Calhoun and/or other government officials would appreciate hearing from Poinsett while he was in Mexico, which was then reputedly a "very unsettled" nation. Observe, immediately above this transcription, that Calhoun wrote to Poinsett on 8/8/1822 about a matter of official business and addressed that letter also to Charleston. See also, herein, Poinsett's letter of 8/20 from Charleston to Calhoun, who is not known to have answered that letter.

From William Clark, St. Louis, 8/9. In reply to Calhoun's letter of 7/1, Clark states that the license granted to [William H.] Ashley and [Andrew] Henry [to trade, trap, and hunt on the Upper Missouri] "will not produce any disturbance among the Indian tribes with whom we have much intercourse." It will be in the interest of Ashley and Henry "to cultivate the friendship of the more distant Tribes by a regular & conciliatory course, which if pursued will most probably strengthen the confidence those Tribes may have in our government." Clark acknowledges receipt of the copy of a talk of the Shawnee Chiefs concerning an exchange of lands. Clark explains that a negotiation was begun in 1820 by [Pierre] Menard "for the exchange of their [the Shawnees'] Claims at Cape Girardeau for lands on the waters of White River." The negotiations were never concluded because the demands of the Indians were too high. "The Tribe have abandoned their lands at Cape Gerredeau [*sic*] and are scattered on the waters of White River." Some of their Chiefs have recently expressed a desire for a settlement. Clark informed them that "the government would decide upon the allowance to be made to them, and untill that decision was made no decisive answer could be given to them." Clark would like to know Calhoun's views on the subject to aid in further negotiation. "The other Subjects contained in your letter shall be strictly attended to, and every precaution taken to prevent the vexatious and predatory conduct of the Indians which has been complained of by Gen[era]l [Duff] Green." LS in DNA, 1, C-80 (M-221:95).

From John Floyd, St. Marys, [Ga.,] 8/9. He acknowledges Calhoun's letters of 6/17, 7/9, and 7/19. [John Alfred] Cuthbert has informed Floyd that Cuthbert has declined his appointment [to be a commissioner for a treaty with the Eastern Cherokees]. Floyd has been assured that the $34,989.07 have been deposited in the Bank of Darien, [Ga.]. Floyd fears that the treaty will be delayed until early in 1823. ALS in DNA, 1, F-23 (M-221:95).

To J[oel] R. Poinsett, Charleston, S.C., 8/9. "I transmit herewith a copy of the report of the Board of Engineers upon the subject of your communication of the 21st ultimo relating to the lines of defence for the City of Charleston." FC in DNA, 21, 1:314.

From W[illiam] Ward, Choctaw Agency, 8/10. Although he has not yet received the two drafts mentioned in Calhoun's letter of 6/12, Ward has paid, from funds on hand, for the improvements [abandoned] by the Choctaws. He has paid to [Cyrus] Kingsbury $5,000 and to the Chiefs their part of the annuity; the balance will be paid in 9/1822 "at the Trading house, where I expect they will receive a part in the Factory Goods." The Choctaws in council have requested the removal of the Agency "into the nation fourthwith [*sic*]." ALS in DNA, 77 (M-271:4, frames 239–240).

To James E[dward] Colhoun, [Philadelphia?]

War Dep[artmen]t, 11th August 1822

Dear James, I some time since informed you, that I had written to my factors to ascertain whether funds could not be obtained from the South at a less discount by drawing on Charleston [S.C.] instead of the Branch Bank [of the United States] in Savannah. By a letter, which I received a few days since from them, I learn that exchange between Augusta [Ga.] and Charleston is usually from 2 to 5 per cent discount, which added to the discount here of one per cent would occasion a loss on a bill of from 3 to 6 per cent. I apprize you of the fact in order that you might determine, whether to obtain funds by drawing through the Branch Bank [of the United States] here with so heavy a loss, or through some other means. I think it quite probable, that by consulting Mr. [Langdon] Cheves you might make some more advantageous arrangement. I have determined on my part to avoid drawing, if possible, till I can avoid the loss.

We are all well. The city is healthy, and should it continue so, we will probably remain here till some time in Sept[embe]r when we propose to take a short excurs[ion] for exercise and relaxation. With affection, J.C. Calhoun.

ALS in ScCleA.

From Th[omas] M[ann] Randolph, [Governor of Va.,] "Monticello," 8/11. He recommends Dabney Overton Carr, a son of Col. Samuel Carr, for an appointment to be a Cadet. Samuel Carr did militia duty during the War of 1812 and is a son of a sister of [Thomas] Jefferson. The applicant, aged 15, possesses "a very considerable degree of capability" and "great vivacity of character." ALS in DNA, 15, 1822, 109 (M-688:22, frames 165–166).

[2nd] Lt. L[ouis] A. Rigail, Cantonment Sand Hills near Augusta, Ga., to [George] Bomford, 8/11. Rigail has learned that the gun stocks at [Adam] Carruth's [former] armory are too short for the barrels that require stocking in Augusta. Carruth has two U.S. muskets that have been sent to him as patterns, and Rigail asks if he can obtain those two. Rigail would like also to receive the surplus paper, lead, and gunpowder that are at Carruth's. ALS in DNA, 31, 1822, R.

From [Bvt.] Maj. W[illiam] J. Worth

Camp Calhoun, West Point, August 11th 1822

I avail myself of the privilege contained in the general Army regulations in addressing you directly and respectfully solicit your attention to the accompanying documents.

I think Sir ten years [of] reputable service should have shielded a soldier from so wanton an attack upon his professional pride and feelings as that conveyed in [Bvt.] Major General [Alexander] Macomb[']s letter [to me of 8/5] and its accompanyment [*sic*]. In this and the following remarks, I desire to be distinctly understood as expressing the belief that the offensive paper in question is wanting in your authority—that it is penned in misapprehension of your orders, else based on a former decission [*sic*] since which the relative state of things are [*sic*] much altered. From the spirit of the Major General[']s letter, it is to be infer[r]ed that there has been a contest for the supremacy at this Post; this is not the fact—no officer junior to myself has had the indiscretion to interfere with my authority. I flatter myself that my duty is too familiar to suffer such an act to pass with impunity.

The Major General[']s decission requires of me, (if it requires any thing,) to place myself subject to the orders of a junior officer, as it contains nothing authorising my absence from the station.

There is, I am aware a law, of an old date, which at all times devolves the command of this post on officers of Engineers only. When this law was passed, the Corps of Engineers was undoubtedly supposed competent to furnish *all* the officers required for the purposes of the institution—the history of the institution however proves this to have been an error, inasmuch as the government have [*sic*] found it necessary from time to time to send officers of other arms & grades of services hither.

A subsequent regulation however, which *was* a law and did in effect ["devolve the" *canceled*] re-organize the institution, directs that "there shall be a *permanent* Superintendent *selected* from the Corps of Engineers &c. &c." I consider Maj. [Sylvanus] Thayer Superintendent therefore whether he [be] present or temporarily absent—but waiving the question of Superintendency, which is not [at] all involved in the present case, it appears, during the period of encampment, when the academic functions of the institution are suspended, the Professor present or absent, as they list, the *permanent* Sup[erintenden]t is authorized to absent himself, the command devolves of course on the officer next in rank. In the present instance however it was specially delegated—had this not been in virtue of my commission, standing in that relation to the Superintendent, I should have assumed and exercised it.

That my services are at all times subject to the disposition of the government there is no doubt, but I must be allowed, [*two words, possibly* "to question," *almost illegible*; "the" *interlined*] right of its subordinate agents, to impose upon me duties incompatible with a due regard to my rank and character.

According to the decission of General Macomb wherein he observes, that the *contents* of [1st] Lieutenant [George] Blaney's letter had been laid before the Sec[retar]y &c. &c., an officer of the line of the Army cannot serve at this post, without becoming accessory to his own dishonor—by the operation of the law as here construed, a Cadet of yesterday may be clothed with the privileges and high prerogatives of an officer of Engineers to dav and in virtue thereof assert his right to command an officer, older perhaps in service than he in years. I feel warranted in the remark that there is not one ["the" *canceled*] American officer who could yield obedience to such a command. I am by [no] means unmindful of the distinction confer[r]ed in assigning my present station and have endeavored by zeal corresponding with the importance of my duties to manifest a just appreciation of its advantages; neither should I be insensible of the misfortune of being removed; nevertheless, if this question cannot be arranged more in accordance with the principles and usages of service, I shall be compelled, reluctantly, to beg to be withdrawn from among a privileged order and allowed to resume my duties in the line of the Army. I therefore solicit a consideration of the case in the hope and belief that it will result in finally settling a question the agitation of which, evidently has a tendency to disturb the harmony of the institution.

ALS with Ens in DNA, 30, 340. NOTE: One of the Ens was Macomb's letter to Worth dated 8/5, of which a PC appears herein. Two other Ens were CC's of documents indicating that Worth had been ordered on 7/2 to take command of the Military Academy and that on 7/3 he had done so. Compare, herein, the next document and related letters dated 8/20 and 8/24.

[Bvt.] Maj. W[ILLIAM] J. WORTH to [Alexander] Macomb

Camp Calhoun, West Point, Aug[us]t 11th 1822

I have received your letter of the 5th instant enclosing a copy of your communication to [1st] Lieut[enant George] Blaney, purporting to be the decission [*sic*] of the Hon[ora]ble Sec[retar]y for the Department of War on a question of command, from which it is to be infer[r]ed that there has been a contest for the command of this Post. Let me assure you Sir, that the Lieutenant has been altogether too discreet to interfere with my authority; if he had been so forgetful of his own interest I should very promptly have adopted in his case the most summary measures known to the service.

I do not deem myself called, in any [*illegible*; intimation?] to reply to this communication, (as it will be refer[r]ed directly [by me] to the Sec[retar]y at War,) and should not do so, but for the possibility that silence on my part might be construed into an acquiescence in the doctrine which it seems intended to establish by this decission.

I yield to no man in service Sir in deference for, and in an un-hesitating obedience to the laws, & profess a most particular veneration for those having a direct reference to the obligations of my profession, but must be allowed to add that, while it pleases God to continue my understanding & the President [James Monroe] my commission, I stand ready to sacrifice it and the reward of ten years [of] service, sooner than place, or suffer myself to be placed, directly or indirectly, subject to the orders or controul even by inference of my junior officer—or any officer over whom the *laws* entitled me to the honor of rank.

If your document was intended as an intimation to me to relinquish the command, it was altogether too imperfect as it contained nothing authorizing my absence from the Post, and I can hardly persuade myself that it was intended, I should bend the knee to my junior altho I must confess to the latter alternative it would seem (so far as it admits of any definite construction,) to direct my attention.

I have addressed the Sec[retar]y on the subject and meantime so I shall continue to exercise the command of this Post—untill relieved by a superiour or ordered to devolve the command upon a junior officer; in the latter event myself relieved from further service at the Post.

Ere this reaches you however Maj. [Sylvanus] Thayer will have returned and resumed his command.

ALS in DNA, 221, 442. Note: Compare, herein, the letter from Macomb to Calhoun dated 8/24 and that from Calhoun to Worth dated 8/20.

Winfield Scott to C[hristopher] Vandeventer

Aug[us]t 12th, 1822

Dear Major: Mr. [Charles] Vignoles, civil engineer, will have the pleasure of calling on you with this note. He has in hand a map of the two Floridas, nearly finished; but before he closes his labours, he wishes to avail himself of any surveys, partial or general, which may have been collected in the War Department. He has a letter to Major [Isaac] Roberdeau. Will you have the goodness to present him to the Secretary of War—if the latter be yet in Washington? The latter will probably patronize the map to the extent of a subscription for some copies.

Mr. Vignoles is skil[l]ful in his profession & worthy of the attentions which I take the liberty to solicit for him. Yours with great esteem, Winfield Scott.

ALS in DNA, 228.

To Thomas Bennett, Governor of S.C., Charleston

Department of War, August 13th 1822

I have the honor to acknowledge the receipt of your letter of the 30th Ultimo.

I do not know whether the views of the Board of Engineers comprehend the occupation of the site of Fort Johnson and the continuance of Castle Pinckney ["in" *interlined*] its present state or with alteration as their project for the defence of Charleston Harbour has not yet been reported. I am therefore unable to afford the information you desire with respect to the probability of a retrocession of Fort Johnson to the State. The report of the Board of Engineers will be received next fall. Should it recommend the abandonment of Fort Johnson, it will then rest with Congress to determine whether or not the retrocession desired may be granted. Its decision at the last session with regard to Castle Clinton in New York Harbour would encourage a belief that no opposition would be made to a proposition of the same nature respecting Fort Johnson.

Orders will be immediately issued for the requisite arrangements to be made at Castle Pinckney for the reception and preservation of the powder that it may be desirable to deposit there.

FC in DNA, 3, 11:424 (M-6:11).

To John Clark, Milledgeville, 8/13. [James Monroe] has authorized the War Department to receive until 1/1/1823 claims that have been examined by [James P.] Preston. FC in DNA, 72, E:312 (M-15:5); CC in DNA, 77 (M-271:4, frames 269–271).

From John Le Conte, New York [City], 8/14. He encloses a long report by himself, by J[oseph G.] Swift, and by [Simon] Bernard as members of the Board of Visitors of the Military Academy and comments at length on several aspects of the work of the Board of the Academy. ALS with En in DNA, 222, F-66.

Contract of Eli Whitney, 8/15. With Calhoun's approbation, George Bomford and Whitney, who is described as a resident of New Haven, agree that Whitney is to manufacture and to deliver there, in equal installments through five years beginning on 1/1/1824, 15,000 muskets with bayonets, ramrods, and flints. For each he is to receive $12; but this price can be adjusted to equal the cost of making similar products in the U.S. Armories. An appended notation indicates that models were delivered to Whitney on 1/2/1823. FC in DNA, 331, 1:164–167.

To Lewis Cass, Detroit, 8/16. Calhoun encloses a copy of a speech by a Potawatomi Chief. If the causes assigned by the Chief are true explanations of the Indians' trips to Canada [to receive presents from the British], Calhoun believes that these causes can be removed and ought to be. But, since the subject is one with which Cass is well acquainted, he is authorized to answer in whatever way and with whatever measures he judges to be proper. LS with En in DNA, 76 (M-1:11, pp. 276–287); FC in DNA, 72, E:309 (M-15:5).

Alexander Macomb to S[tephen] Pleasonton, 8/16. Samuel L. Gouverneur's letter of 8/15, "which you laid before the Sec[retar]y of War with a recommendation in favor of granting to Mr. Gouverneur copies of the papers therein requested has been referred to this dep[artmen]t." At [Calhoun's] direction, Macomb encloses those documents concerning [Samuel] Hawkins's sureties and "the substitution of Tapia for Brick Masonry at Mobile Point." FC in DNA, 21, 1:316.

From Joseph Lovell, 8/17. He reports, with statistical evidence, that during approximately 1819–1821 about one-fourth of all deaths in the Army have occurred at or near Baton Rouge, where fewer than a twelfth of the soldiers have been stationed. "As this post has been so exceedingly sickly for nearly three years, & different reasons have been assigned for it, the above facts are reported with a view to a full investigation of the circumstances, that the real causes may be ascertained & suitable measures taken to obviate them." ALS in DNA, 16, 1822, L-27 (M-567:3, frames 619–622); FC in DNA, 242, 2:305.

From T[homas] F[orsyth], Fort Armstrong, 8/18. Game is not plentiful near the Mississippi River. The Sauk and Fox Indians who lack horses and arms enough to make summer hunts west of the river, therefore, mine lead north of Fort Armstrong. This is especially true of the Foxes. They find many traders, amply supplied with goods, who are eager to purchase the lead. "I cannot see how the major part of the Foxes and some of the Sauks could exist without these mines. The Fox Indians have always been and continue so to be very jealous of these mines. They will not allow white person[s] to work any of them and it is my opinion if the whites will insist on working them some accidents must take place." The principal ones of these mines are beside the Fever River; and, because of the failure of the Indians' corn crop near Fort Armstrong last summer, more families than usual are at work in the mines this year, earning an abundance of provisions and clothing that they receive from the traders in exchange. The Sauks are angry at the Sioux, who killed a peaceful Sauk hunter last winter, and have asked Forsyth to write to [Lawrence Taliaferro], the Indian Agent at St. Peters. He has done so, delivering an offer of a renewal of the peace that was agreed upon last year if the Sioux Chiefs will meet with the Sauks for that purpose but threatening to renew the warfare if the Sioux Chiefs do not come to Fort Armstrong by autumn. FC's in WHi, Draper Collection, Thomas Forsyth Papers, 4:103–105 and 7:96–97 (published microfilm, series T, vols. 1–9).

To [former] Col. WILLIAM DUANE, Philadelphia

Department of War, August 19th 1822

I have received your letter of the 15th instant [*actually* 7/15 (ALS in DNA, 1, D-21 [M-221:95])] offering to dispose of your military Library.

The Library attached to this Department is very imperfect, particularly as a military one, and I would be very happy were it in my power to enlarge it by adding your collection to it. There is, however, no appropriation at my disposal, which could be applied to that purpose[,] the one for maps, plans, and books being so far exhausted as not to be more than sufficient to meet the demands on it.

FC in DNA, 3, 11:424 (M-6:11).

To William P. "Duvall [*sic*; DuVal]," [Governor of Fla. Territory,] Pensacola, 8/19. Calhoun acknowledges DuVal's letter of 7/18 ["Duplicate" LS in DNA, 1, D-22 (M-221:95); PC in Carter, ed., *Territorial Papers,* 22:491–492]. "The [new] Indian Agent [Gad Humphreys] has been ordered to repair to Florida immediately and report himself to you for instructions. A copy of the order is enclosed." The War Department has always desired that the Fla. Indians should join the Creeks in Ga., but the people of Ga. objected so strenuously that it was decided not to unite the tribes without the sanction of Congress. Measures were taken to concentrate the Indians of Fla. at the point in Fla. designated by [Andrew] Jackson in his letter of 9/20/1821 [to Calhoun (Abs in *The Papers of John C. Calhoun,* vol. VI)], but the Indians refused to meet Capt. [John R.] Bell at the appointed time. The appropriation for such a treaty was made too late by Congress for negotiations to be held in the spring, and the hot, sickly climate and farming activities of the Indians prevented a meeting during the summer. As soon as [Humphreys] arrives, DuVal will assemble the Indians and make final arrangements for their concentration at the selected place. "The means for conciliating the Indians and facilitating the accomplishment of the object of the meeting are already in the Indian Country (as you will observe by the enclosed extract of a letter from Capt. Bell) and orders have been given to Capt[ai]n Bell to place these means at your disposal, and also to deliver over to your order the sum of $298.34 which remains in his hands, to be applied to the same object, if it should be necessary." Additional funds for the expenses of DuVal's Superintendency will be sent from the Treasury pursuant to DuVal's submission of quarterly estimates to the War Department. The documents laid before Congress relating to the accounts of the various Superintendents and Agents of Indian Affairs are too voluminous to be copied for DuVal's use, but specific ones can be extracted and sent to DuVal if he will point them out. Calhoun agrees that a road from Pensacola to St. Augustine is important and that troops might be usefully employed in its construction, but the project would involve so much expense that "it cannot be done without the authority of Congress." FC in DNA, 72, E:310–311 (M-15:5); PC in Carter, ed., *Territorial Papers,* 22:508–509.

To [former Lt. Col.] Gad Humphreys, Indian Agent, Marcellus, N.Y., 8/19. Calhoun directs Humphreys to make "immediate arrangements" for his departure for Fla. and to report to the Governor, [William P. DuVal,] who will instruct Humphreys in his duties and who will supply him with the necessary funds. Humphreys will also execute and send his bond to the War Department "and state the probable time of your departure. Any omission, or unreasonable delay on your part, to comply with the above order, will be considered as a resignation of your office, and a new appointment will be made." FC in DNA, 72, E:311 (M-15:5); PC in Carter, ed., *Territorial Papers*, 22:509–510.

To Gad Peck, Cincinnati, 8/19. His son, [Robert T. Peck,] will be allowed to take a reëxamination next month for admission into the Military Academy. FC in DNA, 13, 1:151–152 (M-91:1).

To Capt. John R. Bell, St. Augustine, 8/20. Calhoun has received Bell's letters of 7/9 [*not found*] and 7/16 [ALS in DNA, 1, B-69 (M-221:95)]. [William P. DuVal] "has been instructed to receive of you the money and property remaining in your hands, belonging to the Indian Department and you will accordingly deliver them to his order. A copy of the statement of the property enclosed with your letter of the 9th has been transmitted to the Governor [DuVal]." FC in DNA, 72, E:311 (M-15:5).

To William P. [DuVal], 8/20. "I enclose herewith for your information, a copy of a statement which I have received from Captain [John R.] Bell of the property belonging to the Indian Department remaining in his hands, and to which I referred in my letter of yesterday." FC in DNA, 72, E:311 (M-15:5).

To N[INIAN] EDWARDS, "Private"

War Dep[artmen]t, 20th Aug[us]t 1822

Since I wrote to you last your several communications of the 13th June, 5, 14, 27th ["and the 27th Inst." *canceled and* "July" *interlined; none found*] have been received. I take much interest in Mr. [Daniel Pope] Cook's election, and shall wait with great impatience to learn the result. He is honest, capable and bold; just such a man as the times require. His absence from Congress would be a serious loss.

Since the return of the President [James Monroe] to the city, I have urged on his attention the subject of making appointments to the offices, to which you referred, and brought before him the names which you mentioned. He took the names down, and informed me, that so soon as he had finished the investigation of the proceedings of the court-martial in the case of Lie[utenan]t Abbott, which he was then investigating, he would attend to the subject; and requested me so to inform you.

I do trust, that he begins to feel the necessity of taking a decided stand. I agree with you that it is much easier to put down the opposition when its existence is once acknowledged, than to prove to the satisfaction of the people its existence. Until the President shall uniformly make the distinction between friends and foes in his appointments, this cannot be done. If he will not see the opposition, or acts, as if he did not, the country will be incredulous as to its existence. These ideas, I have urged on him. That he fully ["understands" *canceled and* "comprehends" *interlined*] the opposition, I cannot doubt; and do hope, that he will act in such a manner, as to leave no dou[b]t on the minds of the people, that he knows what is the actual state of things. For myself, I care far less for my own prospects than I do for the welfare of the administration. Identified as I am with it, and approving its policy, I shall use every effort to maintain it in the good opinion of the people. The new paper here, [the Washington *Republican and Congressional Examiner*,] if supported by a decided course on the part of the Pres[iden]t, will aid much in bringing out the opposition. You will see that its tone is decisive and that it knows what it is about.

Since the adjournment no great change has occurred on this side of the Mountains. Pennsy[lvani]a is firm. The sym[p]toms in Maryland, Deleware [*sic*], New Jersey, Connecticut and the New England States presently appear favourable. In Virginia and North Carolina they are also fully as much so as at the adjournment. The same cannot be said of New York. [Martin] Van Beuren [*sic*] for the present has taken his stand in favour of Mr. [William H.] C[rawfor]d, as being most suitable to his purpose of opposing the administration. The [New York] Advocate, which is under his influence, has made a demonstration, the same way. It has not openly taken his ground but leaves no doubt as to his course. It is, however, the opinion of [editor Mordecai M.] Noah (I have it from a letter of his to a particular friend of his) that neither Mr. C[rawfor]d, or myself will be elected, but that some third person, whom he does not name, will be. With this impression his Zeal will not be great and he will take care at least for the present not to commit himself too fully to prevent him from going back.

It seems by the papers that Tennessee has put Gen[era]l [Andrew] Jackson in nomination. What will be the effects of this step, particularly in the West? It is certainly adverse to Mr. [Henry] Clay, but how will it effect [*sic*] others? We now exhibit the extraordinary fact of five persons, from the slave holding States, being before the people for the highest office in their gift, and but one from the non slave holding States. This gives Mr. [John Quincy] Adams great advantages, if he knew how to improve them.

It is strange after the appointment of [Jesse B.] Thomas, that Mr. C[rawfor]d should have appointed [Walter] Lowrie's brother to inspect the land offices. He wants discretion in an extra-ordi[nar]y degree, and ought to be made to feel the effects of it in this case. I am told he has conferred an appointment on another brother of Lowrie. If any evidence could be had of Thomas having electioneered for him while engaged in making his inspection the last year, it would have a strong effect on the publick mind. His intrigue and management would make his election dangerous to the country.

The appointments to South America will not be made unless something should occur till after the next meeting of Congress. On many accounts it would be imprudent to make them now.

I am much gratified with your statement as to the publick feelings in the West in relation to the subject of lead mines. You have seen the course adopted by the [War] Dep[artmen]t, and I hope it is such as to meet your approbation. That [Thomas Hart] Benton has been counteracted I attribute to you, who alone fully understood the subject in the Senate and had the energy to meet it boldly. Benton had been long in maturing his plan of attack and no doubt anticipated much success from it against the administration.

Your friend [Charles] Fisher of North Carolina, I see is elected a member of the State Legislature. I mention the fact, so that you might avail yourself of it in your correspondence with him. North Carolina will doubtless become the scene of much political intrigue on the part of Mr. C[rawfor]d and his friends. It is as yet unoccupied ground. Yours Truely [*sic*], J.C. Calhoun.

ALS in ICHi. NOTE: The five Presidential nominees whom Calhoun mentioned as being associated with slave States were himself, Henry Clay, William H. Crawford, Andrew Jackson, and William Lowndes.

From Joseph Hawkins, Philadelphia, 8/20. He offers his invention [of a cannon designed to be loaded at the breech] to his country. The invention is not finished but can be tested at a cost of about $500 in the presence of Army officers. It is so effective that Army officers will oppose its adoption, because it might result in a reduction of the Army's personnel. "I am willing to engage in the prosecution of this design immediately upon being furnished with a sufficient sum of money to subsist on until the object is completed and then would willingly retire on a reasonable salary." ALS in DNA, 35, In-1b-1.

From Edwin James, [M.D.,] Philadelphia, 8/20. He requests a commission to serve as an Army physician. ALS in DNA, 241, J. (He was appointed to be an Assistant Surgeon as of 1/27/1823 and served for more than 10 years. Heitman, *Historical Register*, 1:569).

From J[oel] R. Poinsett, Charleston, [S.C.,] 8/20. "I enclose a note [to myself dated 8/19] received from Mr. [Jacob N.] Cardozo and will be obliged to you to remind Mr. [John Quincy] Adams of the application made in favor of the gentleman," [Jacob Moïse, Editor of the *Southern Patriot*, for an appointment to be the U.S. commercial agent in Jamaica or Barbadoes or Antigua]. ALS with En in DNA, 103, Moïse (M-439:12, frames 15–18).

To [Bvt.] Maj. W[illiam] J. Worth, West Point

Department of War, August 20th 1822

I have received your communication of the 11th instant with its enclosures.

Previous to transmitting the letter of the 31st Ultimo to [1st] Lieu[tenan]t [George] Blaney, General [Alexander] Macomb submitted it for the sanction of this Department, and on examination of the act of the 16th March 1802, I felt myself compelled by its provisions[,] however reluctantly, to designate the senior Officer of Engineers present as the Superintendent, although junior in rank to yourself. I am aware that the institution at its commencement had far more limited bases than what the existing laws contemplate, but I cannot conceive that the provisions of the act referred to, are on that account obsolete. The inconvenience resulting from the particular provision in this case, has been so severely felt, that application has been made to Congress by this Department to have it repealed, so that the Officers of the Corps of Engineers should have no preference over any others that might be detailed to do duty at the institution. From the want of time, or some other cause, the act has not been repealed, and so long as it exists on the statute book, its provisions must be respected.

I duly appreciate the feelings which a provision so anomalous is calculated to excite, but it is only in the power of Congress to apply an adequate remedy.

FC in DNA, 3, 11:425 (M-6:11).

To [Lt.] Col. A[bram] Eustis, St. Augustine, 8/21. "Your letter of the 23d ultimo [ALS with Ens in DNA, 1, E-18 (M-221:95); PC with Ens in Carter, ed., *Territorial Papers*, 22:495–498], enclosing a copy of a letter [dated 7/19] from Captain [Peter] Pelham to you, and of your reply [on 7/21] to the same, has been received." Calhoun approves of Eustis's "taking charge of the affairs of the Indians during the absence of Captain Pelham" and answers the 10 questions posed by Eustis. Calhoun encloses "copies of the law of intercourse [with the Indians of 1802] and the supplementary law passed at the late session of Congress, for your information and government." Eustis will correspond with Governor [William P.] DuVal. [Gad Humphreys,] the Indian Agent, should arrive in Fla. soon to relieve Eustis of these duties. FC in DNA, 72, E:312–313 (M-15:5); PC in Carter, ed., *Territorial Papers*, 22:512–513.

From Charles John Steedman

St. James's, So[uth] C[arolina,] August 21st, 1822

Permit me to call your attention to the undecided question of the Barracks at Haddrils Point and as I have obtained the periods they were in possession of the Troops in the service of the United States, I would respectfully suggest as a ready mode of settlement, the same as governed in the demand of the State for damages sustained by the erection of the Forti[fi]cations on the neck. If you approve of this mode, I will be obliged to you to name a Gentleman on the part of the General Government and another will be immediately named on the part of the State by the Governor [Thomas Bennett].

ALS in DNA, 262, 10333.

To William P. [DuVal], Pensacola, 8/22. "I enclose herewith, for your information and direction, a copy of a letter [dated 8/21] to [Lt.] Col. [Abram] Eustis, who has charge of Indian Affairs at St. Augustine during the absence of Captain [Peter] Pelham, the Sub-Agent, to whom a furlough has been granted in consequence of the weak state of his health." FC in DNA, 72, E:313 (M-15:5).

From Alexander Macomb

Engineer Department, Washington, August 22d 1822

I have attentively purused [*sic*] the *Memoire phisique, historique, politique et militaire sur quelques isles de la Mediterranée et particulièrement sur l'Isle d'Elba,* and find it written with great perspicuity giving an account of the History, productions, population, soil, resources, revenue and political and military advantages of those islands, which form the Tuscan archipellago [*sic*]. As an historical memoir, it is mighty interesting, especially in its details of the events, which took place at the Island of Elba; as a military memoir, it is still more important—it points out the great advantages, which the Island of Elba possesses as a naval station, particularly the Bay and Harbour of its capital, Porto ferrajo [*sic*; Portoferraio], which are capable of sheltering a large f[l]eet from the violence of the sea and perfectly secure against all weathers. The fortifications are also represented as very strong and in good condition—the details on this head are very minute; the Barracks and casemates are extensive enough to contain upwards of two thousand men & the Magazines and store houses in proportion. With a small expense Porto ferrajo might be rendered impregnable; as it is, the writer says, it is one of the strongest fortresses in Europe. On the whole the memoir is written with great latent [*sic*; talent] and ability and is highly creditable to its author.

ALS in DLC, James Monroe Papers, vol. 31, 5770 (Presidential Papers Microfilm, Monroe Papers, Reel 8).

To R[obert] C[arter] Nicholas

Department of War, August 23d 1822

Your letter of the 12th ultimo enclosing your estimate for the two last quarters of this year, has been received.

I have directed the amount of your estimate to be remitted to you, and also the following sums additional, to wit, $1,892 to pay for improvements under the Treaty of 1818, and $500 to be paid to Mr. Robert Bell, on account of buildings for the school in the Chickasaw nation, making the whole sum remitted $5,492.

The letter addressed to you on the 3d June was in the nature of a circular to the Superintendents, and Agents, of Indian Affairs and there may be some parts of it which are not entirely applicable to your Agency. It was presumed, however, that such parts only as were applicable would engage your attention.

The prohibition contained in the 7th Article of the Treaty of [9/20/]1816 relative to licenses to trade in the Chickasaw Nation is considered to extend to the government as well as the Agent. It is quite probable that it may have an injurious effect on the nation, but until the Article of treaty in question is abrogated, it will not be in the power of the Department to apply any adequate remedy.

The Department has no controul over the operations of the Treasury, and is not responsible for its delays or the manner in which its drafts are made. But it has always been presumed that its remittances on warrants ["and" *canceled and* "or" *interlined*] requisitions from this Department were made with as little delay as possible, and by drafts on such places as would be as convenient to the persons for whom they were intended as the arrangements of the Treasury would possibly admit of and which it is supposed has been done in making the remittance to you to which you refer.

I enclose herewith a blank bond of precisely the same form with the one formerly given by you in the penalty of ten thousand dollars. From the tenor of the bond it is perfectly clear that you and your securities together, are not bound to the United States for any more than the single sum of ten thousand dollars. Your case is not peculiar[;] all the Indian Agents thro' whom annuities of more than $10,000 are paid, have been required under the late Act, to give new bonds in the penalty of $20,000. The annuity paid thro' you is considerably the largest of any, and consequently the greater the necessity for increased security. You will therefore execute the enclosed bond, as soon as your convenience will permit, and transmit it to this Department.

It is usual to apportion the sum annually appropriated by Congress, among the several Superintendents and Agents for Indian Affairs, in order to keep the expenditures within the appropriation. It is not intended however that the whole sum to which the Superintendents and Agents are respectively limited, should be expended unless it should be absolutely necessary, and estimates are therefore required to enable the Department to check and control the disburs[e]ments.

The conduct of the Indians towards their Slaves is deeply to be regretted—the more so, because of the want of authority in the Government to restrain and punish it. There is no other mode to bring them to a proper sense of duty on this subject than by spirited remonstrance. The wickedness and cruelty of the custom which you represent prevails among the Indians in relation to this class of people, ought to be set before them in the most odious colors. It is degrading to themselves, and distructive [*sic*] to their interest. The government views it with [*one word canceled*] indignation and regret, and hopes upon a proper representation of its enormity, it will be abandoned.

FC in DNA, 72, E:313–314 (M-15:5).

To [John Clark, Governor of Ga., Milledgeville,] 8/24. "Major [Freeman] Walker and Mr. [John Alfred] Cuthbert having declined to act as commissioners to hold a treaty with the [Eastern] Cherokees, Duncan G. Campbell Esq[ui]r[e] and Gen[era]l David Meriwether have been appointed by the President [James Monroe] to join Gen[era]l [John] Floyd in the contemplated negotiation." LS in PHi; FC in DNA, 72, E:315 (M-15:5).

To John Floyd, [St. Marys, Ga.,] 8/24. [Freeman] Walker and [John Alfred] Cuthbert have declined to act as commissioners to hold a treaty with the [Eastern] Cherokees. Duncan G. Campbell and David Meriwether have been appointed "to join you in the contemplated negociation, and they are instructed to communicate with you upon the subject." FC in DNA, 72, E:315 (M-15:5).

From ALEXANDER MACOMB

Engineer Department, August 24th 1822

I take the liberty of laying before you a letter [dated 8/11] which I have received from [Bvt.] Major [William J.] Worth, and which is in reply to a letter from me, communicating your decision in regard to the exclusive right of the Officers of the Corps of Engineers to command at West Point. The temper and language of Major Worth's letter, evince such a degree of insubordination and Contempt of authority, as to call for a corrective, and I have been considering what mode ought to be adopted in this case; there appear to me but two modes, the one his arrest & trial, the other his removal from the Military Academy with orders to join his Regiment. The former, although it might be attended with some trouble and expense would tend to check a disposition to cavil about orders and instructions, which I am sorry to find is gaining ground in the service. The latter would be a sufficient mark of displeasure, and at the same time, would, I believe produce a beneficial effect on the institution. In case the latter mode should be adopted, I would beg leave to recommend to your consideration [Bvt.] Lt. Col. [John De Barth] Walbach as a proper person to supply his place. He is well calculated for it, possesses the proper knowledge of Tacticks, etiquette, police and military subordination, with manners peculiarly military & dignified; and it has been a universal remark that there is no officer in the service, better qualified to instruct young officers, than Col. Walbach, which quality he has so often evinced in regard to those who have been placed under his command. I feel confident he would willingly accept the situation provided he could receive the pay & emoluments of his Brevet, and that, I think, the law would warrant.

He would come with the present decision before him & thus save all further difficulty on that account.

As you have so frequently enjoined on me the necessity of compelling the most prompt obedience to the Laws & Regulations from the Officers under my command, I should conceive it my duty to place Major Worth in arrest for such a departure from military propriety, but believing that no beneficial result will eventuate from such a course at present, & taking into consideration the unhappy effects which Courts-Martial generally produce in the service, I should recommend as the most summary procedure, his removal from West Point.

LS with En in DNA, 221, 442. Note: Calhoun permitted Worth to remain at the Military Academy; he continued to be the Instructor of Tactics in 1823, 1824, and 1825. William A. Gordon, *A Compilation of Registers of the Army* . . . (Washington: James C. Dunn, printer, 1837), pp. 236, 250, and 266.

To R[eturn] J. Meigs, Calhoun, Tenn., 8/24. Calhoun informs the [Eastern] Cherokee Agent that [Freeman] Walker and [John

Alfred] Cuthbert have declined to serve as commissioners to hold the proposed treaty and that Duncan G. Campbell and David Meriwether have been appointed to join [John] Floyd in the planned negotiation. FC in DNA, 72, E:316 (M-15:5).

To David Meriwether, [former Representative from Ga.,] Athens, 8/24. He and Duncan G. Campbell have been appointed to serve with [John] Floyd as commissioners to hold a treaty with the [Eastern] Cherokees. Calhoun encloses a commission for Meriwether and instructions for the guidance of the three. Meriwether will correspond with the other two. Governor [John] Clark [of Ga.] has been informed about these appointments. LS owned in 1953 by Caroline Lewis Lovett of Philadelphia; FC in DNA, 72, E:315 (M-15:5). A similar letter of the same date was addressed to Campbell at Washington, Ga. FC in DNA, 72, E:316 (M-15:5).

To Enoch Parsons, President, Branch Bank of the United States and Agent for Paying [U.S.] Pensioners [in Conn.], Middletown, 8/24. Calhoun transmits to Parsons up-dated lists of [Conn.] pensioners "containing all the additions, alterations, transfers, &c. which have taken place for the last six months." These lists show that $53,970.51 are payable to Revolutionary, invalid, and half-pay pensioners on 9/[4]. "The appropriation having fallen short of the sum actually necessary, the full amount due to the Pensioners in your Agency, cannot now be transmitted." Parsons will receive $44,628, "which, it is believed, will be sufficient to meet all demands that may be made prior to the meeting of Congress. Should it not, however, be sufficient, you will first reserve a sufficient sum to meet the payments to Invalids and Half-Pay Pensioners, after which, the Revolutionary Pensioners will be paid out of any funds which may remain in your hands, whether originally intended to pay Revolutionary Pensioners, or not." LS in CtY.

To John Jacob "Aster [*sic*; Astor]," New York [City]

Department of War, August 26th 1822

Your letter of the 14th instant [ALS in DNA, 1, A-19 (M-221:95)] was duly received.

I enclose herewith a copy of the act of Congress passed at

the last Session to amend the act to regulate trade and intercourse with the Indian Tribes &c. to the first and second sections of which and the accompanying extract of a letter from this Department to Governor [Lewis] Cass, I refer you for the information which you request as to the late regulations prescribed by this Government relative to the Trade with the Indians.

FC in DNA, 72, E:317 (M-15:5).

To William Ward, Choctaw Agency, 8/26. Calhoun acknowledges Ward's letters of 7/14 [*not found*] and 7/22. Calhoun approves Ward's bond and urges him "to keep your expenditures for the year, within the limit assigned you, as it is very desirable that there should be no arrearages at the close of the year. All expenses attending the purchase of the three setts [*sic*] of Black Smith's tools for the Choctaw Nation which you have ordered from New Orleans, at the request of the Chiefs, must be paid out of the Annuity." Calhoun encloses an extract from a letter to [Jeremiah] Evarts for referral to [Cyrus] Kingsbury. Calhoun instructs Ward to forward his accounts and vouchers, the receipt of which is necessary before Ward can receive money for expenses during the third quarter of 1822. FC in DNA, 72, E:316 (M-15:5).

To David Brearl[e]y, Indian Agent, Ark. Territory, 8/27. Calhoun is remitting $1,000 as U.S. aid for construction of the buildings of the school for the Western Cherokees. When the actual cost of the structures shall have been ascertained and certified, an additional allotment may be sent. When the school shall actually have students, a tuition grant will be made to it under the established regulations. FC in DNA, 72, E:318 (M-15:5).

[1st] Lt. William H. Chase, Rigolets, [La.,] to [Alexander] Macomb, 8/27. "On removing the articles belonging to the late U.S. steam boat Western Engineer, a trunk was discovered having on it the direction of the late Dr. [William] Baldwin, who was formerly attached to the Expedition up the Missouri [under Stephen H. Long]. As this trunk may be of some consequence to his [Baldwin's] family I have communicated the circumstance to you so that they [the members of Baldwin's family] may be enabled to obtain their property. Direction for the forwarding of the trunk shall be immediately complied with by some safe conveyance." LS in DNA, 223, 1014.

From Richard M. Johnson, [Senator from Ky.,] Great Crossings, [Ky.,] 8/27. "Capt. [*sic*; 2nd Lt. Clark] Burdine has just arrived from the lead mines on his way to the City of Washington. The duty which he has performed is a most important one to the Nation. It has been difficult & hazardous, and it has terminated much to the credit & advantage of the Country." Johnson recommends Burdine for a promotion and speaks well of Burdine's brother, Reuben Burdine, who has been a faithful Clerk in the Paymaster General's office. ALS in DNA, 1, J-30 (M-221:96).

To Josiah Meigs, 8/27. Calhoun encloses a report by [Lewis] Cass [dated 7/17] concerning the public reservation at Fort Wayne. Calhoun approves the recommendation by Cass that the site of the fort, plus 30 acres of land adjoining but not so located as to interfere with "the building lots, or with the proper location of a village," be withheld from public sale. Calhoun suggests that the appropriate surveyor should be instructed accordingly. LS in DNA, 87, Ind. Military Reservations, box 97; FC in DNA, 72, E:318 (M-15:5); CC in DNA, 282, Mich. (Fort Wayne).

To JASPER PAR[R]ISH, Sub-Agent, Six Nations, Canandaigua, N.Y.

Department of War, August 27th 1822

Your letter of the 13th instant [LS with En in DNA, 1, P-61 (M-221:96)] has been received.

I am sorry to hear of the violent opposition made by Red Jacket and others in the Seneca nation to the establishment of schools among them; but as they are, by our laws considered an independent people, the government cannot exercise any authority to produce a more favorable disposition towards such establishments. This however, is a very desirable point to be gained, and ought not to be relinquished without an effort. Great reliance is placed on your discretion and good management, to which is mainly ascribed the improvements that have already been made in the Six Nations, and strong hopes are entertained that you will ultimately be able to overcome the prejudices which still exist among a portion of the Indians against schools and other measures for their civilization and happiness.

FC in DNA, 72, E:317 (M-15:5).

To William P. [DuVal], Pensacola, 8/28. Calhoun answers DuVal's letter of 8/3 [LS with Ens in DNA, 1, D-29 (M-221:95); PC in Carter, ed., *Territorial Papers,* 22:501–505]. Calhoun approves DuVal's preparations for negotiations with the Indians; Calhoun wrote on 8/19 about that subject; he authorizes DuVal to serve as a commissioner or to name someone else, preferably Capt. [John R.] Bell. Calhoun requests an estimate of the cost of the treaty, because funds are limited, but gives assurance that the negotiations will not be charged against DuVal's regular funds. Calhoun sends funds for payment of the salary of [Stephen] Richards as an Interpreter. Calhoun points out that a payment of $1,000 was made in 1818 to an Indian for Seminole War services and that no further payment can be just. If DuVal will submit an estimate of the cost of opening a road between Pensacola and St. Augustine, Calhoun will try to approve that project. FC in DNA, 72, E:318–320 (M-15:5); PC in Carter, ed., *Territorial Papers,* 22:518–519.

To Thomas Swan[n, U.S. District Attorney,] Alexandria, [D.C.]

War Dept., Aug. 28th 1822

A large number of Claims have [*sic*] been presented to the 3rd Auditor [Peter Hagner] under the Act authorizing the payment for property lost in the Seminole Campaign [of 1817–1818], which have strong appearances of being fraudulent. The circumstances which have come to the knowledge of the Auditor lead him to suspect them to have been fabricated by an old offender who from the representation of the person presenting them now [*one word, possibly* "present," *canceled*?] is at ["present at" *canceled*] Charlott[e]sville[,] Albemarle [County,] Va. The object of the Government is if possible to arrest the offender. In the execution of this purpose your presence here [*one interlined word, possibly* "in," *canceled*] would be most desirable. If that be impracticable be pleased to state by return of mail what measures should immediately be taken. The absence of the Attorney Gen[era]l [William Wirt; "here" *canceled*], occasions me to give you this trouble in this state of the business.

LS in ScU-SC, John C. Calhoun Papers. NOTE: Swann answered on 9/17.

From Lewis Cass

Detroit, Aug. 29, 1822

I have the honour to transmit to you the report of Mr. [Charles C.] Trowbridge respecting the proper sites for the establishments upon the St. Joseph and the Grand River provided for by the fourth article of the treaty of Chicago. I transmit also an extract from my letter of yesterday to the Rev. Mr. [Isaac] McCoy on the same subject.

In an experiment whose success depends so much upon the feelings and opinions of the Indians, I think it adviseable [*sic*] that other considerations should yield to their wishes. Whether, therefore, they are influenced in the preference they give to the spot which, in the opinions of Mr. McCoy and of Mr. Trowbridge, offers the least advantages, by a desire to occupy it themselves or by any other motive less friendly and obvious, still a prudent regard to the consequences requires that their representations should be favourably received. Nor do I suppose the difference between the places is such as to justify any sacrifice to a choice.

Under those circumstances, I take the liberty of recommending that the establishment for the Potawatamies be located on the prairie near the head of the rousseau des pères, if the consent of the Indians can be obtained. But, if not, that it [be] located upon the spot pointed out by them on the southern bank of the St. Joseph, near the old fort.

I would also recommend that the establishment for similar purposes upon the Grand River be fixed at the place indicated by Trowbridge, being on the north bank of that river and about fifteen miles above the mouth of the Kaupauquash.

LS with En in DNA, 1, C-100 (M-221:95); FC in DNA, 76 (M-1:5, pp. 81–82). Note: Calhoun replied on 9/18.

To J[ames] E[dward] Colhoun, [Philadelphia?]

War Dept., 29th Aug[us]t 1822

You had better let me know when to draw in your favour a week before hand, and state the amount. The exchange, I understand is very disadvantageous, and I would advise you not to draw more than would be absolutely necessary, till some private opportunity may occur to remit funds.

We are all well and would be glad to see you.

[P.S.] My factors are L.C. Cant[rell] & Co., Augusta, Georgia.

ALS in ScCleA.

To William Clark, St. Louis, 8/30. Calhoun answers his letters of 7/24 and 7/28 [LS's in DNA, 1, C-76 and C-77 (M-221:95)]. No extra funds have been allotted to Clark for the emigration of the Kickapoos and the Delawares; but Calhoun explains that a surplus of more than $10,000 in [Richard] Graham's hands is to be applied to that purpose. These Indians should be removed as soon as possible, because they impose an extreme expense upon the government in their present, temporary locations. "The continuance of the war between the Osages and the [Western] Cherokees and the commencement of a new one between the Sacks and Foxes and Sioux, notwithstanding the efforts to preserve peace, are much to be regretted; but it is believed that the government will never be able to put an end to Indian wars entirely without authority to use the military force for that purpose, which appeared to be the impression of Congress at the last Session, during which a bill was reported to that effect, but not finally acted on. It is hoped it will be taken up and passed at the next Session." Clark's proposed outlays for a combination Sub-Agent and Clerk and for his office arrangements are approved on condition that the costs do not exceed normal and present expenditures; he is granted a stationery allowance but none for fuel. A remittance of $300 is being sent for the salary of former Sub-Agent [John] Ruland. FC in DNA, 72, E:320–321 (M-15:5).

From LEWIS CASS

Detroit, August 31st 1822

I have the honour to acknowledge the receipt of your letter of the 31 ult[im]o. Col. Stockton, to whom the publick buildings at Fort Gratiot were committed, yet remains in possession of them. It appears to me that it would not be proper to evict him, because nothing has occurred on his part to render such a measure necessary. The Indian school, established by the [Northern] missionary society, occupies a part of the buildings under him and, I presume, will, without hesitation, be permitted to do so. Besides, the permanent location of this school at that spot is doubtful, as many considerations will eventually render its removal into the Indian Country adviseable. A change, therefore, of the possession of these works would be temporary and would probably render some other arrangements necessary ere long. I am, therefore, of the opinion that no change should at present be made.

LS in DNA, 1, C-109 (M-221:95); FC (dated 8/30) in DNA, 76 (M-1:5, pp. 83–84).

To Alexander Hamilton, St. Augustine

Department of War, 31st August 1822

Your letter of the 30th ultimo [ALS with Ens in DNA, 1, H-65 (M-221:95)], marked private, with the correspondence therein referred to, has been received.

A very unfavorable impression exists here in relation to the character of [Horatio S.] Dexter, whose unauthorized proceedings among the Indians were represented to this Department by General [Andrew] Jackson during the last year, who stated that he had in consequence of them directed his [Dexter's] removal from the Indian Country, which it was presumed had been done. If he still continues his unauthorized proceedings the provisions of the law of intercourse ought to be enforced against him, and upon a proper representation of his conduct to the Indian Agent, [Gad Humphreys,] or to [Lt.] Col. [Abram] Eustis who is fully authorized to act in the case during the absence of the Agent, I have no doubt that the notice which a violation of the law and the interest of government require, will be promptly taken of him.

FC in DNA, 72, E:322 (M-15:5). Note: Two other, cryptic letters had been written to Calhoun by Hamilton and may have been related to his attitude toward Dexter. These letters were dated 7/24 [ALS in DNA, 1, H-36 (M-221:95)] and 7/28 [ALS with Ens in DNA, 1, H-65 (M-221:95)].

SEPTEMBER 1822

Typically, the past, the present, and the future were involved in Calhoun's thoughts. All three were reflected in letters from and to Jacob Brown on the 20th; he thanked Calhoun for considerate treatment of his protracted illness, and Monroe evinced the administration's concern lest Brown's absence provoke criticism. On the 6th Calhoun assured Jasper Parrish that hostility of the "Pagan party" against Christian schools was viewed "with marked disapprobation." On the same day the faculty of Yale College conferred upon Calhoun the honorary degree of Doctor of Laws. On the 23rd, looking to the future, Calhoun's estimates of the War Department's financial needs for 1823 were requested. "I do not doubt," Calhoun wrote that day, "that we are on the eve of a political struggle, for which we ought to prepare in time to meet [it]."

From the Society of United Brethren, Bethlehem, Pa., 9/——. This report, requested by Calhoun on 3/4 for the information of the Senate, relates the progress made by the Society in its efforts to civilize and to convert to Christianity the Indians occupying a tract of land granted to them by Congress near the Muskingum River in O. (The report was prepared by the Rev. Lewis D. Schweinitz and signed by President C.G. Hueffell for the Directors of the Society. The enclosures consist of two long reports, one undated and the other dated 4/16/1822, by John Heckewelder to the President and Directors of the Society of United Brethren.) PC with Ens in Senate Document No. 3, 17th Cong., 2nd Sess.; PC with Ens in *American State Papers*: *Indian Affairs*, 2:372–391.

From W[illiam] H[enry] Harrison, Northbend, [O.,] 9/2. He argues that he should have been consulted about the device for the medal [voted to him by Congress in 1814], because he was in command of the whole campaign involved. He approves the choice made by [Isaac] Shelby of the incident to be portrayed on Shelby's medal but suggests that the proposed design for his own medal should be revised. PEx in Item 67 of the catalogue for Sale 2297 on 10/13/1964 by the Parke-Bernet Gallaries, Inc., New York City.

From Z[echariah] Lewis, [Domestic Secretary of the United Foreign Missionary Society,] New York [City], 9/2. "In behalf of the Managers of the United Foreign Missionary Society," Lewis quotes a long extract from a letter dated 8/22 from the Rev. T[homson] S. Harris, Superintendent of the "Missionary Establishment at Seneca, near Buffalo." Harris's letter reports that pagan Indians threaten the removal of missionaries at the Society's mission in the same legal manner by which a Baptist teacher was removed by the District Attorney "at the instance of the pagan party as complainants." [Jasper] Parrish has advised that application be made "without delay to the Secretary of War—that orders be forwarded to the Agent, from the President of the United States, [James Monroe,] to interfere in the business, & to tell the pagan party, that they must relinquish their attempts to remove the Missionaries from their lands." Parrish thinks this procedure would have the desired effect, and he can inform the General Council of the Six Nations of it, if the letter can be received by 9/15. Lewis requests that such a letter be sent, and he informs Calhoun that "at the Seneca village, we have more than twenty of the Indian children, living in the Mission Family, & receiving a course of instruction correspondent with the suggestions contained in your Circulars." ALS in DNA, 1, L-21 (M-221:96).

To Young King and Other Deputies of the Christian Party of the Six Nations, Seneca Mission House, near Buffalo

Department of War, Washington, 2d September 1822

Brothers, I have received your communication of the 21st ultimo [LS in DNA, 1, S-118 (M-221:96)], and am glad to find that you are determined to adhere to the institutions and policy which have led you to your present state of civilization and happiness, notwithstanding the opposition of some of your own people. While you continue to pursue this wise course, you will always receive the approbation and support of the government, which rejoices in your prosperity.

Brothers, It is with regret I learn the determination of the

Council which you state was lately held at Tenewanda, by your Brothers of the opposite party. These determinations evince a settled opposition to the wishes of the government, as well as to your and their own best interests. No communication from that Council has been received. If one should be received, or a deputation should come on, nothing will be done without a proper regard to your civilization and welfare.

Brothers, The confidence which you repose in the government will never be disappointed. It will always listen with a willing ear to the voice of its good children, and protect them in their just rights and previledges [*sic*]. I am glad ["your present Agent (Jasper Parrish) and Interpreter (Horatio Jones) have your confidence," *interlined*;] they have also the confidence of the government, and will never be taken from you while you wish them to remain among you.

FC in DNA, 72, E:322 (M-15:5).

To John Nelson, [Representative from Md.,] Frederick, Md.

Department of War, September 5th 1822

Your several letters of the 30th of last month have been duly received.

With regard to the appointment of your Brother Doct[or Arthur?] Nelson as an Agent for the Superintendence of the lead mines of Missouri, I have to state to you that until some legislative provision be made for the appointment, and the compensation of such Agents, I do not find myself sufficiently authorized to make them. The business of the mine lands was formerly confided by the Treasury Department to the Receivers and Registers of the General Land Office, without, it would appear, any additional compensation for such service.

Application will be made early in the next session of Congress for a legislative act, to embrace the above and other measures connected therewith. In the mean while, your Brother's application will be preserved on file, for future recurrence thereto.

From the report of the 3d Auditor, [Peter Hagner, dated 9/4 (FC in DNA, 53, 27:53)] you will perceive that the papers of Captain [Joseph S.] Nelson transmitted by you to this Department [on 8/30 (ALS in DNA, 1, N-13 [M-221:96]))] have been laid before him, and from the circumstances attending his accounting there is, I regret to say, little or no chance for their being admitted. It would have afforded me much satisfaction to have been enabled to have offered you more encouragement on this subject, but the difficulties seem at present insuperable.

FC in DNA, 3, 11:428 (M-6:11).

To Matthew Lyon, Little Rock, 9/6. Calhoun answers Lyon's appeal of 7/20 [ALS in DNA, 1, L-20 (M-221:96); PC in Carter, ed., *Territorial Papers,* 19:451–453] for new employment—an appeal made because the abolition of the Factory system will leave Factor Lyon jobless. Calhoun assures Lyon that, when he was appointed, "so early and radical a change in the system was not expected." Calhoun applauds Lyon's written support of the Indian schools program and says that it would be pleasing to continue Lyon in U.S. employment; but no Indian Agency or Sub-Agency is vacant. FC in DNA, 72, E:323 (M-15:5); PC in Carter, ed., *Territorial Papers*, 19:457.

To Jasper Parrish, Canandaigua, N.Y.

[Department of War, September 6, 1822]

I have consulted the President of the United States [James Monroe] relative to the conduct of the party in the Six Nations called the "Pagan party," towards the establishments which have been made amongst them for the education of the children and other purposes connected with their civilization and happiness, and I have it in charge from him to direct you to say to this party, that he views their conduct with marked disapprobation; That the institutions in the Six Nations, having been established with the consent of a number of the most respectable Chiefs, and with the approbation of the government, a continuance of the violent opposition which they have lately manifested towards them, and in particular any attempts to remove them, against the wish of so many of their own people, and that of the government, will be considered as highly unjust to the former and disrespectful and offensive to the latter; That if they do not choose, themselves, or their children, to profit by them, it is an act of selfishness and injustice to attempt to deprive those of their people that do, of the benefit of them; That he sincerely hopes they will take these things into consideration, and that a regard for justice and respect for the government, if not for their own interests, will induce them to pursue a more wise and liberal course, towards institutions having in view their present & future welfare.

Given under my hand and the seal of the War Office of the United States, at the City of Washington, this sixth day of September, 1822. J.C. Calhoun.

LS in DLC, United States: Indians; FC in DNA, 72, E:323–324 (M-15:5).

From Peter Hagner, 9/7. Pursuant to a House resolution of 5/7 [DS in DNA, 1, R-211 (M-221:94)] concerning Ordnance bureau expenditures for buildings and repairs since 1798, Hagner encloses and discusses three documents requested by Calhoun. He regrets that the reports cannot be more complete, but many records were destroyed by the "Enemy" in "1813 [*sic*; 1814]." LS with Ens in DNA, RG 233, 17A-D1; FC in DNA, 53, 27:66–67; PC with Ens in House Document No. 111, 17th Cong., 2nd Sess.; PC with Ens in *American State Papers: Military Affairs*, 2:513–514.

To Z[echariah] Lewis, New York [City], 9/7. "I have received your letter of the 2d instant relative to the conduct of the Pagan party in the Six Nations, and laid it before the President, [James Monroe,] who directed that instructions be given to the [Sub-] Agent, [Jasper Parrish,] agreeably to your request. Instructions have been given [on 9/6] accordingly, a copy of which is enclosed." FC in DNA, 72, E:324 (M-15:5).

From Lewis Cass, Detroit, 9/8. He encloses a recommendation by Henry R. Schoolcraft, Indian Agent at Sault Ste. Marie, that a building be constructed there for the Agent's quarters. Cass suggests that perhaps the soldiers there can do the construction work. LS with En in DNA, 1, C-118 (M-221:95); FC in DNA, 76 (M-1:5, pp. 86–87); PC with En in Carter, ed., *Territorial Papers*, 11:264–266. (Calhoun answered on 10/3.)

To James E[dward] Colhoun, Philadelphia

War Dep[artmen]t, 9 Sept[embe]r 1822

You will find herewith inclosed five notes of the Branch Bank of [the United States in] Washington for $100 each agreeably to list. I was under the necessity of sending notes, as I could not procure d[ra]ft on Phila[delphia]; however, these notes, the Cashier informs ["me," *interlined*] pass current in that City, at par. Yours affectionately, J.C. Calhoun.

[P.S.] Please to acknowledge the receipt of the money.

LS in ScCleA.

To Mority Fürst, Philadelphia, 9/9. Calhoun replies to Fürst's letter of 9/5 [LS in DNA, 1, F-28 (M-221:95)] by stating that "no money can be remitted on your account for engraving the dies of the medal for General [Alexander] Macomb, without the sum to be remitted is approved by Mr. [Joseph] Hopkinson." FC in DNA, 3, 11:429 (M-6:11).

To Solomon Sibley, [Delegate from Mich. Territory,] Detroit, 9/9. Calhoun answers Sibley's letter to [James Monroe dated 8/18 (ALS in DNA, 1, S-106 [M-221:96])], which enclosed a petition of Joseph La Frambois[e] for a transfer to his sister, Josette La Frambois[e], of the section of land that was granted to him by the Treaty of Chicago. Calhoun has checked the relevant provision of that treaty and asks, before making a decision, for assurance that Joseph is the person who was named in the treaty. LS in MiD; FC in DNA, 72, E:325 (M-15:5). (Compare Sibley's letter to Calhoun dated 3/8/1823.)

To [former Lt. Col.] Gad Humphreys, Marcellus, N.Y.

Department of War, 10th Septem[be]r 1822

No answer having been received from you to my letter of the 19th ult[im]o, and the presence of the Indian Agent in Florida being indispensable, I am under the necessity of stating to you that unless your bond is forwarded, and the Department apprized of your departure for Florida, by the first of October, you will be considered as having resigned your office and a new appointment will be immediately made.

FC in DNA, 72, E:326 (M-15:5).

To William Ward, Choctaw Agency, 9/10. Calhoun acknowledges Ward's letter of 8/10 and expresses apprehension because Ward had not received the draft for $14,135; it was mailed on 6/17 and should have reached Ward by mid-July. Ward should stop payment on it, by the Branch Bank of the United States in Louisville, to anyone but himself. Steps will be taken this autumn to have the Agency moved to a site within Choctaw boundaries; Ward is to report to Calhoun the merits of the site suggested by the Chiefs. FC in DNA, 72, E:325–326 (M-15:5).

To the Cashier of the Branch Bank of the United States at Louisville, 9/11. Because William Ward had not received by 8/10 a draft dated 6/17 for $14,135, Calhoun requests that payment be stopped, unless Ward or someone properly authorized by him should present it for payment. FC in DNA, 72, E:326 (M-15:5).

Degree awarded to Calhoun, 9/11. The faculty of Yale College confers upon Calhoun the honorary degree of Doctor of Laws. This document, written in Latin, is signed by Jeremiah Day and by Elizur Goodrich as President and Secretary, respectively, of the faculty. Photostat of a DS in CtY, Yale Memorabilia.

To John Clark, [Governor of Ga.,] Milledgeville, and William Carroll, [Governor of Tenn.,] Murfreesboro

Department of War, 12 Septem[be]r 1822

The Cherokee Indians on the Arkansaw being desirous to have laid off for them the vast quantity of land to which they are entitled under the treaty of the 8th July 1817, it becomes necessary in order to comply with their wish, first to ascertain the quantity of land ceded by said treaty to the United States. I have therefore to request you will furnish me with a statement of the number of acres contained in that part of the cession which lies within the limits of Georgia, [and of Tenn., respectively,] which, it is presumed, may be easily ascertained from the surveys made by the State.

FC in DNA, 72, E:327 (M-15:5). Note: A marginal notation indicates that an identical request, changing only the name of the State, was written on 10/15/1822 to Governor Gabriel Holmes of N.C. at Raleigh.

To Walter Leake, Governor of Miss., Natchez, 9/12. Because the State of Miss. may have some interest in the contemplated move "next fall" of the Choctaw Agency to some point within the Indian boundaries, Calhoun requests that Leake present his opinion of a site suitable both to the State and to the Indians. FC in DNA, 72, E:326 (M-15:5).

From Winfield Scott, Elizabethtown, N.J., 9/12. He reiterates forcefully his claim to temporary command of the Army during [Jacob] Brown's illness. ALS in DNA, 1, S-120 (M-221:96).

To Joseph Hopkinson, Philadelphia, 9/13. Calhoun encloses a copy of a letter [dated 9/2] from [William Henry] Harrison to the War "Department and an extract of one from [former] Col. [Charles S.?] Todd to the General concerning a device for the General's medal." Calhoun asks Hopkinson to report the progress made on the medal and, if no medal has been formed, that Hopkinson correspond with Harrison, if necessary, for additional information concerning "the incidents which he may desire should enter into the piece." FC in DNA, 3, 11:429 (M-6:11).

John H. Hall, Harpers Ferry, to George Bomford, 9/14. Hall sends a copper flask. If it earns Bomford's approval, more can be made easily. "The insertion of the bullet tube in the body of the flasks will enable us to give them a handsome form & will afford an opportunity for a better spring than that formerly used & will also enable us to make the flasks at less expense than was at first contemplated." ALS in DNA, 31, 1822, H.

From A[YERS] P. MERRILL, Assistant Surgeon

Fort San Carlos de Barrancas, 15 September 1822

The greatest inconvenience is experienced at this post for the want of a Hospital. The men suffer extremely from exposure and want of care. Many of them have had their constitutions destroyed, and some have lost their lives, because no comfortable place was provided to receive them when sick, where they could have the common attentions of a Hospital. Notwithstanding the Regulations expressly make it the primary duty of the commanding officer of troops to provide for the comfort of the sick; and notwithstanding the frequent representations of the necessity of a Hospital at this Post, to the commanding officer, and Surgeon General, [Joseph Lovell,] and also to the commanding General [Jacob Brown] and ["As(sistan)t" *interlined*] Inspector General, still the subject has been neglected, even when philanthropic motives would have impelled the most unfeeling witness to afford assistance. The expense to be incurred in the erection of a building has been the prominent excuse for this neglect, when the rents which have been paid by the Quarter Master for old, confined, dangerous, and inconvenient buildings for the accommodation of the sick, would more than have paid all the expenses of building a good and spacious Hospital.

The troops are now sickly, and men affected with malignant fevers are obliged to be crowded together in a small confined room, which will only contain six or seven, and suffered to remain in the rooms of the ["men" *canceled*] Companies, badly attended, and communicating disease to those around them.

Another cause of disease and death which produces no small degree of mortality at this post, is the danger in the communication with Pensacola, in consequence of two Bayous which frequently compel the men to swim. Almost a daily intercourse is kept up by land, and besides producing colds and fevers from fording them in cold weather, of which we had a great many instances last winter, it is not unfrequently the case that men are drowned. Eight or nine have lost their lives in this way during the last year. Officers and men are alike exposed. Flatboats could be placed upon both these water courses for twenty or thirty dollars, & bridges, probably for three hundred dollars.

A great regard for the good of the Army, & motives of humanity, are the inducements which determine me to make these representations direct to the War Department.

ALS in DNA, 1, M-107 (M-221:96). NOTE: An AES dated 10/17 by [Capt.] T[rueman] Cross reads: "Annexed is an extract of a letter [dated 8/27 and] addressed to the Q[uarte]rmaster at Pensacola, advising of the order of the War Dep[artmen]t to remove the 4th Reg[imen]t to the vicinity of Barrancas. It will be seen that it contains the necessary instructions on the subject of a Hospital." The extract states: "The necessary Stone Houses, and a *suitable building* for *the accommodation* of *the sick* should also be erected at Barrancas as early as practicable after the troops move thither."

From George Boyd, Michilimackinac, [Mich. Territory,] 9/16. He encloses "a statement of my accounts as Indian Agent to the 1st instant—together with additional vouchers, in relation to items objected to in a former account rendered to the 1st of October 1821." Boyd "believed that when my certificate of Honor was attached to my general account of Expenditures, that my oath would not also be required to establish certain items of the same account," as has been required by [William Lee]. Almost no funds have been received at the Agency for 1822. "To remedy the evils growing out of the late law, in relation to disbursing Officers of the Government, who have been found indebted to the U[nited] States, without the means of settling their accounts (and in which predicament unfortunately I stand)[,] the Governor of this Territory [Lewis Cass] has written to me the inclosed letter [*not found*], received the 1st of the present month [in which Cass proposed that Cass receipt the bills in his name]." Boyd, however, believes that "the law in question, has only a direct bearing on the immediate salary of the Officer—and does not prohibit him from drawing for the sums necessary & proper for the use of the Agency over which he has controul. By annexing[,] however, the individual voucher to each Bill drawn, not on account of salary, but for the other objects connected with the Agency, I should imagine that all the scruples of the law would at once be obviated—and I shall accordingly delay any answer to the Governor on this head, until I shall have the pleasure to receive your Commands on the subject." Boyd complains that a draft for $775 for the construction of quarters for the Agent has been rejected, although both Calhoun and Cass have approved the expenditure. He discusses at length the quality, cost, and condition of the "100 stands of arms deposited by me [in 1816] at Greenleafs point [*sic*], together with those Indian Arms turned over to Mr. [Thomas L.] McKenney." McKenney rejected the arms some 18 months after delivery and required repairs, which Boyd claims were unnecessary. [William] Lee, according to Boyd, states that McKenney has informed Calhoun that the arms are worthless even as gifts to Indians. Boyd denies this, maintaining that they are of good quality and requesting Calhoun to "direct the Arms in question to be received at their cost as the property of the U[nited] States." He also encloses an abstract of trading licenses issued between 9/1/1821 and 8/31/1822. (The Ens consist of the abstract of licenses and of a copy of a letter of 9/15 [*sic*; 9/16] from Boyd to Cass.) ALS with Ens in DNA, 77, 5242 (M-271:4, frames 23–32).

To Ninian Edwards, Edwardsville, Ill., 9/16. Calhoun acknowledges Edwards' letters of 8/24 [ALS's in DNA, 1, E-29 and

E-30 (M-221:95)]. Several applicants are seeking appointment as the government's agent at the lead mines, but the War Department has no authorization to make such an appointment. Calhoun believes that the obvious need will cause Congress to make provision for such an agent, and he will then be able to consider Edwards' recommendation of [William] Kinnes. Orders were given for the Peoria Sub-Agency [of James Latham] to be transferred to [William] Clark's Superintendency; but when that Sub-Agent was appointed, there was no Superintendent of Indian Affairs at St. Louis, and the Sub-Agent was therefore made responsible to [Lewis] Cass. Calhoun regrets Edwards' inconvenience arising from trouble over the pay of an Interpreter; that trouble will be corrected. FC in DNA, 72, E:328 (M-15:5).

From G[ad] Humphreys, I[ndian] A[gent for Fla. Territory], Pittsfield, Mass., 9/17. He encloses his bond [for $10,000]. ALS in DNA, 1, H-88 (M-221:95).

From Return J. Meigs, Cherokee Agency, 9/17. He transmits his promised accounts and explains several details concerning them, including his hope that Congress will yet act favorably upon his petition presented to the last session for relief from the obligation to repay to the U.S. the $2,000 that were stolen from him. FC in DNA, 75 (M-208:9).

From Thomas Swann, Alexandria, [D.C.,] 9/17. "I returned from the Country last night to this place and found your letter here of the 28th ult[imo]. It is now perhaps too late to afford the assistance which you requested. If however I should be wanted, or could render any service in the matter to which you alluded, be pleas[e]d to say so, and I will attend you forthwith." ALS in DNA, 1, S-122 (M-221:96).

To Lewis Cass, Detroit, 9/18. Answering Cass's letter of 8/29, Calhoun approves the sites for the establishments called for by the Treaty of Chicago and proposed by [Charles C.] Trowbridge and by [Isaac] McCoy; "I perfectly agree with you that, in fixing upon the sites . . . , the opinions and feelings of the Indians should be respected." LS in DNA, 76 (M-1:11, pp. 438–441); variant FC in DNA, 72, E:330 (M-15:5).

To William P. [DuVal], Pensacola, 9/18. [Gad] Humphreys, the Agent for Indian Affairs in Fla., will be enroute to that [Territory] by 10/1. "I hope he will arrive in time to make under your directions, such preliminary arrangements as may be necessary for the meeting" with the Indians that DuVal has scheduled for 11/20. FC in DNA, 72, E:331 (M-15:5).

To Mority "Fürtz [*sic*; Fürst]," Philadelphia, 9/18. Calhoun returns the likenesses and reverses for the medals for [Jacob] Brown and [Peter B.] Porter and requests Fürst to state for which likeness each reverse is intended, since both commemorate the same three battles. FC in DNA, 3, 11:430 (M-6:11).

To Gad Humphreys, Indian Agent [for Fla. Territory], Marcellus, N.Y., 9/18. Calhoun expresses pleasure that Humphreys, as he wrote on 9/9 [ALS in DNA, 2, H-1820 (*sic*; [M-222:21])], will depart for Fla. by 10/18 at the latest. "You will by no means delay it beyond that period, as the Governor [William P. DuVal] has appointed a meeting with the Indians at St. Marks on the 20th November next, and it is indispensable that you should be at your post as soon as practicable, in order to make such preliminary arrangements for the meeting as the Governor may deem necessary. You will forward your bond previous to your departure." FC in DNA, 72, E:330–331 (M-15:5); PC in Carter, ed., *Territorial Papers*, 22:532–533.

To Lawrence Taliaferro, Indian Agent, St. Peters on the Upper Mississippi, 9/18. Calhoun answers Taliaferro's letter of 7/15 [ALS in DNA, 1, T-35 (M-221:96)]. Calhoun rejoices that the Sauks, Foxes, and Sioux are not conspiring to attack U.S. Army posts. He regrets the heavy losses by a Mississippi flood suffered by the tribes of Taliaferro's Agency; but no relief can be afforded unless it can be squeezed out of his authorized expenditures. LS in MnHi, Lawrence Taliaferro Papers (published microfilm, roll 1, document 46); FC (dated 9/17) in DNA, 72, E:330 (M-15:5); PC (dated 9/17) in Carter, ed., *Territorial Papers*, 11:267.

From W[illiam] Ward, Choctaw Agency, 9/19. He acknowledges Calhoun's letter of 8/26. Ward has forwarded his accounts and vouchers to the War Department, but the balance against him has been reduced by the payment of some claims. [William Lee] has charged against Ward the $14,135 that Ward has not yet received, the draft having obviously been lost in the mails. ALS in DNA, 77 (M-271:4, frames 245–247).

From Jacob Brown, Philadelphia, 9/20. He thanks Calhoun for his letter of 7/2. "It has been my fixed determination, if my strength would permit, to be with you in the course of October, when all doubt as to my command in the Army would be removed. I hope it is impossible for me to be a stumbling block in your path through the excess of good feeling, with which, as a politician, you are troubled. If you err, it will, I am sure, be in consequence of your solicitude for a deeply afflicted friend." FC in DLC, Jacob Brown Papers, Letterbooks, 2:216–217.

James Monroe to [Jacob] Brown, Philadelphia, 9/20. Monroe states the concern that he has felt for Brown's health since the beginning of Brown's illness. "It has also been equally my object to regulate the command of the Army with the utmost delicacy and kindness to you under a firm conviction that it was due to your merit." He has been supported by Calhoun and the officers next in command. In determining what course to pursue at this time, it is thought best to grant a further indulgence to Brown so as not to hazard his health, and the next in command will perform the duties of Brown's office. "It is presumed that this arrangement had better be made at this time than any later period before the meeting of Congress." But Monroe will take no step until he hears from Brown. CC in DLC, Jacob Brown Papers, Letterbooks, 2:217–218.

To William P. [DuVal], Pensacola, 9/20. Calhoun encloses some licenses [to trade with Indians] received by Calhoun from a recent Acting Governor of Fla. [Territory]; Calhoun does so because he believes "that you should be apprized of them, in order to prevent any improper use of them." FC in DNA, 72, E:331 (M-15:5).

From Mority Fürst, Philadelphia, 9/20. The impressions that Fürst received with Calhoun's letter of 9/18 were slightly bruised; therefore, Fürst will supply new impressions to replace the damaged ones. LS in DNA, 1, F-30 (M-221:95).

From William Wirt, 9/21. He decides that a statute of 5/7, repealing part of a statute of 3/2/1821, does nothing more than that and does not alter Wirt's opinion of 12/29/1821 that Bvt. Maj. Gens. [Edmund P.] Gaines and [Winfield] Scott are entitled to pay at their brevet ranks if they command Divisions. Whether or not they command Divisions is a question for the War Department to decide. LS in DNA, 2, W-1822 (M-222:23); FC in DNA, 113, B:92–93 (T-412:2); FC in DNA, 311, 1:275–276.

From Joseph Nourse, Register, Treasury Department, 9/23. He asks that the "usual Estimates for the year 1823" be prepared and transmitted to his office so that they can be submitted to Congress. LS in DNA, 1, N-17 (M-221:96).

From P[ETER] B. PORTER, "Private"

Buffaloe [*sic*], Sept. 23d 1822

Mr. [Jasper] Parrish & Mr. [Horatio] Jones [Interpreter] have shewn me a printed paper, purporting to be the "Proceedings of an Indian Council held at Tonewanta [*sic;* Tonawanda] on the 8th of August 1822," and have requested me to express to you my opinion of the character of this paper & of the consideration to which it is entitled, which I cheerfully do.

Of many, and indeed of most, of the topics treated of, & made the subjects of complaint against Mr. Parrish, I have no particular personal knowledge; but, from my acquaintance with most of the Chiefs—from my knowledge of their affairs generally—from the representations I have heard respecting the council at Tonewanta, and from the complexion of the paper itself, I have no hesitation in beleiving [*sic*] it to be a tissue of misrepresentations. It commences by stating a deliberate falsehood, to wit, that the number of Indians assembled at the Council was 2,608—whereas I am satisfied from the information I have received that the number could not have exceed[ed] 2 or 300, & that many of them were *Canadian* Indians, who had been sent for for this express purpose. As to Mr. Parrish's fidelity in paying over the annuities, I can only say that he has always sustained, and I have reason to beleive justly, the reputation of being *uncommonly* carefull, exact & particular in the discharge of this part of his duty—always making it a point not only to take receipts from the Indians for the sums he pays, but to have some respectable white man present to count the money & attest to the correctness of the transaction.

The difficulties now existing amongst our Indians, are principally to be ascribed to *Red Jacket*, who is a man of great talents, and a great *Intriguer*. I am myself satisfied that the surest & shortest mode of restoring harmony amongst them, will be a steady

& stern perseverance in the course of policy indicated in your late letters to Mr. Parrish, & which he has shewn me.

ALS in DNA, 1, P-88 (M-221:96).

To Samuel L. Southard, [Senator from N.J.]

Washington, 23d Sept. 1822

I would be happy to gratify [2nd] Lieut[enant William?] Cook in his laudable desire of improving himself, if it could be done with propriety; but I cannot imagine any mode by which it can be effected, unless by detailing him as an assistant professor at West Point, which, however, is never done without the request of the Superintendent [Sylvanus Thayer]. If he [Cook] can obtain his [Thayer's] request, I will gratify him with pleasure.

I am much gratified to learn that New Jersey is firm on the side of the administration. Her position greatly increases her natural weight. I cannot doubt, that it was intended by certain individuals to make the city of New York and throug[h] it the State, the centre of a formidable opposition. The soundness of the adjacent States will present formidable obstacle[s] to this scheme. A united voice in the Senate of the Union on the part of Jersey, is highly important, and it seems to me, that it would be wise to take measures to effect it. I do not doubt, that we are on the eve of a political struggle, for which we ought to prepare in time to meet [it]. An opposition originating where the present does must soon bring on a crisis, which, I think must take place before the termination of the next session. With prudence and vigour the result need not be fear[e]d. The people are sound, and the opposition has nothing to stand on.

We hear but little, but what is known to the publick. We have formed a convention with Great Britian [*sic*; "at" *canceled*] in regards to the slaves taken away at the end of the war [of 1812], which provides for a board of four individuals, two of a side, to set [*sic*] at this place, to adjust the value &c. The ["commission" *canceled and* "Ministers" *interlined*] to S[outh] America will not be appointed, till after the meeting of Congress [during 1822–1823]. Mr. [William] Wirt's health is so far restored, that he will probably not think of one of the appointments.

The President [James Monroe] will firmly maintain his political course. The appointment of Judge [John] McLean of Ohio, an able and firm friend of the present policy, [to be the Commissioner of the General Land Office,] I look upon as an earnest of his decision to regard the existing state of things in making his selections.

As distinct from any interest, which I may be ["said" *canceled and* "supposed" *interlined*] to have, I look on the approaching crisis, as a very important one, and yourself, as one calculated to take a lead honorable to yourself and useful to the country. [Martin] Van Buren will certainly lead the opposition in the Senate, and no one in that body is so well calculated to take the opposite side as yourself.

I will at all times be happy to hear from you.

ALS in NjP, Samuel L. Southard Papers.

Jacob Brown, Philadelphia, to [James Monroe,] 9/24. In reply to Monroe's letter of 9/20, Brown states that prior to the receipt of the letter he had, with the approval of his physicians, made arrangements to proceed to Washington. He assumes that this will meet Monroe's approval. FC in DLC, Jacob Brown Papers, Letterbooks, 2:218.

To William H[enry] Harrison, Cincinnati

Department of War, September 24th 1822

In relation to the device for your medal, I enclose herewith a copy of a letter from Mr. [Joseph] Hopkinson, the President of the Academy of Fine Arts at Philadelphia, to whom the execution of the medals has been confided, by which you will see Col. [Charles S.] Todd was mistaken in his communication to you as to the causes of the delay. I have, however, to regret that any delay has occur[r]ed in consulting you respecting the device which should be adopted, and can only account for it by a conviction in my mind that you had been consulted during the winter you were here. But, as you will perceive by Mr. Hopkinson[']s letter, no delay in the execution of the medal has as yet occurred because of having no device deci[s]ion, as the medals voted in 1814 are not yet completed, there being but one artist employed upon them, it being impossible to obtain more. The urgency too on the part of Governor [Isaac] Shelby to have his finished because of his advanced life, is another reason for the delay which has occurred in relation to you. The Governor[']s is but just completed; and with no other effect on yours but in the advantage of a choice of incidents. But this it is believed may be compensated to you by selecting others, of as much prominence and importance in the battles to be thus commemorated, won under your command. Mr. Hopkinson has been requested to correspond with you upon the device which may be desired[?].

The expense stated by Mr. Hopkinson appears great, but there is no disposition on the part of the Executive to for[e]go the introduction of any proper event into the medal, and which may enhance the value of it to you on that account.

There can be no objection to your causing such notice to be taken of the delay in the completion of your medal in the public prints as you may desire and will direct.

FC in DNA, 3, 11:431–432 (M-6:11).

Joseph Hawkins, Philadelphia, to James Monroe, 9/24. Hawkins describes (and offers on undisclosed terms) his invention of a cannon designed to be loaded at the breech. He states that he has already written on this subject to Calhoun and to other members of the Cabinet but has received no reply. ALS in DNA, 35, In-1b-1; ALS in DNA, 35, In-4 & 5-15. (Each version has variant endorsements indicating that Monroe referred this letter and that it was answered [by George Bomford] for Calhoun.)

To Joseph Hopkinson, Philadelphia

Department of War, September 24th 1822

I have received your letter of the 19th instant [ALS in DNA, 1, H-82 (M-221:95)], and have transmitted a copy of it to [former Maj.] General [William Henry] Harrison as bringing the whole subject before him, and that you may also have my views respecting it, I transmit herewith a copy of my letter [of today] to the General. Upon the design of the device I request you to correspond directly with the General, as you will see I have intimated to him that you would.

FC in DNA, 3, 11:431 (M-6:11).

From JOHN JOHNSTON

Piqua, [O.,] Sept. 24, 1822

When I was out among the Indians in July and Aug. paying them their annuities[, I] was taken with the Bilious fever and after reaching home lay four weeks. I am now able to walk about a little and begin to experience some of the feelings of health. Your letter of the 7th of Aug. came here when I was not in a situation to make up my accounts or reply to it. My vouchers up to the 30th June last has [*sic*] been since forwarded thro' Gov[erno]r [Lewis] Cass and no doubt they have reached the Treasury before this; including Annuities for 1822 they amounted to $17,748.35. Having been a long time in the service, [I] was ever attentive to the standing regulations of the Department but I had received no funds from Sept. 1821 until after the adjournment of the last session of Congress, and it was several weeks after before monies were placed at my disposal to pay off the expences of the Agency. This was the cause why my accounts could not be rendered sooner. While on this subject I take the liberty of remarking that our means are too limited; for want of money to pay them I have been oblidged [*sic*] to discharge the two strikers in the Blacksmiths['] shops, at Wapaghkonetta and Upper Sandusky, and in the present situation of these Indians, this kind of assistance was highly necessary. Gov[erno]r Cass, who is a most able and faithful officer, has made the most equitable division of the funds among the different Agencies but the ag[g]regate amount does not enable him to do justice to all.

I am in constant arrangement with the Indians who are emigrating westward of the Mississippi and to the country beyond Green Bay. Several parties from this Agency have gone in both directions the present year. This subjects me to expense, and it is unavoidable. I am in arrears about $250 on this head.

In reply to that part of your letter of the 19th April last, which relates to the payment of part of the Shawaneese Annuity to the portion of that Tribe who reside westward of the Mississippi, I have to state that the Shawaneese on the Mississippi seperated [*sic*] from their nation and moved there immediately after the Revolutionary War under the advice and direction of a noted incendiary named Laramie, that they have continued seperate ever since, that they had no share or agency in any of the Treaties by which annuities have been secured to their nation, that the Chiefs utterly refuse to have their annuity divided and a part paid at any other place than that designated by Treaty. This opinion was unanimously expressed in the national Council at Wapaghkonetta in July last, and it fully accords with my observation and experience in relation to this people. The whole nation will ere long move westward. The principal Chiefs are very aged men. The Black Hoof who is upwards of 90 years old is by reason of age and infirmity against moving. The old men will soon die. The nation will then leave this country and join their friends over the Mississippi. Until then it is recommended that their annuity be paid as heretofore.

ALS in DNA, 1, J-49 (M-221:96); CCEx in MoSHi, Richard Graham Papers.

To William Ward, Choctaw Agency, 9/24. Calhoun acknowledges Ward's letters and enclosures of 8/26 [*not found*] and 9/2 [ALS with En in DNA, 77 (M-271:4, frames 241–244)]. Calhoun authorizes payments to emigrant Choctaws for improvements appraised after their departure but disallows a claim for improvements made after ratification of the Choctaw treaty. He directs payments to Puckshunnubbee specified in the treaty. Calhoun approves Ward's proposed sale of surplus blankets that have proved not to be needed because the number of emigrants has proved to be smaller than was expected but will expect strict records about the sale. FC in DNA, 72, E:333 (M-15:5).

To Lewis Cass, Detroit, 9/25. Calhoun acknowledges Cass's letters of 8/30 [LS in DNA, 1, C-108 (M-221:95); FC in DNA, 76 (M-1:5, p. 85); and LS in DNA, 16, 1822, C-67 (M-567:2, frames 140–144); FC in DNA, 76 (M-1:5, p. 84)], 8/31 (PC under that date herein), and 9/5 [LS in DNA, 1, C-115 (M-221:95); FC in DNA, 76 (M-1:5, p. 86)]. Calhoun authorizes continuance of the occupation by an Army officer and by the Indian mission school, until further orders, of the public buildings at Fort Gratiot, [Mich.]. But if the school should remain there permanently, the U.S. cannot give grants to it, because "the regulations which have been adopted in relation to such institutions, require that they should be located in the Indian Country." [James Monroe] has approved two petitions for permission to sell lands granted to Indians by the Treaty of Chicago on 8/29/1821. [Henry B.] Brevoort's bond for service as Indian Agent at Green Bay has been approved. LS in DNA, 76 (M-1:11, pp. 454–457); FC in DNA, 72, E:333–334 (M-15:5).

To William Clark, St. Louis, 9/25. "Agreeably to the request of the Stockbridge Chiefs, made through their Deputy," Solomon [U. Hendrick,] "I transmit to you a speech from them to the Delawares, which you will deliver, or put it in the hands of Mr. [Richard] Graham for that purpose, in the manner requested in the enclosed extract of a letter" from Hendrick, "accompanied by such remarks as may be deemed calculated to induce the Delawares to do what is just in the business to which the speech relates. The answer of the Delawares will be transmitted to this Department as soon as obtained." FC in DNA, 72, E:334 (M-15:5).

From William Clark, St. Louis, 9/26. In reply to Calhoun's letter of 8/30, Clark states that the funds that have been allotted to him will not be overspent. The war between the Sauks, Foxes, and Sioux continues; some unsuccessful exertions have been made to effect a peace between them. [Richard] Graham has returned from a visit to all the tribes of his Agency. Because of illness, Graham is unable to make a report relative to the progress he has made in selecting a tract of land for the Delawares and the prospects of getting the Delawares and the Kickapoos permanently located. The treaty obligations to support a Factory have been relinquished by the Osages, the Sauks, and the Foxes for slightly more than $3,000 in goods. ALS in DNA, 1, C-135 (M-221:95).

To William Clark, St. Louis, 9/26. Calhoun encloses some accounts, submitted by [Pierre] Menard, of expenses attending the emigration of the Delawares. These outlays cannot be refunded without the special sanction of the War Department. Calhoun asks Clark to obtain additional information about them from Menard and to give his own opinion about them. FC in DNA, 72, E:335 (M-15:5).

From P[eter] Pelham, Sub-Agent, Philadelphia, 9/26. He left St. Augustine on 7/24; Capt. [John R.] Bell declined to take temporary charge of Indian affairs in Fla., but [Lt.] Col. [Abram] Eustis "readily consented" to do so. "It was my wish to have laid before you a detailed statement of the ultimate intentions of the government with respect to the lands to be assigned to them." "This duty, extreme illness compelled me to leave to the respectable gentleman who releived [*sic*] me." Col. [Gad] Humphreys, [newly appointed Indian Agent,] will visit Pelham "in a few days," when Pelham will communicate to Humphreys the information that Pelham has about the Fla. Agency. Pelham's letter will be delivered by [Moses Elias] Levy, who has recently purchased lands in East Fla. for the purpose of extensive cultivation. "He has already introduced the sugar cane with all the valuable productions of the West Indies that can possibly find a congenial soil & climate in Florida. With a philanthropy superior to the selfish views of a mere land speculator, he is devoting his labour, to the laudable object of converting an uncultivated wilderness, now traversed only by the savage, or solitary traveller, into fields of plenty, and the abodes of industry and happiness." Levy feels confident "that any obstacles which may be thrown in his ["way" *interlined*] by the ill advised conduct of the Indians will receive that attention from you which you are known never to refuse." ALS in DNA, 1, L-31 (M-221:96).

To [Peter B.] Porter, Black Rock, N.Y.

Dep[art]m[en]t of War, 26 Sep[tembe]r 1822

Although I am inclined to think that the charges made against Captain [Jasper] Parrish, the Agent to the Six Nations, in the enclosed proceedings of a Council lately held at Tonawanta [*sic*; Tonawanda, a Seneca settlement on Tonawanda Creek in Niagara County, N.Y.], are without foundation, yet, as it is the rule of this Department whenever charges are made against any officer under its control, to institute an enquiry through some person in whom it has confidence into the truth of them, I have taken the liberty to request you confidentially to examine into the charges against Capt. Parrish, and report to me your opinion touching them.

FC in DNA, 72, E:335 (M-15:5).

From Sam[ue]l Wragg

Charleston [S.C.,] 26 Sept[embe]r 1822

My son [2nd Lt. Samuel Wragg, Jr.] wrote some time ago to request the favor of a continuance of his furlough to the 1st Dec[embe]r. As his letter may miscarry I take the liberty to ask that favor for him. He must not shrink from any duty he has to perform on account of risk, but if it be consistent with the arrangements of your office to allow an extension of his furlough

I should be glad of it on account of the sickly state of Pensacola & because we wish him to see some of his friends at George Town [S.C.].

ALS owned in 1960 by Harvey S. Teal of West Columbia, S.C.

To Maj. JAMES MERIWETHER, Athens, Ga.

Dep[art]m[en]t of War, 27 Septem[be]r 1822

From the circumstances of the late General David Meriwether having been frequently employed in holding Indian treaties, his name was put upon the Commission for holding the proposed treaty with the [Eastern] Cherokees by mistake of the Clerk when in fact it was intended to have appointed you. It being understood the General is dead, I ["now" *interlined*] enclose you a Commission as was first intended with a copy of the instructions given for the government of the Commissioners. The papers referred to in the copy were transmitted to Gen[era]l [John] Floyd with the original instructions. You will ["be" *interlined*] pleased immediately on receipt of this, to notify this Department of your acceptance or non acceptance of the enclosed Commission. In case of the former you will correspond with General Floyd & Mr. [Duncan G.] Campbell in relation to the object of your appointment, of which they will be apprized, as also Gov[erno]r [John] Clark.

FC in DNA, 72, E:336 (M-15:5).

From James Miller, [Governor of Ark.,] Crystal Hill, 9/27. He acknowledges Calhoun's letters of 5/29, 6/21, and 6/22 and the enclosed statute regulating trade with the Indians. Miller has negotiated a treaty of peace between the Osages and [the Western] Cherokees and encloses a copy. [The unratified treaty of 8/9/1822 can be found as a DS in DNA, 80 (T-494:8, frames 41–46).] Miller is "in very ill health," but he will forward his accounts, answer Calhoun's letters, and cash the War Department drafts which he has received as soon as he can. Because of growing disaffection among the Cherokees for white people, Miller has given permission for two Chiefs and their interpreter to visit Washington. ALS in DNA, 77 (M-271:4, frames 175–178); PC in Carter, ed., *Territorial Papers*, 19:460–461.

From Capt. J[ohn] L[ind] Smith, Engineer Department, 9/27. Capt. Thomas F. Hunt, Assistant Deputy Quartermaster General, has written that the U.S. steamboat *Western Engineer* has been sold at auction and that the net proceeds of $874.75 have been deposited in the New Orleans Bank of the United States. FC in DNA, 21, 1:326–327.

From Ab[raha]m Bradley, Jr., [Assistant Postmaster General]

General Post Office, [Washington,] Sept. 28th 1822

Maj. Hunter runs a Stage 3 times a week between Cheraw S.C. & Godfrey[']s Ferry[,] the point where the great Southern mail crosses the Pee Dee. That Gentleman does not receive sufficient support for his Stages from Passengers & the town of Cheraw does not produce much postage and the revenue of this Department will not warrant an encrease [*sic*] of expenditure in carrying the mail. All that can be paid on that acc[oun]t would be five hundred dollars[,] the price of carrying the mail once a week.

The Citizens of Cheraw are anxious of having a more frequent communication with the South & to have Maj. Hunter[']s establishment supported & have proposed that three of the seven mails per week sent from Fayetteville [N.C.] to Godfrey[']s Ferry on the direct route 88 miles be sent by Cheraw (137 miles) & the difference of pay ([$]300.00) transferred to Maj. Hunter.

The Messrs. Maillets carry the mail from Fayetteville to Camdem [*sic;* S.C.] & it is proposed that they should expedite their travel & connect with Maj. Hunter at Cheraw so as to complete the conveyance from Fayetteville by Cheraw to Godfrey[']s. This proposition will be acceded to on the part of this office and the only doubt is whether the M[ess]rs. Mailets [*sic*] will consider the encreased number of Passengers which they may obtain on this account as an indemnification for the encrease of expedition.

The utmost time that can be allowed for carrying the mail the 137 miles will be from 3 A.M. to 4 A.M.[,] say 25 hours. From this time will have to be deducted 1½ hours to allow Passengers time to eat & an hour will be lost in waiting & changing horses & Stages, leaving only 22½ hours for travel. This will be too difficult & severe on the horses as there will be 6 hours of the night too dark to travel faster than 4 miles an hour & it will require 7 miles an hour for the rest of the time. Hence it is hardly probably [*sic*] Mr. Hunter[']s object can be effected. An extension of the time would delay the arrival at Charleston[,] S[outh] C[arolin]a.

FC in DNA, 161, 1821–1822:361.

To John Clark, Milledgeville, 9/28. Calhoun answers Clark's letter of 9/10 [ALS in DNA, 1, C-110 (M-221:95); FC in G-Ar, Governors' Letterbooks, 1821–1829:66–67] recommending David Adams to replace David Meriwether in the commission to negotiate a treaty with the [Eastern] Cherokees and urging that the commission be made active promptly. Calhoun explains that James Meriwether has been appointed and expresses a hope that no delay will occur. FC in DNA, 72, E:336–337 (M-15:5).

From Edmund P. Gaines

Fort Atkinson, Council Bluffs, September 28, 1822

I have the honor to transmit herewith a communication from [Bvt. Brig.] Gen[era]l [Henry] Atkinson, enclosing a memorial addressed by [Bvt.] Colonel Henry Leavenworth to the President of the United States, [James Monroe,] soliciting the attention of the President to the circumstance of his (the memorialist['s]) having been twice brevetted in the year 1814—his last brevet being senior to any that has not been followed by promotion; and considering a brevet commission equal to a promise by the Government that the rank which it confer[r]ed in the Army should be confer[r]ed in the line when it could be done without injury to the service or prejudice to the rights of others, he therefore respectfully intimates his wish to fill the vacant Colonelcy of Artillery.

Having been a member of the board of General officers at the reduction of the Army in April and May 1821, when an officer was duly selected by the board, I can not with propriety express an opinion in relation to any candidate for the Colonelcy in question; but it affords me pleasure to state, from my knowledge of Colonel Leavenworth prior and subsequent to the battles of Chippawa [*sic*] and Bridg[e]water [Canada] (where the display of his skill and gallantry is known to have secured to him the warmest approbation of his General and his Country) that he is well qualified for the command he solicits.

His military mind, zeal, and vigilance are equalled by few Officers of my acquaintence; and his whole deportment as an officer and Gentleman I have found to be highly exemplary.

P.S. Col. Leavenworth has explained entirely to my satisfaction the only questionable act of his life, within my knowledge, which was, as to the propriety of his writing a letter published in 1815 by General [Eleazer W.] Ripley. If either were blameable, it was the latter. E.P.G.

ALS with En in DNA, 11, 1502 (M-566:12). NOTE: The enclosure is an ALS dated 9/25/1822 from Leavenworth to Monroe.

[1st] Lt. William H. Chase, Rigolets [Pass, La.,] to Alexander Macomb, 9/30. Chase appeals for an Army physician to be stationed there, because a fever (not entirely like the yellow fever epidemic in New Orleans) has stricken fatally more than 20 percent of his small working force, which is entirely out of reach of medical aid. ALS in DNA, 223, 1059.

J[ames] M[onroe] to [John C.] Calhoun and [William] Wirt, 9/30. "Mr. Calhoun & Mr. Wirt are requested to meet Mr. [John Quincy] Adams here to day at one o[']clock. Mr. Adams is apprized of the proposed meeting." (An EU indicates that this request involved a "Cabinet meeting.") ALI in ScHi.

From [2nd] Lt. J[OHN] R. WILCOX, 5th Infantry Regiment

Frankfort, Kentucky, Sept. 30th 1822

In compliance with your order of the first of July I left West Point on the 19th of the same month to proceed to St. Peters, my route being by the way of Buffalo and Pittsburgh to this place, intending to avail myself of your permission of the date of July 22d to visit my friends, reserving only sufficient time to arrive at my Post before the commencement of Winter, but on the 27th of July I was attacked by the Bilious fever at the little Town of Erie in Pennsylvania and confined to my Room untill the 15th of August. I then proceeded to the residence of my Mother's family, stayed 5 days, and arrived at this place on the 10th of the present month, where I was again taken Ill of the same fever and have not been able to leave my Room untill 3 days since.

I shall again attempt to proceed on my Journey on the 4th of October but from my state of extreme weakness I cannot hope to reach St. Louis before the 20th, at which time the season will be so far advanced that it, together with my weak state of health, will I fear render my further progress this season impracticable, in which conjuncture I have taken the liberty to make this statement and urge you will forward me instructions to St. Louis by which I may be guided.

ALS in KyLoF, Edward C. Thurman Collection. NOTE: An AEU indicates that an answer may have been written, probably by someone other than Calhoun, on 10/10. Calhoun's "order" of 7/1, assigning Wilcox to the 5th Infantry Regiment, has not been found. Wilcox wrote to Calhoun on 7/9 and again on 7/15. ALS's in DNA, 16, 1822, W-51 and W-55 (M-567:5, frames 676–678 and 684–686, respectively).

To Elisha Wood, [Executive Office, State of Ga.,] Milledgeville, 9/30. Calhoun answers Wood's letter of 9/18 [ALS in DNA, 77 (M-271:4, frames 258–260)] notifying Calhoun that Wood has been appointed to pay to Georgians the sums that are due under their claims against the Creeks. Calhoun cautions Wood that he must obtain and submit clear proofs of heirship when the claimants have died; discusses a few specific claims; and offers to give "cheerfully" other counsel. FC in DNA, 72, E:337 (M-15:5).

OCTOBER 1822

AN INVITATION TO SPEND THE COMING WINTER IN WASHington was coupled with Calhoun's announcement to one of his brothers-in-law on the 8th that Calhoun's mother-in-law had purchased the Georgetown home now known as "Dumbarton Oaks." Annual reports from missionaries about Indian schools on both sides of the Mississippi began to be written on the 1st. Eastern Cherokees proclaimed flatly on the 24th that "we will never cede away any more lands." With astonishing mildness, Calhoun commented on the 28th that Jedidiah Morse's *Report* about Indian affairs "contains a good deal of interesting information in relation to our Indian population not heretofore published." Calhoun foresaw on the 5th a struggle against "unprincipled" opponents; ahead lay a contest "between cunning and wisdom . . . political virtue and vice."

From [the Rev.] John S. Hudson, Fort Gratiot, Mich. Territory, 10/——. He presents the first annual report of the Saginaw Mission, founded under the auspices of the Northern Missionary Society of the State of New York and located at Fort Gratiot. Hudson tells of the early efforts to open this school for the Chippewas and of expenditures amounting to more than $8,000. Favorable results have been obtained at Fort Gratiot under the Lancasterian method of teaching, but efforts to establish the mission at Saginaw have met with much misfortune. Upon arrival at Fort Gratiot in 2/1822, the missionaries opened a school for white children, but Indians refused to attend it until June. The present number of Indian children enrolled is 11 boys and six girls, ranging in age from five to 22. Success of a school among the Chippewas depends only upon securing adequate financial support. The new venture has not yet had time to secure much money from the sponsoring Society, and Hudson requests government support. Additional schools will be established among two other tribes in Mich. when funds can be procured. ALS in DNA, 77 (M-271:4, frames 134–137).

From the Rev. Alfred Finney and the Rev. Cephas Washburn, "Dwight, Cherokee Nation, Arkansas Territory," 10/1. They present the second annual report of the Dwight mission school, to whose staff two women have been added. About 40 acres of bottom land have been prepared for farming, and another 20 to 30 acres can be cultivated with little labor other than fencing. They describe the buildings and report that expenses at the mission have amounted to $16,499.4025, exclusive of what has been spent by the [American] Board [of Commissioners for Foreign Missions] and not reported to the mission. Cash on hand totals $643.615. The mission must depend for some time upon the aid of the American Board and the government. The buildings needed most immediately are a sawmill, a gristmill, and a schoolhouse for girls. The value of the property belonging to the mission, exclusive of its buildings, is itemized to a total of $9,655.31. The school was opened on 1/1/1822, and attendance "soon increased to more than fifty." The two superintendents express satisfaction with the progress of the Indian children under the Lancasterian system and expect to play a large role in civilizing the [Western] Cherokees. Not having received any government aid following the submission of their first annual report, they suppose that the report was unsatisfactory, but they express a hope that this report will result soon in a remittance. LS in DNA, 77 (M-271:4, frames 100–106).

To Joseph Hopkinson, Philadelphia, 10/1. Answering Hopkinson's letter of 9/28 [ALS in DNA, 1, H-89 (M-221:95)], Calhoun approves [Thomas] Sully's device for [Andrew] Jackson's medal. Calhoun has had Sully's fee sent to him. FC in DNA, 3, 11:433 (M-6:11).

From the Rev. Ard Hoyt, Brainerd, Cherokee Nation, 10/1. His annual report for the schools at Brainerd, Taloney, and Creek Path shows that the missionary staff consists of 26 adults and 16 minor children; that the Cherokee pupils boarded at Brainerd have included 52 boys and 32 girls; that 19 students have left after having learned at least to read and write; that 12 new pupils have begun their studies; and that expenditures have been $7,632, excluding gifts from the American Board of Commissioners for Foreign Missions and others. ALS in DNA, 77 (M-271:4, frames 141–145).

From Henry R. Schoolcraft, Sault Ste. Marie, [Mich. Territory,] 10/1. He acknowledges a note of 5/8 [from Christopher Vandeventer to Schoolcraft (ALS with En in DLC, Henry R. Schoolcraft Papers, vol. 3, 477)] and its enclosed copy of a Senate resolution of 5/8 concerning copper mines near Lake Superior. Schoolcraft reports how difficult it is to get adequate information on the subject and encloses a related report on "the prejudices and superstitions of the Indian tribes." He also encloses a copy of his report of 11/6/1820 [Abs in *The Papers of John C. Calhoun*, 5:427–428] and other statements and correspondence related to copper mines. Schoolcraft reports at length upon the high quality of copper samples that "continue to be brought" to him and states that he does not expect difficulty in extinguishing the Indian titles to the land. Schoolcraft believes the copper deposits to be abundant, of great value, and potentially beneficial both to the Indians and to the government. ALS with Ens in DNA, RG 46, 17A-E6 (M-200:6); PC in DLC, Henry R. Schoolcraft Papers, vol. 3, 479–482; PC with Ens in Senate Document No. 5, 17th Cong., 2nd Sess.; PC with Ens in *American State Papers*: *Public Lands*, 3:565–575.

From the Rev. William F. Vaill, Union, Osage Nation, 10/1. In this annual report Vaill names the 16 adults at the mission, states their duties and those of some of the 12 hired men, and reports upon the activities of the past year, including discouraging efforts to erect a sawmill. The seven Indian children at the mission are progressing nicely, and prospects of success are even greater with the restoration of peace among the Indians. Mission expenses during the past year totaled $6,700 and will remain high until the mission can supply all of its meat and flour. The $700 received from the U.S. in 1820 have "been faithfully applied," and the mission requests continuation of this aid. The value of the property of the mission, according to an enclosed estimate, is $24,512.88. LS with En in DNA, 77 (M-271:4, frames 220–226).

From William Elliot, Washington, 10/2. He reiterates his former accusations of unstable financial practices by Peter Morte. Elliot charges that Morte was arrested under four or five lawsuits for nonpayment of debts; that Morte caused Elliot to lose the bail that Elliot provided for Morte; and that Morte deeded to William Brent the property given by Morte as security to Elliot. Elliot requests permission to attach Morte's property "to satisfy these demands." An EU reads: "Ans[were]d by the Sec[re]t[ar]y [of War] verbally [that is, orally]." ALS in DNA, 30, 373.

To Col. Hugh Brady, Commanding Officer, Sault Ste. Marie, 10/3. He is to furnish quarters within the Army's cantonment to [Henry R.] Schoolcraft, if possible; otherwise, Brady is to furnish men from the garrison to assist in the construction of quarters for Schoolcraft. FC in DNA, 72, E:339 (M-15:5).

To Lewis Cass, Detroit, 10/3. Calhoun answers affirmatively Cass's request of 9/8. Calhoun stipulates that the costs of the proposed building for [Henry R.] Schoolcraft, Indian Agent at Sault Ste. Marie, must be paid from funds allotted to Cass for Indian affairs and discusses some details about temporary accommodations for Schoolcraft and the best permanent site for the new Agency building. LS in DNA, 76 (M-1:11, pp. 474–477); FC in DNA, 72, E:338–339 (M-15:5).

From Nat[haniel] Cutting, Section of Bounty Lands, 10/3. He encloses two reports about the transactions of his office, the first covering the period of 2/1–10/31/1821 and the second that of 10/31/1821–10/1/1822. His illness delayed the preparation of the former. Cutting also encloses copies of his communications with John Chandler, [Senator from Me.,] "relative to the *'Canadian Volunteer'* Cases which yet remain suspended in this Office." (Under Calhoun's instructions, Cutting asked Chandler on 5/13 to ascertain the validity of the claims of approximately 30 residents of Me. Chandler requested on 8/3 a copy of Cutting's communication of 5/13, because the original letter was obliterated by rain; and Cutting enclosed on 8/31 to Chandler a copy of the letter of 5/13.) ALS with Ens in DNA, 1, C-120 (M-221:95).

[Bvt. Col.] H[enry] Leavenworth, Fort Atkinson, Council Bluffs, to [Thomas S.] Jesup, 10/3. [John E.] Wool and [Edmund P.] Gaines have been pleased by their recent inspections there. Four large buildings have been constructed there at a cost not above $400. Leavenworth solicits Jesup's influence in behalf of Leavenworth's desire to be promoted [to the Colonelcy of an Artillery Regiment]. ALS with 3 Ens in DNA, 43, Leavenworth.

From W[illiam] Ward, Choctaw Agency, 10/3. He acknowledges Calhoun's letter of 9/10. Ward has not yet received the draft for $14,135. Consequently, he has been unable to pay pressing obligations of his Agency. He fears that it is too late to stop payment on the draft if it were taken from the mails, but he will, nevertheless, write to the Branch Bank of the United States at Louisville. ALS in DNA, 77 (M-271:4, frames 248–249).

ANDREW JACKSON to James Monroe

Hermitage[,] Oct[o]b[e]r 4th 1822

I have just rec[eive]d under cover of a letter to me from [former] Col[one]l Wm. King, the enclosed letter, with a request that I should give you my opinion of him as a military man—and forward the same to you, with his to your ad[d]ress.

My several communications which I have no doubt you have rec[eive]d will have given to you that opinion Col[one]l King now requests I should make known to you—but least [*sic*] the multiplicity of business with which you are necessarily surrounded should have caused my sentiments heretofore expressed of Col[one]l King to have escaped your recollection I will here barely state, that Col[one]l King as a military man possesses as much merit as any officer of his grade in any army; and I am sure all his military acquaintance will subscribe to this opinion. Col[one]l King stands high in the estimation of his fellow citizens of Alabama—as a test of which he has been brought forward ["forward" *canceled*] as a candidate for Senator in Congress for that State—and his friends are sanguine of his success.

I have thought it due to Col[one]l King to say this much, and leave to your better Judgment [*sic*] the result of his application. Mrs. J[ackson] unites with me in a tender of our good wishes to you, your Lady, and family, and believe me to be . . . .

ALS with En in DNA, 1, J-132 (M-221:96); CC in DNA, 8. NOTE: The enclosure is an ALS dated 8/1 from King to Monroe in which King requests restoration to his former position in the Army. A variant ALS and a copy of the En can be found in DNA, 1, K-47 (M-221:96).

From [the Rev.] CYRUS KINGSBURY

Mayhew, Choctaw Nation, Oct. 4, 1822

A few days since I received from the Agent, Col. [William] Ward, an Extract of a letter from the Sec[retary] of War to Mr. [Jeremiah] Evarts dated 29th June 1822. In this extract it was stated, that "Two-thirds of the expense of the buildings, as estimated by Mr. Kingsbury, for the new establishment at the French Camps or Newell, in the Choctaw Nation, will be allowed, and a further allowance, at the rate of $350 a year, commencing from the 1st of July next, is made for tuition, to be paid thro' the Indian Agent, Quarter yearly."

It has occurred to me, that my letter of June 5th might have been misunderstood. I perceive it was ambiguous. The last paragraph commencing with, "I avail myself of the present opportunity to certify the commencement of the school at *this place*," had reference to *Mayhew*, where the letter was dated, & not to the school at the French Camps. You will excuse me for making this explanation. As no appropriation has been made for the current expenses at Mayhew, I was apprehensive my letter had been misunderstood.

The number of scholars at Mayhew at the close of the last term was 47. It is proposed the present term to take 50 boys, & 15 girls. The whole number of boys that can be admitted was entered on the list by their parents before the close of the last term. The school is now collecting, but some are detained by sickness.

The number of scholars at the French Camps the last term was 14. The present number is 20 & may perhaps during the term be increased to 25 or more.

In addition to the buildings included in my estimate for the latter school, it is thought necessary to build a school house the ensuing winter. In my former letter, I suggested that a school house would be needed, if the school should be prospered. The expense of the school house is estimated at $250. It is respectfully submitted whether this estimate, may not be added to the one in my letter of June 5th, & two-thirds of it, be paid from the civilization fund.

P.S. The severe affliction we have experienced by sickness, and the death of Mrs. Kingsbury, have prevented me from collecting from the different stations the facts necessary to make the Annual Report [to you]. I am on the eve of starting for the six towns to make arrangements relative to the school there. Immediately on my return I will make out the Report. C.K.

ALS in DNA, 77 (M-271:4, frames 158–161). NOTE: Calhoun answered on 11/8.

TO N[INIAN] EDWARDS

War Dep[artmen]t, 5th ["Sept." *canceled*] Oct[obe]r 1822

I have since my last to you ["received your" *interlined*] several favours from the 3d August [*not found*] to the 14th Sep[tembe]r [*not found*] and I am very happy to learn from the last, that your health, which had been bad, has improved. I hope by your next to hear of its entire restoration.

The President [James Monroe] left this [city] for Albemarle [County, Va.,] a few days since, and will probably be absent till the 20th of this month. I forwarded ["to" *canceled*] your letter to him on the day [on] which I received it. He has not yet made the appointments, for reasons which I suppose he has communicated to you as he informed me, that he would write to you on the subject. Had returns of the survey been made the appointments would doubtless have been made ["also" *interlined*]. None, however, has been received, and I believe no reason has been assigned for the delay. Without the official returns, the President felt a delicacy in acting.

That he has taken his stand to support ["the" *canceled and* "his" *interlined*] administration, I cannot doubt. It is high time that he should. If longer delayed the worst ["of" *interlined*] consequences must result. With firmness, his administration must terminate in a manner honorable to himself and fortunate for the country. Without it the very reverse must follow.

The Republican [a Washington, D.C., newspaper edited by Thomas L. McKenney] has already effected a prodigious change. The *administration* is no longer assailed by the papers which support Mr. [William H.] C[rawfor]d. This they dare not do while he remains a *member* of the administration. His present attempt is to attribute the *dissention* [*sic*] to those who *expose* the opposition, and not to him and his friends, who have been the *authors* of it. A few articles in the Western papers anticipating this course and showing its futility would be of *much service*.

Things have reached, or will at least at the next session, reach a crisis. This then is an important moment. No one can have a greater influence or render to the country more important service than yourself. The struggle is between cunning and wisdom; ["&" *interlined*] political virtue and vice. The opposition to the administration is unprincipled, and its overthrow by such an opposition would give a fatal example. Much will depend on the course pursued by the States, and they again will be much under the influence of the messages of the respective governors. You know [John] Adair [Governor of Ky.], [Alexander] McNair [Governor of Mo.] and several others and have it, I would suppose, in your power to give a right direction to their messages. If no more can be done, it would be a great point for them to come out in favour of the adm[inistratio]n but still more *to notice* the opposition to it. In fact, I think, it would be decisive. If you correspond with [George?] Jackson [of O., former Representative from Va.,] much of the same kind might be done through him. In the South it can be easily attended to.

[Daniel Pope] Cook's election has afforded much gratification. He not only has talents but is bold and resolute. The reëlection of [Jesse B.] Thomas would have a very bad effect. You must run but one, and if necessary, you ["to" *canceled*] ought to come to an understanding. As connected with this subject, I hope the return of the surveys may be received in time to make the appointments before it is too late to have the proper effect. The Pres[iden]t directed their return forthwith. I do not in the least doubt that he will select the very respectable gentlemen whom you recommended.

You must take care of your health. It is valuable not only to yourself and family but to the country. To give a right direction at this moment to our politicks is of the highest importance to the lasting interest of this Republick. Almost as much depends on it as on the late war.

ALS in ICHi, Ninian Edwards Papers.

From G[ad] Humphreys, New York [City], 10/6. He explains the reason for his delay in departing for his position [as Indian Agent for Fla. Territory]. Because of his "inability to procure the necessary pecuniary means," Humphreys has only recently obtained passage on a vessel scheduled to leave this place on 10/13. [William P.] DuVal has been informed about the delay in Humphreys' arrival. ALS in DNA, 1, H-122 (M-221:95).

To David Barton, [Senator from Mo.,] St. Louis, 10/7. Calhoun answers Barton's request of 9/6 [ALS in DNA, 1, B-115 (M-221:95)] for extinguishment of the title of the Kansas tribe of Indians to certain lands by explaining that available funds are totally inadequate to finance any such treaty and cession and that the initiation of any such effort must await a Congressional appropriation. FC in DNA, 72, E:339 (M-15:5).

From William Carroll, [Governor of Tenn.,] Murfreesboro, 10/7. Pursuant to Calhoun's letter of 9/12, which requested "a statement of the number of acres of land within the limits of

Tennessee ceded to the United States by the [Eastern] Cherokee Indians, under the Treaty of" 7/8/1817, Carroll reports that the quantity is 1,000 square miles, of which more than 200,000 acres are "an entire bed of mountain." LS in DNA, 77 (M-271:4, frames 35–36). Calhoun wrote to Carroll an acknowledgment on 10/25. FC in DNA, E:348 (M-15:5).

To Joseph Hopkinson, Philadelphia, 10/7. Calhoun acknowledges Hopkinson's letter of 10/5 [ALS with En in DNA, 1, H-97 (M-221:95)]. Calhoun has forwarded Hopkinson's letter to [William Henry] Harrison [dated 10/3 (CC in DNA, 1, H-97 [M-221:95])]. "I also approve of the device proposed, which you need not forward for my inspection." FC in DNA, 3, 11:433 (M-6:11).

To John Johnston, Indian Agent, Piqua, O.

Dep[art]m[en]t of War, Oct[obe]r 7, 1822

I have received your letter of the 24 Ult[im]o and regret to find that sickness has prevented your usual punctuality in rendering your accounts. The excuse is a very sufficient one and I hope the delay will oc[c]asion no difficulty. Your health I am happy to hear is mending.

The very limited appropriation which was made for the Indian Department for the last year and which became exhausted before the year was more than half out, and the delay in Congress to make the appropriation for this year until the last hour of the session, will furnish you with the reasons why you were left without funds for so long a period as you have mentioned.

In relation to your remark that "our means are too limited" I have to state that in the apportionment of the appropriation for this year, by this Department, as liberal an allowance was made for the Superintendency of Gov[erno]r [Lewis] Cass as it would admit of, and altho' I am aware that the allowance is scant it is not in the power of this Department to extend it. No pains must therefore be spared so to manage your means tho' limited as to prevent the accumulation of arrearages at the close of the year which on every account it is desirable to avoid.

For the reasons you have assigned, no change will be made for the present in the payment of the Shawanoese annuity.

FC in DNA, 72, E:340 (M-15:5).

To J[ohn] E[wing] Colhoun, [Pendleton, S.C.?]

War Dep[artmen]t, 8th Oct[ober] 1822

We were gratified to learn by your favour of the 9th Sep[tembe]r [*not found*] that you were all well and that your crops were so good. I fear cotton must be very low. Tho' the consumption is increasing and the importation from India has nearly ceased, yet the quantity grown has increased so much beyond the consumption, that I see no prospect, but such a declension of price, as will check the growth. We have had one of the most intense drought[s] that I have ever known. We now have rain, but it is too late. Crops of every description are short through this part of the Union.

We have enjoyed good health, tho there has been a good deal of sickness in the city, which, however, I believe has been more healthy than any place within 100 miles of it. We have not left this city on an excursion as we expected to have done, but will take a trip to the country some time during the month.

James [Edward Colhoun] was well when we last heard from him. He will probably be with us shortly. Your mother [Floride Bonneau Colhoun] has bought a splendid establishment in Georgetown [D.C.] at $10,000. The price is low, but as she has no need of it, I fear she will in the long run find it dear.

You say nothing of your elections. I hope that you will succeed and that you will take care not to send us [Elias] Earle [former Representative from S.C.] again. He does no honor to the State; it however ["may" *interlined*] be wrong for me to offer an opinion on a Congressional election in any case.

If you could make your arrangement to bring on Mrs. [Martha Maria Davis] Colhoun ["to" *canceled*] and to spend the next winter ["with" *interlined*] us we would be much gratified. Our house is large and we should experience not the least inconvenience. I think that you both would find a few months agreeable in Washington.

Floride [Colhoun Calhoun] and her mother and the children desire to be remembered to you & Mrs. Colhoun most affectionately. It is now vacation and Andrew is with us. He has grown to be [a] stout boy. Yours affectionately, J.C. Calhoun.

ALS in ScCleA. Note: The home in Georgetown that had been purchased with some of the money of Calhoun's mother-in-law was the mansion that has been known in the twentieth century as "Dumbarton Oaks."

To Mority Fürst, Philadelphia, 10/8. Calhoun has referred a copy of Fürst's letter of 10/6 [LS in DNA, 1, F-35 (M-221:95)] to [Joseph] Hopkinson, who will reply to Fürst's "application relative to the reverses of the Medals for Generals [Andrew] Jackson and [William Henry] Harrison." FC in DNA, 3, 11:434 (M-6:11).

To Richard Graham, St. Louis, 10/8. Calhoun encloses for Graham's information an extract from a letter [of 9/24] from [John] Johnston to himself. "For the reasons assigned by Mr. Johnston, it is not deemed advisable to make any change for the present in the payment" of the annuity to the Shawnees. LS in MoSHi, Richard Graham Papers; FC in DNA, 72, E:340 (M-15:5).

To Joseph Hopkinson, Philadelphia, 10/8. Calhoun encloses "a copy of a letter [dated 10/6 to Calhoun] from Mr. [Mority] Fürst, expressing a wish to be employed in executing the reverses of the medals for Generals [Andrew] Jackson and [William Henry] Harrison. He has been referred to you for an answer to his application." FC in DNA, 3, 11:433 (M-6:11).

To William H. Crawford

Dep[art]m[en]t of War, 10 Oct[obe]r 1822

I enclose herewith a certificate of the President of the Tombeckbe Bank [at St. Stephens, Ala.?] (which has been transmitted to this Department) by which you will see, that the Treasury Draft sent to Col. [Robert Carter] Nicholas for the Chickasaw annuity, has been paid in paper instead of specie. This will create considerable embarrassment and expense in the payment of the annuity; as the Indians are extremely averse to receiving paper money however current and it will consequently be necessary to convert the paper into specie before the payment can be made satisfactorily and according to treaty. Considerable difficulty was experienced in obtaining proper funds for the Treasury draft for the Chickasaw annuity of the last year, and ["a" *interlined*] recurrence of a similar difficulty this year, induces me to advise the Treasury Department of the fact, in order that such funds, as are indispensably necessary may be provided to meet the Treasury drafts, for annuities, at the Banks on which they are drawn, without which it will be impossible for this Department to comply with the treaty stipulations in relation to the payment of annuities.

FC in DNA, 72, E:340–341 (M-15:5).

To Richard Cutts, 10/10. Calhoun requests "a report shewing the amount of accounts if any, which are suspended in settlement for want of appropriations." LS in DNA, 63, 1822:208; FC in DNA, 3, 11:435 (M-6:11). Cutts replied on 10/12 that no accounts were suspended for that reason. LS in DNA, 1, C-130 (M-221:95).

C[hristopher] Vandeventer to Richard Cutts, 10/10. "The Secretary of War directs me to apply to you for a statement of the several appropriations for the War Dep[artmen]t shewing the balance unexpended under each head on the first of this month. You will furnish it without delay." LS in DNA, 63, 1822:209; FC in DNA, 3, 11:434 (M-6:11). Cutts replied on 10/11, supplying the requested information. LS with DS in DNA, 1, C-127 (M-221:95).

To Peter Hagner, 10/10. Calhoun requests "an Estimate of the sum required for arrearages and for the half-pay pensions to Widows and Orphans payable through your Office for 1823." FC in DNA, 3, 11:434 (M-6:11). Hagner replied on 10/14 that $30,000 plus any unexpected balance as of 12/31/1822 would be sufficient to pay arrearages prior to 7/1/1815 during 1823 and that $20,000 would cover half-pay pensions during 1823. FC in DNA, 53, 27:197.

To Thomas [S.] Jesup, 10/10. Calhoun directs Jesup to report "the amount of Clothing required for the troops in the year 1823, allowing the amount now on hand as applicable to the issues of the coming year." LS in DNA, 41, 1821–1822, S-100; FC in DNA, 3, 11:435 (M-6:11); Abs in DNA, 46, 3:S-100.

From Richard M. Johnson, [Senator from Ky.,] Great Crossings, [Ky.,] 10/10. His nephew, E.P. Johnson, has furnished a horse, a saddle, and a bridle to [2nd] Lt. [Clark] Burdine to enable him "to proceed on his way to the lead mines." Richard M. Johnson urges Calhoun to pay the bill for $140 as soon as possible. ALS in DNA, 1, J-53 (M-221:96).

To William Lee, 10/10. Calhoun requests "an Estimate of the sum required for arrearages, and payable through your Office for 1823." FC in DNA, 3, 11:434 (M-6:11).

To Gad Peck, Cincinnati, 10/10. "The request in your letter of the 30th ult[imo (ALS in DNA, 30, 372)] that your son [Robert T. Peck] may be re-appointed as Cadet for next year, [because he received notification that he had been granted the privilege of reëxamination too late for him to report for it last month,] will be complied with, and a new warrant will be transmitted to you," as a substitute for the original, "as soon as the latter may be returned." FC in DNA, 13, 1:166 (M-91:1).

From G[eorge] Bomford, 10/11. As directed by Calhoun and pursuant to a House resolution, Bomford states that three civilian Clerks are employed in the office of the Ordnance Department and that one Sgt. is detached from the Army to serve therein as a Messenger; that all are needed for the work and that none is engaged in unrelated activities; that fewer employees would be insufficient; and that the organization and expenditures of the office are governed by its effort to be as efficient and as economical as possible. FC in DNA, 32, 3:254.

To G[eorge] Bomford, [Jacob] Brown, James L. Edwards, George Gibson, Joseph Lovell, A[lexander] Macomb, and [Nathan Towson], 10/11. Calhoun requests their estimates of the funds that will be needed during 1823 by their respective offices and for their respective Army services. FC in DNA, 3, 11:435 (M-6:11); LS (Lovell's copy) in DNA, 245, 1:122; LS (Macomb's copy) in DNA, 221, 454; LS (Towson's copy, dated 10/10) in DNA, 292, 1-2338; CC (of Brown's copy) in DNA, 17, 1:26; Abs (of Gibson's copy, dated 10/10) in DNA, 192, vol. 2.

To V[irgil] Maxcy

War Dep[artmen]t, 11th Oct[obe]r 1822

I have just received your favour of the 8th Inst[ant; *not found*] and regret very much to hear of the indisposition of Mrs. Maxcy. I trust that she will experience a speedy restoration of her health.

Neither of the Naval Commissioners have [*sic*] returned.

The Post Master Gen[era]l [Return J. Meigs, Jr.] is decidedly my friend; but he is much absent which gives to Mr. [Abraham] Bradley, [Jr.,] his assistant, a great control over the office, who is supposed to be favourable to Mr. [William H.] C[rawfor]d.

From the return of the Frederick district, I presume that either

[John] Lee, or [Thomas Contee] Worthington is elected. The latter I am told is sound.

We shall not be able to leave here till after the formation of the Com[missar]y contracts, which probably will not be completed till the 20th. As soon as the time and rout[e] is [*sic*] fixed, ["we" *canceled and* "I" *interlined*] shall inform you. Is it healthy at West River? Yours truly, J.C. Calhoun.

ALS in DLC, Galloway-Maxcy-Markoe Papers, vol. 32. NOTE: Lee served as a Representative from Md. during 1823–1825, Worthington during 1825–1827.

To R[obert] C[arter] Nicholas, "now in Lexington, Ky.," 10/11. His letter of 9/14 [ALS in DNA, 1, N-18 (M-221:96)] has been received. Calhoun regrets "very much" that Nicholas accepted banknotes rather than specie in payment of a Treasury draft to cover the Chickasaws' annuity. A treaty failed to specify payment of their annuity in specie, but they have a "known aversion" to paper money, "however current" it may be. Calhoun had been confident that Nicholas was aware that he should offer nothing but specie in payment of the annuity. "I conceive that you acted wrong in taking notes for the draft." No legal remedy can be invoked against the white man "who deceived you in relation to the whiskey which he was employed to destroy," but Calhoun approves Nicholas's determination to demand a refund of its full value and points out that Nicholas should be more careful in "the future selection of your agents." FC in DNA, 72, E:341–342 (M-15:5).

Jonathan Barnard, Tazewell, Tenn., to James Monroe, 10/12. Barnard, an elderly, almost blind Revolutionary veteran, suggests some rules for the Army and Navy and illustrates proposed military and naval strategy by creating fictitious battles whose participants on both sides report their reactions by letter to Calhoun. Barnard would consider a note of approval from any of Monroe's aides to be a signal honor. ALS in DNA, 101 (M-179:55).

From 1st Lt. William G[ibbs] McNeill

Newark, New Jersey, October 12th 1822

Having just been apprized thro the public prints of the death of Cap[tai]n [Hugh] Young of the Top[ographica]l Eng[ineer]s, I beg leave to renew my application for an appointment in that Corps.

The enclosed is a copy of the letter I had the honor to address ["you" *interlined*] about a year since, [on 7/10/1821,] which as it is expressive of my claims I have thought it proper to remind you of. It was then accompanied by the recommendations of Gen[era]l [Joseph G.] Swift, Gen[era]l [Simon] Bernard, Colonel [Joseph G.] Totten and Major [John J.] Abert; these Gentlemen have had every opportunity of judging of my qualifications, so I do not consider it requisite to furnish additional testimony of the satisfactory manner in which I have performed the duties of Ass[istan]t Top[ographica]l Eng[inee]r, during the five years that I have acted in that capacity.

I will however add, Sir, that as I have in a great measure forfeited all claim to distinction in my own Corps from never having served with it, I confidently trust that I shall now receive this appointment, for which I have so long and so assiduously endeavoured to qualify myself.

I am still under the impression, Sir, that I once rec[eive]d what I considered equivalent to your promise that when a vacancy should occur that [*sic*] I should have the preference, but if in your opinion my claims do not bear a favourable comparison with those of other applicants, I wa[i]ve any advantage that might result from your recollection of it.

ALS with En in DNA, 11, 12542 (M-566:109, frames 1050–1053). NOTE: A PC of the letter from McNeill to Calhoun dated 7/10/1821 appears in *The Papers of John C. Calhoun,* 6:251–252.

From Reod[olphus] Malbone, Clerk, Chickasaw Agency, 10/12. Acting in the absence of Agent [Robert Carter Nicholas], Malbone encloses a certificate by himself dated 10/10 that the report of the Rev. Thomas C. Stuart, Superintendent of the Chickasaw mission school of the Synod of S.C. and Ga., is substantially correct and that Stuart can complete the construction of the school buildings to qualify for a government grant. ALS with En in DNA, 77 (M-271:4, frames 168–170).

From N[athan] T[owson], 10/12. "I have the honour to report that when I returned to the Pay Department in May last, there were in this Office, in addition to the Paymaster General, 3 Clerks and 1 Messenger. By requiring the Paymaster who is stationed at this place occasionally to perform the duty of clerk, in addition to that of Paymaster (for which he is to receive no compensation) I have been enabled to reduce the number of Clerks to two, and I do not think the public interest would be served by any further reduction. On the subject of the *efficiency* of the gentlemen in this Office, perhaps the best recommendation they can have, is the statement of the facts, that they have been a long time in the Office, and that they were selected and retained, out of the number of Clerks that were employed in the Department. I believe none of the gentlemen are [*sic*] engaged in any other *pursuit or profession* unless the circumstance of Mr. [Andrew] Ramsay's owning a Coal Yard can be so considered. Mr. Ramsay informs me that he has an Agent who attends to the business for him and I can certify that he is never absent from his duty during Office hours or when required to be here without permission." FC in DNA, 291, 15:502.

To Col. "Abraham [*sic*; Abram]" Eustis, St. Augustine, 10/14. Calhoun has received Eustis's letter of 9/15 [ALS in DNA, 1, E-44 (M-221:95)]. [Gad] Humphrey[s] expects to arrive in Fla. [Territory] in time to attend the treaty negotiations to be held on 11/20; therefore, it will not be necessary for Eustis to attend. FC in DNA, 72, E:343 (M-15:5).

To [former] Capt. ALDEN PARTRIDGE, Norwich, Vt.

[Washington,] 14th Oct[obe]r 1822

Mr. Calhoun tenders his thanks to Capt. Partridge for ["an" *canceled and* "the" *interlined*] opportunity of perusing the Journal of the late excursion of the corps under his command, and sincerely wishes him success in an undertaking, which he views with much interest.

He has long believed, that in a free country, the duty of defending which attaches to every citizen capable of bearing arms, the military art, which teaches the mode of performing to the best advantage so essential a duty, ought to constitute a branch of education in all of our siminaries [*sic*], and he hopes that the success of the institution under his charge [that is, under Partridge, the "American Literary, Scientific and Military Academy" at Norwich,] may contribute to introduce, what he believes would be a great improvement, in our literary institutions.

In the present advanced state of military science, a defusion [*sic*] of its knowledge is the only mode, by which we can reconcile a small military establishment with the safety of the country, a thing so desirable under our institutions.

ALU in N; typescript in DLC, Carnegie Institution of Washington Transcript Collection.

To John Clark, [Governor of Ga.,] Milledgeville, 10/15. Calhoun acknowledges Clark's letter of 10/4 [LS in DNA, 77 (M-271:4, frames 61–62); FC in G-Ar, Governors' Letterbooks, 1821–1829:69], which enclosed "the report of the Surveyor General of the number of acres contained in that part of the cession made by the Cherokees to the U[nited] States, before the treaty of the 8th July 1817, within the limits of Georgia." FC in DNA, 72, E:344 (M-15:5).

From G[ad] Humphreys, Washington, 10/15. He requests an advance against his salary for the purpose of paying a balance that he owes to the U.S. ALS in DNA, 1, H-104 (M-221:95).

To George Bomford, [Jacob] Brown, George Gibson, Thomas S. Jesup, [Joseph Lovell], Alexander Macomb, and [Nathan Towson], 10/16. "You will accompany your estimates for 1823 [requested on 10/10 and 10/11] with an estimate of the amount of funds you will require to meet the expenses of your Department up to the end of the present quarter (31st of December next)." FC in DNA, 3, 11:436 (M-6:11); LS (Bomford's copy) in DNA, 31, 1822, War Department; LS (Gibson's copy) in DNA, 43, Calhoun, 513; LS (Jesup's copy) in DNA, 41, 1821–1822, S-104; LS (Lovell's copy) in DNA, 245, 1:124; LS (Macomb's copy) in DNA, 221, 455; LS (Towson's copy) in DNA, 292, 1-2339; CC (Brown's copy) in DNA, 17, 1:26–27.

To J. C. Gilleland

Washington, 16th October 1822

I rec[eive]d your letter of the 9th inst[ant; *not found*] by yesterday's mail, which I hasten to answer. I had certainly received an impression through your letter to Mr. [Samuel D.] Ingham, as well as the one to myself, to which my last was a reply, that an impression existed at Pittsburg[h,] with many, that less than justice had been done, by me to Doct[or Hanson] Catlett, while more than justice had been done to Major [Abram R.] Woolley. The object of my reply, as well as my communication to Mr. Ingham was to remove such impression as I was perfectly conscious, that there was not the least foundation for it, having most conscientiously, through every stage, acted according to what I believed to be the strictest dictates of justice in regard to both. My communications were made private, because I had to refer to facts, and correspondence, which it would be improper for me to make publick; and you have acted correctly, in so considering my letter to you, as well as the communication through Mr. Ingham.

I am now happy to infer from your letter that yourself, and other respectable citizens of Pittsburg[h], as well as the Doctor himself are satisfied, that I have acted justly and correctly in relation to this affair; you however seem to think, that I ought to give to the Doctor a statement which he could use, showing in what light, I have viewed his conduct, particularly in relation to the charges preferred by him against the Major. I have as a general rule declined in every instance of which I have any recollection, giving any opinion such as is requested in relation to the conduct of the Officers of the Army, on principles which appear to me to be correct, unless when officially called on to give such opinion. Independently however, of the general rule, there are reasons for declining in this case which, I am sure you must on reflection consider satisfactory.

If the Doctor has sustained any injury, it has not been by any act of this Department, but by the decision of the Court-Martial which tried Major Woolley. By the rules and articles of War, the decision of the Court referred itself for confirmation, not to this Department, but to the Officer ordering the Court. I then, could have no controul over it; and consequently whatever opinion I might entertain, as to its correctness, must from the nature of the case, be extra judicial and private. To give such a statement, as you suggest, would be to pronounce an opinion, or rather a censure on the Court, without having by law any right to do so, or to express it differently, to render myself justly liable to censure, while undertaking to censure the Court, which would be manifestly improper.

In the mean time the acts of the Department both before and since have been governed by what it considers the real state of the facts, in connection with both of these Officers, and its opinion must be inferred from its acts.

I have been thus minute from a sincere desire that I might be judged from the real state of the facts, by which in every act of my publick life, I have been content to rise or sink.

FC in DNA, 3, 11:437 (M-6:11); CC in ScU-SC, John C. Calhoun Papers.

To William Ward, Choctaw Agency, 10/16. Calhoun regrets to learn from Ward's letter of 9/19 that the draft for $14,135, which was mailed on 6/18, had not yet been received. It appears that a draft mailed on 6/28 for the payment of claims arising from the Pensacola campaign has also been lost in the mails. As soon as sufficient time passes, duplicate drafts will be issued. Ward will advise the War Department of anything he may learn about the original drafts. FC in DNA, 72, E:344 (M-15:5).

From [Bvt.] Maj. J[OHN] J. ABERT

Mount Holly, N.J., Oct. 17, 1822

Altho' I have done myself the honor on two or three occasions of addressing letters to you in favour of [1st] Lieut[enant] W[illiam] G. McNeill, my very valuable assistant, I will rather risk the appearance of being importunate by addressing you again, than that my silence should by any accident operate to the disadvantage of so excellent an Officer.

This Gentleman, after passing through the course of studies at the Military Academy with great credit to himself, about five years ago, was ordered to join me, and has continued acting as an Assistant Topographical Engineer ever since, and without meaning to disparage the pretensions of others, I may safely say, that excepting the Topographical Officers, he has rendered more valuable services to the Topographical department than any other officer of the Army.

Contemplating when first he joined me to become a Topographical officer, he has waived all the advantages of his own Corps, an[d] has devoted himself to the duties of this, under my personal observation, with an intelligence and an industry that I can never too highly praise, and has acquired a knowledge of these duties and a facility in executing them, which have often excited my admiration, and which have allowed me frequently to entrust to him the most important parts of a survey which he has in all instances performed to my entire satisfaction and in justice to him I must declare it as my opinion, that there are no Topographical duties, with which in my experience I have become acquainted, but what Lieut[enant] McNeill will be found adequate to perform and to the satisfaction of the department.

In addition to these powerful claims of merit and of services, I cannot forbear intimating how admirable an excitement would be created among the acting assistants to the Corps, if the road to preferment was open to their exertions, and on the contrary how heartsickening it would be for an officer to experience that no services or qualifications would entitle him to the favour of government; in behalf therefore of the well doing of the Topographical department, allow me Sir most respectfully to solicit your friendly consideration of the case.

ALS in DNA, 11, 12542 (M-566:109, frames 1056–1057).

To William H. Crawford

Department of War, October 17th 1822

I transmit herewith a copy of a letter from the Pay Master General, [Nathan Towson, dated 10/16 (ALS in DNA, 1, P-102 [M-221:96])] and an extract of one from Pay Master [Thomas] Wright to him, by which it will be seen, that not only a loss to a considerable amount will be sustained by the troops, but great inconvenience was experienced on the part of the Pay Department in paying the troops in the funds in which the Bank at Tombeckbe [at St. Stephens, Ala.?] paid the Treasury drafts.

In noticing this additional instance of loss and inconvenience experienced by the refusal of this Bank to pay in specie or U.S. Bank paper, I have to express my hope, that effectual steps will be taken by the Treasury Department to prevent a recurrence of the same evil in future, as it is manifestly unjust to pay those to whom the public are indebted, but in the legal currency of the Country.

FC in DNA, 3, 11:438 (M-6:11).

From [Lt. Col.] Abr[a]m Eustis, St. Augustine, 10/17. Having been unofficially informed that Governor [William P.] DuVal has left Fla. Territory, Eustis submits copies of his correspondence with the Governor on the subject of Indian affairs. Eustis believes that "the present state of affairs may be deemed such as to require the immediate interference of the Government." The enclosures consist of three letters from Eustis to DuVal dated 9/10, 9/15, and 10/16; one letter dated 8/24 from DuVal to Eustis; and two letters dated 10/5 and 10/8 from Horatio S. Dexter to Eustis, copies of which were enclosed by Eustis to DuVal on 10/16. The Seminoles have been delayed in attending the proposed meeting on 11/20, because of a report that two tribes of Indians have declared war on the Seminoles. Mecanope, "the Pond Governor," will not leave his nation until he has ascertained the truth of the report. ALS with Ens in DNA, 1, E-48 (M-221:95); PC in Carter, ed., *Territorial Papers*, 22:547–550.

From T[homas] F[orsyth], St. Louis, 10/17. He encloses his accounts for the quarter that ended on 9/30 and an estimate of his expenses during the present quarter. He wants to be informed whether he will receive soon a remittance or is to issue a check against the War Department for funds. The expenses that he now reports for the summer quarter were increased because the Iowa Indians visited St. Louis and [William] Clark—a fact that required extra outlays for merchandise and provisions. Those Indians never visit "my Agency" and "therefore receive very little of the bounty of the U[nited] States." FC in WHi, Draper Collection, Thomas Forsyth Papers, 4T111 (published microfilm, series T, vols. 1–9).

From J[oseph] G. Swift

New York [City], 17 Oct. 1822

[1st] Lieut[enant William G.] McNeill of the Artillery, who from the time of his Promotion at the Military Academy to the present, has been employed upon Topographical duty, is a promising young officer in whose welfare I feel much interest. He entered the Army by my recommendation & under my Command, & has uniformly discharged the duties of his station with much ability & entirely to the satisfaction of his superior officers. I learn that a vacancy has occurred in the Topographical Corps by the death of Capt. [Hugh] Young. I beg leave to present to your consideration the merits of Lieut[enant] McNeill for this vacancy. Should his wishes meet your approbation I have not a doubt that he would fulfil[l] the duties of Captain of Topographical Engineer[s] with entire satisfaction to the Public.

ALS in DNA, 11, 12542 (M-566:109, frames 1058–1060). Note: Hugh Young had died on 1/3/1822. McNeill was commissioned as a Bvt. Capt. and

Assistant Topographical Engineer as of 1/27/1823. Heitman, *Historical Register,* 1:679 and 1067.

From Col. M[athew] Arbuckle, Fort Smith, [Ark. Territory,] 10/18. He encloses a copy of his letter of 12/22/1821 to Jacob Brown questioning at length his 7th Infantry Regiment's transfer in 1821 after four years of continuous frontier duty. Arbuckle encloses also James Gadsden's letter of 3/26/1822 to himself stating that Calhoun "conceives an official notice" of Arbuckle's protest to Brown "unnecessary, and permits me to dispose of the document as I may deem proper." Arbuckle takes offence at what Gadsden wrote, questions his authority as Adjutant General to "give any instructions whatever for the Government of the Army," reviews in self-defense his decisions in leading his Regiment from Fort Scott to posts in the West, and seems to reveal that other issues and documents may be involved in this disagreement. ALS with Ens in DNA, 16, 1823, A-15 (M-567:6, frames 34–46).

From the Rev. JOHN GAMBOLD

Springplace, Cherokee Nation, 18th October, 1822

In Conformity to the Regulations of Government, respecting Schools for the Instruction of Indian Youth &c., I have the honor to report:

That the School for Children of the Cherokee Nation established in this Place, continues to afford Prospects of Usefulness; the number of Scholars during the year past has been, and at present is, twenty, viz: 17 males and 3 females, all of whom are boarded at the Expence of the Mission. Two Boys & on[e] Girl have left the School, and 2 other Boys & 1 Girl have filled their Places. Five of the oldest Boys have been at home all Summer, to assist their Parents in Cultivating their Crops; others were employed by their Parents in similar Labors for a shorter time, and then returned to School. The Scholars, as usual, have been instructed in Spelling, Reading, Writing, Bible history, Geography, Arithmetic, and in the most essential points of our holy Religion; most of them have committed to memory the 10 Commandments, the Creed, the Lord[']s Prayer, Scripture texts & Hymns. Six of them can read well; and five write plain & legibly. The Boys have been occasionally employed in the Labors of the field, and the Girls in Sewing, Knitting and other domestic Occupations.

The following Persons are employed in this Institute: the Rev[eren]d John R. Smith, as Teacher & Man[a]ger of the Concerns, with his Lady, Mr. Joseph Gambold, (who on Acc[oun]t of his advanced Age, being near 70 Years old, intends to return to North Carolina this autumn), one hired Young Man, and one Negroe [*sic*] Woman near 60 Years old.

On the small farm of this Institu[t]e have been raised for the Subsistence of the family & School nearly 500 bushels of Corn, a considerable Quantity of Oats, and a large Supply of sweet & Irish potatoes & Vegetables.

The Expenditure for the Maintenance of this School, during the year past, amounts to something above 500 Dollars—other Expences have been incurred and defrayed by the Directors of the Society residing in Salem, North Carolina, which I cannot ascertain—of this expenditure Government has kindly paid 300 Dollars, the Residue has been supplied by the Society of the United Brethren for propagating the Gospel among the Heathen. The Property on hand consists of 2 work horses & 1 Colt, 50 head black Cattle, 22 hogs, 1 Waggon, 2 Ploughs & other farming Utensils.

N.B. Probably the number of Cattle & Hogs may be considerably greater than here stated, but as they roam at large in the forest, I cannot venture to set down more than what have been seen lately and are known to exist.

That our feeble Efforts to do some Good to the Cherokee Nation may by the blessing of God prove beneficial to this People as well as to the United States, is the Wish & Aim of your humble servant, John Gambold.

ALS in DNA, 1, G-50 (M-221:95).

From Thomas S. Jesup, Hagerstown, Md., 10/20. "I have been detained here since the 18th by the illness of my wife." She has a fever but may be able to resume the trip in two or three days. "Be assured I shall make no unnecessary delay." ALS in DNA, 1, J-52 (M-221:96).

From Jasper Parrish, Sub-Agent

Canandaigua, Oct. 21st 1822

At a general council of the Six Nations held at Buffalo on the 18th ult[imo] (there was a general attendance of both Christian and Pagan parties) I explained to the Chiefs the contents of your most interesting letter of the 6th ult[imo] as also your letter to Young King and Capt. Pollard of the 2nd. After a long consultation and deliberation on the subject, they could not agree on any general plan or course to persue [*sic*], and while one party are [*sic*] determined on receiving s[c]hooling and instruction in the arts of civilization, the other party are opposing every measure towards instructions for their present or future welfare.

The Chiefs of both Christian and Pagan parties have united in making application to you through my Agency to obtain permission for a delegation to visit the seat of government this winter. Red Jacket[']s wishes are to ascertain from his great father the President, [James Monroe,] what the great object is at this time, with Government and the Missionary societys [*sic*] of taking so much pains to civilize and Christianize them. They are also wishing to come to an understanding with government respecting the Green Bay purchase, being at present much divided in opinion upon that subject. The Christian party appear to have the utmost confidence in Government.

Should you think proper to permit a deligation [*sic*] of four or six Chiefs with an Interpreter to visit the seat of Government this winter, I have no hesitation in believing it will be attended with a good effect in bringing about a reconciliation among themselves, and I take the liberty of suggesting that an equal number of both parties be represented, which may tend to harmonize them towards each other.

LS in DNA, 1, P-117 (M-221:96).

From [Lt. Col.] Abr[a]m Eustis, St. Augustine, 10/22. He encloses a copy of his letter [dated 10/22] to William P. DuVal, in which Eustis reported that Mecanope, "the Pond Chief," and five other head men have visited Eustis. "They represent the alarm, which detained them at home, as communicated by my letter[s] to you of the 16th & 17th ins[tan]t to have been discovered to be wholly without foundation. I enclose a copy of a Talk, which I gave them this morning, & they will leave this place tomorrow." ALS with Ens in DNA, 1, E-51 (M-221:95).

To C[allender] Irvine, Philadelphia, 10/22. Calhoun encloses an estimate by [Thomas S. Jesup] of the amount of clothing that will be needed by the Army during 1823. Calhoun directs Irvine to submit an estimate of the appropriations that will be needed in 1823 to enable Irvine to supply that clothing. FC in DNA, 3, 11:440 (M-6:11). (Irvine answered on 10/28 and 11/8.)

Charles Vignoles, New York [City], to [Christopher] Vandeventer, 10/22. Vignoles requests permission to make copies of Capt. [John] Le Conte's map of the St. Johns River and of an Army officer's descriptive letter dated 7/1821 about Fla., both for the purpose of contributing to the projected pamphlet by Vignoles about Fla. ALS with En in DNA, 228.

To Lewis Cass, [Detroit]

Department of War, 23 Oct[obe]r 1822

In the execution of that part of the act passed at the last session of Congress relative to licenses to trade with the Indians, should licenses be granted by yourself or any of the Indian Agents within your Superintendency to trade with Indian tribes within the Superintendency of Gen[era]l [William] Clark at St. Louis, (which includes all the Agencies on the Mississippi and Missouri,) it will be proper that the General should be regularly apprised thereof for the information of himself and the Agents under his control. You will therefore direct the Indian Agents within your Superintendency to give immediate notice to General Clark of all such licenses, with the name and description of the persons to whom they may be issued, and the number, names and description of the persons (if any) who will be employed by them respectively in the transaction of the business with the Indians.

As there is nothing in the late act to which the regulations adopted under the act of 1816, in relation to the employment of Foreign boatmen or interpreters, and communicated to you on the 25[th] March 1818, are repugnant, they will be considered as still in force, and the American trader may be permitted to avail himself of the services of Foreigners on the terms and conditions therein specified.

P.S. The within order has been given at the request of Gen[era]l Clark, believing it would facilitate his duties with respect to trade with the Indians. Should an order to him to furnish you with similar information be of any advantage to you, it will be given upon an intimation from you to that effect.

LS in DNA, 76 (M-1:11, pp. 515–518); FC in DNA, 72, E:346 (M-15:5). NOTE: Cass answered on 11/7. An Abs of Calhoun's letter to Cass dated 3/25/1818 appears in *The Papers of John C. Calhoun*, 2:209.

To William P. DuVal, Governor of Fla. Territory, 10/23. Calhoun approves DuVal's suggestion of 9/22 [LS in DNA, 1, D-52 (M-221:95); PC in Carter, ed., *Territorial Papers*, 22:533–534] that the proposed treaty negotiations with the Indians, scheduled for 11/20, be postponed. Calhoun encloses copies of letters [dated 10/23] to [George] Walton and Col. [Abram] Eustis to show "the course adopted by the Department upon the subject." FC in DNA, 72, E:347 (M-15:5). (DuVal answered on 11/27.)

To [Lt.] Col. "ABRAHAM [*sic*; ABRAM]" EUSTIS, St. Augustine

Dep[art]m[en]t of War, Oct[obe]r 23d 1822

I have received a letter from Governor [William P.] Duval [*sic*] in which he states that owing to the sickly state of New Orleans, Pensacola and Fort St. Marks, the proper supplies for the Treaty contemplated to be held with the Florida Indians at the latter place, the 20th November next, could not be procured in time, and therefore suggests the propriety of postponing the treaty for the present. The suggestion of the Governor is approved, and you will immediately inform the Indians, by sending expresses among them, that the treaty has been postponed to a more favorable season and that as soon as convenient, a suitable time will be fixed upon, for assembling them, of which, they will be duly notified.

FC in DNA, 72, E:347 (M-15:5). NOTE: Eustis answered on 12/3.

To Col. FERRIS PELL, Washington

Department of War, October 23d 1822

The charge made by the State of New York, for the repairs of Arms will be settled without involving the accounts of Military Stores which passed between the State and the United States, during the late War; and the amount found due for repairs, will be paid as soon as the Agent of the State, shall be authorised, and will give his assent, to the following principle of adjusting the balances, which may be found due to either the State, or the United States, on a final settlement of the property account—viz: Any balance of Arms to be carried to the account of Arms apportioned under the law of 1808, for arming the Militia; and any balance of Ammunition, camp Equipage, or other Military stores, to be repaid in Articles of like kind as far as may be practicable, and where impracticable to be charged at their value to the account for Arming and Equipping the Militia.

As it has been found impracticable to determine whether the Arms upon which repairs have been made by the State, were damaged while in the service of the United States, the claim for those repairs will be adjusted as follows viz: In lieu of the charges heretofore made, the State will be allowed forty-five Cents for each stand of Arms issued in good order, and an additional allowance of ten Cents per month for the time said Arms were in service, subject to the following limitations.

1st. For any arms issued by the State to officers of the United States Army or to Volunteers in the service of the United States, or to Militia, and Cavalry in service, and which have been charged to the United States, in the property account, no allowance for repairs will be made.

2d. Where arms have been more than once issued, and without having undergone repairs between the first and subsequent issues the allowance of forty-five cents will be made upon the first issue only.

3d. Where arms have been issued by the United States, to the State or its Militia, or when arms have been issued by the State, to any troops in the service of the United States, they are presumed to have been in good order, when issued, unless the contrary be shown. But where arms have been issued by the State, to Militia not in the service of the United States, proof of their good condition is required to establish the allowance of forty-five cents per stand.

4th. The amount to be allowed upon these principles, shall not exceed the sum actually paid by the State for the repairs of Arms.

To establish the number of arms issued, and the time said Arms were in service, the regular returns and vouchers of issue and receipt should be produced; in cases where such vouchers cannot be obtained, the best evidence the nature of the case will admit should be produced, and if satisfactory will be admitted.

FC in DNA, 3, 11:440–441 (M-6:11); CC in DNA, 262, 7758.

To George Walton, Secretary [and Acting Governor] of Fla. Territory, 10/23. Having approved Governor [William P.] DuVal's suggestion [of 9/22] that the contemplated treaty negotiations with the Indians be postponed, Calhoun reports that Col. [Abram] Eustis has been directed [on 10/23] to notify the Indians of the postponement and instructs Walton not to take any steps towards holding the negotiations. Should the Indian Agent, [Gad Humphreys,] arrive during DuVal's absence, Walton "will inform him of the postponement of the treaty, and give him such instructions as you may deem necessary upon the subject." FC in DNA, 72, E:347–348 (M-15:5); PC in Carter, ed., *Territorial Papers*, 22:554.

From John Ross and other Members of the [Cherokee] National Committee

New Town, [Eastern] Cherokee Nation, October 24th 1822

Brother, We hasten to lay before you the sentiments of the Cherokee People on the subject of the contemplated Treaty for the extinguishment of their title to lands, for the benifit [*sic*] of the State of Georgia. Brother you will perceive that nothing official has been communicated to us either by our Agent or the commissioners on the subject of the contemplated Treaty, altho' the public newspapers have announced the appropriation of Congress and the appointment of Commissioners by our Father the President of the United States [James Monroe] for the purpose of holding a Treaty with us for lands. Brother, our Nation have [*sic*] made cession after cessions of lands to the United States until our limits have become very circumscribed. It was to have been hoped that our White Brethren of the frontier States would have been sattisfied [*sic*] and become contented with the last extensive cession of land which our Nation made to the United States and that they would have said—Red Brethren, we will now let you repose in tranquil[l]ity and enjoy the fruits of the soil, which gave you births & mouldered the bones of your Ancestors, but alas what has been the tone of their voices? More land, more land, the whol[e] limits of ["our" *interlined*] chartered limits. Yes Brother such are [*sic*] their avariciousness, that we despair of ever sattisfying their desires. If we had ["not" *canceled*] but one mile square left they would not be sattisfied unless they could get it. We have been told that the State of Georgia have [*sic*] got the Gen[era]l Government bound to her in strong terms to extinguish the Indian titles to lands within her chartered limits. But we hope that the United States will never forget her obligation to our Nation of an older date than her promises to the State of Georgia. By the Treaty of Tellico [of] 1798 the United States have [*sic*] solemnly guarenteed [*sic*] forever to our Nation this Country which have [*sic*] been bestowed upon our ancestors by the Great Creator of ["all" *canceled and* "this" *interlined*] World for the inher[i]tance of our posterities—money was not pledged as a security for the guarentee, but this Country, & no other. Brother we now declare to you in words with an unchang[e]able heart that we will never cede away any more lands. We therefore come upon a determined resolution to meet no Commissioners on the subject of making a Treaty of cession. It would be wrong in us to run the Government of the United States to any unnecessary expense in meeting them, when we have no disposition and are determined not to sell one foot of land. Brother we are bound by the strongest ties of justice[,] humanity and affection to ourselves, our Wives, our children, our friends & our fellow Citizens, to hold fast to our Country & lay the foundation for the permanent happiness of our posterities. We hope and trust that they will improve and enjoy all the blessings of Civilization & refinement on this our soil which contains the relics of Our Fore Fathers —the advancements making by our Nation towards attaining that happy state of condition, induces a flattering hope that Complete success will ultimately be realized. Brother we have full Confidence in the magnanimity of your Government and trust that no undue advantage will be permitted the adjoining States, to be taken of our Nation in the circumscribed ["limits" *canceled*] Country reserved by us in the late treaty. Brother we have repeatedly complained to your Government of the injuries done to our Nation by our white Brethren of the frontier States, in direct violation of the good faith solemnly pledged by your Government to our Nation in our Treaties. There appear[s] to be a great relaxation in enforcing those obligations. Intruders of considerable numbers have been tolerated to remain ["on" *interlined*] our lands to secure their crops from year to year, and in place of removing off when their crops were secured, it has been only a stimulant for others to move on our lands. Brother our obligations have always been strictly observed on our part and the least possible departure from it has never been permitted to pass without observation. All those violations certainly constitute a reasonable and just ["ob" *canceled*] claim against your Government. If a strict observance was pursued by our venerable Agent, [Return J. Meigs,] there could not have occur[r]ed so many causes of complaint. We cannot altogether impute it to his wilfull neglect, but the natural relaxation attending the infirmities of old age in a great leading cause. We have made communications to our Father the President & several letters written to your Department by our Head Chiefs laying before you our Grievances. We must now beg your perticular [*sic*] attention to those communications, as we have never heard any thing from you in reply. Our lands on the frontier are thickly settled by Intruders from the adjoining States and we now again beg you to have them removed without delay; their crops are now secured and no reason can be given why they should be indulged any longer—they do not only injure us by living on our lands, but by stealing or arbitrarily driving off stocks of property belonging to our citizens. And those intruders are generally of the lowest grade in society, such as introduces all varieties of vices into our Country; ["this" *canceled*] it cannot but be readily perceived that such characters will unhappily imbibe ruinous habits in demoralizing the reputation of our Citizens. We cannot but believe it would mortify the feelings of our Father & Brother to see our Children sinking into those bad practices and laying aside the excellent qualities which they are receiving from a moral & religious education. We take you by hand with the utmost Brotherly friendship and beg ["that" *interlined*] our words may be laid before our Father the President so that the voices of his red children may enter his ears.

LS with En in DNA, 77 (M-271:4, frames 52–60). NOTE: Numerous members of the National Committee signed this letter or affixed their marks in approval of it. Among these were Path Killer, Principal Chief; Going Snake, Speaker; Maj[o]r Ridge, Speaker; George Lowrey; and Ch[arles] R. Hicks. The En is a resolution of 10/23 by the Cherokee Nation in Committee and Council not to meet any U.S. Commissioners and not to cede any part of the Cherokee lands.

To John Floyd, Commissioner, St. Marys, Ga., 10/25/"1823 [*sic*; 1822]." Calhoun acknowledges Floyd's letter of 10/4 [ALS in DNA, 1, F-40 (M-221:95)] and informs Floyd that, "in consequence of the death of Gen[era]l [David] Meriwether, his son Major James Meriwether, has been appointed to join you and Mr. [Duncan G.] Campbell in the intended negociation with the [Eastern] Cherokees. He was instructed to correspond with you & Mr. Campbell in relation to the objects of your commission." FC in DNA, 72, E:348–349 (M-15:5).

From Callender Irvine, Philadelphia, 10/28. Answering Calhoun's letter of 10/22, Irvine promises to submit the requested budget estimates for 1823 as soon as practicable. (He did on 11/8.) ALS in DNA, 1, I-55 (M-221:95); FC in DNA, 45, 389:397.

To V[IRGIL] MAXCY

Washington, 28th Oct[obe]r 1822

I have received your several communications with their enclosures. The letters to Maj. [George] Peter and Mr. [George] Hay were transmitted to them. The one to the latter being open, I read it, as you requested; and I have no doubt it will be well received.

I herewith return the letter from Gen[era]l [Robert Goodloe] Harper, which I have read with much interest. His reflections are judicious, and prove him to be master of the whole subject. The line between the Republicans and Radicals will finally be distinctly drawn, and they will become the national parties, when sides may be selected by all. As it regards subscription to the paper ["two" *canceled*] the caution which he suggests is very proper, but it ought to be remembered, that two things are desirable, to obtain patronage for the editor and ["to" *interlined*] diffuse light, and that the former may be useful where the latter is not required. The signatories[?] are improving in New York, and I am strongly of the impression, that the individuals who have taken up the Treasury candidate [William H. Crawford] cannot support themselves there much longer.

How overwhelming the distress of the Howard family! We sympathize most sincerely with you. Yours truly, J.C. Calhoun.

ALS in DLC, Galloway-Maxcy-Markoe Papers, vol. 32.

To the Rev. JEDIDIAH MORSE, D.D., New Haven

Dep[art]m[en]t of War, 28 Oct[obe]r 1822

I have received your letter of the 18th inst[ant; *not found*] accompanied by a printed copy of your report on Indian Affairs. As soon as the number of Copies subscribed for by this Department is received, the amount of the subscription will be remitted to you.

The report contains a good deal of interesting information in relation to our Indian population not heretofore published and I hope the addition [*sic*; edition] will prove more profitable to you than you seem to anticipate.

FC in DNA, 72, E:349 (M-15:5).

From N[athan] T[owson], 10/28. Pursuant to Calhoun's order of 10/11, "I have the honour her[e]with to submit an Estimate for the year 1823 shewing under the several heads of expenditure, the amount of funds that will be required for the disbursements of the pay department for that year. The only material difference betwe[e]n this and the preceding Estimate, is in the article of forage. Experience has shewn that Officers prefer receiving *money* of the Paymaster in lieu of forage, to receiving *forage* in *kind*, of the Quartermaster. I have therefore estimated for the full amount they are entitled to receive from this department. There is also a small difference in the amount of the brevet compensation of the supernumerary Lieutenants of the Military Academy. I have also the honour to enclose an Estimate of the expences of the Paymaster General[']s Office, for the year 1823." FC in DNA, 291, 16:1.

From N[athan] T[owson], 10/28. "Agreeably to your instructions [of 10/16] I have the honour to report, that from the best examination in this Office, it required on the first day of the present quarter 277,000 dollars to complete the entire disbursements of the Pay Department for the year 1822, and that for the disbursements from the present day, it will require 240,000 dollars." FC in DNA, 291, 15:516.

From Thomson S. Harris and James Young, "Seneca Mission House," [near Buffalo, N.Y.,] 10/29. They report the progress of their school, which is operated by the United Foreign Missionary Society. Staff members and their families total six persons. Pupils formerly lived with the Indians and were day students; but 20 now live in buildings that were completed on 7/1. The plan of education, the necessity for operating a farm, and the school's expenses are among the topics discussed. U.S. financial assistance is requested. LS (in Harris's script) in DNA, 77 (M-271:4, frames 125–130).

To William Ward, Choctaw Agent, 10/29. Calhoun acknowledges Ward's letter of 10/3. Calhoun has ordered $3,242.50 sent to

Ward for his Agency's expenses during the last half of the year and for allowances to schools for the Choctaws. If nothing is heard within a few days about the two lost drafts, duplicates will be sent to Ward. Calhoun instructs Ward to submit his accounts and vouchers as quickly as possible after the receipt of these drafts, because they stand charged to him from the dates on which they were first issued. FC in DNA, 72, E:350 (M-15:5).

From JOSEPH LOVELL

Surgeon Gen[era]l[']s Office, Oct. 30th 1822

I have the honour to submit for your consideration the enclosed report of Dr. [J. Ponte Coulant] M[a]cMahon relative to the removal of troops from Camp Hope [West Fla.] to the Barrancas, & the causes of disease at the latter place. The summer & autumnal complaints peculiar to many of the Southern posts are usually of such a violent type & so little under the control of Medicine, that every practicable arrangement should be made to prevent there [*sic*] occurrence by choosing healthy positions; & in addition to these it appears that the want of a supply of vegitables [*sic*] & of good water has produced the scurvy at the Barrancas, which renders it still more desireable [*sic*] that the troops should be kept for as long a period as possible at a more eligable [*sic*] position while stationed in that country. I would also suggest the propriety of furnishing some fresh vegitables, potato[e]s perhaps, as part of the ration, at those posts where they cannot be obtained in the vicinity & where diarrhea, Dysentery & scurvy usually add materially to the mortality produced by the peculiar diseases of the Country.

ALS with En in DNA, 1, S-159 (M-221:96); FC in DNA, 242, 2:319–320.

From the Rev. J[EDIDIAH] MORSE

New Haven, Oct. 30th 1822

I forwarded to you, a few days ago, a copy of my Ind[ia]n Report. A box containing the no. of your subscript[io]n, & more, were [*sic*] ship[pe]d for Washington last Saturday, & I hope will reach Washington in safety & soon. You will please to send for 30, or more if you wish, to Messrs. Davis & [Peter] Force, to whom the box is directed, on its arrival. You will of course send one to Gov[ernor

Lewis] Cass, & one to each of the Ind[ia]n Agents at Mackinaw, Green Bay, Council Bluffs, & [the] Floridas.

Knowing the interest you feel in the welfare of the Columbian College, I take the liberty to enclose a copy of my son's Geog[raph]y designated for Colleges, Academies & higher schools, & request you to forward it to the Presid[en]t or some other of the Instructors of that Institution, for examination, as a Classical book, with the Atlas (wh[ic]h I believe I gave them last winter, if not, one may be had at Davis & Force's on my acc[oun]t) & then to be deposited at their College Library.

I wrote you, that the state of my financies [*sic*] would not admit of my intended visit to Washington this autumn, to attend the annual meet[in]g of our Ind[ia]n Society. My actual expenditures, & necessary neglect of my affairs, during my absences, will go near to make me a bankrupt.

I shall write you ag[ai]n on this subject of the Society soon. In the mean time I am yours truly, J. Morse.

ALS in DNA, 1, M-119 (M-221:96). NOTE: Morse's "Ind[ia]n Report" was published as *A Report to the Secretary of War of the United States on Indian Affairs, Comprising a Narrative of a Tour Performed in the Summer of 1820* . . . (New-Haven: printed by S. Converse, 1822). His "son's Geography" was published as a book by Jedidiah Morse and Sidney Edwards Morse, *A New System of Geography, Ancient and Modern . . . with an Atlas* . . . (23rd ed. Boston: Richardson & Lord, 1822), which was a revision of Jedidiah Morse's *Geography Made Easy* (1st ed. New Haven: printed by Meigs, Bowen and Dana, [1784], and of later editions). Concerning these geographies, see Joseph Sabin and others, *Bibliotheca Americana: a Dictionary of Books Relating to America, from Its Discovery to the Present Time* (29 vols. New York and Portland, Me.: 1868–1936), 12:412–413. Columbian College has become George Washington University. Calhoun answered on 11/7.

To A[NDREW] JACKSON, "The Hermitage," Nashville

Department of War, October 31st 1822

I have received your favor of the 14th instant [*not found*] recommending Mr. Samuel J. Hays to fill a vacancy in the Military Academy occasioned by the death of Cadet W[illia]m Overton and accompanied by a letter from [former] Col. [Robert] Butler to you requesting of you the recommendation abovestated and expressing his consent as the natural Guardian of Mr. Hays to his signing articles as required by Law binding him to serve five years, should he be appointed.

In answer I have to inform you that vacancies at the Military Academy are not filled as they occur but are provided for by appointments at two stated periods viz. the first in February or March for those existing and in anticipation of those expected from the graduation of the 1st Class in the June following & from casualties up to that date, & the second in July and August for non-acceptances, delinquencies in reporting and rejections of the appointments of the first period. Also that there are two stated periods of admission adapted to the periods of appointment viz. in June for the first and in September for the second. Wherefore you will perceive your application and recommendation in behalf of Mr. Hays cannot be acted upon before February next but I beg you to be assured they will receive particular attention.

LS in DLC, Andrew Jackson Papers, 11500 (Presidential Papers Microfilm, Jackson Papers, Reel 31); FC in DNA, 13, 1:167–168 (M-91:1).

NOVEMBER 1822

Creditable new efficiencies were reported to Calhoun by three of his bureau chieftains. On the 14th George Gibson wrote that, although rations had been improved, they had cost about one-third less in three recent years than in the preceding three. George Bomford asserted on the next day that muskets manufactured in 1822 would cost about one-fifth less than did those produced in 1817 but were better. And on the 28th Dr. Joseph Lovell rejoiced that mortality among soldiers was proportionately less than among comparable civilians but that medical costs were barely above the level of 1807, "though the Army is twice as large, and the posts nearly double in number." To James Monroe on the 27th Calhoun himself wrote a good report. He wanted on the 10th "a good house servant" but dared not "cause discontent" among those he already had.

John H. Hall, Harpers Ferry, to George Bomford, 11/1. Hall asks Bomford to support Hall's idea for educating the approximately 400 children of the workmen at that place. He asks the government to have the Paymaster deduct a small sum from the pay of the workmen to pay the tuition of all the children. At present there is a school; but, because of the high tuition and the prejudices excited against it by "interested & base calumniators," it has not had much support. A year ago, "there were, probably, not ten persons at Harpers ferry favorably disposed to its establishment." The school has also had to struggle "against a general impression that the principal agents of the Government at this place are against it & are gratified by opposition to it." ALS in DNA, 31, 1822, H.

From [former Col.] A[rthur] P. Hayne

Charleston, So[uth] Ca[rolina], 1st Nov[embe]r 1822

I beg leave to solicit your Patronage in behalf of Doctor William H. Simmons, to fill the vacancy occasioned by the death of Doctor

[James C.] Bronaugh [former Assistant Surgeon General of the Army] in the *"Council of Appointment"* of the Floridas. Doctor Simmons is a gentleman of commanding Talents, and possesses the strictest integrity of character. He is a native of Charleston, but has for the last *eighteen* months resided in *East Florida.* Maj[o]r [James] Hamilton [Jr.] (the Intendant [of Charleston]) will address Mr. [James] Monroe in his behalf.

ALS in DNA, 103, Simmons (M-439:15, frames 513–516).

From Callender Irvine, Philadelphia, 11/1. [Thomas S. Jesup], in his estimate of clothing that will be needed for the coming year, has failed to include any clothing for the Engineers at West Point and any caps and ornaments for certain Regiments that have received no recent issues of them. Irvine supposes that he should make provisions for these needs. FC in DNA, 45, 389:402.

From Joseph Lovell, 11/1. He reports his disbursements and balance as of 9/30 and the Army's illnesses during the quarter that ended on 6/30. Two of every three deaths in the Army occurred at Baton Rouge and are attributable to a drought and to the continuance until 6/15 of the soldiers' hard labor. Lovell estimates the Army's medical expenses in 1823. LU with En in DNA, 1, S-163 (M-221:96); FC with En in DNA, 243, 1:140–142.

Isaac Shelby to R[ichard] M. Johnson

November 1st 1822

I have received by a circuitous route two small boxes containing the representations of Medals, which I presume have been forwarded by the War department in pursuance of the Resolution of Congress voting ["a" *canceled*] Gold Medals to General [William Henry] Harrison & myself for the deliverment on the Thames [during the War of 1812].

The composition of the medals received, is so different from that mentioned in the resolution, that I doubt whether it is intended by the Secretary of War, that these medals shall be considered as a compliance with the resolution; if they are so, I ask the favour of you to return them to the President, [James Monroe,] as a bauble not worth acceptance or preservation.

As no letter accompanied the packet containing them, I am left to conjecture for what purpose they are intended. I hope you will not take the trouble to bring these boxes back to me.

LS in DNA, 1, S-189 (M-221:96). NOTE: Compare Calhoun's letter of 11/23 to Shelby.

From [Col.] John E. Wool, [Inspector General,] St. Louis, 11/1. "I conceive it my duty to apprise you, that in consequence of extreme ill health, it will be impracticable for me to complete my tour of inspection as contemplated when I took leave of you in May last." Because of his illness, Wool has been unable to inspect the posts on the Arkansas and Red Rivers. "I am in hopes however to be able to re-commence my tour of inspection in the course of 12 or 14 days, that is, as far as Baton Rouge and New Orleans. From thence I shall return to the North, under the expectation that I shall never be obliged to re-visit this Country of Sickness and death." ALS in DNA, 1, W-123 (M-221:96).

From WILLIAM DRAYTON

Charleston, [S.C.,] 2d Nov[embe]r 1822

I am very desirous of placing at West Point one of my sons, [Thomas Fenwick Drayton,] who has lately attained his sixteenth year. Permit me therefore to request that he may be considered as among the applicants for admission, & also to beg the favor of you to inform me when I shall be able to know whether he is to be regarded as being upon the list of those who will be for examination in September next.

ALS in DNA, 15, 1820, 118 (M-688:14, frames 447–448). NOTE: Calhoun replied on 11/9.

To S[AMUEL] D. INGHAM, "Confidential"

Washington, 2d Nov[embe]r 1822

I received your favour of the 27th Inst[ant; *not found*] yesterday, and as you have touched on a most interesting point, I am induced thus promptly to offer you my opinion, as it ["is" *canceled and* "has been" *interlined*] formed on much reflection and a full view of facts.

You know, that I am wholly devoted to *the cause* and that I consider myself as but one, in relation to it. With these conceptions, I can speak as dispationately [*sic*] as if I was not interested.

I do not doubt, but that the friends of Mr. [John Quincy] Adams ought to be conciliated, but *the mode* and *time* are very important. To me it is certain, that the election will turn on the support ["and" *canceled and* "or" *interlined*] opposition to the Administration, and that ultimately the country will be rallied on these points. I do not doubt, but that the friends of ["the Admn" *canceled*] Mr. Adams will be with the adm[inistratio]n as well as Gen[era]l [Andrew] Jackson's, and that the strongest on our side ["might" *or* "must" *canceled*] ought to be selected. I am however decidedly of the opinion, that any step *at this time particularly in your State* which would strengthen Mr. Adams, at my expense, or to express it differently, which would have the appearance of yielding me up for him, would be fatal to the common cause. I will explain why. Mr. [William H.] C[rawfor]d's whole embarrassment is from me. I devide [*sic*] the South with him. I do much more. He cannot attack me without attacking Mr. [James] Monroe and the adm[inistratio]n. I am identified with ["him" *canceled and* "Mr. Monroe" *interlined*] on all points since 1812. Mr. Adams is not so identified and may be attacked *seperately* [*sic*], and *at present fatally, if I were out of the way.* They are sensible of this and have directed almost their whole effort against *me*, and any thing which would in appearance weaken me *now*, would work fatally to aid their purpose. Again; the least appea[ran]ce of uniting our forces would certainly produce the opposite union, which for many reasons ought *now* to be prevented, if possible. At present Mr. [Henry] Clay's friends are in conflict with Mr. C[rawfor]d's, and Mr. [De Witt] C[linto]n's are, to my knowledge, preparing to direct their effort against him [Crawford] in New York and I suppose Ohio. This had better go on, as long as possible.

Things cannot do better than they are now doing, and if no improper step is made Mr. C[rawfor]d's failure is certain. He is under a distructive [*sic*] cross fire, which will compel him to change his ground, which he cannot do, but at the greatest risk. Clay & Clinton attack him as a member of the adm[inistratio]n; & the friends of the latter, as a Radical. He has no support to sustain these attack[s]. No paper support[s "him" *interlined*] in all of the West, and, *out of* Georgia, not more than two or three in all of the South. He has many favourable to him in the North, but not more than three in that quarter, I mean North of this, that will undertake to defend him. The true line of policy at present is to support the adm[inistratio]n and to point out *by arguments the objections to Mr. C[rawfor]d.* None of his papers are [*sic*] furnishing arguments in *his favour* and it will result, that his opponents will be armed every where with those against him, while his friends will have none to defend him. Were we *near* the election, the parade, which his friends make of his strength would ["be" *canceled*] require notice, but as it is, it will only make his ruin the more certain. *Discussion is our instrument,* under which he must sink, of which so many symptoms now exist. Even in North Carolina, the symptoms are against him. But one paper in that State has given any indication in his favour, while three or four have taken the opposite side. In fact out of Georgia and Virginia in the last of which he is loosing [*sic*] ground, he has but little strength except at the Cuostom [*sic*] house of New York.

My advice is to make no move for the present. Congress will soon be in session, at which time the tone of the country can be ["seen" *canceled and* "heard" *interlined*], and our course taken on a full knowledge of facts.

I am surprised that Mr. Frankes[?] should calculate on me. I gave him a civil answer, and told him, that so many of my friends would be candidates, that I could not take the least part, which answer I have given to all who have applied to me. The choice is important, and I am very sorry that you cannot be present. I still hope circumstances will permit you. If you can, you must be present.

An article in the F[ranklin] Gaz[et]te as to the prospect of Mr. C[rawfor]d would be of some use, at this moment. Could you not prepare one, which would touch on the points that I have al[l]uded to as showing his weakness. Yours truly, J.C. Calhoun.

[P.S.] Penn[sylvani]a if firm will certainly control the election.

ALS in ScU-SC, John C. Calhoun Papers.

To W[illiam] Wigton, Dryden, N.Y., 11/2. In response to an inquiry [*not found*] from Wigton, Calhoun explains that a committee of Congress objected to the proposed increase in payment from $1 to $3 per day for certain members of the court-martial [that tried N.Y. militia delinquents]. The bill that Congress approved provided the increased pay for only those members of the court whose accounts had not been settled, but another bill will be presented to

Congress during the next session to provide for the other members of the court. FC in DNA, 3, 11:441–442 (M-6:11).

To Jasper Parrish, Sub-Agent, Six Nations, 11/4. In answer to Parrish's letter of 10/21, Calhoun declines to grant permission for a delegation of Indians to visit Washington during the winter, both because of the [low] "state of the appropriation for the Indian Department" and because of the "great press of public business which constantly occupies the attention of this Department during the session of Congress." Calhoun will not object to a visit next spring or summer if the object of the visit is considered important enough to justify the expenses associated with it. FC in DNA, 72, E:351 (M-15:5).

From George Walton, Secretary and Acting Governor of Fla. Territory, "Near Pensacola," 11/4. He expects that the public buildings there will be placed under his authority soon. "It seems, that some little doubt exists, as to what buildings, if any, should be considered of a *military* character. All the public buildings, except the prison and Hospital, were included within the old British Fort. Under the Spanish Government, the plan of that part of the town has been changed. The block houses now stand on the street, or on the public square, and excepting their *form*, they have nothing of a military character." Because the U.S. troops have left Pensacola, it would be better to leave these buildings unoccupied. Walton discusses Indian affairs, particularly the contemplated treaty at St. Marks scheduled for 11/20. He requests instructions on this subject, in the absence of Governor [William P.] DuVal. ALS in DNA, 1, W-129 (M-221:96); PC in Carter, ed., *Territorial Papers*, 22:556–560.

From J[AMES] L. E[DWARDS, Chief Clerk]

Pension Office, Nov[embe]r 5, 1822

It would appear from a memorandum in the Office of the 3d Auditor, [Peter Hagner,] that the 2nd Comptroller [Richard Cutts] has decided that after the allowance of an Invalid Pensioner had been reduced, under the act of the 3d March 1819, the same may again be increased, on the production of a certificate under oath, from two reputable Surgeons, provided the pension when so increased, do not exceed the rate at which the Pensioner was originally paid. The power of increasing as well as granting pensions on original claims, is vested exclusively in this Department. I therefore apprehend that there may have been some mistake in the application of some of the regulations which the Comptroller may have made as to the manner and form of keeping the Pension Agents['] accounts; for, this, by law, is all that he can do. His duties as prescribed by the 9th Section of the Act of the 3d ["March" *canceled*] March 1817, extend no farther than controlling the settlement of accounts. If such a decision has been made, I presume it has been made without due consideration of its consequences. I will merely state one case out of many which may very naturally arise from the operation of such a rule, to shew how productive it would be of imposition on the government. A.B. for example, an Invalid Pensioner residing in New York, was seven or eight years ago placed on the pension list on account of a flesh wound at the rate of eight dollars per month, but in September 1821, the Surgeons examine him and find that he is only one-fourth, instead of being totally, disabled. His pension is consequently reduced from eight to two dollars per month: but, not long after the first examination has taken place, from some cause or other he gets disabled—goes to the same Surgeons who before examined him, and they certify that he is again totally disabled. This they may do with propriety, and still the pensioner by law be entitled to no more than two dollars per month. Thus it is seen, by the operation of such a rule, that a man may receive $72 per annum, or more, which he is not legally entitled to. The Act of the 3d March 1817 simply requires the Surgeon's testimony as to the degree of disability, in a case where the claim has been previously established at the War Department—and in every case of the kind where a reduction may have taken place, a new examination should be had at the War Department before an increase can be made—otherwise it would be impossible to prevent imposition.

FC in DNA, 91, 12:390. NOTE: The next page in the same source contains a letter from Edwards to Cutts dated 11/5, written by order of Calhoun, directing Cutts to discontinue his new practice because it left "much room . . . for defrauding the government." Cutts wrote apologetically to Calhoun on 11/11 [LS in DNA, 1, C-154 (M-221:95)], explaining that the practice had been used in only one instance involving $11.25 and "in the hurry of business, . . . without reflecting that it belonged entirely to the War Department to decide on the increase of pensions."

To Thomas Forsyth, Indian Agent, Fort Armstrong, [Ill.,] 11/5. Calhoun has received Forsyth's letter of 9/19 [ALS in DNA, 1,

F-43 (M-221:95); FC's in WHi, Draper Collection, Thomas Forsyth Papers, 4:153–155 and 6:18–20; incomplete FC in WHi, Draper Collection, Thomas Forsyth Papers, 7:106]. A copy of it is being sent to [William] Clark, "who, as Superintendent of Indian Affairs is vested with discretionary power to act upon the subjects to which it refers." LS in WHi, Draper Collection, Thomas Forsyth Papers, 1:67; FC in DNA, 72, E:352 (M-15:5).

To George Bomford

Department of War, November 6th 1822

You will report a statement of the work done at the Armories and Ordnance depots distinguishing the amount and expenditure of each from the 1st of January to the 1st of October last, the amount of moneys drawn for the same period, and remitted to disbursing Officers, and the amount of accounts rendered by them, and settled in the same period, the comparative expense of manufacturing a musket now, and in 1817—the measures which have been taken as to the lead mines—number of applications for leases—number of leases granted—the prospect of Utility to the Government, to which you will add what further measures are in your opinion necessary to render the mines productive.

LS in DNA, 31, 1822, War Department; FC in DNA, 3, 11:444 (M-6:11). Note: Bomford replied on 11/12 and 11/15.

To J[acob] Brown, 11/6. Calhoun asks Brown to report the organization of the Army, its force and distribution, the tours of inspection made since 1/1, and the results and costs of the recruiting service during 7/1–9/30. FC in DNA, 3, 11:444 (M-6:11); CC in DNA, 17, 1:27. Brown replied on 11/25. LS with 5 DS's by Brown and Charles J. Nourse (dated 11/9 and 11/12) in DNA, RG 233, 17A-D1; FC with Ens in DNA, 6, 2:64–70 (M-127:2); FC in DLC, Jacob Brown Papers, Letterbooks, 2:219–220; FC (of the letter of 11/12) in DNA, 12, 6:260–261 (M-565:6, frame 426); PC's with Ens in Senate Document No. 1 and House Document No. 2, 17th Cong., 2nd Sess.; PC with Ens in *American State Papers: Military Affairs*, 2:450–457; PC in *Niles' Weekly Register*, vol. XXIII, no. 17 (December 28, 1822), pp. 268–269. (Calhoun summarized Brown's more important remarks in his letter of 11/27 to [James Monroe].)

To Col. George Gibson

Department of War, November 6th 1822

You will report as soon as practicable the amount of money drawn and remitted to the disbursing officers of your Department from the commencement of the present year to the termination of the third quarter, the amount of accounts of disbursements rendered by each, with a comparative view of the expense of the Department since its establishment at this place compared with the rate of expenditure immediately preceeding [*sic*] that period.

LS in DNA, 43, Calhoun, 512; FC in DNA, 3, 11:443 (M-6:11). Note: Gibson replied on 11/14. LS with 2 DS's in DNA, 1, S-206 (M-221:96); LS with Ens in DNA, RG 233, 17A-D1; FC with Ens in DNA, 6, 2:92–96 (M-127:2); PC's with Ens in Senate Document No. 1 and House Document No. 2, 17th Cong., 2nd Sess.; PC with Ens in *American State Papers: Military Affairs*, 2:467–469.

To C[allender] Irvine, Philadelphia

Department of War, November 6th 1822

You will report the amount of money drawn from the appropriation for clothing in the three first quarters of the present year, and an estimate of the amount you will require for the fourth quarter of the year, the amount of the accounts of disbursement rendered for the three first quarters for settlement, the price of the various articles which enter into the supply of the Army provided by your Department (compared with the prices of similar articles in 1817).

The estimate of funds for the fourth quarter should accompany your estimate for 1823 which may be rendered before the [other] statement[s] required above.

FC in DNA, 3, 11:443 (M-6:11). Note: Irvine submitted a partial reply on 11/8 [LS in DNA, 2, I-1822 (M-222:23); FC in DNA, 45, 389:407], stating that an additional $20,000 would enable him to liquidate all existing debts and to pay for all deliveries that will be made during the present quarter. His main report, dated 11/14 [LS with Ens in DNA, RG 233, 17A-D1; FC in DNA, 45, 389:409–417; FC in DNA, 6, 2:97–100 (M-127:2), CC with Ens in DNA, 1, P-136 (M-221:96); PC's with Ens in Senate Document No. 1 and House Document No. 2, 17th Cong., 2nd Sess.; PC with Ens in *American State Papers: Military Affairs*, 2:470–472], contained 6 DS's dated 11/12.

To [Thomas S. Jesup], 11/6. This letter duplicates that written today to George Gibson. LS in DNA, 41, S-115; FC in DNA, 3, 11:443 (M-6:11). (T[rueman] Cross replied on 11/16.)

To [Joseph Lovell], 11/6. "You will report as soon as practicable the amount of money drawn and remitted to the disbursing Officers of your [Medical] Department from the commencement of the present year to the termination of the third quarter; the amount of accounts of disbursements rendered by each, with a comparative view of the expenditure of the Department since its establishment at this place, with preceding expenditures." LS in DNA, 245, 1:126; FC in DNA, 3, 11:443–444 (M-6:11). (Lovell replied on 11/8.)

To A[LEXANDER] MACOMB, Chief Engineer

Department of War, November 6th 1822

You will report as early as practicable the application of the appropriation of last Session, for fortifications to the several works, & the expenditure necessary for their completion. The works remaining to be commenced according to the plans of the Board of Engineers, the estimate of the Board for those works, & the progress of the Board of Engineers in its labours, comprehending the operations of the Topographical Engineers from the commencement of this year. The condition of the Military Academy, including its present numbers and the number which graduated last year. The amount drawn for the three first quarters of this year under the several heads of appropriation and the amount of accounts rendered and settled in the same period.

LS in DNA, 221, 461; FC in DNA, 3, 11:443 (M-6:11). NOTE: Macomb replied on 11/14. LS with En in DNA, RG 233, 17A-D1; FC with En in DNA, 6, 2:71–76 (M-127:2); FC with En in DNA, 21, 1:338–340; CC with En in DNA, 1, E-53 (M-221:95); PC's with En in Senate Document No. 1 and House Document No. 2, 17th Cong., 2nd Sess.; PC with En in *American State Papers: Military Affairs*, 2:457–460; PC in *Niles' Weekly Register*, vol. XXIII, no. 17 (December 28, 1822), pp. 269–270.

To James Miller, Little Rock, Ark. [Territory], 11/6. Calhoun rejoices over the treaty of peace between the [Western] Cherokees and the Osages, reported in Miller's letter of 9/27. Calhoun regrets Miller's illness and the resultant delay in the submission of his accounts; they should be transmitted, if practicable, before Congress convenes. Calhoun approves Miller's having granted permission for a deputation of two Cherokees and one interpreter to visit Washington; "but as the winter is always the most busy season with the

Department, it would be preferred that such visits should be made in the spring or summer when there is more leisure to attend to them, and should the proposed deputation not have started before this reaches you, you will for this reason postpone their visit until then." FC in DNA, 72, E:353 (M-15:5); PC in Carter, ed., *Territorial Papers*, 19:467.

To S[TEPHEN] PLEASONTON, [Fifth Auditor]

Dep[art]m[en]t of War, 6th Nov[embe]r 1822

I transmit herewith a letter of the President of the U.S. Branch Bank [at New York City, Isaac Lawrence, dated 11/4; *not found*] respecting a suit commenced against Jacob S. Arden for the recovery of pension money fraudulently obtained from the United States.

I have no doubt of the guilt of Arden & I deem it important, as an example that [*sic*] not only that he should be convicted criminally but that a judgment be obtained against him in the civil suit; and therefore hope the Government will afford every aid to the officers of the Bank compatible with its interest in obtaining a recovery.

FC in DNA, 3, 11:444 (M-6:11). NOTE: Compare the letter of 11/8 to Lawrence from James L. Edwards.

To L[ittleton] W[aller] Tazewell, [former Representative from Va.,] "present," 11/6. Calhoun replies to Tazewell's note of 11/6 [*not found*] by requesting that an application and other information be placed on file concerning the young man whom Tazewell recommends for an appointment to the Military Academy. The next appointments will be made in 3/1823. FC in DNA, 3, 11:445 (M-6:11). (Compare the letter of 11/11 from Tazewell to Calhoun.)

From Lewis Cass, Detroit, 11/7. In accordance with Calhoun's letter of 10/23, Cass has informed William Clark about all licenses granted within Cass's Superintendency to traders who will deal with Indians in Clark's. It is unlikely that any licenses have been issued in Clark's for trade within Cass's; but, if there be any, Cass's local Agent should be informed by Clark. "Not seeing any reason to suppose that the instructions in relation to foreign interpreters and Boatmen were abrogated by the late law, I directed the Agents, some time since, to continue to execute them as usual." LS in DNA, 1, C-161 (M-221:95); FC in DNA, 76 (M-1:5, p. 113); PC in Carter, ed., *Territorial Papers*, 11:278.

To the Rev. JED[IDIA]H MORSE, D.D., New Haven

Department of War, 7th Novem[be]r 1822

I have to acknowledge the receipt of your letter of the 30th ultimo.

The copy of a Geography which you enclosed to me for the Columbian College, has been forwarded agreeably to your request.

LS in CtY; FC in DNA, 72, E:354 (M-15:5).

From [Bvt.] Brig. Gen. H[enry] Atkinson, St. Louis, 11/8. He encloses three copies of an "arrangement entered into with Mr. [George C.] Sibley relative to the public buildings &c. at Fort Osage, the terms of which I hope will meet your approbation." (Sibley is given charge of the public buildings, etc., at Fort Osage.) Atkinson returned to St. Louis for the purpose of closing his public accounts, which were forwarded to [William] Lee "last week." ALS with En in DNA, 1, A-34 (M-221:95).

From J[ames] L. Edwards, 11/8. Pursuant to Calhoun's order, written to Edwards by C[hristopher] V[andeventer] on 11/7 [FC in DNA, 3, 11:445 (M-6:11)], Edwards reports that during 1822 there have been paid $1,353,308.58 to pensioners for Revolutionary service, $303,094.24 to invalid pensioners, and $12,689.30 to half-pay (or commutation) pensioners. LS in DNA, RG 233, 17A-D1; FC in DNA, 6, 2:71 (M-127:2); FC in DNA, 91, 12:392; PC's in Senate Document No. 1 and House Document No. 2, 17th Cong., 2nd Sess.; PC in *American State Papers: Military Affairs*, 2:457; PC in *Niles' Weekly Register*, vol. XXIII, no. 17 (December 28, 1822), p. 269.

From Callender Irvine, Philadelphia, 11/8. As Calhoun ordered on 10/22, Irvine submits estimates that he will need during 1823 for clothing purchases $107,201.01 and for office expenses $7,330. FC in DNA, 45, 389:404–406.

To the Rev. Cyrus Kingsbury

Dep[art]m[en]t of War, 8 Nov[embe]r 1822

Your letter of the 4th Ult[im]o was duly received.

Remittances have been made to Mr. [William] Ward, the Choctaw Agent, on account of the buildings and tuition at the School at Newell. The remittance for tuition embraced the whole amount allowed to the end of this year; and that for buildings two-thirds of your estimate, including the estimate for the additional building mentioned in your letter now before [me].

I sincerely regret the the [*sic*] very severe affliction which has prevented you from making your annual report at the usual period. No inconvenience, however, will result from the delay if the report be received by the meeting of Congress.

FC in DNA, 72, E:354 (M-15:5).

J[ames] L. E[dwards] to [Isaac Lawrence], President, U.S. Branch Bank, New York [City]

Pension Office, Nov[embe]r 8th 1822

In answer to your letter of the 4th inst[ant; *not found*] respecting a suit commenced against Jacob S. Arden for the recovery of pension monies fraudulently obtained from the U[nited] States, the Secretary of War has directed me to inform you that he has no doubt of the guilt of Arden, and deems it important, as an example that he should not only be convicted criminally, but that a judgment be obtained against him in the Civil Suit; and therefore will afford every aid to the officers of the Bank compatible with the interest of the government in obtaining a recovery. He thinks it most expedient for you to take the advice of counsel as to the restoration of $2,500 placed in the Marshal's hands. You are authorised to incur, on the part of the United States, any expense which may be proper in defence of the expected suit against the Bank, the Marshal, or yourself.

FC in DNA, 91, 12:392. Note: Compare Calhoun's letter of 11/6 to Stephen Pleasonton.

From Joseph Lovell, 11/8. Pursuant to Calhoun's order of 11/6, Lovell reports that no money has been advanced for medical expenses this year and that no accounts remain to be tendered for settlement. He encloses a tabular report of the expenses of the Medical Department in certain years; it shows the economy of the Army's present Medical Department as contrasted with that before 1818. ALS with En in DNA, 1, S-204 (M-221:96); LS with En in DNA, RG 233, 17A-D1; FC in DNA, 242, 2:322; PC's (dated 11/28) with En in Senate Document No. 1 and House Document No. 2, 17th Cong., 2nd Sess.; PC (dated 11/28) with En in *American State Papers: Military Affairs*, 2:467.

From James Miller, "Post of Arkansaw [*sic*]," 11/8. "In addition to the two Chiefs and Interpreter of the [Western] Cherokee Tribe, a delegation chosen by them to visit Washington to come to a full understanding of all their demands against the U[nited] States," Miller recommends another Chief, Walter Webber. He has much influence over the Indians and is "much esteemed" by white people. ALS in DNA, 1, M-172 (M-221:96).

To William Ward, [Choctaw Agency,] 11/8. Calhoun acknowledges Ward's letter of 10/10 [ALS with Ens in DNA, 77 (M-271:4, frames 250–255)]. Calhoun has ordered a remittance of $666.66 to Ward to cover two-thirds of the cost, estimated by the Rev. [Cyrus] Kingsbury, of the construction of additional buildings for the Indian school at Newell. The accounts of Mingo [that is, Chief] Mushulatubbee have evidently not reached Calhoun; if duplicates are sent, properly certified, they will receive prompt attention. FC in DNA, 72, E:355 (M-15:5).

To William Drayton, Charleston, S.C., 11/9. Answering Drayton's letter of 11/2 seeking the admission of his son [Thomas Fenwick Drayton] to the Military Academy, Calhoun states that appointments will be made in 2/1823 and that appointees will report to West Point in 6/1823. Calhoun asks "the first name of your son, and [requests] a statement of his qualifications, or a letter to that effect from his teachers." FC in DNA, 13, 1:169 (M-91:1). (William Drayton replied on 11/19.)

To V[IRGIL] MAXCY, [Baltimore]

Washington, 10th Nov[embe]r 1822

The servant, from your description, would exactly suit us, but Mrs. [Floride Colhoun] Calhoun is of the opinion, that so high a price, as he asks, would not fail to cause discontent with the other servants, particularly our cook, whose services are no less important to us than that of a good head servant. Under this impression we decline making any offer for him. We are, however, very much obliged to you for the information and would be very glad to obtain a good house servant could one be obtained on suitable terms. Yours truely [*sic*], J.C. Calhoun.

ALS in DLC, Galloway-Maxcy-Markoe Papers, vol. 32. NOTE: Calhoun wrote on the envelope, below Maxcy's name: "Should Mr. M[axcy] not be in Baltimore Mrs. Maxcy will please open the letter."

From M[ARTIN] D. HARDIN, [former Senator from Ky.]

Locust Hill, [Ky.,] Nov. 11th 1822

I saw a sample of the impression of the die with which the medal for Gov[ernor Isaac] Shelby is to be struck. The features are as good as usual ["for" *canceled*] on such occasions, but the back of the head and sho[u]lders are quite too small. Is it past alteration?

If any figure on the other side were intended to represent him, it has the same fault.

By the large, the old Governor rec[eive]d this sample by an indirect channel from *Shelbyville* post office, where it had been missent, under your frank & without any letter of advice accompanying it. This coming at a time he was not in good humour about some other matters, had like to have made an unfavourable impression.

He will when ready reply to W[illia]m C. Preston[']s publication. Preston improperly imputes to Shelby more than he said or intended. I learn, for I have not seen him, that ["he will" *canceled*] he will put put [*sic*] this right, & then justify what he did say.

ALS in DNA, 1, H-137 (M-221:95).

To the Rev. LEWIS D. SCHWEINITZ, Bethlehem, Pa.

Dep[art]m[en]t of War, 11 Nov[embe]r 1822

I have received your letter of the 23 ult[im]o [*not found*] transmitting a report of the President and Directors of the Society of

United Brethren, accompanied by sundry documents, relative to certain lands on the Muskingum [River] in the State of Ohio and the Christian Indians formerly settled there and for whose benefit said lands were granted in trust to said Society, prepared in pursuance of a letter to you from this Department of the 4th of March last enclosing copies of two resolutions of the Senate of the U[nited] States requesting information in relation to said lands & Indians.

I have examined the report & accompanying documents with as much attention as the current business of the Department would permit and think the information communicated satisfactorily answers the several enquiries embraced by the resolutions of the Senate. I am fully impressed with the belief that the trust confided to the Society has been faithfully administered and it will give me pleasure to promote its wishes on this subject in any way that I can with propriety.

As it is not probable that anything will be done with the report, by Congress, but to refer it to a committee, until after the holidays, it will not perhaps be necessary for you to come on here, as you propose, before the 1st of January, or to transmit the vouchers to which you refer before that period. Should anything however occur which would demand your presence with the vouchers earlier, due notice will be given to you. On your arrival here I should be happy to see you and afford you any facility in my power in the transaction of your business with Congress.

FC in DNA, 72, E:355–356 (M-15:5). NOTE: Compare Calhoun's letter to James Monroe dated 11/30.

From LITT[LETO]N W[ALLER] TAZEWELL

Washington, Nov[embe]r 11, 1822

I beg leave to request that this recommendation of mine of Mr. Henry Allmand of Norfolk in Virginia, who is desirous of being received as a Cadet in the Military Academy at West-Point, may be placed on file in your office, to the end that his application may not pass unnoticed next March, when the appointments of Cadets for 1823 is to be made.

I am not accurately informed of Mr. Allmand's age or proficiency in his studies; his particular friends will in due season supply the requisite documents as to these points, but I suppose him to be about fifteen at this time, and that his progress in his classical and other studies is equal to that of any boy of that age in Virginia.

Mr. Allmand is the son of a very respectable gentleman now deceased, who formerly resided in Norfolk, and was my near neighbour. Our vicinity, and the circumstance that he has been an intimate associate of my own sons, two of whom are very nearly of his age I should think, have given me a good opp[ortunit]y of observing him particularly and well. And I very confidently assure you, that I regard him as a young gentleman of much merit and good promise, well deserving the patronage of the guardians of the excellent institution of which he wishes to become a member, and one who most probably will do it honor hereafter.

LS in PHi.

From George Bomford, 11/12. In compliance with one of Calhoun's orders of 11/6, Bomford reports upon lead mines in the U.S., concentrating upon developments subsequent to his report of 5/3. He reiterates that there appear to be vast quantities of lead ore in Mo. and Mich. Territories, as was reported to Calhoun on 3/30. Bomford recommends that Congress authorize the appointment of agents for the principal mining districts in the two Territories and provide adequate funds for their salaries and for surveys of Mich. Territory. Bomford contemplates applying for the transfer of some Military Academy graduates to serve as topographical surveyors in the mining districts. LS in DNA, 1, O-44 (M-221:96); LS in DNA, RG 233, 17A-D1; FC in DNA, 33, pp. 60–63; FC in DNA, 6, 2:77–79 (M-127:2); DS in DNA, RG 233, 18A-C19.2; PC's in Senate Document No. 1 and House Document No. 2, 17th Cong., 2nd Sess.; PC in *American State Papers*: *Military Affairs,* 2:460–461; PC in Carter, ed., *Territorial Papers,* 11:291–293.

To Col. Marinus Willett, New York [City]

Department of War, 12th Novem[be]r 1822

Your letter to the President [James Monroe] of the 4th instant, [*not found,*] recommending [former Bvt.] Major G[erard] D. Smith for the appointment of Indian Agent, has been referred to this Department. I have also received a letter from Major Smith, enclosing letters from you and Mr. Morgan addressed to me, upon the same subject.

These letters afford sufficient evidence of the claims and fitness of Major Smith for the appointment which he solicits, but there is at present no vacancy in that branch of the Indian business under the control of this Department. The appointment held by the late Colonel [Matthew] Lyon was that of Factor and connected with the system of Indian Trade which was abolished by an act of Congress passed during the last session.

The application of Major Smith will be placed upon file, and should an Indian Agency become vacant, I shall take pleasure in submitting his name to the President, with those of other candidates, for such office.

LS in NNC; FC in DNA, 72, E:356 (M-15:5). NOTE: Compare Calhoun's letter of 11/18 to Smith.

From Callender Irvine, Philadelphia, 11/13. Pursuant to Congressional resolutions of 4/16 and 5/17, he reports that three Clerks and one Messenger are employed full-time in his office. He considers all three essential to efficiency. FC in DNA, 45, 389:409.

To William Clark, St. Louis, 11/14. Calhoun acknowledges Clark's letter of 10/17 [ALS with Ens in DNA, 1, C-155 (M-221:95)]. Calhoun is pleased that [Richard] Graham has negotiated a treaty of peace between the Osages, Delawares, and Shawnees. Clark is to set a deadline by which white settlers must vacate the Delawares' lands and is to use force thereafter for the removal of any who linger longer. The Kickapoos' annuity for 1822 can be withheld until that for 1823 can be paid at the same time, in whatever form will be satisfactory to the Kickapoos, who do not want specie. Although Graham has stated that only one Sub-Agent is needed and has chosen one, Calhoun authorizes payment of [George C.] Sibley's salary as Sub-Agent for work elsewhere. Clark can expect to receive some instructions from [William Lee]. FC in DNA, 72, E:358–359 (M-15:5).

From George Gibson, 11/14. As ordered, he submits comparative figures as to the cost of subsisting the Army. He paid out $217,070.39 to contractors and to Assistant Commissaries of Subsistence during 1/1–9/30; $206,340.41 have been accounted for, with eight reports from distant posts yet due for the past quarter. Costs totaled $2,361,453.97 in the three years ending 5/31/1819 and $1,575,933.20 during the three years ending 5/31/1822—and this despite the fact that under the new system food has been provided for hospitalized soldiers who were excluded from the subsistence expenses of the old system and despite the great improvements in the quality of the ration. FC in DNA, 191, 3:172, with an earlier draft ("not sent") on p. 168.

From Capt. J[ohn] L[ind] Smith, Engineer Department, 11/14. He estimates that the Army Engineers will need in 1823 appropriations totaling $500,000 for fortifications and $15,150 for the Military Academy. The former figure includes $81,500 for Fort Delaware, $45,500 for Fort Washington, $90,000 for Fort Monroe, $70,000 for Fort Calhoun, $100,000 for the fort at Chef Menteur, and $50,000 for that at Mobile Point. FC in DNA, 21, 1:334.

From Capt. J[ohn] L[ind] Smith, Engineer Department, 11/14. He reports that unexpended balances of the appropriations for fortifications as of today amount to tens of thousands of dollars, most of which will be expended before 4/1/1823 in payments for current operations. FC in DNA, 21, 1:335.

From George Bomford, 11/15. Complying with one of Calhoun's orders of 11/6, Bomford submits statements showing the number of muskets produced in the armories between 1/1 and 9/30, the expenditures of those months, and comparative costs of muskets in 1817 and 1822. Muskets produced in 1822 will cost about $2.00 less per stand than those made in 1817 and are superior to the earlier weapons. LS with Ens (dated 11/13 and 11/14) in DNA, 1, O-45 (M-221:96); LS with Ens in DNA, RG 233, 17A-D1; FC with Ens in DNA, 6, 2:79–84 (M-127:2); FC in DNA, 32, 3:262–263; PC's with Ens in Senate Document No. 1 and House Document No. 2, 17th Cong., 2nd Sess.; PC with Ens in *American State Papers*: *Military Affairs*, 2:461–463.

2nd Lt. C[lark] Burdine, Fever River, [Ill.,] to [George] Bomford, 11/15. Burdine summarizes the progress of the lead mines. He is being pressed by many individuals for the right to work the mines, but the area has not been properly surveyed yet. Several of the lessees, he has learned, have been subleasing their claims. He asks for instructions about these matters and whether applicants should be allowed to select their own places to dig. He complains of a lack of assistance. Burdine thinks that the yield of the mines will be greater than the Ordnance Department anticipated. ALS in DNA, 31, 1822, B.

To William Clark, St. Louis, 11/15. Pursuant to Clark's letter of 10/25 [LS with En in DNA, 1, C-156 (M-221:95)], Calhoun protests that [James] Latham's estimate of expenses at the Peoria Sub-Agency during 9/18–12/31 is much too high and must be reduced; Calhoun suggests in what particulars. FC in DNA, 72, E:359 (M-15:5).

To William H. Crawford, 11/15. Calhoun encloses the War Department's requests for appropriations in 1823, which total $4,814,067.75. FC in DNA, 171, 2:[49–55].

To [Nathan Towson], 11/15. Calhoun directs Towson to prepare a statement showing the amount of money remitted to disbursing officers during the first three quarters of 1822, the amount of "the accounts rendered for settlement for the same period, and the period to which the several Corps of the Army have been paid." LS in DNA, 292, 1-2347; FC in DNA, 3, 11:446 (M-6:11).

From the Rev. Robert Bell, "Beach Meeting house, Sumner C[oun]ty," Tenn., 11/16. He presents his annual report. Fifteen boys and six girls attend the Charity Hall school for the Chickasaws and are doing well. Expenditures during the year have been $608, and the property belonging to the school is worth about $1,700. Because little money is in circulation, it has been necessary to receive donations in produce, and this cannot be disposed of until "towards Christmas." It is impossible to ascertain accurately what funds can be applied to the school, but Bell estimates the amount at between $700 and $1,000. There is insufficient money to admit all the Indian children whose parents wish them to attend; consequently, the Cumberland Missionary Board requests $500 in government aid. ALS in DNA, 77 (M-271:4, frames 13–14).

From Capt. T[rueman] Cross, Assistant Quartermaster General, 11/16. In the absence of [Thomas S. Jesup], Cross answers Calhoun's letter to [Jesup] of 11/6. Cross subunits reports of remittances and disbursements made through the first three quarters of 1822 and a comparative view of Quartermaster expenditures in 1817 and 1822, showing a saving of 24% in 1822. There will probably be no cases of delinquency in accounts by Quartermaster officers this year. Cross calls attention to the "extension of our military frontier several thousand miles" since 1817, along the Red, Arkansas, Missouri, and Mississippi Rivers. LS with Ens in DNA, RG 233, 17A-D1; FC with Ens in DNA, 6, 2:84–88 (M-127:2); FC in DNA, 42, 4:328–330 (M-745:2, frames 462–463); FC in DNA, 50, vol. 2; CC with Ens in DNA, 1, Q-85 (M-221:96); PC's with Ens in Senate Document No. 1 and House Document No. 2, 17th Cong., 2nd Sess.; PC with Ens in *American State Papers: Military Affairs*, 2:463–465. (Canceled versions dated 11/14 precede each of the FC's.)

To John E[arle] Frost, [Washington]

Department of War, November 16th 1822

As it appears by the report of Mr. [Nathaniel] Cutting [Chief Clerk of the Section of Bounty Lands in the War Department] that the business in this Department on which you have been engaged is nearly completed I have to notify you that your services as Clerk in this Office will not be required after the 31st of December next.

In communicating this decision to you, it is proper to remark that it has not been formed upon any preference for the qualifications of others over yours, but upon the rule that those retire first whose business is first first [*sic*] completed. It affords me pleasure to accompany this notification, with an expression of my approbation of your conduct while in this Department and of my wishes that you may be prosperous in whatever pursuit you may engage [in].

FC in DNA, 3, 11:446 (M-6:11).

To Joseph McMinn, New Canton (Hawkins County), Tenn., 11/16. Calhoun writes to McMinn pursuant to a letter from the latter to [William Lee] dated 8/23. The instructions under which McMinn was authorized to sell certain public property in 1820 implied that he was expected to collect payments due for sales on credit. Calhoun wants McMinn to make "every proper exertion to collect the money [due] on the notes" and will allow to him "reasonable compensation" for this service. "You will not, however, in the progress of the business bring any suits on the notes until you have advised this Department of the failure of other steps to obtain the money and received its instructions." FC in DNA, 72, E:360 (M-15:5).

2nd Lt. C[lark] Burdine, Fever River, [Ill.,] to [George] Bomford, 11/17. Burdine reports the progress of the lead mines. He complains that he has no assistance and lacks instructions. He has had several applications for leases, but there has not been time properly to survey the lands. He asks for detailed instructions. LS in DNA, 31, 1822, B.

To V[IRGIL] MAXCY

War Dept., 17th Nov. 1822

I received your favour of the 13th Inst[ant; *not found*] this morning.

I am glad that Col. [Talbot] Chambers is so sound. He is an important man, and I have no doubt, considering his standing and the natural [*or possibly* "material"] strength of the Republican side, that he must hold [Edward] Lloyd in check.

If a nomination can be obtained by a respectable majority it would be an important event; but nothing ought to be put to hazard. The expression of the opinion of the Legislature would have a very desirable effect or even a favourable notice of the adm[inistratio]n by the Governor in his Message. The crisis is at hand. I see the Radicals are afraid to make it yet, and are holding in; we on the contrary ought to bring it to an issue as soon as possible. The President[']s [James Monroe's] message I have no doubt will favour the making of the issue this winter.

I hope great care will be taken in the selection of the Gov[erno]r. Should one of Radical principles be elected, it will embarrass you much.

If I should see [Dr. Joseph] Kent I will improve your suggestion; but I fear that I may not ["be" *canceled*] see him in time; and you had better, if it can be done in the mean time, to [*sic*] attend to it through some other channel, ["if one" *canceled*] should ["one" *interlined*] offer itself. Yours truly, J.C. Calhoun.

ALS in DLC, Galloway-Maxcy-Markoe Papers, vol. 32.

From the Rev. C[yrus] Kingsbury, Mayhew, Choctaw Nation, 11/18. He has learned from an extract of a letter of 6/29 from Calhoun to Jeremiah Evarts that two-thirds of the estimated cost of the buildings at a contemplated school will be paid by the government. "If that estimate was not altered by Mr. Evarts after I saw him, it was for two thousand dollars. For various reasons, confirmed by experience, we are of opinion that smaller schools, will be more usefull [*sic*] in proportion to the expense than large ones, especially in connection with the large ones already in operation. It has therefore been determined to reduce the first establishment in the S.E. District one-half, from the former plan." Kingsbury encloses "a plan of the buildings on the reduced scale," for which the present estimate is $1,000. He hopes that "the other half of the former estimate, will be allowed for a second school in the same District, so soon as we shall be able to commence it." Long desirous that a committee should examine minutely the schools in the Choctaw Nation and report upon them to the Government, to the American Board [of Commissioners for Foreign Missions], and to the public, Kingsbury discusses its membership and suggests that the members be appointed jointly by the President [James Monroe] and the American Board. ALS with En in DNA, 77 (M-271:4, frames 162–166).

From Joshua Shaw, Philadelphia, 11/18. He has invented an improved method of obtaining the firing of charges in pistols and rifles—so much better that it will double the effectiveness of any Army unit and proportionately improve the certainty with which hunters can kill game. It is practically impervious to damp weather. He wants to sell this invention to the Army, although he considers it useless to attempt to patent it, and has sent samples to Calhoun and to others. ALS in DNA, 35, In-6-32.

To [former Bvt.] Maj. Gerard D. Smith, New York [City]

Dep[art]m[en]t of War, 18 Nov[embe]r 1822

I have received your letter of the 14th inst[ant; *not found*] and in reply have to state that under the act of Congress passed at the last session abolishing the Factory system [of Indian trade], several persons were appointed by the Treasury Department (which is charged with the execution of said act) as its agents to repair to the several Factories for the purpose of receiving of the respective

Factors the merchandise in their possession and winding up the business with them.

The appointment held by the late [that is, former] Maj. [George] McGlassin was one of this description & is merely temporary. I have, however, submitted your application for the vacancy to the consideration of the Secretary of the Treasury [William H. Crawford].

FC in DNA, 72, E:360–361 (M-15:5).

2nd Lt. C[lark] Burdine, Fever River, [Ill.,] to [George] Bomford, 11/19. Burdine recommends that the area of the lead mines be surveyed in a regular order, to avoid disputes with the lessees and conflict with the Indians. He complains of the drunkenness of his soldiers. ALS in DNA, 31, 1822, B.

To Duncan G. Campbell, Washington, Ga.

Dep[art]m[en]t of War, 19 Nov[embe]r 1822

I have received a letter from Gen[era]l [John] Floyd tendering his resignation as one of the Commissioners to hold a treaty with the [Eastern] Cherokee nation, which has been accepted. Gen[era]l Floyd has been requested to forward to you all the papers in his possession connected with the Commission; and as the President [James Monroe] does not deem it necessary to appoint another Commissioner in the place of the General, Major James Meriwether & yourself will proceed with the negociation [*sic*]. The Department has not yet been apprized of your acceptance. In order that the Commissioners may be apprized of the temper of the Cherokee nation with respect to the proposed treaty, I herewith enclose a Copy of the proceedings of a national Committee and Council upon the subject which have been recently communicated by the Chiefs to this Department.

FC in DNA, 72, E:361 (M-15:5).

To John Clark, [Governor of Ga.,] Milledgeville

Dep[art]m[en]t of War, 19 Nov[embe]r 1822

I have received a letter from Gen[era]l [John] Floyd tendering his resignation as one of the Commissioners to hold a treaty with the

[Eastern] Cherokee nation, which has been accepted. The President [James Monroe] does not deem it necessary, at this time, to appoint another Commissioner in the place of the General, but has directed that the other Commissioners Messrs. [Duncan G.] Campbell & [James] Meriwether be instructed to proceed with the negociation [*sic*], and they have been instructed accordingly.

FC in DNA, 72, E:362 (M-15:5).

From William Drayton

Charleston, [S.C.,] 19th November 1822

My son's Christian name is Thomas [Fenwick]. His qualifications for entering the Military Academy I am not otherwise able to state, than by saying that he has received a classical education in Pen[n]sylvania, until within about eighteen months, that he has been under a private tutor in England: I have already written to his Teacher to instruct him in those branches of knowledge which I have been informed are absolutely requisite to an admission at West Point. I can send no certificate of my son's progress in his studies, as he is in Europe. I had understood that the nomination by the government was conditional, & that the applicant could not be received, unless, upon an examination, he should be proved to possess the qualifications specified in the Secretary's appointment. If I am in error, will you have the goodness to correct me, & also to communicate to me by what day in the month of June it will be necessary for my son to repair to West Point, should he be appointed a Cadet in February next.

The qualifications for admission at the Military Academy, as I obtained them from [2nd] Lieut[enant Samuel] Wragg, who was educated there, are, "to be able to read distinctly & pronounce correctly, to write a fair legible hand, & to perform, with facility & accuracy, the various operations of the general rules of arithmetic, both simple & compound, of the rules of reduction, of single & compound proportion & also of vulgar & decimal fractions."

With many apologies for the trouble I occasion you, I am, my dear Sir, most respectfully . . . .

ALS in DNA, 15, 1820, 118 (M-688:14, frames 444–446).

To JOHN FLOYD, St. Marys, Ga.

Dep[art]m[en]t of War, 19 Nov[embe]r 1822

I have received your letter of the 26th Ult[im]o [LS in DNA, 1, F-45 (M-221:95)] tendering your resignation as Commissioner to hold a treaty with the [Eastern] Cherokee nation & regret that circumstances have rendered it necessary for you to withdraw from the Commission. Your resignation is accepted and you will be pleased to transmit all the papers in your possession connected with the Commission to Duncan G. Campbell Esq[ui]r[e] at Washington, Wilkes Co[unty,] Ga., who has been informed of your resignation and requested to take charge of them.

FC in DNA, 72, E:361 (M-15:5).

To Maj. JAMES MERIWETHER, Athens, Ga.

Dep[art]m[en]t of War, Nov[embe]r 19, 1822

I have received a letter from Gen[era]l [John] Floyd, tendering his resignation as one of the Commissioners to hold a treaty with the [Eastern] Cherokee nation, which has been accepted. Gen[era]l Floyd has been requested to forward all the papers in his possession connected with the Commission to Duncan G. Campbell, Esq[ui]r[e], at Washington, Wilkes County, Geo[rgi]a, and as the President [James Monroe] does not deem it necessary to appoint another Commissioner in the place of the General, Mr. Campbell & yourself will proceed with the negociation [*sic*]. The Department has not been apprized of your acceptance.

FC in DNA, 72, E:361–362 (M-15:5); LS offered as Item 404 in Catalog 4 (*ca.* 10/1962) by Paul C. Richards, 1023 Beacon St., Brookline, Mass.

From Nathaniel B. Dodge, Superintendent, Harmony Mission, Harmony, [Ark. Territory,] 11/20. He submits a six-page, first annual report of the mission to the autumn of 1822. It was established [in 1819] by the United Foreign Missionary Society of N.Y. for the benefit of the Osages. After almost five months of travel, the 41 staff members arrived on 8/2/[1819]; illnesses cost several lives before Christmas. The school was opened in 1/1820 and has had a fluctuating number of students; the present number is 10, some of whom are doing quite well. "On the whole we think the school [is] in a flourishing state." Dodge describes its location, its buildings, its livestock, and the duties of its staff. He describes Osage men as being indolent; he proposes to combat that disposition by setting an industrious example and by employing Indians as laborers. His greatest hope for tribal improvement lies, however, in the "rising generation." For the benefit of the mission the Indians have set aside "not less than 15 or 20,000 acres." ALS in DNA, 77 (M-271:4, frames 91–97).

From John Floyd, Milledgeville, Ga., 11/20. He has traveled to that place under an expectation that he would meet "the Commissioners authorised to hold the Contemplated Treaty, with the Creek, and [Eastern] Cherokee Indians." Floyd brought with him all papers concerning that business. "I therefore wait your instructions, for the direction I shall give to them. Your answer will reach me at this place." ALS in DNA, 1, F-49 (M-221:95).

From Davis & [Peter] Force, Washington, 11/21. They inform Calhoun that they have received 30 [printed] copies of Dr. [Jedidiah] Morse's Indian report. LU in DNA, 1, D-62 (M-221:95).

From Joseph Lovell, 11/21. Dr. [Walter V.] Wheaton, Surgeon at the Sault of St. Mary, has recommended that all-wool fabrics shall be used in uniforms furnished to soldiers there, where the temperatures fall far below zero. Lovell approves and adds that the same change should be made for all posts on the Missouri, the Upper Mississippi, the Great Lakes, Plattsburg, and posts east of Newport, R.I. (Appended is a memo by T[rueman] Cross dated 11/27, partly approving.) ALS in DNA, 43, Sault [Ste.] Marie; FC in DNA, 242, 2:324.

From Return J. Meigs

Cherokee Agency, 22nd November 1822

I enclose to you the copy of a letter [dated 10/26 and] addressed to me by the Cherokee National Council & National Committee; the contents of which they request me to communicate to the Georgia Commissioners for holding a treaty with them, the present year, which I shall do as soon as possible, but think it my duty first to communicate it to you.

Their declaration not to meet the Commissioners is little short of a declaration of independance [*sic*], which they never lose sight of, which I have frequently mentioned formerly in my letters to you. Such a declaration I consider as disrespectful to the United States Commissioners & to the Government, & inconsistent with their standing, and dependant circumstances.

Their pretence of having obtained the sentiments of the people is a bubble; for the populace are governed by a few leading men, who fabricate their political catechism.

Indeed their government is an aristocracy, consisting of about 100 men, called Chiefs, and these Cheifs [*sic*] are controlled by perhaps twenty speculating individuals; some of these individuals are making fortunes in trade by merchandise, a considerable portion of which merchandise is whiskey and other ardent spirits. The tendency of the conduct of these individuals is to perpetuate barbarism, by encouraging indolence.

The United States are now giving their children a lettered education. It may be a question, whether these children will retain their acquirement after they shall have been turned back into Indian Society of 10,000 souls only, scattered over a wilderness of 10,000,000 of acres of land?

If it shall once be admitted that the Cherokees are an independant people, I can hardly conceive our obligations to expend thousands & thousands of dollars to bring them to a state of refinement, while in many parts of the United States, the children of our citizens are destitute of instruction in letters from the inability of their parents.

If they should persist in their resolution, "never again to dispose of one foot more of land," the citizens of Tennessee, Georgia, & Alabama would probably, hardly be restrained long, from taking possession of their respective claims: this would be regretted by the government. And I think still, if the United States Commissioners will invite the Cherokees to a conference for the purpose of making some friendly arrangements, having for their object the advantage of both parties, that the Cherokees would meet them & take them by the hand, & the prospect would be greater of succeeding than if their rash resolutions had never been made.

I have written once to Mr. Freeman [Walker], and twice to General [John] Floyd, and have received one letter from him. He urges me to write freely to him. In my letters to him, I have kept in mind what I thought were your sentiments in relation to arrangements with the Indians.

Some untoward circumstances have retarded this buisness [*sic*], so that I am not informed of the time or place of meeting. February or early in March next would do very well. The persons here, who offered to contract, have every thing ready; and they want no advances from Government to enable them to provide [rations].

ALS with En in DNA, 1, M-175 (M-221:96).

To Jacob Brown, 11/23. Pursuant to a House resolution of 4/16 asking the Secretary of War and the heads of four other executive departments to report the number of their respective office employees and Messengers "and whether any of them, and if any, how many of them, are unnecessary, inefficient or engaged in other pursuits or professions in no wise relating to the public service" and whether any economies can be contrived, Calhoun orders Brown to submit a report about these matters insofar as the Adjutant General's office is concerned. CC in DNA, 17, 1:27. (An appended note says that Brown complied with this order on 11/25; see his letterbook, 6:265.)

From William Lee, 11/23. He submits a statement, with a recapitulation, of the unsettled War Department accounts in his office as of 3/4/1817, the amount settled since then, and the amount remaining unsettled as of 9/30/1822. DS in DNA, 1, L-93 (M-221:96).

To Isaac Shelby, Danville, Ky.

Department of War, November 23d 1822

Under cover of a letter [*not found*] from Col. [Richard M.] Johnson, I have this day received yours to him of the 1st instant, and regret to find that you supposed that the designs of the medals in plaster enclosed to you should have been considered as a compliance with the resolution granting a Gold medal for your distinguished services. They were put under cover to you merely to show the design of the medal, which is now in execution, in the belief that it would afford some gratification to form an opinion from them of the appearance of the medal when completed. I hope it will speedily be completed in a style well calculated to commemorate the glorious events for which it is intended.

LS in KyU; variant FC in DNA, 3, 11:447 (M-6:11).

To J[OSEPH] G. SWIFT, [New York City]

Washington, 23d Nov. 1822

I received in the due course of the mail your private letter [*not found*] in relation to Capt. [Frederick] Lewis. I would be very much gratified, that some arrangement could be made by which he could be provided for out of the corps; but I can not think of any thing by which it can be effected. The late reduction of the Army threw so many meritorious officers on the Department, that any vacancy however inconsiderable the emolument has been taken up by them, and many still remain to be provided for.

It is impossible to give to Capt. Lewis any command adequate to his rank. I want confidence in him, and if I had, as there is a debt against him on the books of the Treasury, he can not be charged with any command which would require an advance am[oun]t of money.

ALS in NWM.

From George Gibson, 11/25. Pursuant to a House resolution of 4/16, Gibson reports that two Clerks are employed in the office of the Commissary General of Subsistence, that the work of neither is dispensable, and that each is capable, remarkably attentive to his duties, and free from any employment not related to the service. FC in DNA, 191, 3:172.

From E[dmund] Kirby, "Aid[e]-de-Camp," 11/25. Answering [Calhoun's] communication of 11/23 to [Jacob] Brown, Kirby states, in conformity with the resolution of 4/16 of the House of Representatives, that there are two Clerks in the Adjutant General's office who are vital to its operation and who are engaged in no pursuits that are unrelated to the public service. FC in DNA, 12, 6:265–266 (M-565:6, frames 428–429).

From W[illiam] Ward, Choctaw Agency, 11/25. He has received Calhoun's letter of 10/29 and the drafts for $14,135 and $1,972. Ward discusses briefly some financial matters, states that he has no instructions how to pay the warriors who participated in the Pensacola campaign, and reports the site selected by the Choctaws for the new location of the Agency. Although the site is not in the center of the Choctaw nation, it is on the mail route to

Natchez and appears to be the best possible location. ALS in DNA, 77 (M-271:4, frames 256–257).

The Rev. Henry Ford, Elmira, [N.Y.,] to David Woodcock, [Representative from N.Y.,] 11/26. Ford applies through Woodcock to Calhoun for a Cadet's appointment for his pupil, George [W.] Hughes. "Though but very recently acquainted with him personally; I have frequently heard him spoken of as a youth of very grave and sober habbits [*sic*] and much addicted to the improvement of his mind." Ford adds a postscript saying that he was Calhoun's "college mate" [at Yale College, New Haven, Conn.,] and though both men have been widely separated since, "perhaps neither of us have [*sic*] entirely lost a remembrance of the sympathies and endearments of our alma mater." (An AEI by Calhoun reads, "To be particularly attended to." For a summary of Hughes' Army career see Heitman, *Historical Register*, 1:552.) ALS in DNA, 15, 1823, 187½ (M-688:26, frames 40–42).

To M[artin] D. Hardin, Locust Hill, Ky., 11/26. Calhoun has forwarded an extract from Hardin's letter to Calhoun dated 11/11 to [Joseph] "Hopkinson in the hope that it is not too late to effect the alteration suggested." Calhoun regrets that [Isaac] Shelby misunderstood the object of the sample [medal], but Calhoun has written to Shelby [on 11/23] "on the subject, and [I] hope he will be satisfied with the explanation given." FC in DNA, 3, 11:447–448 (M-6:11).

To Joseph Hopkinson, Philadelphia, 11/26. Calhoun encloses an extract from [Martin D.] Hardin's letter [dated 11/11] concerning [Isaac] Shelby's medal. "Should you think that any alteration for the better can be made at this time, you will be pleased to give such directions in relation to it as may be deemed advisable." FC in DNA, 3, 11:448 (M-6:11).

From J[oseph] McIlvaine, [U.S. District Attorney for N.J.,] Burlington, N.J., 11/26. He encloses a committee report from the N.J. legislature explaining its reasons for not ceding the Pea Patch Island to the U.S. He describes his efforts to have the matter reconsidered by the legislature and by the Governor, [Isaac H. Williamson]. Despite McIlvaine's effeorts to have the lawsuit [by Dr. Henry Gale against Maj. Samuel Babcock for the title to the

Pea Patch Island] tried in the U.S. Circuit Court, it appears that it will be heard before the N.J. Supreme Court. PC's with Ens in *American State Papers: Military Affairs,* 5:487–488, and *Public Lands,* 6:439–441.

From J[oseph] McIlvaine, Burlington, N.J., 11/26. He submits his account for legal services falling outside of his ordinary duties [as U.S. District Attorney for N.J.] in regard to litigation brought by [Henry] Gale against Maj. [Samuel] Babcock in the N.J. Supreme Court over the U.S. claim to the Pea Patch [Island] and for McIlvaine's services in the N.J. legislature during eight days [in trying to get the State to cede the Pea Patch to the U.S.]. LS in DNA, 30, 387.

From William P. DuVal

Nov[embe]r 27th 1822[,] Bards Town, Kentucky

I had the honor a few days since of receiving your letter of the 23d of October on the subject of postponing the Treaty which was to have been held on the 20th of this month with the Florida Indians. The copy of the letters to Col. [Abram] Eustis and [George] Walton on the same subject, have [*sic*] been likewise received.

I feel confidant [*sic*] that the President [James Monroe] and yourself on a full examination of the situation of the Country which ["it" *interlined*] was expected the Indians would occupy, will be convinced that the Indians ought not to be placed in any situation that might enable them, to cut off the communication between East and West Florida. The most valuable and fertile part of Florida is situated on the Suwanny [*sic*] River and running towards the old Allachua [*sic*] Towns, near St. John's river. The whole of this country from the best information I have been able to obtain is uncommonly rich, and will produce better sugar than Louisiana and I believe it is the interest of the United States, as early as possible, to have this country surveyed and brought into market. It will raise a considerable sum. Gen[era]l [Andrew] Jackson has the highest opinion of that region of Florida, and Capt. R[ichard] K[eith] Call who saw much of it represents it to be as fertile as any part of Kentucky or Tennessee.

ALS in DNA, 1, D-69 (M-221:95).

To [James Monroe]

Department of War, November 27th 1822

In compliance with your directions, I herewith transmit statements from the Major General of the Army, [Jacob Brown, dated 11/25,] and the several subordinate branches of this Department, which give in detail the information requested.

In order to render the military organization more complete, the Major General after the late reduction of the Army, under the act of 2d March 1821, was stationed at the seat of the Government, thus bringing the military administration of the Army, as well as its pecuniary, through the several subordinate branches, under the immediate inspection and control of the Government. There is reason to believe that the arrangement will be highly useful.

The report of the Major General herewith transmitted marked A, exhibits the present organization, strength, and distribution of the Army. In the distribution, both in relation to the positions occupied, and the number at each post, regard has been had to the protection of important points, and the discipline of the troops. The Artillery with the exception of four Companies on the Lakes and one at West Point, has been assigned to the Garrisoning of the various fortress's [*sic*] along the line of the Sea Coast, and the important Ordnance depots in the interior; while the Infantry with the exception of a Regiment at Pensacola has been stationed at the important points in the interior, principally on the Upper Lakes, and the Western frontier.

No change has been made in the course of the year in the distribution of the troops with the exception of transferring one Company of Artillery from Fernandina to Charleston Harbour; one Battalion of the 2d Regiment of Infantry from Sacketts [*sic*] Harbour to the Sault of St. Marie, at the outlet of Lake Superior, and the whole of the 7th Regiment from Fort Scott and Bay of St. Louis, to the Arkansaw [*sic*] and Red Rivers, to each of which one Battalion has been assigned.

The Inspector Generals (one of whom [Col. Samuel B. Archer] has been assigned to the Artillery, and the other [Col. John E. Wool] to the Infantry) have in the performance of their duty visited all of the posts and military depots in the course of the year, with the exception of the posts on the Arkansaw and Red Rivers, the inspection of which was prevented by the Inspector [Col. Wool] being severely attacked by a fever while on his tour of

Inspection. In addition to the inspection by the Inspector Generals, the Generals commanding the Departments have inspected, or are in the course of inspection[,] of the whole of their respective commands.

The various articles which constitute the supplies of the Army have been during the year regularly issued, and of a good quality.

The report of the Chief of the Engineers [Alexander Macomb, dated 11/14] marked B exhibits the progress, which has been made in the course of the year in the Erection of fortifications; also the operation of the Board of Engineers and the Corps of Topographical Engineers, and the present condition of the Military Academy, by reference to which it will appear that the important duties assigned to that Department have been performed in a very satisfactory manner.

The report of the Col. of Ordnance [George Bomford, dated 11/12 and 11/15] marked C contains an exhibit of the operations in that branch of service during the last year, comprizing the operations of the Armories, the Ordnance depots, and the measures which have been taken in relation to the lead mines, the superintendence of which has recently been annexed to the Ordnance Department. The report satisfactor[il]y shows, that this important Department is gradually attaining a state of high perfection. The rigid inspection of the various Ordnance depots, which has lately been made the duty of the Inspector of Artillery, will it is believed greatly contribute to improve this important Branch of Service.

The reports of the Quarter Master General [Thomas S. Jesup, dated 11/16 and prepared by Trueman Cross], Pay Master General [Nathan Towson, dated 11/29], Surgeon General [Joseph Lovell, dated 11/28], and the Commissary Generals of Provision [George Gibson, dated 11/14] and Purchases [Callender Irvine, dated 11/14] herewith transmitted marked D, E, F, G, & H exhibit a very satisfactory view of the condition of their respective Departments.

On the 4th of March 1817, there remained unsettled on the Books of the 2d and 3d Auditors, [William Lee and Peter Hagner,] of the sums disbursed through this Department previous to that date $45,111,123.01 which on the 30th of September last was reduced to $4,689,292.95. Since the former period there has been disbursed through this Department $40,887,772.83 of which on the 30th of September last there remained to be settled $6,290,110.60 the greater part of which consist[s] of accounts, in the ordinary and due course of settlement. Of the sum advanced in the year ending the 30th of September 1821 to the Officers under the control of this Department, but $—— remained to be accounted for at the commencement of this quarter.

By reference to the statements in the reports of the subordinate branches of this Department, already referred to, it will appear that there was drawn from the Treasury in the three first quarter[s] of this year on account of the Army, Military Academy, fortifications, and Ordnance $1,930,464.59 and that accounts amounting to $1,737,072.30 have been rendered for settlement, leaving but $193,392.29 to be rendered, all or nearly all of which it is believed will be accounted for before the termination of the quarter, and there is reasonable grounds [*sic*] to believe that the disburs[e]ments of the year will be made without any loss to the government. Nearly the whole amount which is outstanding of the disburs[e]ments of the three first quarters of the year, have been prevented from being accounted for either by the sickness of the disbursing Agents, or the very great distance of the posts at which the disburs[e]ments have been made.

Great reduction has been made in the amount of expenditures in every branch of service, as will appear by reference to the reports already referred to, which contain comparative statements of the present and former rates of expenditure.

All [of] which is respectfully submitted.

LS with Ens in DNA, RG 233, 17A-D1; FC with Ens in DNA, 6, 2:62–70 (M-127:2); PG's with Ens in Senate Document No. 1 and House Document No. 2, 17th Cong., 2nd Sess.; PC with Ens in *American State Papers: Military Affairs,* 2:450–472; PC in *Niles' Weekly Register*, vol. XXIII, no. 17 (December 28, 1822), pp. 267–268; PC in Crallé, ed., *Works,* 5:123–126.

From Joseph Lovell, 11/28. In compliance with Calhoun's instructions of 11/6, Lovell encloses a "comparative table of the expenses of the Medical Department under its different organizations, from 1806 to 1822." Lovell explains that "a perfect system of responsibility for all public property from the period of its purchase to that of its expenditure, has been Established in this Office; that the returns of the Surgeons, of every Article, are regularly rendered and examined, and full receipts required in every case of transfer before their accounts are settled. This with the plan of purchasing adopted, and of paying all bills without advancing money, absolutely precludes the possibility of fraud, extravagance or undue expenditure. It may also be remarked, that during the four last years, our Military Hospitals have been regularly and abundantly furnished with every Article of furniture, medicines, stores &c. necessary for the comfort[,] convenience, and recovery of the sick; to which, as well as to the skill and attention of the Surgeons, the quarterly reports bear ample testimony; for with the exception of two posts, at which there was unusual sickness from accidental causes, the whole number of deaths in the Army for two quarters was but thirty-one, thirteen of which were from casualties, consumption, and sudden hemorrhage, leaving but eighteen from all other diseases in six months; a proportion vastly less than occurs among the same class of men in Civil life in any part of the Country." The enclosure shows that the expenses of the Medical Department have decreased so much that "the appropriation required for 1823 is but $3,000 more than that for 1807, though the Army is twice as large, and the posts nearly double in number." FC with En in DNA, 6, 2:91–92 (M-127:2).

From Alexander Macomb, 11/28. In response to a House resolution of 4/16, Macomb reports the number of persons employed in the Engineer Office and asserts that none of them is "unnecessary, inefficient or engaged in other pursuits or professions in no wise relating to the Public Service." FC in DNA, 21, 1:337.

To C[HARLES] CALDWELL, [M.D.,] Lexington, Ky.

War Department, Nov[embe]r 29th 1822

In compliance with your request, I now transmit the information promised in my letter to you in June last. It would have been finished long since, had the business of the Pension Office allowed the Clerks in that branch of the Department to devote their time to the examination of the various documents necessary to effect the object of your enquiry. In my former communication I stated to you, that the whole numerical force of the Revolutionary Army could not be ascertained, in consequence of the rolls being incomplete. Documents have been discovered in the Treasury Department, shewing the strength of the Army for each year of the War; but from these no satisfactory information could be obtained to aid you in your enquiry, as it cannot be ascertained therefrom, how many different men were actually enlisted, owing to the fluctuations of the Army, arising from the various terms and dates of enlistment. I have therefore transmitted the number of those only who were in the service at the close of the War, of whom 5,543 applied for and obtained pensions under the first act passed for the relief of those who served in the Revolution. Under a subsequent act of Congress, requiring a schedule of property under oath, only 4,648 have been continued on the list, many not having made application a second time, and others having been dropt from the roll on account of their property. Of the number, therefore, who originally obtained pensions as above, it cannot be ascertained precisely how many are now living; but it may be safely estimated that the number of deaths has not exceeded 500. It may be fairly inferred then, that 5,043 are now living. Document No. 1 contains a statement of the number of non-commissioned officers and Privates who were in the Army at the end of the War. The returns of the number of officers are incomplete; but as far as we have been able to ascertain, the number is in the proportion of one to twenty non-commissioned officers, Privates &c. Document No. 2 embraces those who served to the end of the War and are now on the pension list, distinguishing between those who served in the Army and those who served in the Navy. It also shews the States to which the Pensioner belonged during the Revolution, and the States in which they now reside. It is believed, that fewer applications for pensions, in proportion to the number that served, have been made from the Southern than from the Northern States, in consequence of those in the former section of the country being in less indigent circumstances than those in the latter.

FC with Ens in DNA, 91, 12:411–413. NOTE: Document No. 1, described above, was probably prepared under the direction of James L. Edwards, but it contains no date or signature. Document No. 2, also described above, was submitted by Edwards on 11/29.

From Benjamin A. Markley, Charleston, [S.C.,] 11/29. He seeks an appointment to succeed the late John Drayton as [U.S.] District Judge [in S.C.] and requests Calhoun's help, "as without it I could have but little expectation of success." ALS in DNA, 103, Markley (M-439:11, frames 414–416).

From N[athan] Towson, 11/29. "In obedience to your order, I have the honor herewith to submit 'a report of the amount of money drawn ["from the" *canceled*] from the appropriation for the Pay Department and remitted to the disbursing Officers, on account of the payments of the three first quarters of the present year: the periods to which accounts have been rendered, the amount remaining to be accounted for and the periods to which the troops have been paid.' From this report it will be seen that the remittances amount to 693,925.47 dollars. The accounts rendered amount to 611,851.85 dollars, leaving a balance of 82,073.62 dollars to be accounted for. From the reports of Paymasters recently received, I am warranted in stating that *by this time* ["the balance" *canceled*] the balance has been applied to the purposes for which it was intended; and that the whole will be fully accounted for, before the end of the fourth quarter: also, that the troops are paid up to the 31st August with the exception of the Companies in the district paid by Major [Abraham A.] Massias, who was authorized to postpone the Company payments in consequence of the recommendation of the commanding Officers and opinion of the Surgeons; that it would be injurious to the health of the men to receive pay in the sickly season. The Officers in his district have been paid to ["the" *interlined*] last of August. Company payments for the last month of the third quarter (September) do not become due until after the October muster and cannot therefore be made before November. In justice to those Paymasters who have the largest balances to account for, it may be proper to state the causes that have occasioned delay in rendering their accounts. Capt. [Benjamin F.] Larned has been employed in paying [Daniel] *Randall*[']*s* district in the absence of that Paymaster which he has completed to the 31st of August, but it has delayed the payment of his own. Paymaster [Asher] Phillips received funds in July and has made partial payments to the last of August. He was prevented visiting the remote posts in his district, by a severe attack of the fever prevailing at Louisville[,] Ky. He reports that he left Louisville to pay the troops on the Arkansas river, on the 5th of October and that he expects to return by the 18th of Nov[embe]r, when his payments will be completed to the last of August and his accounts rendered. Major [David] Gwynne has also been delayed in making his payments by sickness. He reports however his district paid to the last of August with the exception of two Companies: that he has made arrangements to to [*sic*] have them paid and that his accounts will be rendered as soon as he is sufficiently recovered to attend to business. Paymaster [Charles B.] Tallmadge was not furnished with funds for his present district until the month of August, as the troops he is to pay did not reach their stations on the Lakes till late in the season." LS with En in DNA, 1, P-138 (M-221:96); LS with En in DNA, RG 233, 17A-D1;

FC with En in DNA, 6, 2:88–90 (M-127:2); FC in DNA, 291, 16:8–9; PC's with En in Senate Document No. 1 and House Document No. 2, 17th Cong., 2nd Sess.; PC with En in *American State Papers: Military Affairs,* 2:465–466.

To JOHN CLARK, [Governor of Ga.,] Milledgeville

Dep[art]m[en]t of War, 30 Nov[embe]r 1822

The letter of the 11th inst[ant; *not found*] signed by yourself, Hon. Mr. Talbot & D[uncan] G. Campbell, Esq[ui]r[e], recommending Gen[era]l David Adams to fill the vacancy in the Commission for holding a treaty with the [Eastern] Cherokees occasioned by the resignation of Gen[era]l [John] Floyd, has been received.

My letter to you of the 19th inst[ant,] which I presume you have received, will apprize you of the course which has been adopted by the President [James Monroe] in consequence of the resignation of Gen[era]l Floyd. This course was adopted by him not only to avoid the delay which would necess[ar]ily attend the appointment of a new Commissioner, but with the belief, that the remaining Commissioners could proceed, with less uncertainty and delay, to the execution of the duties of the Commission. Under these circumstances you will see that no new appointment can now, consistently, be made.

FC in DNA, 72, E:362 (M-15:5).

From WILLIAM H. CRAWFORD

Treasury Department, 30th Nov[embe]r 1822

The public funds, during the present year, have accumulated to a considerable amount in the offices of the Bank of the United States at Chil[l]icothe, [O.,] and Louisville. Whatever amount is in those offices which cannot be expended in the Western States, must be transferred to the Atlantic cities. This transfer cannot be effected, according to the existing arrangements with the Bank, in less than four months. It is therefore an object of some importance to ascertain the amount which will be required ["at those offices" *interlined*] for the public service, during the next year. It is presumed that the following expenditures may be made at those offices, consistently with the public interest; viz.

1st. The pay of the Troops stationed on the Western & North Western frontier.

2d. The sums required for the Provisions necessary for their subsistence.

3d. The sums necessary for the discharge of the Military & Revolutionary Pensions in the States of Ohio, Kentucky, Indiana, Illinois & Missouri; & the Indian annuities; &

4th. The expenses of surveying the public land.

I will thank you to inform me what amount, under the three first heads, will be required for the War department.

It is important that as much of the revenue collected in those States should be expended in them as the public service will permit. If the expenditure is made at Chil[l]icothe, & Louisville, the amount so expended is thrown into circulation where it is most useful, and increases the facilities otherwise existing, of making payments into the Treasury. If payment shall be made on account of the foregoing objects, by bills drawn upon the public officers, & payable at this place, or the Eastern Cities, the amount so paid will have to be drawn from the Western offices, by the Bank of the United States, in specie.

ALS in DNA, 1, C-225 (M-221:95). NOTE: Calhoun replied on 1/15/[1823].

From J[AMES] L. E[DWARDS, Chief Clerk]

Pension Office, Nov[embe]r 30th, 1822

In the report which I made some time since concerning the Clerks employed in this Office, I omitted to state particularly the case of Col. David Henley, whose age and infirmities render him incapable of performing much duty. He is not employed in writing, being totally incapacitated for such labor; but he is sometimes usefully employed in the investigation of Revolutionary claims, being well qualified therefor, on account of his knowledge of the service at the interesting period of our struggle for independence. He is 74 years of age, and has been in the service of the United States, except an interval of twelve years, from the year 1775, up to the present time. He filled several offices in the Staff during the Revolution; was aid[e]-de-camp to Lord Sterling [*sic*; that is, William Alexander, Lord Stirling]; at one period, commanded the *elite* of the Army; and has subsequently occupied several important stations under the government.

FC in DNA, 91, 12:412–413.

To the Rev. E[DWARD] EVERETT, [Boston]

Washington, 30th Nov. 1822

I have delayed acknowledging your note [*not found*] accompanying the volume on the state of Europe, till I could give it an attentive perusal. The drudgery of office has so engaged my time, that I did ["not" *interlined*] find sufficient leisure to peruse the work, till very lately.

It treats of a very interesting subject, in a very interesting manner; and, tho' I do not agree with all of the views of the writer, particularly in relation to the Russian power, I have been not only pleased, but instructed.

It is gratifying to witness our American youths, while abroad employing their time so honorably to themselves and usefully to the country; and I trust, that the example placed before them by your brother [Alexander Hill Everett] and Mr. [Theodore] Lyman of your city will be followed by many of them.

ALS in MHi. NOTE: Alexander Hill Everett's book was entitled *Europe: or a General Survey of the Present Situation of the Principal Powers; with Conjectures on Their Future Prospects* (Boston: Cummings and Hilliard, 1822). Theodore Lyman (1772–1849) had written in 1820 a description of the political state of Italy.

To Gen. JOHN FLOYD, Milledgeville, Ga.

Dep[art]m[en]t of War, 30th Nov[embe]r 1822

Your letter to the President [James Monroe] of the 15th inst[ant; *not found*] enclosing a recommendation signed by a majority of the members of the Legislature [of Ga.] in favor of Hugh Montgomery, Esq[ui]r[e], to fill the vacancy in the Commission for holding a treaty with the [Eastern] Cherokees occasioned by your resignation, has been referred to this Department.

After the receipt of your resignation, the President determined not to fill the vacancy which it occasioned, but to let the other two Commissioners proceed with the negociation [*sic*], and in pursuance of this determination the necessary instructions were issued to them. Consequently no new appointment can now, consistently, be made. Lest you may not have received my letter to you of the 19th inst[ant] I herewith enclose a copy.

FC in DNA, 72, E:362–363 (M-15:5).

From Isaac Harby, Charleston, [S.C.,] 11/30. He seeks Calhoun's support for John D. Heath's application for appointment to be the [U.S.] District Judge in S.C. ALS in DNA, 103, Heath (M-439:8, frames 872–873).

From Joseph Lovell, 11/30. He submits his financial report for 1/1–9/30/1822. FC in DNA, 242, 2:325.

To J[OHN] P[ENDLETON] KENNEDY, [later a Representative from Md.,] "Confidential"

[Washington, *ca.* November 30, 1822?]

It is not in my power to give very precise answers to the ["your" *canceled*] inquiries in your note of the 27th Inst[ant; *not found*]. The President [James Monroe] is now deliberating on the appointments to which you refer; but it is not probable, that he will come to any decision till after the arrival of the Minister, who is shortly expected from Mexico. Should he arrive, it is not probable that they will be made till we hear from their governments. I received the pacquet with the letters to which you refer and laid them before the President. They are now filed in the State Department, and will be brought regularly before the President, when he comes to make the appointment to which they refer. I will be happy to give you such information, as you may at any time request.

ALS in MdBP. NOTE: See, herein, Calhoun's letter of 1/21/1823 to Kennedy. Sketches of Kennedy's career report that he was appointed to a diplomatic post in Chile in 1/1823, that he did not report to it for duty, and that he resigned.

To [James Monroe], 11/30. Pursuant to a Senate resolution of 2/22 [DS in DNA, 1, S-352 (M-221:94)] requesting information about "certain Christian Indians, and the lands intended for their benefit, on the Muskingum, in the State of Ohio, granted under an act of Congress of June 1, 1796, to the Society of United Brethren for propagating the Gospel among the Heathen," Calhoun encloses several documents prepared in 9/1822 by the Rev. Lewis D. Schweinitz and John Heckewelder in response to Calhoun's requests of them dated 3/4 [FC's in DNA, 72, E:223 (M-15:5)]. (Monroe relayed this report to the Senate on 12/9.) LS with Ens in DNA, RG 46, 17A-E6; FC in DNA, 6, 2:107–108 (M-127:2); PC with Ens in Senate Document No. 3, 17th Cong., 2nd Sess.; PC with Ens in *American State Papers: Indian Affairs*, 2:372–391.

DECEMBER 1822

DR. JOHN C. CALHOUN WROTE ON THE 2ND HIS ACCEPTANCE of his honorary degree and during the next two days letters indicating that, despite his zeal for internal improvements, he was more willing to recommend for the office of Civil Engineer of Virginia a Topographical Engineer or a former Army Engineer than an active Army Engineer, lest the national interest should suffer. On the 2nd Congress began to meet, and Calhoun congratulated Nicholas Biddle. A week later a much relieved Calhoun announced that the "affair" between one of his supporters and one of William H. Crawford's "is finally ended"—after another duel and another wounding. A Tennesseean suggested on the 21st schools and savings banks for soldiers. The Librarian of the Military Academy spent part of Christmas describing the services that he rendered in that capacity.

From T[APPING] REEVE

Litchfield, [Conn.,] Dec. 1st 1822

Dear respected Sir, Permit me to introduce to your acquaintance a Gentleman [William Greene] who read Law in my office and attended to a course of Lectures there delivered. After admission ["to the bar" *interlined*] he went to Cincin[n]ati and there pursued his Profession as I have been informed with great credit to himself. His object is to procure the Office of [U.S.] Attorney for the District of Ohio the present incumbent [John Crafts Wright] having been Elected a member of Congress, and as Mr. Green[e] has no acquaintance at Washington with any of the Heads of Departments, he requested me to write an introduction to you Sir. I have been long acquainted with Mr. Green[e] and you will find him if I mistake not ["a" *canceled*] not only a Gentleman of Talents but particularly distinguished as such ["a Man of incom" *canceled*], of uncommon industry and unusu[a]l enterprize. I know of no young Gentleman who deserves the esteem of his acquaintances for a frank and manly conduct more than Mr. Green[e]—he will be not only a valuable acquisition to that part of our Country where he lives, but an honour to the Nation. With sentiments of esteem and gratitude your obliged friend, T. Reeve.

ALS in DNA, 103, Greene (M-439:7, frames 855–857). NOTE: An EU reads: "Recommends Mr. Green[e] as Attorney in Ohio." An AEI by Calhoun reads; "Submitted for the consideration of the Sec[retar]y of State [John Quincy Adams]."

From RICHARD WILLCOX, "Private & Confidential"

New York [City], Decem[be]r 1st 1822

As an active interest in the behalf of the suffering Greeks is daily expanding in this country, there appears a fair prospect of introducing the System I had the honor to present to you in July last, into efficient action, as an auxiliary to their emancipation.

But the most ardent wish of my heart being, that this my newly adopted country should possess, and be the promulgator to the World at its own sound discretion, of a System that will ultimately prostrate all others in Warfare, I hope I may be pardoned & stand excused in your mind, of egotism or arrogance, when I take the liberty of assuring you of my deep rooted conviction that if you can find it compatible with your high functions, with your arrangements, and your sober judgment to be the patron & introducer of my Whole System, which you will find to be methodical and intire [*sic*] in all its parts, to the adoption of this republic, you will secure to yourself the highest Station to which man can aspire *That of being Benefactor to the Whole World.* I pray your forgiveness for this Liberty which would not have been taken had I not conceived the highest respect for your superior talents and rising fame.

ALS in DNA, 31, 1822, W. NOTE: The fact that this letter was referred to the Ordnance office seems to indicate that Willcox's "System" was some sort of invention for warfare.

To Philip P[endleton] Barbour, [Speaker of the House of Representatives,] 12/2. In compliance with a House resolution of 4/16 (CC in DNA, 31, 1822, War Department; CC's in DNA, 138, 1820–1825:96 and 100), Calhoun reports that 34 Clerks and four Messengers are employed in the War Department. Clerks in the War Office are Chief Clerk C[hristopher] Vandeventer, Lewis Edwards, Gideon Davis, Samuel S. Hamilton and John P. Fenner; the Messengers are William Markward and Francis Datcher. There are five Clerks, including Chief Clerk Nathaniel Cutting, in the Bounty Land Office; nine Clerks, including Chief Clerk James L. Edwards, in the Pension Office; two Clerks in the Engineer bureau; three Clerks in the Ordnance bureau; two Clerks, including Chief Clerk Nathaniel Frye, [Jr.,] and one Messenger in the Paymaster General's Office; three Clerks and one Messenger in the office of the Commissary General of Purchases; one Clerk in the office of the Surgeon General; two Clerks in the office of the Commissary General of Subsistence; and two Clerks in the office of the Adjutant General. It is believed that one Clerk in the Bounty Land Office and two in the Pension Office can be dispensed with in the near future because of the decrease in the volume of business conducted by those offices. The only inefficient Clerk is 74-year-old Col. David Henley, whose excellent record of service dates back to 1775 and whose recollection of Revolutionary events renders him useful in the examination of Revolutionary claims. The only employee "engaged in other pursuits or professions" is Gideon Davis, whose bookstore in Georgetown is operated "principally by an Agent." It is believed that no more efficient or economical organization of the War Department can be adopted. LS in DNA, RG 233, 17A-E4; FC in DNA, 4, 2:251–252 (M-220:1); PC in House Document No. 5, 17th Cong., 2nd Sess.; PC in *American State Papers*: *Miscellaneous*, 2:983.

To Philip P[endleton] Barbour, 12/2. Pursuant to a House resolution of 5/7 [DS in DNA, 1, R-210 (M-221:94)], Calhoun reports that 18 "active and well qualified Clerks" will be needed through this month but that in the near future one can be discharged from the Bounty Land Office and two from the Pension Office. Fifteen Clerks will be necessary through most of 1823: five in the War Office, four in the Bounty Land Office, and six in the Pension Office. The 15 other Clerks required by the subordinate branches of the War Department are: two by the Engineer Department; three by the Ordnance Department; two by the Paymaster General; three by the Commissary General of Purchases; two by the Commissary General of Subsistence; one by the Surgeon General; and two by the Adjutant General. "It is believed that a less number of Clerks would not be adequate to a prompt and faithful discharge of the duties of the Department." LS in DNA, RG 233, 17A-E4; FC in DNA, 4, 2:252 (M-220:1).

To Nicholas Biddle, [prospective President, Bank of the United States, Philadelphia]

Washington, 2 Dec[em]b[er] 1822

Feeling as I do deep solicitude in the prosperity of the Bank, I have been very much gratified with your nomination to the Presidency of that institution and most sincerely hope, that you may be elected.

. . . . If at any time, I can render aid to the institution, it will afford me much pleasure, and should you be elected, of which there can be no reasonable doubt, the pleasure would be still farther [*sic*] advanced by coöperating, as with the present President [of the Bank, Langdon Cheves], with one for whom I have so great an esteem.

PEx in Reginald C. McGrane, ed., *The Correspondence of Nicholas Biddle Dealing with National Affairs, 1807–1844* (Boston: Houghton Mifflin Company, c. 1919), pp. 28–29.

To Duncan G. Campbell and James Meriwether, [Milledgeville, Ga.]

Dep[art]m[en]t of War, 2nd Dec[embe]r 1822

Gentlemen, I have received your letter of the 20th Ult[im]o [LS with En in DNA, 1, C-175 (M-221:95)] with the copy of your letter [dated 11/22; *sic*] to Col. [Return J.] Meigs, and am happy to find that you are making you[r] preliminary arrangements, by the appointment of a time &c. for holding the contemplated treaty with the [Eastern] Cherokee nation.

The Department, reposing every confidence in your discretion, does not deem it necessary to give you any further instructions upon the subject of the negociation [*sic*].

I enclose herewith copies of letters which were addressed to you after the receipt of Gen[era]l [John] Floyd's resignation at your respective places of residence but which I presume you have not received.

FC in DNA, 72, E:363 (M-15:5).

To the Rev. Jere[mia]h Day, [Yale College, New Haven]

Washington, 2d Dec[embe]r 1822

I have the honor to acknowledge your favour of the 26th Inst[ant; *sic*], covering a Diploma containing the degree of Doctor of Laws.

In accepting so distinguished an honor, I avail myself of the opportunity of tendering to you and the fellows of the College my sincere and grateful acknowledgement, with the assurance, that it will ever be among the objects of my ambition to merit the continuance of your favourable opinion.

Permit me to offer you my acknowledgement individually for the very flattering manner, in which you have communicated the honor, which has been conferred on me. In the prosperity of the venerable and noble institution, over which you preside, and with which I am connected by so endearing a tie, I take the deepest interest. I feel it to be the duty of all of her sons to act in a manner worthy of her illustrious reputation, and that I have, in the opinion of one so capable of forming a correct opinion, in some degree so acted, is to me a source of much gratification.

I have the honor to be with high consideration & affectionate regard your &c. . . . .

ALS in CtY. Note: An Abs of the certificate of the honorary degree appears herein under date of 9/11. Day's covering letter dated the 26th of an undetermined month has not been found.

To [John Gaillard,] President of the Senate, 12/2. Pursuant to a Senate resolution of 4/29 [DS in DNA, 1, S-202 (M-221:96)], Calhoun encloses a statement of the number of pensioners placed on the list through 9/4/1822 under acts of 3/18/1818 and 5/1/1820, showing their length of service and distinguishing between officers and enlisted men. FC with En in DNA, 91, 12:414–415; PC with En in *Annals of Congress*, 17th Cong., 2nd Sess., cols. 10–12; PC with En in *Niles' Weekly Register*, vol. XXIII, no. 15 (December 14, 1822), pp. 232–233; PC with En in *American State Papers: Claims*, 1:873–874.

To G[eorge] Gibson, 12/2. "You will report as soon as practicable, the sum which will be required for your Department on the Western and North Western frontier for the next year." LS in DNA, 43, Calhoun, 520; Abs in DNA, 192, vol. 2. Gibson replied on 12/3 by itemizing $67,550 that would be needed at Western posts for subsistence. FC in DNA, 191, 3:180.

To Thomas S. Jesup, 12/2. Calhoun asks Jesup to estimate what funds will be needed for Quartermaster services on the Western and Northwestern frontiers during 1823. LS in DNA, 41, 1821–1822, S-121. In reply on 12/3, Jesup itemized $54,000 that should be provided at five Western centers. FC in DNA, 42, 4:338 (M-745:2, frame 467); FC in DNA, 50, vol. 2.

To [Joseph Lovell], 12/2. "You will report as soon as practicable, the sum which will be required for your [Medical] Department on the Western and North Western frontier for the next year." LS in DNA, 245, 1:128. Lovell answered on 12/3 that not more than $600 would be needed for purchases of medical supplies in the West during 1823. FC in DNA, 242, 2:326.

To [Nathan Towson], 12/2. "You will report as soon as practicable the sum which will be required for your [Pay] Department on the Western and North Western frontier for the next year." LS in DNA, 292, 1-2348. Towson answered that he would need $380,000 in the West, apportioned as follows: at Baton Rouge, Fort St. Philip, and on the Red River, $80,000; at Louisville and on the Arkansas River, $45,000; at St. Louis, Bellefontaine, and Forts St. Anthony, Crawford, and Edwards, $75,000; at Council Bluffs, $60,000; at Detroit, Saginaw, Green Bay, and Sault Ste. Marie, $120,000. LS in DNA, 1, P-139 (M-221:96); FC in DNA, 291, 16:12.

From J[ames] L. E[dwards], 12/3. "According to the estimate for the year 1823, it is probable that there will be required to pay the Pensioners in the Western and North Western States" $221,312, apportioned as follows: Ky., $68,590; East Tenn., $13,478; West Tenn., $20,858; O., $88,088; Ind., $16,352; Miss., $1,670; Ill., $3,012; Ala., $2,442; Mo., $4,566; and Mich. Territory, $2,256. FC in DNA, 91, 12:417.

From [Lt. Col.] Abr[a]m Eustis, St. Augustine, 12/3. He acknowledges Calhoun's letters of 10/14 and 10/23. "They reached this place, during my absence under the orders of Major Gen[era]l [Winfield] Scott. The latter communication arrived here too late for its object to have been affected [*sic*; effected]; the Indians of East Florida having previously started for St. Marks. I fear that this second disappointment will occasion considerable discontent among them. I have received neither intelligence, instructions, nor funds from Gov[erno]r [William P.] Duval [*sic*]. Rumour says that he has abandoned the Territory, & returned to his residence in Kentucky. I have been compelled to make some small disbursements (about $50) from my private purse. Col. [Gad] Humphreys [newly appointed Indian Agent] has not yet arrived here, & I could hear nothing of him at Charleston." Eustis asks whether compensation will be allowed to him as Acting Indian Agent. ALS in DNA, 1, E-72 (M-221:95).

To M[artin] D. Hardin, Locust Hill, Ky., 12/3. "The enclosed is a copy of a letter [dated 11/30 (ALS in DNA, 1, H-138 [M-221:95])] from Mr. [Joseph] Hopkinson, President of the Academy of Fine Arts in Philadelphia, to whom the superintendence of the execution of the medals was intrusted [*sic*] by the President of the United States [James Monroe,] in relation to Gov[erno]r [Isaac] Shelby['s] medal, by which you will see that it is impracticable to make the alterations in the medal which you suggested." LS in ICHi; FC in DNA, 3, 11:448 (M-6:11).

To [James Monroe], 12/3. In compliance with a Senate resolution of 5/8 [DS in DNA, 1, S-454 (M-221:94)] requesting information about copper mines near the southern shore of Lake Superior, Calhoun submits reports [dated 11/6/1820 and 10/1/1822] from Henry R. Schoolcraft. LS with Ens in DNA, RG 46, 17A-E6 (M-200:6); FC in DNA, 6, 2:101 (M-127:2); PC with Ens in Senate Document No. 5, 17th Cong., 2nd Sess.; PC in *American State Papers: Public Lands*, 3:565–575; PC in Carter, ed., *Territorial Papers*, 11:298.

To George Newton, Washington

Department of War, December 3, 1822

I have the honor to acknowledge the receipt of your communication of the 21st ultimo [ALS in DNA, 30, 384] on the subject of a nomination to you of a suitable person from among the officers of Engineers to fill the vacancy which now exists of Civil Engineer to the State [*sic*; Commonwealth] of Virginia. However much I am disposed to aid in promoting the views of the [Virginia] Board of Public Works in their important undertakings, and indeed to lend every assistance in furtherance of internal improvements in general throughout the Union, I regret that the officers attached to the Engineer Department (qualified for the vacant office) are so disposed of at present as to render it impracticable to dispense with their services without serious inconvenience to the national interest.

FC in DNA, 21, 1:341–342. NOTE: Compare Calhoun's letter to Newton dated 12/4.

To Ab[raha]m H[enry] Schenck, [former Representative from N.Y.,] Fishkill Landing, N.Y., 12/3. Answering Schenck's letter of 11/29 [ALS in DNA, 15, 1822, 56½ (M-688:20)], offering his son Edwin as a candidate for admission into the Military Academy, Calhoun assures the father that the son will be considered next year. Calhoun remembers "with pleasure" his association with Schenck during the 14th Congress and regrets the fact that he missed the visit that Schenck tried to have with Calhoun at West Point. FC in DNA, 13, 1:173 (M-91:1). (Compare the letter from Abr[aha]m H[enr]y Schenck dated 3/23/1823.)

To CHARLES H. SMITH, Norfolk

Department of War, December 3d 1822

I was duly favored with your letter [*not found*] setting forth that a vacancy existed in the Department of Public Works in Virginia which you believe might be filled with advantage by Col. [William] McRee, formerly of the Engineers. I cannot but accord with you in this opinion, but I am not certain that Col. McRee would accept the appointment if offered to him. A friend of Colonel McRee has however, in consequence of your letter, written to him, and if it suits his views to become a candidate for the place of Civil Engineer, I shall be happy to promote them as he is esteemed well qualified to fill the office.

FC in DNA, 21, 1:342.

A General Order by Calhoun, 12/4. "In addition to the present allowance of clothing, there will in future be issued to the troops stationed North of the 40th degree of latitude, five pairs of [woolen] flannel drawers during their term of enlistment—two pairs will be issued the first year, and one pair for each of the third, fourth, and fifth years of service." FC in DNA, 6, 11:449 (M-6:11). With the approval of [James Monroe], this order was published as no. 88 by E[dmund] Kirby, by order of [Jacob] Brown, on 12/11. DS in DNA, 48, 192; FC in DNA, 49, 1:109; FC in DNA, 19, 3:85–86; CC in DNA, 186, 1822–1823:257; CC in DNA, 188.

To Maj. S[TEPHEN] H. LONG, Philadelphia

Department of War, December 4th 1822

I have this day received your letter of the 29th ultimo [*not found*], and have lost no time in laying your application before Mr. [George] Newton of Virginia, from whom I lately received a communication on the subject of filling the Vacancy of Civil Engineer for the State [*sic*; Commonwealth] of Virginia. I have with pleasure given your application such support as I thought it deserved, believing you well qualified to fill the station you solicit.

FC in DNA, 3, 11:449 (M-6:11).

From Return J. Meigs, Cherokee Agency, 12/4. He has received a letter from James "Merriwether [*sic*; Meriwether]" and Duncan [G.] Campbell, Commissioners for holding "the long expected treaty with the Cherokees," requesting Meigs to make arrangements for rations for the Indians and to invite the Indians to assemble on 1/15/1823. "The Contract for rations will be eight cen[t]s p[e]r ration for Meat, Breadstuff, and salt." In spite of the "intemperate resolutions" of the Cherokees not to meet with the Commissioners if their purpose is to obtain land, Meigs presumes that the Indians will "come in freely" as they did in 1817. He suggests that a small military guard be made available to protect the supplies and a "considerable sum of money." ALS in DNA, 1, M-176 (M-221:96).

To GEORGE NEWTON, Norfolk, Va.

Department of War, December 4th 1822

Since I addressed you yesterday on the subject of a Civil Engineer, I have received a letter [dated 11/29] from Major [Stephen H.] Long of the Topographical Engineers requesting that I would lay his name before the Board of publick works as a candidate for the vacant office. As Major Long is esteemed well qualified for the situation, I take particular pleasure in recommending him to the consideration of the Board.

FC in DNA, 3, 11:449 (M-6:11).

To William Ward, Indian Agent, Choctaw Agency, 12/4. Calhoun encloses a letter from the Governor of Miss., Walter Leake, to Calhoun dated 10/15 [ALS in DNA, 1, L-45 (M-221:96)], which should aid in selecting a site for the Choctaw Agency. Calhoun instructs Ward to consult with the Chiefs and to report upon a suitable site. FC in DNA, 72, E:364 (M-15:5).

Alexander Macomb to J[oseph] McIlvaine, Burlington, N.J., 12/5. Macomb is answering for Calhoun a letter of 11/26 from McIlvaine, whose bill "for services rendered and expenses incurred by you in defending the title of the U[nited] States to the Pea Patch Island" is deemed to be reasonable and is to be paid if McIlvaine will mail to Macomb a proper receipt. FC in DNA, 21, 1:342.

From Nicholas Biddle

Phil[adelphi]a, Dec[embe]r 6, 1822

I had the pleasure last night of receiving your letter of the 2d inst[ant], & thank you with great cordiality for the friendly dispositions which dictated it. The course which I have hitherto prescribed to myself, has been neither to seek nor to shun a situation of so much responsibility, but if I am called to share in the administration of the Bank, I shall bring to its service at least a laborious & zealous devotion to its interests. This unfortunate institution has from its birth been condemned to struggle with the most perplexing difficulties, yet even with all its embarrassments it has sustained the national currency & rescued the country from the dominition [*sic*] of irresponsible banks, & their depreciated circulation. The time has perhaps arrived when it may combine its own & the country's security with a more enlarged development of its resources and a wider extension of its sphere of usefulness. To this object to which [*sic*] my own exertions shall be anxiously directed. I have long known and appreciated the manly & decisive services which you have rendered to the same cause—& if I should see any occasion in which the Bank may avail itself of your assistance I shall ask it with the same frankness & sincerity with which I now assure you of the great personal respect & esteem of . . . .

PC in Reginald C. McGrane, ed., *The Correspondence of Nicholas Biddle Dealing with National Affairs, 1807–1844* (Boston: Houghton Mifflin Company, c. 1919), pp. 29–30.

To William Clark, 12/6. Calhoun encloses Joel D. Walker's papers in support of his claim for horses allegedly stolen from him by the Sauks and a copy of a letter [of 12/3] from [David] Barton concerning Samuel Gilbert's claim for property also alleged to have been taken by the Sauks. Calhoun asks Clark to examine these claims and to report to the War Department any information he may have. FC in DNA, 72, E:366 (M-15:5).

To William H. Crawford

Dep[art]m[en]t of War, 6th Decem[be]r 1822

You will see by the enclosed documents that the Collector at Michilimackinac has granted permits for certain boats having on board whiskey to pass from that port to Prairie-du-Chien; and as it is intended by this Department to give orders to carry into effect fully the provisions of the act passed at the last Session of Congress, to amend the act of trade and intercourse of 1802, which relate to the introduction of ardent spirits into the Indian Country, I wish first to ascertain whether any & what instructions have been given by the Treasury Department to the Collectors upon the subject.

I will thank you to return the papers, with the information requested, as soon as convenient.

FC in DNA, 72, E:365 (M-15:5). Note: No reply to this letter has been found.

From Robert Y. Hayne, [later a Senator from S.C.]

Charleston, [S.C.,] 7th Dec[embe]r 1822

When I wrote to you yesterday [*no such letter found*] on the subject of the office of [U.S.] District Judge I was not aware that Mr.

Thomas Lee is willing to accept of it. The accounts received this day from Columbia state that the friends of Mr. Lee have made an application in his behalf. If so, I should suppose there could be no difference of opinion with respect to his superior claims. Indeed I am convinced than [*sic*] none of the Candidates would press their [*sic*] claims in opposition to those of Mr. Lee. His age, character, and standing in the community, his splendid talents, unquestionable integrity, and undeviating Republican principles put him beyond the reach of competition. You know of course that he was for a short time a Judge, and for many years Comptroller General of the State. In all respects he stands on much higher ground than ["any" *interlined*] of the Gentlemen who have been named, & I should consider the Government very fortunate in obtaining the services of such a man. I have also heard today that Mr. L[ionel] H. Kennedy has made an application. He is also a respectable man, of good principles, amiable character, & worthy of public confidence. But on the score of talents and learning I should consider him inferior to several of the applicants. In great haste I am Dear Sir y[ou]rs, Rob[er]t Y. Hayne.

ALS in DNA, 103, Lee (M-439:10, frames 622–624).

From William Carroll, Nashville, [Tenn.,] 12/8. Having recently received the enclosed communication from the Creek Path Cherokee Indians, Carroll replied by giving his opinion that the U.S. will not purchase any of their lands without the approval of at least a majority of the headmen of the nation. The Indians wish, however, to know the disposition of the President [James Monroe] on this subject. LS with En in DNA, 1, C-201 (M-221:95); CC with En in DNA, RG 233, 18A-D1, vol. 263; PC in House Document No. 136, 18th Cong., 1st Sess.; PC with En in *American State Papers: Indian Affairs*, 2:505–506.

From Jacob Brown, Washington, 12/9. He recommends Bvt. Capt. [Edmund] Kirby for the command of the arsenal at Watertown, Mass. "His long service in the staff grade of Major and his faithful services in every grade, wherein he has acted, entitle him to whatever indulgence can be extended to him consistently with the good of the service." LS in DNA, 31, 1822, B; variant FC (dated 12/7) in DLC, Jacob Brown Papers, Letterbooks, 2:227.

From Cadet Reuben Holmes

West Point, Dec. 9, 1822

I take the liberty of begging your indulgence for one moment whilst I do myself the honor to address you on a subject prompted by my own feelings & approved by those of my friends—viz, of asking the favor of a furlough for two years & a half from the time I graduate here, for the express purpose of going through Yale College. My intention is to spend my life in the service of my country & surely, a competent knowledge of those studies not pursued here, would better qualify me to meet its approbation. General information is one grand requisite for an officer, the basis of which can no where, in my opinion, be better & sooner obtained than at Yale College. I wish that this petition may be considered as emanating from pure motives & I pledge my honor that, if it is granted, I will endeavour to evince that no mistaken confidence has been placed in me.

ALS in DNA, 221, 473. Note: In the same file is a similar ALS of 12/9 from Holmes to Alexander Macomb indicating that those two had discussed Holmes's hopes at West Point in person. No answer by Calhoun to Holmes's appeal has been found.

To V[irgil] Maxcy

Washington, 9th Dec[embe]r 1822

I have barely time to say that the affair between [George] McDuffie and [William] Cumming is finally ended. They meet [*sic*] and passed two fires, in the second of which the former received the ball of his antagonist in his left arm. A reconciliation ensued, Cumming agreeing, as it is said, to make the requisite explanation to Capt. Elmore, on account of the manner in which he spoke of him in his statement of the affair at the Saluda mountain. Truely [*sic*], J.C. Calhoun.

ALS in DLC, Galloway-Maxcy-Markoe Papers, vol. 32.

From Jasper Parrish, Canandaigua, [N.Y.,] 12/10. He is glad that Gen. [Peter B.] Porter has been appointed by Calhoun to investigate certain charges made by the Six Nations against Parrish. "I shall hold myself ready to attend to this business whenever called upon" to do so. ALS in DNA, 1, P-152 (M-221:96).

From J[AMES] R[EID] PRINGLE

Charleston, [S.C.,] 10th Dec[embe]r 1822

A few days ago I signed a paper recommending Mr. Toomer as [U.S.] District Judge not knowing at the time Mr. Thomas Lee would accept if appointed. Mr. Lee's integrity[,] honor & great acquirements in conjunction with his having so long possessed the confidence of the community ought certainly to give him a preference over any candidate who could offer. It is unnecessary for me to say more as you are well acquainted with that Gentleman. I feel confident many respectable merchant[s] in this City would cheerfully sign any recommendation of Mr. Lee if he or his friends would ask it of them—indeed *no* appointment would be more fit and would give more general satisfaction. I have understood Mr. Joseph Bennett the brother-in-Law of Judge [William] Johnson has applied for this station[;] no judicious ["person" *interlined*] could for a single moment hesitate between these two Gentlemen. I pray you to excuse my troubling ["you" *interlined*] when I am aware your time is now so much taken up but I was fearful any act of mine could possibly induce a hesitation as to Mr. Lee's appointment. Trusting to your indulgence I am . . . .

ALS in DNA, 103, Lee (M-439:10, frames 625–627).

From JON[ATHA]N RUSSELL, [Representative from Mass.]

Washington, 10th Dec[embe]r 1822

Mr. Shaler, the American Consul at Algiers, has requested me to remind you of his desire to place his nephew, William Shaler Stillwell, as a Cadet, in the Military Academy at Westpoint—and I sincerely hope that his expectations which you have been pleased to encourage, on this subject may not be disappointed.

ALS in PHi.

From JOHN R. WILLIAMS, [Adjutant General of Mich. Territory]

Detroit, Dec[embe]r 10th 1822

I have the honor to transmit herewith, a Return of the Militia of this Territory for the present year, (1822).

It is however a matter of regret to me, that the return is materially incorrect and deficient, particularly in relation to the number of men, which the militia muster Rolls of this Territory should exhibit, if the Officers, whose duty it is to make returns, were made to attend punctually, and perform with more accuracy, that important detail of duty.

Owing to the neglect of Company Officers, three Companies in the 3d Reg[imen]t have not been returned. The return of the Volunteer Reg[imen]t is also defective in an extraordinary degree, as at least one-half the men composing it, two Companies, are not Returned, to wit, the Rifle Company and Infantry. When the Officers of those Companies were commissioned, the men who enrolled in them, were induced to believe that the United States would furnish arms and accoutrements, and that they would only have to procure their uniform. But the Officers having failed in procuring the arms, have become discouraged as well as their men, and have ceased to perform any duty. The men however, who have been enrolled, either in the Rifle or Infantry, still claim exemption from performing duty in the common militia. Thus a considerable number of men, the present year, are not returned.

It is extremely difficult in a population such as our Territory affords, to enforce a due degree of military subordination and punctuality, particularly, in relation to Returns, as many of the Officers are illiterate and consequently, unacquainted with their duties: and a great proportion of them being also poor, the cost of uniform is a tax, which operates as an insurmountable source of difficulty and discouragement; and there being no pay nor emolument attached to militia appointments, few men in times of peace, are disposed to consider it in any other light, than as a heavy tax, both upon their time and means. And in many instances, men entrusted with the highest commands, have given the worst examples of neglect and inattention to duty.

It appears to me, that it is clearly the interest of the United States, on this remote and extended frontier, to put the Militia on a respectable footing. That important object might be attained, by furnishing a few hundred stands of Arms for the Infantry, a sufficient number of Rifles for a Company, and the necessary equipments of swords and pistols for one Company of Cavalry. I feel confident that such a measure, would be productive of the best consequences. It would renovate the military ardour of the whole body of the militia, and resuscitate the feelings and energies of our Officers. Then Commissions in the militia would cease to be considered as mere encumbrances but would be deemed honorable, and therefore be sought after, by men of respectability and talents.

Never perhaps, within so small a population, in the United States, has [*sic*] there been so many militia appointments and resignations, as the records of our military books exhibit for two or three years past, and that spirit, I regret to say, seems constantly to increase, and must be attributed to causes, which have created a feeling of disgust throughout the whole militia.

In justice to my feelings & character, I must here remark, that notwithstanding my exertions and assiduous labours, in the performance of the duties committed to my charge, that [*sic*] the existing state of things forbids, that I should continue in the office, unless a more rigid and strict enforcement of duty, should be subjected to my discretion and authority. I am well satisfied of the inefficacy of General Orders and all the threats and thundering assemblage of words on paper, unless supported by something more formidable. I mean, that under the existing state of things, it is absolutely indispensable, that a few examples of punishment by fine or degradation should be made, to insure a faithful and punctual performance of militia duty, within this Territory. Such a course must however be attended with an increase of duty, which I cannot perform, without manifest injury to my private interest, and consequent injustice to my family. For upwards of four years, I have performed the duties attached to this Office, and furnished the necessary stationary [*sic*], without having yet, received a single cent's compensation. It is true that an appropriation of $160 to be paid out of the Territorial Treasury, was made in my favor, six or eight months ago for stationary & four year's [*sic*] services, on which I have not been able to obtain a single Dollar; and on enquiry, within a few days of the Treasurer, I have been informed, that it was very uncertain, whether it would be paid even, within the next year; as the demands upon the Treasury, (founded on appropriations) are much larger, than the am[oun]t of taxes to be collected, for the year 1823.

I am induced Sir, to mention these facts for your information, and do not hesitate to declare, as my candid opinion, that whatever person fills this Office, I am satisfied that the arduousness of the duties, if properly performed, are [*sic*] too great a tax, for any individual in this community to sustain, without some compensation from the General Government.

It will ever be to me, a source of pride and pleasure, to serve my Country, in any capacity which I may be deemed qualified to sustain, and it is those sentiments and principles, which have influenced me thus far, to continue, subjected to the labours and vexations of this Office, for nearly five years, without any compensation or emoluments.

ALS in DNA, 16, 1822, W-99 (M-567:5, frames 809–815).

To W[illiam] G.D. Worthington, Baltimore, 12/10. Calhoun acknowledges Worthington's letter of 11/27 [ALS in DNA, 1, W-132 (M-221:96)] and its enclosed, certified account of his expenditures as Acting Superintendent of Indian Affairs in Fla. [Territory]. Calhoun returns the account for Worthington to make a more distinct statement of his charges for services and of the sums actually spent. FC in DNA, 72, E:367 (M-15:5).

Resolution by the House of Representatives, 12/11. "Resolved, That the President of the United States [James Monroe] be requested to cause to be laid before the House a Statement shewing the amount of all monies advanced by Government to Agents, Sub Agents, Contractors, Sub Contractors or to individuals" since 1/1/1816 "which have not been accounted for on settlement—and the amount of loss (if any) sustained in each—and whether in all cases on the advancement of money, Security has been taken and the names of the Sureties." This copy of the resolution was attested by M[atthe]w St. Clair Clarke, Clerk of the House. CC in DNA, 1, R-74 (M-221:96).

To [Burwell] Bassett, [Representative from Va.,] 12/12. Calhoun returns a bill concerning the disbursements of public money, having proposed a few alterations and added a recommendation. He encloses a letter on the subject from Paymaster General [Nathan Towson dated 12/12, quoted herein]. LS with En in DNA, RG 233, 17A-E4; FC in DNA, 3, 11:450 (M-6:11).

From Joseph McMinn, New Canton, Tenn., 12/12. He answers Calhoun's letter to him of 11/16. He cannot, because of his health, visit promptly and individually the purchasers of some public property sold in 9/1820, as Calhoun wishes, before opening lawsuits for collection of their unpaid notes. "I have . . . been able to visit the courthouse of the County in which, I reside but once in the last Twelve months." But his health is improved; and, if Calhoun wishes, McMinn can begin in the spring "to travel with a servant and not only more expensively, but more Tardily than a man of sound health." ALS in DNA, 1, M-168 (M-221:96).

To [Enoch Parsons], President, Branch Bank of the United States [and Agent for Paying U.S. Pensioners in Conn.], Middletown, 12/12. James R. Woodbridge of Hartford has been appointed to serve as the conservator of the person and estate of Timothy Olmstead, a Revolutionary pensioner who is "incapable of taking care of himself." Olmstead's pension is payable to Woodbridge. FC in DNA, 91, 12:434; CC in DLC, Carnegie Institution of Washington Transcript Collection.

From N[athan] T[owson, Paymaster General,] 12/12. "I have the honor to submit the following for consideration, on the subject of the bill concerning the disbursements of public monies, so far as it relates to the Pay Department. All disbursing Officers, except those of the pay department, are required to render accounts quarterly! The Paymasters every two months, where it is practicable! As it is only in the power of Paymasters residing near this place, and such as have facilities of travelling to the different posts within their districts, to comply with the law in this respect, I am of opinion, that it would be better to extend the priviledge [*sic*] to them also, of settling accounts quarterly, as the musters which include the last months of the first and third quarters of the year, cannot, agreeably to law, be made until the end of the succeeding months, (April & October,) the payments found in those musters, and which are necessary to complete the business of the 1st and 3d quarters, cannot be made, before the middle of the succeeding quarters! This might be remedied by mustering the troops, either monthly or quarterly. I am of opinion the first would be preferable, as payment could then be made for any number of months most convenient and desirable. On the 2d Section of the bill I beg leave also to observe, that it is not practicable, at one of the remote posts, to make regular quarterly payments, in consequence of the difficulty of travelling in the cold months. Paymasters are therefore not furnished with funds, until after the communication by water is open; but they may always render accounts, within three months after the end of the quarter in which they receive funds; unless prevented by some cause beyond their control. I would therefore respectfully suggest that the time allowed for rendering accounts before dismissing an Officer from service, should have reference, to the time of his receiving funds, and not to the end of any particular quarter. The law already provides, that the President shall dismiss from service, *Paymasters who fail to render accounts for money received more than six months after the receipt thereof!* That period, I suppose to be, a reasonable limitation; but am of opinion that it would be better if the law vacated the Office, and that the President should be authorized to restore such persons as should in his judgement have used due diligence but had been prevented by circumstances which they could not control from rendering their accounts within the time limited. As accounts are, in most cases, rendered to the heads of the Departments to which they belong, and transmitted, after examination, to the accounting Officers of the Treasury Department, it would perhaps be better to substitute some other terms for accounting Officers of the Treasury Department. It should also be provided that the neglect of Officers, to render their accounts regularly, should not be so construed as to release their sureties from the penalty of their bonds: but that they should be held bound, for their official acts, so long as they are continued in service." FC in DNA, 291, 16:15–16; LS in DNA, RG 233, 17A-E4.

From Alexander Hamilton, Washington, 12/13. [William P.] DuVal has issued to Horatio S. Dexter a license to trade with Indians. Dexter has obtained from them, since the cession of the Floridas, large numbers of horses, cattle, and Negroes. A law enacted during the recent session of Congress provides that, in "all trials about the right of property, in which the Indians shall be party on one side and white persons on the other, *the burthen of proof shall rest upon the white person.*" This act "has been virtually abrogated by the legislative council of Florida in prohibiting *Indians* and Negroes from being admitted as witnesses against white persons." ALS in DNA, 1, H-144 (M-221:95).

To William Ward, Choctaw Agency, 12/13. Calhoun acknowledges Ward's letter of 11/21. Calhoun assumes that Ward has received the drafts for $14,135 and $1,972.40 that were mailed on 10/29. "I regret that you have drawn on this Department without previously advising it of your intention to do so and obtaining its authority for that purpose particularly as the appropriation for the Indian Department is not at this time adequate to meet the draft here." Calhoun instructs him to deposit in a Louisville bank sufficient funds to meet Ward's unauthorized draft for $4,440. "In relation to the compensation to be made to Indians for the inconvenience of moving, under the 10th art[icle] of the treaty [of 1820] you will see by reference to that article that the allowances therein specified are made the basis on which allowances in other cases entitled to the benefit of the provision are to be determined. You will accordingly take that as your guide in deciding on the proportion of compensation to which each person is entitled." Calhoun cautions that payments are to be made only to those Choctaws "who have *valuable* or *comfortable houses*." FC in DNA, 72, E:367–368 (M-15:5).

To JEREMIAH EVARTS, Corresponding Secretary, American Board of Commissioners [for Foreign Missions], Boston

Dep[art]m[en]t of War, 14th Dec[embe]r 1822

I enclose herewith an extract of a letter [dated 11/18] which I have recently received from the Rev[eren]d Mr. [Cyrus] Kingsbury. The proposition which it contains [concerning a kind of board of visitors to Kingsbury's Choctaw schools] is considered a judicious one; but before deciding on it, and appointing a Committee (which it is thought adviseable [*sic*] should be appointed entirely by the President [James Monroe]) it is deemed proper to consult the American Board in relation to it and the persons suitable to compose the Committee. For this purpose I will thank you to submit this letter to the board and communicate to me its views upon the subject as soon as convenient.

FC in DNA, 72, E:368 (M-15:5). NOTE: Evarts answered on 1/9/1823.

To the Rev. C[YRUS] KINGSBURY, Superintendent of Schools, Choctaw Nation

Dep[art]m[en]t of War, 14 Dec[embe]r 1822

Your letter of the 18th ult[im]o has been received.

Your idea as to small schools is believed to be a good one, and two-thirds of your estimate for the two schools contemplated to be established in the S[outh] E[ast] district in the Choctaw nation instead ["of" *interlined*] one at first intended, amounting to $1,333.33

will be allowed & paid on the certificate of the Agent [William Ward].

I am much pleased with your proposition for the appointment of a Committee of respectable gentlemen to visit the schools in the Choctaw nation, for the purpose of examining and reporting the state of these institutions, but as the American Board [of Commissioners for Foreign Missions] is immediately concerned, as well as the government, it is deemed proper to ascertain its opinion in relation to the proposition before it is decided on by this Department. For this purpose a letter has been addressed to Mr. [Jeremiah] Evarts at Boston, as the Corresponding Secretary of the Board &c. which it is presumed will be opened and attended to by any other officer of the Board in case of his absence.

As soon as the answer is received, the decision of the Department will be communicated to you.

FC in DNA, 72, E:369 (M-15:5).

Jacob Kunkapot and others of the Six Nations and Stockbridge Indians, Green Bay, to "Great Father [James Monroe]," 12/14. Some French settlers in Green Bay are dissatisfied with a treaty permitting the Iroquois Indians to settle on certain lands, particularly those around the mouth of the Fox River. The French possibly will attempt to induce [Monroe] to disapprove of the treaty. The Indians claim that the French "have no just cause of complaint, as a provision is made in the Treaty (of which our Great Father is doubtless ere this aware) for their peaceful remainder upon the land, as long as they shall see fit." They were invited to attend the Council and to make suggestions relative to the treaty, but "not one of them appeared." The Menominees "treat us as Brothers." They "agree to follow our examples in agriculture &c., and seem fondly to anticipate the day when they shall have become like one of us." LS in DNA, 1, S-249 (M-221:96).

From Col. M[athew] Arbuckle, Fort Smith, [Ark. Territory,] 12/15. He thinks that "a very great error" has been made in an estimate of the quantity of the tract of land known as Lovely's Purchase. A map received from the War Department indicates that the total number of acres is 7,392,000. By actual survey of the land, that figure will probably be found to be grossly overestimated. ALS in DNA, 1, A-86 (M-221:95).

To V[IRGIL] MAXCY

Washington, 15th Dec[embe]r 1822

The course which the Maryland elections have taken is deeply to be regretted. I do not doubt, that the real cause of the election of [*one word*, possibly the surname of John S. Spence, who had been elected a U.S. Representative from Md., *illegible*] and [Samuel] Smith [as U.S. Senator] is to be found in [Edward] Lloyd's intriques and [Dr. Joseph] Kent's indifference. The latter appears at length roused, and speaks in a decided tone. Should these elections tend to call the attention of the State to the real condition of things in relation to the General government they would be still fortunate. Maryland I believe to be perfectly sound; and if so, it is only necessary to identify the Radical party with Mr. [William H.] C[rawfor]d to defeat him, in your State. Of such identity there can be no doubt.

I return Gen[era]l [Robert Goodloe] Harper's letter. It is manifest, that he has taken his opinion of Penn[sylvani]a from the politicks of the city [of Philadelphia]. The Federal party there is the most numerous, and is favourable to Mr. [John Quincy] Adams. Of the general sentiment of the State there can be no doubt. Every country member of every political [persuasion] concur[s] in stating that I am by far the strongest. My [*manuscript mutilated*; temporary?] course is obvious, and is [*manuscript mutilated*] such as I stated to you in [con]versation. It is the strongest of itself, most likely to succeed and, at the same time, the most safe. Judicious articles in the Annapolis paper on Gen[era]l political views, or on more special, would have a good effect.

We have not heard from [George] McDuffie for three days. I think, he will save his arm. Sincerely, J.C. Calhoun.

ALS in DLC, Galloway-Maxcy-Markoe Papers, vol. 32.

From R[ICHARD] GRAHAM, [Indian Agent]

St. Louis, 16th Dec[embe]r 1822

I returned a few days since from St. Charles, [Mo.,] where I have been attending the Legislature for the purpose of getting a law passed to prevent trade & intercourse with the Indians resident in this State & within its jurisdiction, without having first obtained a license from the Agent of Indian Affairs—to effect this I made a map shewing the situation & extent of the Indian lands within this State, & their proximity to the white settlements, and the Lands designed for the Delawar[e]s—a hint from Gen[era]l [Duff] Green, a member from Chariton, to whom I had explained my wishes to obtain such a law—that, the locating of the Indians within the State, had been made use of, as an argument against you, in a kind of caucus which has been held by our legislature, induced me to withhold the map, which the Governer [*sic*; Alexander McNair] had been anxious to obtain—I afterwards learned that attempts had been made to render you unpopular here, by throwing out the idea that you had placed all the Indians on lands within the State & that they would still continue to be sent here from the East side of the Mississippi.

In writing this I am well aware that I may be trespassing too far, but the very high respect & esteem in which I hold your character induces me to give you this information, and to apprize you that the feeling of this State is very much opposed, to the locating of Indians among them.

ALS in DNA, 2, G-1822 (M-222:23).

From Thomas H. Williams and David Holmes, [Senators from Miss.,] and Christopher Rankin, [Representative from Miss.]

Washington City, Dec. 16, 1822

In consequence of the Treaty negociated [*sic*] in October 1820, by Generals [Andrew] Jackson and [Thomas] Hinds with the Choctaw Indians, it becomes necessary to change the *location* of the Choctaw Agency, which has fallen within the limits of the cession made by that Treaty [to the U.S.], and we recommend as a suitable site for that purpose, a position near the Oaknoxabee, on the road leading from Columbus [Miss.] to Natchez.

By an arrangement with the Choctaws which is recognized in the 6th Article of the Treaty of Mount Dexter, dated the 16th of November 1805—The United States were authorized to establish within the said Nation, certain public stands on the road leading from Natchez to Nashville, for the accom[m]odation of the mail carriers and travellers in general. In accordance with this stipulation these establishments were made, and by the Treaty of 1820 two of these establishments have fallen within the country ceded to the United States. Consequently, it becomes necessary that two others should be selected in lieu of them, and proper persons authorized to take charge of them. We therefore recommend that the Agent to the Choctaws, [William Ward,] be instructed to make the said selections, and that they be located on the road leading from Columbus to Natchez. And we respectfully suggest, for the consideration of the Secretary of War, whether it would not be most advisable, that the said Agent in the execution of this trust, should be instructed to consult the views of the Executive authority of the State of Mississippi.

LS (in Williams's script) in DNA, 1, W-144 (M-221:96). NOTE: The Oaknoxabee River was probably that shown on modern maps as the Noxubee, which flows southeastward (into Ala.) through an area near Choctaw County and to the southwest and south side of Columbus. Calhoun answered on 12/19.

From the Rev. John Gambold, Salem, N.C., 12/17. He encloses his report dated 9/30 that he had purchased a building for a new school for [Eastern] Cherokee children about 10 miles from Newtown and a certificate by Return J. Meigs dated 10/24 that this building qualifies for government aid. The Directors of the Society [of the United Brethren for Propagating the Gospel among the Heathen] have recently added their endorsement to this expansion of Gambold's several missionary schools. ALS with Ens in DNA, 77 (M-271:4, frames 108–116).

To C[allender] Irvine, Philadelphia, 12/17. Calhoun sends to Irvine an estimate of additional clothing that will be needed for 1823. If this supply cannot be provided from the funds already requested by Irvine for 1823, "which is desirable, then you will forward an estimate of the additional sum you will require for this object." FC in DNA, 3, 11:457 (M-6:11). On 12/20 Irvine replied that he would be able to supply the [woolen] flannel underclothing without additional funds, provided that he should receive no other unexpected demands for 1823. ALS in DNA, 1, I-78 (M-221:95); FC in DNA, 45, 389:434.

From Sol[omon] Sibley, [Delegate from Mich. Territory,] 12/18. He solicits an appointment as a Cadet for his son, Ebenezer Sproat Sibley, to whom Calhoun offered an appointment during the last session of Congress, when the son was a student in Union College, [N.Y.]. ALS in DNA, 15, 1822, 37½ (M-688:20); draft in MiD, with a variant draft dated 12/15.

From William Clark, St. Louis, 12/19. He acknowledges Calhoun's letters of 11/14 and 11/15. For various reasons, Clark believes that "it would be good policy to place all the Tribes or Bands of Osages under the Control of one Indian Agent." Clark suggests the enactment of a law establishing an Agency for the Osages, Delawares, Shawnees, and Kickapoos. Because the new Agent "will necessarily have to perform fatigueing [*sic*] & hazardous duties in a wilderness Country," his salary should be equal to "the highest Class of Agents." Clark suggests another plan, which he thinks would be even more beneficial. This plan would include the addition of two Sub-Agents for the tribes on the Missouri, one for the Delawares, one for the Kickapoos, one for the Shawnees, and "one Principal Indian Agent for all the Mississippi Tribes above this [place], who Should also visit the Tribes on the Illinois River" as far north as the forks of that river. Additional boats, boatmen, and provisions would also be necessary. Clark reports that the accounts of [Nicholas] Boilvin, Indian Agent at Prairie du Chien, have not been received. Boilvin "has been a useful Agent, but unfortunately does not write English, and knows nothing of accounts." ALS in DNA, 1, C-231 (M-221:95).

From William Eustis, [Chairman, House Committee on Military Affairs,] 12/19. He requests, for the committee, "a statement specifying the nature and extent of the work done and the kind and quantity of materials delivered at the several fortifications under the" 1822 appropriation for the construction of them. ALS in DNA, RG 233, 17A-C16.3; LS in DNA, 30, 393.

To Thomas H. Williams and David Holmes, [Senators from Miss.,] and Christopher Rankin, [Representative from Miss.]

Dep[art]m[en]t of War, 19 Dec[embe]r 1822

Gentlemen, Since the receipt of your letter of the 16th inst[ant] I have received one from the Choctaw Agent, [William Ward,] in which he states that the Chiefs & headmen of the Choctaw nation have in Council "agreed that the Agency should be located between David Shotes [*sic*; Choate's] and the French Camps on the great mail route to Natchez." As I have no map on which the point and that mentioned by you is [*sic*] sufficiently designated to enable me to judge of the difference between them, I will thank you to state how nearly the former accords with the latter.

FC in DNA, 72, E:371 (M-15:5). NOTE: Williams replied on 12/21.

From Alexander Macomb, 12/20. He requests the services of [2nd] Lt. [William Theobald Wolfe] Tone for six to nine months and enumerates five areas in which Tone's services will be useful: studying the military schools of Europe to ascertain their superiorities over those of the U.S., assisting in translating a French work concerning officers in the Engineer service, assisting in formulating a program for "a school of application" for staff officers, establishing a uniform system of tactics for the Cavalry and Light Artillery, and assisting in "translations & memoirs relating to the Military Academy." ALS in DNA, 1, E-60 (M-221:95).

From Henry R. Schoolcraft, Sault Ste. Marie, [Mich. Territory,] 12/20. Schoolcraft recommends William Hoffman, [Jr.,] the son of Capt. William Hoffman, for an appointment as a Cadet. William is about 15 years of age and has "attained a competent knowledge of the preliminary studies." Schoolcraft is personally acquainted with William and considers him to be a very promising youth. Hoffman is a very deserving officer with a large family and no means of support other than his commission. Schoolcraft will appreciate any aid given to Hoffman. ALS in DNA, 15, 1824, 92 (M-688:29, frame 286).

To George Walton, [Secretary and Acting Governor of Fla. Territory,] Pensacola, 12/20. Calhoun acknowledges Walton's letter of 11/24 [*not found*] and approves the measures taken by him to appease the Indians following the postponement of the treaty negotiations originally scheduled for 11/20. Walton's draft for $1,000 to defray the expenses incident to the postponement will be honored when presented. Calhoun hopes that [Gad Humphreys] will have entered by this date upon his duties [as Indian Agent]. FC in DNA, 72, E:371–372 (M-15:5).

From Maj. S[tephen] H. Long, Philadelphia, 12/21. "I embrace the earliest opportunity to transmit a Copy of the 'Account of the Expedition' and will forward eleven others as soon as the work shall have been published, which will complete the dozen ordered in your instructions of Nov. [17,] 1821. I know not yet whether it will be practicable to send you a copy of the letters, belonging to the work, but in case I do not, will transmit it with the eleven copies still due." ALS in DNA, 1, L-50 (M-221:96). Long was referring to Edwin James, compiler, *Account of an Expedition from Pittsburgh to the Rocky Mountains, Performed in the Years 1819 and '20 . . .* (3 vols. Philadelphia: H.C. Carey and F. Lea, 1822–1823).

From Samuel Martin, Kingston, Tenn., 12/21. He makes some suggestions for improvements in the Army, including the operation of a school at every garrison, regulations against alcoholic beverages, and the establishment of "a saving bank" at every command. ALS in DNA, 1, M-177 (M-221:96).

From Thomas H. Williams, [Senator from Miss.,] 12/21. In reply to Calhoun's letter "of yesterday [actually 12/19]," Williams reports, without benefit of maps but from memory of his own travels, that the site proposed by the Miss. delegation in Congress for the new Choctaw Agency is about 60 miles east of "Louis Leflo's, the upper French Camp," [which is in the vicinity of a site proposed by the Choctaws]. ALS in DNA, 1, W-144 (M-221:96).

From Ferris Pell, Washington, 12/22. "I have this morning been assured by Mr. [Peter] Hagner that it will be impracticable for him to enter upon the examination of the State accounts for repairs of Arms at present." Pell feels that the State of N.Y. is entitled to receive now at least part of its claim of about $17,000, because "all the evidence required by the rule is fully furnished." LS in DNA, 262, 7754.

CL[AUDIUS] BERARD to Alexander Macomb

West-Point, December 25th 1822

I wished to avail myself of your late visit at this place, in order to call your attention to a subject, which daily grows of more importance; but your time seemed to be so much engrossed by your minute inspection of the different departments of the Academy, that I did not find an opportunity to have a private conversation with you: I, therefore, take the liberty of addressing you a few lines respecting it.

The Library of the Military Academy, which, in April, 1816,

was confided to my care by Gen[era]l [Joseph G.] Swift, has been increasing ever since; and the trouble and responsibility attached to it, have, of course, become much greater. I have, cheerfully, and I believe, faithfully, attended to it for the space of nearly seven years, without receiving any remuneration. Major [Sylvanus] Thayer, and the Secretary of War, to whom I have applied for obtaining an adequate salary for my services as Librarian, have readily admitted the justice of my claim; but nothing, as yet, has been determined; and, unless it be urged by some influential person at Washington, I am afraid that many more years will pass away before any thing is granted me. I have, consequently, resolved, General, now to solicit your kind mediation in this business, sure that as the Inspector of this Institution, and as one so thoroughly acquainted with all its wants, you will feel disposed to recommend to the Secretary of War the propriety of allowing me a due compensation for performing an additional duty which involves so much labour and responsibility.

ALS in DNA, 14, 346. NOTE: Berard signed this letter over his title as "Librarian of the Mil[itary] Academy." His salaried service there was as "first teacher of the French language." Gordon, *A Compilation of Registers of the Army,* p. 223.

From Bernard Peyton, Adjutant General of Va., Richmond, 12/25. He submits his annual return of the strength of the Va. militia for 1822. ALS in DNA, 16, 1822, P-45 (M-567:4, frames 739–741).

By P[eter] H[agner], 12/26. He feels that sufficient evidence has not been given for a proper settlement of N.Y.'s claim. However, it is his opinion that $6,322.50 may be allowed as an advance, partial payment of the claim. An AES by Calhoun dated 12/27 directs that the amount may be advanced if Col. [Ferris] Pell agrees to certain adjustments of the property accounts between N.Y. and the U.S. DI in DNA, 262, 7759.

From ERASTUS ROOT, [former Representative from N.Y.]

Delhi, [N.Y.,] 26 Dec. '22

My neighbor Mr. Lupton is among the most respectable inhabitants of this county. His ["son," *interlined*] both by precept & example, must be well taught in the moral & civic virtues. I know the youth; He is sprightly, well formed, & has made very good progress in our academy. With very high respect & esteem, your obed[ien]t &c., Erastus Root.

ALS in PHi.

From George Bomford, 12/27. Pursuant to a House resolution of 5/7, Bomford encloses and discusses at length 12 documents, prepared by his office on 11/30, 12/18, and 12/26, including a report of 9/24 to Bomford from Roswell Lee, Superintendent of the U.S. Armory at Springfield, Mass. LS with Ens in DNA, RG 233, 17A-D1; FC in DNA, 32, 3:267–273; PC with Ens in House Document No. 111, 17th Cong., 2nd Sess.; PC with Ens in *American State Papers*: *Military Affairs*, 2:473–507.

S[ylvanus] Thayer, West Point, to Alexander Macomb, 12/27. Thayer encloses the letter [of 12/25] from [Claudius] Berard [to Macomb] "soliciting a reasonable compensation for his services as Librarian in the Mil[itary] Academy. He has most faithfully discharged the duty for the period of seven years & as the situation involves considerable responsibility & requires much of his time & attention, I hope the Secretary of War will think proper to allow him some compensation for his future services." ALS with En in DNA, 14, 346.

From the Rev. Eleazer Williams

Green Bay (Michigan Ter[ritory]), Dec[em]b[e]r 27th 1822

I am happy to have it in my power to state to your Excellency, that according to Government permission, the Delegates of the Stockbridge and Six Nations, have the past season, made a second Treaty with their Brethren here the Menominies—a copy of which has doubtless ere this, reached your Excellency's office. It is expected that a portion of the Six Nations, being influenced by designing persons, will oppose its ratification, though, I feel confident the number will be few, as the principal cause of the heretofore dissenting [pagan] party[']s complaint is, (in case of the last Treaty's ratification) removed.

It is also expected that some few of the French traders, who are somewhat interested will use their endeavours to have the Government refuse to ratify our proceedings, but as we have been instructed by your Excellency, and long had the countenance of the General Government in the business, we give ourselves little uneasiness and rest almost assured that the Six Nations and U[nited] States will not finally have spent several thousand Dollars for nothing by having the great object defeated. At least, so firm am I in this opinion, I have taken my final abode on the spot and have commenced my labours among the Menominies, who appear unusually well pleased with their new neighbours, as well as with my Mission, which is thus far very successful.

I would beg particularly to mention to your Excellency that we have already commenced a school for the Menominies and half-breed French and Indian children, the latter of which, I think are almost or quite as needy as the former. We design if possible to continue this until the children are educated, or as long as the Mission continues, which is established under the permission of Bishop [John Henry] Hobart, tho, without a great pecuniary support, he not feeling himself at liberty to send funds out of his Diocess [*sic*]. We have, however, for the support of the school, entertained no small hopes from your Excellency in as much as your Excellency has been very gracious to other institutions of the kind as well as to give us encouragement thereto.

About thirty of the before mentioned children attend who are making rapid progress, & are very fond of school.

In case your Excellency should not see fit to appropriate something to the benefit of these Heathen Children, I see nothing but the school must stop in the spring as the teacher is now wholly unsupported.

May I hope that your Excellency will do me the favour to answer this as soon as convenient, and much oblige your . . . .

ALS in MoSHi.

From G[eorge] Bomford, 12/28. He reports, in reference to a portion of a House resolution of 1/8, that all arsenals erected since [the War of 1812] are indeed necessary and indispensable. All other information required by the resolution can be found in statements that accompanied Bomford's report of 12/27 to Calhoun. LS in DNA, RG 233, 17A-D1; FC in DNA, 32, 3:274–275; PC in House Document No. 111, 17th Cong., 2nd Sess.; PC in *American State Papers*: *Military Affairs*, 2:475.

Receipt of Ferris Pell, Agent [of N.Y., Washington,] 12/28. Pell has received a requisition for $6,000 issued by the Secretary of War in [partial] payment of claims of the State of N.Y. for expenditures relative to the militia in the service of the U.S. during the War [of 1812]. DS in DNA, 262, 7754.

To John Tod, Chairman, House Committee on Lead Mines, 12/28. Calhoun encloses and explains a bill drafted by himself "for the better regulation of the leasing and working of the mines, and salt springs of the United States." The bill covers a number of minerals, provides for six-year leases (in order to encourage investments of private capital), and seeks to encourage individuals to explore mining districts. FC in DNA, 4, 2:253 (M-220:1).

From S[amuel] D. Ingham, [Representative from Pa.,] 12/29. He submits a proposal from John Fon to sell "a quantity of ordnance." Ingham thinks that it may be in the interest of the U.S. to accept the offer. (An EU indicates that Fon proposed to sell 30 pieces of brass artillery.) ALS in DNA, 31, 1822, I.

From G[eorge] Bomford, 12/30. Pursuant to the House resolution of 12/17 requiring information about the arms now belonging to the U.S., Bomford states that the required data can be found in his reports of 12/27 and 12/28 to Calhoun. LS in DNA, RG 233, 17A-D1; FC in DNA, 32, 3:275–276; PC in House Document No. 111, 17th Cong., 2nd Sess.; PC in *American State Papers: Military Affairs*, 2:473.

From John H. Hall, Harpers Ferry, 12/30. "If the bill for establishing an Armoury on the Western waters should pass at this Session of Congress I shall be desirous of being considered a candidate for the Superintendency of it." There is a letter on file in the War Department from his friends in Portland, Me., including the present Governor, [Albion K. Parris,] which expresses their confidence in Hall's qualifications for such a position. His mechanical skills are well known. He has succeeded in an object which has baffled all others. "*I have succeeded in establishing methods for fabricating arms exactly alike, & with economy, by the hands of common workmen, & in such a manner as to ensure a perfect observance of any established model, & to furnish in the arms themselves a complete test of their conformity to it.*" This will ultimately reduce the expense of manufacturing arms to its lowest possible amount. ALS in DNA, 31, 1822, H.

From David Holmes, [Senator from Miss.,] 12/30. He believes that the best site for the proposed new Choctaw Agency will be "near to the Oaknoxabee on the road leading from Columbus [Miss.] to Natchez." The exact spot on which the buildings should be constructed should be determined by the judgment of the Agent, [William Ward]. ALS in DNA, 1, W-144 (M-221:96).

From William Lee, 12/30. Pursuant to House resolutions of 1/8 and 5/7 pertaining to the production and expenses of the Ordnance bureau, Lee submits six statements giving the desired information. A report on 1822 expenses will be made as soon as it can be completed. LS with Ens in DNA, RG 233, 17A-D1; FC in DNA, 51, 8:221–223; PC with Ens in House Document No. 111, 17th Cong., 2nd Sess.; PC with Ens in *American State Papers*: *Military Affairs*, 2:508–512.

To Joseph McMinn, New Canton, Tenn.

Dep[art]m[en]t of War, 30 Dec[embe]r 1822

I have received your letter of the 12th inst[ant].

As your health will not permit you to attend to the collection of the notes taken for the public property sold by you, you will put the notes into the hands of an Attorney, in whom you have confidence, for collection, with directions to inform the individuals concerned, that if payment be made within a reasonable time (which will be fixed on by the Attorney) current notes of the Banks of the State will be received; but that in default of such payment, the notes will be put in suit and the currency of the State will not be received in payment when judgments are obtained.

You will take duplicate receipts of the Attorney in whose hands you may place the notes, for them, and transmit one to this Department.

With best wishes for the speedy restoration of your health, I am . . . .

FC in DNA, 72, E:373–374 (M-15:5); FC in DNA, 75, 1822–1827:1 (M-208:10). Note: This letter was substituted for another dated 12/27 to McMinn [FC in DNA, 72, E:373 (M-15:5)]. The earlier letter, which was not mailed, differs from the one of 12/30 in the second paragraph: "As your health will not permit you to attend to the collection of the notes taken for the public property sold by you, you are authorized to put the notes into the hands of an Attorney, in whom you have confidence, for collection, with directions not to sue until he has called on the individuals concerned for the amount of their respective accounts, and where a disposition to pay is manifested, allow a reasonable time to make the payment. To prevent further difficulty & delay in the collection, current notes of the Banks of the State may be received in payment."

To R[eturn] J. Meigs, Calhoun, Tenn., 12/30. Calhoun acknowledges Meigs's letters of 11/20 [ALS in DNA, 1, M-174 (M-221:96)], 11/22, and 12/4. Calhoun had been apprized of the proceedings of the [Eastern Cherokee] National Committee and Council by a communication from them. He agrees with Meigs's remarks about these proceedings but hopes, notwithstanding the Indians' declared opposition, to obtain additional cessions of their lands. The enclosed extract from a letter of 11/2 from the Creek Path towns to Governor [William] Carroll [of Tenn.] indicates that "the nation is not unanimous in the declaration not to cede any more lands" east of the Mississippi. Calhoun hopes that Meigs will be able to use this dissenting opinion as a means of convincing other [Eastern] Cherokees that a treaty will be desirable. FC in DNA, 72, E:374 (M-15:5); CC in DNA, RG 233, 18A-D1, vol. 263; PC with En in House Document No. 136, 18th Cong., 1st Sess.; PC with En in *American State Papers*: *Indian Affairs*, 2:505–506.

To [James Monroe], 12/30. In compliance with House resolutions of 1/8 (compare, herein, Calhoun's letter of 4/24 to Philip P[endleton] Barbour), 5/7 [DS in DNA, 1, R-211 (M-221:94); CC in DNA, 31, 1822, War Department], and 12/17 [DS in DNA, 1, R-79 (M-221:96)], requesting detailed information concerning the Ordnance bureau and its expenses since 1817, Calhoun submits reports from George Bomford dated 12/27, 12/28, and 12/30; from William Lee dated 12/30; and from Peter Hagner dated 9/7. These should provide all of the requested information with the exception of expenditures during 1822, which will be reported as soon as possible. LS with Ens in DNA, RG 233, 17A-D1; FC in DNA, 6, 2:101–103 (M-127:2); PC with Ens in House Document No. 111, 17th Cong., 2nd Sess.; PC with Ens in *American State Papers*: *Military Affairs*, 2:472–514.

To William Carroll, [Governor of Tenn.,] Murfreesboro, 12/31. Calhoun acknowledges Carroll's letter of 12/8 and the enclosed "communication, addressed to you from the Creek Path Cherokee Indians." Calhoun encloses an extract from his own letter [of 12/30] to [Return J.] Meigs "to be laid before the Commissioners, who have been appointed to hold a treaty with the [Eastern] Cherokee nation, on their arrival at the Agency where it is intended to hold the treaty; who will, no doubt, give the subject to which it relates due attention." FC in DNA, 72, E:374–375 (M-15:5).

From W[illiam] Eustis, Chairman, [House Committee on Military Affairs,] 12/31. Two members of his Committee, [John] Cocke, [Representative from Tenn.,] and J[ohn Speed] Smith, [Representative from Ky.,] plan to visit the military works at Old Point Comfort and the Rip Raps Shoal. "Any facility which it may be convenient to afford them, on their arrival in that vicinity," will be appreciated. ALS in DNA, 1, E-68 (M-221:95).

From the Rev. J[EDIDIAH] MORSE, *"Confidential"*

New Haven, Dec[embe]r 31, 1822

Respected Sir, The friendly intercourse with which you have indulged me, induces me in few words, to open my heart to you, & to inform you of my present trials.

Six weeks ago, [*one or two words canceled*] while walking the streets, I was suddenly deprived of the use of my limbs & reason, & in that state was carried to the house of a friend, where I was confined for three weeks; & since my return home, the effects of this attack are felt to such a degree, as to confine me principally to my house. My suffering is principally in my limbs.

During my absence on my Indian Mission, my pecuniary affairs, & the property to meet them, became deranged—losses have ensued—wh[ic]h together with the heavy expenses incurred on my journies, & the publication of my Report, have brought me to the verge of *bankruptcy*.

You will easily recollect, Sir, the conversation wh[ic]h passed between us when I received my Commission. My expectation was, that my expenses would be reimbursed, wh[ic]h has been done in part—my time I was willing gratuitously to devote to so good an object. I need not acquaint you, Sir, with the course of events since.

With these facts before you, Sir, I ask, if there is no way in wh[ic]h some relief can be afforded—from either the $10,000 dol[lar] fund—or the fund provided in the Ind[ia]n Act of 1802, now unrepealed—or by Congress taking a No. of my Report, or in any other way. If no relief can be had—then—the consequences cannot be foreseen. They are with that GOD in whom I trust, & to whose service I have endeavored humbly to devote my life. My cause is with Him—he is full of compassion—& will not forsake those who trust in him.

Pardon, Sir, this frank & confidential disclosure of my *real* situation. I beg that this letter may *rest wholly with yourself*. If any thing can be done, I have confidence you will readily do it. With high consideration & respect I am, Sir, y[ou]r ob[edien]t & devoted serv[an]t, J. Morse.

ALS in DNA, 1, M-244 (M-221:96).

To Smith Thompson, Secretary of the Navy, 12/31. "In compliance with your request [of 12/28 (LS in DNA, 1, T-75 [M-221:86]; FC in DNA, 136, 1:131)] for the loan of six 12-pounders on field carriages, [in order to assist the Navy in making effectual a new statute for the suppression of piracy,] I herewith enclose an order in favour of Captain [Samuel] Evans [U.S.N.] for the Artillery and necessary equipment." FC in DNA, 3, 11:455 (M-6:11).

To W[ILLIAM] WARD, Choctaw Agency

Dep[art]m[en]t of War, 31 Decem[be]r 1822

After consulting with the delegation in Congress from Mississippi, it has been determined to fix the Choctaw Agency at "a position near the Oaknoxabee on the road leading from Columbus to Natchez." The selection of the particular spot on which the buildings should be erected is left to your sound discretion.

You will immediately furnish me with an estimate for the buildings, and other expenses which may probably attend the removal of the Agency from the present site to that above designated.

As two of the tavern stands established within the Choctaw nation, under the treaty of 1805, on the road leading from Natchez to Nashville, have by the treaty of 1820 fallen within the Country ceded to the U[nited] States, it is deemed necessary that two others should be selected in lieu of them, within the Choctaw boundary on the road leading from Columbus to Natchez. You will accordingly, consult the Chiefs upon the subject and if not objected to by them, select suitable sites for such stands. In making the selection due regard should be had to the views of the executive authority of the State of Mississippi [Walter Leake].

It is proper to observe that the U[nited] States have paid annually to the Choctaw Nation $100 for each of the stands provided for by the treaty of 1805. If, therefore[,] the above arrangement for two new stands in lieu of those superseded by the treaty of 1820, should not be made, $200 only will hereafter be paid on that account. If the sites should be selected you will report them to this Department; when further instructions in relation to the establishments to be made upon them, will be given to you.

FC in DNA, 72, E:375–376 (M-15:5).

JANUARY 1823

Incoming letters recommended Calhoun's future son-in-law, Thomas Green Clemson, for a Cadetship. And on the 16th Calhoun congratulated one of his brothers-in-law upon having become a father, because "I find my children the great solace of life." Cyrus Kingsbury wrote on the same day another of his always superior reports about his schools for the Choctaws, and a letter of the 29th announced the untimely death of the veteran Agent to the Eastern Cherokees, Return J. Meigs. Almost one-fifth of last summer's new Cadets were not retained at the Military Academy, the Academic Board reported on the 13th. Duff Green sought help on the 3rd for fur traders. Calhoun had decided by the 20th that neither William H. Crawford nor Henry Clay could win the Presidency; the "cause must at least triumph, and I cannot be defeated."

To J[oseph] Hopkinson, Philadelphia, 1/2. Calhoun returns some letters to Hopkinson under an assumption that Hopkinson had sent them to the War Department. Calhoun remarks that "the alterations requested by General [William Henry] Harrison are left to your judgment to be made or not as you may deem fit, provided it does not involve much additional expense." FC in DNA, 3, 11:453 (M-6:11).

From Walter Lowrie, [Senator from Pa.,] 1/2. He requests permission to examine the "missionary reports" [about schools for Indians] made to the War Department during the past six months. ALS in DNA, 1, L-53 (M-221:96).

To [James Monroe], 1/2. Calhoun transmits a report by the Board of Engineers concerning the Ohio and Mississippi Rivers. LS with Ens in DNA, RG 233, 17A-D1; FC in DNA, 6, 2:103 (M-127:2).

From Edward F. Tattnall, [Representative from Ga.,] 1/2. "With regard to the works in the harbor of Savannah, there seems to be every prospect that a partial appropriation could be obtained. On this subject, however, the Chairman of the [House] Committee of Ways and Means, [Louis McLane,] to whom I shall this morning by resolution refer the matter, will address a note to your Department." ALS in DNA, 30, 397.

From W.H. Bedford, Washington, 1/3. In compliance with Calhoun's request, Bedford discusses at length claims for indemnities for property lost [by Tenn. militiamen during the Seminole War of 1817–1818]. He has been authorized to act as an agent in collecting claims totaling approximately $70,000. Although these claims may be defective in form, he insists that they are honest. LS in DNA, 1, B-204 (M-221:95).

From Duff Green

Chariton[, Mo.,] 3rd Jan[uar]y 1823

Circumstances have lately come to my knowledge which induce me to believe that the N[orth] West Company intend[s] to prevent if possible any American Citizens (not connected with them) from trading or trapping on the Missouri River above the Mandan Villages. I am credibly informed that an Agent of that Company has lately visited St. Louis and endeavered [*sic*] by the offer of large salaries to engage Interpreters who speak the language of the Upper Indians.

Gen[era]l W[illia]m H. Ashley and Major [Andrew] Henry have now ninety-seven men at and near the mouth of the Yellow Stone River and intend to take on from one to two hundred more next spring. From the enlarged and extended policy which you have pursued, I feel confident that you will do all in your power to counteract British influence and to protect these enterprising Citizens.

Major Thomas S. Locke has spent several years on the Upper Missouri and speaks the French and S[i]oux very fluently, and has a general knowledge of the Mandans, Ricaries & S[i]oux. He is an intelligent and worthy man, well calculated to obtain influence among savages. I am authorized to state that if you will confer on him the appointments of Sub agent and interpreter he will locate himself among the S[i]oux or Mandans.

ALS in DNA, 1, C-326 (M-221:95). Note: Calhoun replied on 3/18.

From Maj. S[tephen] H. Long, Philadelphia, 1/3. "I transmit by this day[']s mail, six copies of the 'Account' of the late Expedition [to the Rocky Mountains] under my command, being the residue of the Dozen Copies which you have instructed me to furnish to the War Department. They would have been forwarded at an earlier period, but that the publishers could not obtain sufficient supplies from the Binding [plant] to answer the numerous demands for the work." If agreeable with Calhoun, Long plans to travel to Washington for the purpose of adjusting his accounts. ALS in DNA, 1, L-54 (M-221:96).

From Jacob Brown, 1/4. He encloses a letter to himself [dated 1/1] from John Bissell, [Sr.,] soliciting a Cadetship for [John Bissell, Jr.]; Brown supports this application. LS with En in DNA, 15, 1823, 248 (M-688:26, frames 463–465); FC in DLC, Jacob Brown Papers, Letterbooks, 2:220.

To Duncan G. Campbell and James Meriwether, Commissioners

Dep[art]m[en]t of War, 4 January 1823

Gentlemen, In answer to your letter of the 18th Ult[im]o [LS (in Meriwether's script) in DNA, 1, C-210 (M-221:96)] in which you express a doubt whether the time limitted [*sic*] in your Commissions will be sufficient for the discharge of all the duties assigned you, and suggest the expediency of an extention [*sic*] of the Commissions, I have to state that, there will be no limitation to your Commission other than that which the completion of all your duties may prescribe.

FC in DNA, 72, E:376 (M-15:5).

To [James Monroe], 1/4. Calhoun encloses, for Monroe's consideration, the "treaties concluded with the Osage and Sack & Fox tribes of Indians, since the last Session of Congress, for the extinguishment of the treaty obligations on the part of the" U.S. to maintain "trading houses for their benefit." LS in DNA, RG 46, 17B-C1; FC in DNA, 6, 2:103 (M-127:2); PC with Ens in *American State Papers*: *Indian Affairs*, 2:392–393.

To [James Monroe], 1/4. Calhoun submits a list of Army promotions and appointments for Senate confirmation. LS with En in DNA, RG 46, 17B-A2; FC with En in DNA, 6, 2:104–107 (M-127:2).

William Wirt to James Monroe, 1/4. James Johnson and Johnson & Ward have obtained in Ky. a verdict in favor of themselves as defendants. A balance of more than $13,000 has been adjudged to be due from the U.S. to James Johnson. He proposes to use that balance to offset "about $17,000 due from him on a contract with the Navy Department." Monroe has inquired whether the accounting officers would be justified in admitting this offset "on the ground of this finding merely." A Treasury official feels that a suit should be prosecuted for Johnson's debt to the Navy; Wirt agrees, partly because the Ky. verdict is being appealed and may be found to have been in error. The proposed offset could be admissible if the verdict of the Ky. jury constituted a legal claim against the U.S.; but Wirt is convinced that it does not. He is also certain that the verdict would not be acceptable evidence in a court of law if the Navy's suit against Johnson should be prosecuted. CC in DNA, 68, box for 1823.

To David Barton, [Senator from Mo.,] 1/5. In answer to Barton's letter of 1/3 [ALS in DNA, 1, B-192 (M-221:95)], Calhoun reports that he has not received the [Senate] resolution [concerning the leasing and working of lead mines] to which Barton referred. Calhoun encloses copies of a bill and a reply made [on 12/28/1822] to a similar request by [John] Tod. FC in DNA, 3, 11:454 (M-6:11).

From Joseph Hopkinson, Philadelphia, 1/5. In reply to Calhoun's letter of 1/2, Hopkinson states that it is too late to make any changes in Gen. [William Henry] Harrison's medal. ALS in DNA, 1, H-163 (M-221:95).

To J[ames?] Gibbon, Richmond, 1/6. Calhoun acknowledges Gibbon's letter of 12/27/1822 (ALS in DNA, 30, 395) concerning [Lt.] Col. [Charles] Gratiot's experiments at Old Point Comfort with samples of waterproof cement furnished by Gibbon. A copy of Gratiot's report will be furnished to Gibbon when it arrives. FC in DNA, 21, 1:347.

From S[AMUEL] D. INGHAM, JAMES BUCHANAN, JOSEPH HEMPHILL, and Fifteen Other Representatives from Pa., WILLIAM MILNOR, [former Representative from Pa.,] and C[AESAR] A[UGUSTUS] RODNEY, [Senator from Del.]

Washington, 6th Jan[uar]y 1823

Thomas Green Clemson, of Philadelphia, being desirous of entering the Military Academy at West Point, as a Cadet, we beg leave respectfully to recommend ["him" *interlined*] to you for that situation, when the next appointments may be made. He is a young man of 16 years of age, of respectable connexions [*sic*], and has already made considerable progress in his education, and we confidently hope, he will do credit both to him self and the institution, should he be favoured by the appointment.

LS in DNA, 15, 1823, 177 (M-688:25, frames 482–483). NOTE: The editor has discovered no evidence that Clemson, who was to become a son-in-law of Calhoun, was ever offered a Cadet's warrant. The fact that he was recommended for such a warrant was discovered neither by the author of the sketch of him in the *Dictionary of American Biography* nor by his biographers, Alester G. Holmes and George R. Sherrill, *Thomas Green Clemson: His Life and Work* (Richmond: Garrett and Massie, Inc., c. 1937). Transcriptions of letters from Levi Ellmaker to Calhoun dated 1/8 and 1/17 in support of Clemson's application appear herein.

From L[OUIS] MCLANE, Chairman, [House] C[ommittee on] W[ays] and M[eans]

Washington, Jan. 6, 1823

At an early period of the present Session, there was refer[r]ed to the Committee of Ways and Means a Memorial from the Legislature of the Arkansas Territory, requesting an appropriation for the extinguishment of the title of the Quapaw Indians to certain lands within that territory; which Memorial was subsequently refer[r]ed to the Secretary of War.

I am now instructed by the Committee of Ways and Means to call your attention to the subject, and to request you to furnish such remarks as you may think proper to communicate in relation thereto.

The Committee particularly desire[s] to be informed, whether, in your opinion, it will be proper to open a negotiation for the extinguishment of the Quapaw title, whether it be probable that such negotiation may result in a favorable treaty, and what amount of appropriation will be required for the purposes of such negotiation.

ALS in DNA, 2, M-1823 (M-222:23). NOTE: An EU in an unidentified hand, probably written by someone as a suggestion as to the nature of a reply to be made by Calhoun, apparently reads: "From the situation and quality of the soil of the Quapaw lands I think it would be advisable to make the purchase. I have no means of ascertaining the precise am[oun]t that will be necessary to hold a treaty but from the best estimate I can form presume that $5,000 will be sufficient."

From [former Maj. Gen.] Peter B. Porter, Albany, "January 6th 1822 [*sic*; 1823]." In compliance with Calhoun's instructions, Porter submits this report relative to his investigation of certain charges against [Jasper] Parrish, Iroquois Indian Agent, contained in a printed document entitled, "The proceedings of the great Indian Council at Tonewanta [*sic*; Tonawanda] in August 1822." During a meeting between Porter and 10 or 12 Chiefs of the Pagan party, an attempt was made to prove misconduct on the part of Parrish; however, no proper evidence was presented. Since then Porter has heard that the Indians plan to go to Washington during either the winter or the spring to present their complaints to [James Monroe]. Pollard, the principal Chief of the Christian party, has informed Porter that the Indians in his tribe are "entirely satisfied with the official integrity & good conduct of their Agent." They are convinced that the charges against Parrish are groundless. Porter concludes: "On the whole, I have not discovered, in the course of the enquiries I have made, any reasonable ground to suspect that there is any solid foundation for any of the charges exhibited against Mr. Parrish in the printed hand bill." ALS in DNA, 1, P-215 (M-221:96).

From EDWARD F. TATTNALL, [Representative from Ga.]

House of Rep[resentative]s, Jan[uar]y 6th 1823

Having seen an advertisement in a Georgia paper (which I take the liberty of enclosing) stating that a treaty with the Cherokee

Nation is "contemplated to be held on the 15th Inst[ant]," I shall be much obliged to you if you will inform me who are the United States' Comm[issione]rs for the purpose of holding such treaty. Gen[era]l [John] Floyd, Maj[o]r [James] Merriwether [*sic*; Meriwether] & Mr. D[uncan] G. Campbell of Georgia were, I understand, some time since appointed by the President [James Monroe]. ["Each of" *canceled.*] These Gentlemen were candidates to represent their several counties in the State Legislature & consequently at the time of the rec[ei]pt of their appointments deemed themselves not qualified to hold these app[ointmen]ts. The two latter Gentlemen I have understood ["determined to" *interlined*] delay their acceptance of their app[ointmen]ts until after the adjournment of the Legislature when their disqualification would cease, but the former Gentleman (Gen[era]l Floyd) made known his inability to accept, soon after he received his app[ointmen]t. Gen[era]l F[loyd]'s *refusal* to accept was for the same reason which operated to produce the *delay* of acceptance with the other Gentlemen. I hope therefore that his name (if his place has not been already supplied) may be embraced in the nomination which may be made to the Senate during this session, & that he may, without delay, receive a reappointment from the President. His service would be of the most essential character in effecting the object of holding the contemplated treaty.

ALS with En in DNA, 8. NOTE: Calhoun replied on 1/8.

Smith Thompson, William H. Crawford, and J[ohn] C. Calhoun to [Philip Pendleton Barbour], 1/6. In compliance with a House resolution of 12/22/1822, the Commissioners of Naval Hospitals submit a statement [from Fourth Auditor Constant Freeman, dated 11/19/1822] showing the amount of funds due to the Naval Hospital Fund and the unexpended balance in that Fund. They refer the House for further information to their report of 12/21/1821 [Abs in *The Papers of John C. Calhoun*, 6:579–580]. Agents appointed to select possible sites for hospitals have not yet made their report. The Commissioners comment that they would be able to fulfill their responsibilities better if the money originally set aside for the Naval hospitals were available. FC with En in DNA, 125, 4:23–24; PC with En in House Document No. 20, 17th Cong., 2nd Sess.; PC with En in *American State Papers*: *Naval Affairs*, 1:853.

From JOEL YANCEY, [later a Representative from Ky.]

Richmond, January 6th 1823

I am here at my brother's, waiting to get a passage to Key West with Commodore [David] Porter, as I frankly acknowledge that I deem it unsafe to go there in an unarmed vessel, on account of the seas in that neighbourhood being so infested with pirates: I hope they will shortly be effectually extirpated. If that Island is defended well, I think it will ["be" *interlined*] a very important place of deposit, and a brisk place of business. I need not ["point out" *interlined*] to you the necessity of its being defended by a military force, for your superior information on such subjects, together with your desire to promote the best interests of every quarter of our Union, will have demonstrated to you the utility of that position, & that it is very vulnerable; and consequently needs fortifying. You'll please to excuse the liberty I take, but I thought from the short acquaintance I had the honour of forming with you while at Washington City, that you were very willing to communicate with any person of good character, and to receive and attend to any suggestions that might be salutary. I shall take the liberty to write to you again, when I arrive at my post of destination; in the meantime please to accept assurances of my esteem & believe me to be Sir . . . .

LS in DNA, 228.

To CHARLES CALDWELL, [M.D.,] Lexington, Ky.

War Department, 7th Jan[uar]y 1823

I have had the pleasure of receiving your letter of the 19th [of December, 1822; *not found*] and regret that owing to an oversight in the Pension Office, document No. 1 was not transmitted with my letter of the 29th of November last. It is now enclosed. I am pleased to hear of the flourishing condition of the medical school in the West; and I have not the least doubt from the present favourable appearances that it will attain to that point of perfection to which it is desirable to bring it.

FC in DNA, 91, 12:485.

From N[imrod] Farrow, Strother's Hotel, Washington, 1/7. He has returned to Washington for the purpose of presenting his claims before Congress, and he anticipates that justice will be done. He has many things he would like to discuss with Calhoun in a personal interview. Farrow discusses the subject of a Negro slave whom he purchased in 1819 and sent to Dauphin Island; the Negro has traveled more than 2,000 miles on foot to see Farrow, who, according to the Negro, was "his proper master." The Negro was arrested a short distance from Farrow's residence and jailed. If it is agreeable with Calhoun, Farrow will have the Negro released from jail into Farrow's custody. ALS in DNA, 30, 398.

Joseph Lovell, Surgeon General's Office, to Maj. S[tephen] H. Long, Philadelphia, 1/7. "In reply to your letter of the 3d inst[ant], I am directed by the Secretary of War to state, that should Dr. [Edwin] James accept the appointment for which he has been nominated to the Senate it will be necessary for him to repair to Belle Fontaine [Mo.] as soon as possible, as a Surgeon is required there immediately. From that place he would probably be ordered in the spring to Prairie du Chien for duty." FC in DNA, 242, 3:1.

From G[eorge] Bomford, 1/8. In compliance with a Senate resolution of 12/23, Bomford reports that about 3,500 muskets are required annually for the "Militia of the West" and explains how he arrived at that figure. He also reports that the total number of arms in the various depots is 357,262, of which 65,854 are in Western depots, which now require 23,500 to fulfill their proper proportion based upon population. If his calculations applied only to muskets, the principal weapon of the West, the deficiency there would be about 31,000. The average number of arms manufactured annually is 38,000, of which 9,500 should be sent to the West. A total of 85,418 weapons has been transported to the Western States and Territories between 1812 and 1822, inclusive, with an average of 7,765 annually. The cost of transportation has been estimated at $1 per stand, but better roads and lower prices in general may now reduce it to $.75. Bomford discusses the relative costs of manufacturing arms in the West and East and estimates that it would require three years and $200,000 to erect an armory in the West. Although about 60,000 weapons were manufactured during the [War of 1812], the supply was critical at the end of the war, with at least 240,000 muskets having been "expended." Nearly "eight years of peace, have been required, to make good losses occasioned by a

War of less than three years['] duration." The long frontier will require distribution of large numbers of arms. Another war might find us unable to manufacture a sufficient number. If it should be decided to build an armory in the West, it should increase its capacity gradually over five or six years, by which time it could train a sufficient number of skilled workmen and equal the present armories in size. If an additional armory of equal size were built, about 50,000 weapons could be produced annually. LS in DNA, RG 46, 17A-F4; FC in DNA, 32, 3:277–281; PC in House Document No. 83, 17th Cong., 2nd Sess.; PC in Senate Document No. 18, 17th Cong., 2nd Sess.; PC in *Annals of Congress*, 17th Cong., 2nd Sess., cols. 1310–1314; PC in *American State Papers: Military Affairs*, 2:523–524.

From Levi Ellmaker

Washington, Jan[uar]y 8th 1823

In addition to the almost unanimous recommendation by the delegation in Congress [from Pa.], of Tho[ma]s Green Clemson of Phil[adelphi]a for a Cadet[']s commission at West Point, I beg leave respectfully to state that from an intimate & long acquaintance with his very respectable family in Lancaster Co[unt]y & in Phil[adelphi]a, & from my particular knowledge of himself, & the proficiency he has made in his education, I believe him entirely worthy of the appointment which he is very desirous to obtain.

He is an orphan, & on that account I hope entitled to a favourable consideration from you.

ALS in DNA, 15, 1823, 177 (M-688:25, frame 484).

From J[ames] Hamilton, Jr., [Representative from S.C.,] 1/8/"1822 [*sic*; 1823]." "I beg leave to request that you will do me the favor ["of" *canceled*] to have placed on the List of Applicants for Appointments in the Military Academy at the West Point the following young Gentlemen": Thomas [Fenwick] Drayton of Charleston, S.C.; Thomas Gregorie of Beaufort, S.C.; —— Lawton of Colleton District, [S.C.]; and [Richard B.] Screven of Beaufort District, [S.C.]. ALS in DNA, 15, 1820, 118-119-120-121 (M-688:14). (Hamilton had taken his seat in the House two days earlier.)

To Edward F. Tat[t]nall, [Representative from Ga.]

Dep[art]m[en]t of War, 8 January 1823

I have received your letter of the 6th instant.

Previous to the meeting of the Legislature of Georgia Gen[era]l [John] Floyd sent in his resignation to the President, [James Monroe,] who aware of the value of the services of the General received it with much regret. The President would with great pleasure again put him on the Commission but the time appointed for holding the treaty is too near at hand to allow him to render any service. Besides, after the resignation of the General, Mr. [Duncan G.] Campbell and Major [James] Meriwether were informed that the vacancy occasioned thereby would not be filled, but that the negociation [*sic*] would be confided entirely to them; and the appointment of another Commissioner now, would have the appearance of a want of that confidence in them, to which their talents & respectability entitle them.

FC in DNA, 72, E:377 (M-15:5).

From [Lewis Cass]

Washington, Jan[uar]y 9, 1823

I have the honour to acknowledge to acknowledge [*sic*] the receipt of the papers submitted to you by Mr. [Solomon] Sibley respecting the claims of the proprietors of the Bridges across the Rivers Rouge & Ecorces against the United States for the passage of the Indians over those bridges.

Previous to my leaving Detroit the original books were brought to me, and I have no reason to doubt either their accuracy or the correctness of the transcripts. The river Aux Ecorces enters the Detroit river at the distance of nine miles and the River Rouge at the distance of five miles from the Town. The country is flat, and all the tributary streams attain the level of the strait long before they affect [*sic*] a junction with it. Of course they cannot be forded for some miles above their mouths, and artificial means are required to cross them. The subject is already so familiar to you that I need not advert to the various causes which induce the Indians to visit Detroit. It is sufficient to say that great numbers of them every year and at all times in the year resort to that place, led by business or necessity, curiosity or unbroken usage for a long series of years. A considerable portion of these Indians cross these bridges and, as is well known, without the means of paying toll. Formerly, boats were kept in which they could transport themselves free of expense, but the erection of the bridges has destroyed the ferries, and boats are no longer found there. When the Indians arrive at these bridges, if the United States do[es] not pay the expense, they must return, procure a passage by force, or pledge some valuable article for the toll. We cannot alter the habits of the Indians. Improvident they are, and improvident they will be. In the attainment of almost every object, the proportion between the value of the means and the end is entirely disregarded. I venture to say that not an Indian would be prevented from passing these bridges by any consideration of expense and that his blanket, his gun or article of clothing or subsistence would, if necessary, be pledged without any hope of redeeming it.

As to the alternative of crossing by force, it is certainly to be depreciated [*or* deprecated]. The rights of property are at all times insecure with them, and no inducement should be held out for them to violate the rights of our citizens.

The custom of pledging their property is as ruinous to the Indians, and we cannot aid them more effectually than by taking from them all temptation to this improvident practice. There is such a total disregard of consequences and such a childish sacrifice of property, on one side, and such destitution of moral principle, on the other, that every thing is abandoned for the most temporary objects and gratifications. The most sacred duties are forgotten, & nakedness & starvation are hazarded for the most trifling reasons.

I had the honour last year to state to you the situation of these bridges, and, in consequence of your opinion, I stated to the proprietors that compensation should be made to them. The amount, however, was kept wholly undeterminate. I ought also to mention that the Indians have repeatedly requested that this road, as they express themselves, should be kept clear: that is, that a free passage should be allowed them. And at one of the treaties they applied earnestly for the insertion of a stipulation to that effect.

With respect to the amount to be paid, it must be [a] matter of opinion. The charge as it stands is, I think, too high. If one hundred dollars a year were allowed for each bridge since the period of their erection, it would be a reasonable compensation, and the amount hereafter can only be determined by a comparison of the future with the past.

FC in DNA, 76 (M-1:5, pp. 117–119).

From Jeremiah Evarts

Boston, Jan. 9, 1823

Your letter of Dec. 14th inclosing a copy of a letter from the Rev. Mr. [Cyrus] Kingsbury, did not reach me till the 23rd of that month; after which date I was not able to lay your proposal before the Committee of our Board till yesterday.

It appears to the Committee, that important advantages may result from such a Board of Visitors as was proposed by Mr. Kingsbury.

If the President [James Monroe] should see fit to appoint the persons named by Mr. Kingsbury, the appointment would be perfectly acceptable to us. Mr. Postlethwaite is a man of great respectability & worth. Mr. Dinsmore, as I have always understood, is a great friend to Indian improvement. Of the other gentlemen we know nothing; but we have the fullest confidence that Mr. Kingsbury would not mention any other than suitable persons.

After the President shall have made the appointment, you will confer an obligation upon me by communicating the list of the gentlemen appointed, & their places of residence.

I presume it will be proper for our Board to write to the same gentlemen, expressing our wishes that the intentions of government, in this respect, may be fully executed.

Permit me to mention, that in my letter to yourself, dated June 28, 1822, ["I" *interlined and* "requesting" *changed to* "requested,"] among other things, that $316.67 might be paid on account of the four youths at Cornwall, & that your answer was favorable to my request in this & other particulars. As the bank was closed, & I was obliged to leave Washington soon, you proposed to make the remittance by letter. The subject probably escaped your recollection, in the multitude of concerns to which your attention was called, as no remittance has been received.

I will thank you to cause a check on the U.S. Bank in this place, payable to my order, to be forwarded; & the proper vouchers shall be returned.

I am happy to add, that the four youths, on their return to their native country, have excited a very pleasing interest in the places through which they passed; and that many gentlemen in Charleston [S.C.] & Augusta, [Ga.,] who formerly doubted, as to the practicability of civilizing the Indians, are now fully convinced that it is not only practicable but an imperious duty.

ALS in DNA, 1, E-126 (M-221:95).

Samuel S. Hamilton, [Clerk,] War Department, to [Josias W.] King, [Clerk,] State Department, 1/9. "The Secretary of War wants a copy of the Commission of Robert Houston (certified by the Sec[retar]y of State [John Quincy Adams]) who was appointed about the 12 March 1819 comm[issione]r to run the lines under the [Eastern] Cherokee treaty of Feb[ruar]y 1819 and to lay off certain reservations granted by said treaty. Will you have the goodness to prepare the copy, get it certified with the seal of the Dept. of State affixed & send it to this Dept., as soon as you conveniently can[?] It is wanted to be used as evidence in suits depending in the courts of N[orth] Carolina for some of these reservations." ALS in DNA, 101 (M-179:56).

To [James Monroe], 1/9. Pursuant to a Senate resolution [of 12/23/1822 (DS in DNA, 1, S-287 [M-221:96])] requesting information concerning arms issued to Western militia troops, the estimated cost of erecting a Western armory, etc., Calhoun encloses a report [of 1/8 by George Bomford]. FC in DNA, 6, 2:108 (M-127:2); FC in DNA, 4, 2:254 (M-220:1).

To George Walton, Secretary and Acting Governor [of Fla. Territory,] Pensacola, 1/9. Answering Walton's letter of 12/8/1822 [ALS with En in DNA, 1, W-152 (M-221:96); PC with En in Carter, ed., *Territorial Papers*, 22:576–579], enclosing a copy of [Thomas] Wright's letter of 12/7/1822 to Walton, Calhoun applauds their success in reconciling the Seminoles to the postponement of treaty negotiations. But the conduct of an Interpreter has been "highly improper"; he should be replaced immediately, and the name of the new Interpreter should be reported to Calhoun. FC in DNA, 72, E:378 (M-15:5).

To Joseph M. White, Pensacola, 1/9. Calhoun acknowledges White's letter of 12/1/1822 [ALS in DNA, 1, W-151 (M-221:96); CCEx in DNA, RG 233, 17A-E4; PC in House Document No. 51, 17th Cong., 2nd Sess.; PC in *American State Papers*: *Indian Affairs*, 2:411] recommending removal of the Seminoles from areas of white settlement in Fla. (The same recommendation was repeated in a letter from White dated 12/23/1822 [ALS with En in DNA, 1, W-163 (M-221:96)], which enclosed a petition dated 9/15/1822 and signed by "a respectable number of Farmers" who resided beside the Apalachicola River, including Edmund Doyle and six others.) Calhoun replies that White's wishes coincide with those of the government. The subject has been submitted to Congress by President [James Monroe], and Calhoun has no doubt that the necessary authority will be given for making such arrangements "as sound policy and humanity may require." FC in DNA, 72, E:378 (M-15:5).

Memoranda concerning the Western Cherokee Delegation to Washington, [*ca.* 1/10]. These two documents comprise "Subjects to be adjusted with the delegation from the Arkansaw Cherokees" and a "*Memorandum* relative to the ann[uit]y of 1818 & 1819." DU's in DNA, 77, 5302 (M-271:4, frames 318–320).

From [former Bvt. Brig. Gen.] James Miller, [Governor of Ark. Territory,] Temple, [N.H.,] 1/10. He intended to have been in Washington long ago, while enroute on his return trip to Ark., but explains that illness has prevented him from traveling. He will begin the trip as soon as there is any prospect that he will be able to complete it. He feels confident that the ordinary business of his office is being transacted faithfully by the Secretary of the Territory, [Robert] Crittenden. But Miller does not expect to reach the Territory in time to pay the annuities to the Indians. ALS in DNA, 1, M-273 (M-221:98).

To John Cocke, Chairman Pro Tempore, House Committee on Military Affairs, 1/11. In reply to Cocke's letter of 1/8 [ALS in DNA, 1, C-224 (M-221:95)] requesting plans with accompanying explanations of Forts Monroe and Calhoun, Calhoun states that [Alexander Macomb] will present the original plans and explanations to the committee whenever it may desire. Copies cannot be prepared in less than a month. LS in DNA, 228; FC in DNA, 4, 2:255 (M-220:1).

To William Eustis, Chairman, House Committee on Military [Affairs], 1/11. In answer to Eustis's request of 1/4 [LS in DNA, 1, E-70 (M-221:95); CC in DNA, RG 233, 17A-C16.3; CC in DNA, 31, 1823, E], Calhoun encloses a report from George Bomford dated 1/11 (LS with Ens in DNA, RG 233, 17A-C16.3; FC in DNA, 32, 3:282–284; CC with Ens in DNA, RG 233, 14C-B1, 158:184–188). Bomford reports in detail upon arrangements for the repayment of loans of gunpowder to various individuals, explains the advantages accruing to the Ordnance bureau by having made the loans, and remarks that only $12,000 remain to be accounted for from some $7,000,000 appropriated to the bureau. LS with Ens in DNA, RG 233, 17A-C16.3; FC in DNA, 4, 2:254 (M-220:1); CC with Ens in DNA, RG 233, 14C-B1, 158:184–188; PC with Ens in House Report No. 67, 17th Cong., 2nd Sess.; PC with Ens in *American State Papers*: *Military Affairs*, 2:525–527.

From J[OHN] MASON [of Georgetown, D.C.]

Columbian Foundery [*sic*], Jan[uar]y 11th 1823

As some objections exist on the part of Colo[nel George] Bomford as [to] the exterior dimensions of twenty-["three" *interlined*] 12-p[ounde]r Guns executed at my Foundery and proved by order of the Ordinance [*sic*] Department in July and Nov[embe]r 1821—relative to which objections I have left a statement with him (in March last)—if you will permit the amount of the price of said Guns to be passed to my credit in the War Department—I hereby consent that the whole matter shall yet be subject to your descision [*sic*].

ALS in DNA, 2, M-1823 (M-222:23). NOTE: An EU, evidently written by a filing Clerk, seems to read: "Relative to objections made to the interior [*sic*] dimensions of some of his Guns."

To [Samuel L. Southard, Senator from N.J.,] 1/11. "The Secretary of War presents his compliments to Judge Southard and, agreeably to his request, sends him a blank for ["Revolutionary" *canceled and* "increase of" *interlined*] pensions &c." LU with 2 Ens in NjP, Samuel L. Southard Papers.

From Black Fox, John McLamore, Walter Webber, and James Rogers, [Western Cherokee Delegation,] Washington, 1/12. These Cherokees explain in detail the controversy concerning a bond entered into by some Cherokee Chiefs with John D. [Chisholm] and [Samuel] Moseley. They maintain that the Cherokees are obligated for only a small portion of the total bond and that the Eastern Cherokees are liable for the balance. LS (signed by Rogers and to which Black Fox, McLamore, and Webber affixed their marks) in DNA, 77 (M-271:4, frames 316–317).

From Lewis Cass, Washington, 1/12. "I have the honour to suggest to you the names of Henry and —— Baker, sons of Major [Daniel?] Baker of the United States Army, as candidates for admission to the United States Military Acadamy [*sic*]. Mr. [Walter L.] Newberry, of New York, now living at Detroit, is also a candidate for admission to the same institution. They are all promising young men and will do honour to any profession in life which they may adopt." LS in PHi.

From Lewis Cass, Washington, 1/12. He suggests reissuance of orders for the construction of a building for the Indian Agent at Michillimackinac—a building for which materials were bought but which has not yet been constructed; [Alexander] Macomb can specify the exact site. [The Rev. Isaac] McCoy has reported that a Mr. Sears will probably not accept appointment to conduct a missionary school beside the Grand River; McCoy has named a successor to Sears who is unknown to Cass. Therefore, Cass suggests that Calhoun ask the Baptist Missionary Society, principal supporter of the enterprise, to choose the successor to Sears. LS in DNA, 1, C-353 (M-221:95); FC in DNA, 76 (M-1:5, p. 120); PC in Carter, ed., *Territorial Papers,* 11:330–331.

To Robert Houston, Knoxville, 1/13. It appears that no copy of Houston's commission to survey the boundaries under the [Eastern] Cherokee Treaty of 1819 was retained by the War Department [and the State Department]. Application has been made to the War Department for a certified copy of it to be used in lawsuits for reservations surveyed under Houston's direction. He is requested to return the original commission to the Department to be recorded; and, if he wishes, it will then be returned to him. FC in DNA, 72, E:379–380 (M-15:5).

To R[ichard] M. Johnson, [Senator from Ky.,] 1/13. Calhoun answers his inquiry of 1/8 [ALS in DNA, 1, J-91 (M-221:96)] as to the compensation to which Governor [William P.] DuVal of Fla. Territory is entitled for his services as Superintendent of Indian Affairs there. Territorial Governors are required by law to serve as Superintendents of Indian Affairs, but the statutes have provided no specific compensation to them as such. The War Department has refunded their actual expenses as Superintendents and has granted to them extra compensation for duties performed in addition to their duties as Superintendents (for example, for negotiating treaties with Indians). Both the expenses and the duration of the negotiation must be certified in each instance. DuVal will be paid accordingly. FC in DNA, 72, E:379 (M-15:5).

Report of the Academic Board of the U.S. Military Academy, West Point, 1/13. This Board reports the names and home States of 76 students who were conditionally admitted in 1822, have now passed the examination and demonstrated satisfactory "moral and military conduct," and are recommended to receive Cadets' warrants; of two students of similar status who "have declined to be examined"; of six students of similar status who were absent from the examination because of illness or with permission; and of 11 students who are not recommended for warrants and for permission to remain at West Point "either because of deficiency in their studies, or because their conduct has not been satisfactory," or both. DS (signed by S[ylvanus] Thayer as Superintendent and President of the Board and by Thomas Picton as Secretary of the Board) in DNA, 14, 351.

To TIMO[THY] PITKIN, [former Representative from Conn.,] Farmington, Conn.

War Department, 13th January 1823

I have the honor to acknowledge the receipt of your letter of the 13th ultimo, [*not found*,] stating your desire to have your son William [H. Pitkin] placed, at a proper age, in the Military Academy.

The name of your son will be registered on the list of applicants, and noted for particular attention; and I hope it will be in my power, when he shall have arrived at a suitable age, to appoint him a Cadet. The legal age is between fourteen and twenty-one. Fourteen is generally much too young. I should greatly prefer ["the age of" *canceled*] seventeen, at which age, if proper attention have been paid to his education, a young man, from his previous acquirements and consequent confidence in himself, will be able to pass with comparative ease through the course of academic studies.

You can repeat your application annually till your son shall have reached a suitable age, when it will be particular[l]y attended to.

LS in CSmH; FC in DNA, 13, 1:170 (M-91:1). NOTE: William H. Pitkin entered the Academy in 1826 but did not graduate. *Register of Graduates and Former Cadets, United States Military Academy . . . 1802–1946*, p. 125.

To George Bomford, George Gibson, Thomas S. Jesup, and A[lexander] Macomb, 1/14. Calhoun requests statements in duplicate of all contracts made in their respective bureaus during 1822. FC in DNA, 3, 11:455 (M-6:11); LS (Bomford's copy) in DNA, 31, 1823, War Department; LS (Gibson's copy) in DNA, 43, Calhoun, 533; LS (Jesup's copy) in DNA, 41, 1823–1824, S-6; LS (Macomb's copy) in DNA, 221, 478.

From John Clark, [Governor of Ga.,] Milledgeville, 1/14. He encloses "a report and resolutions adopted . . . by the Legislature at their last Session, which, with this letter, I request you to lay before the President [James Monroe]." Clark discusses at length the claims of Ga. citizens against the Creeks for Negroes and other property stolen or destroyed and urges prompt attention to this matter. LS in DNA, 77 (M-271:4, frames 329–338); FC in G-Ar, Governors' Letterbooks, 1821–1829:85–88; CCEx in DNA, RG 233, 17A-D1. (Calhoun answered on 2/13.)

To W[illiam] Lee, Second Auditor, 1/14. Calhoun requests a statement of the amounts that have been paid by the U.S. for the acquisition of Indian titles to lands in Ga., under the agreement of 4/24/1802 between the U.S. and Ga., from then until now. This statement is to show the costs of [negotiating] the several treaties, the payments made to Indians in purchasing their lands, and the expenses of running the boundary lines of the several cessions. FC in DNA, 72, E:380 (M-15:5).

From Alexander Macomb, 1/14. In compliance with Calhoun's request of 1/14, Macomb encloses duplicate statements of all contracts made during 1822 by the Engineer Department. FC in DNA, 21, 1:349.

To Thomas Metcalfe, [Representative from Ky.,] 1/14. Calhoun answers Metcalfe's letter of 1/13 [ALS in DNA, 1, M-196 (M-221:96)], written as Chairman of the House Committee on Indian Affairs; states that the requested information concerning outlays by the U.S. for Indian lands under the compact of 1802 between Ga. and the U.S. will be submitted as soon as practicable; and requests a copy of the earlier inquiry made of the State Department by Metcalfe concerning the Indians in Fla., because, contrary to the State Department's assurance, that inquiry was not referred by it to Calhoun. FC in DNA, 72, E:380 (M-15:5).

From [former Brig. Gen.] W[illiam] H. W[inder?], Baltimore, "Jan[uar]y 14, 1822 [*sic*; 1823]." He expresses his concern about the dilapidated condition of Fort Covington, because the situation there may injure Calhoun's reputation. ALI in DNA, 1, A-70 (M-221:95).

To William H. Crawford, "January 15th 1822 [*sic*; 1823]." Answering Crawford's letter of 11/30/1822, Calhoun itemizes a total of $704,864 that will be needed in the Western States and Territories north of La. and Tenn. for War Department expenditures during 1823. FC in DNA, 171, 2:[57].

From H[enry] A[lexander] S[cammell] Dearborn, [later a Representative from Mass.,] Boston, "Jan[uar]y 15, 1822 [*sic*; 1823]." He recommends the bearer, Alexander Paris, for some government employment. Paris "is the most distinguished architect among us. He was at the head of the Corps of Artificers during the war." He has "plan[n]ed & erected many public & private edifices, in various parts of the country; [he] was the architect of the National Arsenal at Watertown, [Mass.]." Paris was associated with the construction of the fortification in Portland during 1807–1808. ALS in DNA, 30, 403.

To W[ILLIAM] H[ENRY] HARRISON, Chillicothe, [O.]

Department of War, January 15th 1823

The Secretary of War[']s compliments to General Harrison, and [Calhoun] herewith transmits the casts of his [Harrison's] medal now in the Artist[']s [Mority Fürst's] hands. So soon as the medal is struck it will be disposed of agreeably to the General[']s directions.

FC in DNA, 3, 11:455 (M-6:11).

Petition of Eleanor Lawrance of New York City to the Senate and the House of Representatives, 1/15. This "Memorial" appeals for "just" compensation originating in the Army's occupation of her farm on Long Island in 1813. An accompanying statement itemizes the farm's cost of $7,000 plus interest thereon from 6/1813 at seven percent per annum, totaling about $4,100; deducts $3,500 that she has been paid by the War Department and $4,150 that she has received from sale of the farm; and claims about $3,450 as being still due, plus interest on that sum from 4/1822. (By an EU, this copy of the petition was referred to Calhoun.) DS in DNA, 25, 134.

To "Lewis [*sic*; Louis]" McLane, Chairman, House Committee on Ways and Means, 1/15. Calhoun acknowledges McLane's letter of 1/10 [ALS in DNA, 1, L-60 (M-221:96)], which inquired about the necessity of an appropriation for improving the defenses of the harbor at Savannah. Calhoun encloses a report from the Board of Engineers [by Joseph G. Totten to Alexander Macomb dated 1/7 (CC in DNA, RG 233, 18A-C19.1)], notes the dilapidated condition of existing works, stresses the military, commercial, and agricultural importance of the city, and suggests that a "partial appropriation for the collection of materials may be usefully applied" before the next session of Congress, when the Board of Engineers will report an estimate of the total cost. LS with En in DNA, RG 233, 18A-C19.1; FC in DNA, 4, 2:255 (M-220:1).

Resolution by the Senate, 1/15. "Resolved, That the Petition of Eleanor Lawrance of the City of New York, be referred to the Secretary of the Department of War, to consider and report thereon to the Senate." Attested by Charles Cutts, Secretary of the Senate. DS in DNA, 1, S-283 (M-221:96).

From Lewis Cass

Washington, Jan[uar]y 16, 1823

At the request of Governor [Return J.] Meigs, [Jr.,] I have the honour to submit for your consideration the facts connected with his services in the organization of the troops which marched from Ohio to Detroit in June 1812.

The requisition for calling out, assembling and organizing these troops was made upon him as Governor of Ohio by the War Department. In the execution of this duty, he was compelled to visit different parts of the State & personally to superintend the necessary operations. The arrangement was one which could not be carried into effect at the bureau. Every thing connected with the subject was new, and officers & men were to be collected from all quarters, advances of money made, arms, provisions, and clothing procured. Governor Meigs proceeded on the receipt of his orders to Zanesville, made arrangements for the levying and marching of the troops from that quarter, continued his journey to

Chillicothe, executed a similar duty, & from there proceeded to Cincinnati. He there provided for the raising of another Regiment & procured and delivered tents, arms, ammunition, provision, blankets & other supplies. He then accompanied the Troops to Dayton, where all the forces were collected, and officered & organized the whole. After that, he proceeded to Urbana, where the troops finally parted from him.

I was personally acquainted with a great part of his exertions during this time, and I was a witness of the expense he was compelled to encounter. The nature of these exertions & the amount of the expenses may be estimated by a consideration of the extent of Country he was compelled to travel over, by the strong desire there was on the part of the Government that this force should consist of volunteers rather than drafted Militia, by the total absence of all military organization, & by the want of all the necessary supplies.

Had Governor Meigs issued his orders in the usual manner through the Adjutant General and left to the moral influence or legal obligations of others their execution, the force, if collected at all, which is doubtful, would not have reached the place of rendezvous till after the period assigned for operations had passed away. In fact, the active personal exertions of an influential, zealous man were indispensibly [*sic*] necessary, and these exertions could not have been made without a sacrifice of time & money.

During subsequent years of the war the same services were required & performed, but as they did not fall so much within my personal observations, I forbear calling your attention to them.

LS in OHi. NOTE: On the reverse of this letter is a statement made by L[evi] Barber, Thomas R. Ross, Joseph Vance, and J[ohn] Sloan, [Representatives from O.,] dated 2/26, concurring in the statements made by Cass. They assert that "if compensation has not already been made [to Meigs], we think it altogether proper [that] it should be made."

From [Lewis Cass], Washington, 1/16. "The proprietors of the Toll bridges alluded [to] in my letter of the 9th inst[ant] claim $1,363.695. I have the honour to submit for your consideration the propriety of allowing them $1,000, being at the rate of $100 for each bridge per year, since the year 1817, and excluding that portion of that year in which they were [im]passable. This allowance will settle their claim to the 1st of January 1823. I also submit the propriety of allowing $75 for each bridge for every year hereafter, during which the Indians may resort to Detroit, as they have heretofore done." FC in DNA, 76 (M-15:5, p. 121).

From William Clark, St. Louis, 1/16. He acknowledges Calhoun's letters of 11/14, 11/15, and 12/6/1822. Clark reports that he has informed the white settlers on lands assigned to the Delaware Indians that they must move before 5/1. [William H.] Ashley has returned from his trading establishment at the mouth of the Yellowstone River and has informed Clark that most of the Indians there are friendly. British traders have recently established a trading post that is located nearer to the Mandans than the trading posts formerly established by the British. Clark regrets that U.S. military posts were not extended to the Yellowstone River. A show of strength would have improved relations with the Indians and produced checks on the British traders. ALS in DNA, 1, C-266 (M-221:95).

To J[OHN] E[WING] COLHOUN, Charleston, [S.C.]

Washington, 16th Jan[uar]y 1822 [1823]

Dear John, We congratulate you most sincerely on the birth of your son, and hope that you may enjoy all of the anticipated happiness that such an event is calculated to inspire. To be placed in the relation of father is among the greatest changes which we experience through life, and tho' it has its anxieties, it is not without its preponderance of happiness. I find my children the great solace of life, and midest [*sic*] all of the anxiety which must occasionally be felt, there is still that which makes you feel how much more happy you are with them and how disconsolate you would be without them.

When you see James [Edward Colhoun] say to him there appears to be no prospect of selling his Georgetown [D.C.] property but at a great sacrafice [*sic*]. Mr. Blunt, who it was expected would purchase is dead, and there has been no offer at any price.

We are all well, and Floride [Colhoun Calhoun] and your mother [Floride Bonneau Colhoun] desire their love to you and Mrs. [Martha Maria Davis] Colhoun and sincerely hope that she will continue to do well. What do you intend to call your son? Yours sincerely, J.C. Calhoun.

ALS in ScCleA; PEx in Jameson, ed., *Correspondence*, p. 205.

From [the Rev.] CYRUS KINGSBURY

Mayhew, C[hoctaw] N[ation], Jan. 16, 1823

I have the honour herewith to transmit the Annual Report of the schools in this nation. The great delay which has attended it, was occasioned by several successive journies [*sic*], on business relating to the schools, and by which I was detained much longer than had been expected. Measures will be taken hereafter, to have the Report more promptly made.

It will be seen by the report, that the buildings at Mayhew, have cost upwards of $6,000. This is a great expense, but I think it will not be judged by candid persons, that there has been any extravagence [*sic*], on the supposition that the school is to be a large one, & permanent. The number of buildings mentioned in my estimate for Mayhew, have [*sic*] been completed, with the exception of a little inside work ["in two of them" *interlined*] which is not necessary to the buildings being used for the purposes intended. They are now all comfortable, & what has already been done on each, considerably exceeds the estimate. Several other buildings not included in the estimate, but which have been found necessary, have also been erected & completed.

I have requested the Agent [William Ward] to certify these facts, presuming that the school will now be entitled to the balance of the appropriation towards the buildings at this place, amounting to $1,000, as stated in the letter of the Sec[retary] of War, dated 2d Oct. 1821.

It is respectfully submitted whether any additional appropriation can be made on account of buildings at this school, as was done for those at Brainerd & Elliot[t]. Also whether an annual allowance can be made on account of the current expenses at Mayhew.

It ought perhaps to have been stated in the Report, that the schools have had to encounter much opposition. This has arisen principally from the misrepresentations of unfriendly white people. These have not had much influence in the neighbourhood of the schools, & with those who have visited them, but in distant parts of the nation considerable prejudices have been excited.

Some of the Chiefs say there are so many stories, they do not know which to believe. If they could hear the opinion of their great Father, the President, [James Monroe,] they think they should be satisfied. It would probably very much hasten the progress of civilization, if a few of the most intelligent, could visit

Washington, & hear the advice of the President, on this subject, so deeply interesting to them.

ALS with En in DNA, 77 (M-271:4, frames 691–708). NOTE: The enclosed ALS report of 1/15 contains an interesting account of a typical morning's activity in 4/1822 at the school at Elliott: "A little after day light, the horn was blown by the Cook, who rises about 4 o'clock to prepare breakfast. This horn is a signal for the family to rise. The interval between this & breakfast, is occupied in making fires, washing, & other preparations. Frequently the children are ready in season to spend ["to spend" *repeated and then canceled*] a short time in reading at their several rooms before the bell rings, which is about half an hour before sunrise. The family including children, & all others in health assemble in the Hall for breakfast, which consists of Coffee, (¾ rye) corn bread, meat, potatoes, &c. After breakfast the family unite in reading a portion of Scripture, singing a Hymn & prayer. By this time the sun is 20 minutes, or ½ an hour high. On leaving the hall the whistle is blown, a signal for the boys to prepare for work. About 20 boys with their axes, followed Mr. [Elijah] Bardwell to the wood where they are engaged in clearing land. The timber is not heavy. They cut it all down, & cut it suitable for rails, for rolling, & for firewood, on about an ["about an" *repeated and then canceled*] acre in a week. Fifteen or 20 other boys were with Mr. [Cyrus] Byington, chopping wood at the house, ["clearing &" *interlined*] leveling the yard, & doing various other work. At the house occupied by the female school, the Teacher, Miss [Hannah] Thacher, with two Choctaw girls, were quilting a bed quilt. In another part of the room two small girls were picking cotton; two others were carding & one was spinning. In another room, two of the girls were sewing, with Mrs. [Elijah] Bardwell. In a third were two girls with Mrs. [Joel] Wood, one was ironing clothes, the other was sewing. In the Kitchen two girls were washing dishes, & preparing vegetables for dinner. At a ¼ before 9, the horn blew for the scholars to leave their work & prepare for school. In 15 minutes the horn blew the second time, for the school to begin. Mr. [Joel] Wood[,] the teacher, had been employed during the morning in making pens, ruling writing books, & making other preparations for the prompt discharge of his various duties. The school was opened by reading a portion of Scripture, singing an hymn, in which the scholars united, & prayer. The school is divided into nine classes, & is taught on the [Joseph] Lancasterian plan. One class was in the Alphabet, 3 in easy spelling lessons, one in easy reading lessons, & 4 in the Testament, English Rreader [*sic*], Geography & Christian Orator. Most of the scholars could write a legible hand. In the course of the forenoon there ["was" *interlined*] an exercise for speaking English, for the benefit of those not acquainted with it." Kingsbury relates, in regard to the school at Elliott, that "about the last of May, one of the Chiefs, who had five children in the school, & whose little daughter had been punished for misconduct, came & expressed much displeasure at the way in which the children were treated. He complained that they worked too much on the farm. He wished them to learn to read & write, & to learn trades. He also charged the Missionaries with misconduct in several other particulars. This talk had an unfavourable effect upon the school, & for a time weakened its government, particularly as it respected the large scholars. It soon became necessary to dismiss two of them. By taking a decided stand, order was again restored, & the schools went on in the usual way." Later letters from Kingsbury to Calhoun, dated 2/14/1823, 10/30/1823, and 1/6/1824, tend to indicate that the disaffected Chief was a Capt. Cole.

From Alexander Macomb, 1/16. He submits duplicate copies of the "Report of the Board of Engineers of a Reconnaissance of the Ohio & Mississippi Rivers" conducted in the last quarter of 1821. LS with En in DNA, RG 233, 17A-D1; FC in DNA, 21, 1:349; PC with En in House Document No. 35, 17th Cong., 2nd Sess. (The report had been prepared for Macomb on 12/22/1822 by Brig. Gen. Simon Bernard and Maj. Joseph G. Totten [DS in DNA, RG 233, 17A-D1; FC in DNA, 22, 479–493; PC with En in House Document No. 35, 17th Cong., 2nd Sess.; PC with En in *American State Papers: Commerce and Navigation*, 2:740–746].)

To the Rev. William Staughton, President, "Baptist B[oar]d &c.," Philadelphia, 1/16. Calhoun encloses an extract from "a letter from Gov[erno]r [Lewis] Cass, in order that the Baptist Missionary Society may name a suitable person to succeed Mr. Sears, as suggested by the Governor; which it is desirable should be done with as little delay as possible." FC in DNA, 72, E:381 (M-15:5).

Assignment of contract by John Bulkley, 1/17. Acting in his own name and as attorney for John Berry and Seth Hunt, Bulkley conveys to Howes Goldsborough of Havre de Grace, Md., their rights in the contract that they received from Jacob Lewis & Company on 4/6/1822 for delivery of stone at Old Point Comfort and the Rip Raps Shoal. CC in DNA, 227, 1:26–27.

From John Clark, Milledgeville, 1/17. He encloses a resolution of the Ga. legislature on 11/15/1822 "upon the subject of running the line between this State, and Alabama, which I will thank you to lay before the President of the United States [James Monroe] for his decision." LS with En in DNA, 1, C-390 (M-221:95); FC in G-Ar, Governors' Letterbooks, 1821–1829:90.

From Levi Ellmaker

Philad[elphi]a, Jan[uar]y 17, 1823

When I had the honour of dining with you last week, you suggested the propriety of being made more particularly acquainted with the education & qualifications of Thomas Green Clemson, who has applied for the appointment of Cadet in the Military Academy at West Point.

He has been principally educated at the University of Pa. He has studied English Grammer [*sic*] & arithmetic, & has some knowledge of algebra, has read all the books usually taught in Latin, including Ca[e]sar Delphini, Virgil & Horace—in Greek, Graeca Minora & Xenophon. His mind is thoughtful, inquisitive & aspiring—he is 16 years of age & well grown, being 5 f[ee]t 8 in[ches] in height, healthy & active.

I have no doubt, should he be appointed, he will fully justify the Expectations of the Institution and do honour to himself.

ALS in DNA, 15, 1823, 177 (M-688:25, frames 485–486). Note: In the same file can be found a letter from Ellmaker in Philadelphia dated 2/13 to someone who is not identified but who was probably a Congressman from Pa. In this letter Ellmaker reviewed his efforts in behalf of Clemson and asked his addressee to confer with Calhoun by way of "calling his attention particularly to Mr. Clemson" at a time when appointments were soon to be made.

From S[amuel] D. Ingham, [Representative from Pa.,] 1/17. He submits the names of —— Calvin, Campbell Meredith, and [John Clements] Stocker, [Jr.,] as applicants for Cadets' appointments. ALS in DNA, 15, 1823, 132–134 (M-688:25, frames 170–171).

From Horatio Seymour, [Senator from Vt.,] 1/17. In behalf of the [Senate] Committee on the Militia, he requests information relative to "the estimated expense of one year[']s clothing" for a soldier. ALS in DNA, 1, S-435 (M-221:96).

From Edward F. Tattnall, [Representative from Ga.,] 1/17. He requests, either for himself or for [Louis] McLane, [Chairman of the House Committee on Ways and Means,] "an estimate of the amount which would be required for the *partial* & *temporary* repairs of one of the Forts" in Savannah Harbor, either Fort Wayne or Fort Jackson. This would "prevent the *recurrence* of the insults of the armed privateers, that so frequently visit that port for the purpose of obtaining supplies, & of *recruiting men.*" Fort Jackson should be repaired. "A new (perhaps temporary) platform & a few gun carriages as well as rough temporary quarters for the Garrison, would be all that would be required." He believes that "an appropriation of money at this time for the purpose of purchasing materials to be employed some time hence" in the erection of permanent defenses for Savannah "can afford no relief in respect to the inconveniences & humiliating aggressions to which that place is almost monthly subjected." ALS in DNA, 30, 404.

From Lt. Col. George Bomford

Ordnance Dep[artmen]t, Jan[uar]y 18, 1823

In obedience to your directions to report to you upon that part of the call of the House of Representatives of the 6th inst[ant] which relates to the Lead Mines of the U[nited] States I have to state that this Dep[artmen]t is not in possession of more information upon the subject than is contained in the former reports made to your Dep[artmen]t on the 30 March & 12 Nov. last. From the former of said report[s] I therefore beg leave to quote the following:

"From those documents (received from the Gen[era]l Land Office) it would appear that Lead ore is computed to commence at mine a la motte in the County of *Geneveive* [*sic*], Missouri, extending in a northern direction as far as Mine a Dutrique, below Prairie du Chien, on the west side of the Mississip[p]i, and probably across the River at that place, averaging in breadth about 25 miles from east to west; that most of the Mines worked were in Washington County, St. Louis dist[an]t about 35 Miles south of the river Missouri, their extent about 50 miles in circumference, the whole number being stated at 33 to 45. Mines of lesser magnitude were worked in various sections of the late Missouri territory, and other Districts on the Mississip[p]i, of the actual value of which there appears no precise or authentic account from the papers received. There are also in the State of Illinois numerous mine Lands, and chiefly in the district ceded by the Sacs & Fox Indians—others within the U.S. Reservations. The leases which appear to have been formerly granted have expired; and it is stated by respectable persons that there are at present no Mines known to be worked in any of the mining Districts under any regular leases or authority, but that many in the last year were worked in the State of Missouri without such authority, & chiefly by new settlers or emigrants [immigrants]. There does not appear among the papers now produced, any account of what has been the actual receipt, by the U[nited] States, of the Mineral raised from the numerous discoveries of Lands producing it; and indeed it would appear that no Rents have been received from them. The number of Applicants up to the present time amount[s] to upwards of eighty, mostly from the State of Missouri; and with very few exceptions for the mine lands in the north west or Michigan territory. No Leases have yet been granted, for the reasons, for the reasons [*sic*] already stated." With regard to the old Leases granted, and the measures formerly pursued in relation to the Lead mines, it is presumed a Report thereof will more properly come from the Gen[era]l Land Office, under whose direction they took place; and for this purpose the papers received at this Dep[artmen]t from that Office will be returned in order to enable the Commissioner [John McLean] from those and other Records which may remain in the Treas[ur]y Dep[artmen]t to give the further information relative to the points in question which may seem desirable.

FC in DNA, 33, 1:68–69.

To [John Gaillard] and Philip P[endleton] Barbour, 1/18. Pursuant to a statute of 4/20/1818, Calhoun encloses a report about War Department Clerks and their salaries during 1822. LS with En in DNA, RG 46, 17A-F4; LS with En in DNA, RG 233, 17A-E4; FC with En in DNA, 4, 2:256 (M-220:1); PC with En in House Document No. 34, 17th Cong., 2nd Sess.

From James W[illiam] McCulloch, Collector's Office, Custom House, Baltimore, 1/18. He introduces James Madison Burn and recommends him for an appointment to be a Cadet. "The youth appears modest & sufficiently intelligent; has progressed well in arithmetic, & has [done] some reading in ancient & modern history. He is between 14 & 15 years of age. His father [James Burn] is a respectable man, of old standing, in the place, & the oldest officer of the Revenue in this District. His uniform correctness & good character entitle him to any offices [that is, services] of this kind from me." (The editor has found no evidence that the younger Burn ever received an appointment.) ALS in DNA, 15, 1823, 309 (M-688:27, frames 381–382); CC in DLC, James Madison Papers, vol. 70 (Presidential Papers Microfilm, Madison Papers, Reel 20).

George Bomford to John McLean, Commissioner, General Land Office

Ordnance Department, January 18th 1823

As the object of the call of the House of Representatives of the 6th instant, as far as it relates to the Lead mines, (referred to this Department by the Hon. Secretary of War,) embraces information required to be given, which is not in possession of this Office, otherwise than in the papers rec[eive]d from the General Land Office; and as those refer to, and give an account of Leases and other transactions, which took place whilst the same was under the direction of the Dep[artmen]t of the Treasury (thro' the above Office), I deem it to be the most correct course, to return to you the papers together with several plats of Surveys, in order that you may be enabled, from an examination thereof, and other documents which may remain in the Treasury Department, to add the information they may be found to contain.

FC in DNA, 33, 1:67.

From [former Col.] Robert Butler, near Nashville, 1/19. He encloses a copy of his letter [dated 1/19] to Col. R[oger] Jones. (In reply to Jones's suggestion of 12/26/1822 that a scheme was being plotted in Washington to have Butler accept an appointment to serve as Adjutant General and then resign in order that [James Gadsden] could be appointed, Butler assured Jones on 1/19/1823 that Butler would never accept the appointment under such circumstances. "With regard to my accepting the Appointment with the intention to *continue* in the office, should it be offered me, I will" reply in the affirmative, unless "a civil appointment adequate to the support of my family" is offered.) ALS with En in DNA, 1, B-231 (M-221:95).

From G[eorge] Bomford, 1/20. He reports the names and salaries of each Clerk in the Ordnance Department during 1822. John Morton, William Riddall, Thomas G. Ringgold, J.T. Alexander, and R[euben] Burdine received a total of $2,950. "The place of Mr. Ringgold has been occupied by Mr. Alexander, & since by Mr. Burdine, who will remain until the return of Mr. Ringgold from Green Bay." FC in DNA, 32, 3:284.

From Howes Goldsborough, Havre de Grace, [Md.,] 1/20. "After I had the pleasure of seeing you at Washington, I went to New York [City,] where I have obtained from Messrs. [John] Bulkley & Co., a regular transfer of thier [*sic*] contract. As I may be detained two or three days before I return to Washington, I have thought it my duty to advise you [of] the result of my journey." ALS in DNA, 30, [405].

To John McLean, 1/20. "On the subject of the resolution of the House of Representatives of the 6th instant, referred to this Department by you," Calhoun encloses a report from [George Bomford dated 1/18 concerning the leasing of lead mines]. FC in DNA, 3, 11:456 (M-6:11).

To V[IRGIL] MAXCY

War Dept., 20th Jan[uar]y 1823

I am so much engaged that I can do little more than acknowledge your very agreeable favour of the 17th Inst[ant; *not found*]. There can be no doubt, that Maryland is sound from the facts which you have stated, which concur with Dr. [Joseph] Kent's information. It is a great point gained and must be rendered secure.

A statement of the opinion of Maryland in relation to Mr. [William H.] C[rawfor]d either by a letter to be published in the paper here, or what is better an article in the Annapolis paper would have a desirable effect else where.

The Radicals cannot succe[e]d and Mr. C[rawfor]d's defeat I consider certain. He is going down rapidly, but cannot go too low for the publick interest. I do not think [Henry] Clay can become formidable. The West is too much divided, and if it were not it is too weak and young to carry the Presidential ["yet" *canceled*] election yet. My friends were never in better sperits [*sic*]. The cause must at least triumph, and I cannot be defeated. With the firm position of Pennsylvania my ultimate prospect is good.

Of [William H.] Winder I have the highest opinion, and he is now completely adopted in the Republican family. It is perhaps better than even his election to Congress. He and [Ezekiel Forman] Chambers must have a most decisive weight in your State.

My true position is fully understood by you, and as far as you can by conversation and correspondence safely make it known, it ought to be done. It will be manifest in six months that I am the only man from the slave holding States that can be elected.

If you can have a safe opportunity Mrs. [Floride Colhoun] Calhoun wishes the shoes to be sent by it, instead of the mail.

I forgot to say that MacDuffie [*sic*; George McDuffie] is doing well and expects to be ["home" *canceled and* "here" *interlined*] in February.

I will speak to Col. [Thomas L.] McKenney as you requested.

I am much pleased with Col. [*one word illegible*] and only regret that his stay has been so short, that I could not extend my acquaintance with him further.

I will be happy to have an opportunity to extend my knowledge personally with your principal citizens, and I trust you will afford me similar opportunities whenever you can. Your friend, J.C. Calhoun.

ALS in DLC, Galloway-Maxcy-Markoe Papers, vol. 32.

From JAMES PLEASANTS, JR., [Governor of Va.]

Executive Department, Richmond, Jan[uar]y 20th 1823

By an advice of [the Executive] Council [of Va.] bearing date on the 18th inst[ant] it becomes my duty to communicate to you some information on the situation of those important sections of our State, in the immediate neighbourhood of the Bellona Arsenal, belonging to the United States. It gives me particular pleasure that you are the individual with whom I have to confer on this subject, as you are, I know, well acquainted with it, and can immediately appreciate, indeed, anticipate my ideas on it; and I am sure, as far as it is in your power, [you] are perfectly disposed to do every thing which propriety may dictate. The Bellona Arsenal is situated on the Southern Bank of James River, about 12 miles above Richmond, in a country of great slave population, added to which is the immediate neighbourhood of the coal mines on both sides [of] the river, where a body of not less perhaps, than 2,000 able bodied slaves might be embodied on a short notice, indeed, may be said to be embodied in their ordinary occupation of mining. The nominal force of United States troops at the Arsenal, is I believe, a Captain's guard, or one Company. I have not the means of entirely correct information, but it is believed from sickness and other casualties, the actual force seldom, particularly at this time exceeds forty or thereabouts.

It is respectfully suggested, that such a force is inadequate to the defence of this important point, should a serious attempt be made to get possession of it; and though I do not know that there is reason to apprehend any thing particular at this, more than at other times, yet those entrusted with the safety of the State, ought not to lose sight of a state of things so serious as this is or might become. I am acquainted with the correspondence between this and the Department of War which has heretofore taken place on this subject, and without particular reference to it, beg leave to ask the attention of the Secretary to it at this time, well knowing his means to be limited, but believing the military depots in our slave holding districts to be at all times objects of serious attention, and that the Government of the United States as far as it may have conduced to encrease the risque, though acting with perfect propriety in doing so, will be disposed to afford the means of diminishing it, I leave the subject at this time to your [consideration] and am . . . .

ALS in DNA, 31, 1823, P; FC in Vi, Executive Letterbooks, 1/2/1823–10/2/1830, pp. 6–7. Note: For the earlier correspondence to which Pleasants referred, in which his predecessor as Governor of Va., Thomas Mann Randolph, had evinced a similar concern that arms in Bellona Arsenal should be protected against any possibility of being used in an insurrection by Negro slaves, see *The Papers of John C. Calhoun*, 6:56–57, 72, 84, and 88–89. Calhoun answered Pleasants on 2/6.

From N[athan] T[owson], 1/20. He reports the names of six Clerks employed in the Paymaster General's office during 1822 and the salary paid to each. FC in DNA, 291, 16:36.

To Philip P[endleton] Barbour, 1/21. Pursuant to a House resolution of 1/15 [DS in DNA, 1, R-109 (M-221:96)], Calhoun encloses a report from [Jacob] Brown [dated 1/20 (LS in DNA, RG 233, 17A-E4; FC in DLC, Jacob Brown Papers, Letterbooks, 2:221–222) about the strategic value and the estimated cost of the military road under construction between Plattsburg and Sackets Harbor, N.Y.]. LS with En in DNA, RG 233, 17A-E4; FC in DNA, 4, 2:257 (M-220:1); PC with En in House Document No. 33, 17th Cong., 2nd Sess.; PC with En in *American State Papers: Miscellaneous*, 2:987–988.

To [former Lt. Col.] Robert Carr, Adjutant General of Pa., Philadelphia, 1/21. Calhoun acknowledges Carr's letter of 1/17 [LS in DNA, 15, 1823, 176 (M-688:25, frames 475–477)] and, "a few days previously, the return of the Militia of the Commonwealth of Pennsylv[ani]a for the year 1822, which is perfectly satisfactory & sufficient." Carr's son, John B. Carr, will be considered when this year's appointments to the Military Academy are made, in February or March. FC in DNA, 13, 1:183 (M-91:1). (The editor has discovered no evidence that John B. Carr ever received an appointment as a Cadet.)

Joseph M. Hernandez, [Delegate from the Territory of Fla.,] to John Quincy Adams, 1/21. Hernandez encloses a copy of a letter dated 12/11/1822 from Lt. Col. Abr[a]m Eustis to Waters Smith, Mayor of St. Augustine, and Smith's reply of 12/26, both of which relate to the controversy between the civil and military authorities in St. Augustine about certain public property. According to Hernandez, the City Council[men] of St. Augustine "consider themselves, & very justly, entitled to a considerable portion" of the land claimed by Eustis. A resolution submitted by Hernandez concerning similar property in Pensacola has been referred by the House of Representatives to the Committee on Lands. Hernandez asks that the enclosures be transmitted to [James Monroe] to prevent Eustis from interfering until a final decision is made. ALS with Ens in DNA, 1, H-267 (M-221:95).

To J[ohn] P[endleton] Kennedy

Washington, 21st Jan[uar]y 1823

In answer to your letter of the 12th Dec[embe]r [*not found*], I am happy to inform you that the President [James Monroe] has nominated you as Secretary of Legation to the Mission to Chili [*sic*], the climate of which, I have no doubt, ["that" *canceled*] you will find highly congenerial [*sic*] to your constitution.

The appearetly [*sic*] sound state of the politicks of Maryland has afforded to all of the real friends of the country much pleasure and affords strong reasons to hope that the policy of the present administration will be fully sustained.

ALS in MdBP.

To Joseph Pearson, [former Representative from N.C.,] Washington

War Department, January 21st 1823

I have just received the report of the Academic Board of the Military Academy on the January examination, and I regret very much to find that your brother [Giles William Pearson] has failed to pass that examination.

I have directed [Bvt.] Major [Sylvanus] Thayer to provide him with his transportation and such an allowance of pay as will enable him to return home. As it may be satisfactory to you to know the grounds of his failure, the enclosed copy of the decision of the Board in the case of your brother is transmitted for your information.

I avail myself of this occasion to assure you of the respect and esteem with which I remain . . . .

FC in DNA, 13, 1:184 (M-91:1). Note: Compare Calhoun's letter to Joseph Pearson dated 1/27.

To Dr. James Spann, Augusta, Ga., 1/21. Calhoun reports that Spann's nephew, Cadet Albert J. Dozier, was tried in 12/1822 by a court-martial and was sentenced to dismissal from the Military Academy. FC in DNA, 13, 1:184 (M-91:1).

To Charles J[ohn] Steedman, Charleston, S.C., 1/21. Calhoun announces the academic failure and dismissal of his son, Thomas Steedman, at the Military Academy. FC in DNA, 13, 1:184 (M-91:1).

From Thomas Thorpe, [Superintendent of the War and Navy Departments' Buildings]

Washington, Jan[uar]y 21st 1823

In obediance [*sic*] to a duty that I conceive indispensable, I wish to communicate facts that exist at the building occupied, by the War Department, and [which] is under my superintendance [*sic*].

From the commenc[e]ment of the occupation of that building, there has [*sic*] been from 10 to 12 men employed as messengers, that are inlisted soldiers, there has been almost, a continual changing of those men, some for the cause of drunkenness, others for misdemeanors of another nature.

From the circumstance, that persons in our country, who has [*sic*] to inlist, in order to live, we cannot expect to find many that are men of varasity [*sic*] and standing, such as ought to have charge of the public offices. At this time the Q[uarte]r M[aster] Gen[era]l's Dep[artmen]t, Subsistance [*sic*] dep[artmen]t[,] Serg[ean]t [*sic*; Surgeon] Ge[nera]l[']s dep[artmen]t[,] Pension office, Ordnance Dep[artmen]t, [Mr. Nathaniel] Cutting[']s office, and the Engin[ee]r Dep[artmen]t are attended by those men, who have access to all these rooms at all times Sundays not excepted, the building is not altogether fire proff [*sic*], and I am fearfull [*sic*] with all the precautions I am capable of using; if this state of things should continue the public may suffer loss.

ALS in DNA, 1, T-92 (M-221:96). NOTE: Calhoun replied on 1/28.

From Duncan G. Campbell and James Meriwether, New Town, [Cherokee Nation,] 1/22. These commissioners write that they have made very little progress in their mission [to hold a treaty to obtain a cession of land from the Eastern Cherokees]. "This nation manifests a stronger reluctance and obstinacy . . . than on any previous occasion." Only one Chief has visited the commissioners, and he was "of subordinate grade and influence. A few of the Nations have come in, but all pursue an independent course, and positively decline drawing rations." Believing it impossible to accomplish the commissioners' goal before their commissions expire, they request that plans be made to renew their commissions or to appoint successors. They enclose a circular sent by them and the commissioners for Ga., Thomas Glasscock and James Blair, to the Cherokee Chiefs. LS with DS in DNA, 1, C-262 (M-221:95); PEx in *American State Papers*: *Public Lands*, 3:626.

To William Eustis, Chairman, [House] Committee on Military Affairs, 1/22. In reply to Eustis's letter of 1/4 [ALS in DNA, RG 233, 17A-C16.4; LS in DNA, 1, E-71 (M-221:95)] "requesting a statement of the payments made in each year to Officers of the Army on account of transportation, since the last reduction of the Army," Calhoun encloses a statement prepared by [Peter Hagner on 1/21 (LS with En in DNA, RG 233, 17A-E4; FC in DNA, 53, 28:224; PC with En in House Document No. 38, 17th Cong., 2nd Sess.)]. In reply to Eustis's letter of 1/17 [LS in DNA, 1, E-75 (M-221:95)] "respecting the allowances of interest made to public officers or agents on money advanced by them for the public service," Calhoun encloses a letter and enclosures from [Peter Hagner dated 1/22 (FC in DNA, 53, 28:226)]. Calhoun encloses also a "statement specifying the nature and extent of the work done, and the kind and quality of materials, delivered [to] the several Fortifications under the appropriation for the year 1822," prepared by [Alexander Macomb on 1/17 (LS with Ens in DNA, RG 233, 17A-E4; FC in DNA, 21, 1:350–351; PC with Ens in House Document No. 39, 17th Cong., 2nd Sess.)]. FC in DNA, 4, 2:257 (M-220:1).

From N[athan] T[owson], 1/22. "I have the honour to report for the information of the Military Committee of the Senate, that none of the Paymasters whose appointments are submitted to the Senate for confirmation, are considered in arrears to the United States. They are all charged with public money at this time, for current disbursements: but there is every reason to believe that it will be faithfully accounted for. The pay department required a full settlement of accounts before recommending any Paymaster to the President for reappointment. None of those now submitted to the Senate, were [*sic*] found in arrears when their term of Office expired except Capt. J[acob] W. Albright who had a balance against him on final settlement of 926.22 dollars. His appointment was of course suspended until that amount was paid to the Treasury of the United States." FC in DNA, 291, 16:36–37.

To Philip P[endleton] Barbour and [John Gaillard], 1/23. Pursuant to an act of 3/3/1809, Calhoun submits a statement of contingent expenses during 1822, prepared by [William Lee on 1/22 (LS in DNA, 1, L-66 [M-221:96]; FC in DNA, 51, 8:246; DS in DNA, RG 233, 17A-E4; DU in DNA, RG 46, 17A-F4)]. LS with DS in DNA, RG 233, 17A-E4; LS with DU in DNA, RG 46, 17A-F4; FC in DNA, 4, 2:257 (M-220:1); PC with Ens in House Document No. 41, 17th Cong., 2nd Sess.

From Samuel Dakin, New Hartford (Oneida County), N.Y., 1/23. As the attorney for the Stockbridge Indians, he has been requested to ascertain the amounts of money that have been paid by the government to Solomon U. Hendrick and to John Sergeant, Jr. "There is much suspicion, among the Indians of this tribe, that Hendrick and Sergeant have practiced some frauds" when Hendrick and Sergeant have acted as agents for the Indians. It is the wish of this tribe that no grant of land be made to any white man or society of white men within the tract of land purchased for the Indians at Green Bay. "If any petition or request, purporting to be executed by" the Indians should be presented to any branch of the government, the Stockbridge Indians hope that their superintendents or their attorney will be informed of it before any definite action is taken. ALS in DNA, 1, D-154 (M-221:95).

From Capt. J[ames] H. Hook, Washington, 1/23. Having carefully examined [Thomas] Thorp[e]'s letter of 1/21 to Calhoun, Hook states the procedures that he will institute to increase the safety of the public buildings. Thorp[e]'s fears for the security of these buildings "appear to be excited," and his "assertions respecting the want of character in the orderlies generally would have applied better if made a year since." Hook lists the orderlies and the buildings to which they are assigned. ALS in DNA, 1, H-191 (M-221:95).

From [James] Lloyd, [Senator from Mass.,] 1/23. He called upon [James Monroe] recently as a member of a committee seeking compensation to Mass. and Me. for their militias' services during the War of 1812. Apprehensive that certain papers had not been made available for Calhoun's consideration, Lloyd left with [Monroe] a recapitulation of the circumstances of the claim. Lloyd asks Calhoun to obtain this "historical sketch" from [Monroe]. LU in DNA, 2, L-1823 (M-222:23); CC in DNA, RG 233, 18A-D1, vol. 260; PC's with Ens in Senate Document No. 43 and House Document No. 83, 18th Cong., 1st Sess.; PC with Ens in *American State Papers*: *Military Affairs*, 3:11–18.

From N[inian] Edwards, [Senator from Ill.,] 1/24. He has mentioned to [James Monroe] the possibility of asking for an appropriation for extinguishing the Indian title to certain lands in Mo. "This subject produces a most unreasonable excitement in that State." [David] Barton, [Senator from Mo.,] "has just introduced a resolution to enquire into the propriety of appropriating a sum of money for the object alluded to—probably some set speeches may be made." Edwards mentions these circumstances in order that any action taken "may be done to the best advantage." ALS in DNA, 1, E-86 (M-221:95).

From George Gibson, 1/24. As ordered, he submits "a list of 'all newspapers, Journals and other periodical publications, charts and instruments & maps and prints, taken at the public expense'" in Gibson's office, together with "a Catalogue of 'all books, which have been purchased at the public expense' for this Department, from the commencement of the Commissariat to the present date." FC in DNA, 191, 3:214.

From Joseph Lovell, 1/24. He lists various articles purchased for the Surgeon General's office since its establishment [in 1818] with its contingent funds. One of these articles, a map of Mexico, "was taken for the War office & is I presume now there." FC in DNA, 243, 1:143.

To [William Wirt]

War Department, 24 January 1823

The Secretary of War requests the opinion of the Attorney General on the following points.

Jacob Lewis & Co. in the year 1819 entered into a contract with the U[nited] States for supplying 80,000 perches of stone at Old Point Comfort; and they procured Messrs. J[ohn] Bulkley & Co. as their sureties for the faithful execution of the same. Messrs. Lewis & Co. finding difficulties in the fulfil[l]ment of their contract requested that their sureties might be permitted to complete it, and thereby redeem the advances made by the U[nited] States on account of the said contract, which J. Lewis & Co. were unable to do. J. L[ewis] & Co. were willing in case the Government would consent to the securities continuing the contract, to make a complete transfer of the same to their said securities, which was accordingly done, the Attorney General being of opinion that the transfer might be legally made with the consent of the Secretary of War. Thereupon the said securities, J. Bulkl[e]y & Co., were informed that the contract ["with" *canceled*] of J. Lewis & Co. had been duly transferred to the said securities, and that the Secretary of War, under that opinion, acceded to their proposition for the execution of the contract agreeable to the original conditions, and to their continuing therein as long as there should be ["satisfactory" *interlined*] evidence of their ability to comply with the requisitions which might be made upon them respecting it.

Messrs. Bulkley & Co. finding it impossible to comply with further requisitions, now propose to transfer their right in the contract to Mr. H[owes] Goldsborough, and do make the transfer agreeably to the paper herewith transmitted for your inspection.

Doctor [Francis] Le Baron, one of the firm of J. Lewis & Co., the original contractors, now objects to this transfer, notwithstanding he had before assented thereto.

Will such transfer be legal if the Government consent thereto?

LS in DNA, 25, 120.

From William Wirt, Attorney General, 1/24. "I am of the opinion, on the statement you have done me the honor to submit for my opinion to-day, that Messrs. [John] Bulkeley [*sic*; Bulkley] &

Co. have the same power over the contract for stone at Old Point Comfort which Jacob Lewis & Co. had before their transfer of it to Messrs. B[ulkley] & Co. What that power is and what the legal nature and consequences of the transfer [are] may be seen by reference to my opinion of the 16 March '22 in this case and my opinion of the 20 Sept. 1821, with relation to the transfer of [Samuel] Hawkins' contract. Doct[or Francis] Le Baron's objection comes too late: he had previously parted with all control over the subject." The transfer sent for Wirt's inspection is "insufficient. It is the act of one partner only and not in the course of partnership transactions. One partner can do any act which falls within the purposes which it is the object of the association to accomplish, but one partner alone cannot do an act which virtually dissolves and annihilates the association." "To do this, the partner who acts must have a special power of attorney from the rest of the firm authorizing him to do the act: and even if such a power did exist in this case (which does not appear by the documents sent me) still this transfer would be imperfect, because although John Bulkley professes to act with the name of the company, the terms of transfer are all in the singular number." ALS in DNA, 30, 407; FC in DNA, 113, B:115 (T-412:2).

From Lewis Cass

Cumberland, [Md.,] Jan[uar]y 25, 1823

I have the honour to request that the unexpended balance of the appropriation for the support of the Blacksmiths, teachers, &c., under the Chicago treaty may be remitted to me at Detroit.

I received when in Washington a note from Mr. [Samuel S.?] Hamilton enclosing a letter from Mr. Connelly respecting the Sac Indian exhibiting [that is, who was being exhibited] as a curiosity in Georgetown. I made an effort to see the Indian but was not successful. I, however, saw the person in whose custody he is, and I have no doubt but the Indian is anxious to return to his Country.

This spectacle is certainly not a very desirable one, in the immediate vicinity of the Government, and I cannot but recommend that some person be employed to convey him to Erie or Cleaveland [*sic*] and secure him a passage to Detroit, where I can make the subsequent arrangements for him.

LS in DNA, 1, C-341 (M-221:95); FC in DNA, 76 (M-1:5, p. 124).

To William Ward, Choctaw Agency, 1/25. His bill for $3,440 in favor of Henry Randall, Agent for the U.S. at the Choctaw trading house, has been submitted for payment by the War Department. "I have to request you will without delay forward to me as directed by my letter of the 13th of December last your draft on the Louisville Bank, to enable me to meet it." FC in DNA, 72, E:382 (M-15:5).

To P[ATRICK] FARRELLY, [Representative from Pa.]

Department of War, January 27th 1823

I have the honor of advising you in answer to the application of Col. Robert Carr, Adjutant General of the Pennsylvania militia, that directions have been given to the Ordnance Officer for the supply of Artillery swords. There are no Riflemen or Cavalry at present in the service of the United States, neither have any systems of exercise or maneuvre, been recognized for such Corps. [Henri Dominique] Lallemand['] s Treatise has lately been introduced as the system for the Artillery arm, [and] directions have been given for the forwarding of a copy of that work to Col. Carr, together with a copy of the General regulations for the Army.

FC in DNA, 3, 11:457 (M-6:11).

To [John Gaillard], 1/27. In compliance with a Senate resolution of 1/15 concerning the petition of Mrs. Eleanor Lawrance [for compensation for her property confiscated during the War of 1812], Calhoun states that his views about the petition are contained in correspondence that accompanies it. He encloses other relevant documents. LS in DNA, 25, 134; LS in DNA, RG 46, 17A-F4; FC in DNA, 4, 2:258 (M-220:1).

To Charles Hooks, Representative [from N.C.], 1/27. Calhoun acknowledges Hooks's letter of 1/22 (ALS in DNA, 30, 406) "requesting that the report of the Engineers on the Survey of the Coast of No[rth] Carolina made two years ago, might be forwarded to him." It "is not customary to send the reports of the Engineers out of the Department, as they are very valuable & important"; but Hooks may examine the survey at his convenience in either the War or Engineer office. FC in DNA, 21, 1:352.

To JOSEPH PEARSON, Washington

War Department, Washington, 27 Jan[uar]y 1823
Since I addressed you on the 21st instant conveying to you the decision of the Academic Board in relation to your brother Giles W[illiam] Pearson, I have the pleasure to inform you that a subsequent report has been received, which is more favorable to him, a copy of which is enclosed for your gratification. Should you desire that he be reappointed, you are requested to signify your pleasure to this Department; and he shall be reappointed, agreeably to the recommendation of the Academic Board, to join the Academy with the next fourth class.

FC in DNA, 13, 1:186–187 (M-91:1). NOTE: Joseph Pearson replied quite gratefully, [apparently from Washington,] on 1/27, indicating that Giles William Pearson would accept the proffered reappointment. ALS in DNA, 30, 410. He did accept a reappointment on 4/16/1823. ALS in DNA, 15, 1822, 46 (M-688:20). (The same file and microfilm have several documents of 1821 and 1822 concerning Giles William Pearson.) For documents indicating that the Cadet had failed for a second time, see Joseph Pearson's letter to Calhoun dated 7/10/1824 (ALS with En in DNA, 30, 627) and letters of 7/26/1824 from Calhoun to Joseph Pearson and from J[ohn] L[ind] Smith to [Sylvanus] Thayer in DNA, 13, 1:329 (M-91:1). Giles William Pearson did not graduate. *Register of Graduates and Former Cadets, United States Military Academy . . . 1802–1946* (New York: [1946]), p. 122.

To Capt. J[ames] H. Hook, Washington, 1/28. "I approve of the arrangements respecting the orderlies attached to the several Offices in this building, suggested in your letter of the 23d instant, and you will accordingly take the necessary steps to give it effect." FC in DNA, 3, 11:457 (M-6:11).

To Thomas Metcalfe, Chairman, House Committee on Indian Affairs, 1/28. Answering Metcalfe's request of 1/15 [ALS in DNA, 1, M-197 (M-221:96)], Calhoun encloses information about Indian land titles in Fla. Pursuant to Metcalfe's request of 1/13, Calhoun submits also partial information about the extinguishment of Indian titles to lands in Ga. under the compact of 1802 with that State. LS (misdated 1/28/1822) with Ens in DNA, RG 233, 17A-E4; FC (dated 1/27/1823) in DNA, 72, E:382 (M-15:5); PEx with Ens in House Document No. 51, 17th Cong., 2nd Sess.; PEx with Ens in *American State Papers*: *Indian Affairs*, 2:411–416.

From W[illiam] Plumer, Jr., [Representative from N.H.,] 1/28. "I take the liberty, agreeably to your request, to remind you of the bill respecting frauds on the U.S. which you were so good as to promise to send me, but which I have not yet received." (An AEI by Calhoun directs [Peter] Hagner "to furnish a copy of the bill which he prepared for Col. [John] Williams, [Senator from Tenn.]." An AEI by Hagner indicates that he has "mislaid or lost the original draft of the Act." Hagner believes that two copies have been furnished to [Samuel L.] Southard, [Senator from N.J.,] one by [Calhoun] and one by Williams. "Will the Sec[retar]y of War request Judge Southard to return one copy or shall I do so[?]") ALS in DNA, 1, P-192 (M-221:96).

To Thomas Thorp[e], Superintendent of Public Buildings

Department of War, January 28th 1823

Captain [James H.] Hook has been directed to give effect to the following arrangement respecting the orderlies on duty at the several Offices in this building.

The orderlies will have free access to the Offices to which they belong for the purpose of cleaning them, and extinguishing the fires in the afternoon, which will be completed as soon as the Officers and Clerks leave them, and for making fires in the morning which must be done before 9 O[']Clock in the morning—and no office will be opened after it be closed in the afternoon, unless by order of the Chief of the Office. You will attend at the closing and opening of the Offices.

FC in DNA, 3, 11:457 (M-6:11).

To William Ward, Choctaw Agency, 1/28. Calhoun directs Ward to deliver to James C. Dickson the iron chest that is understood to belong to the Agency if the Agency does not need it; but if it cannot be spared, Ward is to report that fact to Calhoun. FC's of two drafts of this letter (neither of which has been canceled) in DNA, 72, E:382–383 (M-15:5).

From D[uncan] G. Campbell, Cherokee Agency, 1/29. He informs Calhoun of the death of [Return J.] Meigs. "What will be the effect of this catastrophe upon our negotiations, we are unable to say. We hope however that the circumstance will not retard us. Our previous difficulties were sufficiently formidable. The Chiefs have not yet Cowered. They are now in Council, and will probably meet us, en masse, or by deputation in a few days." A nephew of the deceased Agent has "deposited in the hands of the Commissioners the sum of $1,222, said to belong to the Missionary fund. This will be disposed of as you may direct." ALS in DNA, 1, C-269 (M-221:95).

From Alexander Macomb, 1/29. In reply to a House resolution of 1/17 (DS in DNA, 30, 411) concerning the expediency of repairing the fort at Smithville, N.C., or of erecting new fortifications at a more suitable site, Macomb reports that it would be better to erect entirely new fortifications for defending the entrance into the Cape Fear River. A survey of possible sites has not yet been received. Although Smithville is classified as being of the second priority, a fort there is important. LS in DNA, RG 233, 17A-E4; FC in DNA, 21, 1:354–355.

To Reuben H. Walworth, Member, House Committee on Military Affairs, 1/29. Calhoun answers Walworth's inquiry of 1/28 (ALS with En in DNA, 30, 411) concerning the fort at Smithville, N.C., by enclosing the letter to Calhoun from Alexander Macomb dated 1/29. LS with En in DNA, RG 233, 17A-E4; FC in DNA, 4, 2:259 (M-220:1).

To "Lewis [Louis]" McLane, Chairman, House Committee on Ways and Means, 1/30. "Since the annual estimates of appropriations for this year were submitted, it has been ascertained that the sum of $9,500 in addition to the sum of $120,857 will be required for the cloathing [*sic*] of the Army, making the sum of $136,357 necessary to be appropriated for 1823." An additional $5,000 will be required to pay the Creek annuity under the treaty of 1/8/1821. Calhoun suggests the propriety of a general provision for paying this annuity "instead of making annual appropriations in each year for each instalment as it becomes due." Calhoun submits an estimate [of 1/16/1823 by William Lee (DS in DNA, 1, L-94 [M-221:96])] of $1,088.89 as payment for the services of Beekman M. Van Buren as a member of the court-martial for N.Y. militia delinquents. Calhoun also proposes the purchase for $8,500 of a tract of land adjoining the Military Academy. As the enclosed report [from Alexander Macomb of 1/30 (LS with Ens in DNA, RG

233, 18A-C19.1; FC in DNA, 21, 1:355)] shows, acquisition of this tract, upon which there is located a "publick House" [tavern], is of "great importance to the character and efficiency of the Military Academy." FC in DNA, 4, 2:258 (M-220:1).

From Joseph McMinn, New Canton, Tenn., 1/30. He acknowledges Calhoun's letter of 12/30/1822. "The mode you have adopted with the Debtors meets my entire approbation; it affords them an opertunity [*sic*] of Discharging their notes in the only Currency now in circulation in this State." "Your instructions shall be promptly attended to, and due notice given of the progress, that may be made." ALS in DNA, 1, M-220 (M-221:96).

To [James Monroe], 1/30. In compliance with a Senate resolution of 1/28 [DS in DNA, 1, S-288 (M-221:96)] asking for "the instructions to the Commissioners nominated to treat with Indians for the extinguishment of Indian titles" in Ga., Calhoun encloses copies. LS with En in DNA, RG 46, 17B-C2; FC in DNA, 6, 2:108–109 (M-127:2). (The En is a copy of instructions from Calhoun to John Floyd, Freeman Walker, and John A. Cuthbert dated 6/15/1822.)

From Col. J[OSIAH] SNELLING

Fort St. Anthony, [later in Minn.,] Jan[uar]y 30th 1823

I beg leave to solicit your interest in favour of Serg[ean]t W[illia]m P. Roberts of the 5th Reg[imen]t of Inf[antr]y who is desirous to be admitted into the Military Academy at the next annual examination; a train of misfortunes brought this young man into the service about two years ago, since which his conduct has acquired him the esteem of every officer in the corps. He is uncommonly well educated, free from bad habits and possesses talents of a superior order; he is a native of Connecticut & now about nineteen years of age.

ALS in PHi. NOTE: The editor has discovered no evidence that Roberts ever became a Cadet.

From W[illiam] Hickey, [Clerk, Pension Office,] Washington, 1/31. Calhoun directed on 11/20/1822 that all claims to pensions for invalids should be suspended except those from claimants under the statute of 2/4/1822 who offer medical certificates given by Army Surgeons at the time of discharge and from those who submit satisfactory proof of having been wounded in action. Hickey believes it to be his duty to discuss these requirements now, while Calhoun is attempting to formulate general regulations for invalid pensions and before the suspended applications will be reconsidered, probably after the adjournment of Congress. The most pertinent question is the nature of the disability. Hickey reviews all relevant statutory statements concerning disabilities from 6/7/1785 through 2/4/1822. He is alarmed that efforts in behalf of claimants to invalid pensions have been comparatively ignored since 1818 and that the routine, easy task of copying letters has monopolized the Clerks' work; indeed, claims by disabled veterans would have been neglected altogether but for Calhoun's inherent benevolence and generosity of heart. The invalid claims business increases and becomes more difficult daily; it necessitates checking muster rolls. Because of Hickey's experience with pensions, he asks Calhoun to give him the responsibility of processing the pending claims. In deciding what disabilities should entitle an applicant to a pension, Calhoun will find help in Hickey's summary of the statutes, in former Attorney General [Richard] Rush's opinion concerning that of 3/16/1802, and in Surgeon General [Joseph Lovell's] opinion as to that of 5/17/1822. Hickey encloses a report of the "Number of Deaths of Invalid and Revolutionary Pensioners reported in 1822." ALS with En in DNA, 1, H-144 (M-221:97).

To R[UFUS] KING, Senator [from N.Y.]

War Department, [Friday,] Jan[uar]y 31, 1823

The Secretary of War presents his compliments to Mr. King, and in answer to his note of yesterday [LU in DNA, 30, 414] stating that the report on Mrs. [Eleanor] Lawrance's petition, called for by the Senate, had not been received, although he had understood directions for it to be sent had been given on Monday last, has the honor to inform him that the packet in which the report was contained, addressed to the President of the Senate, [John Gaillard,] was deposited in the post office on Monday last, by the Messenger of the War Department. The Secretary of War regrets that any delay in its receipt should have occurred, and would be very sorry if it should be attended with the consequences apprehended by Mr. King.

FC in DNA, 21, 1:357.

To James Lloyd, [Senator from Mass.,] 1/31. The President [James Monroe] has considered the claims of Mass. for the service of her militia during the War of 1812, and [Peter Hagner] has been directed to audit the claims "in conformity to principles which have been established and applied in the settlement of similar claims." Calhoun reminds Lloyd "that the settlement must be subordinate to the general views in relation to the constitutional power of the general government over the militia of the State, which were taken by the Department when the accounts were originally presented and discussed on its [*sic*] general merits." Lloyd will receive soon some "abstracts of the rules under which the settlement of the accounts [of other States] have been made." FC in DNA, 3, 11:458 (M-6:11); CC in DNA, RG 233, 18A-D1, vol. 260; PC's in Senate Document No. 43 and House Document No. 83, 18th Cong., 1st Sess.; PC in *American State Papers: Military Affairs*, 3:18.

From L[ouis] McLane, 1/31. "As it will be impracticable for the Committee of Ways & Means to report a Bill making appropriations for Fortifications, for the present year, until I receive your answer to my letter on that subject, calling for a designation of the sum required for each object, and the nature & progress of the works, I have to beg your early attention to this subject." (Copies of eight letters dated 6/8/1818–3/11/1820 from William Lee to Col. James R. Mullany are also found in this file. They discuss Mullany's accounts, mentioning specifically a balance due from Mullany to the U.S. government of $8,951.95.) ALS in DNA, 1, M-216 (M-221:96).

To "Lewis [Louis]" McLane, Chairman, House Committee on Ways and Means, 1/31. In reply to McLane's letter of 1/29 [LS in DNA, 1, M-200 (M-221:96)], Calhoun transmits [Thomas S. Jesup's] detailed estimate [of 10/9/1822 (DS in DNA, RG 233, 18A-C19.2)], which explains "the nature of items of expenditure for which the sum of $297,148 in addition to the unexpended balance, is required" for the Quartermaster bureau during 1823. Calhoun encloses [George Bomford's] estimate [of 1/31 (DS in DNA, RG 233, 18A-C19.2)] and explanations concerning the $360,000 "required for National Armories, for the current expenses of the Ordnance, and for Arsenals." The $90,000 for contingent Indian affairs expenses will be used for salaries, supplies such as agricultural implements and iron and steel for blacksmith shops, transportation of annuities, rations for Indians, the travel expenses of Indian deputations to Washington, medical aid to sick Indians, and other expenses that cannot be anticipated. In regard to arrearages prior to 7/1/1817, for which $35,000 are asked, Calhoun replies that they arose almost wholly out of the War [of 1812]. The enclosed statement [from William Lee of 1/31 (DS in DNA, RG 233, 18A-C19.2)] "furnishes the names of the members of the [N.Y.] Militia General Court-Martial of which General [Gerard] Steddiford was President, whose accounts have been rendered and settled since the last session of Congress, as well as the names of those members whose accounts have not been finally settled for want of an appropriation for which Estimates have been made, and which have been transmitted to the Committee." In reply to another letter of 1/29 from McLane (LS in DNA, 30, 413), Calhoun encloses a report [from Alexander Macomb of 1/29 (LS in DNA, RG 233, 18A-C19.2; FC in DNA, 21, 1:357)] "relative to the distribution of the Estimate of $500,000 for fortifications for 1823" and supplying additional data concerning the progress of the fortifications for which appropriations have been made. LS with Ens in DNA, RG 233, 18A-C19.2; FC in DNA, 4, 2:259–260 (M-220:1).

From James Monroe

[*Ca.* January 31, 1823?]

I have examined with attention the subject which has been submitted to me, and am of opinion, that the employment of a certain number of [Army] officers in the bureaux of the Department of War, is economical and conducive to the public interest. Their knowledge of the various duties of the Department, acquired by military experience, enables them to render services to which others would be less competent. This practice, therefore, which was adopted at an early period, appears to me to have been judicious, and ought to be adhered to. In making the selection, care should be taken not to interfere with the calls of the service, or to extend the detail further than may be absolutely necessary, and to give to those thus employed a reasonable compensation only, having regard to the salaries allowed by law to Clerks performing similar duties, to be paid out of the contingent fund of the Army. Those who have been disabled by wounds, or otherwise, ought to be preferred.

CC in DNA, 2, P-1823 (M-222:23).

From [James Monroe, *ca.* 1/31?]. He asks Calhoun to prepare a message [for Monroe to submit to Congress] proposing an appropriation for the extinguishment of Indian titles to lands in Mo. and in Ark. [Territory]. ALU in DNA, 1, P-202 (M-221:96).

From [the Rev.] William Staughton, Philadelphia, 1/31. He reports that the [American Baptist] Board of [Commissioners for Foreign] Missions will select, "as early as possible," a "suitable substitute" to replace Mr. Sears. ALS in DNA, 1, S-307 (M-221:96).

FEBRUARY 1823

CALHOUN PLEADED ON THE 23RD FOR HELP IN HIS PRESIDENTIAL campaign: "it will be necessary to remove the impression of my withdrawal" from the race; a nomination by Pennsylvania would counteract that erroneous idea. On the 14th the missionary to the Choctaws wrote, "The objects & plan of the schools are I believe better understood now, than at any former period." On the 12th and the 26th Calhoun exchanged "talks" with a Western Cherokee deputation. Letters from George Graham on the 6th and the 22nd sought to liquidate the Factory system of Indian trade before the first of May. Better maps and geographies, a promotion for Sylvanus Thayer, the finances of Calhoun's mother-in-law, an employee who was absent without leave, a larger garrison for Bellona Arsenal—these are some of the other topics that concerned Calhoun.

From [2nd] Lt. C[lark] Burdine, Fever River, Ill., 2/1. Three lessees are digging for lead and are finding it in large quantities. Burdine transmits a weather report for last month and a census of the civilized persons who live near the mines. He has almost recovered from his illness and may soon be able to travel. ALS in DNA, 31, 1823, B.

From [1st] Lt. W[illiam] S[cott] Colquhoun of the 7th Infantry [Regiment], Fort Smith, 2/1. He discusses the reasons for recent hostilities between the [Western] Cherokees and the Osages. Indians of "the latter nation on the Osage river under *White Hair* declare that they never acceded to the treaty of Fort Smith and may therefore be considered at open war with the Cherokees. Those on the Arkansaw river have much reason to be dissatisfied." First, they were coerced into signing the treaty. Second, they "were not put in possession of Tom Graves the white Savage who murdered the Osage prisoners that had been put under his charge." Third, an attack made upon them during a journey to Fort Smith can be attributed to Choctaws, Cherokees, and white men. The Osages have "openly declared vengeance against Graves." Graves has charged recently that the Osages killed one of his men. "Hunters have been very successful this winter and large quantities of skins have pass[e]d this place. Herds of Buffalo have been within 15 miles of us all the winter nearly and none of us have [*sic*] had a shot at them. The weather has been very cold." If it "had not been for the Skin of an immense Buffalo I should have suffered much having been for the most part badly quartered." Colquhoun had hoped to be able to report in this letter his adventures to the falls of the Verdigris. The sudden departure of Col. [Mathew] Arbuckle for Baton Rouge and the unwillingness of Capt. [William] Davenport, Colquhoun's present commanding officer, to interfere in Indian affairs prevented Colquhoun from going. ALS in DNA, 1, C-376 (M-221:95).

To [John Gaillard] and Philip P[endleton] Barbour, 2/1. In compliance with a statute of 5/1/1820, Calhoun encloses a detailed statement [by Richard Cutts of 1/31 (LS in DNA, 1, C-254 [M-221:95]; DS in DNA, RG 46, 17A-F4)] of appropriations and expenditures during 1822, with a column showing the balances that can be spent in 1823. LS with En in DNA, RG 46, 17A-F4; LS in DNA, RG 233, 17A-E4; FC in DNA, 4, 2:260 (M-220:1); PC with En in House Document No. 55, 17th Cong., 2nd Sess.

To Peter Hagner, 2/1. Calhoun sends to Hagner a copy of Calhoun's letter of 1/31 to James Lloyd and directs Hagner to adjust "as early as practicable" the claim [of Mass. for the services of her militia during the War of 1812]. FC in DNA, 3, 11:458 (M-6:11); CC in DNA, RG 233, 18A-D1, vol. 260; PC's in Senate Document No. 43 and House Document No. 83, 18th Cong., 1st Sess.; PC in *American State Papers*: *Military Affairs*, 3:18.

[Bvt. Maj.] S[tephen] H. Long, Philadelphia, to C[hristopher] Vandeventer, 2/1. "The subject of this communication is one to which my pursuits in the discharge of official duties, have forcibly drawn my attention. An astronomical Survey of the country, which is the subject alluded to, remains not only a desideratum as it respects almost every part of our inland frontier, but is peculiarly so in the interiour and most populous parts of the United States, if we except a very few of our principal cities, and here & there a solitary point. So defective is our Geography in the essentials of *Latitude* and *Longitude*, that I have little hesitation in asserting, that within the limits of our territory, these elements have not been determined with any considerable precision at more than eight or ten points; and that these points are so disconnected by any intermediate surveys, that very little advantage can result therefrom, in the construction of maps of the intervening country. Yet there is no subject of science in regard to which a more general interest and a more eager curiosity is so uniformly excited. In the course of my travels I have observed that almost every man, whether literate or illiterate, with whom I took occasion to converse on the subject has manifested a strong desire to know the Lat[itude] and Long[itud]e of his residence, or at least of some point in its neighbourhood. But I have been still more forcibly struck with the defects in the Geography of the country while engaged in compiling the large Manuscript Map now on file in the Topographical Office at Washington. In the prosecution of this work I consulted the most approved Maps of the different States and Territories, but invariably found them so discordant in their meridians and parallels of Latitude, that it was necessary, especially in the former, to deviate materially from the delineations, and in some instances to give a very different configuration to a portion of the country. In fact, the distortion was so great on some occasions, that errors of no less magnitude than from 10 even to 30 or 40 miles in distance are to be apprehended. No measure can be adopted for the remedy of these mistakes, with any prospect of success, but that of ascertaining the Lat[itude] & Lon[gitude] at a variety of points in dif[f]erent parts of the country, so situated as that the intermediate spaces between them respectively, are traversed by boundaries, or other lines of known extent. This step having been taken, the Maps of the several States may be corrected accordingly, and arranged in symmetric order, so as to form one entire and accurately digested Map of the U[nited] States, which should serve as a standard map of the country, to be kept ["as a" *canceled*] in the Topographical Office, as a document to be referred to on any suitable emergency. Such a Map embracing none but surveys well authenticated, on a scale of ten geographical miles to the inch, has been for some time a subject of interest & consideration with Maj. [Isaac] Roberdeau and myself, and I am strongly induced to wish, that the steps proper and necessary for its construction, may be taken. The part I have been and still am desirous to act in this undertaking, is, to be employed in ascertaining the Lat[itude] and Lon[gitud]e of the points alluded to, and in delineating maps of the several States and Territories conformably to these results, and preparatory to the construction of the large map above mentioned; in ascertaining the heights of mountains, and in ["preparing" *can-*

celed] furnishing a compendious account of the Topography, soil and productions of the country. In the performance of these services, I should need the aid of one or more assistants, and should wish that [1st] Lt. [Andrew] Talcott of the Corps of Eng[inee]rs, particularly might be associated with me. I trust that in all my views connected with this subject, I am influenced by ["motives of" *canceled*] patriotic motives, and I have no doubt they will meet your concurrence and approbation. Our sentiments in relation to the person who would most effectually promote the interests of the nation, should it fall to his [Calhoun's] lot to fill the chair of the President, are I believe perfectly concordant. Our favourite candidate has established an imperishable reputation whenever his measures have been recognised and felt. But his operations hitherto have been more immediately directed to the *out-posts* of the political camp. It now only remains, that he attack the *main fortress*, or in other words, that he carry his operations to the very doors of the sovereign people, and convince them of the usefulness and efficacy of his measures; and I know of no way in which this is so likely to be accomplished, as by adopting the plan above pointed out, which would require no extra appropriation to put it in practice, and would be exclusively an exertitive [*sic*] measure. There are very few places in the U[nited] States, where instruments requisite in taking accurate Astronomical observations can be had; and still fewer where persons are to be found competent to the performance of such operations, and to making accurate deductions therefrom. The mariner is satisfied with his deductions of Lat[itude] and Longitude, if he is enabled thereby to arrive in sight of his destined port. But his calculations are but illy adapted to geodesic operations, where an error of a single minute would materially affect the interests of a State or Territory. As an example, we have only to recur to the circumstances connected with the establishment of the boundary line, between the U[nited] States and L[ower] Canada on the 45th deg[ree] N[orth] Lat[itude]." Long lists 39 inland places for which he believes that neither the latitude nor the longitude has been accurately determined and for which it would be desirable to do so. They include Columbia, S.C.; Columbus, O.; Concord, N.H.; Cumberland Gap, [Tenn.]; Detroit, Mich.; Erie, Pa.; Fort Howard at Green Bay; Frankfort, Ky.; Harpers Ferry; Indianapolis, Ind.; Milledgeville, Ga.; Nashville; Pittsburg[h]; Raleigh or Fayetteville, N.C.; Richmond, Va.; and Sackets Harbor, [N.Y.]. The same need is true also of certain boundaries. "It would be well also to ascertain the Lat[itude] &

Lon[gitude] of many points along our maritime coast." "In addition to the services ["above" *canceled*] contemplated as above, a general statistical account of the several States and Territories, may readily be furnished, which might prove of great importance in forming a correct idea of of [*sic*] the resources and strength of the country. Whether it should be my fortune to be engaged in carrying such a plan into effect or not, I think you will agree with me in regard to the utilitty [*sic*] of the measure, and should be very glad of your aid and influence in bringing it about. Your favour of 28th ult[imo; *not found*] has been received. Your children are all spending the day with us, and are very well. Marcia has not the Spanish grammar but I will see that she is provided with one, as you request. I have consulted one of our best Phrenologists in regard to a Phrenological Cast. He thinks no reliance can be placed on them, but recommends a real scull [*sic*], marked and numbered '*secundum artem.*['] He said he had a cast at my disposal, but he considered it useless. The cost of such a one as he recommended, will be from 5 to 10 dollars, according to the quality and style of its preparation. I have as yet heard nothing from Virginia to be relied on, but shall probably have that matter put to rest in a very few days. I understand that Col. McCrea [former Lt. Col. William McRee] is a candidate; consequently my prospects are not very flattering. Marcia has no *Historical List*, and I know not the course you would prefer. Please furnish the list, both *antient* [*sic*] *& modern* and I will take the steps necessary to supply the books. I arrived in safety after a fatiguing journey thro' the mud, and had the satisfaction to find all well at home." ALS in DNA, 1, L-118 (M-221:96).

From Joseph Lovell, 2/1. He makes his quarterly report about his finances through 12/30/1822 and about soldiers' illnesses through 9/30/1822. Deaths declined to 37, but returns have not been received from the posts that are usually most sickly, such as Baton Rouge, the Barrancas, and those occupied by the 1st Infantry and by the Red River portion of the 7th Infantry. LS with En in DNA, 2, L-1823 (M-222:23); FC with En in DNA, 243, 1:144–148.

To Philip P[endleton] Barbour, 2/4. Pursuant to a statute of 4/21/1808, Calhoun encloses statements by George Bomford dated 1/14/1823 (FC in DNA, 32, 3:284); by George Gibson dated 1/22/1823; by Callender Irvine dated 11/12/1822; by Thomas S.

Jesup dated 12/31/1822 [DS in DNA, 1, Q-107 (M-221:96)]; and by Alexander Macomb (not dated). These report all contracts made by the War Department during 1822. LS with Ens in DNA, RG 233, 17A-E4; FC in DNA, 4, 2:261 (M-220:1); PC with Ens in House Document No. 60, 17th Cong., 2nd Sess.

From JOHN E. BONNEAU

Charleston, [S.C.,] 4th Feb[ruar]y 1823

Your letter dated 28th ["ult(im)o" *canceled; not found*] has just come to hand, & [I] hasten to reply to it. John E[wing] Colhoun has not said a syllable to me on the subject of your drawing on account of Mrs. [Floride Bonneau] Colhoun. He is now at his plantation in Pendleton, but is expected here about 15 Ins[tan]t. Mrs. [Martha Maria Davis] Colhoun is still here not having yet got out from her confinement. She is well & also, her son. You can draw on me for Eight hundred & forty Dollars at such sight as that, the draft should not become payable before the 10th or 15th of next month. I make this stipulation, as the time agreed upon for the pay[men]t of the rent of the ferry, say $1,000, is not until the 1st of March, and in general, engagements of this kind are not as punctually attended to as those with the banks; so that, I have endeavoured, consider[in]g these circumstances, to fix as short a period as possible. The reason of *$840* being stated as the am[oun]t to be drawn for, is in consequence of my having been compelled the last year to purchase a *new flat & rope* &c. for the ferry, it being absolutely & indispensably necessary.

As soon as the rent is paid Mrs. Colhoun shall be furnished with a statement of her account. I have rented the ferry for the present season, say from 1 March 1823 to 1 March 1824, to Colo[nel] Jno. Bryan, who has engaged to pay $1,000 at the expiration of the said term, being precisely the same terms [on which the ferry] was rented the last year.

We are all well, except my sister Mrs. Cox, who still continues very unwell. Do remember us to Mrs. Colhoun & Floride [Colhoun Calhoun] & [I] remain Dear Sir with great Respect . . . .

[P.S.] James [Edward] Colhoun is still here & well—he purposes remain[in]g until about [the] 20th Inst[ant].

ALS in ScU-SC, John C. Calhoun Papers. NOTE: This letter was postmarked at Charleston on 2/4 and was mailed to Calhoun in Washington.

From D[avid] Brearley, Indian Agent [in Ark. Territory, Washington,] 2/4. "With respect to the Cotten [*sic*] Gin, should you think proper to award it to the Indians, I am of opinion, that a house, and Machinery necessary to put ["it" *interlined*] in opperation [*sic*], can be erected for five Hundred dollars." ALS in DNA, 77 (M-271:4, frame 279).

Performance bond of Howes Goldsborough, 2/4. He promises to pay $15,000 to the U.S. if he does not fulfill the contract [for delivery of stone at Hampton Roads, Va.,] initially issued on 3/7/1819 to Jacob Lewis & Company, a firm that "failed in the execution of their part of the said contract," which fact enabled its sureties to sell the contract to Howes Goldsborough on 1/17/1823. CC in DNA, 227, 1:27–28.

To [James Monroe], 2/4. Pursuant to a House resolution of 1/28 [DS in DNA, 1, R-122 (M-221:96)], Calhoun reports that measures were undertaken to execute the Choctaw treaty of 10/18/1820 but that many Indians have refused to emigrate to the west of the Mississippi, largely because of the many white settlements in the Western lands ceded to the Choctaws. Calhoun encloses extracts from correspondence and other documents that explain the situation. "The Department has no information that will enable it to say whether the difficulties have diminished or increased by the delay in the execution of the Treaty." FC in DNA, 6, 2:109 (M-127:2); CC with Ens in DNA, RG 233, 17A-D1; PC with Ens in *American State Papers*: *Indian Affairs*, 2:393–397.

From Alexander Macomb, 2/5. Since Macomb recommended on 1/30 that Calhoun request an appropriation of $8,500 for the purchase of Oliver Gridley's farm, which adjoins the Military Academy, Macomb has received from [Sylvanus] Thayer a letter [dated 1/28 (CCEx in DNA, RG 233, 18A-C19.2)] stating that the property cannot "be had for less than $10,000." The proposed purchase is so important that Macomb asks Calhoun to request $10,000. LS with En in DNA, RG 233, 18A-C19.2; FC in DNA, 21, 1:361–362.

From John O'Fallon, Adjutant General of M[o]., St. Louis, 2/5. He encloses the annual returns of the militia of Mo. for 1822 and apologizes for the incompleteness of the report, which is attributable to the imperfect organization of the militia, the incapacity of the officers, and the "lameness" of the militia laws of the State.

The State is divided into two Divisions, four Brigades, and 30 Regiments. ALS in DNA, 16, 1823, O-2 (M-567:8, frames 423–424).

From T.L. Conkling, Herkimer, N.Y., 2/6. Because he believes that a bill now pending in Congress will authorize an Army movement to the mouth of the Columbia River, he applies for an appointment to serve as a Topographical Engineer, surveyor, or otherwise in the expedition. ALS in DNA, 8, 272.

[George Graham to the Factors at the Prairie du Chien, Fort Armstrong, and Osage Factories]

Indian Office, George Town, [D.C.,] Feb[ruar]y 6th 1823

I am specially directed by the Secretary of the Treasu[ry, William H. Crawford,] to instruct you to remove all the goods and other property [in] your possession to St. Louis, so soon as your spring sales may be over, which it is presumed will be by the 1st of May. Previous to your removal you will offer to the Indian Agent any goods in your possession which may be suitable and required for Indian purposes for the present year, or for the year 1824, at such reasonable prices as you and the Agent may agree upon, payable by drafts on the War Department, out of the appropriations for the years 1823 and 1824 respectively. On your arrival at St. Louis you will call upon Gen[era]l [William] Clark, Superintendent of Indian Affairs, furnish him with an inventory of the goods then on hand, and tender to him any portion of them which he thinks can be disposed of for Indian purposes, in the present year, or in the year 1824 at such prices as you and himself may agree upon, taking his drafts on the War Department for the amount payable in due proportions out of the appropriations for the years respectively within which he proposes to use the goods. The residue of the goods you will dispose of at auction giving reasonable notice of the sale on a credit not exceeding twelve months for notes satisfactorily endorsed. As you cannot be presumed to have such personal acquaintance at St. Louis as to enable you to judge of the goodness of the paper offered, you must take every possible precaution to guard against any ultimate loss to the U[nited] States, by requiring satisfactory certificates of the public officers or other known characters, as to the sufficiency of the security offered.

Of the Factory buildings you will make the best disposition you can, and if they cannot otherwise be disposed of, you will turn them over to the Indian Agent. You will also deliver to the Indian Agent the evidences of such debts as may be due the Factory when you leave it, taking his duplicate receipts for the same, the debts to be collected under such instructions as he may receive from the Secretary of War. You are authorized to assure him that an adequate compensation for his trouble will be allowed. In making your sales at the Factory you are not to be regulated by the Invoice prices of the goods; you will dispose of them at such fair prices as can be obtained for them, taking payment in cash, furs & peltries.

CC in DNA, 1, G-123 (M-221:95); CC in DNA, 76 (M-1:12, pp. 97–100).

From [Thomas S. Jesup], 2/6. As ordered, he submits a list of the publications purchased for the use of his office since its establishment "in this city, June 1818." He explains the reference value of the maps, statistical and geographical works, Congressional documents, law books, and newspapers thus purchased. FC in DNA, 42, 4:419–420 (M-745:2, frames 507–508); FC (dated 2/6/1824) in DNA, 50, vol. 3.

From John McCurdy, New York [City], 2/6. He has sent to [George] Gibson the new bonds that Calhoun has been "so indulgent as to permit me to exchange for those on file." McCurdy asks Calhoun to instruct Gibson to send McCurdy's contracts without delay. He signs himself with "grateful thanks for your attention & politeness; & with a fervent wish that you may long continue to enjoy health, & public confidence." ALS in DNA, 43, McCurdy.

To "Lewis [Louis]" McLane, Chairman, House Committee on Ways and Means, 2/6. Calhoun answers the questions posed in McLane's letter of 2/4 [LS in DNA, 1, M-217 (M-221:96)]. In explaining the difference between the 1822 appropriation and the estimate for 1823, Calhoun states that $90,000 were requested in 1822 and 1823 as the minimum amount for meeting the contingent expenses for the Indian Department but that the 1822 appropriation was for only $75,000. It is believed that the 1822 appropriation will be sufficient since various economies have been instituted; nevertheless, "there will be nothing left for contingencies or casualties which is always desirable in appropriations of this kind to prevent arrearages. The expense of the Indian Department for the year 1823 will be increased by the appointment of a Superintendent at St. Louis, and an Indian Agent in Florida, and the establishment of an Agency at the Sault of St. Marie at the outlet of Lake Superior. It is also believed that the expenses of the Indian Department will be considerably increased by the abolition of the Factories, which were much resorted to by the Indians, by making the Agencies the sole place and resort for them in the future." The nature of contingent expenses makes it impossible to predict them, except for the salaries of interpreters and blacksmiths, which should amount to about $15,000 and $14,000, respectively. A report from [William Lee] concerning contingent expenses for the first three quarters of 1822 will be submitted to Congress within a few days; meanwhile, Calhoun refers to a report submitted to the last session of Congress. In relation to the authority and reasons for employing Clerks in the offices of the Adjutant General, Ordnance bureau, Commissary General of Subsistence, Engineer bureau, and Surgeon General, Calhoun refers to acts of 4/20/1818 and 3/2/1821 for authority to employ Clerks in the Ordnance and Adjutant and Inspector General's offices. Authority for Clerks in the other offices may be found in the various annual appropriation bills starting with the one of 3/3/1819. The reason most of the offices were not included in the act of 4/20/1818 is that they were created after that date. All the Clerks are "indispensably necessary" to the public service. Calhoun discusses at length the salary of Beekman M. Van Buren as a member of the court-martial [for N.Y. militia delinquents]. FC in DNA, 4, 2:261–263 (M-220:1).

To "Lewis [Louis]" McLane, Chairman, House Committee on Ways and Means, 2/6. Calhoun encloses a report [of 2/6 from Alexander Macomb] and recommends that $8,000 be appropriated for repairs to Fort Jackson [at the Savannah, Ga., harbor]. LS with En in DNA, RG 233, 18A-C19.2; FC in DNA, 4, 2:265 (M-220:1).

From Alexander Macomb, 2/6. The Board of Engineers reports that, "if either of the works in the Harbour of Savannah be repaired, a preference should be given to Fort Jackson, as it would completely defend the inner harbour." Because that fortification "enters into the system of defence contemplated for Savannah, it may be made a permanent and respectable work." Macomb therefore recommends that Congress be asked to appropriate $8,000 for the repair of Fort Jackson. LS in DNA, RG 233, 18A-C19.2; FC in DNA, 21, 1:362.

To James Pleasants, Jr., Richmond

Department of War, February 6th 1823

I have the honor to acknowledge the receipt of your Excellency[']s letter of the 20th of last month, and have given to it, its due consideration.

It affords me great pleasure that the subject which the Executive Council [of Va.] have [*sic*] had under consideration has been placed in your hands, and that I have to confer thereon with an individual whose ideas I can duly appreciate, and you do me justice in believing in my disposition to promote the views which have been stated in your communication. I have therefore to inform you that measures will be immediately taken to have the Company of Artillery now stationed at the Bellona Arsenal increased to a full [authorized] Establishment, and maintained there at that additional complement, and the same precautions taken by that force as if in the presence of an Enemy during a state of War. Two additional pieces of Light Artillery will also be placed at that station, suitably equipped for active service. The flints also will be removed from the small Arms, and so disposed of as to prevent the Arms being used in case of their falling into improper hands. Every other measure of precaution and defence will be strictly enjoined and enforced for preserving the works against any attack, and securing the munitions deposited there; to which would be added a further augmentation of force, if our very limited means did not forbid it.

I wish your Excellency, and the Honorable Council to be assured of the continued disposition of this Government to extend every means of assistance and protection within its power to remove every cause of apprehension.

FC in DNA, 3, 11:460 (M-6:11).

To John Williams, Chairman, Senate Committee on Military Affairs, 2/6. Calhoun approves the draft of a bill that was enclosed with Williams's letter of 2/3 [ALS in DNA, 1, W-177 (M-221:96)] and refers to a report concerning estimates for ordnance supplies required for new fortifications that was submitted on 1/31/1822 to the House of Representatives. Calhoun suggests that [cannon] carriages should be included in the list of supplies named in the bill. LS in DNA, RG 46, 17A-D9; FC in DNA, 4, 2:263–264 (M-220:1); FC in DNA, 32, 3:286–288; PC in Senate Document No. 30, 17th Cong., 2nd Sess.; PC in *American State Papers: Military Affairs*, 2:529–530.

From Winfield Scott, New York [City], 2/7. The fact that [Bvt.] Maj. [Sylvanus] Thayer, Superintendent of the Military Academy, is junior in rank to Maj. [William J.] Worth, commander of the Corps of Cadets, "presents an anomaly in military service." To correct this, Scott suggests that the brevet rank of Lt. Col. be conferred on Thayer. "If any officer, since the peace, has earned a brevet, Major Thayer is certainly that individual. The Academy has been placed in a state of the most perfect organization & efficiency under his administration, & has, in the last five years, given to the Army a majority of the good officers in it." ALS in DNA, 1, S-406 (M-221:96).

From 22 "peacemakers, Chiefs & wa[rr]iors" of the Stockbridge Indians, New Stockbridge, [N.Y.,] 2/7. They request that their annuity be paid to the Governor of the State of N.Y., who would forward it to the Superintendents of the Stockbridge. In the past, their annuity has been paid to [Jasper] Par[r]ish, who has given it to the [Solomon U.] Hendrick family. That family and the [John] Serge[a]nt families have always taken the money, and "the poor people of this town have never as yet recieved [*sic*] any benifit [*sic*] there from." LS (some with their marks) in DNA, 1, S-356 (M-221:96).

From N[athan] T[owson], 2/7. "On examining the bill reported for making appropriations for the Military service of the United States for the year 1823 I find the amount contemplated by the bill, to be appropriated under the head of pay of the Army and subsistence of the Officers, to be less by 35,540 dollars than was estimated. As the above sum is precisely the amount required for 'double rations, compensation of 20 Supernumerary 2d Lieutenants graduates of the Military Academy and brevet pay of such Officers ["as such Officers" *canceled*] as are entitled to it by law,' I presume those items have been omitted in forming the bill and have therefore taken the liberty respectfully to call your attention to the subject." FC in DNA, 291, 16:46.

J[ohn] Elliott and Nicholas Ware, [Senators from Ga.,] and Joel Abbot, A[lfred] Cuthbert, George R. Gilmer, R[obert] R. Reid, Edward F. Tattnall, and Wiley Thompson, [Representatives from Ga.,] to James Monroe, 2/8. Frequent applications by citizens of Ga. for "a further extension of the time in which to exhibit their claims under the late treaty of [1/8/1821] with the Creek Indians" prompt these members of Congress to request an extension and to explain the "peculiar circumstances" that make the request seem reasonable. LS in DNA, 77, 5033 (M-271:4, frames 646–648).

Resolution by the House of Representatives, 2/8. The House requests the submission to it, during the next session of Congress, of stipulated information about salt springs, lead mines, and copper mines—for examples, the value of each and the extent to which each has been made or can be made productive. An EU by C[hristopher] Vandeventer dated 2/13 referred this resolution to [George] Bomford for action. Another EU, dated 11/5/1823, indicates that Calhoun directed Bomford to provide specific information about lead mines, leases of them, and their productivity. Copy in DNA, 31, 1823, War Department.

To "Lewis [Louis]" McLane, Chairman, House Committee on Ways and Means, 2/8. In reply to McLane's letter of 2/5 (ALS in DNA, 30, 417) asking Calhoun to stipulate what appropriations have been made for seven forts, Calhoun encloses a report of 2/6 from Alexander Macomb (LS in DNA, RG 233, 18A-C19.1; FC in DNA, 21, 1:366), who stated that prior to 1821 appropriations for fortifications were general and were allocated by the Presidents but also listed the specific appropriations made since 1820 for the named forts. In addition, Calhoun requests that $1,500 be added to the appropriation for Clerks in the War Department, because the enactment of a pending bill concerning Revolutionary pensioners will necessitate the services of the two Clerks whom Calhoun had stated on 12/2/1822 could be dismissed after the first quarter of 1823. LS with En in DNA, RG 233, 18A-C19.2; FC in DNA, 4, 2:265 (M-220:1).

To James Noble, Chairman, Senate Committee on Pensions, 2/8. In reply to Noble's letter of 2/6 [ALS in DNA, 1, N-32 (M-221:96)], Calhoun states that no record was kept until 8/1818 of the number of applicants for Revolutionary pensions under the statute of 3/18/1818. Since then, however, there have been 27,948 applications under that act, with 2,039 under the statute of 5/1/1820. The number of claims admitted is 18,880, of which 2,328 have been rejected or dropped from the pension rolls under the act of 5/1/1820. There were 12,331 on the pension list on 9/4/1822; the remaining 4,221 have either died or failed to exhibit schedules of property. In 1818 the sum of $104,900.85 was paid under the act of that year; $1,811,328.96 were paid in 1819 and $1,373,849.41 in 1820, when the list was reduced by the act of 5/1/1820. Such pensions cost $1,200,000 in 1821 and $1,833,936.30 in 1822. The higher expenditure in 1822 "arises from the circumstance that in the preceding year, a deficiency was occasioned by a greater number having applied . . . than was anticipated when the estimates were made. $451,836 of the expenditure of the last year was due the Pensioners in the preceding year." Calhoun suggests that the Committee on Pensions limit "the commencement of the Revolutionary Pensions in all cases to the time of completing the testimony, not only in original claims, but where persons have been continued on or restored to the Pension Roll. At present the latter class receive their pay from the 4th March, 1820; and the prospect of receiving the amount of three years['] stipend at one time, opens a door to attempts at fraud, and is no small inducement for many to dispose of their property with a view of receiving pensions." LS in DNA, RG 46, 17A-F4; FC in DNA, 91, 13:57; PC in Senate Document No. 31, 17th Cong., 2nd Sess.; PC in *Annals of Congress*, 17th Cong., 2nd Sess., col. 199; PC in *American State Papers: Claims*, 1:885.

S[YLVANUS] THAYER to Alexander Macomb, "Private"

Military Academy, West Point, 8th Feb[ruar]y 1823

Owing to some accident or other I did not receive your favor of the 22d ultimo until about Three days ago. This delay however did not in the least diminish the pleasure I derived from perusing it, as it was the first intimation I had rec[eive]d of the President[']s [James Monroe's] intention to nominate me as [Brevet] Lieut[enant] Col. By a note from The Hon'ble Rufus King dated 3d inst[ant] & this moment rec[eive]d I am informed that the nomination was confirmed on the morning of that day. You, who have so often experienced similar feelings, will know how to appreciate mine on the present occasion. This distinguished & unexpected honor greatly increases my debt of gratitude to the President & Secretary of War, while it inspires me with a firm determination to merit, as far as an entire devotion to the public service can merit, a continuance of this favorable opinion. If my vanity does not deceive me, the officers of the Institution are highly gratified by this appointment. They consider it in some measure as a compliment to the Academy & an indication of the strong interest felt for it by at least Two branches of the National Legislature.

ALS in DNA, 14, 362.

To Philip P[endleton] Barbour, 2/10. Pursuant to a House resolution [of 1/20 (ADS in DNA, 31, 1823, War Department; FC in DNA, 49, 1:110; CC in DNA, 25, 121; CC in DNA, 48, 193; CC in DNA, 138, 1820–1825:116; CC in DNA, 245, 1:136)] requesting information from the State, Treasury, War, and Navy Departments about newspapers and other periodicals, instruments, charts, maps, and prints purchased at public expense and asking for catalogs of all books so purchased during the past six years, Calhoun encloses 11 statements and comments briefly about major items purchased in 1820 and 1821. The enclosures are reports by: the Department of War, undated; George Bomford, dated 2/8 (FC in DNA, 32, 3:290–291); Jacob Brown, dated 1/24 (FC in DLC, Jacob Brown Papers, Letterbooks, 2:222); George Gibson, dated 1/24; Peter Hagner, dated 1/30 (FC in DNA, 53, 28:262); Thomas S. Jesup, dated 2/5; William Lee, dated 2/[*ca.* 5]; Joseph Lovell, dated 1/24; Alexander Macomb, dated 2/7 (FC in DNA, 21, 1:363–365); Charles J. Nourse, dated 1/27 [FC in DNA, 12, 6:288–289 (M-565:6, frame 440)]; and N[athan] Towson, dated 1/24 (FC in DNA, 291, 16:37). LS with Ens in DNA, RG 233, 17A-E4; FC in DNA, 4, 2:266–267 (M-220:1); PC with Ens in House Document No. 68, 17th Cong., 2nd Sess.

To [George Bomford, Jacob] Brown, [George] Gibson, [Callender Irvine, Thomas S. Jesup,] Joseph Lovell, and [Alexander Macomb], 2/10. Each of their offices is allowed to purchase [at public expense] one daily newspaper; the offices of [Gibson, Jesup, and Macomb] are allowed to buy [at public expense] "as many prices current as may be necessary to a proper and intelligent discharge of their duties." FC in DNA, 3, 11:416 (M-6:11); LS (Bomford's copy) in DNA, 31, 1823, War Department; LS (Gibson's copy) in DNA, 43, Newspapers; LS (Jesup's copy) in DNA, 48, 195; LS

(Lovell's copy) in DNA, 245, 1:148; LS (Macomb's copy) in DNA, RG 77, General and Special Orders, 1817–1824; FC in DNA, 49, 1:110; CC in DNA, 17, 1:28.

To "Lewis [Louis]" McLane, Chairman, House Committee on Ways and Means, 2/10. In answer to that portion of McLane's letter of 2/4 [*not found*] asking whether the estimate of $136,351 for purchases of clothing in 1823 will permit advance purchases to be made for 1824, Calhoun states that it applies only to 1823, as was explained in Callender Irvine's report to Christopher Vandeventer of 2/8 [ALS in DNA, 1, I-110 (M-221:95)] in reply to Vandeventer's letter to Irvine of 2/5 [FC in DNA, 3, 11:459 (M-6:11)]. Because woolen manufacturers prefer advance contracts, Calhoun suggests an additional appropriation of $50,000 if the committee should deem it to be advisable. LS in DNA, RG 233, 18A-C19.1; FC (dated 2/8) in DNA, 4, 2:266 (M-220:1).

From N[athan] Starr, Washington, 2/10. This veteran of almost 30 years of experience in manufacturing arms for the U.S. offers to produce 5,000 rifles per year for five years at a price $1.00 below the lowest price ever paid by the U.S. He has seen the price lowered already by $.50 and claims part credit for improvements used in his plant and at the Springfield Armory. If he does not receive a new contract, he will have to sacrifice his factory. ALS in DNA, 31, 1823, S.

From Thomas H[art] Benton, [Chairman, Senate Committee on Indian Affairs,] 2/11. Benton is instructed by the Committee to inquire about the probable expense of moving a military unit to some point between the mouth of the Yellowstone River and the falls of the Missouri; about the appropriation necessary to "hold treaties" to establish relations of trade and friendship with the Indian tribes beyond the Mississippi; and whether additional Agencies are necessary among those tribes. The Committee also wants to know the government's plans for maintaining peace with the Indians and for preserving the fur trade. ALS in DNA, 1, B-261 (M-221:97).

To William Eustis, Chairman, [House] Committee on Military [Affairs], 2/11. Calhoun answers Eustis's letter of 2/6 [LS in DNA, 1, E-90 (M-221:95); CC in DNA, 332, p. 34], which requested information about expenditures of the 1822 appropriation for arming the militia and about the extent of contracts that will be payable under the 1823 appropriation. Calhoun encloses a report from [George Bomford dated 2/11 (LS with 2 DS's in DNA, RG 233, 17A-E4; FC in DNA, 32, 3:291; CC with 2 Ens in DNA, 332, pp. 34–39)]. LS with Ens in DNA, RG 233, 17A-E4; FC in DNA, 4, 2:267 (M-220:1); CC with 3 Ens in DNA, 332, pp. 34–39; PC with Ens in House Document No. 74, 17th Cong., 2nd Sess.; PC with Ens in *American State Papers: Military Affairs*, 2:531–533.

To Thomas Metcalf[e], Chairman, [House] Committee on Indian Affairs, 2/11. "I herewith transmit the statement of the Second Auditor [William Lee] referred to in my letter to you of the 27th [*sic*; 28th] Ultimo and regret that it has been delayed so long. The ascertaining of the expenses of the several treaties, it appears, has been attended with considerable difficulty, which has prevented the Auditor from furnishing me with the statement earlier." FC in DNA, 72, E:383–384 (M-15:5).

From Thomas L. Moore, [Representative from Va.,] 2/11. He asks that the papers previously requested by the House Committee on Military Affairs concerning the petition of R[ichard] Harris and N[imrod] Farrow be furnished "as early as practicable." (*No such written request has been found.*) "Mr. Farrow is very anxious on the subject and the com[mittee] are desireous [*sic*] to act on it immediately." ALS in DNA, 30, 423.

From J[AMES] L. EDWARDS

Pension Office, Feb[ruar]y 12th 1823

It is my duty to inform you that Benjamin L. Beall, a Clerk in this Office, has been absent for several weeks. It is thought very doubtful whether he will return, as he has left the District, and no one knows where he is gone. To spare the feelings of Mrs. Beall, I have not written to her concerning her son; but I am informed by a gentleman who was requested by her to speak to me about him, that she is entirely ignorant of his present place of abode—his occupation, or the cause of his leaving home. Should he not return, and the amendment to the act of the 1st May 1820, now before the Senate, become a law, two Clerks, in addition to those now in this Office, will be wanted for the present year.

LS in DNA, 1, E-91 (M-221:95); FC in DNA, 91, 13:64.

Resolution by the House of Representatives, 2/12. "Resolved, That the President [James Monroe] be requested to communicate to the House a statement, shewing the several classes of expenditures made during the years 1821 and 1822, out of the contingent fund of the Indian Department, so far as the same may be susceptible of classification, stating particularly the amount of each species of expenditure. Also what security is taken for the disbursement or application of money, goods, or labor of persons charged with, or required to render the same for the benefit of Indians under the laws of the United States, and what rules and regulations have been adopted and are now in force to produce economy and accountability in the disbursement of public money by Superintendents of Indian Affairs and Indian Agents, together with such rules and regulations as are now in force concerning trade and intercourse with the Indian Tribes." DS in DNA, 1, R-130 (M-221:96).

From Joseph McMinn

Knoxville, Tennessee, 12 February 1823

I arrived here this evaning [*sic*], but have not been able to learn any thing from the Agency worthy [of] your attention, since the date of my last ["dated" *canceled*; of the] 6th [*sic*; 7th?] inst[ant]. The Indians, I am told are opposed to making any further dispostion, with the Government of their [*sic*] lands, but there [are] so much vagueness, and uncertainty in such reports, as to render them almost unworthy of notice.

The persons who have purchased Cherokee Reservations, are now attending the circuit court here, with some distant expectation that their suits will have an examination at this time, but what may be the result is at this time uncertain, tho I am inclined to the opinion that reservee's title will privail [*sic*].

ALS in DNA, 1, M-246 (M-221:96).

From Alexander Macomb, 2/12. In reply to [William Eustis's] letter of 1/28, which was referred to him, Macomb reports that the contract between [Joseph G.] Swift and N[imrod] Farrow and R[ichard] Harris for construction at [Dauphin Island, Ala.,] was an oral one. Macomb encloses several statements which bear upon the subject and comments that no penalties were placed upon the contractors for many months after the arrival of an Engineer officer. "At the time of discontinuing the advances the work done and materials delivered were not equal to the advances which had been made to the Contractors." LS with Ens in DNA, RG 233, 17A-F2.1; FC in DNA, 21, 1:369–370.

To the WESTERN CHEROKEE DEPUTATION, "now in Washington"

Dep[art]m[en]t of War, 12 Feb[ruar]y 1823

Brothers, I have rec[eive]d your communication of the 7th ult[im]o [*not found*] with attention and after consulting your father, the President, [James Monroe,] who is always willing to listen to the wants of Red Children, and to do them justice, have received his directions to make you the following answer.

Agreeably to your request, immediate measures will be taken for the establishment of the Western boundary according to ["the" *canceled*] Treaty, of the Country ceded to your nation between the Arkansaw & White Rivers, so as to lay off for it a number of acres, equal to the number ceded to the U[nited] States by the treaties of 1817 & 1819, which is ascertained to be about 3,285,710 acres and which is considered the full proportion of Territory, to which the Cherokees West of the Mississippi are entitled to [*sic*] from the old nation, according to their estimated numbers.

As to the out-let to the west, promised you by the President, it is not deemed proper to make any decision in relation to it, until the western boundary is established; after which, the subject will receive due attention and be finally decided upon.

The propriety of all your people settling within your own limits must be obvious to you, as it is equally as objectionable for them to settle on our lands, as for our people to settle on yours. It is expected therefore, that the nation will cause all of its people who have settled on our lands, to be removed as soon as possible, within its own boundaries.

The cession of land of twelve miles square, by the treaty of 1819, to the U[nited] States, to be sold and the proceeds to be applied under the directions of the President to the support of schools in the Cherokee nation on this side of the Mississippi, and of which you claim a part for the benefit of your nation, was made without reference to, or connection with, the treaty of 1817 and is considered and was so intended at the time the treaty of 1819 was made, as so much land ceded over and above the proportion to which the Cherokees on the Arkansaw were entitled, and consequently the claim which you have set up on the part of your nation, for a portion of the proceeds, to be applied for its benefit, or for an equivalent in land on the Arkansaw, cannot consistently with the treaty or in justice to your Brethren in Tennessee, be admitted.

The cotton Gin, to which you refer, will be completed agreeably to your wishes, for the convenience of your nation; and your Agent [David Brearley] will be instructed to take the necessary measures for that purpose, provided that the expense to ["the" *interlined*] Government does not exceed $500, the Sum estimated as sufficient for the object by the Agent; and provided also, that after said Gin is completed and put in operation, it be kept up solely at the expense of your nation, without any further charge whatever upon the Government.

In relation to the allowance of wheels, looms and blacksmith[']s work, your former Agent [Reuben Lewis] was instructed to attend to the wants of your nation on this subject, which it is presumed he did, as far as the funds placed at his disposal would admit of. Your present Agent will be directed to continue to supply you with these articles in the due proportion, but as the appropriation for the Indian Department has for the last two years been very limitted [*sic*], the supply could not be as large as formerly, and was accordingly reduced in the old nation as well as yours. The same reason, that is, the scantiness of the appropriation, will not admit of a compliance with your request for the erection of a mill for the convenience and comfort of the nation.

I have directed the charge of $555.75, which now stands against your annuity for a quantity of corn purchased by your ["former" *interlined*] Agent at the request of the Chiefs in consequence of the supply furnished under the promise of the President not being equal to the wants of the nation to be withdrawn; and I have allowed the whole of the annuity due for 1818 & 1819 amounting to $7,214.56, with the deduction however of the sum of $1,815 advanced to [by?] Governor [Joseph] McMinn to a delegation from your nation in 1818, at the request of the Chiefs; and with the deduction also of the amount due on the bond given by the Chiefs of your nation to John D. Chisholm, which is now held by Mr. [Patrick] Farrelly according to its tener [*sic*] at this time amounting to $1,800, with interest from the time said bond was presented by the Superintendent to the Chiefs in Council and payment was refused.

In relation to the Negro woman and child belonging to a woman of your nation, which, it is represented, were improperly sold by John D. Chisholm the necessary steps will be taken, thro' your Agent, for the investigation of the transaction, in order that justice be done to the parties concerned; of the result of which, you will be duly advised.

Your father the President, is very desirous that your nation and its neighbours the Osages, should be at peace and live in harmony with each other—there is nothing to be gained by war, and much to lose. Governor [James] Miller will be instructed, particularly, to attend to your wishes on this subject, and directed to adopt such measures, in conjunction with the Commanding Officer at Fort Smith as he may judge best calculated to adjust all differences that may arise between you and prevent hostilities in future.

FC in DNA, 72, E:384–386 (M-15:5). NOTE: Members of the deputation, to whom this letter was addressed, were Black Fox, John McLamore, Walter Webber, and James Rogers. They replied on 2/26.

To JOHN CLARK, [Governor of Ga.,] Milledgeville

Dep[art]m[en]t of War, 13 Feb[ruar]y 1823

Your letter of the 14th Ult[im]o with its enclosures has been received.

"The subject of a further extinguishment of the Indian title within the State of Georgia, has been submitted to Congress by the President [James Monroe] and he has agreed to keep open the time for the reception of claims under the late treaty [of 1/8/1821] with the Creek Indians until the 1st day of August next; extending the privilege thus allowed as well to those whose claims were rejected by the late Commissioner [James P. Preston] on account of insufficiency or informality *of proof* only, as to those who have not yet exhibited their claims. Those exhibited before the 1st of January last will be attended to as soon as the President is released from the duties incident to the Session of Congress."

FC in DNA, 72, E:386 (M-15:5); CCEx in DNA, 77, 5035 (M-271:4, frames 865–866). NOTE: The quotation marks in the FC indicate a portion of the letter that was extracted by one of Calhoun's Clerks for inclusion in the CCEx.

To William Eustis, Chairman, [House] Committee on Military Affairs, 2/13. In reply to Eustis's letter of 1/28 (LS in DNA, 30,

412), Calhoun encloses a report [of 2/12 from Alexander Macomb] concerning the claims of N[imrod] Farrow and R[ichard] Harris. Calhoun returns the documents that accompanied Eustis's letter. FC in DNA, 4, 2:267 (M-220:1).

From Jeremiah Evarts

Boston, Feb. 13, 1823

These lines will be delivered to you by Mr. David Brown, a Cherokee youth, who has been at the North [in Cornwall, Conn.] for his education since the spring of 1820. You may have heard of him as the brother of Catharine Brown. He is an amiable & pious young man, & promises to be of great use to his people.

Permit me, Sir, to call your attention to the letter, which I wrote you some time since, respecting the allowance of government to the Foreign Mission School [in Cornwall]; or rather, to the four young men, who studied there.

I am, Sir, with best wishes for your health and happiness, your friend and ob[edien]t ser[van]t, Jer[emia]h Evarts.

ALS in DNA, 1, E-136 (M-221:95). Note: In reference to Evarts' second paragraph, compare, herein, Calhoun's letter to Evarts dated 6/29/1822 and the letter from Evarts dated 1/9/1823.

From John Green

Zanesville, Ohio, Feb[ruar]y 13, 1823

In compliance with your letter [*not found*] on the subject of my brother Isaac Greene [*sic*] I have to state, that the principal reason why I wish to be informed, is, that he has been a long ["time" *interlined*] absent from his father's (with whom I reside) and he is my brother. His age is about 26 years. He was born in Ohio County Virginia. He enlisted as a soldier during the late war in the 27th Reg[imen]t U.S. Infantry, commanded by Capt. Joseph Cairns—volunteered on board of Com[modore Oliver Hazard] Perry's fleet & was in the action on Lake Erie on the 10th Sept. 1813—was wounded in that action & thereby was placed on the pension list.

I hope no other reasons will be required from the War Dept., in order to obtain information of a lost son & brother—especially as this is the only mode now left me or his aged father to receive that information. The place from which we last heard from him, was, between Natchez & Louisville.

ALS owned in 1960 by Harvey S. Teal, West Columbia, S.C. NOTE: EU's on this letter indicate that it was answered on 2/22 (perhaps by James L. Edwards) and that pension payments had not been drawn since 1/1/1821.

From V[IRGIL] MAXCY

Near Annapolis, Feb[ruar]y 13, 1823

I have been requested to mention to you, as a candidate to fill a vacant Clerkship in your Department, Mr. Wm. G. Ridgely, of Maryland. He is a young man of excellent character and I doubt not from the representations made to me of his qualifications for the place he solicits, that he would do credit to the situation. He is a grandson of the late Judge [Samuel] Chase of the U.S. Supreme Court, and a son of Judge Ridgely, late of our State court. His connexions are extensive & highly respectable. As the family have been unfortunate, as well as himself, the appointment would probably be of great importance to them & confer a great obligation.

ALS in DNA, 103, Ridgely (M-439:14, frames 435–436).

To [James Monroe], 2/13. In response to a Senate resolution of 2/11 [DS in DNA, 1, S-403 (M-221:96)], Calhoun submits a War Department report of 2/13 estimating the land in Ga. to which the Indian title has been extinguished by the U.S. since 4/24/1802 and the quantity of land within Ga. "to which the Indian title still remains to be extinguished." A second statement, prepared by [William Lee on 2/10 (DS in DNA, RG 46, 17A-E6)], shows prices paid for the extinguishment of the Indian land titles. LS with Ens in DNA, RG 46, 17A-E6; FC in DNA, 6, 2:110 (M-127:2); PC with Ens in Senate Document No. 35, 17th Cong., 2nd Sess.; PC with Ens in *American State Papers: Public Lands*, 3:622–624.

From Thomas L. Moore, [Representative from Va.,] 2/13. He reiterates his request that copies of documents in the War Department [concerning the petition of Nimrod Farrow and Richard Harris] be forwarded as soon as possible to the House Committee on Military Affairs. The Committee "will be ready to report immediately after the rec[eip]t of the expected communication." ALS in DNA, 30, 426.

To "J[OHN] ELLIOT[T], and others composing the representation in Congress from Georgia"

Dep[art]m[en]t of War, 14 Feb[ruar]y 1823

Gentlemen, Your letter of the 8th inst[ant] addressed to the President, [James Monroe,] has been referred by him to this Department, with directions to inform you, in reply, that for the reasons which you have mentioned, the time for the exhibition of claims, under the late treaty [of 1/8/1821] with the Creek Indians will be extended to the 1st day of August next; and that upon further reflection, as it appears there are some claims which were rejected by the Commissioner [James P. Preston] on account of the insufficiency or informality of the proof, the same time will be allowed to such claimants to produce further evidence in support of their respective claims.

FC in DNA, 72, E:387 (M-15:5).

To [John Gaillard] and Philip P[endleton] Barbour, 2/14. Pursuant to an act of 4/2/1794, Calhoun encloses a statement by George Bomford of 2/13 (FC in DNA, 32, 3:292; DS in DNA, RG 46, 17A-F4; DS in DNA, RG 233, 17A-E4) showing the expenditures of the national armories and the arms manufactured and repaired during 1822. LS with DS in DNA, RG 46, 17A-F4; LS with DS in DNA, RG 233, 17A-E4; FC in DNA, 4, 2:268 (M-220:1); PC with En in House Document No. 69, 17th Cong., 2nd Sess.; PC with En in *American State Papers*: *Military Affairs*, 2:530–531.

From [the Rev.] C[YRUS] KINGSBURY

Mayhew, C[hoctaw] N[ation], Feb. 14th 1823

I have the pleasure to inform you, that at a Council recently holden at Elliot[t], the difficulty which had existed with Capt. Cole, & which was noticed in my late Report, was amicably settled to the satisfaction of both parties. The objects & plan of the schools are I believe better understood now, than at any former period, & the minds of the natives more settled in their favour. Capt. Cole observed that had he known the rules of the school, he should not have felt the dissatisfaction which he did.

Your letter of 14th Dec. has been received. I am truly grateful for the Kind attention which has been paid to the wants & the welfare of these schools. I trust the Agent [William Ward] has before this certified the commencement of the buildings in the S[outh] E[ast] District, & the completion of those at Mayhew.

Permit me here to suggest, that communications to myself, would be received more directly through the Post Office at *Columbus, Mis*[*s*]. By being addressed to the Choctaw Agency, they pass by me 150 miles, & are then sent back.

ALS in DNA, 77, 5036 (M-271:4, frames 709–710). Note: There is no reference by name to Cole in Kingsbury's letter of 1/16/1823 or in its enclosed report of 1/15/1823, but Kingsbury might have been referring to Cole when he mentioned under the earlier date a disaffected Chief who had withdrawn his children from the school.

From L[ouis] McLane, [Chairman, House Committee on Ways and Means,] 2/14. By the treaty of 1/8/1821 with the Creeks, the U.S. agreed to pay a maximum of $250,000 in five annual installments to the citizens of Ga. for their claims against the Creeks. The Representatives from Ga. have requested that the annual installment be inserted into the current appropriations bill. Accordingly, McLane inquires about the balance, if any, still owed to the citizens of Ga. ALS in DNA, 1, M-234 (M-221:96). (Compare Calhoun's letter to George R. Gilmer of 2/15.)

To [James Monroe], 2/14. Pursuant to a House resolution of 12/17/1822 concerning specific expenditures of the Ordnance bureau since 1817, Calhoun submits a report from William Lee dated 1/28/1823 (LS with 4 Ens in DNA, RG 233, 17A-D1; FC in DNA, 51, 8:256). These, together with Calhoun's report of 12/30/1822, should supply all the necessary information. LS with Ens in DNA, RG 233, 17A-D1; FC in DNA, 6, 2:111 (M-127:2); PC with Ens in House Document No. 73, 17th Cong., 2nd Sess.

To T[homas] L. Ogden, New York [City], 2/14. "In compliance with the request contained in your letter of the 10th instant [ALS in DNA, 1, O-78 (M-221:96)], I have addressed a letter [dated 2/14] to Capt. [Jasper] Parrish, which is herewith enclosed unsealed for your perusal. After which you will ["be" *interlined*] pleased to seal and forward it." FC in DNA, 72, E:387 (M-15:5).

From Jasper Parrish, Canandaigua, [N.Y.,] 2/14. The Seneca Chiefs have agreed to wait until spring to send a deputation to Washington for the purpose of settling the differences that exist between the Pagan and the Christian parties. LS in DNA, 1, P-266 (M-221:96).

To Jasper Parrish, Sub-Agent, Six Nations

Dep[art]m[en]t of War, 14 Feb[ruar]y 1823

It has been represented to this Department by the proprietors of the pre-emptive title in the reservation lands within the State of New York, occupied by the Seneca Indians that some opposition having been manifested to the survey of these lands which has been commenced by the proprietors with the consent of the Chiefs, "it was agreed by way of conciliation, that the advice of the President should be asked on the question of the survey and that the conduct of the Indians should be regulated by it." The survey which has been commenced is considered as perfectly harmless to the rights and interests of the Seneca Nation, while it will be advantageous to the proprietors; but the Government does not wish to interfere in the business. You will, however, make such explanations to the Chiefs on the subject, as will induce them to take a favorable view of it, and allow the survey to proceed without further interruption.

FC in DNA, 72, E:386–387 (M-15:5).

From Winfield Scott, New York [City], 2/14. In compliance with Calhoun's "verbal [that is, oral] request," Scott discusses his ideas regarding the establishment of a School of Practice for the U.S. Artillery. The School should consist of from five to ten Companies of Artillery. For the command and superintendence of the School, a Colonel of Artillery would be needed. Two instructors from the Artillery and one from the Engineers should be selected. Workshops, a laboratory, and an arsenal would be indispensable. For various reasons, Scott believes that Fort Monroe, [Va.,] is the best location for the School. The greatest advantage in selecting

Fort Monroe is its military position. Secondarily, it is easily accessible to water, by which most of its students would arrive. "It may be objected to Fort Monroe, that its works are not in a sufficient state of forwardness for the reception of the garrison School. The Companies might be accommodated under tents" until barracks are constructed. ALS in DNA, 1, S-364 (M-221:96).

From W[illiam] G.D. Worthington, Baltimore, 2/14. He presents additional explanation about his claim of $800 against the government for his services as Acting Superintendent of Indian Affairs for East Fla. ALS in DNA, 1, W-206 (M-221:96).

To Philip P[endleton] Barbour, 2/15. Pursuant to a House resolution of 2/6, Calhoun submits a report and statement from Alexander Macomb of 2/14 (LS with DS in DNA, RG 233, 17A-E4; FC in DNA, 21, 1:371–372) concerning expenditures for fortifications. LS with Ens in DNA, RG 233, 17A-E4; FC in DNA, 4, 2:268 (M-220:1); PC with Ens in House Document No. 72, 17th Cong., 2nd Sess. Macomb submitted a supplementary report on 2/14, showing the total expenditures on seven different fortifications prior to 1821 (FC in DNA, 21, 1:372–373). Peter Hagner also submitted to Calhoun on 2/11 a detailed statement in reply to this resolution (LS with DS in DNA, 30, 424; FC in DNA, 53, 28:330).

From L[ouis] William DuBourg, R[oman] C[atholic] Bishop of N[ew] Orleans

Washington, February 15th 1823

Encouraged by the friendly attention with which you have been pleased to honour my advances for the establishment of Catholic missions among the native Indians of Missouri, I gladly meet your kind invitation, in submitting some considerations on that important subject, which, if approved, may serve as a basis of the concessions to be made by Government for the support of those missions.

Whatever may be the merit of the Regulations adopted by Government towards the civilisation of the Eastern tribes, which is better tested by experience than by theory, It is my opinion that their application to the Western and far remote ones would be at least premature. Those Indians as long as they have a wide hunting range open before them, will not easily be brought to set any value on the pursuits of civilized life. They rather show an utter dislike and contempt for occupations, which the exercise of unrestrained liberty leads them to view as servile drudgery; and many of the nations, have positively resisted the Introduction among them of teachers of our Arts and Sciences, whilst the few who have admitted them evince no disposition to avail themselves of their services.

I should then, with due deference, think that, for those distant nations at least, the work of civilisation should commence with humanising them by the kind doctrines of Christianity, instilled into their minds, not by the doubtful and tedious process of books, but by familiar conversations, striking representations, and by the pious lives of their spiritual teachers. Men, disenthralled from all family cares, abstracted from every earthly enjoyment, inured to fatigue and self denial, living in the flesh as if strangers to all sensual inclinations, are well calculated to strike the man of nature as a supernatural species of beings, entitled to his almost implicit belief—thus become masters of his Understanding, their unremitting charity will easily subdue the ferocity of their hearts, and by degrees assimilate their inclinations to those of their fellow Christians.

I would therefore be for abandoning the whole management of that great work to the prudence of missionaries, as the best judges of the means to be progressively employed to forward the great object of their own sacrifices. Such at least always was the policy observed in Catholic Indian missions, the success of which, in almost every instance answered, and often surpassed, every prudent expectation.

Upon these principles, I would be willing to send a few missionaries, by way of trial at least, among the Indians of Missouri, should Government be disposed to encourage the undertaking. The appropriation of monies for that object being, I understand, very limited, and in a great measure already disposed of, I feel extremely delicate in prof[f]ering any specific demand. I would only beg leave to observe that hardly a less sum than two hundred Dollars per annum would suffice to procure to a missionary the indispensible [*sic*] necessaries of life.

With this abridged view of the subject, I beg you will have the goodness to inform me, Sir, whether and to what extent Government would be willing to favour my scheme.

1st. What allowance, It would grant to each missionary.

2ly. To how many that support might be extended.

3d. In case establishments could me [*sic*; be] made, what help would be afforded towards them, either in money or Lands.

LS in DNA, 77, 5039 (M-271:4, frames 432–435). NOTE: Calhoun replied on 2/20.

From Jere[miah] Elkins, Washington, 2/15. It is his desire to publish in book form "the few remaining fragments of the official letters [and other documents] of our Naval & Military Officers of the Revolutionary War." If any of those letters and documents are filed in the War Department, Elkins would like permission to copy them. ALS in DNA, 1, E-93 (M-221:95).

To George R. Gilmer, [Member,] House [Committee on Ways and Means], 2/15. In answer to Gilmer's letter of 2/14 [ALS in DNA, 1, G-104 (M-221:95)], Calhoun states that no additional appropriation is required to effect "the provision of the late treaty [of 1/8/1821] with the Creek Indians relative to the claims of the citizens of Georgia against" the Creeks. The total sum owed to the citizens of Ga. by the Creeks is estimated at $88,702.62. FC in DNA, 72, E:388 (M-15:5); CC in DNA, RG 233, 18A-C19.2.

To Peter Hagner, 2/15. "You will prepare a statement of the amount expended in constructing the military road leading from Plattsburg to Sacketts [*sic*] Harbour [both in N.Y.] as early as practicable." FC in DNA, 3, 11:461 (M-6:11); CC in DNA, 77 (M-271:4, frames 871–872).

To HENRY JOHNSON, [Senator from La.]

Dep[art]m[en]t of War, 15 Feb[ruar]y 1823

Agreeably to your [oral?] request of this morning, I have to state for the information of the Committee on Indian Affairs in the Senate that the views of the Government in relation to the line of the land ceded to the Choctaws, by the treaty of the 18th October 1820 as fixed by that treaty are, that the line should be so altered as to interfere in the least possible manner with the white settlements in the Territory of Arkansaw. A very good conception of a line that will effect this object, may be formed from the report of the Commissioner appointed to run out the line, under the late

Treaty, a copy of which accompanied a report, from this Department relative to the execution of that Treaty, which was transmitted to the House of Representatives by the President [James Monroe] a few days ago, and to which, to prevent the delay which the preparation of copies to accompany this letter would occasion, I would respectfully refer the Committee. If, however, the Committee cannot obtain a sight of that report another copy will be prepared and transmitted for its information, with as little delay as possible.

With regard to the disposition of the Choctaws to emigrate to the Country ceded to them west of the Mississippi, and the Sum that will be [*one word canceled*] necessary to hold a new treaty to procure an alteration of the line referred to, upon which points the Committee also request to be informed, I have to state, that there appears to be at present, from the information which this Department has on the subject, great reluctance to emigrate at all; it is probable, however, when an alteration is made in the line as proposed, emigration to some extent may take place; tho', it is believed, while it depends as it does, on the will of the Indians themselves, there is very little prospect of its ever being commenced with much spirit. As to the sum necessary to hold a new treaty, there is a sufficiency for the object remaining of the appropriation to carry into effect the treaty of the 18th Oct[obe]r 1820, and I would respectfully suggest the propriety, instead of making a new appropriation, of authorizing the President to apply it to holding such treaty, if the committee should deem it expedient. The balance remaining is $34,945.

FC in DNA, 72, E:388–389 (M-15:5).

To "Lewis [Louis]" McLane, Chairman, [House] Committee on Ways and Means, 2/15. The enclosed report [from Alexander Macomb of 2/14 (ALS in DNA, RG 233, 18A-C19.2)] supplies the information requested by McLane's letter of 2/13 (ALS in DNA, 30, 425), which had pronounced Macomb's report of 2/6 to be unsatisfactory, because it stated the amount of appropriations, not of expenditures, for fortifications. ALS with En in DNA, RG 233, 18A-C19.2; FC in DNA, 4, 2:268 (M-220:1).

To L[ouis] McLane, 2/15. Calhoun acknowledges McLane's letter of 2/14 [LS in DNA, 1, M-229 (M-221:96)] containing a memorial from the Ala. legislature requesting the extinguishment of Indian land titles in Ala. Calhoun has no information on the subject for the committee, but he encloses several papers revealing that the [Eastern] Cherokees have been reluctant recently to cede land. Calhoun refers McLane to a report [of 2/13 by Calhoun to Monroe] concerning the extinguishment of Indian titles in Ga. LS with Ens in DNA, RG 233, 17A-C26.2; FC in DNA, 72, E:387–388 (M-15:5); PC with Ens in *American State Papers: Public Lands*, 3:625–626.

To [Louis] McLane, 2/15. In reply to McLane's letter [of 2/14 (ALS in DNA, 1, M-230 [M-221:96])], Calhoun states that [Peter Hagner] will prepare a statement of the costs of the military road from Plattsburg to Sackets Harbor. "The road has been constructed by the labour of the troops." LS in DNA, RG 233, 18A-C19.2; FC in DNA, 4, 2:268 (M-220:1).

[Bvt. Lt. Col.] S[ylvanus] Thayer, West Point, to Alexander Macomb, 2/15. Thayer encloses an ALS to himself from D[avid] B[ates] Douglass dated 2/15 expressing Douglass's continued desire, upon suggestion of [Claudius] Crozet, to exchange professorships with Crozet, as they sought permission about a year ago to do. Thayer adds that Crozet has reiterated his desire for the exchange. Douglass wrote: "Should it be necessary, as was suggested by the Secretary of War, to consider it in the light of a mutual resignation and reappointment, I have no objection." ALS with En in DNA, 14, 364.

From W[illiam] Ward, Choctaw Agency, 2/15. He estimates at about $3,250 the costs of constructing a new Agency and of removing from the old site to the new. Ward has not yet been able to ascertain the Chiefs' attitude toward the proposed two taverns for travelers and mail along the road through the new site. The Choctaws have asked Ward to report that they want the land west of the Mississippi that has been ceded to them surveyed and its boundaries defined, in accordance with treaty stipulations. ALS with En in DNA, 1, W-3 (M-221:98).

From Stevenson Archer, [former Representative from Md.,] Bel Air, Md., 2/16. "Several of my neighbours are desirous of being informed whether it is the intention of the Department of War to continue the *contract* system for supplying the forts Calhoun &

Monroe with stone," or whether the market will be opened "to all such as may choose to take stone to these fortifications for sale. Should the latter plan be adopted I have little hesitation in saying that there can be supplied from the Susquehannah alone 20,000 perch of *first rate building* stone in one year. Should the Contract system be continued would you have the goodness to inform me whether government would make a contract at this time" for the supply of 20,000 perches of stone for the abovementioned forts? ALS in DNA, 30, 428.

From [Lewis Cass], Washington, 2/16. "Understanding that Mr. [John] Hays, the Indian Agent at Fort Wayne, is about to resign his office, I beg leave to recommend Benjamin B. Kercheval as his successor. He [Kercheval] has resided some years at that place, speaks the Miami language fluently, and would be peculiarly acceptable to the Indians of that tribe. He has also acted as Sub-Agent for nearly two years and during a considerable part of that time, in the absence of Mr. Hays, has discharged the duties of principal Agent. I know him well and can safely recommend him as a faithful, intelligent officer and a high minded, honourable man. I do not believe the office can be better filled." FC in DNA, 76 (M-1:5, p. 125).

From [William Henry] Harrison, Northbend, O., 2/16. "General Harrison has the honour to acknowledge the receipt of the Secretary of War[']s note of the 15th Ultimo with the casts of the medal transmitted with it. He requests that the medal when finished may be committed to the care of any of the members of Congress or other gentleman coming to Cincinnati." ALU in DNA, 2, H-1823 (M-222:23).

To Philip P[endleton] Barbour, 2/18. Pursuant to a statute of 5/6/1822 concerning trade with Indians, Calhoun encloses a report from [William Lee dated 2/18 (LS with Ens in DNA, RG 233, 17A-E4; FC in DNA, 51, 8:293–294) about funds used for the benefit of Indians during the first eight months of last year]. Calhoun submits also copies of the accounts of Superintendents and Agents for Indian Affairs. LS with Ens in DNA, RG 233, 17A-E4; FC in DNA, 4, 2:269 (M-220:1); PC with Ens in House Document No. 80, 17th Cong., 2nd Sess.; PC with Ens in *American State Papers: Indian Affairs,* 2:398–408.

To C[HURCHILL] C. CAMBRELENG, [Representative from N.Y.]

Department of War, February 18th 1823

I have the honor of informing you that the proper Officer had reported Castle Clinton to be no longer required as a Military position for the defence of the harbor, and City of New York, and that orders have been given for dismantling and evacuating that post. When this shall be completed, the other necessary steps will be taken for carrying into effect the act of the 30th March 1822.

I have the honor at the same time of advising you that the retention and preservation of the North Battery at the foot of Hubert Street is considered essentially necessary so long as other defences than the existing ones are incomplete.

FC in DNA, 3, 11:462 (M-6:11).

To John Cocke, [Member,] House Committee on M[ilitary Affairs], 2/18. In reply to Cocke's letter of 2/17 (ALS in DNA, 30, 431), which requested "all the letters from Lieut[enant Horace C.] Story, and Captain [*sic*; Col. James] Gadsden received since April 1820, relative to the fortification on Dauphin Island," Calhoun encloses a report [from Alexander Macomb dated 2/18 (LS with Ens in RG 77, Records of the Office of the Chief of Engineers, Laminated Files; FC in DNA, 21, 1:373)]. FC in DNA, 4, 2:269 (M-220:1).

From Nat[haniel] Cutting, Section of Bounty Lands, 2/18. He reports the results of an investigation relative to "certain *Fraudulent procedures* under the '*Canadian Volunteer*' Act" that were suspected of some individuals in Me. John Chandler, [Senator from Me.,] was authorized to make an inquiry into the matter. He elicited the aid of his son, John A. Chandler, who "entered into the Spirit of the business with alacrity & pursued it with ardour." He has acquired "satisfactory proof that *Thirty*, out of *Thirty-five* Cases committed to his investigation, were spurious, and ["were" *interlined*] wont to *impose* upon *Government* & to *pillage* the *Public Patrimony*." Whether the other five cases were legitimate remains undecided. Cutting encloses a letter from John Chandler covering his son's account for expenses. Even though John A. Chandler was not an agent of the government, Cutting recommends that Chandler's claim for expenses be paid. "The aggregate, is *One hundred* & five dollars; the quantity of Land thus rescued from the grasp of a few impudent Speculators, amounts to Nine Thousand Six Hundred Acres!" ALS in DNA, 1, C-274 (M-221:95).

To Thomas H[art] Benton, [Senator from Mo.,] 2/18. In reply to Benton's letter of 2/14 [ALS in DNA, 1, B-254 (M-221:95)], Calhoun states that claims tendered under the second article of the treaty of 9/25/1818 with the Osages have been received and that they will be acted upon "as soon as the Department has a little leisure." Since more than $3,000 remain of the appropriation to carry into effect this article of the treaty, "no legislative aid will be necessary." FC in DNA, 72, E:391 (M-15:5).

From Callender Irvine, Philadelphia, 2/19. He acknowledges Calhoun's regulation of 2/10 limiting newspaper subscriptions. Irvine argues that he buys more varied items than the Quartermaster, Engineer, and Subsistence bureaus, which are allowed to subscribe to an unlimited number of newspapers or prices current. The Purchasing bureau should be allowed the same privilege, partly because "there is an advantage in taking several newspapers other than the information derived from them, as a very considerable deduction is made from the customary charge of inserting advertisements to subscribers." ALS in DNA, 1, I-117 (M-221:95); FC in DNA, 45, 389:457. (Calhoun answered on 2/22.)

From John Clark, Milledgeville, 2/20. Having been informed that [Return J.] Meigs died on 1/28, Clark reiterates his former recommendation of Daniel Newnan to succeed Meigs as Agent to the [Eastern] Cherokees. Newnan is qualified and is indigent. FC in G-Ar, Governors' Letterbooks, 1821–1829:99–100.

To Bishop [Louis William] DuBourg "of New Orleans, now in Washington City," 2/20. In reply to DuBourg's letter of 2/15, Calhoun states that President [James Monroe] has approved a U.S. grant of $200 each towards the annual support of as many as three [Roman Catholic] missionaries, if they should be sent by DuBourg to the remote Mo. Indian tribes beyond the Osages and the line of military posts. The funds will be paid quarterly, beginning when the missionaries "shall actually set out in the prosecution of their duties." The enclosed printed regulations reveal the conditions under which the government will aid in paying for the necessary buildings. Calhoun stipulates what reports must be made and directs the missionaries to secure passports from William Clark in St. Louis. FC in DNA, 72, E:392 (M-15:5).

From Daniel Groves, Edward Coleman, Jonah Brewster, James Robertson, Stephen Duncan, and 20 other members of the Pa. Senate, Harrisburg, 2/20. They petition that [former] Maj. Peter Mühlenberg, [Jr.,] be appointed to the "Office of Pay Master in Case of a Vacancy," with rank not inferior to his former status. LS in DNA, 11, 10550 (M-566:91).

From Solomon U. Hendrick, "Deputy of the Stockbridge Tribe," Washington, 2/20. He reports that deputies from the [Six Nations] arrived at Green Bay on 9/1/1822 and held councils with the Menominees and the Winnebagoes. The latter tribes have ceded to the [Six Nations] "all the lands owned by them situated from the lower line of the Territory ceded to us last year including all islands in the Bay." At the direction of his Chiefs, Hendrick presents the treaty of 9/23/1822 to Calhoun for [James Monroe's] approval. He also encloses a letter from John Sergeant to Lewis Cass, who preceded Hendrick to Washington. CCEx in DNA, 77 (M-271:4, frames 766–767). (Calhoun answered on 3/13.)

From J[OHN] BROOKS, [Governor of Mass.]

Medford, Mass., Feb[ruar]y 21st 1823

I understand that James Varnum Gale of Concord in New Hampshire is a candidate for admission into the academy at West Point, & that he is well recommended for that purpose. Knowing nothing myself of his qualifications, I can only say that he is a grandson of Colonel James Varnum of Dracut in this State, who was an officer in the Revolutionary army of great merit, that he entered the service of his country on the memorable 19th of April 1775, & distinguished himself for his bravery & good conduct at the battle of Bunker's Hill, at the Heights of Harlem, & at the capture of Gen[era]l Burgoine [*sic*; John Burgoyne] & his army, & is now a citizen of great respectability, & a magistrate of Massachusetts. On this ground I particularly recommend the young man for admission into the academy.

LS in PHi.

From Mority Fürst, Philadelphia, 2/21. He reports that a likeness of [James] Miller has been engraved and that Fürst needs a likeness of [Eleazer W.] Ripley. LS in DNA, 1, F-88 (M-221:95, incorrectly filmed after E-86).

To Robert Houston, Knoxville, 2/21. Calhoun acknowledges Houston's letter and enclosures of 1/30 [ALS in DNA, 1, H-223 (M-221:95)]. "The purpose for which the Commission was wanted having been completed, it is herewith, with the letters of instruction, which you enclosed with it, returned to you." FC in DNA, 72, E:392 (M-15:5).

To "Lewis [Louis]" McLane, Chairman, [House] Committee on Ways and Means, 2/21. In addition to the information furnished by Calhoun's letter of 1/15 to McLane, Calhoun encloses a statement prepared by Peter Hagner on 2/20 [LS in DNA, 1, H-224 (M-221:95); FC in DNA, 53, 28:374; DS in DNA, RG 233, 18A-C19.1] concerning the amount of money "expended upon the military road leading from" Plattsburg, N.Y., to Sackets Harbor, N.Y. LS with DS in DNA, RG 233, 18A-C19.1; FC in DNA, 4, 2:270 (M-220:1).

From Alexander Macomb, 2/21. He reports that Fort Griswold, [Conn.,] must be rebuilt to be effective in defending New London, [Conn.]. The Board of Engineers has estimated that the principal work will cost $108,379.58 and a new battery and tower $23,850.83. Fort Griswold is listed in the second category of fortifications to be repaired; therefore, Macomb recommends no appropriation for it until work shall have been begun on the more urgent projects. If, however, an appropriation should be provided now, Macomb suggests that it be for the amount needed to build the battery and tower. LS and CC in DNA, RG 233, 18A-C19.1; FC in DNA, 21, 1:376–377.

To R[obert] R. Reid, [Representative from Ga.,] 2/21. In reply to Reid's "note" of 2/21 [ALU in DNA, 1, R-144 (M-221:96)], Calhoun states that President [James Monroe] "has extended the time for the presentation of the claims of Citizens of Georgia against the Creek Indians, under the late treaty, to the 1st of August next." Calhoun refuses to let Reid have the papers constituting the claim of [Asa] Newsom [in behalf of the estate of Solomon Newsom], because these records should not be removed from the U.S. archives;

Calhoun explains that the claim was rejected because it did not include an oath required by regulations. Calhoun offers to let Reid examine the records in the War Department for the purpose of learning how to perfect the claim. FC in DNA, 72, E:393 (M-15:5).

From Winfield Scott, New York [City], 2/21. He recommends that a permanent name be selected "for the new Fortress at The Narrows, that has recently been garrisoned. It is, at present (I presume, by mere accident) called Fort *Diamond,* a designation that will not re-call to the country, or to the garrison, any endearing or animating recollection whatever." "In harmony with our general practice . . . I have the honour to propose that a name may be selected from our history for the work, worthy of a fortress of the first class." "The name, La Fayette, is, in this respect, unappropriated, for altho' many particular States have complimented it in the designation of counties, cities, &c., &c., the United States, as one, have not followed the example." An EU reads: "There have been several forts called after the illustrious Fayette." ALS in DNA, 30, 434.

To R[euben] H. Walworth, [Member, House Committee on Military Affairs,] 2/21. The enclosed report [of 2/20 from Alexander Macomb (LS with En in DNA, RG 233, 17A-F2.1; FC in DNA, 21, 1:376)] complies as far as is practicable with Walworth's request of 2/14 [ALS in DNA, 1, W-187 (M-221:96) for information concerning a petition by Nimrod Farrow and Richard Harris]. LS with Ens in DNA, RG 233, 17A-F2.1; FC in DNA, 4, 2:269 (M-220:1).

To W.H. Bedford, "Present," 2/22. Calhoun acknowledges Bedford's letter of 2/18 [LS in DNA, 1, B-259 (M-221:95)] and replies that the points arising from [Peter Hagner's] "adjustment of the claims of the Officers [of the Tenn. militiamen] for their losses in the Seminole campaign" [of 1817–1818] refer themselves as legal questions to [Richard Cutts] for decision. "Should he however entertain any doubts in relation to them he will take the opinion of the Attorney General [William Wirt] respecting them." FC in DNA, 3, 11:464 (M-6:11).

From GEORGE GRAHAM

Indian Office, George Town [D.C.,] February 22nd 1823

The Secretary of the Treasury [William H. Crawford] having decided to close all the Factories on the 1st of May next, instructions have been issued to the agents, to sell at public sale all the property then remaining on hand, except such as may be required by the Indian Agents or Superintendents for public purposes. I enclose you an extract from the letter [of 2/6] addressed to the Agents at [the] Prairie du Chien, Fort Armstrong, and Osage Factories, and request that you will give such instructions to Gen[era]l [William] Clark and the Indian Agents, as you may think the circumstances require. A great sacrifice will be necessarily made of these goods by a sale at public auction; and as a large portion of them are well calculated for Indian purposes, it would be very desirable that the public Agents should be instructed to take as many of them as the public service may require for the present and the next year.

Similar instructions have been given to the other Agents. Mr. Ringgold the Agent at Green Bay has been directed to repair to Detroit, for the purpose of selling at auction such of the goods under his charge, as he cannot otherwise dispose of. It is expected that the Agents at the Choktaw [*sic*] Factory and at those on the Arkansaw and Red River will be able to sell at their respective Factories at auction, such of the goods as they cannot dispose of to the Indian Agents or others at private sale previous to the 1st of May.

LS with En in DNA, 1, G-123 (M-221:95); CC (of the En only) in DNA, 76 (M-1:12, pp. 101–104).

To Joseph M. Hernandez, [Delegate from the Territory of Fla.,] 2/22. Calhoun encloses an estimate of the cost of constructing a road from Pensacola to St. Augustine by using Army labor. The cost is greater than the War Department is willing to incur without authority from Congress; but, because the road is considered important to the people of Fla., Calhoun encloses two letters from Acting Governor [George Walton] on the subject, and, if Hernandez considers it expedient, he may use the letters to obtain an appropriation. Since these letters are originals, Calhoun asks that they be returned as soon as Hernandez is through with them. FC in DNA, 72, E:393–394 (M-15:5); PC in Carter, ed., *Territorial Papers,* 22:628–629.

To C[allender] Irvine, Philadelphia, 2/22. In reply to Irvine's letter of 2/19, Calhoun states that Irvine "will be put on the same footing in relation to prices current as" [Thomas S. Jesup, Alexander Macomb, and George Gibson], "as specified in my regulation of the 10th instant, and in future will take such prices current as may be necessary to an intelligent discharge of your duties—reporting the number which you take to this Department." FC in DNA, 3, 11:463 (M-6:11).

To L[ouis] McLane, Chairman, [House] Committee on Ways and Means, 2/22. Calhoun requests an appropriation of $29,600 for a purchase of land surrounding Fort Washington, [Md.,] from William Dudley Digges, with the understanding, to which Digges has acquiesced, that the approximately $16,350 owed by Digges to the estate of Robert Brent, former Paymaster General of the Army, will be deducted from the payment for the land, in order that Brent's estate can pay what it owes to the U.S. LS in DNA, 281, Md. (Fort Washington), 41.

To "Lewis [Louis]" McLane, 2/22. In answer to McLane's letter of 2/21 (ALS in DNA, 30, 433) inquiring about the usefulness of Fort Griswold, Conn., and the propriety of appropriating funds for repairs there, Calhoun encloses a report [by Alexander Macomb dated 2/21]. ALS in DNA, RG 233, 18A-C19.1; FC in DNA, 4, 2:270 (M-220:1).

To Joseph McMinn, "Cherokee Agency near Calhoun," Tenn., 2/22. Calhoun acknowledges McMinn's letter of 2/7 [ALS in DNA, 1, M-245 (M-221:96); CC in DNA, 75 (M-208:9)], written while McMinn was enroute to the Agency. Calhoun approves McMinn's intention to take charge of the Agency because of the death [on 1/28] of [Return J.] Meigs; but a new Agent will be appointed promptly. Calhoun expresses his pleasure that McMinn's health has been restored sufficiently to enable him to collect the debts owed to the U.S. by the purchasers of the public property sold by McMinn; Calhoun hopes that all debts will soon be paid. FC in DNA, 72, E:394 (M-15:5); FC in DNA, 75, 1822–1827:1–2 (M-208:10).

From Jasper Parrish, Canandaigua, [N.Y.,] 2/22. He informs Calhoun that a group of Seneca Indians who have gone to Washington were not authorized to do so, either by the majority of the Seneca Chiefs or by Parrish. The unauthorized deputation was persuaded "to make this hasty movement, by a few white people, residing at Batavia," who seek the appointment of a new Agent and the payment of the annuities at Batavia. "They have been tampering with the Indians for three or four years past, to obtain this object." LS in DNA, 1, P-242 (M-221:96).

From John Williams, [Chairman, Senate Committee on Military Affairs,] 2/22. A majority of the members of the Committee agrees to "the propriety of confer[r]ing Brevet rank [as a Lt. Col.] on Major [Sylvanus] Thayer." Williams suggests that the nomination be sent "as soon as convenient." ALS in DNA, 1, W-202 (M-221:96).

From Duncan Dobbins & Co.

Louisville, Kentucky, Februa[r]y 23rd 1823

We herewith lay before you our ac[count] amounting to $94.69 being a balance due to us since *December 1821* for goods furnished [the] steam Boat *Western Engineer* on ac[count] of the United States. We have repeatedly endeavor'd to get this ac[count] settled but all to no purpose, owing we presume to our not applying to the proper ["purposes" *canceled and* "persons" *interlined*]. We therefore, Sir, take the liberty of addressing you on this subject well knowing from your established character in this section of the Union, that you will act in the case, with promptitude & justice. The debt tho small is long & justly due, & is to us a matter of considerable importance.

We send you *signed* duplicate accounts & also bills of particulars as taken from our books, which we hope is quite sufficient to enable you to remit to us the amount at this place.

LS with Ens in DNA, 30, 427. Note: The enclosures indicate that the merchandise was furnished during 10/1821–12/1821.

To V[IRGIL] MAXCY

Washington, 23d Feb[ruar]y 1823

I have received your three last letters but have not answered them for the want [of] time. I am sorry you cannot visit us before the close of the session, and particularly that your visit should have been prevented on account of the state of Mrs. Maxcy's health. I hope that it may so improve still as to enable you to ride up the last of the week. I wish to see you much, before Congress rises. The real state of things here is not much known to the country. If I am not in a mistake we have reached an important point. I have never been stronger in Congress; and it will be necessary to remove the impression of my withdrawal. This may be effectually done at Harrisburgh [*sic*]. My friends think it ought to be done, and such is my own opinion, in which almost the whole delegation ["from Pena" *interlined*] concur. I have but little doubt but a movement will be made at Harrisburgh. You see the importance of the moment. Should it take place and be properly managed, it must go far to decide the question which now agitates the country. [George M.?] Dallas is here and is heartily with us.

Still hoping to see you I will add no more for the present, except to say that I have read the two letters with [*one word canceled and* "interest" *interlined*] which you enclosed and which I herewith return. Sincerely, J.C. Calhoun.

ALS in DLC, Galloway-Maxcy-Markoe Papers, vol. 32.

From W[illiam] Ward, Choctaw Agency, 2/23. He acknowledges Calhoun's letters of 1/25 and 1/28. Ward replies that he forwarded to Calhoun on 1/16 "The Treasur[e]r[']s D[ra]ft on the Bank [of] Darien (Georgia) for $3,242.50 in Lieu of my check on Louisville Ky. as I had no funds in that Bank." In regard to Calhoun's "Order in favour of James C. Dickson Esq[ui]r[e] for the Agency Iron Chest," Ward maintains that retention of the chest at the Agency is necessary for the safekeeping of the specie which must be kept there to meet the demands of Indians for improvements "and troubles of moving." It is 120 miles to the Natchez bank and the new location of the Agency will be 100 miles farther away. Ward certifies that construction has begun on buildings for a mission school "under the Directions of the Rev. Mr. C[yrus] Kingsbury" in the southeast part of the Choctaw Nation. ALS in DNA, 77, 5047 (M-271:4, frames 841–843).

From John E[wing] Colhoun

Charleston, [S.C.,] Feb[ruar]y 24th 1823

Doctor Edward [W.] North[,] brother of Mr. John North of Pendleton, [S.C.,] who[m] you know, is desirous of placing his son at the Military Academy of West Point. He ["is now at Cambridge College," *canceled*] is a lad of fourteen or fifteen, said to be very steady and of some promise. Should there be a vacancy, and you could possibly give him the appointment, it will no doubt be a source of great satisfaction to his father[,] who is one of our most worthy citizens. Very sincerely yours, John E. Colhoun.

ALS in DNA, 15, 1823, 130 (M-688:25, frames 165–166).

From Thomas S. Jesup, 2/24. He discusses in great detail the question of brevet rank, "which for the last nine years has produced so much difficulty in the Army." A correct interpretation of the statute of 7/6/1812 authorizing the conferring of brevets and of other laws provides the key to a proper understanding of the problem. Distinctions are made between the right of a brevet officer to command and his right to pay at his brevet rank; upon the latter there is a statutory limitation. "It is of vital importance to the service that the question be promptly settled," and it "is perhaps not now practicable to do complete justice" to all brevet officers in all respects, but justice can be granted to them in respect to their commands. The small, dispersed condition of the Army makes brevet rank "peculiarly adapted to our situation." With this long essay are filed several documents. One itemizes the pay received by nine officers who serve in seven Army bureaus in Washington. Another is an ADS by James Monroe, undated, reading: "I have examin[e]d with attention the subject which has been submitted to me and am of opinion, that the employment of a certain number of officers, in the bureaus of the department of war, is economical & conducive to the public interest. Their knowledge of the various duties of the department, acquir[e]d by military experience, enables them to render services, to which others, would be less competent. This practice, therefore, which was adopted, at an early period, appears to me to have been judicious, & ought to be adher'd to. In making the selection, care should be taken not to interfere with the calls of the service, or to extend the detail, further, than may be absolutely necessary, & to give to those thus employed a reasonable compensation only, having regard to the salaries allowed by law to Clerks, performing similar duties, to be paid, out of the contingent fund of the Army. Those who have been disabled by wounds, or otherwise, ought to be preferr[e]d." Additional documents in the file concern the right of Col. [John R.] Fenwick to be considered the commander of the post at Pensacola and to brevet pay since 12/1821, as opposed to a counter claim of Col. [Duncan Lamont] Clinch to the same since 5/1822. ALS with Ens in DNA, 1, Q-133 (M-221:96); FC (dated 3/12/1823) in DNA, 42, 4:462–469 (M-745:2, frames 529–532); FC (dated 3/12/1823) in DNA, 50, vol. 3; CC and CCEx (each dated 3/12/1823 and the latter with a unique footnote) in DLC, Thomas Sidney Jesup Papers; CC (of the Monroe document) in DNA, 2, P-1823 (M-222:23).

From Will[iam] F. Pendleton, Richmond, 2/24. He applies for appointment to be the Agent to the [Eastern] Cherokees. He relates his past contacts with Indians, who "were very fond of me. I am at present a member of the Privy Council [of Va.] and a Director of the Literary Fund, but both of them will not enable me to do that which if known to a feeling heart would excite sympathy." ALS in DNA, 77 (M-271:4, frame 729).

From James Pleasants, Jr., [Governor of Va.,] Richmond, 2/24. He recommends William F. Pendleton of Richmond to be appointed Agent to the [Eastern] Cherokees. ALS in DNA, 77, 5049 (M-271:4, frames 727–728).

To Lewis Williams, Chairman, [House] Committee on Claims, 2/24. Calhoun replies at length to Williams's letter of 2/12 [ALS in DNA, 1, W-201 (M-221:96)] concerning the claim of [former] Col. James R. Mullany for pay and emoluments as Quartermaster General of the Northern Division during the last seven months of 1818. Calhoun returns the papers supporting the claim and encloses documents substantiating his rejection of it. (He based his decision, in part, upon a report submitted to him by Peter Hagner on 2/19 [FC in DNA, 53, 28:378].) FC in DNA, 4, 2:270–271 (M-220:1).

William Dudley Digges, [Washington, to James Monroe, *ca.* 2/25]. Digges needs money. He reviews the prospect, under a decision by arbiters, that he might receive $29,600 from the U.S. for land adjacent to Fort Washington, [Md.]—a prospect stymied by the [House] Committee on Ways and Means about eight days before the imminent adjournment of Congress. Though $46,000 are being appropriated for fortifications at the Fort, no more than about $7,000 can be expended without acquiring Digges's land. So he asks that the purchase from him be authorized from that fund or from any contingent funds. He owes about $16,000 of what he would receive and could retain only about $13,000. ALS in DNA, 281, Md. (Fort Washington), 71.

From S[amuel] D. Ingham, [Representative from Pa.,] and William Findlay, [Senator from Pa.,] 2/25. These Congressmen recommend Jefferson Van Horne, son of "Gen. [*sic*; former Capt.]" Isaac Van Horne of O., as a candidate for a Cadet's appointment. LS in DNA, 15, 1823, 203 (M-688:26, frame 217).

From Alexander Macomb, 2/25. He recommends that Maj. [Isaac] Roberdeau of the Topographical Engineers be promoted to the brevet rank of Lt. Col. (According to Heitman, *Historical Register,* 1:834, Roberdeau was promoted, as requested, on 4/29.) ALS in DNA, 1, E-110 (M-221:95).

From Jacob Brown, 2/26. He encloses a letter of 2/15 to himself from former Lt. Col. Robert Carr, Adjutant General of Pa., who seeks a Cadet's appointment for his son, John B. Carr, and another letter from A[mbrose] Spencer, former Chief Justice of N.Y., in support of [Alexander Jenkins] Center for the same purpose. (Center was appointed a Cadet in 1823. Heitman, *Historical Register*, 1:292. John B. Carr apparently was not appointed.) LS with En in DNA, 15, 1823, 176 (M-688:25, frames 478–481); FC in DLC, Jacob Brown Papers, Letterbooks, 2:223.

From [the Western Cherokee Delegation]

Washington, February 26th, 1823

We have read your talk which you say our Father the President [James Monroe] directed you to make to us on the 12th inst[ant], and we are willing to believe that he will listen to the wants of his red children & attend to them, and he may rest assured that such assurances are always consoling to us. We trust that measures will speedily be taken to give us suitable conveyances of all the lands due to us from the United States with correct metes & bounds, so that we may plainly understand everything; not only about the land, but also respecting the western *outlet* agreeable to the President's promise, and we shall take due care to keep our people within our own limits & in all respects be guided by the treaty of 1817, and shall expect our Father the President to do the same with his people: and notwithstanding what you have said relative to the twelve miles square, we can not as yet see why we should not have our proportion of it or the proceeds. We desire you to thank the President for his good intentions for sending us the cotton gin & he may rely upon it that when delivered to us, it shall be kept in good repair at the charge of the nation. We are sorry to hear that no additional allowance is to be made for wheels, looms &c. as we think they tend much to our progress in civilization & learn us to walk straight in the path which the President has so often directed us. By the treaty of 1817, it was agreed that we should have all the benifits [*sic*] we had in Tennessee. We there had mills &c. & think it now just that we should have them on the Arkansaw. We presume if our Father the President could be made fully sensible of the great suffering we undergo for the want of a corn & saw mill, he would rather that some part of his great family should be deprived of the luxuries with which he furnishes them, than to have us continue longer in want of these articles which are necessary to the sustenance of life. We thank the President for blotting out the charge [to] us of $555.75 cents, which was made for corn. We never expected he would demand payment of us for the corn. We had justice in allowing us the annuities of 1818 & 1819, amounting as you say, to $7,214.56, with the deduction however of the sum of $1,855 said to be advanced to Gov[ernor Joseph] McMin[n]. We now wish to talk very plain to you about John D. Chisholm's bond. We never thought it was right for Chisholm or any of his assigners [*sic*] to bring this bond as a charge against the nation & if by any misunderstanding, our Chiefs have ever agreed he might, it is still less intelligible to us, what right has the President to take this bond & charge it to us in payment of the annuities due to us from him. A great [number of] individuals of the President's people come into our nation & get furs & go away & never pay us. If the President will pay us the debts his people contract with us, we then might [think] it right for him to take our money to pay ["our money to pay" *repeated*] the debt of Chisholm or [Patrick] Farrel[l]y. In short we do not see what the President has to do with the business at all—let Farrel[l]y collect it either from the nation or whoever else owes him, but if as you [say], our nation has become bound to pay this debt & you consider it as a national debt, what right has the President to demand interest? You tell us as relating to our annuities which have been due four or five years, that no interest is to be allowed us, because it is a national debt, & if no interest be allowed on [a] national debt, you certainly have no right to demand interest of us—for the sole ground, on which you demand interest of us is, as you say, that the Chisholm debt has become a debt against the nation and if interest is not allowed in the one case, we do not understand why it should not [*sic*; be] in the other. And if we allow any thing for the debt of Chisholm or Farrel[l]y, we still think the value of the Negro woman & child, he took away, ought to be deducted from the debt. We thank our Father the President for being desirous that we should live in peace with all our neighbors; but defensive war is sometimes necessary. Of this the President has lately set us an example by going to war himself & that we believe under very just provocations. Such was our late case with the Osages, all which we made known to Gov[ernor James] Miller before we went to war & we then had permission to make war, as we presume, he has informed the President. And in no instance have we been or mean to be the offending party. The peace with the Osages was made under the multitude of injuries, they had done us without any suitable compensation for the same, in obedience to the wishes of the President expressed to us through Gov[ernor] Miller, at a moment when we were sure of complete victory.

We conclude by saying that we still hope justice may be done to our nation & that Gov[ernor] Miller may be directed to see that the Cherokees be remunerated for the injuries they have sustained by the depredation of the Osages; & we pray you to tell the President we wish to obey him in all things & shew him respect in every subject & to convince him that we are as much attached to the laws of the United States as the white men are & intend to be as good citizens, and pray him as soon as he consistently can to take us under the same patronage and treat us in the same manner as his white children, so that we may enjoy the liberty of freemen.

LS in DNA, 77, 5053 (M-271:4, frames 321–324). NOTE: This letter was signed by Black Fox, John McLamore, Walter Webber, and James Rogers, the first three of whom affixed their marks.

From Capt. R[ufus] L[athrop] Baker, Bellona Arsenal, [Va.,] 2/27. He discussed recently in Washington with [James Monroe] the unhealthiness of that garrison during summers and autumns. [Monroe] suggested that the troops be encamped a mile or two away from the [James] River's fogs. Baker tells how he would maintain a guard at the Arsenal and approves the plan. He is constructing gun carriages for mounting four small cannon in the buildings. Baker has corresponded recently with [Winfield Scott] and with Virginia's Adjutant General about "the defence of this post against the Blacks of the Country." Because plans for Baker's family are involved, he asks whether he is likely to be continued in command of the Arsenal "a year or two longer." ALS in DNA, 31, 1823, B.

From Alexander Macomb, 2/27. "A mutual application for an exchange of Professorships has been made by David B[ates] Douglass, Professor of Mathematics, and Claude [*sic*; Claudius] Crozet, Professor of Engineering, both attached to the Military Academy. As the exchange is thought beneficial to the Institution, Major [Sylvanus] Thayer[,] the Superintendent[,] has recommended the same, in which I fully concur." ALS in DNA, 1, E-111 (M-221:95); FC in DNA, 21, 1:379.

From David L. Morril, [Senator from N.H.]

Senate Chamber, Feb. 27th 1823

At the request of Mr. Benjamin Gale, of Concord N.H. I transmit the enclosed Documents to your Department, believing them deserving your consideration & notice.

ALS in PHi. Note: The enclosures probably recommended James Varnum Gale for an appointment to be a Cadet and probably included the letter to Calhoun from J[ohn] Brooks dated 2/21, a transcription of which appears herein.

From David Brown, Washington, 2/28. He expresses his concern about the selection of a new Indian Agent for the [Eastern] Cherokees to replace the deceased [Return J.] Meigs. "If I mistake not, dear Sir, your theory is, with regard to the aboriginal inhabitants of this land to promote their happiness & in all your dealings with them to do them justice." "But, my dear Sir, how can you promote their happiness by sending them your officers who are regardless of humanity, religion, to act as a medium between your gover[n]ment & that of the Indian tribes? How much good do you do them when you send your gove[r]nors & commissioners . . . [who] use all the threats & compulsions of an enemy[?] How can your sensual & speculating agents promote the happiness of the Indians[?]" Indian Agents "should be men of veracity & truth—men who will be obedient to your just demands & who will seek the true interest of the Long oppressed aborigines." "I have made these observations because an aboriginal blood runs in my veins. I have seen the unhappy condition of my fathers." "I flatter myself that a happier day is daw[n]ing in the Cherokee Nation. Schools, court houses, places of public worship, are established in the nation. My countrymen are now rapidly advancing toward civilization & religion. In a few years when we shall be capable & when we are admitted under the government of the United States, I hope you shall see an aborigine in Congress who will act in the capacity of a representative from the Cherokee Nation." ALS in DNA, 1, B-280 (M-221:95).

To John Holmes, [Member,] Senate Committee on Finance, 2/28. In reply to Holmes's letter of 2/27 [*not found*] enclosing a Senate resolution [of 2/20 (DS in DNA, 1, S-390 [M-221:96])] "respecting the expediency of making an appropriation to complete the Barracks and other buildings commenced at Baton Rouge," Calhoun encloses an estimate and report by Thomas S. Jesup dated 2/28 [LS with En in DNA, RG 233, 18A-C19.2; FC in DNA, 42, 4:442 (M-745:2, frame 519); FC in DNA, 50, vol. 3] explaining that "the sickness and mortality" of the troops caused unexpected expenses in procuring materials and labor at Baton Rouge and forced costs above the estimated outlay. LS with Ens in DNA, RG 233, 18A-C19.2; FC in DNA, 4, 2:272 (M-220:1).

From [Thomas S. Jesup,] 2/28. "Should an appropriation be made to complete the Barracks at Baton Rouge," [Jesup] recommends Lt. Col. [Zachary] Taylor to superintend the construction. "His rank, industry, energy, and talent for business would enable him to command every assistance from the troops without those difficulties to which an officer of less rank, or different character, would be liable." FC in DNA, 42, 4:442 (M-745:2, frame 519); FC in DNA, 50, vol. 3.

C[hristopher] Vandeventer to E[leazer] W. Ripley, New Orleans, 2/28. Vandeventer informs Ripley, as Calhoun has directed, that "the execution of your Medal is suspended for want of your likeness." FC in DNA, 3, 11:466 (M-6:11).

To Samuel L. Southard, [Senator from N.J.,] 2/28. In reply to Southard's letter of today (ALS in DNA, 30, 436), Calhoun expresses regret over the necessity that compels Southard to return "so suddenly" to his home. Calhoun also encloses an appointment as Cadet for John [D.] Westcott of N.J. and asks Southard to "give it its proper direction." LS in NjP, Samuel L. Southard Papers; FC in DNA, 13, 1:195 (M-91:1).

MARCH 1823

Congress adjourned on the 3rd, doubtless much to Calhoun's relief. On the 26th he assured a donor that he had planted some grape vines "with care," because "the success of the vine" was important to "our commerce and morals." The next day he summarized to a supporter some "topicks for arguments to sustain" his Presidential candidacy —among them "my uniform Republican course" and "my habits of industry and business." On the 30th he wrote that two of his rivals were not gaining in public favor, advocated acquisition of Cuba as a means of protecting American liberty, and avowed the maxim that one should "do right and fear not." One of his letters of the 18th ordered compliance with a new statute requiring annual financial reports but did not relax the War Department's own requirements calling for more frequent accountability.

From [2nd] Lt. C[lark] Burdine, Fever River, Ill., 3/——. None of his questions written since his "second arrival" there [in the autumn of 1822] has been answered. He feels quite handicapped. ALS in DNA, 31, 1823, B.

To [John Gaillard], 3/1. Pursuant to a Senate resolution of 2/27, Calhoun encloses a statement showing the number of disabled officers and enlisted men from the War of 1812 placed on the pension lists since the last session of Congress. The list includes their names, State or Territory, the amount of each pension, where paid, the date on which each application was allowed and how far before that date each pension began, the degree of disability, and the evidence upon which each disability was ascertained. (Also enclosed were CC's of letters to Calhoun from William Wirt dated 7/19/1822 and from James L. Edwards dated 12/11/1822.) LS with Ens in DNA, RG 46, 17A-F4; FC with En in DNA, 91, 13:93–97; PC with Ens in Senate Document No. 43, 17th Cong., 2nd Sess.; PC with Ens in *American State Papers*: *Claims*, 1:893–894.

From Jacob Brown, Washington, 3/3. He states his opinions that on 12/1/1821, under authority of the general regulations of the

Army, Col. [John R.] Fenwick was properly placed in command of the forces at Pensacola; that Fenwick's right to command has never been disputed; and that, although Congress repealed those regulations, his command was continued by Presidential proclamation as being not in conflict with "positive legislation." LS in DNA, 1, Q-133 (M-221:96); FC in DLC, Jacob Brown Papers, Letterbooks, 2:223.

From Lawrence Taliaferro, Washington, 3/3. He states his intention to call on Calhoun next Friday morning to discuss the hostile feelings of the Indians. ALS in MnHi, Lawrence Taliaferro Papers (published microfilm, roll 1, document 51).

To [Mathew?] Carey, [Philadelphia?]

War Dept., March 4th 1823

The Secretary of War presents his compliments to Mr. [Mathew?] Carey and sends agreeably to his request, a statement prepared at the Gen[era]l Land Office, of the quantity &c. of Lands relinquished under the act of 2d March 1821. This statement would have been sent on the return of mail, but the pressure of business at the close of the session [of Congress] prevented. He hopes it may yet be in time.

ADU in MH.

To James Miller, Little Rock, 3/4. Calhoun reports that the Western Cherokee delegation is about to return to Ark. Territory and encloses a copy of his answer [of 2/12] to the subjects submitted by the delegation for the decision of the War Department. Calhoun thinks the visit to Washington will be beneficial both to the Western Cherokee Indians and to the government. Calhoun instructs Miller about procedures to be followed in surveying their boundary line. Miller will pay particular attention to the last paragraph of Calhoun's reply to the Indians, and Miller will adopt the measures necessary "to effect the desire of the [Western] Cherokee Nation." Since the U.S. has agreed to erect a [cotton] gin for the Indians, "the allowance for wheels, looms &c. for the present year cannot of course be as liberal as usual, and such is the understanding with the Deputation." The [Western] Cherokee annuities for

1818, 1819, and 1823 have been paid to [David] "Brearley their Agent, who attended them to Washington." FC in DNA, 72, E:396 (M-15:5); CCEx in MHi; PC in Carter, ed., *Territorial Papers*, 19:498–499.

W.H. Bedford, Washington, to James Monroe, 3/5. Bedford complains about the delay and the "frivolous" objections made to the claims for losses by residents of Tenn. who served as militia-men during the Seminole War [of 1817–1818]. Bedford feels that objections were made because of incorrect form rather than of improper claims. He charges [Peter Hagner] and "a British Clerk" in Hagner's office with improper handling of the claims. As agent for the claimants, Bedford will return to Tenn. and endeavor to give the claimants an explanation, but he urges that the decision be reconsidered. ALS in DNA, 1, B-287 (M-221:95).

From Simeon North, Washington, 3/5. He offers to manufacture 10,000 rifles during 1823–1827 for $14.50 each. Because this would bring to North an average income $30,000 per year less than "has ever been set apart [by the U.S.] for my Establishment for ten years past," he hopes that this bid will be considered reasonable. ALS in DNA, 31, 1823, N.

To James Pleasants, [Jr.,] Governor of Va., [Richmond,] 3/5. Calhoun recommends Isaac Briggs for the position of Civil Engineer of Va. LS in DLC, Isaac Briggs Papers.

To Lewis Cass, Detroit

Dep[art]m[en]t of War, 6 March 1823

The arrangement proposed by the Treasury Department which is referred to in the enclosed paper [George Graham's letter to Calhoun dated 2/22] for the disposition of a portion of the Goods at the several Factories, has been acceded to by this Department; and you will give the necessary instructions to the Indian Agent at Green Bay, to carry the same into effect, restricting his purchases to such goods only as are of a suitable kind and quality for Indian purposes, and which can be had at the Factory near him on as advantageous terms as elsewhere, and to an amount not exceeding in any event that which, according to the most moderate and economical annual allowance at his Agency for this purpose, will be sufficient for the years 1823 & 1824. The amount of the purchases made by the Agent will be considered as constituting a part of the sums that may be allotted to him for his expenses in each of those years, and will be deducted therefrom in due proportion. Should any goods be required for Indian purposes at Detroit, or at those Agencies which have no Factory near them, you are authorized to take them of the Factory Agents after ["their" *canceled*] his removal to Detroit, under the restrictions above mentioned.

To enable the Department to retain a sufficient amount out of the sum assigned for the expenses of your Superintendency to meet the drafts which may be drawn on it by the Indian Agent or yourself, in pursuance of this arrangement, you will furnish, as soon as practicable, an estimate of the probable amount of Goods that will be purchased of the Factory for Indian purposes within your Superintendency. Those purchased at the request of the Indians for annuities, you will pay for out of funds which will be remitted to you for the payment of the annuities.

The Department has no objection to the arrangement which it is proposed to make with the Indian Agents for the collection of the debts that may be due to the Factories; and should the Agent at Green Bay find it convenient to undertake that duty, he is at liberty to do so, on the terms and in the mode which he and the Factory Agent may agree upon; with this understanding, however, that he is to look to the Treasury Department only for any additional compensation to which he may consider himself entitled for the performance of said duty.

LS with Ens in DNA, 76 (M-1:12, pp. 93–104); FC in DNA, 72, E:397 (M-15:5).

From Joseph McMinn, Cherokee Agency, 3/6. He reports the murder of an Indian by two white men. "We have been attentively engaged in the examination of the papers of this Agency, more particularly on the subject of the accounts between Col. [Return J.] Meigs Dec[ease]d and the United States, which accounts present obstacles that cannot fail to perplex, if not to render the final adjustment at this office uncertain." McMinn asks Calhoun to report what items in the account submitted by Meigs on 9/17/1822 are considered acceptable and tells how an executor has begun to administer the estate. ALS in DNA, 1, M-319 (M-221:96); draft in DNA, 75 (M-208:9).

To James Miller, Little Rock, 3/6. Calhoun directs Miller to give to the Western Cherokees' Indian Agent, [David Brearley,] instructions similar to those written on 3/6 by Calhoun to William Ward concerning the closing of the Indian Factories. FC in DNA, 72, E:398 (M-15:5).

To William Ward, Choctaw Agency

Dep[art]m[en]t of War, 6 March 1823

The arrangement proposed by the Treasury Department which is referred to in the enclosed papers, for the disposition of a portion of the goods at the several Factories, has been acceded to by this Department. You will accordingly take such goods of the Factory near you as you may want for Indian purposes at your Agency, in the present and ensuing year, provided they can be had there of a suitable kind and quality and on as advantageous terms as elsewhere, limiting your purchases to an amount not exceeding in any event that which according to your usual annual expenditure for this purpose, will be sufficient for both these years. The amount of the purchases which you may make will be considered as constituting a part of the sum allowed for the expenses of your Agency in those years respectively, and will be deducted therefrom in due proportions to meet the drafts which you may draw on the Department in pursuance of this arrangement.

It will, therefore, be necessary for you to advise the Department without delay of the probable amount of your purchases.

Should you purchase any goods of the Factory at the request of the Indians, on account of their annuity, you will pay for them out of the funds which will be remitted to you for the annuity.

The Department has no objection to the arrangement which it is proposed to make with the Indian Agents for the collection of the debts that may be due to the Factories; and should you find it convenient to undertake that duty, you are at liberty to do so on the terms and in the mode which you and the Factory agent may agree upon; with the understanding that you are to look to the Treasury Department only, for any additional compensation to which you may consider yourself entitled for the performance of this duty.

FC in DNA, 72, E:398–399 (M-15:5). Note: Similar letters to William Clark and to George Gray dated 3/6 appear in the same letterbook, pp. 399–401.

From D[avid] Brearley, Washington, 3/7. "In my Estimate [of 2/4], for the Amount requisite, for putting the Cotten [*sic*] Gin into opperation [*sic*], I did not take into view the cost of the Gin." ALS in DNA, 77 (M-271:4, frame 280).

From Brig. Gen. [Simon] Bernard, "Private"

New York [City], March 8th 1823

Whether the rumours of an occupation of Cuba by Great Britain are founded or not, the consequences of such an undertaking would be too serious not to deserve some investigations even on the mere ground of hypothesis. The importance of the subject, and its near connection with the task to which I am associated induce me to hope that you will receive with indulgence the following observations which I very respectfully submit to you.

The power of Great Britain rests chiefly on her Navy, her Auxiliaries, and her ultra-marine Positions. While the Navy shelters the territory of England from foreign invasions, it maintains unmolested the intercourse between the metropolis and the whole world; it exercises over the other navies the proper control to insure the continuance of its relative superiority. By means of Auxiliaries, England is enabled to wage war throughout the old continent without endangering her own territory or disturbing her industry at home: Turkey in Europe, Piedmont, Portugal, Holland, Hanover afford to England the means of meddling with the political concerns of Europe, of favoring her commercial interests, of exciting quarrels and jealousies the consequences of which are to benefit English industry.

As to her ultra-marine Positions, time and circumstances having taught England how greatly her insular position had contributed to her safety and power, she applied herself to enlarge the field of her influence by the occupation of islands conveniently situate to that effect. Already she has entrapped the old continent in that system: St. Helena, with the Cape of Good Hope, and Mauritius Island insure her communication with India, where auxiliaries make and support her conquests; whilst Gibraltar commands the entrance of the Mediterranean, the Ionian islands control the Adriatic Gulf and Malta overlooks the outlet of the Black Sea: thus are thwarted the hopes entertained by some European nations to open, through that quarter, a commercial intercourse with India; the islands of Jersey and G[u]ernsey, on the very coasts of France, watch at once on

Brest and Cherbourg, the two great French naval depots on the Ocean; from the rock of Heliogoland, the British navy ["controls" *interlined*] the outlets to the sea of the Ems, Elbe and of the celebrated canal of Holstein [*footnote*: "This canal connects the Baltic with the Northern Sea; it admits vessels of 9½ feet draught; from two to three thousand sails pass yearly through it, and most of the commerce of the North is carried through that inland communication."]: that insular position checks, therefore, in time of emergency, the ["water" *interlined*] communications of Germany and Poland to the sea; besides, it could command the very opening of the grand projected canal, which would unite the Elbe to the Rhine, the Rhine to the Meuse, the Meuse to the Scheldt, that is to say, the Northern Sea to the English channel, the Baltic to the Mediterranean, St. Petersbourg to Paris. [*Footnote*: "That canal was projected by the French under the empire: the section from the Rhine to the Meuse is nearly finished; that from the Meuse to the Scheldt is but sketched in a few places; the uncouth political division of the territory of lower Germany will, very likely, ("prevent" *interlined*) the section from the Rhine to the Elbe from being soon executed."] It would be superfluous to enter in ["a" *interlined*] more minute examination respecting the properties of those positions; it suffices to mention the names of those strong and well situate holds to show ["all" *interlined*] their importance for Great Britain.

England having, by this time, thus completed her system of ultra-marine positions against the eastern hemisphere, analogy authorizes and makes it reasonable to believe that the British cabinet will not suffer such a work of policy to lie unfinished in its relations against this continent; and will ["on the contrary" *interlined*] avail itself of future events to carry it toward completion. Already, Canada is a permanent and continental auxiliary of Great Britain against the Union, and Bermuda a central ["and" *interlined*] insulary position overlooking, in the Western Ocean, the two Americas. But this latter position is yet too far for the object in contemplation; Great Britain wants a point nearer to the continent, in order to exercise a more effectual control: on that ground Cuba deserves the most earnest attention.

The island of Cuba is possessed of numerous and excellent harbours; it abounds with timber for naval constructions; its Capital, Havana, is defended by strong fortifications and protected against hurricanes. Should England, under any plausible pretence, occupy that island, the external commerce and carrying-trade of the Mexican Empire would fall into her hands; she could, in progress of time, create, in that quarter, political feelings hostile to the Union; she could control the whole commerce of the gulf of Mexico; in fine her line of naval operations would be shortened of 5,000 miles. The Union having, on her coasts south of the Chesapeak[e], no harbour for line battle ships, the British, being masters of Cuba, could, in time of war, blockade the outlets of the Mississip[p]i; thus leaving to this noble stream no other safe communication to the sea than that intended through New York by means of canals: [a] circumstance which could perhaps ["tend to" *interlined*] alter materially the connection now existing between the respective interests of the States. With Cuba the British Navy could prevent any communication by sea between the States on the Atlantic and those on the gulf of Mexico, harass the intercourse between the manufacturing States and South America, keep in continual alarms the Southern States, threaten with expeditions the vulnerable points of the maritime frontiers; finally try any attempt which would involve the Union into expenses and difficulties the consequences of which cannot easily be for[e]seen.

Sometime before the rupture of the Treaty of Amiens, the illustrious [William] Pitt [the Younger] said, (in Parliament) alluding to the French, that England had every thing to apprehend from a nation which sailed out of her ports under the shelter of tempests: it was, indeed, a handsome compliment to the navies of both nations; but, what is not to be dreaded from the English nation and the firmness of her cabinet, when we reflect that Malta alone had cost [*one word canceled*] her ten years of war, an increase of debt of three hundred millions sterling, and a material alteration in her political institutions! If, after such a tremendous struggle, Russia, owing to a train of events which it was impossible to foresee, has assumed the first rank among the continental Powers of Europe; yet, on the other hand, it is worthy of remark that, this very same rock of Malta is, at this moment, the ["point" *interlined*] on which the English nation relies to prevent Russia from extending her dominions farther to the south, creating a Navy in the Black Sea, and associating to her Empire the Greek provinces, nurseries of numerous and skil[l]ful sailors.

Here, I ought perhaps to stop and dismiss the subject, but fully confident in your kind dispositions towards me, I will investigate it a little further and show that among the ancients as well ["as" *interlined*] among the moderns, the nations, which knew better how to take advantage of the three means [*one word canceled*] just pointed out, were those which attained the highest degree of power. To that effect the long contest between Rome and Carthage affords a proper field for illustration.

During the first Punic war the Romans took possession of Sicily, gained there a powerful ally and built a navy to support their occupation. Then they were enabled to carry war into Africa, where the Carthaginians were soon obliged to sue for peace: it was granted with heavy restrictions on their navy and the cession of all the islands between Italy and Africa.

At the beginning of the second Punic war, Hannibal formed the project of invading Italy; but the Carthaginians had then a navy inferior to that of the Romans; these were covered on the side of Africa by Sicily, Corsica and Sardinia. In that state of things, Hannibal had but two lines of operations left to his choice: one through Liguria, the other through the Pirenees [*sic*] and Alps; he followed the latter, and after a march of five months, during which he lost half his army, he entered Italy. Asdrubal, sent ten years afterward to join him, took the same line, but the Romans could easily prevent the junction by taking post between the two armies and engaging one of them with superior forces: Asdrubal was defeated. Three years after Mago landed in Liguria and thus shortened in a great degree ["the" *interlined*] line of operations; but, still the same difficulty existed as to the junction with the main army; and though Mago maintained his ground, yet he could not effect his object. Finally he and Hannibal were compelled to leave Italy and go to the relief of Carthage. What a difference could have been brought in so long and so obstinate a contest, if, from the beginning of that war, the Carthaginians had been masters of Sicily with auxiliaries in that island! Hannibal could then have ["sallied" *interlined*] from that position, to invade Rome, with ["the" *interlined*] certainty of receiving, through the shortest way, supplies and reinforcements. During this war, defensive on the side of the Romans, Fabius acquired, a prudence and perseverance, a reputation which has since become proverbial in defensive warfare; but he kept Rome, perhaps, too long ["a while" *interlined*] sheltered under his shield, for, after the taking of Syracusa [*sic*], which made again the Romans masters of Sicily, he does not appear to have perceived the advantages he could derive out of it, especially that of passing from the defensive to the offensive war. It was to the genius of Scipio that appertained the thought as well as the execution of such a transition: after having previously gained auxiliaries in Africa, he organized in Sicily the expedition against Carthage, and compelled the proud rival of Rome to submit to the most distressing conditions. Whether Fabius was born with a genius of a temporizing nature only, or that he apprehended that the success of Scipio would ["undervalue" *interlined*] his own, or that his feelings were wounded by his having not, the first, thought of the plan, certain it is that he strenuou[s]ly opposed Scipio's undertaking, and exerted the best of his abilities to counteract the execution of it.

As to the third Punic war, it could be but fatal to the Carthaginians: they were deprived of navy and auxiliaries; the Romans had both, and ["besides" *interlined*] were firmly established in Sicily. What was left to Carthage? Submission or despair. She tried the first; but most treacherously deceived, she resorted to the last with a sublime resignation; and, after an heroic agony, her inhabitants, her history, her litterature [*sic*], her monuments were all for ever buried under her ruins.

Here, I close ["up" *canceled*], those views: they were suggested by my devotedness to this noble Palladium of rational liberty. If every generous mind cherishes the highest concern for the welfare of the Union, what must not feel one, who is so much indebted to her liberality and hospitality!

CC in DLC, James Monroe Papers, vol. 32, 5894–5896 (Presidental Papers Microfilm, Monroe Papers, Reel 8).

Pension regulations issued by Calhoun, datelined in the Pension Office, 3/8. A statute of 3/1, supplementary to the statutes of 3/18/1818 and 5/1/1820 for Revolutionary pensions, has given to Calhoun the power to restore to pension lists the name of any veteran whose name has been removed, provided that the veteran can satisfy Calhoun that the former pensioner is now in "such indigent circumstances as to be unable to support himself without the assistance of his country, and that he has not disposed of or transferred his property . . . with a view to obtain a pension." In order to carry out this authorization, "public notice" is given that the evidence required for restoration to the pension lists is to be a schedule of the claimant's property, to be sworn to before a court of record. In every instance of a transfer of real estate, "authenticated copies of the deed of conveyance should be exhibited," as well as the names of the persons to whom the property was sold, the time of the sale, and the amount of money or property received in return. Any applicant who is unable to appear in a court will swear before a judge that he has a disease or bodily disability. A model of the required declaration as to an applicant's possessions is annexed. PC with En in the Washington, D.C., *Daily National Intelligencer,* April 3, 1823, p. 4, col. 4. Many other printings of this document appear in earlier and later issues of *ibid.*, some of them (for example, in the issue of March 11, 1823, without specifying the day of the month); and the same lack of detail is true also of the PC with En in *Niles' Weekly Register*, vol. XXIV, no. 9 (May 3, 1823), pp. 141–143.

From Sol[omon] Sibley, Washington, 3/8. A section of land was mistakenly granted by the Treaty of Chicago to Joseph La Framboise rather than to his sister, Josette. "This error was made known to the Commission[er]s, by the Indians too late" to be rectified. Joseph was advised to petition [James Monroe] for a transfer of the land from Joseph to Josette. ALS in DNA, 1, S-510 (M-221:96).

W[infield] Scott, New York [City], to [Christopher] Vandeventer, 3/9. "Some time since, General Paez, of Colombia, sent two sons & a nephew to this country for the purpose of being instructed in free principles & in military science—with a personal request (by letter) that I would, to a certain degree, superintend their education. They have now been, for —— months at a School or private academy in Penn[sylvani]a." Scott has been informed that the boys will soon be transferred to [Alden] Partridge's school [in Norwich, Vt.]. "Now as I know that P[artridge] is cursed with genius & eccentricity in equal quantities, that he never did, & never can, impart more than a superficial knowledge of any branch of learning, & that he has not one practical military idea in his head, I am anxious to save these young Colombians from the mischief of falling into such hands. Will it not be possible to have them *attached* to the Military Academy—say for two years or a *full term*? They might have warrants, in order to subject them to martial law, but be *supernumeraries* & without pay." Money "can be placed in the hands of the Treasurer of the Academy for the payment of all charges &c., & I will undertake to interest Majors [*sic*; Bvt. Lt. Col. Sylvanus] Thayer and [Bvt. Maj. William J.] Worth in their behalf. I am confident that by giving the benefit solicited the U[nited] States government would gratify, in the highest degree, that of Colombia, without violating any law of our own, or doing the sligh[t]est disservice to our Academy. Please enquire of Mr. Calhoun whether it be practicable or not, to grant the warrants?" "I have heard some indistinct acc[oun]ts of a nomination, &c., which have given me much uneasiness. Major [Charles J.] Nourse, who was much interested in the success of the party, has promised to give me the particulars." An AEI by A[lexander] M[acomb] reads: "I can see no impropriety in this particular instance in granting the request of Gen. Paez under the proposition herein contained." ALS in DNA, 30, 439.

To David Brearley, Indian Agent, Washington

Dep[art]m[en]t of War, 10 March 1823

I enclose for your information a copy of my answer on the several points submitted by the [Western] Cherokee delegation for the consideration and decision of the Department; and also a copy of my letter [of 3/4] to Gov[erno]r [James] Miller.

Your attention is particularly called to that part of my answer to the Delegation which relates to a claim for a Negro woman and child alleged to have been improperly taken from a Cherokee woman by John D. Chisholm.

I enclose an extract of a letter from Mr. [George] Graham to the Agent in charge of the Factory on the Arkansaw [*sic*] relative to the Cotton Gin at the Factory. You are authorized to purchase the Gin of the Agent on the best terms you can, provided the whole expense thereof including the sum of $500, estimated by you to be necessary to put it into operation, does not exceed $700.

The money will be paid to you here [*one word canceled and* "for" *interlined*] the balance of annuities due for the years 1818 & 1819 & the annuity due for the present year.

The subject of Missionaries was mentioned by the Delegation, but, as it was not urged, nothing has been said upon it in the letter [to] Gov[erno]r Miller; it having, however, since been mentioned, you are instructed to inform them that I am happy to find them so well disposed on this subject, that every necessary encouragement & protection will be afforded, by the Government, to the Missionaries amoung [*sic*] them, and that it will contribute towards the Schools which they may establish in the Cherokee Nation on the Arkansaw their due proportion according to the contribution for the same object in the old nation.

FC in DNA, 72, E:401 (M-15:5).

From WILLIAM CARROLL, [Governor of Tenn.]

Nashville, March 10th 1823

Since Gen[era]l [Andrew] Jackson has declined accepting the mission to Mexico, a number of Gentlemen have recommended Colo[nel] Henry Crabb as a suitable person to fill that appointment.

Colo[nel] Crabb is an eminent lawyer of extensive political information and is destined (if he lives) to be one of the most distinguished citizens of the West. Should the President [James Monroe] be disposed to make a selection from Tennessee, I know of no person whose appointment would more generally meet the approbation of the people than that of Colo[nel] Crabb.

LS in DNA, 103, Crabb (M-439:5).

From L[ouis] William DuBourg, "Monastery of the Visitation at George Town," [D.C.,] 3/10. Although Calhoun's letter of [2/20] approved [$200 each for the annual support of three Roman] "Catholic Missionaries for the Indian tribes of the upper Missouri and Mississippi [Rivers]," DuBourg's "second verbal [that is, oral] application" secured from Calhoun a promise to support four missionaries, for which DuBourg now seeks written confirmation. He asks also that William Clark in St. Louis be informed of the aid to the missionaries and invited "to assist in conveying them to their respective destinations." Their departure will be somewhat delayed, in order better to equip and to staff "the three posts designated by you, viz. Council bluffs, River St. Pierre and Prairie du chien. When this latter circumstance is fully ascertained, I will have the honor of addressing you for an extension of patronage." ALS in DNA, 77 (M-271:4, frames 436–437).

From William F. Hay, Secretary to the U.S. Commissioners, n.p., [*ca.* 3/10]. He encloses a journal of the proceedings during 1/1823 and 2/1823 of Commissioners Duncan G. Campbell and James Meriwether, who negotiated with the [Eastern] Cherokee Indians. ALS with En in DNA, 1, F-102 (M-221:95).

From Peachy R. Taliaferro, Orange, [Va.,] 3/10. He accepts "with pleasure" his appointment to be a Cadet. ALS in DNA, 15, 1822, 72½ (M-688:21).

To William Clark, St. Louis

Dep[art]m[en]t of War, 11 March 1823

Upon the application of Bishop [Louis William] DuBourg of New Orleans, permission has been given him to send among the remote tribes of Indians on the Mississippi & Missouri a number of Missionaries not exceeding *four* and I herewith enclose for your information copies of my letters to the Bishop.

It is believed that the Missionaries will besides preparing the way for their [that is, the Indians'] ultimate civilization be useful in preventing the commission of outrages and preserving peace with the tribes ["among" *interlined*] which, they may fix ["with" *canceled*] themselves. You will accordingly give them passports with letters to the Indian Agents, and every other facility, particularly in ["the" *canceled*] transportation, as you can conveniently and cheaply furnish, to enable them to prosecute their respective missions.

FC in DNA, 72, E:402 (M-15:5).

To Bishop [Louis William] DuBourg "of New Orleans," 3/11. Calhoun acknowledges DuBourg's letter of 3/10 and agrees "to extend the encouragement, promised in my letter to you of the 20th ultt[im]o [*sic*], to *four* Missionaries instead of *three* as stated in that letter." Calhoun also encloses a copy of his requested letter [dated 3/11] to [William] Clark. FC in DNA, 72, E:402 (M-15:5).

From R[ichard] Graham, St. Louis, 3/11. As authorized by Calhoun's letter of 12/31/1822, Graham has paid $207.20 to Jacques Metté for the latter's services as Interpreter during the first half of 1820; Graham encloses Metté's receipt. ALS in DNA, 1, G-157 (M-221:95); draft in MoSHi, Richard Graham Papers.

From Elisha P. Swift, Secretary, Western Missionary Society of Pa., Pittsburgh, 3/11. He applies for federal aid to the school maintained for a year for the Ottawa Indians in O., beside the Miami of the Lakes, by the Society, which was founded in 1804 by the Presbyterian Synod of Pittsburgh specifically for the civilization of the Indians, was incorporated in 1810, and suffered cessation of its work in northern O. during the War of 1812. Swift provides all information about the Society's project that is required by the regulations governing the fund for the civilization of the Indians. He claims the approval of [Lewis] Cass and of Sub-Agent Benjamin F. Stickney. Swift encloses an evaluation of the school's property, signed on 1/11/1823 by Stickney and two others and certified on 1/17/1823 by Samuel Tait, Superintendent of the school. Appended to this application is an AES by Francis Herron, the Society's President, approving it. ALS with En in DNA, 77 (M-271:4, frames 782–789). (Calhoun answered on 5/1.)

From [the Western Cherokee Delegation], Washington, 3/11. These Cherokees express their appreciation for the many kindnesses shown to them during their visit to Washington and ask for another letter from Calhoun concerning their lands and an appropriation for those "Cherokees who may choose to remove to the Arkansaw." They discuss the recent hostilities with the Osages and profess a sincere desire to remain at peace, requesting that troops fulfill their obligation under the 1822 treaty to maintain the peace. Although some white people seek to turn the Cherokees away from the missionaries and their schools, the Delegation has resolved "to follow their example & do all we can for the promotion of ["the" *canceled*] civilization, virtue & religion among our people," who "are now rapidly adopting the manners & customs of Europeans & we fondly hope that the time is not far distant, when we the Cherokees shall enjoy all the blessings of civilization, and live under the happy government of these United States." (This letter was signed by James "Rodgers [*sic*; Rogers]," Black Fox, John McLamore, and Walter Webber, the last three of whom affixed their marks. No written reply to it has been found.) LS in DNA, 77, 5066 (M-271:4, frames 325–328).

From Richard Bland Lee, Washington, 3/12. This former government employee applies for appointment to the commission, the authorization of which was initiated by a bill introduced in the Senate by [James] Barbour of Va. on 2/21, to adjust the claims of Richard Harris and Nimrod Farrow for damages sustained by them in connection with their contract for the building of fortifications on Dauphin Island. Lee encloses a copy of the bill. ALS with En in DNA, 8, 1824, 123.

Order by Alexander Macomb, by order of Calhoun, 3/12. "An extra allowance of ten dollars per month will be made to the officer doing the duty of Librarian at the Military Academy [Claudius Berard] who will under the direction of the Superintendent [Sylvanus Thayer] be held responsible for the books and other property belonging to the Library." FC in DNA, 18, 1:44; FC in DNA, 284, 1:107.

To V[IRGIL] MAXCY, Annapolis, "Confidential"

Washington, 12th March 1823

I have just heard from Mr. [George M.?] Dallas. The question of taking up the nomination of ["Govr." *canceled and* "Prest." *interlined*] was tried on presenting the name of Gen[era]l [Andrew] Jackson, by the delegates from Westmoreland [County, Pa.], who had been instructed to that effect. My friends were prepared to bring my name forward if the question should be entertained; but there appeared such aversion to the subject both on account of the want of authority in the members and the fear that it might distract their State election, that they thought it prudent not to bring my name forward, at all, so that even the appearance of an abortive attempt has been avoided. It was fully ascertained that I had ⅔ of the convention against all of the other candidates combined; and my friends in the State were never in better sperits [*sic*].

Arrangements must be made to bring out the next Legislature at the com[mencemen]t of the session; and in the mean time as much sperit given both to correspondence and papers, as may be practicable.

It is certain that the election is with Pen[nsylvani]a & New York. If they unite they choose their man; if they divide their respective candidates must become the rival candidates. This simple view combined with my known strength in Pen[nsylvani]a places me on high ground. The idea must be scouted that I have withdrawn, or that there is the least foundation for it[s] assertion. You must attend to the An[n]apolis Paper. It is the most important in the State.

Mrs. [Floride Colhoun] Calhoun has been very unwell but is much better. Truly, J.C. Calhoun.

[P.S.] Will you please to give to Gen[era]l [Robert Goodloe] Harper the substance of this letter.

ALS in DLC, Galloway-Maxcy-Markoe Papers, vol. 32. NOTE: This letter was forwarded from Annapolis to Maxcy in Baltimore, in the care of a Col. Howard. Mrs. Calhoun's illness may have been related to the fact that John C. Calhoun, Jr., was born in 1823.

To [THOMAS J.] ROGERS, [Representative from Pa.,] "Private & Confidential"

Washington, 12th March 1823

Dear Gen[era]l, Tho' what was intended at Harrisburgh [*sic*] has not succeeded, yet by judicious management nothing has been lost. Still every day proves the importance of Pen[nsylvani]a taking, and avowing her stand. There is strength enough in the State, which if it could be made manifest ["itself" *interlined*] to the Union by some act would go far to decide the Presidential contest. A very large portion of the Union is looking to her for direction and will follow her if she acts in time. She and New York have the principal influence at present. Should they unite the object of their choice must succeed; and should they divide the candidates which they may respectively support, must become the great rival candidates. My friends look to Pen[nsylvani]a and Mr. [William H.] C[rawfor]d's to New York and, I fear, that on [Martin] Van Buren's return an effort will be made to obtain some expression for his favourite. Should Penn[sylvani]a give a previous expression, it would effectually control all attempts in New York, and put Mr. C[rawfor]d out of the question. Hence its importance. Could not something be done in the counties, when they come to act on the Gov[erno]r's nomination? And could it not be so managed as to induce the Republicans of the Legislature to make some expression of their opinion before the adjournment? I have written to the same effect to [Samuel D.] Ingham and [George M.?] Dallas, but you must consider it in the light of suggestion rather than advice.

ALS in CSmH.

From LEWIS CONDICT, [Representative from N.J.]

Capitol Hill, 13th March 1823

When I last had the pleasure to see you, I intended to mention to you the case of my friend, Bernard Smith, at Little Rock. You recollect our former conversation concerning him. His family are there with him, & they are truly in a very deplorable condition. The place is sickly, provisions & other essentials are enormously high, his salary very small, sales of land in that quarter amount to nothing, & of course no perquisites—without the means of returning & [with] the almost certainty of starvation if he remains, what can the poor fellow do? He is as *upright* & as *honest* a man as breathes, worthy of any confidence you may repose in him, & highly respectable for his acquirements & good sense. We were school boys together in our early life, & I have known him well, ever since, & will vouch for his integrity.

Can you not, & *will* you not, furnish him some employm[en]t in your Departm[en]t which may relieve him from his present distress? Excuse my importunity—it is very painful to me I assure you. I hope in a day or two to be able to travel homeward. Yours most respectfully, Lewis Condict.

ALS in DNA, 8, 275.

To Solomon U. "Hendricks [*sic*; Hendrick], present"

Dep[art]m[en]t of War, 13th March 1823

I have laid before the President of the U[nited] States [James Monroe] the instrument of writing entered into between the Stockbridge, Oneida, Tuscarora, St. Regis, and Munsee tribes or nations of Indians and the Menomenees [*sic*], on the 23d September 1822, which you handed to me and now return it, endorsed as you will see, by the President.

The talk which you left at the Department some time ago for the Delewares [*sic*], was transmitted to Gen[era]l [William] Clark Superintendent of Indian Affairs at St. Louis to be communicated to them through their Agent. No answer has yet been received upon the subject either from Gen[era]l Clark or the Agent. As soon as an answer is rec[eive]d your nation will be made acquainted with the purport of it.

I have at your request directed $75 to be advanced to you out of the annuity of your nation for your expenses on your return from Washington, which Capt. [Jasper] Parrish will be directed to deduct accordingly.

FC in DNA, 72, E:402–403 (M-15:5).

To V[irgil] Maxcy, Baltimore

Washington, 13th March 1823

I wrote you yesterday, but directed to Annapolis, giving an account of the proceedings at Harrisburgh [*sic*]. Gen[era]l [Andrew]

Jackson's name was brought forward by the delegates from Westmoreland, which my friends thought a suitable opportunity to test the sense of the convention on the P[residentia]l nomination. The temper appeared very adverse to the consideration of the subject, on the grounds of the want of power, and the danger that it might distract the State nomination. Under these circumstances they ["indisposed" *canceled*] thought it unadvisable ["not" *interlined*] to act, tho' fully prepared, and have managed with so much prudence, as to loose [*sic*] nothing. It was well ascertained, that at least ⅔ were in my favour against all of the other candidates combined; and that Mr. [William H.] Crawford had but one friend in the convention. My friends in that State were never more determined or in better sperits [*sic*], than at present.

You are at liberty to apprize Gen[era]l [Robert Goodloe] Harper of the contents of this communication.

I do not think that we ought to be discouraged by the want of the nomination. There can be no rational doubt of the ["temper" *canceled and* "opinion" *interlined*] of the State in my favour. Even my enemies grant the fact. Occupying so strong a ground, my chance must be considered as among the very best. There is a simple mode of viewing the subject, which has always appeared to me to be very strong. It is acknowledged by all that the election will turn on New York and Pen[nsylvani]a. If united their candidate must succeed. If divided their respective candidates must become the great rival candidates. Examine, and you will find, that not one of the candidates can succeed unless he obtains one, or the other of these powerful States. The very fact, that I am certain of one of them, when no other candidate is of the other, gives me great advantage in the contest, which added to the fact that the interest, which supports [John Quincy] Adams, Jackson and much of [Henry] Clay's interest is better disposed towards me than any other candidate should either not run, puts my chance, if I am not mistaken, on ["the" *canceled*] ground stronger, than that of any other candidate.

These grounds ought to be taken extensively in correspondence, and the idea of my withdrawing scouted.

You would do well to prepare some article for the Annapolis paper, showing that it is the true interest of Maryland to act with Pen[nsylvani]a and the other mid[d]le States. That your interest is the same as hers, and that it is ["a" *interlined*] fortunate circumstance that that [*sic*; "this" *interlined*] great Democratick State is free from the sleight [*sic*] taint of Radicalism and ["that" *inter-*

lined] constitutes the safest basis on which to rally the Republican party, both from position and character, in which you might point out the unity of interest, that belongs to the mid[d]le States and its harmony with those of the rest of the Union.

I may be mistaken, but it appears to me my prospect was never better. I stand on the great Republican cause, free alike from the charge of Federalism or Radicalism.

If you can obtain any support for the paper here it would be desirable. A thousand or even five hundred dollars would be at present important to the editor [Thomas L. McKenney]. Mr. Cox the Mayor of Georgeto[w]n would endorse for the editor. He has very extensive possessions but not a command of cash at present. Without some support, I fear the editor may encounter insurmountable difficulties. [*Mutilated*; I have] no doubt, but my friends in Caro[lina] will make an effort in his fav[our] but it may not be adequate, or in time. If relieved ["now" *interlined*], the establishment has a fair prospect, in future. I think it very important.

I am rejoiced to learn that Mrs. G[alloway] is so much better. Mrs. [Floride Colhoun] Calhoun has been very unwell but is now better. I will be happy to form an acquaintance with Mr. Howard, as I have a high opinion of his character. I am yours Truly, J.C. Calhoun.

ALS in DLC, Galloway-Maxcy-Markoe Papers, vol. 32.

From Horatio Jones, Interpreter, Genesee (Livingston County), [N.Y.,] 3/14. "At the request of the Chiefs of the Christian party of the Seneca Nation of Indians, I take the Liberty to inform you that the visit made you by Red Jacket and two other Indians of the Pagan Party is unauthorized by the Nation in General." Jones complains about "the improper interference of the People of Batavia [N.Y.] between the Indians and their Agent Jasper Par[r]ish." ALS in DNA, 1, J-130 (M-221:96).

To Jasper Parrish, Sub-Agent for Indian Affairs, Six Nations, N.Y.

Dep[art]m[en]t of War, 14 March 1823

I transmit herewith, for your information, a copy of a talk which I have given to Red Jacket, Major Berry and Corn Planter, Chiefs of the Seneca nation, who are on a visit to Washington, and will leave it tomorrow morning.

Your attention is particularly called to that part of the talk which relates to a Blacksmith, and to the annuity. The money will soon be remitted to you for the annuity and you will purchase the goods (after obtain[in]g a list from the Indians of the articles they want) and distribute them in the mode pointed out in the talk. It would be proper to have the name of the person who may attend at the distribution of the goods to the receipts of the Indians, as a witness. These precautions are not taken because there is any doubt of the correctness of your conduct, but to prevent the complaints of a people, who it appears, from their suspicious and jealous disposition, are ["pretty" *canceled and* "very" *interlined*] difficult to deal with.

I have advanced to Solomon U. Hendricks [*sic*; Hendrick] who has been on here to get the President['] s [James Monroe's] assent to the late Treaty concluded with the Menominees at his request out of the annuity $75 for his expenses on his return home. I have also advanced to Red Jacket &c. at their request out of the annuity $200 for the same purpose. When you pay the annuity you will be careful to charge the proper tribes with their advances. The advance made to Hendricks is perhaps properly chargeable in due proportion to all the tribes concerned in the treaty before mentioned.

[Enclosure]

To Red Jacket, Major Berry, and Cornplanter, Seneca Chiefs

Brothers, I heard with an attentive ear the talks which you have made to me and have since carefully reflected upon the several points upon which you complain, and now make you the following answer.

That with respect to a Blacksmith, the treaty of the 11th of Nov[embe]r 1794 with the Six Nations made ample provision by an annuity of $4,500 for this object among others, and if no Blacksmith has been employed for the benefit of your nation the [Sub-] Agent [Jasper Parrish] will be instructed to see that you are furnished with your due proportion of Blacksmith['] s work, to be paid for out of your annuity above mentioned.

That as regards the annuity usually paid to you, which you state to be less in quantity latterly than formerly it is presumed the difference may have arisen from the goods having been purchased and forwarded by the Superintendent of Indian Trade [Thomas L. McKenney] whose office was kept at this place as the law then prescribed; but as the Indian Trade department was abolished by Congress about a year ago, the money will now always be remitted to your Agent to be laid out in such goods as you may wish him to purchase at New York [City] or any other place where they can be had of a suitable quality and on the best terms.

Your requests to have ["the" *interlined*] copies of the treaties with the Six Nations, with which you were formerly furnished, renewed, is granted. But, as the Department is very busy, and it will take some time to prepare the copies, they cannot be given to you now, but will be forwarded to you by mail as soon as there is sufficient leisure to attend to them.

You state that Captain Parrish, your Agent, is going contrary to orders, and wish him and Capt. [Horatio] Jones the Interpreter to be put aside. Capt. Parrish has been for many years acting as your Agent, and some of the Chiefs of the Six Nations have recently expressed themselves satisfied with his conduct and also with that of the Interpreter and wish them continued. But as the Government has no desire to protect the Agent when he acts wrong, the printed copy of the proceedings of the great Indian Council held at Tonewanta [*sic*; Tonawanda] in August last which was transmitted to this Department and contained charges against Capt. Parrish similar to those which you have now made, was enclosed to Gen[era]l Peter B. Porter, a gentleman of great respectability, and who is well known to your nation, in order that he might investigate the charges, which he did; and it appears by the report which he has made to this Department that the charges were not well founded. The government considers itself bound to sustain its Officers while their conduct is correct; but if any charges are brought against the Agent or ["the" *interlined*] Interpreter, and supported by proper evidence, they will be immediately displaced. But, to remove all ground of complaint in future on the subject of the annuity the Agent will be directed to call on you for a list of such goods as you may want your annuity paid in, to purchase them in New York [City] or any other convenient place on the best terms they can be had, and to distribute them among you in the presence of some respectable person in whom you have confidence.

As to the Ministers who are among you, whom you state have caused a division in your Council, they are not personally known to the government but they usually are some of our best men, whose object is of a very different character—it is to give you good advice, which if attended to, instead of dividing and making you enemies to each other, will unite you in the bonds of friendship and peace. You say there are two paths—one for the Whiteman, and another for the red man. This was the case and did well enough many years ago, when the red people were numerous and roamed at large over this great island, and lived upon game, with which it then abounded; but now that their numbers have become small, confined to narrow limits, and game scarce, if not voluntarily done, necessity will eventually compel the Red man to leave his path and travel in that of the whiteman—to abandon his accustomed habits and pursuits for those of civilized life.

As to your objection to remove to Green Bay, it is entirely at your option to go or stay; the Government will never take any steps to compel you to do either; you are at perfect liberty to follow your inclination in this respect. But it is believed that your interest would be promoted by a removal to that country. The distance which it would place between you and the white settlements would prevent the collisions which now frequently happen between you; the various tribes composing the Six Nations, which are now scattered over several distinct and distant reservations could there be united in one body on one tract of country owned in common by all, where game is plenty and where your settlements would be, for many years to come, unmolested by the too near approach of those of the white people. What I now say is not intended to urge you to move; it is only offered to your consideration in the way of advice, and you are free to adopt or reject it, according to your inclination.

You complain of the white settlers cutting your timber without your consent, and stealing your horses & cows. This furnishes evidence of the truth of what I have just said to you. Surrounded as you now are by the white people, bad men will, in spite of the law and all our efforts to prevent it, sometimes trespass upon you. The Department is, however, disposed to extend to you the justice which the law allows, and if you will exhibit a specific statement of the depredations which have been committed upon your property, with the necessary evidence to support it, it will be considered by the Department and such reparation ordered as may appear to be proper.

I take this opportunity to mention that the proprietors of the right to purchase your lands are as much interested as yourselves to prevent the timber from being cut down and destroyed, and for the better securing it against depredations they are desirous to have the land surveyed. As this measure will not affect your rights in the smallest degree, and will be advantageous to the proprietors, it is presumed you will have no objection to permitting them to proceed with it.

You have now finished your business, and I hope satisfactorily. I have allowed you $150, out of the Indian fund to pay your expenses home; if you think that is not sufficient and wish an advance from your annuity, I will direct it to be made to a reasonable amount.

Given under my hand and the Seal of the War Office of the United States at the City of Washington this fourteenth day of March in the year of our Lord 1823.

FC with En in DNA, 72, E:403–406 (M-15:5).

To P[ETER] B. PORTER, Black Rock, N.Y.

Department of War, 14th March, 1823

Red Jacket, Major Berry and Cornplanter, Chiefs of the Seneca nation, have been here, and in a talk which I gave them, I stated the substance of your report upon the charges exhibited by them against Captain [Jasper] Parrish, the Agent, which you made at the request of this Department. They expressed a desire to have a copy of your report, to which I replied that I did not consider it proper to give them a copy without your consent. I, however[,] informed them that I would enclose a copy to you, with a request, if you should have no objection to it, to hand it to them. In compliance with this promise a copy is herewith enclosed.

LS in NBu; FC in DNA, 72, E:403 (M-15:5). NOTE: The last sentence is omitted from the FC version of this letter.

From [2nd] Lt. C[lark] Burdine, Fever River, Ill., 3/15. He explains that the circular to him dated 10/1/1822 can enable lead-mine lessees to claim unconscionable tracts on the basis of an alleged right of private surveys. He hopes that no such claim will be recognized and that only official surveys made under this direction will be considered acceptable. ALS in DNA, 31, 1823, B.

To T[HOMAS] L. OGDEN, New York [City]

Dep[art]m[en]t of War, 15 March 1823

Your letter of the 1st inst[ant (ALS with En in DNA, 1, O-80 [M-221:96])] was duly received.

Nothing final upon the subject of the removal of the Seneca Nation to Green Bay, has grown out of the recent visit of Red Jacket to Washington. He appears to be inveterately opposed to removal and declared it to be his intention to live and die on the lands he now occupies. The Department, however, stated its views upon the subject and urged upon him as far as it thought proper, the advantages of changing his present residence for one more remote from the white settlements.

The Department took occasion also to mention to Red Jacket the survey which the proprietors wish to have made, and suggested to him the expediency of permitting the survey to proceed, as it would be an advantage to the proprietors and no injury to him.

Solomon U. Hendricks [*sic*; Hendrick] of the Stockbridge nation has also been here with the treaty to which you refer, concluded in September last between the New York Indians and the Menominees, which has been approved in part, by the President, [James Monroe,] with which Hendrick appeared to be satisfied.

FC in DNA, 72, E:406–407 (M-15:5). NOTE: Ogden's enclosure of 3/1 was a CCEx from Robert Troup to [Ogden?] concerning the proposed survey.

To DUNCAN G. CAMPBELL, Washington, Ga.

Dep[art]m[en]t of War, 17 March 1823

The appointment of Major [James] Merriwether [*sic*; Meriwether] and yourself as Commissioners to hold a treaty with the [Eastern] Cherokees, was submitted to the Senate, at the late session of Congress, by the President, [James Monroe,] and received the advice and consent of that body; and I accordingly enclose you a new Commission made out in due form.

You will continue your efforts, in the way you may judge best calculated to effect the object to bring about a treaty with the Cherokees. I think it probable their aversion to hold a treaty may be conquered by a little perseverance and judicious management.

Governor [Joseph] McMinn, of Tennessee, has been appointed to succeed Colo[nel Return J.] Meigs, as Cherokee Agent, and he has been instructed to correspond with you and to obey your instructions upon all points connected with the negociation [*sic*]. He is also instructed to seize every suitable occasion to dispose the Indians favorably for the negociation.

Congress at the last Session appropriated $50,000 for the purpose of purchasing certain tracts of land, reserved to Indians in fee [simple], by the treaties with the Creek Indians of the 9[th] August 1814 & of the 8th Jan[uar]y 1821, and by the treaties with the Cherokee Indians of 8 July 1817 & of the 29[th] Feb[ruar]y 1819. In order to carry into full effect the views of Congress in making the appropriation you will consider the authority given, in my first letter of instructions to the Commissioners, for the extinguishment of the Indian title to the reservations taken under the treaties referred to with the Cherokees, as extending also, to the reservations taken under the treaties referred to, with the Creeks. You are authorized to draw on this Department for such sums, not exceeding the amount appropriated as you may find necessary to effect this object.

I enclose an act of Congress relative to advances by which you will be regulated on the subject.

FC in DNA, 72, E:407–408 (M-15:5).

To John Clark, Milledgeville, 3/17. Pursuant to Clark's request of 3/3 [ALS in DNA, 1, C-321 (M-221:95); FC in G-Ar, Governors' Letterbooks, 1821–1829:103], Calhoun reports that "$17,740.73 for the payment of the second instal[l]ment due for the claims allowed under the late treaty [of 1/8/1821] with the Creek Indians will be remitted to you from the Treasury." FC in DNA, 72, E:407 (M-15:5). Receipt of this remittance was acknowledged by Clark on 4/1. LS in DNA, 1, C-360 (M-221:95); FC in G-Ar, Governors' Letterbooks, 1821–1829:109.

From L[ouis] William DuBourg, B[isho]p of N[ew] Orleans

Conv[en]t of the Visit[ati]on,
Geo[rge]town, [D.C.,] March 17th 1823

The liberal encouragement which the Government has, at my request, consented to extend to [Roman] Catholic Missions among the remote Indian tribes on the Missouri & Upper Mississip[p]i, having induced me to bestow upon that important subject all the attention to which it is entitled, I have the honour to submit to your consideration a plan of operation, which the most serious reflections have presented to me as best calculated to insure permanency to that Establishment, to enlarge its sphere of usefulness.

The basis of that plan would be the formation, (on an eligible spot near the confluence of those two large streams,) of a *Seminary*, or nursery of Missionaries, in which young Candidates for that holy function, would be trained to all its duties; whilst it would also afford a suitable retreat for such, as, thro' old age, infirmity, or any other lawful cause, would be compelled to withdraw from that arduous Ministry. The chief studies pursued in that Seminary would be: the manners of the Indians, the Idioms of the principal Nations, and the arts best adapted to the great purpose of civilization. And, in order to facilitate the attainment of some of these objects, I would at once try to collect in that Institution some Indian youths of the most important tribes, whose habitual converse with the *Tyros* of the Mission, would be mutually of the greatest advantage for the promotion of the ultimate object in contemplation. The result of that Kind of Noviciate would be a noble emulation among the Missionaries, uniformity of System, a constant succession of able & regularly trained Instructors, and a gradual expansion of their sphere of activity.

I am willing to give for that establishment a fine & well stocked Farm of mine, situate in the rich valley of Florissant, about one mile from the river Missouri & fifteen from St. Louis.

Seven young Clergymen, from 22 to 27 years of age, of solid parts & an excellent classical Education, are now ready to set off at the first signal, under the guidance of two Superiors & Professors, and with an escort of a few faithful Mechanics & husbandmen, to commence that foundation. I calculate at about two years the time necessary to consolidate it, and to fit out most of those highly promising Candidates for the duties of the Missions, after which they will be anxious to be sent in different directions, according to the views & under the auspices of Government, whilst they will be replaced in the Seminary by others, destined to continue the noble Enterprise.

So forcibly am I struck with the happy consequences likely to result from the execution of that project, that I hesitate not to believe that Government, viewing it in the same light with myself, will be disposed to afford me towards its completion that generous aid, without which I would not be warranted to undertake it. Personal sacrifices to the extent of my very narrow abilities will be cheerfully made. I also depend upon assistance from other quarters: But, besides this being precarious, I hope, that, taking into view the considerable expence attending the voyage to such a distance, of from 12 to 16 persons, the necessary constructions to be made, and the entire support of the Establishment, Government will be induced to assume upon itself a portion of the burden. It has already condescended to allow $800 per annum for four Missionaries: But it was on the supposition that they would be *immediately* sent to the Mission; and in the proposed plan, the opening of the Mission would take place but two years after the commencement of the Seminary: Yet, tho' not actually employed among the tribes, the Missionaries, whilst yet in their Novitiate, would not be the less profitably engaged in the cause; since, besides having a Number of young Indians to feed, to educate, to maintain, they would be laying the foundation of far more extensive usefulness for the future.

The true object, therefore, of this memoir, is, to demand, that the allowance, granted by Government, increased, if possible, to *one thousand Dollars,* per Annum, (on account of the great additional expence, incident on the present Scheme,) should be paid from the first onset, on my pledging myself, as I solemnly do, that, at latest, in two years from the commencement, I will send out five or six Missionaries, and successively as many more as Government may then be disposed to encourage.

For the attainment of the object of collecting some Indian boys in the Seminary, it would be of great service, Sir, that you should please to invite Gen[era]l [William] Clarke [*sic*; Clark] & Col. [Benjamin] O'Fallon to lend me their assistance.

LS in DNA, 77 (M-271:4, frames 438–440). NOTE: Calhoun answered on 3/21.

To Joseph McMinn, Cherokee Agency, 3/17. Calhoun appoints McMinn to be the Agent to the [Eastern] Cherokees, as successor to the late [Return J.] Meigs; asks McMinn to execute his bond; gives him instructions, including some special ones about finances; acknowledges his letter of 2/19 [LS in DNA, 1, M-265 (M-221:96); FC in DNA, 75 (M-208:9)] reporting that the Cherokees did not meet the treaty commissioners, although the Cherokees confess that they should have done so, because the young Indians are taught to believe that the U.S. wants to seal the doom of their nation by such treaties. FC in DNA, 72, E:409–410 (M-15:5); FC in DNA, 75, 1822–1827:2–4 (M-208:10).

To James Meriwether, Athens, Ga., 3/17. "I enclose for your information a copy of a letter [dated 3/17] from this Department" to [Duncan G.] Campbell. FC in DNA, 72, E:408 (M-15:5).

To [George Bomford, George Gibson, Thomas S. Jesup, and Alexander Macomb], 3/18. They are each to inform their subordinates about the recent statute "concerning the disbursement of public money," which is to be strictly enforced; but existing regulations that require more frequent [financial] returns are not to be relaxed. [James Monroe] intends to report to the next session of Congress, as to the recent statute, statements revealing the condition of each branch of the military service; reports through the first three quarters of this year must be promptly submitted and each bureau "put in the best possible condition." FC in DNA, 3, 11:466–467 (M-6:11); LS (Bomford's copy) in DNA, 31, 1823, War Department; LS (Gibson's copy) in DNA, 43, Calhoun, 534; LS (Jesup's copy) in DNA, 41, 1823–1824, S-33; LS (Macomb's copy) with En in DNA, 221, 497; CC with En in DNA, 285; CC (of Gibson's copy) in PHi.

To [Superintendents of Indian Affairs] Lewis Cass, William Clark, William P. DuVal, and James Miller; to [Indian Agents] John Crowell, G[eorge] Gray, Joseph McMinn, R[obert] C[arter] Nicholas, and William Ward; and to [Indian Sub-Agent Jasper] Parrish, 3/18. Calhoun sends to them copies of the statute concerning the disbursement of public money that was enacted during the past session of Congress, and he assures them that the provisions of this law will be strictly enforced. The statute of 5/6/1822 concerning Indian trade requires that the accounts of Superintendents and Agents of Indian Affairs shall be settled annually as of 9/1; that copies of these accounts shall be submitted to Congress at the opening of each session; and that the names of any defaulters must thus be reported. Therefore, "you will see the importance of a prompt rendition and settlement of all accounts for Indian expenditures," of your reporting as soon after each 9/1 as is practicable, and of putting "the Indian Department . . . in the best possible condition." LS (Cass's copy) in DNA, 76 (M-1:12, p. 129); FC in DNA, 72, E:410 (M-15:5); FC (McMinn's copy) in DNA, 75, 1822–1827:4–5 (M-208:10); CC (of Cass's copy) in In; CC (of Cass's copy) in DLC, Henry Rowe Schoolcraft Papers, Correspondence, A:31; CC's in DNA, 76 (M-1:66, p. 57, and M-1:70, pp. 341–342, 345); PC in Carter, ed., *Territorial Papers,* 19:501–502.

From the Rev. James B. Finley, Upper Sandusky, [O.,] 3/18. As its Superintendent, he reports the progress of the Indian school there that was begun in 1821 and is sponsored by the Methodist

Episcopal Church. Almost all of the 30 boys and 15 girls "are spelling in from two to five Syllabals [*sic*]." A farm provides agricultural training for the boys, and the girls are learning the household arts. Finley encloses both an estimate of the cost of the mission's buildings and a certificate of 3/21 by John Shaw, Sub-Agent for the Wyandots. ALS with Ens in DNA, 77 (M-271:4, frames 551–560).

To Duff Green, Chariton, Mo., 3/18. Answering Green's letter of 1/3, Calhoun says: "It would give me pleasure to comply with your wishes relative to Major [Thomas S.] Locke, particularly as I have no doubt his services would be valuable in the quarter in which it is proposed to locate him; but as there is a specific appropriation for the pay of Sub-Agents, which does not exceed in amount the pay of those now in service, I am at present thereby precluded from making any new appointments." FC in DNA, 72, E:409 (M-15:5).

To Col. N[athan] Towson, Paymaster General

Dep[art]m[en]t of War, 18 March 1823

You will communicate to the officers and agents of your Department copies of the act "concerning the disbursement of Public Money" passed at the last session of Congress, or such parts of it as relates [*sic*] to them, for their information and direction; and you will instruct them that the provisions of the act will be strictly enforced; and that, in those cases where existing orders and regulations require returns to be made for shorter periods than are specified in the act, it is not intended there shall be any relaxation of the orders or regulations.

The President [James Monroe] designs at the opening of the next session of Congress to accompany his Message with statements similar to those exhibited last year, showing the condition of each branch of the military service. You will therefore see the importance of a prompt rendition and settlement of all public accounts, and particularly that the money remitted in the three first quarters of the present year be accounted for as soon after the expiration of that period as practicable, and that your Department be in the best possible condition.

LS in DNA, 292, 1–2362.

To an Unknown Addressee, "Private"

War Dep[artmen]t, 18th March 1823

I regret exceedingly, that the indisposition of Mrs. [Floride Colhoun] Calhoun will prevent me from making my visit to the South, as I had informed you, at least till after she is confined ["which" *interlined*] will make it late.

I would have been very happy to spend several days in Salisbury in order to converse with yourself, [Charles] Fisher [former Representative from N.C.] and my other friends in that quarter. We have reached the moment to act, and concert and activity are required. I have deliberately reviewed the whole gro[un]d, and I am under the sober conviction, that with proper efforts we must succeed. Did I not think so, I would not ask the effort of my friends in a cause, ["in" *interlined*] which, tho' it is preëminently the cause of the country, I am so prominent. On North Carolina the contest will greatly depend. Mr. [William H.] Crawford and his friends, you know, have counted on her with great certainty, as necessarily following in the track of Virginia ["and" *canceled*] under the direction of Mr. [Nathaniel] Macon [Senator from N.C.]. I am satisfied, that nothing can throw your State so much in the background, as the impression, that she was the mere appendage of the Ancient Dominion, and this point Mr. B[artlett] Yancey [former Representative from N.C.] and the rest of Mr. C[rawfor]d's friends acknowledged in 1816 in the contest against Mr. [James] Monroe. You need no suggestion from me how to act, but it appears to me that the gro[un]d might be taken with advantage both in your papers and correspondence of supporting the Carolina candidate. The two States were originally one, and ought probably never to have been seperated [*sic*]. Their character and interest are the same; and if they should act together North Carolina, as being the greater, must have ["a" *canceled*] proportionally greater influence. The two Carolinas acting with Pen[nsylvani]a and being supported by the policy of the Gen[era]l Adm[inistratio]n and the soundness of their cause could scarcely fail of success. You may safely assume that Pennsylvania will support me. It was ascertained, beyond doubt, that ⅔ of the convention which lately meet [*sic*] at Harrisburgh [*sic*] were decidedly for me against all other candidates combined. A nomination did not take place only because, the members supposed it would be a strethch [*sic*] of their power, as they were elected for a specifick pu[r]pose, and that it might under such circumstances tend to distract the State nomination. Considering the great weight of that State, her steady character, sound Democratical ["of" *canceled*] sentiment, and central position, ["that" *canceled*] she ["will" *canceled and* "must" *interlined*] ultimately control the whole of the center States and have a most decided influence on the election. The two Carolinas may act safely with her.

Much will depend on the Western Carol[in]ian. It ought to take a decided stand. An expression from it of any strength in the State would tend to ["str" *canceled*] animate ["of" *canceled*] our friends, and to repel the attempt, made, with so much art, to hold out the idea, that I have withdrawn.

I trust your Congressional elections will be attended to, and that we will have the pleasure of seeing you and Fisher both in the next Congress. Dr. [James S.] Smith [former Representative from N.C.] declines being a candidate; if Mr. [Josiah] Crudup, [Representative from N.C.,] who is a most worthy man, is not a candidate, care ought to be taken to bring forward some one of sound political sentiment. Will [William] Davidson [former Representative from N.C.] be a candidate? Cannot Maj[o]r [Daniel M.] Forney, or his father, or some sound man be brought forward in that district?

Your election of members of the Legislature will doubtless be attended to also. It is of great, I may say almost decisive importance. You can ["however" *interlined*] better judge how to act in this important crisis, I may with truth say of the country, than what I can advice [*sic*] you.

For myself, I feel but little solicitude, but for the success of the principles and policy, for which I have ever contended, I feel great interest.

Mr. [George] McDuffie [Representative from S.C.] will pass through Salisbury on his return a few weeks hence, and is [*two or three words missing*] meeting you there [*the remainder of the manuscript is missing*].

ALU (incomplete) in NcU, Southern Historical Collection, Charles Fisher Papers; PC in A.R. Newsome, "Correspondence of John C. Calhoun, George McDuffie and Charles Fisher, Relating to the Presidential Canpaign of 1824," in the *North Carolina Historical Review*, vol. VII, no. 4 (October, 1930), pp. 477–479. NOTE: The identity of the addressee and his residence are unknown; the institution that preserves this incomplete document has speculated that it may possibly have been written to Philo White, the Editor of the *Western Carolinian*, at Salisbury, but Calhoun's hope, expressed in the fourth paragraph from the end, of "seeing you and Fisher both in the next Congress" militates against that assumption, partly because Salisbury could not be represented by two residents of the same Congressional district. Mrs. Calhoun was doubtless "confined" in connection with the birth of John Caldwell Calhoun, Jr. (1823–1855). Meriwether, ed., *The Papers of John C. Calhoun*, 1:433.

To J[oseph] M. Hernandez, Washington, 3/19. Pursuant to Hernandez's letter of 3/11 (PC in Carter, ed., *Territorial Papers*, 22:642–645), Calhoun has ordered the Army officer at St. Augustine to open a road between there and St. Mary's; when the cost of that is known, orders will be given to develop other roads farther south in the Territory of Fla. "if it can be done with propriety." A survey is planned for next summer of the area between St. Augustine and Pensacola; it will result in sufficient plans and estimates of costs "to enable you I hope to get the consent of Congress at the next session for opening a road between these places." Commissioners will be appointed promptly to locate the Indians south of Charlotte Harbor, if enough good land can be found there, or at least south of Tampa Bay. FC in DNA, 72, E:410–411 (M-15:5); PC in Carter, ed., *Territorial Papers*, 22:651–652.

To Samuel L. Southard, [Trenton, N.J.,] "Private"

Washington, 19th March 1823

I am sure you will attribute my silence to its true cause, the great pressure of official duties, and a long private correspondence, which had been wholly suspended on my part, during the session of Congress.

Mr. [Samuel D.] Ingham and his friends did not calculate on his success at Harrisburgh [*sic*] with any certainty; and in fact, he was ["wholly" *canceled*] indifferent, believing his situation in Congress not less eligible at present. Shultze [*sic*; John Andrew Shulze, Governor of Pa., 1823–1829] is with him in the State politicks, and very hearty in the cause, on the national question. Mr. [George M.] Dallas informs me, that, after much pains, it was ascertained, that fully ⅔ of the convention was in my favour, against all of the other candidates combined; and if the body had proceeded to nominate at all, there was no question of a decided majority in my favour, but that the general disinclination to act at all ["was so great" *interlined*] principally on the ground, that the members had been elected for a specifick purpose, and that they ought not to take up another ["subject" *interlined*], that it was thought advisable not [to] agitate the ["subject" *canceled and* "question" *interlined*]. He is of the impression, that the support of the State may be assumed with perfect certainty.

The rumour you heard, in regard to Maj[o]r [Christopher] Vandeventer's nomination, is not without foundation. He was nominated Naval agent at New York [City], and rejected in a very thin [U.S.] Senate, and again renominated [*sic*] at the request, as I understand, of some of the Senators. The hour being a late one and some of the body desiring farther [*sic*] information the nomination was not acted on. When ["the" *interlined*] rejection took place most of the Senators, who usually act with the adm[inistratio]n, Col. [Richard M.] Johnson, Gov[erno]r [Ninian] Edwards and many others were absent. It was doubtless partly, at least, on political grounds, that he was rejected.

Judge H[enry Brockholst] Livingston [an Associate Justice of the U.S. Supreme Court] died [*one word canceled*] yesterday. His death creates a very important vacancy on the Bench. Should it be filled, as I suppose it will, I trust, we shall soon have the pleasure of seeing you. I will give you the earliest information, with the addition, should it be necessary, of any aid in my power.

As to political prospects, my friends were never more sanguine; and I may add active. Our cause has never yet been presented to the publick. The foundation (laid, I think, I may say, in truth and patriotism) being now secure, it only remains to rear the superstructure. I would not ask the coöperation of my friends, tho I sincerely believe that it [is] the cause of the country, did I not ["believe" *canceled*] think, after a cool and careful survey of my circumstances, that to ensure success, nothing but their activity is wanting. Your State, tho' not large, is important, as being intimately connected with the States, Pen[nsylvani]a & New York, on which the election must turn. Your weight, if exerted in time, must decide Jersey; but, I do think, no time is to be lost. Much may be done by correspondence, and much by short, but judicious articles in your leading Republican papers. Mr. [Martin] Van Buren, it is believed, returned after full consultation with Mr. [William H.] C[rawfor]d, to come out for him openly and actively; and even to obtain, if possible, a nomination at Albany. Any demonstration in Jersey would tend to check his efforts. I do not believe he can succeed, but every precaution ought to be taken.

I have been gradually lead [*sic*] to write you a long letter; and for fear, it should be longer, I must abstain from some reflections, which, I intended to make, on the late news from Europe. In great haste.

ALS in NjP, Samuel L. Southard Papers. NOTE: An AEU by Southard indicates that this letter was received by him on 3/23 and that it was answered on 3/31.

To the Rev. EDWARD EVERETT, Boston

Department of War, March 20th 1823

I this day recieved [*sic*] your letter of the 14th Inst[ant; ALS in DNA, 15, 1824, 103 (M-688:29, frames 415–417)] stating that your brother [E.H. Everett] would be unable, by absence from the country, to avail himself of an appointment to the Military Academy for the current year.

Agreeably to your request, I take pleasure in enclosing you herewith an appointment for 1824 in his favor, which I hope a safe return to his friends may enable him to accept.

LS in MHi; FC in DNA, 13, 1:202 (M-91:1).

From JACOB BROWN

[Washington,] 21st March 1823

I have deemed it my duty to communicate for your consideration suggestions, which have occurred to me in reflecting on the local condition of the Army and the state of its discipline.

In a view of the relation, which the Army holds, with the geographical boundaries of the country, the consideration of greatest prominence is its extreme subdivision. That such a state is unfriendly to discipline by removing the immediate impulses of competition is unquestionable; and it should be the object of our military arrangements to obviate, as far as is compatible with the public security, the inconveniences inseparable from dispersion.

I am strongly impressed with the wisdom of the policy, which has extended our military forces far to the West, and has effectually restrained the hostile dispositions of the savages by a show of strength in the bosom of their retirement. This frontier I conceive to be effectually guarded by the five posts of St. Marys, Green Bay, Prairie du Chien, St. Anthony and Council Bluffs. The positions within this line, intended as frontier occupations, do not appear to possess the facilities for offensive or protecting purposes, which should belong to them in order to justify their maintenance with our limited means. As our posts in the North West are intended merely as a defence against savages and the command of the fur-trade within our limits, those alone which are indispensable in this point of view deserve to be maintained; and they should be maintained in full strength.

It is the custom of savages never to leave behind them a fortified post, and it is but recently that this practice has been abandoned in the warfare of civilised nations. In wars with the savages then, our external occupations would neutralize the utility of those within them.

I would assume as a first principle in the regulation of our North-Western defences, that no position should be occupied, which is not strong enough to resist any force of savages, and which is not provided with supplies ["of men and munitions" *canceled*] for at least a year. Feeble positions invite attack, and it is important in savage warfare to preclude the minutest advantage. The observation, that success stimulates the spirit & efforts of assailants, applies with peculiar force to the savage character.

In passing from the North Western to the Atlantic border a different combination of circumstances demands a different order of military arrangement. A dense population, numerous towns of great commercial importance, and a greater facility of access into the heart of our settlements require a variety of fortified positions; and, on the other hand, the ability of reinforcing them, on any sudden emergency, by the militia of the country obviates the necessity of keeping large bodies of regular troops combined for action. But the dispersion of our forces and their great subdivision still hold the objection of hostility to the interests of discipline and improvement of every species. Such posts as Eas[t]port in Maine and Smithville in North Carolina can be of little service either in peace or war. The latter is deemed useless in any state of the country; and the former can only be serviceable in peace by aiding the Revenue officers in the execution of their duties—in war it is almost certain of being captured. Under governments like our own, where the different members of the Union have a voice in all its social arrangements, I am aware that a reference must be had to opinions, which are entertained by the inhabitants of different sections of the country relative to their own security. But the institution of a school of practice, which you have contemplated, would, it is hoped and believed, afford, in the view of the public, a sufficient ground for the relinquishment of several positions of the character last mentioned. With regard to the importance of such an establishment, there can be but one opinion among military men. It would seem to be almost in vain that military education is fostered, if it is to terminate with the course of studies at West Point. The knowledge acquired there being almost ["purely" *interlined*] of a theoretical character, a scientific course of practice directed with great care and ability appears to be necessary to confirm it. The custom of withdrawing graduates from the Military Academy to be immured in small garrisons, where they are of necessity consigned to inaction—a custom inevitable without a school of practice—would be corrected by such an institution, and all the benefits, which naturally belong to the course of study at West Point, would be preserved. The importance of this consideration cannot, I conceive, be too strongly urged.

If the small posts within the external line of defence in the North West be abandoned and the garrisons united to their Regiments, which I would advise, as soon as it can conveniently be done—the posts on the Atlantic coast, which are not of indispensable utility, be relinquished and the garrisons concentrated for the organization of a school of practice; the Army will then possess all the facilities for the preservation of its discipline, the improvement of its science and the extension of its character, which are attainable under the difficulties incident to its limited numbers and the vast territory, over which it is spread.

LS in DNA, 1, B-297 (M-221:95); FC in DLC, Jacob Brown Papers, Letterbooks, 2:224–226.

To L[ouis] William DuBourg, [Georgetown, D.C.]

Dep[art]m[en]t of War, 21 March 1823

I have received your letter of the 17th inst[ant] and submitted it to the President [James Monroe] for his consideration and directions, who has instructed me to inform you, in reply, that believing the establishment of a school on the principles which you have suggested is much better calculated to effect your benevolent design of extending the benefits of civilization to the remote tribes and with it the just influence of the government, than the plan you formerly proposed for the same object, he is willing to encourage it as far as he can with propriety and will allow you at the former rate of $800 per annum to be paid quarter yearly, towards the support of the contemplated establishment. No advance, however, can be made, consistently with the regulations, until the establishment has actually commenced its operations, with a suitable number of Indian youths, of which fact, and the number of pupils, the certificate of Gen[era]l [William] Clark will be the proper evidence.

A copy of this letter will be sent to Gen[era]l Clark with instructions to give proper orders to the [*sic*] to such of the Indian Agents under his charge as you may think necessary to facilitate the collection of the Indian youths to be educated, to afford every aid in his power to promote the success of the establishment.

FC in DNA, 72, E:414 (M-15:5).

From Maj. S[TEPHEN] H. LONG, "Private"

Philadelphia, March 21, 1823

I again take the liberty to trouble you with a private communication, on the subject of my last, and beg you will regard the peculiarity of my circumstances as an acceptable apology.

I am indirectly solicited by a member of the Board of Public Works of Virginia, to signify to that institution, that I will serve in the capacity of Civil Engineer, in case I should be elected. But, having been recently informed that the office is supplied by an *Annual Election*, I am disposed to doubt whether such a step would be advisable, inasmuch as it might lead to the loss of my present station, with the prospect only, of serving for a single year in the capacity just mentioned. Since the duties of both stations are nearly allied, and since the services to be performed in Virginia may be regarded as appropriate to an officer of my Corps, I beg leave to ask, whether it will be compatible with the regulations of the War Department, to allow me a furlough of six months or a year, in case I should receive the Virginia appointment, that I may be able to decide with greater safety as to the propriety of continuing on that service. With the understanding that I shall receive no compensation from the U[nited] States during the period of the furlough, or so long as I may continue in the Virginia service?

The indulgences with which I have already been favoured, altho' I have never enjoyed one of this description, would seem to preclude the propriety of asking any more, yet, the desire of promoting the welfare of a rising family, on one hand, and the fear of being thrown out of employment on the other, have induced me to make the inquiry above stated.

I beg you will favour me with a reply by an early opportunity, while I remain Dear Sir with the highest respect . . . .

ALS in DNA, 228. NOTE: This letter was answered on 3/27 by I[saac] Roberdeau.

To James Miller, Little Rock, 3/21. He will receive $1,500 to cover the annuities due to the Quapaws and to the Osages, plus $2,500 to cover the cost of distributing those annuities. "The Cherokee annuity has been paid here, of which you have been already apprized." He will be allowed about the same sum that he was authorized to spend last year from the Indian Department's appropriation, viz: the Agent's salary, $1,500; the Sub-Agent's salary, $500; for presents to the Indians, $500; and for contingencies, including all other expenses, $3,000. Calhoun urges economy upon Miller. FC in DNA, 72, E:412–413 (M-15:5); PC in Carter, ed., *Territorial Papers*, 19:502–503.

From L[OUIS] WILLIAM DUBOURG, B[isho]p of N[ew] Orleans

Monastery of the Visitation, Geo[rge] Town, [D.C.,]
March 21st [*sic*; probably the 22nd] 1823

Permit me to intrude once more on y[ou]r Kindness, and present to you some reflections, which occurred to me on the subject of y[ou]r communications of yesterday [3/21].

That the bounty granted by Government to our contemplated Indian Establishment at Florissant [Mo.] should commence to be *paid* only from the moment it will be in activity, that is to say, to take in some Indian youths, appears to me perfectly consistent with your high responsibility. But I cannot help thinking that consistently with y[ou]r general regulations on the Indian mission, it should begin to *run* from the actual setting off of the missionaries. I suppose it was y[ou]r understanding; For the Establishment being considered by Government in the same light with all others, it should also be assimilated to them in this respect—and in fact, great expenses are necessary to prepare for the accom[m]odation of the missionaries and of the Indian boys, for which we ask nothing of Government. Then Until these can be collected, ["the" *interlined*] missionaries must be supported, and it is impossible to say how many months it may take to effect that purpose, this circumstance not depending on us but on the efficiency of the Superintendant [*sic*; William Clark] and [Indian] Agents to procure them. I hope then that you will have the goodness to express in y[ou]r message that the contribution of $800 will commence to *run* from the time of departure of our Gentlemen, which will be at latest in one month from this, altho' no part of it is to be paid until the Seminary is put into activity.

ALS in DNA, 77 (M-271:4, frames 441–442).

To [LOUIS WILLIAM DUBOURG, Georgetown, D.C.]

[Department of War, March 23, 1823]

The Secretary of War[']s compliments to the Rev[eren]d Dr. DuBourg, [and the Secretary] acknowledges the receipt of his [DuBourg's] note of yesterday's date, and informs him in reply, that under all the circumstances he thinks it proper to defer for the present a decision on the point therein suggested for his consideration.

FC in DNA, 72, E:414 (M-15:5).

From ANDREW JACKSON

Hermitage, March 23rd 1823

I have lately seen Mr. W[illiam] Smith[']s address to the citizens of So[uth] Carolina. The manner in which he has introduced the name of that high minded[,] meritorious officer Colo[nel James] Gadsden before the public, is as wicked as the production is weak. I have thought that justice to Colo[nel] Gadsden might require that the public should know the estimation in which I held Colo[nel] Gadsden[']s military merits whilst serving with me—and that it was ["me" *altered to* "I"] that urged his claims to the Adjutant Gen[era]l[']s office without his knowledge ["or approbation commencing" *interlined*] from the moment I was advised by you that Colo[nel Robert] Butler (agre[e]able to my wishes) would be provided for in the line of the Army. My letters will shew, that I did this ["from a conviction of his talents & military merit," *interlined*] with an eye single to the ["public good(,) the" *interlined*] wellfare [*sic*] of the Army, and ["thereby" *interlined*] to promote the public service.

It being intimated to me that Mr. [George] McDuffie [Representative from S.C.] intends to reply to Mr. Smith, I would sug[g]est the propriety, that he might be furnished with extracts from my letters to you that bear upon the above points. They would be furnished by me, but the enemies of Colo[nel] Gadsden might say that they were furnished (by me) for the occasion—coming from your Department with their dates & time of receipt, will foreclose such intimations as those, & they will be duly appreciated by the public. You will see Colo[nel] Gadsden['s] reply to Mr. S[mith] in the Nashville Gazzett [*sic*] of the 21st instant. This reply must make him feel—and bring to his view the adage of, "O that mine enemy might write a Book."

Accept assurances of my friendship & Esteem. Andrew Jackson.

Autograph draft, signed, in DLC, Andrew Jackson Papers, 11632 (Presidential Papers Microfilm, Jackson Papers, Reel 32).

From Abr[aha]m H[enry] Schenck, "Fish Kill" Landing, [N.Y.,] 3/23. He encloses his son Edwin's acceptance of his appointment to be a Cadet [dated 3/18] and consents to his son's assumption of the obligation to serve for five years. ALS with En in DNA, 15, 1822, 56½ (M-688:20).

To Joseph McMinn, Calhoun, Tenn., 3/24. McMinn will receive $12,970, to be applied as follows: $10,000 for the [Eastern] Cherokees' annuity; $1,280 for an allowance to the "Cherokees in lieu of rations at the distribution of the annuity"; $1,190 for Agency expenses during the first quarter of 1823; and $500 for allowances to the schools at Brainerd, Spring Place, and Valley Towns. McMinn will pay nothing to [Return J. Meigs's] estate, because any sum due to the late Agent will be paid upon the settlement of his accounts. McMinn "will take great care" that his expenditures do not exceed $4,760 during 1823. Calhoun encloses Jeremiah Archer's claim and instructs McMinn to pay it from the Cherokee annuity, unless McMinn should see some strong objection to its payment. FC in DNA, 72, E:471 (M-15:5); FC in DNA, 75, 1822–1827:5–6 (M-208:10).

To William Ward, Choctaw Agency, 3/24. The sum of $13,952.50 is being remitted to Ward. He is to pay $387.50 as an allowance to the schools at Elliot[t] and Newell; $1,115 are to cover his Agency's expenses during the first quarter of 1823; and the remaining $13,450 constitute the Choctaws' annuity (including the annuities to the three principal Chiefs, the annual allowance for Light Horsemen, and all other allowances authorized by treaties). The appropriation for Indian affairs for 1823 is "about the same" as was last year's; Ward's Agency allowance will be unchanged, "and you will take great care that your disbursements do not exceed that amount. Your estimates for the buildings for the Agency on the new site, has [*sic*] been received, and a remittance will be made for that object, as soon as it is ascertained what has been usually allowed at the other Agencies for the same purpose." FC in DNA, 72, E:415 (M-15:5).

From Jacob Brown, 3/25. He encloses the application of Capt. [William] Hoffman for an appointment of his son, William Hoffman, [Jr.,] to be a Cadet. Brown supports the application, claiming that young Hoffman is a promising lad of 16 who has all qualifications for admission into the Academy. (According to Heitman, *Historical Register*, 1:535, young Hoffman was appointed in 1825.) LS in DNA, 15, 1824, 92 (M-688:29, frame 285); FC in DLC, Jacob Brown Papers, Letterbooks, 2:226.

To William Clark, St. Louis, 3/25. "I transmit for your information and direction the enclosed copy of a letter [dated 3/21] from this Department to Bishop [Louis William] DuBourg of New Orleans." FC in DNA, 72, E:417 (M-15:5).

Bishop L[ouis] William DuBourg, Washington, to Count J[acques?] de Menou, "Chargé d'affaires of H.M.C.M.," 3/25. Having to leave for Mo. "before the departure of the Missionaries intended for the Indian seminary at Florissant in said State," DuBourg requests de Menou to give official notification to Calhoun of the date on which the missionaries shall actually leave [for Mo.]. ALS in DNA, 77 (M-271:4, frame 722).

From Bvt. Maj. Gen. Edmund Pendleton Gaines, Louisville, Ky., 3/25. He asserts his claim to precedence in rank over Bvt. Maj. Gen. Winfield Scott; Gaines requests an investigation of their status. ALS in DNA, 1, G-199 (M-221:95).

To V[IRGIL] MAXCY, "Private"

Washington, 25th March 1823

I am so much occupied, that ["you must" *interlined*] excuse me, if I write you very short letters. I am bringing up my correspondence and writing to all of my friends, which occupies every moment. The cause is starting well, and much now may be effected by correspondence.

I enclose ["an extract of" *interlined*] a letter from [Micah] Sterling which gives you the state of things in New York. I do not doubt, that before the next session a great impression will be made in that State. My information from Pen[nsylvani]a is also good. It is not improbable, that a move will still be made in that State, before the rising of the Legislature.

A few numbers ought for[th]with [to] appear in the Annapolis paper turning the attention of the State towards me. You will know how to execute, ["it" *canceled*] so as to suit the taste of Maryland, as you know my grounds. As a slave holding State, as well as a mid[d]le State, it is import[ant "to" *canceled and* "for" *interlined*] Maryland to act in concert with Penn[sylvani]a.

Now is the *time to write*. The foundation being fully laid, every one can aid in rearing the superstructure on so good a basis. [William] Gaston and [John] Stanly [former Representative from N.C.] and other distinguished gentlemen, who belonged to the Federal party in North Carolina, ought to be written to without delay. By acting in concert, but with prudence, they may every where turn the Congression[a]l and State election there in my favour. This is ["an" *interlined*] important point, which you can attend to, with effect. The aid of Pearson, through the Gen[era]l [Robert Goodloe Harper] might be called in with effect. Dr. Watkins, the secretary of the Board, is with us, and can do much in Baltimore. He will write to [Peter?] Little, Stuart, and the sheriff.

[Samuel] Barnes['s] paper [in Frederick, Md.,] ought to be efficiently attended to; and I hope that something may be done for the paper here. I am drawn out to a long letter in spite of myself. Truly, J.C. Calhoun.

[P.S.] The Virginia papers show favourable symptoms. [William H.] C[rawfor]d will fail there, if I do not mistake. Give as much encourage[men]t throug[h] correspondence and the papers to Pen[nsylvani]a as possible. Short articles that I have the best prospects of taking Maryland, or that she will act in concert with Pen[nsylvani]a & other mid[d]le States would have a happy effect.

You might write short letters to Maj[o]r [Christopher] Van D[evente]r to be published in the Rep[ublica]n to that effect.

ALS in DLC, Galloway-Maxcy-Markoe Papers, vol. 32.

From Ferris Pell, Albany, 3/25. "As my official integrity has been wantonly and bitterly assailed, . . . be pleased to peruse the enclosed Memorial, and form your own opinion upon the facts it discloses." The memorial discussed Pell's duties as Agent for settling the claims of the State of N.Y. against the U.S. and his efforts to obtain "reasonable compensation" for his services. ALS with En in DNA, 1, P-276 (M-221:96).

To Col. G[EORGE?] GIBBS

Washington, 26th March 1823

I am very much obliged to you for the grape cuttings, which I received in very good order, and have planted with care. I take great interest in the success of the vine, both as connected with our commerce and morals; and I do not doubt, but of the varieties ["some one" *interlined*] will be found, at last, which will rival in its products the best imported wines.

I am much obliged to you for the information which you obtained from Dr. Le Barron [*sic*; Francis Le Baron], and will immediately take measures to obtain for the government so desirable an acquisition.

ALS in NHi, Miscellaneous Papers, Calhoun.

To James Lloyd, [Senator from Mass.,] 3/26. Calhoun encloses copies of all papers in the War Department that contain rules adopted in the settlement of accounts of States against the U.S. for disbursements during the War of 1812. The rules are considered, however, to be "subordinate to the general principles connected with the constitutional powers of the general government over the militias of the States, which were established by the Department when the accounts . . . were originally presented and discussed on their general merits." Because Mrs. Calhoun's illness will probably prevent Calhoun from making a trip southward during next summer, the agents of [Mass.] may present their claim at their convenience. FC in DNA, 3, 11:467 (M-6:11); CC in DNA, RG

233, 18A-D1, vol. 260; PC's in Senate Document No. 43 and House Document No. 83, 18th Cong., 1st Sess.; PC in *American State Papers: Military Affairs*, 3:18. Lloyd answered from New York [City] on 4/7 that the abovementioned rules had been forwarded to the Governor of Mass., [John Brooks]. ALS in DNA, 1, L-108 (M-221:96).

To George Walton, Secretary and Acting Governor of Fla. [Territory], Pensacola, 3/26. Walton's letters of 1/9 [LS with En in DNA, 1, W-239 (M-221:96); PC in Carter, ed., *Territorial Papers*, 22:597–598], 1/31 [LS with Ens in DNA, 1, W-229 (M-221:96); PC with Ens in Carter, ed., *Territorial Papers*, 22:606–609], and 2/20 [LS with En in DNA, 1, W-240 (M-221:96); PC with En in Carter, ed., *Territorial Papers*, 22:626–628] have not been answered earlier because of "the great press of business in the Department." Walton's bill for $480.88 to pay Interpreter [Stephen] Richards' salary and other expenses will be paid when it is presented. Calhoun is glad that [Gad] Humphreys has entered upon his duties as Indian Agent, and Calhoun approves Walton's instructions to Humphreys. Walton's estimate for construction of a road between Pensacola and St. Augustine was immediately sent to the Delegate from Fla. Territory, [Joseph M.] Hernandez, but it was impossible to get a statute enacted so late in the session of Congress. Calhoun explains that there is no specific salary for Walton as Acting Superintendent of Indian Affairs, but Calhoun instructs Walton to submit an account of his expenses in that capacity. Although Calhoun would like to approve Walton's estimate of expenses, it is necessary to restrict Indian expenses in Fla. to $3,500 for 1823, to be apportioned as follows: $1,500 for pay of the Agent; $500 for pay of the Sub-Agent, [Peter Pelham]; $500 for presents to Indians; and $1,000 for contingencies. Half of this amount is sent now for expenditures during the first half of 1823, and Calhoun hopes that Walton can "make it adequate to the object." (Walton's En of 1/9 was an undated estimate of expenses, signed by Walton. His Ens of 1/31 were an LS of instructions dated 1/21 from Walton to Gad Humphreys, an ADS estimate dated 1/30 by Capt. Daniel E. Burch of the expense of opening a road between Pensacola and St. Augustine, and a CC of Walton's letter of 1/30 to Burch on that subject. The En of 2/20 was a CC of a letter of 2/5 to Walton from Gad Humphreys, who announced that a storm prevented his reaching St. Marks.) FC in DNA, 72, E:417–419 (M-15:5); PC in Carter, ed., *Territorial Papers*, 22:654–655.

Samuel S. Hamilton, [Clerk,] War Department, to Josias W. King, State Department, Washington, 3/27. "I am directed by the Secretary of War to request that a Commission may be made out for Colonel James Gadsden of South Carolina, & Mr. Bernard Segui, of Florida [Territory], who have been appointed by the President of the U.S. Commissioners to hold a treaty with the Indians in the Territory of Florida. I will thank you to attend to it as soon as convenient, and when the Commission is signed transmit it to this Dept." LS in DNA, 103, Gadsden (M-439:7, frames 108–109).

[Maj.] I[saac] Roberdeau to Maj. [Stephen H. Long, Philadelphia]

Washington, March 27, 1823

Dear Major, I am directed by the Secretary of War to inform you that he has received your letter of the 21st instant, and that the President [James Monroe] is willing to allow you a furlough for six Months ["for the purpose you mention" *interlined*]. You['d] better, perhaps, if your intention is to visit Richmond, come here on the way, where such arrangements may be made, as ["may" *canceled and* "are" *interlined*] be [*sic*] necessary under these Circumstances.

[P.S.] In presenting the above to ["the" *canceled*] Mr. C[alhoun] for his ["app" *canceled*] inspection, he observed that he thought you would be wrong in accepting it [that is, the proffered position in Va.]. The same observation he once made ["to me" *canceled*], when it was contemplated to propose it to me, for, independently of other considerations, there will be always more or less insecurity in the tenure of the Office which I consider by no means counterbalanced, by the present increase of Salary—but I have fully expressed my Notions to you heretofore. Gen[era]l [Alexander] Macomb wishes also to see you, on the subject of a proposed expedition—as well as on this subject. So you had better come on, and by all means stay with me. Come in the Line that reaches George Town [D.C.] from Baltimore, which the mail does not, & it will land you at my house. We are &c. . . . .

ALS in DNA, 228.

To S[AMUEL] L. SOUTHARD, [Trenton, N.J.,] "Private"

Washington, 27th March 1823

The President [James Monroe] has offered, as I knew he would when I conversed with you, the vacancy on the Bench to Judge [Smith] Thompson, but it is still uncertain whether he will accept. Should he not, it would be gratify[ing] to me to bring your ["claim" *canceled*] name before him for the place. Of your fitness for the office, I entertain not the least doubt, and in sustaining you I ["would" *canceled and* "should" *interlined*] not only gratify private feelings, but have the satisfaction of advancing the publick interest at the same time. In fact, it has always been a maxim with me to connect myself with those only in publick life, who deserve the publick confidence.

I am anxious to learn, whether you received my answer to your former communication. You mention nothing by which I can infer that you have received it.

It seems to me that [New] Jersey, if she is not determined to follow passively the adjoining States, ought to give some indication of her course. Any thing from her would encourage and sustain Pen[nsylvani]a.

ALS in NjP, Samuel L. Southard Papers. NOTE: An AEU by Southard indicates that this letter was answered.

To M[ICAH] STERLING, "Confidential"

Washington, 27th March 1823

Your letter from on board of the Steam Boat [*not found*] cheered us much, and tho' appearances are not so flattering at Albany yet we have no reason to despond. My friends are now sanguine and active, and a few months will show the effects. I could not well move earlier. Much was to be done to lay the foundation; the admin[istratio]n to be sustained; the Radicals exposed and prostrated, and all objections to my political course and administration of the [War] Dept. to be met and refuted. All this is now done, and I may add effectually done. It only now remains to rear the superstructure; and with so solid a foundation, and such abundant materials, and I may add with so many & so intelligent [supporters] to coöperate over every portion of the country, it cannot be difficult. I have been much engaged in bring[ing] up my correspondence and impressing these ideas so as to put all in motion. Having determined to move it is important that the impulse should be widely given. My friends must now all write, and write constantly wherever it can be done with safety. You can do much in this as well as in other ["ways" *canceled*] particulars, as you are master of the ground. In rearing the superstructure all can contribute.

My past services, my identity with the late war, & with the adm[inistratio]n, my uniform Republican course, my habits of industry and business, the distinctness of my political principles, and the openness and candour which even my enemies concede to me all furnish topicks for arguments to sustain the cause. My election would strengthen and invigorate the Rep[ublica]n party, Mr. [William H.] C[rawfor]d's would distract it and Mr. J[ohn Quincy] Adams would endanger its existence by giving the occasion of rearing up a successful party against it.

[Henry] Wheaton writes with sperit [*sic*] from New York [City]; and my correspondence from the South and West is very flattering. D[aniel] Webster is still with me; and is quite certain that if Mr. Adams does not take New York, that [*sic*] New England will not rally on him but myself. This for yourself only.

I hope that you have arrived safely, and found all well. Sincerely, J.C. Calhoun.

ALS in ScU-SC, John C. Calhoun Papers.

From William Wirt

Office of the Attorney General, March 27, 1823

Had I been called on, *a priori*, to give a construction to the several acts of Congress which are the subject of Mr. [Nathaniel] Cutting[']s letters of the 21 May 1821 and 30 January 1823, of Maj[o]r Cha[rle]s J. Nourse of the 20th of January 1823, and Mr. J.W. Murray[']s of 22nd December 1822, I should have had no hesitation in expressing the opinion that it was not the intention of Congress to incorporate Negroes and People of colour with the Army any more than with the militia of the U.S. But the acts of Congress under which this body of people of colour are understood to have been raised during the late war uses no other terms of description as to the recruits than that they shall be "able bodied, effective" men (act [of the] 24th Dec[embe]r 1811 "for completing the existing military establishment," and act [of] 11 Jan[uar]y 1812 "to raise an additional military force") or "free, effective able bodied men" (act [of] Dec[embe]r 10th 1814 making further provision for filling the ranks of the Army of the U.S.). As either of these descriptions was satisfied by the persons of colour in question; as the recruiting officers who are *quoad* [*sic*] *hoc* the agents of the U.S. recruited these persons on a contract for the pay and bounty stipulated by law; as the officers of Government recognized them as a part of the Army by their regular returns of this Corps, who received, 'til the close of the war, the same pay and rations with other troops, were subject to the same military law and performed the same military services, it seems to me that a practical construction has been given to the law on this particular from which it is not in the power of the government justly to depart. I think therefore that they ought to receive the promised land bounty. But without some further and more explicit declaration of the purpose of Congress, I would not recommend a repetition of such contracts, on any future occasion, or laws worded like those under consideration—by which I mean, not merely the three laws which I have cited, but the whole military system of the United States, militia included.

The papers are returned; and I remain, Sir, ...

FC in DNA, 113, B:126–127 (T-412:2).

From [2nd] Lt. C[lark] Burdine, Fever River, Ill., 3/28. Lessees of the lead-mine lands complain that thieves are stealing their wood, and Burdine has issued a ban on such thievery that he wants the War Department to approve. Bad weather has prevented smelting this month by the lessees and almost all of it attempted by Indian traders. ALS in DNA, 31, 1823, B.

To John Hays, Fort Wayne, 3/28. Calhoun acknowledges Hays's resignation of 2/24 [ALS in DNA, 1, H-272 (M-221:95)] and accepts it with regret. "I think it due to you, to state that your public duties have been performed to the entire satisfaction of this Department." Funds for the annuities for this year have already been sent to Hays, and he will continue to serve until they have been paid. Then, upon notification, Gen. John Tipton of Corydon, Ind., will assume the duties of Indian Agent at Fort Wayne. Tipton was recommended by the members of Congress from Ind. before Hays's recommendation of [Benjamin B.] Kercheval arrived. FC in DNA, 72, E:419 (M-15:5).

To John Tipton, Corydon, Ind., 3/28. Calhoun appoints Tipton to succeed John Hays as Indian Agent at Fort Wayne, when Hays shall have completed paying the "Indian annuity for this year." Tipton will be commissioned when his nomination shall have been ratified [by the Senate]. His annual salary will be $1,200. He is given other instructions. LS in In; FC in DNA, 72, E:419–420 (M-15:5).

From W[ILLIAM] H[ENRY] HARRISON

Northbend, [O.,] 29th March 1823

I have to solicit the favour of having a near relation of mine put on the list of Cadets at the Academy of West Point. His name is John R[ichard] Randolph the son of my nephew Richard K. Randolph a Citizen of the State of Rhode Island residing at New Port. This youth has not yet reached his fourteenth year & will be kept at school until that period arrives. He has been recommended to you by the Representatives of Rhode Island as well as by Mr. [William] Hunter formerly a Senator from that State who will be able to give a better account of his acquirements than I can.

I do not know that it will or ought to give any weight to the pretentions [*sic*] of this youth to state that he is one of the nearest Collateral Relatives of Peyton Randolph the President of the first [Continental] Congress who left no issue[,] my aunt (his wife) never having any children.

P.S. My nephew the father of the youth in whose favour I write is the son of Peyton Randolph of Wilton ["with" *interlined*] whose Patriotic Character the President [James Monroe] is well acquainted.

ALS in DNA, 15, 1823, 43 (M-688:23, frames 453–455). NOTE: John Richard Randolph entered the Military Academy in 1825 but did not graduate with his class in 1829. *Register of Graduates and Former Cadets, United States Military Academy . . . 1802–1946*, p. 124.

To [Nathaniel] Cutting, [Chief Clerk, Section of Bounty Lands, *ca.* 3/30]. "Mr. Cutting will conform to the within decision of the Att[orne]y Gen[era]l," [William Wirt, written to Calhoun on 3/27, concerning the right of free Negroes who have served in the Army to receive bounty lands]. AEI in DLC, John C. Calhoun Papers.

To A[NDREW] JACKSON

Washington, 30th March 1823

Incessant application to official duties since the commencement of the late session of Congress compelled me to suspend wholly my private correspondence, which I hope you will accept as an apology for [my] not acknowledging your favour of the 12th Dec[embe]r last, [*not found,*] at an earlier period.

I find few with whom, I accord so fully in relation to political subjects, as yourself. I have a thorough conviction, that the noble maxim of your's [*sic*], to do right and fear not is the very basis, not only of Republicanism, according to its true acceptation, but of all political virtue; and, that he who acts on it, must in the end prevail. The political gamblers will fail. The cause of the Georgian [William H. Crawford] is, if I mistake not, rapidly declining. It has no foundation in truth, and can only be prop[p]ed by false pretexts [*or possibly* "prete(n)ses"]. Should he fail in New York, as I think he must, he will have not the least prospect of success.

Mr. [Henry] Clay, I think, is not advancing on this side of the mountains, tho' his friends speak confidently of his strength to the West. They expect him to be nominated in Louisiana, during this session.

Our news from Europe has been interesting, and I expect will be still more so by the next arrival. It is not improbable, that a mighty contest has commenced ["there" *interlined*] not for commerce, nor territory, but to crush every vestige of liberty on the continent of Europe. In its progress, ["as" *canceled*] it will probably approach our shores, as Cuba will be involved in all likelyhood [*sic*] in the course of events. That England looks to that Island, and will be ready to seize on it, if a favourable opportunity offers, can hardly be doubted, and that such an event would be full of danger to this Union, is not less clear. I deem the moment important, and do think the country ought to be prepared for the worst. Without Cuba our confederacy is not complete; and with it in the hands of the English, the best line of communication between the extreme parts, would be intercepted.

Say to Col. [James] Gadsden, if you please, that I will write him in a few days; and that the President [James Monroe] has selected him to treat with the Indians in Florida, which I hope he may find convenient to accept. I think his chance of being confirmed ["as Adjutant Gen(era)l" *interlined*] at the next session is good.

ALS in DLC, Andrew Jackson Papers, 11638–11639 (Presidential Papers Microfilm, Jackson Papers, Reel 32); PC in Bassett, ed., *Correspondence of Andrew Jackson,* 3:193–194.

To E[DMUND] P. GAINES, Louisville

Department of War, March 31st 1823

I have received your letter of the 11th instant [ALS with Ens in DNA, 1, G-136 (M-221:95)], covering a copy of one [dated 12/15/1822] from the Governor of Texas [José Felix Trespalacioss] to Lieu[tenan]t Col. [James B.] Many [and a copy of Many's reply of 2/1/1823], complaining of certain Acts of a band of Spaniards and Americans, injurious to the border inhabitants of both Countries, and intimating your intention of giving orders to our Commandants on the Texas frontier to preserve harmony with the Governor and his people, which I have submitted to the President, [James Monroe,] who directs that you adopt such measures as may with propriety be taken, as will maintain harmony and protect as far as practicable the property of the inhabitants on both sides of the line.

FC in DNA, 3, 11:468 (M-6:11); CC in DNA, RG 98, Western Department, Letters Sent, 1:209–210.

SYMBOLS

The following symbols have been used in this volume as space-savers to designate the natures or forms in which papers of John C. Calhoun have been found and the depositories and record groups in which they are preserved.

A-Ar —Alabama Department of Archives and History, Montgomery, Ala.
Abs —abstract (a summary)
ADI —autograph document, initialed
ADS —autograph document, signed
ADU —autograph document, unsigned
AEI —autograph endorsement, initialed
AES —autograph endorsement, signed
AEU —autograph endorsement, unsigned
ALI —autograph letter, initialed
ALS —autograph letter, signed
ALU —autograph letter, unsigned
CC —clerk's copy (usually not for retention in the office of origin)
CCEx —clerk's copy of an extract
CLU —University of California at Los Angeles Library, Los Angeles, Calif.
CSmH —Henry E. Huntington Library and Art Gallery, San Marino, Calif.
Ct —Connecticut State Library, Hartford, Conn.
CtLHi —Litchfield Historical Society, Litchfield, Conn.
CtW —Olin Memorial Library, Wesleyan University, Middletown, Conn.
CtWa —Watertown Library, Watertown, Conn.
CtY —Yale University Library, New Haven, Conn.
CU —University of California Library, Berkeley, Calif.
DCI —Carnegie Institution of Washington, Washington, D.C.
DI —document, initialed
DLC —The Library of Congress, Washington, D.C.
DNA —The National Archives, Washington, D.C.

In citations within this book, the first number following each use of "DNA" is an editorial device referring to a specific series of records within a specific Record Group. For example, a document cited as being in "DNA, 3, 10:223–224" can be found on pages 223–224 of volume 10 in the series known as Letters Sent by the Secretary of War Relating to Military Affairs within Record Group

DNA (*continued*)

107, which consists of Records of the Office of the Secretary of War. The editor's code numbers like the "3" of this example are identified in the following list.

Any effort to locate a specific document, in person or by mail, by referring to such an editorial code number will provide the staff of the National Archives with insufficient information to enable it to render promptly the service desired. Instead, every such request should cite the Record Group by both name and number, the name of the specific series of records within that Record Group, and all document or file numbers or volume and page numbers that follow the editorial code number. For instance, one should not ask the National Archives staff for "DNA, 11, 14431"; instead, one should ask for the letter from Samuel D. Ingham to John C. Calhoun dated June 21, 1820, which is to be found in file number 14431 in the series of manuscripts known as Letters Received by the Adjutant General's Office, 1805–1821, that comprises part of Record Group 94, consisting of the Records of the Adjutant General's Office.

Certain series of records in certain Record Groups have been published, in whole or in part, in microcopies that are offered in the *List of National Archives Microfilm Publications, 1968*, and by some supplementary announcements. In these instances the corresponding microcopy number appears in the following list parenthetically after the name of the series of records—for example, "(M-222)" or "(T-494)." When such a reference in this volume is followed by a colon and an additional number—for instance, "(M-91:1)"—the second number specifies the relevant roll of microfilm in the indicated microcopy. Some users of this volume will find it more convenient to locate a wanted document in such a microfilm than in manuscript.

Some editorial code numbers and corresponding names of series of records have been included in the following list that are not cited within this book. These inclusions have been made for their value as a record of manuscripts within which documents related to other periods of Calhoun's life have been discovered. If inclusive dates appear immediately after the name of a series of records, the specified years may indicate the period for which that series has been searched for Calhoun documents or has been microfilmed rather than the years with which that series begins and ends.

For the most comprehensive information that is available within one set of covers about the Record Groups, see the *Guide to the Records in the National Archives* (Washington: U.S. Government Printing Office, 1948). More detailed analyses of the contents of eight Record Groups relevant to Calhoun have been published by the National Archives in its series of near-print releases entitled

DNA (*continued*)

Preliminary Checklist and *Preliminary Inventory.* These eight, listed in the order in which they appear below, are Record Groups 107, 94, 75, 59, 46, 233, and 99. When an "Entry" number appears parenthetically in the following list, it refers to the description in the corresponding *Checklist* or *Inventory* of the series of records thus designated.

Record Group 107—Records of the Office of the Secretary of War

1—Letters Received by the Secretary of War, Registered Series, 1801–1860 (M-221; Entry 33. The corresponding Registers have been published in M-22 and are described in Entry 34.)

2—Letters Received by the Secretary of War, Unregistered Series, 1789–1860 (M-222)

3—Letters Sent by the Secretary of War Relating to Military Affairs, 1800–1861 (M-6; Entry 2)

4—Reports to Congress from the Secretary of War, 1803–1870 (M-220; Entry 21)

5—Confidential and Unofficial Letters Sent by the Secretary of War, 1814–1847 (M-7; Entry 7)

6—Letters Sent to the President by the Secretary of War, 1800–1863 (M-127; Entry 5)

7—Miscellaneous Papers Relating to Accounts, 1829–1865 (Entry 49)

8—Personnel Papers, 1838–1912: Applications for Appointment (Entry 83)

Record Group 94—Records of the Adjutant General's Office

11—Letters Received by the Adjutant General's Office, 1805–1821 (M-566; Entry 12)

12—Letters Sent by the Adjutant General's Office (Main Series), 1800–1890 (M-565; Entry 1)

13—Records Relating to the U.S. Military Academy, 1812–1867 (M-91; Entries 206, 207, 219)

14—Correspondence Relating to the Military Academy, 1819–1866 (Entry 212)

15—Application Papers of Cadets, 1805–1866 (M-688; Entry 243)

16—Letters Received by the Adjutant General's Office (Main Series), 1822–1889 (M-567; Entry 12)

17—Record of Regulations and Orders Received from the Secretary of War, 1821–1829 (Entry 50)

18—Military Academy Orders, 1814–1867 (Entry 219)

19—Orders and Circulars, 1797–1910 (Entry 44)

DNA (*continued*)

20—U.S. Military Academy: Papers Relating to Appointments on the Board of Visitors, 1823–1866 (Entry 251)
(Additional series within this Record Group begin with editorial code number 261.)

Record Group 77—Records of the
Office of the Chief of Engineers

21—Miscellaneous Letters Sent, 1812–1848

22—Reports on Fortifications and Topographical Surveys, Surveys, 1812–1823

23—Letters and Papers Received (Irregular Series), 1789–1831: Miscellaneous Letters Received, 1813–1818

24—Case and Drawer Bulky Package File, 1789–1877

25—Letters and Papers Received (Irregular Series), 1789–1831: Miscellaneous Papers Received

26—Plans for Removal of Obstructions from the Mississippi and Ohio Rivers, 1824–1826

27—Letters Received by the Board of Engineers for Fortifications, 1825–1830

28—Letters Sent by the Office of the Chief of Engineers Relating to Internal Improvements, 1824–1830 (M-65)

29—Letters and Papers Received (Irregular Series), 1789–1831: Fortification Papers, 1815–1818

30—Letters Received, 1819–1825: Referred
(Additional series within this Record Group begin with editorial code number 221.)

Record Group 156—Records of the
Office of the Chief of Ordnance

31—Letters Received, 1812–1894

32—Letters to the War Department, 1817–1825

33—Letters Sent Relating to Mineral Lands, 1821–1860

34—Lead Mines: Leases, vol. I, 1824–1825

35—Records Relating to Inventions

36—Records Relating to Experiments

37—Letters Sent by the Military Storekeeper, Springfield, Mass., Armory

38—Letterbooks of the Watervliet Arsenal, 1819–1824

39—Letters Sent by the Superintendent, Springfield, Mass., Armory

40—Letters, Endorsements, and Circulars Sent ("Miscellaneous Letters"), 1812–1889
(Additional series within this Record Group begin with editorial code number 331.)

DNA (*continued*)

Record Group 92—Records of the
Office of the Quartermaster General

41—Letters Received, 1818–1825

42—Letters Sent, 1818–1825 (M-745)

43—Consolidated Correspondence File

44—Maj. James H. Hook's Papers: Letters, 1818–1821

45—Commissary General of Purchases: Letters Sent, 1817–1825

46—Registers of Letters Received, 1818–1825

47—Philadelphia Supply Agencies: Coxe and Irvine Papers

48—General and Special Orders of the Adjutant General's Office and Other Offices and Bureaus of the War Department, 1818–1840

49—General and Special Orders of the Adjutant General's Office and Other Offices and Bureaus of the War Department, 1818–1835 (2 vols.)

50—Records of Thomas S. Jesup: Letters and Reports Sent, 1818–1826

Record Group 217—Records of the
United States General Accounting Office

51—Second Auditor: Letters Sent

52—Second Auditor: Letters Sent Relating to Property, 1818

53—Third Auditor: Letters Sent

54—Third Auditor: Congressional Letterbooks

55—Fourth Auditor: Letters Received

56—Fourth Auditor: Letters Sent

57—Fourth Auditor: Letters from the Secretary of the Navy, 1818

58—Fifth Auditor: Letters Sent

59—First Comptroller: Miscellaneous Letters Sent, 1817–1844

60—First Comptroller: Miscellaneous Letters Received

61—First Comptroller: Diplomatic, Consular, and Miscellaneous Letters

62—First Comptroller: Letters from the Third Auditor

63—Second Comptroller: Letters Received

64—Miscellaneous Letters and Papers, *ca.* 1804–1899

65—Records of Richard Bland Lee, Commissioner of Claims

66—Miscellaneous Records of the Third Auditor

67—Second Comptroller: Letters Received Relating to Pensions

Record Group 75—Records of the
Bureau of Indian Affairs

71—Letters Received by the Office of Indian Affairs, 1824–1881 (M-234 and Entry 79, with the Registers in M-18 and Entry 75)

DNA (*continued*)

72—Letters Sent by the Secretary of War Relating to Indian Affairs, 1800–1824 (M-15; Entry 2)

73—Letters Sent by the Superintendent of Indian Trade, 1806–1823 (M-16; Entry 4)

74—Letters Sent by the Office of Indian Affairs, 1824–1881 (M-21; Entry 84, with the Registers in Entries 80–82)

75—Records of the Cherokee Indian Agency in Tennessee, 1801–1835 (M-208; Entries 1041–1057)

76—Records of the Michigan Superintendency of Indian Affairs, 1814–1851 (M-1; Entries 1120–1139)

77—Letters Received by the Office of the Secretary of War Relating to Indian Affairs, 1800–1823 (M-271; Entry 1)

78—Special Files of the Office of Indian Affairs, 1807–1904 (M-574; Entry 98).

79—Letters Received by the Superintendent of Indian Trade, 1806–1824 (T-58; Entry 3)

80—Documents Relating to the Negotiation of Ratified and Unratified Treaties with Various Tribes of Indians, 1801–1869 (T-494; Entries 103–104)
(Additional series within this Record Group begin with editorial code number 271.)

Record Group 49—Records of the General Land Office

81—Miscellaneous Letters Received, 1838–1842

82—Miscellaneous Letters Sent, 1796–1889 (M-25)

83—Letters Sent: Indian Lands, 1840–1842

84—Letters Sent: Preëmption Bureau, 1846–1847

85—Journal and Report of James Leander Cathcart and James Hutton, Agents Appointed by the Secretary of the Navy to Survey Timber Resources between the Mermentau and Mobile Rivers, November, 1818–May, 1819 (M-8)

86—Division D, Mails and Files, Letters Received, 1801–1909

87—Division K, Abandoned Military Reservations Files

Record Group 15—Records of the Veterans Administration

91—Letterbooks of the Pension Office: General, 1812–1831

92—Letterbooks of the Pension Office: Original Cases, 1827–1832

93—Revolutionary War Pension Files

94—Miscellaneous Papers Relating to Pensions and Bounty Land Warrants, 1813–1875

95—Case Files of Pension and Bounty Land Warrant Applications Based on Revolutionary War Service, 1800–1900

96—Letters Sent, 1831–1866 (in chronological volumes)

DNA (*continued*)

Record Group 59—General Records of the Department of State

101—Miscellaneous Letters of the Department of State, 1789–1906 (M-179; Entry 102)

102—Domestic Letters (Sent), 1784–1906 (M-40; Entry 99)

103—Applications and Recommendations for Office; Letters Received, 1797–1901 (M-439 and others; Entry 331)

104—State Department Territorial Papers: Florida, 1777–1824 (M-116; Entry 879)

105—Accounting Records; Miscellaneous Letters Sent, 1832–1916 (Entry 202)

106—Diplomatic Instructions of the Department of State, 1785–1906 (M-77; Entry 1)

107—Diplomatic Despatches, 1789–1906 (a different microcopy for each distinct country or area from which the despatches were sent; Entry 8)

108—Consular Despatches, 1789–1906 (a different microcopy for each distinct country or area from which the despatches were sent; Entry 78)

109—Notes from Foreign Legations, 1789–1906 (a different microcopy for each distinct nation or area having a legation in Washington, D.C.; Entry 26)

110—Letters Received from the Fifth Auditor and Comptroller, 1829–1862 (Entry 216)

Record Group 60—General Records of the Department of Justice

111—Letters Received in the Office of the Attorney General, 1818–1843

112—Letters Sent by the Department of Justice: General and Miscellaneous, 1818–1904 (M-699)

113—Opinions of the Attorney General, 1818–1844 (T-412)

114—Drafts and Copies of Opinions, 1818–1824

Record Group 45—Naval Records Collection of the Office of Naval Records and Library

121—Letters Sent by the Secretary of the Navy to Officers, 1798–1868 (M-149; Entry 1)

122—Miscellaneous Letters Sent by the Secretary of the Navy ("General Letter Book"), 1798–1886 (M-209; Entry 3)

123—Letters to Federal Executive Agents: Nominations for Appointment of Officers, 1798–1824 (Entry 4)

124—Letters to Federal Executive Agents: Letters to the Secretary of the Treasury, 1798–1821 (Entry 4)

DNA (*continued*)

125—Letters to Congress, 1798–1886 (Entry 5)

126—Letters to Members of Congress, 1820–1831 (Entry 9)

127—Letters Sent by the Secretary of the Navy to the President and Executive Agencies, 1821–1886 (M-472; Entry 10)

128—Miscellaneous Letters Received by the Secretary of the Navy, 1801–1884 (M-124; Entry 21)

129—Letters from Federal Executive Agents, 1837–1886 (M-517; Entry 29)

130—Reports of the Secretary of the Navy to Congress, 1811–1820 (Entry 174)

131—Board of Navy Commissioners: Miscellaneous Letters Sent, 1815–1842 (Entry 217)

132—Letters Received by the Secretary of the Navy from Commanders, 1804–1886 (M-147; Entry 23)

133—Letters Received by the Secretary of the Navy from Captains, 1807–1861, 1866–1885 (M-125; Entry 24)

134—Letters Received by the Secretary of the Navy from Officers below the Rank of Commander, 1802–1886 (M-148; Entry 22)

135—Board of Navy Commissioners: Miscellaneous Letters Received, 1814–1842 (Entry 219)

136—Letters to Federal Executive Agents: Letters to the Secretary of War, 1798–1824 (Entry 4)

137—Letters to the Board of Navy Commissioners, 1815–1829 (Entry 8)

138—Board of Navy Commissioners: Letters from the Secretary of the Navy, 1814–1842 (Entry 222)

139—Board of Navy Commissioners: Letters to the Secretary of the Navy, 1815–1842 (Entry 213)

140—Letters Sent Conveying Appointments and Orders and Accepting Resignations, 1813–1842 (Entry 284)

Record Group 53—Records of the
Bureau of the Public Debt

141—Legal Papers in the Office of the Register of the Treasury, 1784–1876

142—Second Bank of the United States, Baltimore Branch: Letterbook, 1817–1835

143—Estimates and Statements, 1811–1839

Record Group 46—Records of the
United States Senate

References are cited in accordance with the practice used in *Preliminary Inventory* No. 23. For example, you may be told that a given manuscript is "in DNA, RG 46, 16A-D1," and you can find it by using that guide.

DNA (*continued*)

Record Group 28—Records of the
Post Office Department

161—Letters Sent by the Postmaster General, 1789–1836 (M-601; Entry 2)

Record Group 203—Records of the
Office of the Chief of Finance (War)

171—Letters Sent to the Secretary of the Treasury, 1817–1819

Record Group 98—Records of
United States Army Commands

181—6th U.S. Infantry: Letters Sent, 1817–1826

182—Northern Division: Militia Delinquents Reported to the Secretary of War, 1818–1819

183—Northern Division: Orderly Books, 1815–1820

184—Records of Edmund P. Gaines, vol. 2, 1817–1819

185—Eastern Department: Letters Sent, 1819–1826

186—Eastern Department: Order Books, 1821–1826

187—8th Military Department: Letters Sent, 1817–1821

188—8th Military Department: Order Book, 1820–1823

Record Group 192—Records of the
Office of the Commissary General of Subsistence

191—Letters Sent, 1818–1820

192—Miscellaneous Correspondence and Reports, 1818–1907

Record Group 233—Records of the
United States House of Representatives

References are cited in accordance with the practice used in *Preliminary Inventory* No. 113. For example, you may be told that a given manuscript is "in DNA, RG 233, 16A-G13.1," and you can find it by using that guide.

Record Group 206—Records of the
Office of the Solicitor of the Treasury

211—Letters Received: War Department

212—Letters Received: Miscellaneous

213—Letters Written

214—Letters Sent

215—Letters of Debts and Suits

Record Group 77—Records of the
Office of the Chief of Engineers

221—Letters Received, 1819–1825: Miscellaneous

DNA (*continued*)

222—Letters and Papers Received (Irregular Series), 1789–1831: Miscellaneous Papers Relating to the Military Academy, 1813–1831

223—Letters Received, 1819–1825: Engineers

224—Letters Received, 1826–1866 (File C)

225—Buell Collection of Historical Documents Relating to the Corps of Engineers, 1801–1819 (M-417)

226—Correspondence Relating to Proposed Locations of the National Road, 1825–1826

227—Central Office, Contracts: Bonds Provided by Contractors Engaged in the Construction of Fortifications and Public Buildings and the Furnishing of Supplies, 1817–1841

228—Topographical Bureau: Correspondence of the Topographical Officer Stationed in Washington, D.C., 1818–1826

229—Boards and Commissions, Internal Improvements: Letters Received, 1824–1831

230—Letters of Col. Joseph G. Totten, 1803–1864
(Additional series within this Record Group begin with editorial code number 281.)

Record Group 26—Records of the
United States Coast Guard

231—Lighthouse Bureau: Miscellaneous Correspondence, 1785–1852

Record Group 112—Records of the
Office of the Surgeon General (Army)

241—Letters Received, 1818–1889

242—Letters and Endorsements Sent, 1818–1889

243—Reports to the Secretary of War Relating to Office Activities, Personnel, and Expenditures, 1818–1894

244—Orders Issued by the Surgeon General, the Secretary of War, and the Adjutant and Inspector General ("Orderly Book"), 1818–1819

245—Orders from the Secretary of War, Forms, and Resolutions of Congress, 1816–1837

Record Group 125—Records of the
Office of the Judge Advocate General (Navy)

251—Records of General Courts-Martial and Courts of Inquiry of the Navy Department, 1799–1867 (M-273)

Record Group 94—Records of the
Adjutant General's Office

261—Orders, 1824–1854 (Entry 49)

262—War of 1812: Miscellaneous Records (Entry 125)

DNA (*continued*)

Record Group 75—Records of the
Bureau of Indian Affairs

271—Miscellaneous Cherokee Removal Records, *ca.* 1820–1854 (Entry 222)

Record Group 77—Records of the
Office of the Chief of Engineers

281—Land Papers, 1794–1916

282—Miscellaneous Papers Relating to the Acquisition of Land, 1820–1882

283—Letters and Papers Received (Irregular Series), 1789–1831: Letters Relating to the Military Academy, 1813–1818

284—Orders of the Engineer Department, the U.S. Military Academy, and the War Department, 1811–1874

285—Fort Monroe, Va., Engineer Office: Letters Received from the Engineer Department, 1820–1825

Record Group 99—Records of the
Office of the Paymaster General

291—Letters Sent, 1808–1889 (Entry 1)

292—Letters Received, 1799–1894 (Entry 7)

Record Group 56—Records of the
Office of the Secretary of the Treasury

301—Letters and Reports to Congress, Series E, 1825–1839

Record Group 153—Records of the
Office of the Judge Advocate General (War)

311—Opinions of the Attorney General, 1821–1870

312—Court-Martial Case Files, 1809–1938

Record Group 93—Revolutionary War
Records Collection (War Department)

321—Miscellaneous Numbered Records ("Manuscript File")

322—Miscellaneous Unnumbered Documents

Record Group 156—Records of the
Office of the Chief of Ordnance

331—Contracts for Ordnance and Ordnance Supplies, 1812–1910

332—Records concerning Arming and Equipping of Militia, 1808–1853 (1 vol.)

DNA (*continued*)

Record Group 127—Records of the United States Marine Corps

341—Letters Received, 1818 (collection assembled by the Historical Section)

342—Letterbook, January 22, 1817–April 24, 1820

DNDAR —Daughters of the American Revolution Library, Washington, D.C.
DS —document, signed
DU —document, unsigned
EI —endorsement, initialed
En —enclosure
Ens —enclosures
ES —endorsement, signed
EU —endorsement, unsigned
Ex —extract
ExU —extract, unsigned
FC —file copy (usually in the form of a letterbook copy retained in the office of origin)
FU —University of Florida Library, Gainesville, Fla.
GAHi —Atlanta Historical Society, Atlanta, Ga.
G-Ar —Georgia Department of Archives and History, Atlanta, Ga.
GEU —Emory University Library, Atlanta, Ga.
GHi —Georgia Historical Society, Savannah, Ga.
GU —University of Georgia Library, Athens, Ga.
Ia-HA —Iowa State Department of Archives and History, Des Moines, Ia.
ICHi —Chicago Historical Society, Chicago, Ill.
ICN —The Newberry Library, Chicago, Ill.
IHi —Illinois State Historical Library, Springfield, Ill.
In —Indiana State Library, Indianapolis, Ind.
InHi —Indiana Historical Society, Indianapolis, Ind.
InU —Indiana University Libraries, Bloomington, Ind.
KHi —Kansas State Historical Society, Topeka, Kan.
KyLoF —The Filson Club, Inc., Louisville, Ky.
KyU —University of Kentucky Library, Lexington, Ky.
LI —letter, initialed
LNHT —Howard-Tilton Memorial Library, Tulane University, New Orleans, La.
LS —letter, signed
LU —letter, unsigned
MB —Boston Public Library, Boston, Mass.
MBAt —Boston Athenaeum, Boston, Mass.

MdAA —Maryland Hall of Records, Annapolis, Md.
MdBJ —Johns Hopkins University Library, Baltimore, Md.
MdBP —Peabody Library, Baltimore, Md.
MdHi —Maryland Historical Society, Baltimore, Md.
MeHi —Maine Historical Society, Portland, Me.
MeLB —Bates College Library, Lewiston, Me.
MH —Harvard University Library, Cambridge, Mass.
MHi —Massachusetts Historical Society, Boston, Mass.
MiD —Detroit Public Library, Detroit, Mich.
MiDW —Wayne State University Library, Detroit, Mich.
MiU-C —William L. Clements Library, University of Michigan, Ann Arbor, Mich.
MnHi —Minnesota Historical Society, St. Paul, Minn.
MnM —Minneapolis Public Library, Minneapolis, Minn.
MoHi —State Historical Society of Missouri, Columbia, Mo.
MoKiT —Northeast Missouri State Teachers College, Kirksville, Mo.
MoSHi —Missouri Historical Society, St. Louis, Mo.
MWA —American Antiquarian Society, Worcester, Mass.
MWelC —Wellesley College Library, Wellesley, Mass.
MWiW-C—Chapin Library, Williams College, Williamstown, Mass.
N —New York State Library, Albany, N.Y.
NBu —Buffalo and Erie County Public Library, Buffalo, N.Y.
Nc-Ar —North Carolina Department of Archives and History, Raleigh, N.C.
NcD —Duke University Library, Durham, N.C.
NcU —University of North Carolina Library, Chapel Hill, N.C.
NhD —Dartmouth College Library, Hanover, N.H.
NhHi —New Hampshire Historical Society, Concord, N.H.
NHi —New-York Historical Society, New York, N.Y.
NHpR —Franklin D. Roosevelt Library, Hyde Park, N.Y.
NIC —Cornell University Library, Ithaca, N.Y.
NjHi —New Jersey Historical Society, Newark, N.J.
NjMoN —Morristown National Historical Park, Morristown, N.J.
NjP —Princeton University Library, Princeton, N.J.
NN —New York Public Library, New York, N.Y.
NNC —Columbia University Library, New York, N.Y.
NNPM —Pierpont Morgan Library, New York, N.Y.
NRU —University of Rochester Library, Rochester, N.Y.
NWM —United States Military Academy Library, West Point, N.Y.

OCHP —Historical and Philosophical Society of Ohio, University of Cincinnati, Cincinnati, O.

OClWHi —Western Reserve Historical Society, Cleveland, O.

OFH —Hayes Memorial Library, Fremont, O.

OHi —Ohio Historical Society, Columbus, O.

OMC —Marietta College Library, Marietta, O.

PBL —Lehigh University Library, Bethlehem, Pa.

PC —printed copy

PCarlD —Dickinson College Library, Carlisle, Pa.

PDS —printed document, signed

PEx —printed extract

PHarH —Pennsylvania Historical and Museum Commission, Harrisburg, Pa.

PHC —Haverford College Library, Haverford, Pa.

PHi —Historical Society of Pennsylvania, Philadelphia, Pa.

PLS —printed letter, signed

PPAmP —American Philosophical Society, Philadelphia, Pa.

PPiU —University of Pittsburgh Library, Pittsburgh, Pa.

PPL —Library Company of Philadelphia, Philadelphia, Pa.

PSC-Hi —Friends Historical Library, Swarthmore College, Swarthmore, Pa.

PU —University of Pennsylvania Library, Philadelphia, Pa.

PWbWHi—Wyoming Historical and Geological Society, Wilkes-Barre, Pa.

PWcHi —Chester County Historical Society, West Chester, Pa.

R-Ar —Rhode Island State Archives, Providence, R.I.

RHi —Rhode Island Historical Society, Providence, R.I.

RPJCB —John Carter Brown Library, Brown University, Providence, R.I.

Sc-AH —South Carolina Department of Archives and History, Columbia, S.C.

ScC —Charleston Library Society, Charleston, S.C.

ScCCit —The Citadel, Charleston, S.C.

ScCleA —Clemson University Library, Clemson, S.C.

ScFHi —Florence County Historical Society, Florence, S.C.

ScGF —Furman University Library, Greenville, S.C.

ScHi —South Carolina Historical Society, Charleston, S.C.

ScSpW —Wofford College Library, Spartanburg, S.C.

ScU-SC —South Caroliniana Library, University of South Carolina, Columbia, S.C.

T —Tennessee State Library and Archives, Nashville, Tenn.

THi —Tennessee Historical Society, Nashville, Tenn.

TKL —Knoxville Public Library, Knoxville, Tenn.

TxDaHi —Dallas Historical Society, Dallas, Tex.

TxGR	—Rosenberg Library, Galveston, Tex.
TxU	—University of Texas Library, Austin, Tex.
Vi	—Virginia State Library, Richmond, Va.
ViHi	—Virginia Historical Society, Richmond, Va.
ViLxW	—Washington and Lee University Library, Lexington, Va.
ViU	—University of Virginia Library, Charlottesville, Va.
ViW	—College of William and Mary Library, Williamsburg, Va.
VtU	—University of Vermont, Burlington, Vt.
WaPS	—Washington State University, Pullman, Wash.
WHi	—State Historical Society of Wisconsin, Madison, Wis.

BIBLIOGRAPHY

Adams, Charles Francis, ed., *Memoirs of John Quincy Adams, Comprising Portions of His Diary from 1795 to 1848.* 12 vols. Philadelphia: J.B. Lippincott & Co., c. 1874–1877.

American State Papers: Documents, Legislative and Executive, of the Congress . . . . 37 vols. Washington: 1832–1861.

Ammon, Harry, *James Monroe: the Quest for National Identity.* New York: McGraw-Hill Book Company, c. 1971.

Annals of Congress: Debates and Proceedings in the Congress of the United States, 1789–1824. 42 vols. Washington: 1834–1856.

Bassett, John Spencer, ed., *The Correspondence of Andrew Jackson.* 7 vols. Washington: Carnegie Institution of Washington, 1926–1935.

[Benton, Thomas Hart,] *Thirty Years' View; or, a History of the Working of the American Government for Thirty Years, from 1820 to 1850* . . . . 2 vols. New York: D. Appleton and Company, c. 1854–1856.

Biographical Directory of the American Congress, 1774–1949 . . . . House Document No. 607, 81st Congress, 2nd Session. [Washington:] U.S. Government Printing Office, 1950.

Brannan, John, *Official Letters of the Military and Naval Officers of the United States, during the War with Great Britain in the Years 1812, 13, 14, & 15* . . . . Washington: published by the editor, 1823.

Capers, Gerald M., *John C. Calhoun, Opportunist: a Reappraisal.* Gainesville: University of Florida Press, c. 1960.

Carter, Clarence Edwin, and John Porter Bloom, eds., *The Territorial Papers of the United States.* 28 vols. to date. Washington: 1934–present.

Coit, Margaret L., *John C. Calhoun: American Portrait.* Boston: Houghton Mifflin Company, c. 1950.

Crallé, Richard K., ed., *The Works of John C. Calhoun.* 6 vols. Columbia, S.C.: printed by A.S. Johnston, 1851, and New York: D. Appleton and Company, 1853–1857.

Everett, Alexander Hill, *Europe: or a General Survey of the Present Situation of the Principal Powers; with Conjectures on Their Future Prospects.* Boston: Cummings and Hilliard, 1822.

Fisher, Samuel Herbert, *The Litchfield Law School, 1775–1833.* (*Tercentenary Pamphlet Series* No. 21.) [New Haven:] Yale University Press for the [Connecticut] Tercentenary Commission, 1933.

Gordon, William A., *A Compilation of Registers of the Army of the United States, from 1815 to 1831 (Inclusive)* . . . . Washington: printed by James C. Dunn, 1837.

Hay, Thomas Robson, "John C. Calhoun and the Presidential Campaign of 1824," in the *North Carolina Historical Review*, vol. XII, no. 1 (January, 1935), pp. 20–44.

Hay, Thomas Robson, ed., "John C. Calhoun and the Presidential Campaign of 1824: Some Unpublished Calhoun Letters," in the *American Historical Review,* vol. XL, no. 1 (October, 1934), pp. 82–96, and no. 2 (January, 1935), pp. 287–300.

Heilman, Grace E., and Bernard S. Levin, *Calendar of Joel R. Poinsett Papers in the Henry D. Gilpin Collection.* Philadelphia: Historical Society of Pennsylvania, c. 1941.

Heitman, Francis B., *Historical Register and Dictionary of the United States Army, from Its Organization, September 29, 1789, to March 2, 1903.* 2 vols. Washington: U.S. Government Printing Office, 1903.

Holmes, Alester G., and George R. Sherrill, *Thomas Green Clemson: His Life and Work.* Richmond: Garrett and Massie, Inc., c. 1937.

Hopkins, James F., and Mary W.M. Hargreaves, eds., *The Papers of Henry Clay.* 3 vols. to date. [Lexington:] University of Kentucky Press, c. 1959, 1961, 1963.

Hunt, Gaillard, ed., *The First Forty Years of Washington Society, Portrayed by the Family Letters of Mrs. Samuel Harrison Smith (Margaret Bayard), from the Collection of Her Grandson, J. Henley Smith.* New York: Charles Scribner's Sons, c. 1906.

James, Edwin, compiler, *Account of an Expedition from Pittsburgh to the Rocky Mountains, Performed in the Years 1819 and '20 . . . .* 3 vols. Philadelphia: H.C. Carey and F. Lea, 1822–1823.

James, Marquis, *The Raven: a Biography of Sam Houston.* Indianapolis: The Bobbs-Merrill Company, c. 1929.

Jameson, J. Franklin, ed., *Correspondence of John C. Calhoun,* in *American Historical Association Annual Report* for 1899 (2 vols. Washington: U.S. Government Printing Office, 1900). vol. II.

Johnson, Allen, and Dumas Malone, eds., *Dictionary of American Biography.* 22 vols. New York: Charles Scribner's Sons, 1928–1944.

McGrane, Reginald C., ed., *The Correspondence of Nicholas Biddle Dealing with National Affairs, 1807–1844.* Boston: Houghton Mifflin Company, c. 1919.

McKenney, Thomas L., *Memoirs, Official and Personal: with Sketches of Travels among the Northern and Southern Indians: Embracing a War Excursion, and Descriptions of Scenes along the Western Borders.* 2 vols. in 1. New York: Paine and Burgess, c. 1846.

Meriwether, Robert L., and W. Edwin Hemphill, eds., *The Papers of John C. Calhoun.* 6 vols. to date. Columbia: University of South Carolina Press, c. 1959–1972.

Morse, Jedidiah, *Geography Made Easy.* 1st ed. New Haven: printed by Meigs, Bowen and Dana, [1784].

Morse, Jedidiah, *A Report to the Secretary of War of the United States, on Indian Affairs, Comprising a Narrative of a Tour Performed in the Summer of 1820 . . . .* New Haven: printed by S. Converse, c. 1822.

Morse, Jedidiah, and Sidney Edwards Morse, *A New System of Geography, Ancient and Modern . . . with an Atlas . . . .* 23rd ed. Boston: Richardson & Lord, 1822.

Newsome, A.R., "Correspondence of John C. Calhoun, George McDuffie and Charles Fisher, Relating to the Presidential Campaign of 1824," in the *North Carolina Historical Review,* vol. VII, no. 4 (October, 1930), pp. 477–504.

Niles' Weekly Register. Baltimore: 1811–1849.

Parton, Dorothy M., *The Diplomatic Career of Joel Roberts Poinsett.* Washington: Catholic University of America, c. 1934.

Peters, Richard, ed., *The Public Statutes at Large of the United States of America . . .* [Including Private Laws, Indian Treaties, and Treaties with Foreign Powers, 1789–1845]. 8 vols. Boston: Little, Brown and Company, c. 1846.

Prucha, Francis Paul, *American Indian Policy in the Formative Years: the Indian Trade and Intercourse Acts, 1790–1834.* Cambridge, Mass.: Harvard University Press, c. 1962.

Prucha, Francis Paul, *The Sword of the Republic: the United States Army on the Frontier, 1783–1846.* [New York:] The Macmillan Company, c. 1969.

Register of Graduates and Former Cadets, United States Military Academy. [New York:] The West Point Alumni Foundation, Inc., [1946?].

Richardson, James D., *A Compilation of the Messages and Papers of the Presidents, 1789–1902.* 10 vols. [Washington:] Bureau of National Literature and Art, 1903. (Other editions are also available, one being as House Miscellaneous Document No. 210, 53rd Congress, 2nd Session.)

Sabin, Joseph, and others, *Bibliotheca Americana: a Dictionary of Books Relating to America, from Its Discovery to the Present Time.* 29 vols. New York and Portland, Me.: 1868–1936.

Shipp, J.E.D., *Giant Days, or the Life and Times of William H. Crawford, Embracing Also Excerpts from His Diary, Letters and Speeches, Together with a Copious Index to the Whole.* Americus, Ga.: Southern Printers, c. 1909.

Skeen, C. Edward, "Calhoun, Crawford, and the Politics of Retrenchment," in the *South Carolina Historical Magazine,* vol. LXXIII, no. 3 (July, 1972), pp. 141–155.

Washington, D.C., *National Intelligencer,* 1800–1870.

Wiltse, Charles M., *John C. Calhoun.* 3 vols. *Nationalist, 1782–1828; Nullifier, 1829–1839; Sectionalist, 1840–1850.* Indianapolis: The Bobbs-Merrill Company, Inc., c. 1944, 1949, 1951.

Wiltse, Charles M., "John C. Calhoun and the 'A.B. Plot,'" in the *Journal of Southern History,* vol. XIII, no. 1 (February, 1947), pp. 46–61.

INDEX